The Webster-Hayne Debate

on the Nature of the Union

D0074591

Daniel Webster

Robert Y. Hayne

THE WEBSTER-HAYNE DEBATE
ON THE NATURE OF THE UNION

Selected Documents

EDITED BY HERMAN BELZ

LIBERTY FUND
INDIANAPOLIS

This book is published by Liberty Fund, Inc., a foundation established to encourage study of the ideal of a society of free and responsible individuals.

𒀀𒈠𒄄

The cuneiform inscription that serves as our logo and as the design motif for our endpapers is the earliest-known written appearance of the word "freedom" (*amagi*), or "liberty." It is taken from a clay document written about 2300 B.C. in the Sumerian city-state of Lagash.

Portrait of Robert Y. Hayne courtesy of the South Carolina Governor's Mansion and reprinted with permission.
Portrait of Daniel Webster courtesy of Corbis and used by permission.

Library of Congress Cataloging-in-Publication Data

Webster, Daniel, 1782–1852.
  The Webster-Hayne debate on the nature of the Union: selected documents/Daniel Webster, Robert Y. Hayne; edited by Herman Belz.
    p.   cm.
  Includes bibliographical references.
  ISBN 0-86597-272-9 (hc: alk. paper).
  ISBN 0-86597-273-7 (pb: alk. paper)
    1. United States—Politics and government—1829–1837 Sources.
  2. Speeches, addresses, etc., American.   3. Foot's resolution,
  1829.   4. Nullification.   I. Hayne, Robert Young, 1791–1839.
  II. Belz, Herman.   III. Title.
  E381.W3717   2000
  320.473'049—dc21   99-34147

10 09 08 07 00 C 5 4 3 2 1
11 10 09 08 07 P 6 5 4 3 2

Liberty Fund, Inc.
8335 Allison Pointe Trail, Suite 300
Indianapolis, IN 46250-1684

Contents

CONTENTS

FOREWORD

T HE NATURE AND PURPOSE of the federal government was the fundamental issue in the Constitutional Convention of 1787. Rather than settle the issue, however, the ratification of the Constitution made it central to the structure of American politics. From the beginning of national lawmaking and administration in 1789, the nature of the Union has been a major source of controversy in constitutional law and politics. Responding to the need for constitutional construction in organizing the new government, Federalist and Republican politicians in the 1790s advanced centralizing nationalist and decentralizing states' rights arguments to explain the type of authority conferred on the federal head of the American Union. For more than three decades, these arguments were employed by partisans in all sections of the country seeking to advance local, state, and sectional interests.

In January 1830, in a dramatic encounter on the floor of the United States Senate, the debate over the nature of the Union took an alarming turn. The debate moved beyond the exchange of alternative views on how to administer the federal government to accusations and recriminations about the destruction of the federal government and the Union. States' rights and nationalist positions, which previously were adopted without regard to a consistent pattern of sectional identification or alignment, were defined in a way that portended political violence between irreconcilably opposed sections. The event that presented this portent of sectional discord was the debate over the nature of the Union between Daniel Webster of Massachusetts and Robert Y. Hayne of South Carolina.

More than fifty years ago, a study of American political oratory noted that the Webster-Hayne debate had fallen into historical and political neglect. Once regarded as basic texts in the development of American nationality, Webster's speeches were taken out of context and treated as purple patches in teaching declamation to schoolchildren. Hayne's speeches were read even more rarely, and almost never were considered in relation to Webster's.[1] In more recent years, the Webster-Hayne debate has further faded in American memory as social and cultural studies have gained ascendancy in professional historiography. Yet

1. Wilbur Samuel Howell and Hoyt Hopewell Hudson, "Daniel Webster," vol. II in *A History and Criticism of American Public Address,* ed. William Norwood Brigance (1943; reprint, New York: Russell and Russell, 1960), 710 in reprint.

if the need for national unity during the Second World War was a reason for ignoring the disunionism of the antebellum period, the more recent rediscovery of federalism has given new relevance to issues raised in the dramatic encounter of 1830. From a historical point of view, the Webster-Hayne debate provides a case study of the tendency inherent in pre–Civil War federal-system politics toward instability and violence. To the extent that it deals generally with the relationship between liberty and governmental sovereignty, the significance of the debate transcends the immediate historical context and addresses a fundamental problem in modern political theory.

In order to understand the issues raised in the Webster-Hayne debate, it is necessary to reconstruct the historical context in which it occurred. The Federal Union established by the Constitution was a novel political experiment that combined features of both a confederation of sovereign states and a sovereign national government. In a practical sense, the structure was held together by a system of political partisanship that began with the start of federal administration in 1789 and continued for over three decades. The party system was unifying in the sense that the two original parties—Federalists and Republicans—found it in their respective interests to employ either the nationalist or the states' rights construction of the Constitution to administer the federal government, or to criticize the other party's administration of it. The practical effect of this party system was to legitimize their constructions as valid theories in constitutional law. However, the system of partisan competition was destabilizing to the extent that it encouraged shifts in constitutional standpoint and strategy motivated by a desire for partisan advantage at the expense of fidelity to basic constitutional principles and values.

The election to the presidency of Andrew Jackson in 1828 had a realigning effect on American politics. By the mid-1820s, the success of the Republican party under Presidents Jefferson, Madison, and Monroe largely eliminated the Federalist party as an effective political opposition. The Republicans were dominant, but territorial expansion and economic development produced class and sectional factionalism within the party. The election of John Quincy Adams as president over rival Republican candidates Henry Clay, William H. Crawford, and Andrew Jackson—in an election that was decided by the House of Representatives in 1824—reflected this dissension. Jackson, the candidate of the National Republican party, gained the support of dissident elements and won the election of 1828 as the head of a new political organization: the Democratic party.

Depending on the perspective of the observer, Jackson's victory over John Quincy Adams offered the promise or the threat of far-reaching changes in American government and politics.

The opening of the Twenty-First Congress on December 7, 1829, marked the first meeting of the national legislature following Jackson's inauguration in March of that year. The Webster-Hayne debate, extending from January to May 1830, was the most important event to occur in this legislative session. In the course of the debate, twenty-one of the Senate's forty-eight members, in sixty-five speeches, analyzed, evaluated, and offered predictions concerning the changing political, constitutional, and economic conditions of the country. Senator Levi Woodbury of New Hampshire observed that the encounter between Webster and Hayne "seems to have metamorphosed the Senate, not only into a committee of the whole on the state of the Union, but on the state of the Union in all time past, present, and to come."[2]

Jackson's assumption of the executive office brought into view a cluster of fundamental issues in American government and politics that dominated the attention of the political community in Washington, D.C., and much of the country. Principal subjects discussed in the great debate of 1830 were the nature of the Union; the purpose, extent, and limits of the powers of the federal and state governments; the scope and character of the executive power; the role of political parties in the constitutional system; the significance of geo-political and geo-economic sections as constituent parts of the Union; the allocation of resources through policies dealing with land distribution, taxation, improvements to transportation and communication systems; and public finance. Equally controversial subjects were the nature of constitutional construction and interpretation, the locus of authority for deciding the meaning of the Constitution, the role of the Supreme Court and the federal judiciary in the government of the Union, the place of social contract theory in the American political tradition, the scope and effect of majority rule and minority rights in the government of the Union, the relationship between slavery and republican government, and the status of the Indian tribes in the American system of government. Much like a constituent assembly called to assess the fit between existing institutions and a changing social environment, Senate discussion of these issues—to the surprise of observers—unfolded pursuant to the introduction, on

2. *Register of Debates in Congress*, 21st Cong., 1st sess., February 24, 1830, 179.

December 30, 1829, of a resolution by Senator Samuel A. Foot of Connecticut concerning federal land policy.

Foot proposed that the committee on public lands inquire into the expediency of abolishing the office of Surveyor General and temporarily limiting the sale of public lands to those lands already on the market. Western senators viewed the resolution as a hostile measure intended to stop the growth of Western states by keeping Eastern workers from moving west, thus assuring a labor supply for New England manufacturers. Senator Thomas Hart Benton of Missouri immediately attacked Foot's resolution. He attracted the support of Senator Robert Y. Hayne of South Carolina, who, on behalf of Southern interests, saw an opportunity, through cooperation with Western members, to shift federal tax policy away from the high protective duties adopted by Congress in 1828, referred to as the "tariff of abominations." Therefore, on January 19, 1830, Hayne entered the discussion.

Having dealt specifically with the public lands, the debate to this point had been concerned with gauging the effect of the new Democratic administration on existing federal policies. Jackson's election signified repudiation of the centralizing program of federal bank, tariff, and internal improvement policies, known as the American System, enacted by the Adams administration. The constructive work of setting the federal government safely on a states' rights course—the purpose for which Jackson was elected—remained to be accomplished. This objective was complicated by the presence within the Democratic party of conflicting Northern, Western, and Southern interests. Just how complicated and unsettled the political situation was could be seen in the fact that Jackson's vice president, John C. Calhoun of South Carolina, had served as vice president under John Quincy Adams. By rejecting the American System, Calhoun between 1824 and 1828 became a champion of state sovereignty, joined the emerging Democratic coalition, and was reelected as vice president on the Jackson ticket. Thus resulted the extraordinary circumstance which saw Calhoun, the erstwhile colleague of Webster and now a leader with Hayne of the South Carolina antitariff movement, presiding as president of the Senate over the Webster-Hayne debate.

At the outset, the debate on Foot's resolution was between Western and New England senators and concerned the public lands, emigration, and the national debt. The public debt had long been in process of being reduced, and revenues from the sale of public lands, unless curtailed, would help to eliminate it in about four more years. Only to the extent that states' rights men wanted to pay off the debt and reduce the scope of the federal government, while nationalists wanted to enact spending programs that would maintain the debt and expand the federal government's role, did the discussion have a constitutional dimension.

Hayne's entry into the debate turned the issue of the sale of public lands into a clash between state sovereignty and national sovereignty, and he expounded these sovereignties in terms of rival and irreconcilable theories of constitutional construction and the nature of the federal Union. Although the South Carolina senator earned lasting distinction as a champion of state sovereignty, this rhetorical transformation was Webster's doing, not Hayne's. Webster's political purpose was to defend the sectional interests of New England as the base of the National Republican party and to prevent a Western-Southern alignment in the Democratic opposition. Webster pursued his objective through a rhetorical strategy that ignored Benton, the principal opponent of New England sectionalism, and that provoked Hayne into an exposition and defense of what became the South Carolina doctrine of nullification.

The supporters of nullification had justified it as a form of state interposition based on the compact theory of the Union, which embodied the principles of the Kentucky and Virginia Resolutions of 1798. In the view of South Carolina politicians, nullification was a procedure for deciding the constitutionality of federal measures that would preserve the Union. Webster argued, on the contrary, that the logic, tendency, and practical effect of nullification, if permitted to be developed and employed, would be to destroy the Union and foment lawless, revolutionary violence. As a peaceful alternative to the South Carolina doctrine, Webster offered the theory of the Union as a sovereign national government, created by the people of the United States as a whole, with authority to decide on the lawfulness and constitutionality of its actions.

According to Hayne, the fundamental issue in the debate was "the right of a State to judge of the violations of the Constitution on the part of the Federal Government, and to protect her citizens from the operations of unconstitutional laws." Hayne said that Webster's doctrine—that "the Federal Government is the exclusive judge of the extent as well as the limitations of its powers"—was "utterly subversive of the sovereignty and independence of the States" (speech, January 25, 1830). In Webster's view, the fundamental question was: "Whose prerogative is it to decide on the constitutionality or unconstitutionality of the laws?" He held that the Constitution of the United States "confers on the Government itself, to be exercised by its appropriate Department, and under its responsibility to the People, this power of deciding ultimately and conclusively, upon the just extent of its own authority." The power to decide constitutional disputes was conferred on the "Judicial Tribunals of the United States," headed by the Supreme Court. Webster acknowledged that the people of a state possessed a right of revolution. But, he insisted that no mode existed "in which a State Government, as a member of the Union, can interfere and stop the progress of the General Government, by force of her own laws, under any circumstances whatever" (speech, January 26, 1830).

Hayne gave three speeches and Webster two between January 19 and January 27, 1830. The speeches drew packed galleries to the Senate chamber and attracted national attention. Webster's second reply to Hayne, containing the appeal to "Liberty *and* Union, now and forever, one and inseparable," is regarded in the history of American public address as the most powerful and effective speech ever given in an American legislature. On the strength of this memorable assertion, Webster has often been judged the winner of the debate. However, the practice of verbatim reporting and publication of congressional speeches had not yet begun, and texts were not available for study until several weeks had passed. For this reason, and because partisanship and ideology affected people's views, opinions differed over which speaker actually prevailed. Far from ending discussion, therefore, from a contemporaneous standpoint the effect of the Webster-Hayne encounter was to broaden the debate into a comprehensive review of politics and constitutionalism in the United States since the American Revolution.

From this perspective, it becomes possible to appreciate the importance of the views presented by other senators going beyond the polarizing sectional confrontation between Webster and Hayne. To be sure, Webster secured his immediate objective. By, in effect, accusing Hayne of revolution and treason, Webster isolated South Carolina and blocked the formation of an alliance between the South and West. Webster's masterly parliamentary tactics also removed the onus of disunionist sectionalism from the New England states, where it had lain since the War of 1812, and placed it on the sectional groups constituting the Democratic party. He assured that, for the time being, no significant change would occur in federal policies—especially the protective tariff—of greatest concern to his section.

Yet, by changing the terms of the debate, Webster provoked the responses by other senators that give the debate its landmark significance in constitutional history. The responses included John M. Clayton's nationalist argument for Supreme Court determination of constitutional conflict between the federal government and the states; John Rowan's rigorous and erudite defense of state sovereignty and interposition; and the searching arguments of Thomas Hart Benton, William Smith, and Edward Livingston, seeking in distinctive ways and to varying degrees to define positions in the middle ground that the logic of Webster's and Hayne's theories excluded. Considered altogether, these speeches demonstrate the responsibility for constitutional construction and commitment to constitutional values that were basic features of legislative practice in the nineteenth century. An ethic of constitutional conviction and intelligence that has no counterpart in modern congressional deliberation is evident in the debate on the public lands.

After the Civil War, the Webster-Hayne debate appeared to many as a prophetic foreshadowing of the bloody trauma through which the American people were destined to pass before they could truly become one nation. In this spirit, Woodrow Wilson wrote that the debate marked "the formal opening of the great controversy between the North and the South concerning the nature of the Constitution which bound them together." For the first time on the floor of Congress, said Wilson, distinct statements were presented of the constitutional principles on which North and South were to divide.[3] Although the Civil War was fought over secession rather than nullification, both doctrines rested on the theory of state sovereignty. The North's victory can therefore be seen as a practical judgment that Webster was right, and that as a matter of constitutional law and theory his argument for federal sovereignty settled the issue of the nature of the Union. So many variables affected the outcome of the Civil War, however—not to mention the difference between secession and nullification as constructions of the Constitution—that an equally plausible case can be made that neither Webster's nor Hayne's arguments settled the question of the nature of the Union.

Although some contemporaneous observers believed that the conflict of sectional interests and constitutional philosophies posed in the Webster-Hayne debate could be resolved only by force, most lawmakers and politicians resisted this conclusion. As seen particularly in the speeches of Edward Livingston and Thomas Hart Benton, ambiguity

3. Woodrow Wilson, *Division and Reunion 1829–1889* (New York: Longmans, Green, and Co., 1897), 43–44.

about the nature of the Union could also serve as an incentive to find a constitutional middle ground between the extreme conclusions to which the doctrines of state sovereignty and national consolidation could be taken. In this connection, it is pertinent to consider the factual question of whether the country was in a state of crisis at the time of the Webster-Hayne debate. Professing alarm at South Carolina's actions, Webster claimed that the mere assertion of the doctrine of nullification created a crisis of the Union. Benton and Hayne, objecting to what they viewed as Webster's tactic of wrapping the defense of New England sectional interests in the rhetoric of Unionism, denied that a crisis existed. With stark clarity, the debate revealed that the tension between states' rights and federal authority—a tension inherent in the design of the Constitution—could encourage a multiplicity of political responses.

In an expanding pluralistic society, the federal structure of government created opportunities for bargaining and negotiation between the sections, states, and economic interests that constituted the American political system. Yet, though federalism created a distinctive kind of politics, it did not change the nature of politics. As seen in the Webster-Hayne debate, partisans of rival sections and philosophies of government confronted each other convinced of the legitimacy of their respective interests, the justness of their respective causes, and the correctness of their constitutional arguments. On the one hand, the ambiguity of power relations in the federal Union encouraged bargaining and compromise between the constituent parts of the system because much political history could be cited in support of the belief that compromise was the price of union. On the other hand, should issues arise not amenable to compromise, partisans might conclude, contrary to the official theory of American federalism, that sovereignty could not in fact be divided between the states and the general government. In this view, sovereignty must either be consolidated in the nation or be exercised by the several states. Elevated to the level of constitutional principle, this perception could lead to polarization between the parts of the federal system. Yet if a strategy of polarization were pursued to its logical conclusion, resulting in the violent confrontation anticipated in Webster's second reply to Hayne, there could be no predicting the outcome. As never before, the peril inherent in the structure of federal politics—along with the opportunity and need for responsible statesmanship—appeared in the great debate of 1830.

Senators who spoke after the personal encounter between Webster and Hayne had been concluded were conscious of the historical significance of the debate. Edward Livingston expressed the purpose of the extraordinary deliberation in observing: "The publication of what has been said, will spread useful information on topics highly proper to be understood in the community at large. The recurrence which has been had to first principles is of incalculable use. The nature, form, history, and changes of our Government, imperceptible or disregarded at the time of their occurrence, are remarked; abuses are pointed out; and the people are brought to reflect on the past, and provide for the future."

Profound changes have occurred in American society since the early nineteenth century. Yet, to a remarkable extent, the issues raised in the Webster-Hayne debate remain relevant and controversial in American government and politics. A record of the deliberations of early Republican statements on these issues at a critical moment in the development of the American political tradition has practical worth for Americans today as they reflect on the meaning of republican liberty.

HERMAN BELZ
University of Maryland
1998

NOTE ON THE TEXT

The speeches reprinted in this volume are taken from the edition published by the firm of Joseph Gales and William M. Seaton under the title *Debate on the Subject of the Public Lands: Daniel Webster and Robert Hayne. Original Printings of Webster and Hayne's Speeches of January 20, 21, 26, and 27, 1830,* followed by speeches of five others. Gales and Seaton did not print Hayne's speech of January 19, 1830. I have included it because, according to Webster's account, it was this speech that caused him to take part in a debate he previously had had no intention of entering. Gales and Seaton was a Washington printing firm. Joseph Gales was the editor of the *National Intelligencer* and a close friend of Daniel Webster. Although he had other reporters who covered congressional speeches, Gales, at Webster's request, personally reported the second reply to Hayne. Webster and his political advisors made extensive revisions in the text, and the speech was first printed in the *National Intelligencer,* February 23, 1830. It achieved instant fame, owing in part to Webster's systematic effort to influence public opinion by distributing the speech. Gales and Seaton printed 40,000 copies of it by May, and it is estimated that 100,000 copies had been circulated by the end of the year. The entire record of 65 speeches given in the course of the debate on the public lands can be found in the *Register of Debates in Congress,* published by Gales and Seaton.

BIBLIOGRAPHY

Anonymous. "The Several Speeches Made during the Debate in the Senate of the United States on Mr. Foot's Resolution, by Mr. Hayne of South Carolina and Mr. Webster of Massachusetts." *Southern Review* 6 (August 1830): 140–98.

Baxter, Maurice G. *One and Inseparable: Daniel Webster and the Union.* Cambridge: Harvard University Press, 1984.

Benton, Thomas Hart. *Thirty Years' View.* 2 vols. New York: D. Appleton, 1859.

Current, Richard N. *Daniel Webster and the Rise of National Conservatism.* Boston: Little, Brown, 1955.

Curtis, George Ticknor. *Life of Daniel Webster.* 2 vols. New York: D. Appleton, 1872.

Ferguson, Robert A. *Law and Letters in American Culture.* Cambridge: Harvard University Press, 1984.

Fields, Wayne. "The Reply to Hayne: Daniel Webster and the Rhetoric of Stewardship." *Political Theory* 2 (1983): 5–28.

Freehling, William W. *Prelude to Civil War: The Nullification Controversy in South Carolina 1816–1836*. New York: Harper & Row, 1965.

Fuess, Claude Moore. *Daniel Webster*. 2 vols. Boston: Little, Brown, 1930.

Jervey, Theodore D. *Robert Y. Hayne and His Times*. New York: Macmillan, 1909.

Hockett, Homer Carey. *The Constitutional History of the United States 1826–1876*. New York: Macmillan, 1939.

Howell, Samuel Wilbur, and Hoyt Hopewell Hudson. "Daniel Webster." Edited by William Norwood Brigance. Vol. II of *A History and Criticism of American Public Address*. 1943. Reprint, New York: Russell and Russell, 1960. 665–733 in reprint.

MacDonald, William. *Jacksonian Democracy 1829–1837*. New York: Harper & Brothers, 1906.

McLaughlin, Andrew C. *A Constitutional History of the United States*. New York: D. Appleton-Century, 1935.

Peterson, Merrill D. *The Great Triumvirate: Webster, Clay, and Calhoun*. New York: Oxford University Press, 1987.

Sheidley, Harlow W. "The Webster-Hayne Debate: Recasting New England's Sectionalism." *New England Quarterly* 67 (1994): 5–29.

Smith, Craig R. *Defender of the Union: The Oratory of Daniel Webster*. Westport, Conn.: Greenwood Press, 1989.

Smith, Elbert B. *Magnificent Missourian: The Life of Thomas Hart Benton*. 1958. Reprint, Westport, Conn.: Greenwood Press, 1973.

Weaver, Richard M. "Two Orators." In *The Southern Essays of Richard M. Weaver*, edited by George M. Curtis III and James J. Thompson, Jr. Indianapolis: Liberty Fund, 1987. 104–33.

Wilson, Woodrow. *Division and Reunion 1829–1889*. New York: Longmans, Green, 1897.

Wiltse, Charles M. *John C. Calhoun: Nullifier. 1829–1839*. Indianapolis: Bobbs-Merrill, 1949.

The Webster-Hayne Debate
on the Nature of the Union

Robert Y. Hayne

Robert Y. Hayne was born in South Carolina in 1791 and educated in Charleston. He studied law and was admitted to the bar in 1812. During the War of 1812, he served as an officer in the Third South Carolina Regiment. A member of the State House of Representatives from 1814 to 1818, Hayne was State Attorney General from 1820 to 1822, when he was elected as a Republican to the United States Senate. He was reelected in 1828. Hayne was aligned with John C. Calhoun as a nationalist in the Republican party in South Carolina, and in winning election to the Senate he defeated William Smith, the leader of the radical states' rights Jeffersonian Republicans in South Carolina politics. With Calhoun, his opposition to the protective tariff led him to become a radical advocate of state sovereignty. Hayne was a member of the South Carolina convention that passed the Ordinance of Nullification in 1832. He resigned from the Senate and was elected governor from 1832 to 1834. In the nullification crisis, he commanded a force of 25,000 South Carolina volunteers with caution and restraint. Hayne was mayor of Charleston from 1835 to 1837, and he was president of the Louisville, Cincinnati & Charleston Railroad at the time of his death in 1839.

Speech of Mr. Hayne,

of South Carolina

[January 19, 1830]

The following resolution, moved by Mr. Foot, of Connecticut, being under consideration:

"Resolved, That the Committee on Public Lands be instructed to inquire into the expediency of limiting for a certain period the sales of the public lands to such lands only as have heretofore been offered for sale, and are subject to entry at the minimum price. And also whether the Office of Surveyor General may not be abolished without detriment to the public interest."

M R. HAYNE SAID THAT, IF THE GENTLEMEN who had discussed this proposition had confined themselves strictly to the resolution under consideration, he would have spared the Senate the trouble of listening to the few remarks he now proposed to offer. It has been said, and correctly said, by more than one gentleman, that resolutions of inquiry were usually suffered to pass without opposition. The parliamentary practice in this respect was certainly founded in good sense and sound policy, which regarded such resolutions as intended merely to elicit information, and therefore entitled to favor. But [said Mr. H.] I cannot give my assent to the proposition so broadly laid down by some gentlemen, that, because nobody stands committed by a vote for inquiry, that, therefore, every resolution proposing an inquiry, no matter on what subject, must pass almost as a matter of course, and that, to discuss or oppose such resolutions, is unparliamentary. The true distinction seems to be this: Where information is desired as the basis of legislation, or where the policy of any measure, or the principles it involves, are really questionable, it was always proper to send the subject to a committee for investigation; but where all the

---

material facts are already known, and there is a fixed and settled opinion in respect to the policy to be pursued, inquiry was unnecessary, and ought to be refused. No one, he thought, could doubt the correctness of the position assumed by the gentleman from Missouri, that no inquiry ought ever to be instituted as to the expediency of doing "a great and acknowledged wrong." I do not mean, however, to intimate an opinion that such is the character of this resolution. The application of these rules to the case before us will decide my vote, and every Senator can apply them for himself to the decision of the question, whether the inquiry now called for should be granted or refused. With that decision, whatever it may be, I shall be content.

I have not risen, however, Mr. President, for the purpose of discussing the propriety of instituting the inquiry recommended by the resolution, but to offer a few remarks on another and much more important question, to which gentlemen have alluded in the course of this debate—I mean the policy which ought to be pursued in relation to the public lands. Every gentleman who has had a seat in Congress for the last two or three years, or even for the last two or three weeks, must be convinced of the great and growing importance of this question. More than half of our time has been taken up with the discussion of propositions connected with the public lands; more than half of our acts embrace provisions growing out of this fruitful source. Day after day the changes are rung on this topic, from the grave inquiry into the right of the new States to the absolute sovereignty and property in the soil, down to the grant of a pre-emption of a few quarter sections to actual settlers. In the language of a great orator in relation to another "vexed question," we may truly say, "that year after year we have been lashed round the miserable circle of occasional arguments and temporary expedients." No gentleman can fail to perceive that this is a question no longer to be evaded; it must be met—fairly and fearlessly met. A question that is pressed upon us in so many ways; that intrudes in such a variety of shapes; involving so deeply the feelings and interests of a large portion of the Union; insinuating itself into almost every question of public policy, and tinging the whole course of our legislation, cannot be put aside, or laid asleep. We cannot long avoid it; we must meet and overcome it, or it will overcome us. Let us, then, be prepared to encounter it in a spirit of wisdom and of justice, and endeavor to prepare our own minds and the minds of the people, for a just and enlightened decision. The object of the remarks I am about to offer is merely to call public attention to the question, to throw out a few crude and undigested thoughts, as food for reflection, in order to prepare the public mind for the adoption, at no distant day, of some fixed and settled policy in relation to the public lands. I believe that, out of the Western country, there is no subject in the whole range of our legislation less understood, and in relation to which there exists so many errors, and such unhappy prejudices and misconceptions.

There may be said to be two great parties in this country, who entertain very opposite opinions in relation to the character of the policy which the Government has heretofore pursued, in relation to the public lands, as well as to that which ought, hereafter, to be pursued. I propose, very briefly, to examine these opinions, and to throw out for consideration a few ideas in connexion with them. Adverting first, to the past policy of the Government, we find that one party, embracing a very large portion, perhaps at this time a majority of the people of the United States, in all quarters of the Union, entertain the opinion, that, in the settlement of the new States and the disposition of the public lands, Congress has pursued not only a highly just and liberal course, but one of extraordinary kindness and indulgence. We are regarded as having acted towards the new States in the spirit of parental weakness, granting to froward children, not only every thing that was reasonable and proper, but actually robbing ourselves of our property to gratify their insatiable desires. While the other party, embracing the entire West, insist that we have treated them, from the beginning, not like heirs of the estate, but in the spirit of a hard taskmaster, resolved to promote our selfish interests from the fruit of their labor. Now, sir, it is not my present purpose to investigate all the grounds on which these opposite opinions rest; I shall content myself with noticing one or two particulars, in relation to which it has long appeared to me, that the West have had some cause for complaint. I notice them now, not for the purpose of aggravating the spirit of discontent in relation to this subject, which is known to exist in that quarter—for I do not know that my voice will ever reach them—but to assist in bringing others to what I believe to be a just sense of the past policy of the Government in relation to this matter. In the creation and settlement of the new States, the plan has been invariably pursued, of selling out, from time to time, certain portions of the public lands, for the highest price that could possibly be obtained for them in open market, and, until a few years past, on long credits. In this respect, a marked difference is observable between our policy and that of every other nation that has ever attempted to establish colonies or create new States. Without pausing to examine the course pursued in this respect at earlier periods in the history of the world, I will come directly to the measures adopted in the first settlement of the new world, and will confine my observations entirely to North America. The English, the French, and the Spaniards, have successively planted their colonies here, and have all adopted the same policy, which, from the very beginning of the world, had always been found necessary in the settlement of new countries, viz: A free grant of lands, "without money and without price." We all know that the British colonies, at their first settlement here, (whether deriving title directly from the crown or the lords proprietors) received grants for considerations merely nominal.

The payment of "a penny," or a "pepper corn," was the stipulated price which our fathers along the whole Atlantic coast, now composing the old thirteen States, paid for their lands, and even when conditions, seemingly more substantial, were annexed to the grants; such for instance as "settlement and cultivation." These were considered as substantially complied with, by the cutting down a few trees and erecting a log cabin—the work of only a few days. Even these conditions very soon came to be considered as merely nominal, and were never required to be pursued, in order to vest in the grantee the fee simple of the soil. Such was the system under which this country was originally settled, and under which the thirteen colonies flourished and grew up to that early and vigorous manhood, which enabled them in a few years to achieve their independence; and I beg gentlemen to recollect, and note the fact, that, while they paid substantially nothing to the mother country, the whole profits of their industry were suffered to remain in their own hands. Now, what, let us inquire, was the reason which has induced all nations to adopt this system in the settlement of new countries? Can it be any other than this; that it affords the only certain means of building up in a wilderness, great and prosperous communities? Was not that policy founded on the universal belief, that the conquest of a new country, the driving out "the savage beasts and still more savage men," cutting down and subduing the forest, and encountering all the hardships and privations necessarily incident to the conversion of the wilderness into cultivated fields, was worth the fee simple of the soil? And was it not believed that the mother country found ample remuneration for the value of the land so granted in the additions to her power and the new sources of commerce and of wealth, furnished by prosperous and populous States? Now, sir, I submit to the candid consideration of gentlemen, whether the policy so diametrically opposite to this, which has been invariably pursued by the United States towards the new States in the West has been quite so just and liberal, as we have been accustomed to believe. Certain it is, that the British colonies to the north of us, and the Spanish and French to the south and west, have been fostered and reared up under a very different system. Lands, which had been for fifty or a hundred years open to every settler, without any charge beyond the expense of the survey, were, the moment they fell into the hands of the United States, held up for sale at the highest price that a public auction, at the most favorable seasons, and not unfrequently a spirit of the wildest competition, could produce, with a limitation that they should never be sold below a certain minimum price; thus making it, as it would seem, the cardinal point of our policy, not to settle the country, and facilitate the formation of new States, but to fill our coffers by coining our lands into gold.

Let us now consider for a moment, [said Mr. H.] the effect of these two opposite systems on the condition of a new State. I will take the State of Missouri, by way of example. Here is a large and fertile territory, coming into the possession of the United States without any inhabitants but Indians and wild beasts—a territory which is to be converted into a sovereign and independent State. You commence your operations by surveying and selling out a portion of the lands, on long credits, to actual settlers; and, as the population progresses, you go on, year after year, making additional sales on the same terms; and this operation is to be continued, as gentlemen tell us, for fifty or a hundred years at least, if not for all time to come. The inhabitants of this new State, under such a system, it is most obvious, must have commenced their operations under a load of debt, the annual payment of which must necessarily drain their country of the whole profits of their labor, just so long as this system shall last. This debt is due, not from some citizens of the State to others of the same State, (in which case the money would remain in the country) but it is due from the whole population of the State to the United States, by whom it is regularly drawn out, to be expended abroad. Sir, the amount of this debt has, in every one of the new States, actually constantly exceeded the ability of the people to pay, as is proved by the fact that you have been compelled, from time to time, in your great liberality, to extend the credits, and in some instances even to remit portions of the debt, in order to protect some land debtors from bankruptcy and total ruin. Now, I will submit the question to any candid man, whether, under this system, the people of a new State, so situated, could, by any industry or exertion, ever become rich and prosperous. What has been the consequence, sir? Almost universal poverty; no money; hardly a sufficient circulating medium for the ordinary exchanges of society; paper banks, relief laws, and the other innumerable evils, social, political, and moral, on which it is unnecessary for me to dwell. Sir, under a system by which a drain like this is constantly operating upon the wealth of the whole community, the country may be truly said to be afflicted with a curse which it has been well observed is more grievous to be borne "than the barrenness of the soil, and the inclemency of the seasons." It is said, sir, that we learn from our own misfortunes how to feel for the sufferings of others; and perhaps the present condition of the Southern States has served to impress more deeply on my own mind, the grievous oppression of a system by which the wealth of a country is drained off to be expended elsewhere. In that devoted region, sir, in which my lot has been cast, it is our misfortune to stand in that relation to the Federal Government, which subjects us to a taxation which it requires the utmost efforts of our industry to meet. Nearly the whole amount of our contributions is expended abroad: we stand towards the United States in the relation of Ireland to England. The fruits of our labor are drawn from us to enrich other and more favored sections of the Union; while, with one of the finest climates and the richest products in the world, furnishing, with one-third of the population, two-thirds of the whole exports of the country, we exhibit the extraordinary, the wonderful, and painful spectacle of a country enriched by the bounty of God, but blasted by the cruel policy of man. The rank grass grows in our streets; our very fields are scathed by the hand of injustice and oppression. Such, sir, though probably in a less degree, must have been the effects of a kindred policy on the fortunes of the West. It is not in the nature of things that it should have been otherwise.

Let gentlemen now pause and consider for a moment what would have been the probable effects of an opposite policy. Suppose, sir, a certain portion of the State of Missouri had been originally laid off and sold to actual settlers for the quit rent of a "peppercorn" or even for a small price to be paid down in cash. Then, sir, all the money that was made in the country would have remained in the country, and, passing from hand to hand, would, like rich and abundant streams flowing through the land, have adorned and fertilized the whole. Suppose, sir, that all the sales that have been effected had been made by the State, and that the proceeds had gone into the State treasury, to be returned back to the people in some of the various shapes in which a beneficent local government exerts its powers for the improvement of the condition of its citizens. Who can say how much of wealth and prosperity, how much of improvement in science and the arts, how much of individual and social happiness, would have been diffused throughout the land! But I have done with this topic.

In coming to the consideration of the next great question, What ought to be the future policy of the Government in relation to the Public Lands? we find the most opposite and irreconcileable opinions between the two parties which I have before described. On the one side it is contended that the public land ought to be reserved as a permanent fund for revenue, and future distribution among the States, while, on the other, it is insisted that the whole of these lands of right belong to, and ought to be relinquished to, the States in which they lie. I shall proceed to throw out some ideas in relation to the proposed policy, that the public lands ought to be reserved for these purposes. It may be a question, Mr. President, how far it is possible to convert the public lands into a great source of revenue. Certain it is, that all the efforts heretofore made for this purpose have most signally failed. The harshness, if not injustice of the proceeding, puts those upon whom it is to operate upon the alert, to contrive methods of evading and counteracting our policy, and hundreds of schemes, in the shape of appropriations of lands for Roads, Canals, and Schools, grants to actual settlers, &c. are resorted to for the purpose of controlling our operations. But, sir, let us take it for granted that we will be able, hereafter, to resist these applications, and to reserve the whole of your lands, for fifty or for a hundred years, or for all time to come, to furnish a great fund for permanent revenue, is it desirable that we should do so? Will it promote the welfare of the United States to have at our disposal a permanent treasury, not drawn from the pockets of the people, but to be derived from a source independent of them? Would it be safe to confide such a treasure to the keeping of our national rulers? to expose them to the temptations inseparable from the direction and control of a fund which might be enlarged or diminished almost at pleasure, without imposing burthens upon the people? Sir, I may be singular—perhaps I stand alone here in the opinion, but it is one I have long entertained, that one of the greatest safeguards of liberty is a jealous watchfulness on the part of the people, over the collection and expenditure of the public money—a watchfulness that can only be secured where the money is drawn by taxation directly from the pockets of the people. Every scheme or contrivance by which rulers are able to procure the command of money by means unknown to, unseen or unfelt by, the people, destroys this security. Even the revenue system of this country, by which the whole of our pecuniary resources are derived from indirect taxation, from duties upon imports, has done much to weaken the responsibility of our federal rulers to the people, and has made them, in some measure, careless of their rights, and regardless of the high trust committed to their care. Can any man believe, sir, that, if twenty-three millions per annum was now levied by direct taxation, or by an apportionment of the same among the States, instead of being raised by an indirect tax, of the severe effect of which few are aware, that the waste and extravagance, the unauthorized imposition of duties, and appropriations of money for unconstitutional objects, would have been tolerated for a single year? My life upon it, sir, they would not. I distrust, therefore, sir, the policy of creating a great permanent national treasury, whether to be derived from public lands or from any other source. If I had, sir, the powers of a magician, and could, by a wave of my hand, convert this capital into gold for such a purpose, I would not do it. If I could, by a mere act of my will, put at the disposal of the Federal Government any amount of treasure which I might think proper to name, I should limit the amount to the means necessary for the legitimate purposes of the Government. Sir, an immense national treasury would be a fund for corruption. It would enable Congress and the Executive to exercise a control over States, as well as over great interests in the country, nay, even over corporations and individuals—utterly destructive of the purity, and fatal to the duration of our institutions. It would be equally fatal to the sovereignty and independence of the States. Sir, I am one of those who believe that the very life of our system is the independence of the States, and that there is no evil more to be deprecated than the consolidation of this Government. It is only by a strict adherence to the limitations imposed by the constitution on the Federal Government, that this system works well, and can answer the great ends for which it was instituted. I am opposed, therefore, in any shape, to all unnecessary extension of the powers, or the influence of the Legislature or Executive of the Union over the States, or the people of the States; and, most of all, I am opposed to those partial distributions of favors, whether by legislation or appropriation, which has a direct and powerful tendency to spread corruption through the land; to create an abject spirit of dependence; to sow the seeds of dissolution; to produce jealousy among the different portions of the Union, and finally to sap the very foundations of the Government itself.

But, sir, there is another purpose to which it has been supposed the public lands can be applied, still more objectionable. I mean that suggested in a report from the Treasury Department, under the late administration, of so regulating the disposition of the public lands as to create and preserve, in certain quarters of the Union, a population suitable for conducting great manufacturing establishments. It is supposed, sir, by the advocates of the American System, that the great obstacle to the progress of manufactures in this country is the want of that low and degraded population which infest the cities and towns of Europe, who, having no other means of subsistence, will work for the lowest wages, and be satisfied with the smallest possible share of human enjoyment. And this difficulty it is proposed to overcome, by so regulating and limiting the sales of the public lands, as to prevent the drawing off this portion of the population from the manufacturing States. Sir, it is bad enough that Government should presume to regulate the industry of man; it is sufficiently monstrous that they should attempt, by arbitrary legislation, artificially to adjust and balance the various pursuits of society, and to "organize the whole labor and capital of the country." But what shall we say of the resort to such means for these purposes! What! create a manufactory of paupers, in order to enable the rich proprietors of woollen and cotton factories to amass wealth? From the bottom of my soul do I abhor and detest the idea, that the powers of the Federal Government should ever be prostituted for such purpose. Sir, I hope we shall act on a more just and liberal system of policy. The people of America are, and ought to be for a century to come, essentially an agricultural people; and I can conceive of no policy that can possibly be pursued in relation to the public lands, none that would be more "for the common benefit of all the States," than to use them as the means of furnishing a secure asylum to that class of our fellow-citizens, who in any portion of the country may find themselves unable to procure a comfortable subsistence by the means immediately within their reach. I would by a just and liberal system convert into great and flourishing communities, that entire class of persons, who would otherwise be paupers in your streets, and outcasts in society, and by so doing you will but fulfil the great trust which has been confided to your care.

Sir, there is another scheme in relation to the public lands, which, as it addresses itself to the interested and selfish feelings of our nature, will doubtless find many advocates. I mean the distribution of the public lands among the States, according to some ratio hereafter to be settled. Sir, this system of distribution is, in all its shapes, liable to many and powerful objections. I will not go into them at this time, because the subject has recently undergone a thorough discussion in the other House, and because, from present indications, we shall shortly have up the subject here. "Sufficient unto the day is the evil thereof." I come now to the claims set up by the West to these lands. The first is, that they have a full and perfect legal and constitutional right to all the lands within their respective limits. This claim was set up for the first time only a few years ago, and has been advocated on this floor by the gentlemen from Alabama and Indiana, with great zeal and ability. Without having paid much attention to this point, it has appeared to me that this claim is untenable. I shall not stop to enter into the argument further than to say, that, by the very terms of the grants under which the United States have acquired these lands, the absolute property in the soil is vested in them, and must, it would seem, continue so until the lands shall be sold or otherwise disposed of. I can easily conceive that it may be extremely inconvenient, nay, highly injurious to a State, to have immense bodies of land within her chartered limits, locked up from sale and settlement, withdrawn from the power of taxation, and contributing in no respect to her wealth or prosperity. But though this state of things may present strong claims on the Federal Government for the adoption of a liberal policy towards the new States, it cannot affect the question of legal or constitutional right. Believing that this claim, on the part of the West, will never be recognized by the Federal Government, I must regret that it has been urged, as I think it will have no other effect than to create a prejudice against the claims of the new States.

But, sir, there has been another much more fruitful source of prejudice. I mean the demands constantly made from the West, for partial appropriations of the public lands for local objects. I am astonished that gentlemen from the Western country have not perceived the tendency of such a course to rivet upon them for ever the system which they consider so fatal to their interests. We have been told, sir, in the course of this debate, of the painful and degrading office which the gentlemen from that quarter are compelled to perform, in coming here, year after year, in the character of petitioners for these petty favors. The gentleman from Missouri tells us, "if they were not goaded on by their necessities, they would never consent to be beggars at our doors." Sir, their course in this respect, let me say to those gentlemen, is greatly injurious to the West. While they shall continue to ask and gratefully to receive these petty and partial appropriations, they will be kept for ever in a state of dependence. Never will the Federal Government, or rather those who control its operations, consent to emancipate the West, by adopting a wise and just policy, looking to any final disposition of the public lands, while the people of the West can be kept in subjection and dependence, by occasional donations of those lands; and never will the Western States themselves assume their just and equal station among their sisters of the Union, while they are constantly looking up to Congress for favors and gratuities.

What, then, [asked Mr. H.] is our true policy on this important subject? I do not profess to have formed any fixed or settled opinions in relation to it. The time has not yet arrived when that question must be decided; and I must reserve for further lights, and more mature reflection, the formation of a final judgment. The public debt must be first paid. For this, these lands have been solemnly pledged to the public creditors. This done, which, if there be no interference with the Sinking Fund, will be effected in three or four years, the question will then be fairly open, to be disposed of as Congress and the country may think just and proper. Without attempting to indicate precisely what our policy ought then to be, I will, in the same spirit which has induced me to throw out the desultory thoughts which I have now presented to the Senate, suggest for consideration, whether it will not be sound policy, and true wisdom, to adopt a system of measures looking to the final relinquishment of these lands on the part of the United States, to the States in which they lie, on such terms and conditions as may fully indemnify us for the cost of the original purchase, and all the trouble and expense to which we may have been put on their account. Giving up the plan of using these lands forever as a fund either for revenue or distribution, ceasing to hug them as a great treasure, renouncing the idea of administering them with a view to regulate and control the industry and population of the States, or of keeping in subjection and dependence the States, or the people of any portion of the Union, the task will be comparatively easy of striking out a plan for the final adjustment of the land question on just and equitable principles. Perhaps, sir, the lands ought not to be entirely relinquished to any State until she shall have made considerable advances in population and settlement. Ohio has probably already reached that condition. The relinquishment may be made by a sale to the State, at a fixed price, which I will not say should be nominal; but certainly I should not be disposed to fix the amount so high as to keep the States for any length of time in debt to the United States. In short, our whole policy in relation to the public lands may perhaps be summed up in the declaration with which I set out, that they ought not to be kept and retained forever as a great treasure, but that they should be administered chiefly with a view to the creation, within reasonable periods, of great and flourishing communities, to be formed into free and independent States; to be invested in due season with the control of all the lands within their respective limits.

DANIEL WEBSTER

Daniel Webster was born in New Hampshire in 1782. He attended Phillips Exeter Academy, was graduated from Dartmouth College, and taught school in Maine before studying law and being admitted to the bar in 1805. He practiced law in Portsmouth, New Hampshire, and became involved in Federalist party politics. He was elected to Congress as a Federalist and served in the House of Representatives from 1813 to 1817. He was a prominent opponent of the Republican embargo and the War of 1812. In 1816, after being defeated for reelection, Webster moved to Boston. He became a successful constitutional lawyer, making nationalist arguments before the United States Supreme Court in *McCulloch v. Maryland* (1819), *Dartmouth College v. Woodward* (1819), and *Gibbons v. Ogden* (1824). Webster established his reputation as an orator in several patriotic addresses in the 1820s. He was elected to the House of Representatives, serving from 1823 to 1827, and was elected to the Senate in 1827. A spokesman for New England business interests, Webster opposed the protective tariff from 1816 to 1824. As the economic interests of New England manufacturers changed, however, he became a supporter of the protective tariff and voted for the tariff act of 1828. Webster supported Andrew Jackson in the nullification crisis, and opposed him on policy toward the Bank of the United States. As a critic of Jackson's exercise of the executive power, he became a leading Whig politician when that party came into existence in 1834. He was reelected to the Senate in 1833 and 1839, resigning in 1841 to become Secretary of State under William Henry Harrison and John Tyler. Elected to the Senate in 1844, Webster supported the Compromise of 1850. He served in the administration of Millard Fillmore as Secretary of State from 1850 until his death in 1852.

Speech of Mr. Webster,

of Massachusetts

[January 20, 1830]

The following resolution, moved by Mr. Foot, of Connecticut,
being under consideration:

*"Resolved, That the Committee on Public Lands be instructed
to inquire and report the quantity of the public lands
remaining unsold within each State and Territory, and
whether it be expedient to limit, for a certain period, the sales
of the public lands to such lands only as have heretofore been
offered for sale, and are now subject to entry at the minimum
price. And, also, whether the office of Surveyor General, and
some of the Land Offices, may not be abolished without
detriment to the public interest; or whether it be expedient to
adopt measures to hasten the sales, and extend more rapidly
the surveys of the public lands."*

M R. WEBSTER SAID, ON RISING, that nothing had been further from
his intention than to take any part in the discussion of this resolution. It proposed only an inquiry, on a subject of much importance, and
one in regard to which it might strike the mind of the mover, and of other
gentlemen, that inquiry and investigation would be useful. Although [said
Mr. W.] I am one of those who do not perceive any particular utility in instituting the inquiry, I have, nevertheless, not seen that harm would be
likely to result from adopting the resolution. Indeed, it gives no new powers, and hardly imposes any new duty on the Committee. All that the resolution proposes should be done, the Committee is quite competent,
without the resolution, to do, by virtue of its ordinary powers. But, sir, although I have felt quite indifferent about the passing of the resolution, yet

opinions were expressed yesterday on the general subject of the public lands, and on some other subjects, by the gentleman from South Carolina, so widely different from my own, that I am not willing to let the occasion pass without some reply. If I deemed the resolution, as originally proposed, hardly necessary, still less do I think it either necessary or expedient to adopt it, since a second branch has been added to it to-day. By this second branch, the Committee is to be instructed to inquire whether it be expedient to adopt measures to hasten the sales, and extend more rapidly the surveys of the public lands. Now, it appears that, in forty years, we have sold no more than about twenty millions of acres of public lands. The annual sales do not now exceed, and never have exceeded, one million of acres. A million a year is, according to our experience, as much as the increase of population can bring into settlement. And it appears also, that we have, at this moment, sir, surveyed and in the market, ready for sale, two hundred and ten millions of acres, or thereabouts. All this vast mass, at this moment, lies on our hands, for mere want of purchasers. Can any man, looking to the real interests of the country and the people, seriously think of inquiring whether we ought not still faster to hasten the public surveys, and to bring, still more and more rapidly, other vast quantities into the market? The truth is, that, rapidly as population has increased, the surveys have, nevertheless, outran our wants. There are more lands than purchasers. They are now sold at low prices, and taken up as fast as the increase of people furnishes hands to take them up. It is obvious, that no artificial regulation, no forcing of sales, no giving away of the lands even, can produce any great and sudden augmentation of population. The ratio of increase, though great, has yet its bounds. Hands for labor are multiplied only at a certain rate. The lands cannot be settled but by settlers; nor faster than settlers can be found. A system, if now adopted, of forcing sales at whatever prices, may have the effect of throwing large quantities into the hands of individuals, who would, in this way, in time, become themselves competitors with the Government in the sale of land. My own opinion has uniformly been, that the public lands should be offered freely, and at low prices; so as to encourage settlement and cultivation as rapidly as the increasing population of the country is competent to extend settlement and cultivation. Every actual settler should be able to buy good land, at a cheap rate; but, on the other hand, speculation by individuals, on a large scale, should not be encouraged, nor should the value of all lands, sold and unsold, be reduced to nothing, by throwing new and vast quantities into the market at prices merely nominal.

I now proceed, sir, to some of the opinions expressed by the gentleman from South Carolina. Two or three topics were touched by him, in regard to which he expressed sentiments in which I do not at all concur.

In the first place, sir, the honorable gentleman spoke of the whole course and policy of the Government towards those who have purchased and settled the public lands and seemed to think this policy wrong. He held it to have been, from the first, hard and rigorous; he was of opinion that the United States had acted towards those who had subdued the Western wilderness, in the spirit of a step-mother; that the public domain had been improperly regarded as a source of revenue; and that we had rigidly compelled payment for that which ought to have been given away. He said we ought to have followed the analogy of other Governments, which had acted on a much more liberal system than ours, in planting colonies. He dwelt particularly upon the settlement of America by colonists from Europe; and reminded us that their governments had not exacted from those colonists payment for the soil; with them, he said, it had been thought that the conquest of the wilderness was, itself, an equivalent for the soil; and he lamented that we had not followed the example, and pursued the same liberal course towards our own emigrants to the West.

Now, sir, I deny altogether, that there has been any thing harsh or severe in the policy of the Government towards the new States of the West. On the contrary, I maintain that it has uniformly pursued towards those States, a liberal and enlightened system, such as its own duty allowed and required, and such as their interests and welfare demanded. The Government has been no step-mother to the new States; she has not been careless of their interests, nor deaf to their requests; but from the first moment, when the Territories which now form those States, were ceded to the Union, down to the time in which I am now speaking, it has been the invariable object of the Government to dispose of the soil, according to the true spirit of the obligation under which it received it; to hasten its settlement and cultivation, as far and as fast as practicable; and to rear the new communities into equal and independent States, at the earliest moment of their being able, by their numbers, to form a regular government.

I do not admit sir, that the analogy to which the gentleman refers is just, or that the cases are at all similar. There is no resemblance between the cases upon which a statesman can found an argument. The original North American colonists either fled from Europe, like our New England ancestors, to avoid persecution, or came hither at their own charges, and often at the ruin of their fortunes, as private adventurers. Generally speaking, they derived neither succor nor protection from their governments at home. Wide, indeed, is the difference between those cases and ours. From the very origin of the Government, these Western lands, and the just protection of those who had settled or should settle on them, have been the leading objects in our policy, and have led to expenditures, both of blood and treasure, not inconsiderable; not indeed exceeding the importance of the object, and not yielded grudgingly or reluctantly certainly; but yet not inconsiderable, though necessary sacrifices, made for high proper ends. The Indian title has been extinguished at the expense of many millions. Is that nothing? There is still a much more material consideration. These colonists, if we are to call them so, in passing the Alleghany, did not pass beyond the care and protection of their own Government. Wherever they went, the public arm was still stretched over them. A parental Government at home was still ever mindful of their condition, and their wants; and nothing was spared which a just sense of their necessities required. Is it forgotten that it was one of the most arduous duties of the Government, in its earliest years, to defend the frontiers against the Northwestern Indians? Are the sufferings and misfortunes under Harmar and St. Clair not worthy to be remembered? Do the occurrences connected with these military efforts show an unfeeling neglect of Western interests? And here, sir, what becomes of the gentleman's analogy? What English armies accompanied our ancestors to clear the forests of a barbarous foe? What treasures of the exchequer were expended in buying up the original title to the soil? What governmental arm held its aegis over our fathers' heads, as they pioneered their way in the wilderness? Sir, it was not till General Wayne's victory, in 1794, that it could be said we had conquered the savages. It was not till that period that the Government could have considered itself as having established an entire ability to protect those who should undertake the conquest of the wilderness. And here, sir, at the epoch of 1794, let us pause, and survey the scene. It is now thirty-five years since that scene actually existed. Let us, sir, look back, and behold it. Over all that is now Ohio, there then stretched one vast wilderness, unbroken, except by two small spots of civilized culture, the one at Marietta, and the other at Cincinnati. At these little openings, hardly each a pin's point upon the map, the arm of the frontiersman had leveled the forest, and let in the sun. These little patches of earth, and themselves almost shadowed by the over hanging boughs of that wilderness, which had stood and perpetuated itself, from century to century, ever since the creation, were all that had then been rendered verdant by the hand of man. In an extent of hundreds and thousands of square miles, no other surface of smiling green attested the presence of civilization. The hunter's path crossed mighty rivers, flowing in solitary grandeur, whose sources lay in remote and unknown regions of the wilderness. It struck, upon the North, on a vast inland sea, over which the wintry tempests raged as on the ocean; all around was bare creation. It was a fresh, untouched, unbounded, magnificent wilderness! And, sir, what is it now? Is it imagination only, or can it possibly be fact, that presents such a change, as surprises and astonishes us, when we turn our eyes to what Ohio now is? Is it reality, or a dream, that, in so short a period even as thirty-five years, there has sprung up, on the same surface, an independent State, with a million of people? A million of inhabitants! an amount of population greater than that of all the cantons of Switzerland; equal to one third of all the people of the United States, when they undertook to accomplish their independence. This new member of the republic has already left far behind her a majority of the old States. She is now by the side of Virginia and Pennsylvania; and in point of numbers, will shortly admit no equal but New York herself. If, sir, we may judge of measures by their results, what lessons do these facts read us upon the policy of the Government? What inferences do they authorize, upon the general question of kindness, or unkindness? What convictions do they enforce, as to the wisdom and ability, on the one hand, or the folly and incapacity, on the other, of our general administration of Western affairs? Sir, does it not require some portion of self-respect in us, to imagine that, if our light had shone on the path of government, if our wisdom could have been consulted in its measures, a more rapid advance to strength and prosperity would have been experienced? For my own part, while I am struck with wonder at the success, I also look with admiration at the wisdom and foresight which originally arranged and prescribed the system for the settlement of the public domain. Its operation has been, without a moment's interruption, to push the settlement of the Western country to the full extent of our utmost means.

But, sir, to return to the remarks of the honorable member from South Carolina. He says that Congress has sold these lands, and put the money into the treasury, while other Governments, acting in a more liberal spirit, gave away their lands; and that we ought, also, to have given ours away. I shall not stop to state an account between our revenues derived from land, and our expenditures in Indian treaties and Indian wars. But, I must refer the honorable gentleman to the origin of our own title to the soil of these territories, and remind him that we received them on conditions, and under trusts, which would have been violated by giving the soil away. For compliance with those conditions, and the just execution of those trusts, the public faith was solemnly pledged. The public lands of the United States have been derived from four principal sources. First, Cessions made to the United States by individual States, on the recommendation or request of the old Congress. Second, The compact with Georgia, in 1802. Third, The purchase of Louisiana, in 1802. Fourth, The purchase of Florida, in 1819. Of the first class, the most important was the cession by Virginia, of all her right and title, as well of soil as jurisdiction, to all the territory within the limits of her charter, lying to the Northwest of the river Ohio. It may not be ill-timed to recur to the causes and occasions of this and the other similar grants.

When the war of the Revolution broke out, a great difference existed in different States in the proportion between people and Territory. The Northern and Eastern States, with very small surfaces, contained comparatively a thick population, and there was generally within their limits, no great quantity of waste lands belonging to the Government, or the Crown of England. On the contrary, there were in the Southern States, in Virginia and in Georgia for example, extensive public domains, wholly unsettled and belonging to the Crown. As these possessions would necessarily fall from the crown, in the event of a prosperous issue of the war, it was insisted that they ought to devolve on the United States, for the good of the whole. The war, it was argued, was undertaken, and carried on, at the common expense of all the colonies; its benefits, if successful, ought also to be common; and the property of the common enemy, when vanquished, ought to be regarded as the general acquisition of all. While yet the war was raging, it was contended that Congress ought to have the power to dispose of vacant and unpatented lands commonly called Crown lands, for defraying the expenses of the war, and for other public and general purposes. "Reason and justice," said the Assembly of New Jersey, in 1778, "must decide, that the property which existed in the Crown of Great Britain, previous to the present Revolution, ought now to belong to Congress, in trust for the use and benefit of the United States. They have fought and bled for it, in proportion to their respective abilities, and therefore the reward ought not to be predilectionally distributed. Shall such States as are shut out, by situation, from availing themselves of the least advantage from this quarter, be left to sink under an enormous debt, whilst others are enabled, in a short period, to replace all their expenditures from the hard earnings of the whole confederacy?"

Moved by these considerations, and these addresses, Congress took up the subject, and in September, 1780, recommended to the several States in the Union, having claims to Western Territory, to make liberal cessions of a portion thereof to the United States; and on the 10th of October, 1780, Congress resolved, "That any lands, so ceded in pursuance of their preceding recommendation, should be disposed of for the common benefit of the United States; should be settled and formed into distinct republican States, to become members of the Federal Union, with the same rights of sovereignty, freedom, and independence, as the other States; and that the lands should be granted or settled, at such times, and under such regulations, as should be agreed on by Congress." Again, in September, 1783, Congress passed another resolution, expressing the conditions on which cessions from States should be received; and in October following, Virginia made her cession, reciting the resolution, or act, of September preceding, and then transferring her title to her Northwestern Territory to the United States, upon the express condition "that the lands, so ceded, should be considered as a common fund for the use and benefit of such of the United States as had become or should become members of the confederation, Virginia inclusive, and should be faithfully and *bona fide* disposed of for that purpose, and for no other use or purpose whatsoever." The grants from other States were on similar conditions. Massachusetts and Connecticut both had claims to western lands, and both relinquished them to the United States in the same manner. These grants were all made on three substantial conditions or trusts: First, that the ceded territories should be formed into States, and admitted in due time into the union, with all the rights belonging to other States. Second, that the lands should form a common fund, to be disposed of for the general benefit of all the States. Third, that they should be sold and settled, at such time and in such manner as Congress should direct.

Now, sir, it is plain that Congress never has been, and is not now, at liberty to disregard these solemn conditions. For the fulfilment of all these trusts, the public faith was, and is, fully pledged. How, then, would it have been possible for Congress, if it had been so disposed, to give away these public lands? How could they have followed the example of other Governments, if there had been such, and considered the conquest of the wilderness an equivalent compensation for the soil? The States had looked to this territory, perhaps too sanguinely, as a fund out of which means were to come to defray the expenses of the war. It had been received as a fund— as a fund Congress had bound itself to apply it. To have given it away, would have defeated all the objects which Congress, and particular States, had had in view, in asking and obtaining the cession, and would have plainly violated the conditions which the ceding States attached to their own grants.

The gentleman admits that the lands cannot be given away until the national debt is paid, because, to a part of that debt they stand pledged. But this is not the original pledge. There is, so to speak, an earlier mortgage. Before the debt was funded, at the moment of the cession of the lands, and by the very terms of that cession, every State in the Union obtained an interest in them, as in a common fund. Congress has uniformly adhered to this condition. It has proceeded to sell the lands, and to realize as much from them as was compatible with the other trusts created by the same deeds of cession. One of these deeds of trust, as I have already said, was, that the lands should be sold and settled, "at such time and manners as Congress shall direct." The Government has always felt itself bound, in regard to sale and settlement, to exercise its own best judgment, and not to transfer the discretion to others. It has not felt itself at liberty to dispose of the soil, therefore, in large masses, to individuals, thus leaving to them the time and manner of settlement. It had stipulated to use its own judgment. If, for instance, in order to rid itself of the trouble of forming a system for the sale of those lands, and going into detail, it had sold the whole of what is now Ohio, in one mass, to individuals, or companies, it would clearly have departed from its just obligations. And who can now tell, or conjecture, how great would have been the evil of such a course? Who can say what mischiefs would have ensued, if Congress had thrown these territories into the hands of private speculation? Or who, on the other hand, can now foresee what the event would be, should the Government depart from the same wise course hereafter, and, not content with such constant absorption of the public lands as the natural growth of our population may accomplish, should force great portions of them, at nominal or very low prices, into private hands, to be sold and settled, as and when such holders might think would be most for their own interest? Hitherto, sir, I maintain Congress has acted wisely, and done its duty on this subject. I hope it will continue to do it. Departing from the original idea, so soon as it was found practicable and convenient, of selling by townships, Congress has disposed of the soil in smaller and still smaller portions, till, at length, it sells in parcels of no more than eighty acres; thus putting it into the power of every man in the country, however poor, but who has health and strength, to become a freeholder if he desires, not of barren acres, but of rich and fertile soil. The Government has performed all the conditions of the grant. While it has regarded the public lands as a common fund, and has sought to make what reasonably could be made of them, as a source of revenue, it has also applied its best wisdom to sell and settle them, as fast and as happily as possible; and whensoever numbers would warrant it, each territory has been successively admitted into the Union, with all the rights of an independent State. Is there, then, sir, I ask, any well founded charge of hard dealing; any just accusation for negligence, indifference, or parsimony, which is capable of being sustained against the Government of the country, in its conduct towards the new States? Sir, I think there is not.

But there was another observation of the honorable member, which, I confess, did not a little surprise me. As a reason for wishing to get rid of the public lands as soon as we could, and as we might, the honorable gentleman said, he wanted no permanent sources of income. He wished to see the time when the Government should not possess a shilling of permanent revenue. If he could speak a magical word, and by that word convert the whole capital into gold, the word should not be spoken. The administration of a fixed revenue, [he said] only consolidates the Government, and corrupts the people! Sir, I confess I heard these sentiments uttered on this floor not without deep regret and pain.

I am aware that these, and similar opinions, are espoused by certain persons out of the capitol, and out of this Government; but I did not expect so soon to find them here. Consolidation!—that perpetual cry, both of terror and delusion—consolidation! Sir, when gentlemen speak of the effects of a common fund, belonging to all the States, as having a tendency to consolidation, what do they mean? Do they mean, or can they mean, any thing more than that the Union of the States will be strengthened, by whatever continues or furnishes inducements to the people of the States to hold together? If they mean merely this, then, no doubt, the public lands as well as every thing else in which we have a common interest, tends to consolidation; and to this species of consolidation every true American ought to be attached; it is neither more nor less than strengthening the Union itself. This is the sense in which the framers of the constitution use the word consolidation; and in which sense I adopt and cherish it. They tell us, in the letter submitting the constitution to the consideration of the country, that, "in all our deliberations on this subject, we kept steadily in our view that which appears to us the greatest interest of every true American—the consolidation of our Union—in which is involved our prosperity, felicity, safety; perhaps our national existence. This important consideration, seriously and deeply impressed on our minds, led each State in the Convention to be less rigid, on points of inferior magnitude, than might have been otherwise expected."

This, sir, is General Washington's consolidation. This is the true constitutional consolidation. I wish to see no new powers drawn to the General Government; but I confess I rejoice in whatever tends to strengthen the bond that unites us, and encourages the hope that our Union may be perpetual. And, therefore, I cannot but feel regret at the expression of such opinions as the gentleman has avowed; because I think their obvious tendency is to weaken the bond of our connexion. I know that there are some persons in the part of the country from which the honorable member comes, who habitually speak of the Union in terms of indifference, or even of disparagement. The honorable member himself is not, I trust, and can never be, one of these. They significantly declare, that it is time to calculate the value of the Union; and their aim seems to be to enumerate, and to magnify all the evils, real and imaginary, which the Government under the Union produces.

The tendency of all these ideas and sentiments is obviously to bring the Union into discussion, as a mere question of present and temporary expediency; nothing more than a mere matter of profit and loss. The Union to be preserved, while it suits local and temporary purposes to preserve it; and to be sundered whenever it shall be found to thwart such purposes. Union, of itself, is considered by the disciples of this school as hardly a good. It is only regarded as a possible means of good; or on the other hand, as a possible means of evil. They cherish no deep and fixed regard for it, flowing from a thorough conviction of its absolute and vital necessity to our welfare. Sir, I deprecate and deplore this tone of thinking and acting. I deem far otherwise of the Union of the States; and so did the framers of the constitution themselves. What they said I believe; fully and sincerely believe, that the Union of the States is essential to the prosperity and safety of the States. I am a Unionist, and in this sense a National Republican. I would strengthen the ties that hold us together. Far, indeed, in my wishes, very far distant be the day, when our associated and fraternal stripes shall be severed asunder, and when that happy constellation under which we have risen to so much renown, shall be broken up, and be seen sinking, star after star, into obscurity and night!

Among other things, the honorable member spoke of the public debt. To that he holds the public lands pledged, and has expressed his usual earnestness for its total discharge. Sir, I have always voted for every measure for reducing the debt, since I have been in Congress. I wish it paid, because it is a debt; and, so far, is a charge upon the industry of the country, and the finances of the Government. But, sir, I have observed that, whenever the subject of the public debt is introduced into the Senate, a morbid sort of fervor is manifested in regard to it, which I have been sometimes at a loss to understand. The debt is not now large, and is in a course of most rapid reduction. A very few years will see it extinguished. Now I am not entirely able to persuade myself that it is not certain supposed incidental tendencies and effects of this debt, rather than its pressure and charge as a debt, that cause so much anxiety to get rid of it. Possibly it may be regarded as in some degree a tie, holding the different parts of the country together by considerations of mutual interest. If this be one of its effects, the effect itself is, in my opinion, not to be lamented. Let me not be misunderstood. I would not continue the debt for the sake of any collateral or consequential advantage, such as I have mentioned. I only mean to say, that that consequence itself is not one that I regret. At the same time, that if there are others who would, or who do regret it, I differ from them.

As I have already remarked, sir, it was one among the reasons assigned by the honorable member for his wish to be rid of the public lands altogether, that the public disposition of them, and the revenues derived from them, tends to corrupt the people. This, sir, I confess, passes my comprehension. These lands are sold at public auction, or taken up at fixed prices, to form farms and freeholds. Whom does this corrupt? According to the system of sales, a fixed proportion is every where reserved, as a fund for education. Does education corrupt? Is the schoolmaster a corrupter of youth? the spelling book, does it break down the morals of the rising generation? and the Holy Scriptures, are they fountains of corruption? or if, in the exercise of a provident liberality, in regard to its own property as a great landed proprietor, and to high purposes of utility towards others, the Government gives portions of these lands to the making of a canal, or the opening of a road, in the country where the lands themselves are situated, what alarming and overwhelming corruption follows from all this? Can there be nothing pure in government, except the exercise of mere control? Can nothing be done without corruption, but the imposition of penalty and restraint? Whatever is positively beneficent, whatever is actively good, whatever spreads abroad benefits and blessings which all can see, and all can feel, whatever opens intercourse, augments population, enhances the value of property, and diffuses knowledge—must all this be rejected and

25

reprobated as a dangerous and obnoxious policy, hurrying us to the double ruin of a Government, turned into despotism by the mere exercise of acts of beneficence, and of a people, corrupted, beyond hope of rescue, by the improvement of their condition?

The gentleman proceeded, sir, to draw a frightful picture of the future. He spoke of the centuries that must elapse, before all the lands could be sold, and the great hardships that the States must suffer while the United States reserved to itself, within their limits, such large portions of soil, not liable to taxation. Sir, this is all, or mostly, imagination. If these lands were leasehold property, if they were held by the United States on rent, there would be much in the idea. But they are wild lands, held only till they can be sold; reserved no longer than till somebody will take them up, at low prices. As to their not being taxed, I would ask whether the States themselves, if they owned them, would tax them before sale? Sir, if in any case any State can show that the policy of the United States retards her settlement, or prevents her from cultivating the lands within her limits, she shall have my vote to alter that policy. But I look upon the public lands as a public fund, and that we are no more authorized to give them away gratuitously than to give away gratuitously the money in the treasury. I am quite aware that the sums drawn annually from the Western States make a heavy drain upon them, but that is unavoidable. For that very reason, among others, I have always been inclined to pursue towards them a kind and most liberal policy; but I am not at liberty to forget, at the same time, what is due to others, and to the solemn engagements under which the Government rests.

I come now to that part of the gentleman's speech which has been the main occasion of my addressing the Senate. The East! the obnoxious, the rebuked, the always reproached East! We have come in, sir, on this debate, for even more than a common share of accusation and attack. If the honorable member from South Carolina was not our original accuser, he has yet recited the indictment against us, with the air and tone of a public prosecutor. He has summoned us to plead on our arraignment; and he tells us we are charged with the crime of a narrow and selfish policy; of endeavoring to restrain emigration to the West, and, having that object in view, of maintaining a steady opposition to Western measures and Western interests. And the cause of all this narrow and selfish policy, the gentleman finds in the tariff. I think he called it the accursed policy of the tariff. This policy, the gentleman tells us, requires multitudes of dependent laborers, a population of paupers, and that it is to secure these at home that the East opposes whatever may induce to Western emigration. Sir, I rise to defend the East. I rise to repel, both the charge itself, and the cause assigned for it. I deny that the East has, at any time, shown an illiberal policy towards the West. I pronounce the whole accusation to be without the least foundation in any facts, existing either now, or at any previous time. I deny it in the general, and I deny each and all its particulars. I deny the sum total, and I deny the detail. I deny that the East has ever manifested hostility to the West, and I deny that she has adopted any policy that would naturally have led her in such a course. But the tariff! the tariff!! Sir, I beg to say, in regard to the East, that the original policy of the tariff is not hers, whether it be wise or unwise. New England is not its author. If gentlemen will recur to the tariff of 1816, they will find that that was not carried by New England votes. It was truly more a Southern than an Eastern measure. And what votes carried the tariff of 1824? Certainly, not those of New England. It is known to have been made matter of reproach, especially against Massachusetts, that she would not aid the tariff of 1824; and a selfish motive was imputed to her for that also. In point of fact, it is true that she did, indeed, oppose the tariff of 1824. There were more votes in favor of that law in the House of Representatives, not only in each of a majority of the Western States, but even in Virginia herself also, than in Massachusetts. It was literally forced upon New England; and this shows how groundless, how void of all probability any charge must be, which imputes to her hostility to the growth of the Western States, as naturally flowing from a cherished policy of her own. But leaving all conjectures about causes and motives, I go at once to the fact, and I meet it with one broad, comprehensive, and emphatic negative. I deny that, in any part of her history, at any period of the Government, or in relation to any leading subject, New England has manifested such hostility as is charged upon her. On the contrary, I maintain that, from the day of the cession of the territories by the States to Congress, no portion of the country has acted, either with more liberality or more intelligence, on the subject of the Western lands in the new States, than New England. This statement, though strong, is no stronger than the strictest truth will warrant. Let us look at the historical facts. So soon as the cessions were obtained, it became necessary to make provision for the government and disposition of the territory—the country was to be governed. This, for the present, it was obvious, must be by some territorial system of administration. But the soil, also, was to be granted and settled. Those immense regions, large enough almost for an empire, were to be appropriated to private ownership. How was this best to be done? What system for sale and disposition should be adopted? Two modes for conducting the sales presented themselves; the one a Southern, and the other a Northern mode. It would be tedious, sir, here, to run out these different systems into all their distinctions, and to contrast their opposite results. That which was adopted was the Northern system, and is that which we now see in successful operation in all the new States. That which was rejected, was the system of warrants, surveys, entry, and location; such as prevails South of the Ohio. It is not necessary to extend these remarks into invidious comparisons. This last system is that which, as has been emphatically said, has shingled over the country to which it was applied with so many conflicting titles and claims. Every body acquainted with the subject knows how easily it leads to speculation and litigation—two great calamities in a new country. From the system actually established, these evils are banished. Now, sir, in effecting this great measure, the first important measure on the whole subject, New England acted with vigor and effect, and the latest posterity of those who settled Northwest of the Ohio, will have reason to remember, with gratitude, her patriotism and her wisdom. The system adopted was her own system. She knew, for she had tried and proved its value. It was the old fashioned way of surveying lands, before the issuing of any title papers, and then of inserting accurate and precise descriptions in the patents or grants, and proceeding with regular reference to metes and bounds. This gives to original titles, derived from Government, a certain and fixed character; it cuts up litigation by the roots, and the settler commences his labors with the assurance that he has a clear title. It is easy to perceive, but not easy to measure, the importance of this in a new country. New England gave this system to the West; and while it remains, there will be spread over all the West one monument of her intelligence in matters of government, and her practical good sense.

At the foundation of the constitution of these new Northwestern States, we are accustomed, sir, to praise the lawgivers of antiquity; we help to perpetuate the fame of Solon and Lycurgus; but I doubt whether one single law of any lawgiver, ancient or modern, has produced effects of more distinct, marked, and lasting character, than the ordinance of '87. That instrument was drawn by Nathan Dane, then, and now, a citizen of Massachusetts. It was adopted, as I think I have understood, without the slightest alteration; and certainly it has happened to few men, to be the authors of a political measure of more large and enduring consequence. It fixed, forever, the character of the population in the vast regions Northwest of the Ohio, by excluding from them involuntary servitude. It impressed on the soil itself, while it was yet a wilderness, an incapacity to bear up any other than free men. It laid the interdict against personal servitude, in original compact, not only deeper than all local law, but deeper, also, than all local constitutions. Under the circumstances then existing, I look upon this original and seasonable provision, as a real good attained. We see its consequences at this moment, and we shall never cease to see them, perhaps, while the Ohio shall flow. It was a great and salutary measure of prevention. Sir, I should fear the rebuke of no intelligent gentleman of Kentucky, were I to ask whether, if such an ordinance could have been applied to his own State, while it yet was a wilderness, and before Boone had passed the gap of the Alleghany, he does not suppose it would have contributed to the ultimate greatness of that Commonwealth? It is, at any rate, not to be doubted, that, where it did apply, it has produced an effect not easily to be described, or measured in the growth of the States, and the extent and increase of their population. Now, sir, this great measure again was carried by the North, and by the North alone. There were, indeed, individuals elsewhere favorable to it; but it was supported, as a measure, entirely by the votes of the Northern States. If New England had been governed by the narrow and selfish views now ascribed to her, this very measure was, of all others, the best calculated to thwart her purposes. It was, of all things, the very means of rendering certain a vast emigration from her own population to the West. She looked to that consequence only to disregard it. She deemed the regulation a most useful one to the States that would spring up on the territory, and advantageous to the country at large. She adhered to the principle of it perseveringly, year after year, until it was finally accomplished.

Leaving, then, sir, these two great and leading measures, and coming down to our own times, what is there in the history of recent measures of Government that exposes New England to this accusation of hostility to Western interests? I assert, boldly, that in all measures conducive to the welfare of the West, since my acquaintance here, no part of the country has manifested a more liberal policy. I beg to say, sir, that I do not state this with a view of claiming for her any special regard on that account. Not at all. She does not place her support of measures on the ground of favor conferred; far otherwise. What she has done has been consonant to her view of the general good, and, therefore, she has done it. She has sought to make no gain of it; on the contrary, individuals may have felt, undoubtedly, some natural regret at finding the relative importance of their own

States diminished by the growth of the West. But New England has regarded that as in the natural course of things, and has never complained of it. Let me see, sir, any one measure favorable to the West which has been opposed by New England, since the Government bestowed its attention to these Western improvements. Select what you will, if it be a measure of acknowledged utility, I answer for it, it will be found that not only were New England votes for it, but that New England votes carried it. Will you take the Cumberland Road? Who has made that? Will you take the Portland Canal? Whose support carried that bill? Sir, at what period beyond the Greek kalends could these measures, or measures like these, have been accomplished, had they depended on the votes of Southern gentlemen? Why, sir, we know that we must have waited till the constitutional notions of those gentlemen had undergone an entire change. Generally speaking, they have done nothing, and can do nothing. All that has been effected has been done by the votes of reproached New England. I undertake to say, sir, that if you look to the votes on any one of these measures, and strike out from the list of ayes the names of New England members, it will be found that in every case the South would then have voted down the West, and the measure would have failed. I do not believe that any one instance can be found where this is not strictly true. I do not believe that one dollar has been expended for these purposes beyond the mountains, which could have been obtained without cordial co-operation and support from New England. Sir, I put the gentleman to the West itself. Let gentlemen who have sat here ten years, come forth and declare by what aids, and by whose votes, they have succeeded in measures deemed of essential importance to their part of the country. To all men of sense and candor, in or out of Congress, who have any knowledge on the subject, New England may appeal, for refutation of the reproach now attempted to be cast upon her in this respect. I take liberty to repeat that I make no claim, on behalf of New England, or on account of that which I have not stated. She does not profess to have acted out of favor: for it would not have become her so to have acted. She solicits for no especial thanks; but, in the consciousness of having done her duty in these things, uprightly and honestly, and with a fair and liberal spirit, be assured she will repel, whenever she thinks the occasion calls for it, an unjust and groundless imputation of partiality and selfishness.

The gentleman alluded to a report of the late Secretary of the Treasury, which, according to his reading or construction of it, recommended what he called the tariff policy, or a branch of that policy; that is, the restraining of emigration to the West, for the purpose of keeping hands at home to carry on the manufactures. I think, sir, that the gentleman misapprehended the meaning of the Secretary, in the interpretation given to his remarks. I understand him only as saying, that, since the low price of lands at the West acts as a constant and standing bounty to agriculture, it is, on that account, the more reasonable to provide encouragement for manufactures. But, sir, even if the Secretary's observation were to be understood as the gentleman understands it, it would not be a sentiment borrowed from any New England source. Whether it be right or wrong, it does not originate in that quarter.

In the course of these remarks, I have spoken of the supposed desire, on the part of the Atlantic States, to check, or at least not to hasten, Western emigration, as a narrow policy. Perhaps I ought to have qualified the expression; because, sir, I am now about to quote the opinions of one to whom I would impute nothing narrow. I am now about to refer you to the language of a gentleman, of much and deserved distinction, now a member of the other House, and occupying a prominent situation there. The gentlemen, sir, is from South Carolina. In 1825, a debate arose, in the House of Representatives, on the subject of the Western road. It happened to me to take some part in that debate. I was answered by the honorable gentleman to whom I have alluded; and I replied. May I be pardoned, sir, if I read a part of this debate?

"The gentleman from Massachusetts has urged, [said Mr. McDuffie] as one leading reason why the Governments should make roads to the West, that these roads have a tendency to settle the public lands; that they increase the inducements to settlement; and that this is a national object. Sir, I differ entirely from his views on the subject. I think that the public lands are settling quite fast enough; that our people need want no stimulus to urge them thither but want rather a check, at least on that artificial tendency to Western settlement which we have created by our own laws.

"The gentleman says that the great object of Government, with respect to those lands, is not to make them a source of revenue, but to get them settled. What would have been thought of this argument in the old thirteen States? It amounts to this, that these States are to offer a bonus for their own impoverishment—to create a vortex to swallow up our floating population. Look, sir, at the present aspect of the Southern States. In no part of Europe will you see the same indications of decay. Deserted villages, houses falling into ruin, impoverished lands thrown out of cultivation. Sir, I believe that, if the public lands had never been sold, the aggregate amount of the national wealth would have been greater at this moment. Our population, if concentrated in the old States, and not ground down by tariffs, would have been more prosperous and more wealthy. But every inducement has been held out to them to settle in the West, until our population has become sparse; and then the effects of this sparseness are now to be counteracted by another artificial system. Sir, I say if there is any object worthy the attention of this Government, it is a plan which shall limit the sale of the public lands. If those lands were sold according to their real value, be it so. But while the Government continues, as it now does, to give them away, they will draw the population of the older States, and still farther increase the effect which is already distressingly felt, and which must go to diminish the value of all those States possess. And this, sir, is held out to us as a motive for granting the present appropriation. I would not, indeed, prevent the formation of roads on these considerations, but I certainly would not encourage it. Sir, there is an additional item in the account of the benefits which this Government has conferred on the Western States. It is the sale of the public lands at the minimum price. At this moment we are selling to the people of the West, lands at one dollar and twenty-five cents an acre, which are fairly worth fifteen, and which would sell at that price if the markets were not glutted.

"Mr. W. observed, in reply, that the gentleman from South Carolina had mistaken him if he supposed that it was his wish so to hasten the sales of the public lands, as to throw them into the hands of purchasers who would sell again. His idea only went as far as this: that the price should be fixed as low as not to prevent the settlement of the lands, yet not so low as to tempt speculators to purchase. Mr. W. observed that he could not at all concur with the gentleman from South Carolina, in wishing to restrain the laboring classes of population in the Eastern States from going to any part of our territory, where they could better their condition; nor did he suppose that such an idea was any where entertained. The observations of the gentleman had opened to him new views of policy on their subject, and he thought he now could perceive why some of our States continued to have such bad roads; it must be for the purpose of preventing people from going out of them. The gentleman from South Carolina supposes that, if our population had been confined to the old thirteen States, the aggregate wealth of the country would have been greater than it now is. But, sir, it is an error that the increase of the aggregate of the national wealth is the object chiefly to be pursued by Government. The distribution of the national wealth is an object quite as important as its increase. He was not surprised that the old States were not increasing in population so fast as was expected (for he believed nothing like a decrease was pretended) should be an idea by no means agreeable to gentlemen from those States; we are all reluctant in submitting to the loss of relative importance: but this was nothing more than the natural condition of a country densely populated in one part, and possessing, in another, a vast tract of unsettled lands. The plan of the gentleman went to reverse the order of nature, vainly expecting to retain men within a small and comparatively unproductive territory, 'who have all the world before them where to choose.' For his own part, he was in favor of letting population take its own course; he should experience no feeling of mortification if any of his constituents liked better to settle on the Kansas, or the Arkansas, or the Lord knows where, within our territory; let them go, and be happier, if they could. The gentleman says our aggregate of wealth would have been greater, if our population had been restrained within the limits of the old States; but does he not consider population to be wealth? And has not this been increased by the settlement of a new and fertile country? Such a country presents the most alluring of all prospects to a young and laboring man; it gives him a freehold; it offers to him weight and respectability in society; and, above all, it presents to him a prospect of a permanent provision for his children. Sir, these are inducements which never were resisted, and never will be; and, were the whole extent of country filled with population up to the Rocky Mountains, these inducements would carry that population forward to the shores of the Pacific Ocean. Sir, it is in vain to talk; individuals will seek their own good, and not any artificial aggregate of the national wealth. A young, enterprising, and hardy agriculturist can conceive of nothing better to him than plenty of good, cheap land."

Sir, with the reading of these extracts, I leave the subject. The Senate will bear me witness that I am not accustomed to allude to local opinions, nor to compare nor contrast different portions of the country. I have often suffered things to pass which I might, properly enough, have considered as deserving a remark, without any observation. But I have felt it my duty, on this occasion, to vindicate the State I represent from charges and imputations on her public character and conduct, which I know to be undeserved and unfounded. If advanced elsewhere, they might be passed, perhaps, without notice. But whatever is said here, is supposed to be entitled to public regard, and to deserve public attention; it derives importance and dignity from the place where it is uttered. As a true Representative of the State which has sent me here, it is my duty, and a duty which I shall fulfil, to place her history and her conduct, her honor and her character, in their just and proper light, so often as I think an attack is made upon her so respectable as to deserve to be repelled.

Speech of Mr. Hayne,

of South Carolina

[January 25, 1830]

The motion of Mr. Webster to postpone indefinitely,
the resolution proposed by Mr. Foot, concerning the
public lands, being under consideration, Mr. Hayne
addressed the Chair as follows:

MR. HAYNE BEGAN BY SAYING that when he took occasion, two days ago,
to throw out some ideas with respect to the policy of the Government
in relation to the public lands, nothing certainly could have been further from
his thoughts than that he should be compelled again to throw himself upon
the indulgence of the Senate. Little did I expect [said Mr. H.] to be called
upon to meet such as was yesterday urged by the gentleman from Massachusetts [Mr. WEBSTER.] Sir, I questioned no man's opinions; I impeached no
man's motives; I charged no party, or State, or section of country, with hostility to any other; but ventured, I thought in a becoming spirit, to put forth my
own sentiments in relation to a great national question of public policy. Such
was my course. The gentleman from Missouri, [Mr. BENTON] it is true, had
charged upon the Eastern States an early and continued hostility towards the
West, and referred to a number of historical facts and documents in support
of that charge. Now, sir, how have these different arguments been met? The
honorable gentleman from Massachusetts, after deliberating a whole night
upon his course, comes into this chamber to vindicate New England, and; instead of making up his issue with the gentleman from Missouri, on the
charges which he had preferred, chooses to consider me as the author of
those charges; and, losing sight entirely of that gentleman, selects me as his
adversary, and pours out all the vials of his mighty wrath upon my devoted
head. Nor is he willing to stop there. He goes on to assail the institutions and
policy of the South, and calls in question the principles and conduct of the
State which I have the honor to represent. When I find a gentleman of mature age and experience, of acknowledged talents and profound sagacity, pur-

suing a course like this, declining the contest offered from the West, and making war upon the unoffending South, I must believe, I am bound to believe, he has some object in view that he has not ventured to disclose. Why is this? [asked Mr. H.] Has the gentleman discovered in former controversies with the gentleman from Missouri, that he is overmatched by that Senator? And does he hope for an easy victory over a more feeble adversary? Has the gentleman's distempered fancy been disturbed by gloomy forebodings of "new alliances to be formed," at which he hinted? Has the ghost of the murdered Coalition come back, like the ghost of Banquo, to "sear the eye-balls" of the gentleman, and will it not "down at his bidding?" Are dark visions of broken hopes, and honors lost forever, still floating before his heated imagination? Sir, if it be his object to thrust me between the gentleman from Missouri and himself, in order to rescue the East from the contest it has provoked with the West, he shall not be gratified. Sir, I will not be dragged into the defence of my friend from Missouri. The South shall not be forced into a conflict not its own. The gentleman from Missouri is able to fight his own battles. The gallant West needs no aid from the South to repel any attack which may be made on them from any quarter. Let the gentleman from Massachusetts controvert the facts and arguments of the gentleman from Missouri—if he can; and if he win the victory, let him wear its honors: I shall not deprive him of his laurels.

The gentleman from Massachusetts, in reply to my remarks on the injurious operation of our land system on the prosperity of the West, pronounced an extravagant eulogium on the paternal care which the Government had extended towards the West, to which he attributed all that was great and excellent in the present condition of the new States. The language of the gentleman on this topic fell upon my ears like the almost forgotten tones of the tory leaders of the British Parliament, at the commencement of the American Revolution. They, too, discovered, that the colonies had grown great under the fostering care of the mother country; and I must confess, while listening to the gentleman, I thought the appropriate reply to his argument was to be found in the remark of a celebrated orator, made on that occasion: "They have grown great in spite of your protection."

The gentleman, in commenting on the policy of the Government, in relation to the new States, has introduced to our notice a certain Nathan Dane, of Massachusetts, to whom he attributes the celebrated ordinance of '87, by which he tells us, "slavery was forever excluded from the new States north of the Ohio." After eulogizing the wisdom of this provision, in terms of the most extravagant praise, he breaks forth in admiration of the greatness of Nathan Dane—and great, indeed, he must be, if it be true, as stated by the Senator from Massachusetts, that "he was greater than Solon and Lycurgus, Minos, Numa Pompilius, and all the legislators and philosophers of the world," ancient and modern. Sir, to such high authority it is certainly my duty, in a becoming spirit of humility, to submit. And yet, the gentleman will pardon me when I say, that it is a little unfortunate for the fame of this great legislator, that the gentleman from Missouri should have proved that he was not the author of the ordinance of '87, on which the Senator from Massachusetts has reared so glorious a monument to his name. Sir, I doubt not the Senator will feel some compassion for our ignorance, when I tell him, that so little are we acquainted with the modern great men of New England, that, until he informed us yesterday, that we possessed a Solon and a Lycurgus in the person of Nathan Dane, he was only known to the South as a member of a celebrated assembly called and known by the name of "the Hartford Convention." In the proceedings of that assembly, which I hold in my hand, (at page 19) will be found, in a few lines, the history of Nathan Dane; and a little further on, there is conclusive evidence of that ardent devotion to the interests of the new States, which it seems, has given him a just claim to the title of "Father of the West." By the 2d resolution of the "Hartford Convention," it is declared, "that it is expedient to attempt to make provision for restraining Congress in the exercise of an unlimited power to make new States, and admitting them into the Union." So much for Nathan Dane, of Beverly, Massachusetts.

In commenting upon my views in relation to the public lands, the gentleman insists that it being one of the conditions of the grants, that these lands should be applied to "the common benefit of all the States, they must always remain a fund for revenue," and adds, "they must be treated as so much treasure." Sir, the gentleman could hardly find language strong enough to convey his disapprobation of the policy which I had ventured to recommend to the favorable consideration of the country. And what, sir, was that policy, and what is the difference between that gentleman and myself, on this subject? I threw out the idea, that the public lands ought not to be reserved forever as "a great fund for revenue;" that they ought not to be "treated as a great treasure;" but that the course of our policy should rather be directed towards the creation of new States, and building up great and flourishing communities.

Now, Sir, will it be believed, by those who now hear me, and who listened to the gentleman's denunciation of my doctrines yesterday, that a book then lay open before him, nay, that he held it in his hand, and read from it certain passages of his own speech, delivered to the House of Representatives, in 1825, in which speech he himself contended for the very doctrines I had advocated, and almost in the same terms. Here is the speech of the Hon. Daniel Webster, contained in the first volume of Gales and Seaton's Register of Debates, (p. 251) delivered in the House of Representatives, on the 18th January, 1825, in a debate on the Cumberland Road—the very debate from which the Senator read yesterday. I shall read from this celebrated speech two passages, from which it will appear that, both as to the past and the future policy of the Government in relation to the public lands, the gentleman from Massachusetts maintained, in 1825, substantially the same opinions which I have advanced, but which he now so strongly reprobates. I said, sir, that the system of credit sales, by which the West had been kept constantly in debt to the United States, and by which their wealth was drained off to be expended elsewhere, had operated injuriously on their prosperity. On this point the gentleman from Massachusetts, in January, 1825, expressed himself thus: "There could be no doubt, if gentlemen looked at the money received into the treasury from the sale of the public lands to the West, and then looked to the whole amount expended by Government, (even including the whole of what was laid out for the army) the latter must be allowed to be very inconsiderable, and there must be a constant drain of money from the West to pay for the public lands. It might, indeed, be said that this was no more than the refluence of capital which had previously gone over the mountains. Be it so. Still its practical effect was to produce inconvenience, if not distress, by absorbing the money of the people."

I contended that the public lands ought not to be treated merely as "a fund for revenue," that they ought not to be hoarded "as a great treasure." On this point the Senator expressed himself thus: "Government, he believed, had received eighteen or twenty millions of dollars from the public lands, and it was with the greatest satisfaction he adverted to the change which had been introduced in the mode of paying for them; yet he could never think the national domain was to be regarded as any great source of revenue. The great object of the Government in respect to those lands, was not so much the money derived from their sale, as it was the getting of them settled. What he meant to say was, that he did not think they ought to hug that domain as a great treasure, which was to enrich the exchequer."

Now, Mr. President, it will be seen that the very doctrines which the gentleman so indignantly abandons, were urged by him in 1825; and if I had actually borrowed my sentiments from those which he then avowed, I could not have followed more closely in his footsteps. Sir, it is only since the gentleman quoted this book, yesterday, that my attention has been turned to the sentiments he expressed in 1825, and, if I had remembered them, I might possibly have been deterred from uttering sentiments here which, it might well be supposed, I had borrowed from that gentleman.

In 1825, the gentleman told the world, that the public lands "ought not to be treated as a treasure." He now tells us, that "they must be treated as so much treasure." What the deliberate opinion of the gentleman on this subject may be, belongs not to me to determine; but, I do not think he can, with the shadow of justice or propriety, impugn my sentiments, while his own recorded opinions are identical with my own. When the gentleman refers to the conditions of the grants under which the United States have acquired these lands, and insists that, as they are declared to be "for the common benefit of all the States," they can only be treated as so much treasure, I think he has applied a rule of construction too narrow for the case. If, in the deeds of cession, it has been declared that the grants were intended for "the common benefit of all the States," it is clear, from other provisions, that they were not intended merely as so much property: for, it is expressly declared that the object of the grants is the erection of new States; and the United States, in accepting the trust, bind themselves to facilitate the foundation of these States, to be admitted into the Union with all the rights and privileges of the original States. This, sir, was the great end to which all parties looked, and it is by the fulfilment of this high trust, that "the common benefit of all the States" is to be best promoted. Sir, let me tell the gentleman, that, in the part of the country in which I live, we do not measure political benefits by the money standard. We consider as more valuable than gold—liberty, principle, and justice. But, sir, if we are bound to act on the narrow principles contended for by the gentleman, I am wholly at a loss to conceive how he can reconcile his principles with his own practice. The lands are, it seems, to be treated "as so much treasure," and must be applied to the "common benefit of all the States." Now, if this be so, whence does he derive the right to appropriate them for partial and local objects? How can the gentleman consent to vote away immense bodies of these lands—for canals in Indiana and Illinois, to the Louisville and Portland Canal, to Kenyon College in Ohio, to Schools for the Deaf and Dumb, and other objects of a similar description? If grants of this character can fairly be considered as made "for the common benefit of all the States," it can only be because all the States are interested in the welfare of each—a principle which, carried to the full extent, destroys all distinction between local and national objects and is certainly broad enough to embrace the principle for which I have ventured to contend. Sir, the true difference between us, I take to be this: the gentleman wishes to treat the public lands as a great treasure, just as so much money in the treasury, to be applied to all objects, constitutional and unconstitutional, to which the public money is now constantly applied. I consider it as a sacred trust, which we ought to fulfil, on the principles for which I have contended.

The Senator from Massachusetts has thought proper to present in strong contrast the friendly feelings of the East towards the West, with sentiments of an opposite character displayed by the South in relation to appropriations for internal improvement. Now, sir, let it be recollected that the South have made no professions; I have certainly made none in their behalf, of regard for the West. It has been reserved to the gentleman from Massachusetts, while he vaunts his own personal devotion to Western interests, to claim for the entire section of country to which he belongs, an ardent friendship for the West, as manifested by their support of the system of Internal Improvement, while he casts in our teeth the reproach that the South has manifested hostility to Western interests in opposing appropriations for such objects. That gentleman, at the same time, acknowledged that the South entertains constitutional scruples on this subject. Are we then, sir, to understand, that the gentleman considers it a just subject of reproach, that we respect our oaths, by which we are bound "to preserve, protect, and defend, the constitution of the United States?" Would the gentleman have us manifest our love to the West by trampling under foot our constitutional scruples? Does he not perceive, if the South is to be reproached with unkindness to the West, in voting against appropriations, which the gentleman admits, they could not vote for without doing violence to their constitutional opinions, that he exposes himself to the question, whether, if he was in our situation, he could vote for these appropriations, regardless of his scruples? No, sir, I will not do the gentleman so great injustice. He has fallen into this error from not having duly weighed the force and effect of the reproach which he was endeavoring to cast upon the South. In relation to the other point, the friendship manifested by New England towards the West in their support of the system of internal improvement, the gentleman will pardon me for saying that I think he is equally unfortunate in having introduced that topic. As that gentleman has forced it upon us, however, I cannot suffer it to pass unnoticed. When the gentleman tells us that the appropriations for Internal Improvement in the West would, in almost every instance, have failed, but for New England votes, he has forgotten to tell us the when, the how, and the wherefore, this new-born zeal for the West sprung up in the bosom of New England. If we look back only a few years, we will find, in both Houses of Congress, a uniform and steady opposition, on the part of the members from the Eastern States, generally, to all appropriations of this character. At the time I became a member of this House, and for some time afterwards, a decided majority of the New England Senators were opposed to the very measures which the Senator from Massachusetts tells us they now cordially support. Sir, the journals are before me, and an examination of them will satisfy every gentleman of that fact.

It must be well known to every one whose experience dates back as far as 1825, that, up to a certain period, New England was generally opposed to appropriations for internal improvements in the West. The gentleman from Massachusetts may be himself an exception, but if he went for the system before 1825, it is certain that his colleagues did not go with him. In the session of 1824 and 1825, however, (a memorable era in the history of this country) a wonderful change took place in New England, in relation to the Western interests. Sir, an extraordinary union of sympathies and of interests was then effected, which brought the East and the West into close alliance. The book from which I have before read contains the first public annunciation of that happy reconciliation of conflicting interests, personal and political, which brought the East and West together, and locked in a fraternal embrace the two great orators of the East and West. Sir, it was on the 18th January, 1825, while the result of the Presidential election, in the House of Representatives, was still doubtful, while the whole country was looking with intense anxiety to that Legislative hall where the mighty drama was so soon to be acted, that we saw the leaders of two great parties in the House and in the nation "taking sweet counsel together," and in a celebrated debate on the Cumberland Road fighting side by side for Western interests. It was on that memorable occasion that the Senator from Massachusetts held out the white flag to the West, and uttered those liberal sentiments, which he, yesterday, so indignantly repudiated. Then it was that that happy union between the members of the celebrated coalition was consummated, whose immediate issue was a President from one quarter of the Union, with the succession (as it was supposed) secured to another. The "American System," before, a rude, disjointed, and misshapen mass, now assumed form and consistency; then it was, that it became "the settled policy of the Government" that this system should be so administered as to create a reciprocity of interest, and a reciprocal distribution of Government favors—East and West, (the Tariff and Internal Improvements)—while the South—yes, sir, the impracticable South, was to be "out of your protection." The gentleman may boast as much as he pleases of the friendship of New England for the West, as displayed in their support of Internal Improvement; but, when he next introduces that topic, I trust that he will tell us when that friendship commenced, how it was brought about, and why it was established. Before I leave this topic, I must be permitted to say that the true character of the policy now pursued by the gentleman from Massachusetts and his friends, in relation to appropriations of land and money, for the benefit of the West, is, in my estimation, very similar to that pursued by Jacob of old towards his brother Esau; "it robs them of their birthright for a mess of pottage."

The gentleman from Massachusetts, in alluding to a remark of mine, that, before any disposition could be made of the public lands, the national debt (for which they stand pledged) must be first paid, took occasion to intimate "that the extraordinary fervor which seems to exist in a certain quarter [meaning the South, sir] for the payment of the debt, arises from a disposition to weaken the ties which bind the people to the Union." While the gentleman deals us this blow, he professes an ardent desire to see the debt speedily extinguished. He must excuse me, however, for feeling some distrust on that subject until I find this disposition manifested by something stronger than professions. I shall look for acts, decided and unequivocal acts: for the performance of which an opportunity will very soon (if I am not greatly mistaken) be afforded. Sir, if I were at liberty to judge of the course which that gentleman would pursue, from the principles which he has laid down in relation to this matter, I should be bound to conclude that he will be found acting with those with whom it is a darling object to prevent the payment of the public debt. He tells us he is desirous of paying the debt, "because we are under an obligation to discharge it." Now, sir, suppose it should happen that the public creditors, with whom we have contracted the obligation, should release us from it, so far as to declare their willingness to wait for payment for fifty years to come, provided only the interest shall be punctually discharged. The gentleman from Massachusetts will then be released from the obligation which now makes him desirous of paying the debt; and, let me tell the gentleman, the holders of the stock will not only release us from this obligation, but they will implore, nay, they will even pay us not to pay them. But, adds the gentleman, "so far as the debt may have an effect in binding the debtors to the country, and thereby serving as a link to hold the States together, he would be glad that it should exist forever." Surely then, sir, on the gentleman's own principles, he must be opposed to the payment of the debt.

Sir, let me tell that gentleman that the South repudiates the idea that a pecuniary dependence on the Federal Government is one of the legitimate means of holding the States together. A moneyed interest in the Government is essentially a base interest; and just so far as it operates to bind the feelings of those who are subjected to it to the Government; just so far as it operates in creating sympathies and interests that would not otherwise exist; is it opposed to all the principles of free government, and at war with virtue and patriotism. Sir, the link which binds the public creditors, as such, to their country, binds them equally to all governments, whether arbitrary or free. In a free government, this principle of abject dependence, if extended through all the ramifications of society, must be fatal to liberty. Already have we made alarming strides in that direction. The entire class of manufacturers, the holders of stocks, with their hundreds of millions of capital, are held to the Government by the strong link of pecuniary interests; millions of people, entire sections of country, interested, or believing themselves to be so, in the public lands, and the public treasure, are bound to the Government by the expectation of pecuniary favors. If this system is carried much further, no man can fail to see that every generous motive of attachment to the country will be destroyed, and in its place will spring up those low, grovelling, base, and selfish feelings which bind men to the footstool of a despot by bonds as strong and as enduring as those which attach them to free institutions. Sir, I would lay the foundation of this Government in the affections of the People; I would teach them to cling to it by dispensing equal justice, and, above all, by securing the "blessings of liberty to themselves and to their posterity."

The honorable gentleman from Massachusetts has gone out of his way to pass a high eulogium on the State of Ohio. In the most impassioned tones of eloquence, he described her majestic march to greatness. He told us that, having already left all the other States far behind, she was now passing by Virginia, and Pennsylvania, and about to take her station by the side of New York. To all this, sir, I was disposed most cordially to respond. When, however, the gentleman proceeded to contrast the State of Ohio with Kentucky, to the disadvantage of the latter, I listened to him with regret; and when he proceeded further to attribute the great, and, as he supposed, acknowledged superiority of the former in population, wealth, and general prosperity, to the policy of Nathan Dane, of Massachusetts, which had secured to the people of Ohio (by the ordinance of '87) a population of freemen, I will confess that my feelings suffered a revulsion, which I am now unable to describe in any language sufficiently respectful towards the gentleman from Massachusetts. In contrasting the State of Ohio with Kentucky, for the purpose of pointing out the superiority of the former, and of attributing that superiority to the existence of slavery, in the one State, and its absence in the other, I thought I could discern the very spirit of the Missouri question intruded into this debate, for objects best known to the gentleman himself. Did that gentleman, sir, when he formed the determination to cross the southern border, in order to invade the State of South Carolina, deem it prudent, or necessary, to enlist under his banners the prejudices of the world, which like Swiss troops, may be engaged in any cause, and are prepared to serve under any leader? Did he desire to avail himself of those remorseless allies, the passions of mankind, of which it may be more truly said, than of the savage tribes of the wilderness, "that their known rule of warfare is an indiscriminate slaughter of all ages, sexes, and conditions?" Or was it supposed, sir, that, in a premeditated and unprovoked attack upon the South, it was advisable to begin by a gentle admonition of our supposed weakness, in order to prevent us from making that firm and manly resistance, due to our own character, and our dearest interest? Was the significant hint of the weakness of slave-holding States, when contrasted with the superior strength of free States—like the glare of the weapon half drawn from its scabbard—intended to enforce the lessons of prudence and of patriotism, which the gentleman had resolved, out of his abundant generosity, gratuitously to bestow upon us [said Mr. H.] The impression which has gone abroad, of the weakness of the South, as connected with the slave question, exposes us to such constant attacks, has done us so much injury, and is calculated to produce such infinite mischiefs, that I embrace the occasion presented by the remarks of the gentleman from Massachusetts, to declare that we are ready to meet the question promptly and fearlessly. It is one from which we are not disposed to shrink, in whatever form or under whatever circumstances it may be pressed upon us. We are ready to make up the issue with the gentleman, as to the influence of slavery on individual and national character—on the prosperity and greatness, either of the United States, or of particular States. Sir, when arraigned before the bar of public opinion, on this charge of slavery, we can stand up with conscious rectitude, plead not guilty, and put ourselves upon God and our country.

Sir, we will not stop to inquire whether the black man, as some philosophers have contended, is of an inferior race, nor whether his color and condition are the effects of a curse inflicted for the offences of his ancestors. We deal in no abstractions. We will not look back to inquire whether our fathers were guiltless in introducing slaves into this country. If an inquiry should ever be instituted in these matters, however, it will be found that the profits of the slave trade were not confined to the South. Southern ships and Southern sailors were not the instruments of bringing slaves to the shores of America, nor did our merchants reap the profits of that "accursed traffic." But, sir, we will pass over all this. If slavery, as it now exists in this country, be an evil, we of the present day found it ready made to our hands. Finding our lot cast among a people, whom God had manifestly committed to our care, we did not sit down to speculate on abstract questions of theoretical liberty. We met it as a practical question of obligation and duty. We resolved to make the best of the situation in which Providence had placed us, and to fulfil the high trust which had developed upon us as the owners of slaves, in the only way in which such a trust could be fulfilled, without spreading misery and ruin throughout the land. We found that we had to deal with a people whose physical, moral, and intellectual habits and character, totally disqualified them from the enjoyment of the blessings of freedom. We could not send them back to the shores from whence their fathers had been taken; their numbers forbade the thought, even if we did not know that their condition here is infinitely preferable to what it possibly could be among the barren sands and savage tribes of Africa; and it was wholly irreconcileable with all our notions of humanity to tear asunder the tender ties which they had formed among us, to gratify the feelings of a false philanthropy. What a commentary on the wisdom, justice, and humanity, of the Southern slave owner is presented by the example of certain benevolent associations and charitable individuals elsewhere. Shedding weak tears over sufferings which had existence only in their own sickly imaginations, these "friends of humanity" set themselves systematically to work to seduce the slaves of the South from their masters. By means of missionaries and political tracts, the scheme was in a great measure successful. Thousands of these deluded victims of fanaticism were seduced into the enjoyment of freedom in our Northern cities. And what has been the consequence? Go to these cities now, and ask the question. Visit the dark and narrow lanes, and obscure recesses, which have been assigned by common consent as the abodes of those outcasts of the world—the free people of color. Sir, there does not exist, on the face of the whole earth, a population so poor, so wretched, so vile, so loathsome, so utterly destitute of all the comforts, conveniences, and decencies of life, as the unfortunate blacks of Philadelphia, and New York, and Boston. Liberty has been to them the greatest of calamities, the heaviest of curses. Sir, I have had some opportunities of making comparisons between the condition of the free negroes of the North and the slaves of the South, and the comparison has left not only an indelible impression of the superior advantages of the latter, but has gone far to reconcile me to slavery itself. Never have I felt so forcibly that touching description, "the foxes have holes, and the birds of the air have nests, but the son of man hath not where to lay his head," as when I have seen this unhappy race, naked and houseless, almost starving in the streets, and abandoned by all the world. Sir, I have seen in the neighborhood of one of the most moral, religious, and refined cities of the North, a family of free blacks, driven to the caves of the rock, and there obtaining a precarious subsistence from charity and plunder.

When the gentleman from Massachusetts adopts and reiterates the old charge of weakness as resulting from slavery, I must be permitted to call for the proof of those blighting effects which he ascribes to its influence. I suspect that when the subject is closely examined, it will be found that there is not much force even in the plausible objection of the want of physical power in slave holding States. The power of a country is compounded of its population and its wealth; and, in modern times, where, from the very form and structure of society, by far the greater portion of the people must, even during the continuance of the most desolating wars, be employed in the cultivation of the soil, and other peaceful pursuits, it may be well doubted whether slave holding States, by reason of the superior value of their productions, are not able to maintain a number of troops in the field, fully equal to what could be supported by States with a larger white population, but not possessed of equal resources.

It is a popular error to suppose, that in any possible state of things, the people of a country could ever be called out *en masse,* or that a half, or a third, or even a fifth part of the physical force of any country could ever be brought into the field. The difficulty is not to procure men, but to provide the means of maintaining them; and in this view of the subject, it may be asked whether the Southern States are not a source of strength and power, and not to weakness, to the country? whether they have not contributed, and are not now contributing, largely, to the wealth and prosperity of every State in the Union? From a statement which I hold in my hand, it appears that, in ten years (from 1818 to 1827 inclusive) the whole amount of the domestic exports of the United States was five hundred and twenty-one millions eight hundred and eleven thousand and forty-five dollars. Of which, three articles, the product of slave labor, namely, cotton, rice, and tobacco, amounted to three hundred and thirty-nine millions two hundred and three thousand two hundred and thirty-two dollars; equal to about two-thirds of the whole. It is not true, as has been supposed, that the advantages of this labor is confined almost exclusively to the Southern States. Sir, I am thoroughly convinced that, at this time, the States North of the Potomac actually derive greater profits from the labor of our slaves, than we do ourselves. It appears, from our public documents, that, in seven years, (from 1821 to 1827 inclusive) the six Southern States exported to the amount of one hundred and ninety millions three hundred and thirty-seven thousand two hundred and eighty-one dollars; and imported to the value of fifty-five millions six hundred and forty-six thousand three hundred and one dollars. Now, the difference between these two sums, near one hundred and forty millions of dollars, passed through the hands of the Northern merchants, and enabled them to carry on their commercial operations with all the world. Such part of these goods as found its way back to our hands, came charged with the duties, as well as the profits of the merchant, the ship owner, and a host of others, who found employment in carrying on these immense exchanges; and, for such part as was consumed at the North, we received in exchange Northern manufactures, charged with an increased price, to cover all the taxes which the Northern consumer had been compelled to pay on the imported article. It will be seen, therefore, at a glance, how much slave labor has contributed to the wealth and prosperity of the United States; and how largely our Northern brethren have participated in the profits of that labor. Sir, on this subject I will quote an authority which will, I doubt not, be considered by the Senator from Massachusetts as entitled to high respect. It is from the great father of the American System—honest Mathew Carey; no great friend, it is true, at this time, to Southern rights and Southern interests, but not the worst authority, on that account, on the point in question.

Speaking of the relative importance to the Union of the Southern and the Eastern States, Mathew Carey, in the sixth edition of his "Olive Branch," page 278, after exhibiting a number of statistical tables, to show the decided superiority, of the former, thus proceeds:

"But I am tired of this investigation. I sicken for the honor of the human species. What idea must the world form of the arrogance of the pretensions on the one side, [the East] and of the folly and weakness of the rest of the Union, to have so long suffered them to pass without exposure and detection? The naked fact is, that the demagogues in the Eastern States, not satisfied with deriving all the benefit from the Southern section of the Union that they would from so many wealthy colonies; with making princely fortunes by the carriage and exportation of its bulky and valuable productions, and supplying it with their own manufactures, and the productions of Europe, and the East and West Indies, to an enormous amount, and at an immense profit, have uniformly treated it with outrage, insult, and injury. And, regardless of their vital interests, the Eastern States were lately courting their own destruction, by allowing a few restless, turbulent men, to lead them blindfold to a separation, which was pregnant with their certain ruin. Whenever that event takes place they sink into insignificance. If a separation were desirable to any part of the Union, it would be to the Middle and Southern States, particularly the latter, who have been so long harassed with the complaints, the restlessness, the turbulence, and the ingratitude, of the Eastern States, that their patience has been tried almost beyond endurance. 'Jeshurun waxed fat and kicked;' and he will be severely punished for his kicking, in the event of a dissolution of the Union."

Sir, I wish it to be distinctly understood that I do not adopt these sentiments as my own. I quote them to show that very different sentiments have prevailed in former times, as to the weakness of the slave holding States, from those which now seem to have become fashionable in certain quarters. I know it has been supposed, by certain ill informed persons, that the South exists only by the countenance and protection of the North. Sir, this is the idlest of all idle and ridiculous fancies that ever entered into the mind of man. In every State of this Union, except one, the free white population actually preponderates; while in the British West India Islands, where the average white population is less than ten per cent. of the whole, the slaves are kept in entire subjection. It is preposterous to suppose that the Southern States could even find the smallest difficulty in this respect. On this subject, as in all others, we ask nothing of our Northern brethren but to "let us alone;" leave us to the undisturbed management of our domestic concerns, and the direction of our own industry, and we will ask no more. Sir, all our difficulties on this subject have arisen from interference from abroad, which has disturbed, and may again disturb, our domestic tranquillity, just so far as to bring down punishment upon the heads of the unfortunate victims of a fanatical and mistaken humanity.

There is a spirit, which, like the father of evil, is constantly "walking to and fro about the earth, seeking whom it may devour." It is the spirit of false philanthropy. The persons whom it possesses do not indeed throw themselves into the flames, but they are employed in lighting up the torches of discord throughout the community. Their first principle of action is to leave their own affairs, and neglect their own duties, to regulate the affairs and the duties of others. Theirs is the task to feed the hungry and clothe the naked, of other lands, whilst they thrust the naked, famished, and shivering beggar from their own doors; to instruct the heathen, while their own children want the bread of life. When this spirit infuses itself into the bosom of a statesman, (if one so possessed can be called a statesman) it converts him at once into a visionary enthusiast. Then it is that he indulges in golden dreams of national greatness and prosperity. He discovers that "liberty is power;" and not content with vast schemes of improvement at home, which it would bankrupt the treasury of the world to execute, he flies to foreign lands, to fulfil obligations to "the human race," by inculcating the principles of "political and religious liberty," and promoting the "general welfare" of the whole human race. It is a spirit which has long been busy with the slaves of the South, and is even now displaying itself in vain efforts to drive the Government from its wise policy in relation to the Indians. It is this spirit which has filled the land with thousands of wild and visionary projects, which can have no effect but to waste the energies and dissipate the resources of the country. It is the spirit, of which the aspiring politician dexterously avails himself, when, by inscribing on his banner the magical words "liberty and philanthropy," he draws to his support that entire class of persons who are ready to bow down at the very names of their idols.

But, sir, whatever difference of opinion may exist as to the effect of slavery on national wealth and prosperity, if we may trust to experience, there can be no doubt that it has never yet produced any injurious effects on individual or national character. Look through the whole history of the country, from the commencement of the Revolution down to the present hour; where are there to be found brighter examples of intellectual and moral greatness, than have been exhibited by the sons of the South? From the Father of his Country, down to the distinguished chieftain who has been elevated, by a grateful people, to the highest office in their gift, the interval is filled up by a long line of orators, of statesmen, and of heroes, justly entitled to rank among the ornaments of their country, and the benefactors of mankind. Look at "the Old Dominion," great and magnanimous

Virginia, "whose jewels are her sons." Is there any State in this Union which has contributed so much to the honor and welfare of the country? Sir, I will yield the whole question; I will acknowledge the fatal effects of slavery upon character; if any one can say that, for noble disinterestedness, ardent love of country, exalted virtue, and a pure and holy devotion to liberty, the people of the Southern States have ever been surpassed by any in the world. I know, sir, that this devotion to liberty has sometimes been supposed to be at war with our institutions; but it is in some degree the result of those very institutions. Burke, the most philosophical of statesmen, as he was the most accomplished of orators, well understood the operation of this principle, in elevating the sentiments and exalting the principles of the people in slaveholding States. I will conclude my remarks on this branch of the subject, by reading a few passages from his speech "on moving his resolutions for conciliation with the colonies, the 22d of March, 1775."

"There is a circumstance attending the Southern colonies, which makes the spirit of liberty still more high and haughty than those to the Northward. It is, that in Virginia and the Carolinas they have a vast multitude of slaves. Where this is the case, in any part of the world, those who are free are by far the most proud and jealous of their freedom. Freedom is to them not only an enjoyment, but a kind of rank and privilege. Not seeing there, as in countries where it is a common blessing, and as broad and general as the air, that it may be united with much abject toil, with great misery, with all the exterior of servitude, liberty looks among them like something more noble and liberal. I do not mean, sir, to commend the superior morality of this sentiment, which has, at least, as much of pride as virtue in it; but I cannot alter the nature of man. The fact is so, and these people of the Southern colonies are much more strongly, and with a higher and more stubborn spirit, attached to liberty, than those to the Northward. Such were all the ancient commonwealths; such were our Gothic ancestors; such, in our days, were the Poles; and such will be all masters of slaves who are not slaves themselves. In such a people, the haughtiness of domination, combined with the spirit of freedom, fortifies it, and renders it invincible."

In the course of my former remarks, I took occasion to deprecate, as one of the greatest of evils, the consolidation of this Government. The gentleman takes alarm at the sound. "Consolidation," like the "tariff," grates upon his ear. He tells us, "we have heard much, of late, about consolidation; that it is the rallying word for all who are endeavoring to weaken the Union by adding to the power of the States." But consolidation, says the gentleman, was the very object for which the Union was formed; and in support of that opinion, he read a passage from the address of the President of the Convention to Congress (which he assumes to be authority on his side of the question.) But, sir, the gentleman is mistaken. The object of the framers of the constitution, as disclosed in that address, was not the consolidation of the Government, but "the consolidation of the Union." It was not to draw power from the States, in order to transfer it to a great National Government, but, in the language of the constitution itself, "to form a more perfect union;" and by what means? By "establishing justice," "promoting domestic tranquillity," and "securing the blessings of liberty to ourselves and our posterity." This is the true reading of the constitution. But, according to the gentleman's reading, the object of the constitution was to consolidate the Government, and the means would seem to be, the promotion of injustice, causing domestic discord, and depriving the States and the people "of the blessings of liberty" forever. The gentleman boasts of belonging to the party of national republicans. National republicans! a new name, sir, for a very old thing. The national republicans of the present day were the federalists of '98, who became federal republicans during the war of 1812, and were manufactured into national republicans somewhere about the year 1825. As a party, (by whatever name distinguished) they have always been animated by the same principles, and have kept steadily in view a common object—the consolidation of the Government.

Sir, the party to which I am proud of having belonged from the very commencement of my political life to the present day, were the democrats of '98. Anarchists, anti-federalists, revolutionists, I think they were sometimes called. They assumed the name of democratic republicans in 1812, and have retained their name and their principles up to the present hour. True to their political faith, they have always, as a party, been in favor of limitations of power; they have insisted that all powers not delegated to the Federal Government are reserved, and have been constantly struggling, as they are now struggling, to preserve the rights of the States, and prevent them from being drawn into the vortex, and swallowed up by one great consolidated Government. Sir, any one acquainted with the history of parties in this country will recognize in the points now in dispute between the Senator from Massachusetts and myself, the very grounds which have, from the beginning, divided the two great parties in this country, and which (call these parties by what names you will, and amalgamate them as you may) will divide them forever. The true distinction between those parties is laid down in a celebrated manifesto issued by the convention of the federalists of Massachusetts, assembled in Boston, in February, 1824, on the occasion of organizing a party opposition to the re-election of Governor Eustis. The gentleman will recognize this as "the canonical book of political scripture," and it instructs us, that "when the American colonies redeemed themselves from British bondage, and became so many independent nations, they proposed to form a national union." (Not a federal union, sir, but a national union.) "Those who were in favor of a union of the States in this form became known by the name of federalists; those who wanted no union of the States, or disliked the proposed form of union, became known by the name of anti-federalists. By means which need not be enumerated, the anti-federalists became, after the expiration of twelve years, our national rulers; and, for a period of sixteen years, until the close of Mr. Madison's administration in 1817, continued to exercise the exclusive direction of our public affairs." Here, sir, is the true history of the origin, rise, and progress, of the party of national republicans, who date back to the very origin of the Government, and who, then, as now, chose to consider the constitution as having created not a federal but a national union; who regarded "consolidation" as no evil, and who doubtless consider it "a consummation devoutly to be wished," to build up a great "central Government," "one and indivisible." Sir, there have existed, in every age and every country, two distinct orders of men—the lovers of freedom, and the devoted advocates of power. The same great leading principles, modified only by peculiarities of manners, habits, and institutions, divided parties in the ancient republics, animated the whigs and tories of Great Britain, distinguished in our own times the liberals and ultras of France, and may be traced even in the bloody struggles of unhappy Spain. Sir, when the gallant Riego, who devoted himself, and all that he possessed, to the liberties of his country, was dragged to the scaffold, followed by the tears and lamentations of every lover of freedom throughout the world, he perished amidst the deafening cries of "Long live the absolute King!" The people whom I represent are the descendants of those who brought with them to this country, as the most precious of their possessions, "an ardent love of liberty;" and while that shall be preserved, they will always be found manfully struggling against the consolidation of the Government, as the worst of evils.

The Senator from Massachusetts, in alluding to the tariff, becomes quite facetious. He tells us that "he hears of nothing but tariff! tariff! tariff! and if a word could be found to rhyme with it, he presumes it would be celebrated in verse, and set to music." Sir, perhaps the gentleman, in mockery of our complaints, may be himself disposed to sing the praises of the tariff in doggerel verse to the tune of "Old Hundred." I am not at all surprised, however, at the aversion of the gentleman to the very name of tariff. I doubt not that it must always bring up some very unpleasant recollections to his mind. If I am not greatly mistaken, the Senator from Massachusetts was a leading actor at a great meeting got up in Boston in 1820, against the tariff. It has generally been supposed that he drew up the resolutions adopted by that meeting, denouncing the tariff system as unequal, oppressive, and unjust; and, if I am not much mistaken, denying its constitutionality. Certain it is that the gentleman made a speech on that occasion in support of those resolutions, denouncing the system in no very measured terms; and if my memory serves me, calling its constitutionality in question. I regret that I have not been able to lay my hands on those proceedings, but I have seen them, and I cannot be mistaken in their character. At that time, sir, the Senator from Massachusetts entertained the very sentiments in relation to the tariff which the South now entertains. We next find the Senator from Massachusetts expressing his opinion on the tariff as a member of the House of Representatives from the city of Boston in 1824. On that occasion, sir, the gentleman assumed a position which commanded the respect and admiration of his country. He stood forth the powerful and fearless champion of free trade. He met, in that conflict, the advocates of restriction and monopoly, and they "fled from before his face." With a profound sagacity, a fulness of knowledge, and a richness of illustration that has never been surpassed, he maintained and established the principles of commercial freedom on a foundation never to be shaken. Great indeed was the victory achieved by the gentleman on that occasion; most striking the contrast between the clear, forcible, and convincing arguments by which he carried away the understandings of his hearers, and the narrow views and wretched sophistry of another distinguished orator, who may be truly said to have "held up his farthing candle to the sun." Sir, the Senator from Massachusetts, on that, (the proudest day of his life) like a mighty giant bore away upon his shoulders the pillars of the temple of error and delusion, escaping himself unhurt, and leaving its adversaries overwhelmed in its ruins. Then it was that he erected to free trade a beautiful and enduring monument, and "inscribed the marble with his name." It is with pain and regret that I now go forward to the next great era in the political life of that gentleman, when he was found upon this floor, supporting, advocating, and finally voting for the tariff of 1828—that "bill of abominations." By that act, sir, the Senator from Massachusetts has destroyed the labors of his whole life, and given a wound to the cause of free trade, never to be healed. Sir, when I recollect the position which that gentleman once occupied, and that which he now holds in public estimation, in relation to this subject, it is not at all surprising that the tariff should be hateful to his ears. Sir, if I had erected to my own fame so proud a monument as that which the gentleman built up in 1824, and I could have been tempted to destroy it with my own hands, I should hate the voice that should ring "the accursed tariff" in my ears. I doubt not the gentleman feels very much in relation to the tariff as a certain knight did to "instinct," and with him would be disposed to exclaim—

"Ah! no more of that Hal, an thou lov'st me."

But, to be serious, what are we, of the South, to think of what we have heard this day? The Senator from Massachusetts tells us that the tariff is not an Eastern measure, and treats it as if the East had no interest in it. The Senator from Missouri insists it is not a Western measure, and that it has done no good to the West. The South comes in, and in the most earnest manner represents to you, that this measure, which we are told "is of no value to the East or the West," is "utterly destructive of our interests." We represent to you, that it has spread ruin and devastation through the land, and prostrated our hopes in the dust. We solemnly declare that we believe the system to be wholly unconstitutional, and a violation of the compact between the States and the Union, and our brethren turn a deaf ear to our complaints, and refuse to relieve us from a system "which not enriches them, but makes us poor indeed." Good God! has it come to this? Do gentlemen hold the feelings and wishes of their brethren at so cheap a rate, that they refuse to gratify them at so small a price? Do gentlemen value so lightly the peace and harmony of the country, that they will not yield a measure of this description to the affectionate entreaties and earnest remonstrances of their friends? Do gentlemen estimate the value of the Union at so low a price, that they will not even make one effort to bind the States together with the cords of affection? And has it come to this? Is this the spirit in which this

Government is to be administered? If so, let me tell gentlemen the seeds of dissolution are already sown, and our children will reap the bitter fruit.

The honorable gentleman from Massachusetts [Mr. Webster] while he exonerates me personally from the charge, intimates that there is a party in the country who are looking to disunion. Sir, if the gentleman had stopped there, the accusation would "have passed by me as the idle wind which I regard not." But, when he goes on to give to his accusation a local habitation and a name, by quoting the expression of a distinguished citizen of South Carolina, [Dr. Cooper] "that it was time for the South to calculate the value of the Union," and, in the language of the bitterest sarcasm, adds, "surely then the Union cannot last longer than July, 1831," it is impossible to mistake either the allusion or the object of the gentleman. Now I call upon every one who hears me to bear witness that this controversy is not of my seeking. The Senate will do me the justice to remember, that, at the time this unprovoked and uncalled for attack was made upon the South, not one word had been uttered by me in disparagement of New England, nor had I made the most distant allusion, either to the Senator from Massachusetts, or the State he represents. But, sir, that gentleman has thought proper, for purposes best known to himself, to strike the South through me, the most unworthy of her servants. He has crossed the border, he has invaded the State of South Carolina, is making war upon her citizens, and endeavoring to overthrow her principles and her institutions. Sir, when the gentleman provokes me to such a conflict, I meet him at the threshold. I will struggle while I have life, for our altars and our fire sides, and if God gives me strength, I will drive back the invader discomfited. Nor shall I stop there. If the gentleman provokes the war, he shall have war. Sir, I will not stop at the border; I will carry the war into the enemy's territory, and not consent to lay down my arms, until I shall have obtained "indemnity for the past, and security for the future." It is with unfeigned reluctance that I enter upon the performance of this part of my duty. I shrink almost instinctively from a course, however necessary, which may have a tendency to excite sectional feelings, and sectional jealousies. But, sir, the task has been forced upon me, and I proceed right onward to the performance of my duty; be the consequences what they may, the responsibility is with those who have imposed upon me this necessity. The Senator from Massachusetts has thought proper to cast the first stone, and if he shall find, according to a homely adage, "that he lives in a glass house," on his head be the consequences. The gentleman has made a great flourish about his fidelity to Massachusetts. I shall make no professions of zeal for the interests and honor of South Carolina—of that my constituents shall judge. If there be one State in this Union (and I say it not in a boastful spirit) that may challenge comparison with any other for an uniform, zealous, ardent, and uncalculating devotion to the Union, that State is South Carolina. Sir, from the very commencement of the Revolution, up to this hour, there is no sacrifice, however great, she has not cheerfully made; no service she has ever hesitated to perform. She has adhered to you in your prosperity, but in your adversity she has clung to you with more than filial affection. No matter what was the condition of her domestic affairs, though deprived of her resources, divided by parties, or surrounded by difficulties, the call of the country has been to her as the voice of God. Domestic discord ceased at the sound—every man became at once reconciled to his brethren, and the sons of Carolina were all seen crowding together to the temple, bringing their gifts to the altar of their common country. What, sir, was the conduct of the South during the Revolution? Sir, I honor New England for her conduct in that glorious struggle. But great as is the praise which belongs to her, I think at least equal honor is due to the South. They espoused the quarrel of their brethren with a generous zeal, which did not suffer them to stop to calculate their interest in the dispute. Favorites of the mother country, possessed of neither ships nor seamen to create commercial rivalship, they might have found in their situation a guarantee that their trade would be forever fostered and protected by Great Britain. But trampling on all considerations, either of interest or of safety, they rushed into the conflict, and, fighting for principle, periled all in the sacred cause of freedom. Never was there exhibited, in the history of the world, higher examples of noble daring, dreadful suffering, and heroic endurance, than by the whigs of Carolina, during that Revolution. The whole State, from the mountains to the sea, was overrun by an overwhelming force of the enemy. The fruits of industry perished on the spot where they were produced, or were consumed by the foe. The "plains of Carolina" drank up the most precious blood of her citizens! Black and smoking ruins marked the places which had been the habitations of her children! Driven from their homes, into the gloomy and almost impenetrable swamps, even there the spirit of liberty survived, and South Carolina (sustained by the example of her Sumpters and her Marions) proved by her conduct, that, though her soil might be overrun, the spirit of her people was invincible.

But, sir, our country was soon called upon to engage in another revolutionary struggle, and that too was a struggle for principle—I mean the political revolution which dates back to '98, and which, if it had not been successfully achieved, would have left us none of the fruits of the Revolution of '76. The revolution of '98 restored the constitution, rescued the liberty of the citizen from the grasp of those who were aiming at its life, and in the emphatic language of Mr. Jefferson, "saved the constitution at its last gasp." And by whom was it achieved? By the South, sir, aided only by the democracy of the North and West.

I come now to the war of 1812—a war which I well remember was called, in derision, (while its event was doubtful) the Southern war, and sometimes the Carolina war; but which is now universally acknowledged to have done more for the honor and prosperity of the country, than all other events in our history put together. What, sir, were the objects of that war? "Free trade and sailors' rights!" It was for the protection of Northern shipping and New England seamen that the country flew to arms. What interest had the South in that contest? If they had sat down coldly to calculate the value of their interests involved in it, they would have found that they had everything to lose and nothing to gain. But, sir, with that generous devotion to country so characteristic of the South, they only asked if the rights of any portion of their fellow-citizens had been invaded; and when told that Northern ships and New England seamen had been arrested on the common highway of nations, they felt that the honor of their country was assailed; and, acting on that exalted sentiment, "which feels a stain like a wound," they resolved to seek, in open war, for a redress of those injuries which it did not become freemen to endure. Sir, the whole South, animated as by a common impulse, cordially united in declaring and promoting that war. South Carolina sent to your councils, as the advocates and supporters of that war, the noblest of her sons. How they fulfilled that trust let a grateful country tell. Not a measure was adopted, not a battle fought, not a victory won, which contributed in any degree to the success of that war, to which Southern counsels and Southern valor did not largely contribute. Sir, since South Carolina is assailed, I must be suffered to speak it to her praise, that, at the very moment when, in one quarter, we heard it solemnly proclaimed, "that it did not become a religious and moral people to rejoice at the victories of our army or our navy," her Legislature unanimously:

"*Resolved*, That we will cordially support the Government in the vigorous prosecution of the war, until a peace can be obtained on honorable terms; and we will cheerfully submit to every privation that may be required of us, by our Government, for the accomplishment of this object."

South Carolina redeemed that pledge. She threw open her treasury to the Government. She put at the absolute disposal of the officers of the United States all that she possessed—her men, her money, and her arms. She appropriated half a million of dollars, on her own account, in defence of her maritime frontier; ordered a brigade of State troops to be raised; and when left to protect herself by her own means, never suffered the enemy to touch her soil, without being instantly driven off or captured. Such, sir, was the conduct of the South—such the conduct of my own State in that dark hour "which tried men's souls."

When I look back and contemplate the spectacle exhibited, at that time, in another quarter of the Union, when I think of the conduct of certain portions of New England, and remember the part which was acted on that memorable occasion by the political associates of the gentleman from Massachusetts—nay, when I follow that gentleman into the councils of the nation, and listen to his voice during the darkest period of the war, I am indeed astonished that he should venture to touch upon the topics which he has introduced into this debate. South Carolina reproached by Massachusetts! And from whom does the accusation come? Not from the democracy of New England: for they have been, in times past, as they are now, the friends and allies of the South. No, sir, the accusation comes from that party whose acts, during the most trying and eventful period of our national history, were of such a character, that their own Legislature, but a few years ago, actually blotted them out from their records, as a stain upon the honor of the country. But how can they ever be blotted out from the recollections of any one who had a heart to feel, a mind to comprehend, and a memory to retain, the events of that day! Sir, I shall not attempt to write the history of the party in New England, to which I have alluded— the war party in peace, and the peace party in war. That task I shall leave to some future biographer of Nathan Dane, and I doubt not it will be found quite easy to prove that the peace party of Massachusetts were the only defenders of their country, during the war, and actually achieved all our victories by land and sea.

In the mean time, sir, and until that history shall be written, I propose, with the feeble and glimmering lights which I possess, to review the conduct of this party, in connexion with the war, and the events which immediately preceded it. It will be recollected, sir, that our great causes of quarrel with Great Britain were her depredations on Northern commerce, and the impressment of New England seamen. From every quarter we were called upon for protection. Importunate as the West is now represented to be, on another subject, the importunity of the East on that occasion was far greater. I hold in my hands the evidence of the fact. Here are petitions, memorials, and remonstrances, from all parts of New England, setting forth the injustice, the oppressions, the depredations, the insults, the outrages, committed by Great Britain against the unoffending commerce and seamen of New England, and calling upon Congress for redress. Sir, I cannot stop to read these memorials. In that from Boston, after stating the alarming and extensive condemnation of our vessels by Great Britain, which threatened "to sweep our commerce from the face of the ocean," and "to involve our merchants in bankruptcy," they called upon the Government "to assert our rights and to adopt such measures as will support the dignity and honor of the United States."

From Salem, we heard a language still more decisive; they call explicitly for "an appeal to arms," and pledge their lives and property in support of any measures which Congress might adopt. From Newburyport, an appeal was made "to the firmness and justice of the Government to obtain compensation and protection." It was here, I think, that, when the war was declared, it was resolved "to resist our own Government, even until blood!"*

In other quarters, the common language of that day was, that our commerce and our seamen were entitled to protection, and that it was the duty of the Government to afford it at every hazard. The conduct of Great Britain, we were then told, was "an outrage upon our national independence." These clamors, which commenced as early as January, 1806, were continued up to 1812. In a message from the Governor of one of the New England States, as late as the 10th October, 1811, this language is held: "A manly and decisive course has become indispensable—a course to satisfy foreign nations that, while we desire peace, we have the means and the spirit to repel aggression. We are false to ourselves, when our commerce or our territory is invaded with impunity."

About this time, however, a remarkable change was observable in the tone and temper of those who had been endeavoring to force the country into a war. The language of complaint was changed into that of insult, and

*Olive Branch, page 101.

calls for protection, converted into reproaches. "Smoke, smoke;" (says one writer) "my life on it our Executive have no more idea of declaring war, than my grandmother." "The Committee of Ways and Means" (says another) "have come out with their Pandora's Box of taxes, and yet nobody dreams of war." "Congress do not mean to declare war; they dare not." But why multiply examples? An honorable member of the other House, from the city of Boston, [Mr. Quincy] in a speech delivered on the 3d April, 1812, says, "neither promises, nor threats, nor asseverations, nor oaths, will make me believe that you will go to war. The navigation States are sacrificed, and the spirit and character of the country prostrated by fear and avarice;" "you cannot," said the same gentleman on another occasion, "be kicked into a war."

Well, sir, the war at length came, and what did we behold! The very men who had been for six years clamorous for war, and for whose protection it was waged, became at once equally clamorous against it. They had received a miraculous visitation; a new light suddenly beamed upon their minds; the scales fell from their eyes, and it was discovered that the war was declared from "subserviency to France;" and that Congress and the Executive "had sold themselves to Napoleon;" that Great Britain had, in fact, done us "no essential injury;" that she was "the bulwark of our religion;" that where "she took one of our ships, she protected twenty;" and that, if Great Britain had impressed a few of our seamen, it was because "she could not distinguish them from her own." And so far did this spirit extend, that a committee of the Massachusetts Legislature actually fell to calculation, and discovered, to their infinite satisfaction, but to the astonishment of all the world beside, that only eleven Massachusetts sailors had ever been impressed. Never shall I forget the appeals that had been made to the sympathies of the South, in behalf of the "thousands of impressed Americans" who had been torn from their families and friends, and "immured in the floating dungeons of Britain." The most touching pictures were drawn of the hard condition of the American sailor, "treated like a slave," forced to fight the battles of his enemies, "lashed to the mast to be shot at like a dog." But, sir, the very moment we had taken up arms in their defence, it was discovered that all these were mere "fictions of the brain," and that the whole number of the State of Massachusetts was but eleven; and that even these had been "taken by mistake." Wonderful discovery! The Secretary of State had collected authentic lists of no less than six thousand impressed Americans. Lord Castlereagh himself acknowledged sixteen hundred. Calculations on the basis of the number found on board of the Guerriere, the Macedonian, the Java, and other British ships, (captured by the skill and gallantry of those heroes whose achievements are the treasured monuments of their country's glory) fixed the number at seven thousand; and yet, it seems, Massachusetts had lost but eleven! Eleven Massachusetts sailors taken by mistake! A cause of war, indeed! Their ships, too, the capture of which had threatened "universal bankruptcy," it was discovered that Great Britain was their friend and protector; "where she had taken one, she had protected twenty." Then was the discovery made, that subserviency to France, hostility to commerce, "a determination on the part of the South and the West to break down the Eastern States," and especially, (as reported by a committee of the Massachusetts Legislature,) "to force the sons of commerce to populate the wilderness," were the true causes of the war.* But let us look a little further into the conduct of the peace party of New England, at that important crisis. Whatever difference of opinion might have existed as to the causes of the war, the country had a right to expect that, when once involved in the contest, all America would have cordially united in its support. Sir, the war effected, in its progress, a union of all parties at the South. But not so in New England; there, great efforts were made to stir up the minds of the people to oppose it. Nothing was left undone to embarrass the financial operations of the Government, to prevent the enlistment of troops, to keep back the men and money of New England from the service of the Union, to force the President from his seat. Yes, sir, "the Island of Elba! or a halter!" were the alternatives they presented to the excellent and venerable James Madison. Sir, the war was further opposed by openly carrying on illicit trade with the enemy, by permitting that enemy to establish herself on the very soil of Massachusetts, and by opening a free trade between Great Britain and America, with a separate custom house. Yes, sir, those who cannot endure the thought that we should insist on a free trade in time of profound peace, could without scruple claim and exercise the right of carrying on a free trade with the enemy in a time of war; and, finally, by getting up the renowned "Hartford Convention," and preparing the way for an open resistance to the Government, and a separation of the States. Sir, if I am asked for the proof of those things, I fearlessly appeal to cotemporary history, to the public documents of the country, to the recorded opinions and acts of public assemblies, to the

*Olive Branch, pages 134, 291.

declaration and acknowledgments, since made, of the Executive and Legislature of Massachusetts herself.*

Sir, the time has not been allowed me to trace this subject through, even if I had been disposed to do so. But I cannot refrain from referring to one or two documents which have fallen in my way since this debate began. I read, sir, from the Olive Branch of Mathew Carey, in which are collected "the actings and doings" of the peace party of New England, during the continuance of the embargo and the war. I know the Senator from Massachusetts will respect the high authority of his political friend and fellow laborer in the great cause of "domestic industry."

In page 301, et seq. 9 of this work, is a detailed account of the measures adopted in Massachusetts during the war, for the express purpose of embarrassing the financial operations of the Government, by preventing loans, and thereby driving our rulers from their seats, and forcing the country into a dishonorable peace. It appears that the Boston banks commenced an operation by which a run was to be made upon all the banks to the South; at the same time stopping their own discounts, the effect of which was to produce a sudden and most alarming diminution of the circulating medium, and universal distress over the whole country—a distress which they failed not to attribute to the "unholy war."

*In answer to an address of Governor Eustis, denouncing the conduct of the peace party, during the war, the House of Representatives of Massachusetts, in June, 1823, says: "The change of the political sentiment evinced in the late elections forms indeed a new era in the history of our Commonwealth. It is the triumph of reason over passion, of patriotism over party spirit. Massachusetts has returned to her first love, and is no longer a stranger in the Union. We rejoice that, though, during the last war, such measures were adopted in this State, as occasioned double sacrifice of treasure and of life; covered the friends of the nation with humiliation and mourning, and fixed a stain on the page of our history; a redeeming spirit has at length arisen to take away our reproach, and restore to us our good name, our rank among our sister States, and our just influence in the Union.

"Though we would not renew contentions, or irritate wantonly, we believe that there are cases, when it is necessary we should 'wound to heal.' And we consider it among the first duties of the friends of our National Government, on this return of power, to disavow the unwarrantable course pursued by this State during the late war; and to hold up the measures of that period as beacons, that the present and succeeding generations may shun that career which must inevitably terminate in the destruction of the individual, or the party who pursues it; and may learn the important lesson that, in all times, the path of duty is the path of safety; and that it is never dangerous to rally around the standard of our country." —*Note by Mr. H.*

To such an extent was this system carried, that it appears from a statement of the condition of the Boston banks, made up in January, 1814, that with nearly five millions dollars of specie in their vaults, they had but two millions of dollars of bills in circulation. It is added by Carey, that at this very time an extensive trade was carried on in British Government bills, for which specie was sent to Canada, for the payment of the British troops then laying waste our Northern frontier, and this too at the very moment when New England ships, sailing under British licences, (a trade declared to be lawful by the courts both of Great Britain and Massachusetts*) were supplying with provisions those very armies destined for the invasion of our own shores. Sir, the author of the Olive Branch, with a holy indignation, denounces these acts as "treasonable!" "giving aid and comfort to the enemy." I shall not follow his example. But I will ask with what justice or propriety can the South be accused of disloyalty from that quarter. If we had any evidence that the Senator from Massachusetts had admonished his brethren then, he might with a better grace assume the office of admonishing us now.

When I look at the measures adopted in Boston at that day, to deprive the Government of the necessary means for carrying on the war, and think of the success and the consequences of these measures, I feel my pride as an American humbled in the dust. Hear, sir, the language of that day; I read from pages 301 and 302 of the Olive Branch: "Let no man who wishes to continue the war, by active means, by vote or lending money, dare to prostrate himself at the altar on the fast day." "Will federalists subscribe to the loan? Will they lend money to our national rulers? It is impossible. First, because of the principle, and secondly, because of principal and interest." "Do not prevent the abusers of their trust from becoming bankrupt. Do not prevent them from becoming odious to the public, and being replaced by better men." "Any federalist who lends money to Government, must go and shake hands with James Madison, and claim fellowship with Felix Grundy. [I beg pardon of my honorable friend from Tennessee; but he is in good company. I had thought it was 'James Madison, Felix Grundy, and the Devil.'] Let him no more call himself a federalist, and a friend to his country; he will be called by others, infamous," &c.

Sir, the spirit of the people sunk under these appeals. Such was the effect produced by them on the public mind, that the very agents of the Government (as appears from their public advertisements, now before me)

*2d Dodson's Admiralty Reports, 48.—13th Mass. Reports, 26.

could not obtain loans, without a pledge that "the names of the subscribers should not be known." Here are the advertisements: "The names of all subscribers (say Gilbert and Dean, the brokers employed by Government) shall be known only to the undersigned." As if those who came forward to aid their country in the hour of her utmost need, were engaged in some dark and foul conspiracy, they were assured "that their names should not be known." Can any thing show more conclusively the unhappy state of public feeling which prevailed at that day, than this single fact? Of the same character with these measures was the conduct of Massachusetts, in withholding her militia from the service of the United States, and devising measures for withdrawing her quota of the taxes, thereby attempting, not merely to cripple the resources of the country, but actually depriving the Government (as far as depended upon her) of all the means of carrying on the war: of the bone, and muscle, and sinews of war—"of man and steel—the soldier and his sword." But it seems Massachusetts was to reserve her resources for herself; she was to defend and protect her own shores. And how was that duty performed? In some places on the coast neutrality was declared, and the enemy was suffered to invade the soil of Massachusetts, and allowed to occupy her territory, until the peace, without one effort to rescue it from his grasp. Nay, more, while our own Government and our rulers were considered as enemies, the troops of the enemy were treated like friends; the most intimate commercial relations were established with them, and maintained up to the peace. At this dark period of our national affairs, where was the Senator from Massachusetts? How were his political associates employed? "Calculating the value of the Union?" Yes, sir, that was the propitious moment, when our country stood alone, the last hope of the world, struggling for her existence against the colossal power of Great Britain, "concentrated in one mighty effort to crush us at a blow"—that was the chosen hour to revive the grand scheme of building up "a great Northern Confederacy"—a scheme, which, it is stated in the work before me, had its origin, as far back as the year 1796, and which appears never to have been entirely abandoned. In the language of the writers of that day, (1796) "rather than have a constitution such as the anti-Federalists were contending for, [such as we now are contending for] the Union ought to be dissolved;" and to prepare the way for that measure, the same methods were resorted to then, that have always been relied on for that purpose—exciting prejudice against the South. Yes, sir, our Northern brethren were then told "that, if the negroes were good for food, their Southern masters would claim the right to destroy them at pleasure."* Sir, in 1814, all these topics were revived. Again we heard of "a Northern Confederacy." "The slave States by themselves;" "the mountains are the natural boundary;" we want neither "the counsels nor the power of the West," &c. &c. The papers teemed with accusations against the South and the West, and the calls for a dissolution of all connexion with them were loud and strong. I cannot consent to go through the disgusting details. But to show the height to which the spirit of disaffection was carried, I will take you to the temple of the living God, and show you that sacred place (which should be devoted to the extension of "peace on earth and good will towards men," where "one day's truce ought surely to be allowed to the dissensions and animosities of mankind") converted into a fierce arena of political strife, where, from the lips of the priest standing between the horns of the altar, there went forth the most terrible denunciations against all who should be true to their country, in the hour of her utmost need.

"If you do not wish," said a reverend clergyman, in a sermon preached in Boston, on the 23d July, 1812, "to become the slaves of those who own slaves, and who are themselves the slaves of French slaves, you must either, in the language of the day, cut the connexion, or so far alter the national compact as to ensure to yourselves a due share in the Government." (Olive Branch, page 319.) "The Union," says the same writer, (page 320) "has been long since virtually dissolved, and it is full time that this part of the disunited States should take care of itself."

Another reverend gentleman, pastor of a church at Medford, (page 321) issues his anathema—"let him stand accursed"—against all, all, who by their "personal services," or "loans of money," "conversation," or "writing," or "influence," give countenance or support to the unrighteous war, in the following terms: "that man is an accomplice in the wickedness; he loads his conscience with the blackest crimes; he brings the guilt of blood upon his soul, and in the sight of God and his law he is a murderer!"

One or two more quotations, sir, and I shall have done. A reverend doctor of divinity, the pastor of a church at Byefield, Massachusetts, on the 7th of April, 1814, thus addresses his flock [321.] "The Israelites became weary of yielding the fruit of their labor to pamper their splendid tyrants. They left their political woes. They separated; where is our Moses? Where

*Olive Branch, p. 267.

the rod of his miracles? Where is our Aaron? Alas! no voice from the burning bush has directed them here."

"We must trample on the mandates of despotism, or remain slaves forever." [p. 322.] "You must drag the chains of Virginian despotism, unless you discover some other mode of escape." "Those Western States, which have been violent for this abominable war, those States which have thirsted for blood—God has given them blood to drink." [323.]———Sir, I can go no further. The records of the day are full of such sentiments, issued from the press, spoken in public assemblies, poured out from the sacred desk! God forbid, sir, that I should charge the people of Massachusetts with participating in these sentiments. The South and the West had there, their friends—men who stood by their country, though encompassed all around by their enemies. The Senator from Massachusetts [Mr. SILSBEE] was one of them, the Senator from Connecticut [Mr. FOOT] was another, and there are others now on this floor. The sentiments I have read were the sentiments of a party embracing the political associates of the gentleman from Massachusetts. If they could only be found in the columns of a newspaper, in a few occasional pamphlets, issued by men of intemperate feeling, I should not consider them as affording any evidence of the opinions even of the peace party of New England. But, sir, they were the common language of that day; they pervaded the whole land; they were issued from the legislative hall, from the pulpit, and the press. Our books are full of them; and there is no man who now hears me, but knows, that they were the sentiments of a party, by whose members they were promulgated. Indeed, no evidence of this would seem to be required, beyond the fact that such sentiments found their way even into the pulpits of New England. What must be the state of public opinion, where any respectable clergyman would venture to preach and to print sermons containing the sentiments I have quoted? I doubt not the piety or moral worth of these gentlemen. I am told they were respectable and pious men. But they were men, and they "kindled in a common blaze." And now, sir, I must be suffered to remark, that, at this awful and melancholy period of our national history, the gentleman from Massachusetts, who now manifests so great a devotion to the Union, and so much anxiety lest it should be endangered from the South, was "with his brethren in Israel." He saw all these things passing before his eyes—he heard these sentiments uttered all around him. I do not charge that gentleman with any participation in these acts, or with approving of these sentiments; but I will ask why, if he was animated by the same sentiments then, which he now professes, if he can "augur disunion at a distance, and snuff up rebellion in every tainted breeze," why he did not, at that day, exert his great talents and acknowledged influence with the political associates by whom he was surrounded, (and who then, as now, looked up to him for guidance and direction) in allaying this general excitement, in pointing out to his deluded friends the value of the Union, in instructing them, that, instead of looking "to some prophet to lead them out from the land of Egypt," they should become reconciled to their brethren, and unite with them in the support of a just and necessary war? Sir, the gentleman must excuse me for saying, that, if the records of our country afforded any evidence that he had pursued such a course, then; if we could find it recorded in the history of those times, that, like the immortal Dexter, he had breasted that mighty torrent which was sweeping before it all that was great and valuable in our political institutions; if like him he had stood by his country in opposition to his party; sir, we would, like little children, listen to his precepts and abide by his counsels.

As soon as the public mind was sufficiently prepared for the measure, the celebrated Hartford Convention was got up; not as the act of a few unauthorized individuals, but by authority of the Legislature of Massachusetts; and, as has been shown by the able historian of that convention, in accordance with the views and wishes of the party, of which it was the organ. Now, sir, I do not desire to call in question the motives of the gentlemen who composed that assembly: I know many of them to be in private life accomplished and honorable men, and I doubt not there were some among them who did not perceive the dangerous tendency of their proceedings. I will even go further, and say, that, if the authors of the Hartford Convention believed that "gross, deliberate, and palpable violations of the constitution" had taken place, utterly destructive of their rights and interests, I should be the last man to deny their right to resort to any constitutional measures for redress. But, sir, in any view of the case, the time when, and the circumstances under which, that convention assembled, as well as the measures recommended, render their conduct, in my opinion, wholly indefensible. Let us contemplate, for a moment, the spectacle then exhibited to the view of the world. I will not go over the disasters of the war, nor describe the difficulties in which the Government was involved. It will be recollected that its credit was nearly gone; Washington had fallen; the whole coast was blockaded; and an immense force, collected in the West Indies, was about to make a descent, which it was supposed we had no means of resisting. In this awful state of our public affairs, when the Government seemed almost to be tottering on its base, when Great Britain, relieved from all her other enemies, had proclaimed her purpose of "reducing us to unconditional submission," we beheld the peace party of New England (in the language of the work before us) "pursuing a course calculated to do more injury to their country, and to render England more effective service, than all her armies." Those who could not find it in their hearts to rejoice at our victories, sang te deum at the King's Chapel in Boston, for the restoration of the Bourbons. Those who could not consent to illuminate their dwellings for the capture of the Guerriere, could give visible tokens of their joy at the fall of Detroit. The "beacon fires" of their hills were lighted up, not for the encouragement of their friends, but as signals to the enemy; and in the gloomy hours of midnight, the very lights burned blue. Such were the dark and portentous signs of the times, which ushered into being the renowned Hartford Convention. That convention met, and from their proceedings it appears that their chief object was to keep back the men and money of New England from the service of the Union, and to effect radical changes in the Government; changes that can never be effected without a dissolution of the Union.

Let us now, sir, look at their proceedings. I read from "A short account of the Hartford Convention," (written by one of its members) a very rare book, of which I was fortunate enough a few years ago to obtain a copy. [Here Mr. H. read from the proceedings.*]

---

*It appears at p. 6, of "The Account," that by a vote of the House of Representatives of Massachusetts [260 to 90] delegates to this convention were ordered to be appointed to consult upon the subject "of their public grievances and concerns," and upon "the best means of preserving their resources," and for procuring a revision of the constitution of the United States, "more effectually to secure the support and attachment of all the people, by placing all upon the basis of fair representation."

The convention assembled at Hartford, on the 15th December, 1814. On the next day it was

Resolved, That the most inviolable secrecy shall be observed by each member of this convention, including the Secretary, as to all propositions, debates, and proceedings thereof, until this injunction shall be suspended or altered.

On the 24th December, the committee appointed to prepare and report a general project of such measures as may be proper for the convention to adopt, reported, among other things:

"1. That it was expedient to recommend to the Legislatures of the States, the adoption of the most effectual and decisive measures to protect the militia and the States from the usurpations contained in these proceedings." [The proceedings of Congress and the Executive in relation to the Militia and the War.]

It is unnecessary to trace the matter farther, or to ask what would have been the next chapter in this history, if the measures recommended had been carried into effect; and if, with the men and money of New England withheld from the Government of the United States, she had been withdrawn from the war; if New Orleans had fallen into the hands of the enemy, and if, without troops, and almost destitute of money, the Southern and the Western States had been thrown upon their own resources for the prosecution of the war, and the recovery of New Orleans? Sir, whatever may have been the issue of the contest, the Union must have been dissolved. But a wise and just Providence, which "shapes our ends, rough-hew them as we will," gave us the victory, and crowned our efforts with a glorious peace. The ambassadors of Hartford were seen retracing their

---

"2. That it was expedient also to prepare a statement exhibiting the necessity which the improvidence and inability of the General Government have imposed upon the States of providing for their own defence, and the impossibility of their discharging this duty, and at the same time fulfilling the requisitions of the General Government, and also to recommend to the Legislatures of the several States to make provision for mutual defence, and to make an earnest application to the Government of the United States, with a view to some arrangement whereby the States may be enabled to retain a portion of the taxes levied by Congress, for the purposes of self-defence, and for the reimbursement of expenses already incurred on account of the United States."

"3. That it is expedient to recommend to the several State Legislatures certain amendments to the constitution, viz:

That the power to declare or make war by the Congress of the United States be restricted.

That it is expedient to attempt to make provision for restraining Congress in the exercise of an unlimited power to make new States and admit them into the Union.

That an amendment be proposed respecting slave representation and slave taxation."

On the 19th December, 1814, it was proposed "that the capacity of naturalized citizens to hold offices of trust, honor, or profit, ought to be restrained," &c.

The subsequent proceedings are not given at large. But it seems that the report of the committee was adopted, and also a recommendation of certain measures (of the character of which we are not informed) to the States for their mutual defence, and having voted that the "injunction of secrecy, in regard to all the debates and proceedings of the convention (except so far as relates to the report finally adopted) be continued," the convention adjourned *sine die,* but (as it was supposed) to meet again when circumstances should require it. —*Note by Mr. H.*

---

steps from Washington, "the bearers of the glad tidings of great joy." Courage and patriotism triumphed; the country was saved; the Union was preserved. And are we, who stood by our country then; who threw open our coffers; who bared our bosoms; who freely periled all in that conflict, to be reproached with want of attachment to the Union? If, sir, we are to have lessons of patriotism read to us, they must come from a different quarter. The Senator from Massachusetts, who is now so sensitive on all subjects connected with the Union, seems to have a memory forgetful of the political events that have passed away. I must, therefore, refresh his recollection a little farther on these subjects. The history of disunion has been written by one, whose authority stands too high with the American people to be questioned—I mean Thomas Jefferson. I know not how the gentleman may receive this authority. When that great and good man occupied the presidential chair, I believe he commanded no portion of that gentleman's respect.

I hold in my hand a celebrated pamphlet on the embargo, in which language is held in relation to Mr. Jefferson, which my respect for his memory will prevent me from reading, unless any gentleman should call for it. But the Senator from Massachusetts has since joined in singing hosannas to his name; he has assisted at his apotheosis, and has fixed him as "a brilliant star in the clear upper sky;" I hope, therefore, he is now prepared to receive with deference and respect the high authority of Mr. Jefferson. In the fourth volume of his memoirs, which has just issued from the press, we have the following history of disunion, from the pen of that illustrious statesman: "Mr. Adams called on me pending the embargo, and while endeavors were making to obtain its repeal; he spoke of the dissatisfaction of the Eastern portion of our confederacy with the restraints of the embargo then existing, and their restlessness under it. That there was nothing which might not be attempted to rid themselves of it. That he had information of the most unquestionable certainty, that certain citizens of the Eastern States, (I think he named Massachusetts particularly) were in negotiation with agents of the British Government, the object of which was an agreement that the New England States should take no further part in the war, [the commercial war, the 'war of restrictions,' as it was called] then going on, and that, without formally declaring their separation from the Union, they should withdraw from all aid and obedience to them, &c. From that moment [says Mr. J.] I saw the necessity of abandoning it, [the embargo] and, instead of effecting our purpose by this peaceful weapon, we must fight it out, or break the Union." In another letter Mr. Jefferson adds: "I doubt whether a single fact known to the world will carry as clear conviction to it of the correctness of our knowledge of the treasonable views of the federal party of that day, as that disclosed by this the most nefarious and daring attempt to dissever the Union, of which the Hartford Convention was a subsequent chapter; and both of these having failed, consolidation becomes the fourth chapter of the next book of their history. But this opens with a vast accession of strength from their younger recruits, who having nothing in them of the feelings and principles of '76, now look to a single and splendid Government, &c., riding and ruling over the plundered ploughman and beggared yeomanry." — (4 vol. 419, 422.)

The last chapter, says Mr. Jefferson, of that history, is to be found in the conduct of those who are endeavoring to bring about consolidation: ay, sir, that very consolidation for which the gentleman from Massachusetts is contending—the exercise, by the Federal Government, of powers not delegated in relation to "internal improvements," and "the protection of manufactures." And why, sir, does Mr. Jefferson consider consolidation as leading directly to disunion? Because he knew that the exercise by the Federal Government, of the powers contended for, would make this "a Government without limitation of powers," the submission to which he considered as a greater evil than disunion itself. There is one chapter in this history, however, which Mr. Jefferson has not filled up, and I must therefore supply the deficiency. It is to be found in the protest made by New England against the acquisition of Louisiana. In relation to that subject the New England doctrine is thus laid down by one of her learned political doctors of that day, now a doctor of laws, at the head of the great literary institution of the East—I mean Josiah Quincy, President of Harvard College. I quote from the speech delivered by that gentleman on the floor of Congress, on the occasion of the admission of Louisiana into the Union.

"Mr. Quincy repeated and justified a remark he had made, which, to save all misapprehension, he had committed to writing, in the following words: If this bill passes, it is my deliberate opinion that it is virtually a dissolution of the Union; that it will free the States from their moral obligation; and as it will be the right of all, so it will be the duty of some, to prepare for a separation, amicably if they can, violently if they must."

I wish it to be distinctly understood [said Mr. H.] that all the remarks I have made on this subject, are intended to be exclusively applied to a party, which I have described as "the peace party of New England"— embracing the political associates of the Senator from Massachusetts—

a party which controlled the operations of that State during the embargo and the war, and who are justly chargeable with all the measures I have reprobated. Sir, nothing has been further from my thoughts than to impeach the character or conduct of the people of New England. For their steady habits and hardy virtues, I trust I entertain a becoming respect. I fully subscribe to the truth of the description given before the Revolution, by one whose praise is the highest eulogy, "that the perseverance of Holland, the activity of France, and the dexterous and firm sagacity of English enterprise, have been more than equalled by this 'recent people.'" Hardy, enterprising, sagacious, industrious, and moral, the people of New England of the present day, are worthy of their ancestors. Still less has it been my intention to say any thing that could be construed into a want of respect for that party, who, trampling on all narrow, sectional feelings, have been true to their principles in the worst of times—I mean the democracy of New England.

Sir, I will declare that, highly as I appreciate the democracy of the South, I consider even higher praise to be due to the democracy of New England—who have maintained their principles "through good and through evil report," who at every period of our national history have stood up manfully for "their country, their whole country, and nothing but their country." In the great political revolution of '98, they were found united with the democracy of the South, marching under the banner of the constitution, led on by the patriarch of liberty, in search of the land of political promise, which they lived not only to behold, but to possess and to enjoy. Again, sir, in the darkest and most gloomy period of the war, when our country stood single handed, against "the conqueror of the conquerors of the world," when all about and around them was dark, and dreary, disastrous and discouraging, they stood a Spartan band in that narrow pass, where the honor of their country was to be defended, or to find its grave. And in the last great struggle, when, as we believe, the very existence of the principle of popular sovereignty was at stake, where were the democracy of New England? Where they always have been found, Sir, struggling side by side with their brethren of the South and the West, for popular rights, and assisting in that glorious triumph by which the man of the People was elevated to the highest office in their gift.

Who, then, Mr. President, are the true friends of the Union? Those who would confine the federal government strictly within the limits prescribed by the constitution—who would preserve to the States and the people all powers not expressly delegated—who would make this a federal and not a national Union—and who, administering the government in a spirit of equal justice, would make it a blessing and not a curse. And who are its enemies? Those who are in favor of consolidation; who are constantly stealing power from the States and adding strength to the federal government; who, assuming an unwarrantable jurisdiction over the States and the people, undertake to regulate the whole industry and capital of the country. But, Sir, of all descriptions of men, I consider those as the worst enemies of the Union, who sacrifice the equal rights which belong to every member of the confederacy, to combinations of interested majorities for personal or political objects. But the gentleman apprehends no evil from the dependence of the States on the Federal Government; he can see no danger of corruption from the influence of money or of patronage. Sir, I know that it is supposed to be a wise saying, "that patronage is a source of weakness," and in support of that maxim it has been said, that "every ten appointments make a hundred enemies." But I am rather inclined to think, with the eloquent and sagacious orator now reposing on his laurels on the banks of the Roanoke, that "the power of conferring favors creates a crowd of dependants." He gave a forcible illustration of the truth of the remark when he told us of the effect of holding up the savory morsel to the eager eyes of the hungry hounds gathered around his door. It mattered not whether the gift was bestowed on Towser or Sweetlips, "Tray, Blanch, or Sweetheart," while held in suspense they were all governed by a nod; and when the morsel was bestowed, the expectation of the *favors of to-morrow* kept up the *subjection of to-day.*

The Senator from Massachusetts, in denouncing what he is pleased to call the *Carolina doctrine,* has attempted to throw ridicule upon the idea that a State has any constitutional remedy by the exercise of its sovereign authority against "a gross, palpable, and deliberate violation of the Constitution." He called it "an idle" or "a ridiculous notion," or something to that effect; and added, that it would make the Union "a mere rope of sand." Now, Sir, as the gentleman has not condescended to enter into an examination of the question, and has been satisfied with throwing the weight of his authority into the scale, I do not deem it necessary to do more than to throw into the opposite scale, the authority on which South Carolina relies; and there, for the present, I am perfectly willing to leave the controversy. The South Carolina doctrine, that is to say, the doctrine contained in an exposition reported by a committee of the Legislature in December, 1828, and published by their authority, is the good old Republican doctrine of '98, the doctrine of the celebrated "Virginia Resolutions," of that year, and of "Madison's Report," of '99. It will be recollected that the Legislature of Virginia, in December, '98, took into consideration the Alien and Sedition Laws, then considered by all Republicans as a gross violation of the Constitution of the United States, and on that day passed, among others, the following resolution:

"The General Assembly doth explicitly and peremptorily declare, that it views the powers of the Federal Government as resulting from the compact to which the States are parties, as limited by the plain sense and intention of the instrument constituting that compact, as no further valid than they are authorized by the grants enumerated in that compact; and that, in case of *a deliberate, palpable, and dangerous exercise of other powers not granted by the said compact,* the States who are parties thereto, *have the right, and are in duty bound, to interpose, for arresting the progress of the evil,* and for maintaining within their respective limits, the authorities, rights and liberties appertaining to them."

In addition to the above resolutions, the General Assembly of Virginia "appealed to the other States, in the confidence that they would concur with that Commonwealth, that the acts aforesaid [the Alien and Sedition Laws] are unconstitutional, and that the necessary and proper measures would be taken by each for co-operating with Virginia *in maintaining unimpaired the authorities, rights, and liberties,* reserved to the States respectively, or to the people."

The Legislatures of several of the New England States having, (contrary to the expectation of the Legislature of Virginia) expressed their dissent from these doctrines, the subject came up again for consideration during the session of '99–1800, when it was referred to a Select Committee, by whom was made that celebrated report, which is familiarly known as "Madison's Report," and which deserves to last as long as the Constitution itself. In that report, which was subsequently adopted by the Legislature, the whole subject was deliberately examined, and the objections urged against the Virginia doctrines carefully considered; the result was, that the Legislature of Virginia re-affirmed all the principles laid down in the resolutions of '98, and issued to the world that admirable report which has stamped the character of Mr. Madison as the preserver of that Constitution, which he had contributed so largely to create and establish. I will here quote from Mr. Madison's report one or two passages which bear more immediately on the point in controversy. "The resolution having taken this view of the federal compact, proceeds to infer, that, in case of a deliberate, palpable, and dangerous exercise of powers, not granted by the said compact, the States who are parties thereto have the right, and are in duty bound, to interpose for arresting the progress of the evil, and for maintaining, within their respective limits, the authorities, rights, and liberties appertaining to them.

"It appears to your committee to be a plain principle, founded in common sense, illustrated by common practice, and essential to the nature of compacts, that, where resort can be had to no tribunal, superior to the authority of the parties, *the parties themselves must be the rightful judges* in the last resort, whether the bargain made has been pursued or violated. The constitution of the United States was formed by the sanction of *the States*, given by each in its sovereign capacity. It adds to the stability and dignity, as well as to the authority of the Constitution, that it rests upon this legitimate and solid foundation. The States, then, being the parties to the Constitutional compact, and in their sovereign capacity, it follows of necessity, that there can *be no tribunal above their authority*, to decide, in the last resort, whether the compact made by them be violated; and, consequently, that, as the parties to it, they must themselves decide, in the last resort, such questions as may be of sufficient magnitude to require their interposition.

"The resolution has guarded against any misapprehension of its object, by expressly requiring for such an interposition 'the case of a *deliberate, palpable, and dangerous* breach of the Constitution, by the exercise of powers not granted by it.' It must be a case, not of a light and transient nature, but of a nature dangerous to the great purposes for which the Constitution was established.

"But the resolution has done more than guard against misconstruction, by expressly referring to cases of a *deliberate, palpable and dangerous* nature. It specifies *the object of the interposition* which it contemplates, to be solely that of *arresting the progress of the evil* of usurpation, and of maintaining the authorities, rights, and liberties appertaining to the States, as parties to the Constitution.

"From this view of the resolution, it would seem inconceivable that it can incur any just disapprobation from those, who, laying aside all momentary impressions, and recollecting the genuine source and object of the Federal Constitution, shall candidly and accurately interpret the meaning of the General Assembly. If the deliberate exercise of dangerous powers, palpably withdrew by the Constitution, could not justify the parties to it in interposing, even so far as to arrest the progress of the evil, and thereby to preserve the Constitution itself, as well as to provide for the safety of the parties to it, there would be an end to all relief from usurped power, and a direct subversion of the rights specified or recognized under all the State Constitutions, as well as a plain denial of the fundamental principles on which our Independence itself was declared."

But, Sir, our authorities do not stop here—the State of Kentucky responded to Virginia, and on the 10th November, 1798, adopted those celebrated resolutions well known to have been penned by the author of the Declaration of American Independence. In those resolutions the Legislature of Kentucky declare, "that the government created by this compact was not made the exclusive or final *judge* of the extent of the powers delegated to itself: since that would have made its discretion, and not the Constitution, the measure of its powers; but that, as in all other cases of compact among parties having no common judge, each party has an equal right to judge for itself, as well of infractions, as of the mode and measure of redress."

At the ensuing session of the Legislature, the subject was re-examined, and on the 14th November, 1790, the resolutions of the proceeding year were deliberately re-affirmed, and it was, among other things, solemnly declared: "That, if those who administer the General Government, be permitted to transgress the limits fixed by that compact, by a total disregard of the special delegations of power therein contained, an annihilation of the State Governments, and the erection, upon its ruins, of a general *consolidated* Government, will be the inevitable consequence. That the principles of construction contended for by sundry of the State Legislatures, that the *General Government is the exclusive judge of the extent of the powers delegated to it,* stop nothing short of despotism; since the *discretion* of those who administer the Government, and not the *Constitution,* would be the measure of their powers. That the several States who formed that instrument, being sovereign and independent, have the unquestionable right to judge of its construction, and that the *nullification by those sovereignties, of all unauthorized acts, done under color of that instrument, is the rightful remedy.*"

Time and experience confirmed Mr. Jefferson's opinion, on this all important point. In the year 1821, he expressed himself in this emphatic manner: "It is a fatal heresy to suppose, that either our State Governments are superior to the Federal, or the Federal to the State; neither is authorized literally to decide, what belongs to itself, or its co-partner in government. In differences of opinion, between their different sets of public servants, the appeal is to neither, but to their employers, peaceably assembled, by their representatives in Convention."

The opinions of Mr. Jefferson, on this subject, have been so repeatedly and solemnly expressed, that they may be said to have been among the most fixed and settled convictions of his mind. In the protest prepared by him, for the Legislature of Virginia, in December, 1825, in respect to the powers exercised by the Federal Government, in relation to the Tariff and Internal Improvement, which he declares to be "usurpations of the powers retained by the States,—mere interpolations into the compact, and direct infractions of it,"—he solemnly reasserts all the principles of the Virginia Resolutions of '98—protests against "these acts of the federal branch of the government, as *null and void,* and declares that, although Virginia would consider a dissolution of the Union as among the greatest calamities that could befal them, yet it is not the greatest. There is yet one greater—submission to a government of unlimited powers. It is only when the hope of this shall become absolutely desperate, that further forbearance could not be indulged," &c.

In his letter to Mr. Giles, written about the same time, he says.

"I see as you do, and with the deepest affliction, the rapid strides with which the federal branch of our Government is advancing towards the usurpation of all the rights reserved to the States, and the consolidation in itself of all powers, foreign and domestic, and that too by constructions which leave no limits to their powers, &c. Under the power to regulate *commerce,* they assume, indefinitely, that also over agriculture and manufactures, &c. Under the authority to establish Post Roads, they claim that of cutting down mountains for the construction of *roads,* and digging *canals,* &c. And what is our resource for the *preservation of the Constitution?* Reason and Argument?—You might as well reason and argue with the marble columns encircling them, &c. Are we then to *stand to our arms,* with the hot headed Georgian?" No: [and I say no and South Carolina has said no] "that must be the last resource. We must have patience and long endurance with our brethren, &c. and separate from our companions only when the sole alternatives left are a dissolution of our Union with them, or submission to a Government without limitation of powers. Between these two evils, when we must make a choice, there can be no hesitation."

Such, Sir, are the high and imposing authorities in support of "the Carolina doctrines" which in fact, are the doctrines of the Virginia Resolutions of 1798.

Sir, at that day the whole country was divided on this very question. It formed the line of demarcation between the federal and republican parties, and the great political revolution which then took place turned upon the very question involved in these resolutions. That question was decided by the people, and by that decision the Constitution was, in the emphatic language of Mr. Jefferson, "saved at its last gasp." I should suppose, Sir, it would require more self-respect than any gentleman here would be willing to assume, to treat lightly, doctrines derived from such high sources.—Resting on authority like this, I will ask gentlemen whether South Carolina has not manifested a high regard for the Union, when, under a tyranny ten times more grievous than the alien and sedition laws, she has hitherto gone no further than to *petition, remonstrate,* and solemnly *protest* against a series of measures which she believes to be wholly unconstitutional, and utterly destructive of her interests. Sir, South Carolina has not gone one step further than Mr. Jefferson himself was disposed to go, in relation to the very subject of our present complaints,—not a step further than the statesmen from New England were disposed to go, under similar circumstances,—no further than the Senator from Massachusetts himself once considered as within "the limits of a constitutional opposition." The doctrine that it is the right of a State to judge of the violations of the Constitution on the part of the Federal Government, and to protect her citizens from the operations of unconstitutional laws, was held by the enlightened citizens of Boston, who assembled in Faneuil Hall on the 25th January, 1809. They state in that celebrated memorial, that "they looked only to the State Legislature, who were *competent to devise relief* against the unconstitutional acts of the General Government. That your power (say they) is adequate to that object, is evident *from the organization of the Confederacy."*

A distinguished Senator, from one of the New England States, (Mr. HILLHOUSE) in a speech delivered *here,* on a bill for enforcing the embargo, declared "I feel myself bound in conscience to declare, (lest the blood of those who shall fall in the execution of this measure, shall be on my head) that I consider this to be an act which directs a mortal blow at the liberties of my country—an act containing *unconstitutional provisions,* to which the PEOPLE ARE NOT BOUND TO SUBMIT, and to which, in my opinion, they will not submit.

And the Senator from Massachusetts himself, in a speech delivered on the same subject, in the other House, said,—"This opposition is constitutional and legal; it is also conscientious. It rests on settled and sober conviction, that such policy is destructive to the interests of the people, and *dangerous to the being of the government.* The experience of every day confirms these sentiments. Men who act from such motives, are not to be discouraged by trifling obstacles, nor *awed by any dangers.* They know the limits of constitutional opposition up to that limit; at their own discretion, they will walk, and walk fearlessly." How the "being of the Government" was to be endangered by "constitutional opposition" to the embargo, I leave to the gentleman to explain. Thus it will be seen, Mr. PRESIDENT, that the South Carolina doctrine is the republican doctrine of '98; that it was first promulgated by the Fathers of the Faith—that it was maintained by Virginia and Kentucky, in the worst of times—that it constituted the very pivot on which the political revolution of that day turned—that it embraced the very principles the triumph of which at that time "saved the Constitution at its last gasp;" and which New England Statesmen were not unwilling to adopt, when they believed themselves to be the victims of unconstitutional legislation! Sir, as to the doctrine that the Federal Government is the exclusive judge of the extent as well as the limitations of its powers, it seems to be utterly subversive of the sovereignty and independence of the States. It makes but little difference, in my estimation, whether Congress or the Supreme Court, are invested with this power. If the Federal Government, in all or any of its departments, are to prescribe the limits of its own authority; and the States are bound to submit to the decision, and are not to be allowed to examine and decide for themselves, when the barriers of the Constitution shall be overleaped, this is practically "a Government without limitation of powers;" the States are at once reduced to mere petty corporations, and the people are entirely at your mercy. I have but one word more to add. In all the efforts that have been made by South Carolina to resist the unconstitutional laws which Congress has extended over them, she has kept steadily in view the preservation of the Union, by the only means by which she believes it can be long preserved—a firm, manly, and steady resistance against usurpation. The measures of the Federal Government have, it is true, prostrated her interests, and will soon involve the whole South in irretrievable ruin. But this evil, great as it is, is not the chief ground of our complaints. It is the principle involved in the contest, a principle which, substituting the discretion of Congress for the limitations of the Constitution, brings the States and the people to the feet of the Federal Government, and leaves them nothing they can call their own. Sir, if the measures of the Federal Government were less oppressive, we should still strive against this usurpation. The South is acting on a principle she has always held sound—resistance to *unauthorized taxation*. These, Sir, are the principles which induced the immortal Hampden to resist the payment of a tax of twenty shillings— "Would twenty shillings have ruined his fortune? No—but the payment of half twenty shillings, on the principle on which it was demanded, would have made him a slave." Sir, if, in acting on these high motives—if, animated by that ardent love of liberty which has always been the most prominent trait in the Southern character, we should be hurried beyond the bounds of a cold and calculating prudence, who is there with one noble and generous sentiment in his bosom, who would not be disposed in the language of Burke, to exclaim, "YOU MUST PARDON SOMETHING TO THE SPIRIT OF LIBERTY."

Speech of Mr. Webster,

of Massachusetts

[January 26 and 27, 1830]

The resolution of Mr. Foot, of Connecticut, relative to the
public lands, being under consideration, Mr. Webster
addressed the Chair as follows:

Mr. President:

When the mariner has been tossed, for many days, in thick weather,
and on an unknown sea, he naturally avails himself of the first pause in the
storm, the earliest glance of the sun, to take his latitude, and ascertain how
far the elements have driven him from his true course. Let us imitate this
prudence, and, before we float farther, refer to the point from which we
departed, that we may at least be able to conjecture where we now are. I
ask for the reading of the resolution.

[The Secretary read the resolution, as follows:

"*Resolved,* That the Committee on Public Lands be instructed to inquire
and report the quantity of the public lands remaining unsold within each
State and Territory, and whether it be expedient to limit, for a certain period, the sales of the public lands to such lands only as have heretofore
been offered for sale, and are now subject to entry at the minimum price.
And, also, whether the office of Surveyor General, and some of the Land
Offices, may not be abolished without detriment to the public interest; or
whether it be expedient to adopt measures to hasten the sales, and extend
more rapidly the surveys of the public lands."]

We have thus heard, sir, what the resolution is, which is actually before us for consideration; and it will readily occur to every one that it is almost the only subject about which something has not been said in the
speech, running through two days, by which the Senate has been now entertained by the gentleman from South Carolina. Every topic in the wide

---

range of our public affairs, whether past or present—every thing, general or local, whether belonging to national politics, or party politics, seems to have attracted more or less of the honorable member's attention, save only the resolution before us. He has spoken of every thing but the public lands. They, have escaped his notice. To that subject, in all his excursions, he has not paid even the cold respect of a passing glance.

When this debate, sir, was to be resumed, on Thursday morning, it so happened that it would have been convenient for me to be elsewhere. The honorable member, however, did not incline to put off the discussion to another day. He had a shot, he said, to return, and he wished to discharge it. That shot, sir, which it was kind thus to inform us was coming, that we might stand out of the way, or prepare ourselves to fall before it, and die with decency, has now been received. Under all advantages, and with expectation awakened by the tone which preceded it, it has been discharged, and has spent its force. It may become me to say no more of its effect, than that, if nobody is found, after all, either killed or wounded by it, it is not the first time, in the history of human affairs, that the vigor and success of the war have not quite come up to the lofty and sounding phrase of the manifesto.

The gentleman, sir, in declining to postpone the debate, told the Senate, with the emphasis of his hand upon his heart, that there was something rankling *here,* which he wished to relieve. [Mr. HAYNE rose, and disclaimed having used the word *rankling.*] It would not, Mr. President, be safe for the honorable member to appeal to those around him, upon the question, whether he did, in fact, make use of that word. But he may have been unconscious of it. At any rate, it is enough that he disclaims it. But still, with or without the use of that particular word, he had yet something *here,* he said, of which he wished to rid himself by an immediate reply. In this respect, sir, I have a great advantage over the honorable gentleman. There is nothing *here,* sir, which gives me the slightest uneasiness; neither fear, nor anger, nor that, which is sometimes more troublesome than either—the consciousness of having been in the wrong. There is nothing, either originating *here,* or now received *here,* by the gentleman's shot. Nothing original, for I had not the slightest feeling of disrespect or unkindness towards the honorable member. Some passages, it is true, had occurred since our acquaintance in this body, which I could have wished might have been otherwise; but I had used philosophy and forgotten them. When the honorable member rose, in his first speech, I paid him the respect of attentive listening; and when he sat down, though surprised,

and I must say even astonished, at some of his opinions, nothing was farther from my intention than to commence any personal warfare: and
through the whole of the few remarks I made in answer, I avoided, stu-
diously and carefully, every thing which I thought possible to be construed
into disrespect. And, sir, while there is thus, nothing originating *here*,
which I wished, at any time, or now wish to discharge, I must repeat, also,
that nothing has been received *here*, which *rankles*, or in any way gives me
annoyance. I will not accuse the honorable member of violating the rules
of civilized war,—I will not say, that he poisoned his arrows. But whether
his shafts were, or were not, dipped in that, which would have caused
rankling, if they had reached, there was not, as it happened, quite strength
enough in the bow to bring them to their mark. If he wishes now to gather
up those shafts, he must look for them elsewhere; they will not be found
fixed and quivering in the object, at which they were aimed.

The honorable member complained that I had slept on his speech. I
must have slept on it, or not slept at all. The moment the honorable member sat down, his friend from Missouri rose, and with much honeyed commendation of the speech, suggested that the impressions which it had
produced, were too charming and delightful to be disturbed by other sentiments or other sounds, and proposed that the Senate should adjourn.
Would it have been quite amiable, in me, sir, to interrupt this excellent
good feeling? Must I not have been absolutely malicious, if I could have
thrust myself forward, to destroy sensations, thus pleasing? Was it not
much better and kinder, both to sleep upon them myself, and to allow others, also, the pleasure of sleeping upon them? But if it be meant, by sleeping upon his speech, that I took time to prepare a reply to it, it is quite a
mistake; owing to other engagements, I could not employ even the interval, between the adjournment of the Senate, and its meeting the next
morning, in attention to the subject of this debate. Nevertheless, sir, the
mere matter of fact is undoubtedly true—I did sleep on the gentleman's
speech; and slept soundly. And I slept equally well on his speech of yesterday, to which I am now replying. It is quite possible that in this respect,
also, I possess some advantage over the honorable member, attributable,
doubtless, to a cooler temperament on my part: for, in truth, I slept upon
his speeches remarkably well. But the gentleman inquires, why *he* was
made the object of such a reply? Why was *he* singled out? If an attack had
been made on the East, he, he assures us, did not begin it—it was the gentleman from Missouri. Sir, I answered the gentleman's speech, because I
happened to hear it: and because, also, I chose to give an answer to that

speech, which, if unanswered, I thought most likely to produce injurious impressions. I did not stop to inquire who was the original drawer of the bill. I found a responsible endorser before me, and it was my purpose to hold him liable, and to bring him to his just responsibility, without delay. But, sir, this interrogatory of the honorable member was only introductory to another. He proceeded to ask me, whether I had turned upon him, in this debate, from the consciousness that I should find an over-match, if I ventured on a contest with his friend from Missouri. If, sir, the honorable member, *ex gratia modestiae,* had chosen thus to defer to his friend, and to pay him a compliment, without intentional disparagement to others, it would have been quite according to the friendly courtesies of debate, and not at all ungrateful to my own feelings. I am not one of those, sir, who esteem any tribute of regard, whether light and occasional, or more serious and deliberate, which may be bestowed on others, as so much unjustly withholden from themselves. But the tone and manner of the gentleman's question, forbid me that I thus interpret it. I am not at liberty to consider it as nothing more than a civility to his friend. It had an air of taunt and disparagement, a little of the loftiness of asserted superiority, which does not allow me to pass it over without notice. It was put as a question for me to answer, and so put, as if it were difficult for me to answer, whether I deemed the member from Missouri an over-match for myself, in debate here. It seems, to me, sir, that this is extraordinary language, and an extraordinary tone, for the discussions of this body.

Matches and over-matches! Those terms are more applicable elsewhere than here, and fitter for other assemblies than this. Sir, the gentleman seems to forget where, and what, we are. This is a Senate: a Senate of equals: of men of individual honor and personal character, and of absolute independence. We know no masters; we acknowledge no dictators. This is a Hall for mutual consultation and discussion; not an arena for the exhibition of champions. I offer myself, sir, as a match for no man; I throw the challenge of debate at no man's feet. But, then, sir, since the honorable member has put the question, in a manner that calls for an answer, I will give him an answer; and I tell him, that, holding myself to be the humblest of the members here, I yet know nothing in the arm of his friend from Missouri, either alone, or when aided by the arm of *his* friend from South Carolina, that need deter, even me, from espousing whatever opinions I may choose to espouse, from debating whenever I may choose to debate, or from speaking whatever I may see fit to say, on the floor of the Senate. Sir, when uttered as matter of commendation or compliment, I should dissent from nothing which the honorable member might say of his friend. Still less do I put forth any pretensions of my own. But, when put to me as matter of taunt, I throw it back, and say to the gentleman that he could possibly say nothing less likely than such a comparison, to wound my pride of personal character. The anger of its tone rescued the remark from intentional irony, which, otherwise, probably, would have been its general acceptation. But, sir, if it be imagined that by this mutual quotation and commendation; if it be supposed that, by casting the characters of the drama, assigning to each his part: to one the attack; to another the cry of onset; or, if it be thought that by a loud and empty vaunt of anticipated victory, any laurels are to be won here; if it be imagined, especially, that any, or all these things will shake any purpose of mine, I can tell the honorable member, once for all, that he is greatly mistaken, and that he is dealing with one of whose temper and character he has yet much to learn. Sir, I shall not allow myself, on this occasion, I hope on no occasion, to be betrayed into any loss of temper; but if provoked, as I trust I never shall allow myself to be, into crimination and recrimination, the honorable member may, perhaps, find, that, in that contest, there will be blows to take as well as blows to give; that others can state comparisons as significant, at least, as his own, and that his impunity may, perhaps, demand of him whatever powers of taunt and sarcasm he may possess. I commend him to a prudent husbandry of his resources.

But, sir, the Coalition! The Coalition! Aye, "the murdered Coalition!" The gentleman asks, if I were led or frighted into this debate by the spectre of the Coalition—"was it the ghost of the murdered Coalition," he exclaims, "which haunted the member from Massachusetts; and which, like the ghost of Banquo, would never down?" "The murdered Coalition!" Sir, this charge of a coalition, in reference to the late Administration, is not original with the honorable member. It did not spring up in the Senate. Whether as a fact, as an argument, or as an embellishment, it is all borrowed. He adopts it, indeed, from a very low origin, and a still lower present condition. It is one of the thousand calumnies with which the press teemed, during an excited political canvass. It was a charge, of which there was not only no proof or probability, but which was, in itself, wholly impossible to be true. No man of common information ever believed a syllable of it. Yet it was of that class of falsehoods, which, by continued repetition, through all the organs of detraction and abuse, are capable of misleading those who are already far misled, and of further fanning passion, already kindling into flame. Doubtless, it served in its day, and, in greater or less degree, the end designed by it. Having done that, it has sunk into the general mass of stale and loathed calumnies. It is the very cast-off slough of a polluted and shameless press. Incapable of further mischief, it lies in the sewer, lifeless and despised. It is not now, sir, in the power of the honorable member to give it dignity or decency, by attempting to elevate it, and to introduce it into the Senate. He cannot change it from what it is, an object of general disgust and scorn. On the contrary, the contract, if he choose to touch it, is more likely to drag him down, down, to the place where it lies itself.

But, sir, the honorable member was not, for other reasons, entirely happy in his allusion to the story of Banquo's murder, and Banquo's ghost. It was not, I think, the friends, but the enemies of the murdered Banquo, at whose bidding his spirit would not *down*. The honorable gentleman is fresh in his reading of the English classics, and can put me right, if I am wrong; but, according to my poor recollection, it was at those who had begun with caresses, and ended with foul and treacherous murder, that the gory locks were shaken! The ghost of Banquo, like that of Hamlet, was an honest ghost. It disturbed no innocent man. It knew where its appearance would strike terror, and who would cry out, a ghost! It made itself visible in the right quarter, and compelled the guilty, and the conscience-smitten, and none others, to start, with,

> "Pr'ythee, see there! behold!—look! lo
> "If I stand here, I saw him!"

Their eye balls were seared (was it not so, sir?) who had thought to shield themselves, by concealing their own hand, and laying the imputation of the crime on a low and hireling agency in wickedness; who had vainly attempted to stifle the workings of their own coward consciences, by ejaculating, through white lips and chattering teeth, "thou canst not say I did it!" I have misread the great poet, if it was those who had no way partaken in the deed of the death, who either found that they were, *or feared that they should be,* pushed from their stools by the ghost of the slain, or who exclaimed, to a spectre created by their own fears, and their own remorse, "avaunt! and quit our sight!"

There is another particular, sir, in which the honorable member's quick perception of resemblances might, I should think, have seen something in the story of Banquo, making it not altogether a subject of the most pleasant contemplation. Those who murdered Banquo, what did they win by it? Substantial good? Permanent power? Or disappointment, rather, and sore mortification;—dust and ashes—the common fate of vaulting ambition, overleaping itself? Did not even-handed justice ere long commend the poisoned chalice to their own lips? Did they not soon find that for another they had "filed their mind?" that their ambition, though apparently for the moment successful, had but put a barren sceptre in their grasp? Aye, Sir,

"A barren sceptre in their gripe,
"*Thence to be wrenched by an unlineal hand,*
"*No son of their's succeeding.*"

Sir, I need pursue the allusion no farther. I leave the honorable gentleman to run it out at his leisure, and to derive from it all the gratification it is calculated to administer. If he finds himself pleased with the associations, and prepared to be quite satisfied, though the parallel should be entirely completed, I had almost said, I am satisfied also—but that I shall think of. Yes, sir, I will think of that.

In the course of my observations the other day, Mr. President, I paid a passing tribute of respect to a very worthy man, Mr. Dane, of Massachusetts. It so happened that he drew the ordinance of 1787, for the government of the Northwestern Territory. A man of so much ability, and so little pretence; of so great a capacity to do good, and so unmixed a disposition to do it for its own sake; a gentleman who acted an important part, forty years ago, in a measure the influence of which is still deeply felt in the very matter which was the subject of debate, might, I thought, receive from me a commendatory recognition.

But the honorable member was inclined to be facetious on the subject. He was rather disposed to make it matter of ridicule, that I had introduced into the debate the name of one Nathan Dane, of whom he assures us he had never before heard. Sir, if the honorable member had never before heard of Mr. Dane, I am sorry for it. It shows him less acquainted with the public men of the country, than I had supposed. Let me tell him, however, that a sneer from him, at the mention of the name of Mr. Dane, is in bad taste. It may well be a high mark of ambition, sir, either with the honorable gentleman or myself, to accomplish as much to make our names known to advantage, and remembered with gratitude, as Mr. Dane has accomplished. But the truth is, sir, I suspect, that Mr. Dane lives a little too far North. He is of Massachusetts, and too near the North star to be reached by the honorable gentleman's telescope. If his sphere had happened to range South of Mason's and Dixson's line, he might, probably, have come within the scope of his vision!

I spoke, sir, of the ordinance of 1787, which prohibited slavery, in all future times, northwest of the Ohio, as a measure of great wisdom and foresight; and one which had been attended with highly beneficial and permanent consequences. I supposed, that on this point, no two gentlemen in the Senate could entertain different opinions. But, the simple expression of this sentiment has led the gentleman, not only into a labored defence of slavery, in the abstract, and on principle, but, also, into a warm accusation against me, as having attacked the system of domestic slavery, now existing in the Southern States. For all this, there was not the slightest foundation, in any thing said or intimated by me. I did not utter a single word, which any ingenuity could torture into an attack on the slavery of the South. I said, only, that it was highly wise and useful in legislating for the northwestern country, while it was yet a wilderness, to prohibit the introduction of slaves: and added, that I presumed, in the neighboring State of Kentucky, there was no reflecting and intelligent gentleman, who would doubt, that if the same prohibition had been extended, at the same early period, over that commonwealth, her strength and population would, at this day, have been far greater than they are. If these opinions be thought doubtful, they are, nevertheless, I trust, neither extraordinary nor disrespectful. They attack nobody, and menace nobody. And yet, sir, the gentleman's optics have discovered, even in the mere expression of this sentiment, what he calls the very spirit of the Missouri question! He represents me as making an onset on the whole South, and manifesting a spirit which would interfere with, and disturb, their domestic condition! Sir, this injustice no otherwise surprises me, than as it is done here, and done without the slightest pretence of ground for it. I say it only surprises me, as being done here; for I know, full well, that it is, and has been, the settled policy of some persons in the South, for years, to represent the people of the North as disposed to interfere with them, in their own exclusive and peculiar concerns. This is a delicate and sensitive point, in southern feeling; and of late years it has always been touched, and generally with effect, whenever the object has been to unite the whole South against northern men, or northern measures. This feeling, always carefully kept alive, and maintained at too intense a heat to admit discrimination or reflection, is a lever of great power in our political machine. It moves vast bodies, and gives to them one and the same direction. But the feeling is without all adequate cause, and the suspicion which exists wholly groundless. There is not, and never has been, a disposition in the North to interfere with these interests of the South. Such interference has never been supposed to be within the power of Government; nor has it been, in any way, attempted. It has always been regarded as a matter of domestic policy, left with the States themselves, and with which the Federal Government had nothing to do. Certainly, sir, I am, and ever have been of that opinion. The gentleman, indeed, argues that slavery, in the abstract, is no evil. Most assuredly, I need not say I differ with him, altogether and most widely, on that point. I regard domestic slavery as one of the greatest of evils, both moral and political. But, though it be a malady, and whether it be curable, and if so, by what means; or, on the other hand, whether it be the *vulnus immedicabile* of the social system, I leave it to those whose right and duty it is to inquire and to decide. And this I believe, sir, is, and uniformly has been, the sentiment of the North. Let us look a little at the history of this matter.

When the present Constitution was submitted for the ratification of the People, there were those who imagined that the powers of the Government which it proposed to establish, might, perhaps, in some possible mode, be exerted in measures tending to the abolition of slavery. This suggestion would of course attract much attention in the Southern Conventions. In that of Virginia, Governor Randolph said:

> "I hope there is none here, who, considering the subject in the calm light of philosophy, will make an objection dishonorable to Virginia—that at the moment they are securing the rights of their citizens, an objection is started, that there is a spark of hope, that those unfortunate men now held in bondage, may, by the operation of the General Government, be made free."

At the very first Congress, petitions on the subject were presented, if I mistake not, from different States. The Pennsylvania Society for promoting the Abolition of Slavery took a lead, and laid before Congress a memorial, praying Congress to promote the abolition by such powers as it possessed. This memorial was referred, in the House of Representatives, to a Select Committee, consisting of Mr. Foster, of New Hampshire, Mr. Gerry, of Massachusetts, Mr. Huntington, of Connecticut, Mr. Lawrence, of New York, Mr. Sinnickson, of New Jersey, Mr. Hartley, of Pennsylvania, and Mr. Parker, of Virginia,—all of them, sir, as you will observe, Northern men, but the last. This Committee made a report, which was committed to a Committee of the Whole House, and there considered and discussed on several days; and being amended, although in no material respect, it was made to express three distinct propositions, on the subjects of Slavery and the Slave Trade. First, in the words of the Constitution; that Congress could not, prior to the year 1808, prohibit the migration or importation of such persons as any of the States, then existing, should think proper to admit. Second, that Congress had authority to restrain the citizens of the United States from carrying on the African Slave Trade, for the purpose of supplying foreign countries. On this proposition, our early laws against those who engage in that traffic are founded. The third proposition, and that which bears on the present question, was expressed in the following terms:

> "*Resolved*, That Congress have no authority to interfere in the emancipation of slaves, or in the treatment of them in any of the States; it remaining with the several States alone to provide rules and regulations therein, which humanity and true policy may require."

This resolution received the sanction of the House of Representatives so early as March, 1790. And now, sir, the honorable member will allow me to remind him, that not only were the Select Committee who reported the resolution, with a single exception, all Northern men, but also that of the members then composing the House of Representatives, a large majority, I believe nearly two-thirds, were Northern men also.

The House agreed to insert these resolutions in its journal; and from that day to this, it has never been maintained or contended, that Congress had any authority to regulate, or interfere with, the condition of slaves in the several States. No Northern gentleman, to my knowledge, has moved any such question in either House of Congress.

The fears of the South, whatever fears they might have entertained, were allayed and quieted by this early decision; and so remained, till they were excited afresh, without cause, but for collateral and indirect purposes. When it become necessary, or was thought so, by some political persons, to find an unvarying ground for the exclusion of Northern men from confidence and from lead in the affairs of the Republic, then, and not till then, the cry was raised, and the feeling industriously excited, that the influence of Northern men in the public councils would endanger the relation of master and slave. For myself, I claim no other merit, than that this gross and enormous injustice towards the whole North, has not wrought upon me to change my opinions, or my political conduct. I hope I am above violating my principles, even under the smart of injury and false imputations. Unjust suspicions and undeserved reproach, whatever pain I may experience from them, will not induce me, I trust, nevertheless, to overstep the limits of constitutional duty, or to encroach on the rights of others. The domestic slavery of the South I leave where I find it—in the hands of their own Governments. It is their affair, not mine. Nor do I complain of the peculiar effect which the magnitude of that population has had in the distribution of power under this Federal Government. We know, sir, that the representation of the States in the other House is not equal. We know that great advantage, in that respect, is enjoyed by the slave-holding States; and we know, too, that the intended equivalent for that advantage, that is to say, the imposition of direct taxes in the same ratio, has become merely nominal; the habit of the Government being almost invariably to collect its revenues from other sources, and in other modes. Nevertheless, I do not complain: nor would I countenance any movement to alter this arrangement of representation. It is the original bargain—the compact—let it stand: let the advantage of it be fully enjoyed. The Union itself is too full of benefit to be hazarded in propositions for changing its original basis. I go for the Constitution as it is, and for the Union as it is. But I am resolved not to submit, in silence, to accusations, either against myself individually, or against the North, wholly unfounded and unjust—accusations which impute to us a disposition to evade the constitutional compact, and to extend the power of the Government over the internal laws and domestic condition of the States. All such accusations, wherever and whenever made—all insinuations of the existence of any such purposes, I know, and feel, to be groundless and injurious. And we must confide in Southern gentlemen themselves; we must trust to those whose integrity of heart and magnanimity of feeling will lead them to a desire to maintain and disseminate truth, and who possess the means of its diffusion with the Southern public; we must leave it to them to disabuse that public of its prejudices. But, in the mean time, for my own part, I shall continue to act justly, whether those towards whom justice is exercised receive it with candor or with contumely.

Having had occasion to recur to the ordinance of 1787, in order to defend myself against the inferences which the honorable member has chosen to draw from my former observations on that subject, I am not willing now entirely to take leave of it without another remark. It need hardly be said, that that paper expresses just sentiments on the great subject of civil and religious liberty. Such sentiments were common, and abound in all our state papers of that day. But this ordinance did that which was not so common, and which is not, even now, universal; that is, it set forth and declared, *as a high and binding duty of Government itself,* to encourage schools, and advance the means of education; on the plain reason, that religion, morality, and knowledge, are necessary to good government, and to the happiness of mankind. One observation further. The important provision incorporated into the Constitution of the U. States, and several of those of the States, and recently, as we have seen, adopted into the reformed Constitution of Virginia, restraining legislative power, in questions of private right, and from impairing the obligation of contracts, is first introduced and established, as far as I am informed, as matter of express written constitutional law, in this ordinance of 1787. And I must add, also, in regard to the author of the ordinance, who has not had the happiness to attract the gentleman's notice, heretofore, nor to avoid his sarcasm now, that he was Chairman of that Select Committee of the old Congress, whose report first expressed the strong sense of that body, that the old Confederation was not adequate to the exigencies of the country, and recommending to the States to send Delegates to the Convention which formed the present Constitution.—Note I.

An attempt has been made to transfer, from the North to the South, the honor of this exclusion of slavery from the Northwestern territory. The journal, without argument or comment, refutes such attempt. The cession by Virginia was made, March, 1784. On the 19th of April following, a committee, consisting of Messrs. Jefferson, Chase, and Howell, reported a plan for a temporary government of the territory, in which was this article: "that, after the year 1800, there shall be neither slavery, nor involuntary servitude in any of the said States, otherwise than in punishment of crimes, whereof the party shall have been convicted." Mr. Spaight, of North Carolina, moved to strike out this paragraph. The question was put, according to the form then practised: "shall these words stand, as part of the plan," &c. New Hampshire, Massachusetts, Rhode Island, Connecticut, New York, New Jersey, and Pennsylvania—seven States, voted in the affirmative. Maryland, Virginia, and South Carolina, in the negative. North Carolina was divided. As the consent of nine States was necessary, the words could not stand, and were struck out accordingly. Mr. Jefferson voted for the clause, but was overruled by his colleagues.

In March of the next year, (1785,) Mr. King, of Massachusetts, seconded by Mr. Ellery, of Rhode Island, proposed the formerly rejected article, with this addition—*"And that this regulation shall be an article of compact, and remain a fundamental principle of the Constitutions between the thirteen original States, and each of the States described in the Resolve,"* &c. On this clause, which provided the adequate and thorough security, the eight Northern States at that time voted affirmatively, and the four Southern States negatively. The votes of nine States were not yet obtained, and thus, the provision was again rejected by the Southern States. The perseverance of the North held out, and two years afterwards the object was attained. It is no derogation from the credit, whatever that may be, of drawing the ordinance, that its principles had before been prepared and discussed, in the form of Resolutions. If one should reason in that way, what would become of the distinguished honor of the Author of the Declaration of Independence? There is not a sentiment in that paper which had not been voted and resolved in the assemblies, and other popular bodies in the country, over and over again.

But the honorable member has now found out that this gentleman (Mr. Dane) was a member of the Hartford Convention. However uninformed the honorable member may be of characters and occurrences at the North, it would seem that he has at his elbow on this occasion some high-minded and lofty spirit, some magnanimous and true-hearted monitor, possessing the means of local knowledge, and ready to supply the honorable member with every thing, down even to forgotten and motheaten two-penny pamphlets, which may be used to the disadvantage of his own country. But, as to the Hartford Convention, sir, allow me to say, that the proceedings of that body seem now to be less read and studied in New England than farther South. They appear to be looked to, not in New England, but elsewhere, for the purpose of seeing how far they may serve as a precedent. But they will not answer the purpose—they are quite too tame. The latitude in which they originated was too cold. Other conventions, of more recent existence, have gone a whole bar's length beyond it. The learned doctors of Colleton and Abbeville have pushed their commentaries on the Hartford collect so far that the original text-writers are thrown entirely into the shade. I have nothing to do, sir, with the Hartford Convention. Its Journal, which the gentleman has quoted, I never read. So far as the honorable member may discover in its proceedings a spirit, in any degree resembling that which was avowed and justified in those other Conventions to which I have alluded, or so far as those proceedings can be shown to be disloyal to the Constitution, or tending to disunion, so far I shall be as ready as any one to bestow on them reprehension and censure.

Having dwelt long on this Convention, and other occurrences of that day, in the hope, probably, (which will not be gratified) that I should leave the course of this debate to follow him, at length, in those excursions, the honorable member returned, and attempted another object. He referred to a speech of mine in the other House, the same which I had occasion to allude to myself the other day; and has quoted a passage or two from it, with a bold, though uneasy and laboring air of confidence, as if he had detected in me an inconsistency. Judging from the gentleman's manner, a stranger to the course of the debate, and to the point in discussion, would have imagined, from so triumphant a tone, that the honorable member was about to overwhelm me with a manifest contradiction. Any one who heard him, and who had not heard what I had, in fact, previously said, must have thought me routed and discomfited, as the gentleman had promised. Sir, a breath blows all this triumph away. There is not the slightest difference in the sentiments of my remarks on the two occasions. What I said here on Wednesday, is in exact accordance with the opinions expressed by me in the other House in 1825. Though the gentleman had the metaphysics of Hudibras—though he were able

"To sever and divide
"A hair 'twixt North and Northwest side,"

he yet could not insert his metaphysical scissors between the fair reading of my remarks in 1825, and what I said here last week. There is not only no contradiction, no difference, but, in truth, too exact a similarity, both in thought and language, to be entirely in just taste. I had myself quoted the same speech; had recurred to it, and spoke with it open before me; and much of what I said was little more than a repetition from it. In order to make finishing work with this alleged contradiction, permit me to recur to the origin of this debate, and review its course. This seems expedient, and may be done as well now as at any time.

Well, then, its history is this: The honorable member from Connecticut moved a resolution, which constitutes the first branch of that which is now before us; that is to say, a resolution, instructing the Committee on Public Lands to inquire into the expediency of limiting, for a certain period, the sales of the public lands, to such as have heretofore been offered for sale; and whether sundry offices, connected with the sales of the lands, might not be abolished, without detriment to the public service.

In the progress of the discussion which arose on this resolution, an honorable member from New Hampshire moved to amend the resolution, so as entirely to reverse its object; that is, to strike it all out, and insert a direction to the committee to inquire into the expediency of adopting measures to hasten the sales, and extend more rapidly the surveys of the lands.

The honorable member from Maine, [Mr. SPRAGUE,] suggested that both those propositions might well enough go, for consideration, to the committee; and in this state of the question the member from South Carolina addressed the Senate in his first speech. He rose, he said, to give us his own free thoughts on the public lands. I saw him rise, with pleasure, and listened with expectation, though before he concluded, I was filled with surprise. Certainly, I was never more surprised, than to find him following up, to the extent he did, the sentiments and opinions, which the gentleman from Missouri had put forth, and which it is known he has long entertained.

I need not repeat at large the general topics of the honorable gentleman's speech. When he said, yesterday, that he did not attack the Eastern States, he certainly must have forgotten, not only particular remarks, but the whole drift and tenor of his speech; unless he means, by not attacking, that he did not commence hostilities,—but that another had preceded him in the attack. He, in the first place, disapproved of the whole course of the Government, for forty years, in regard to its dispositions of the public land; and then, turning northward and eastward, and fancying he had found a cause for alleged narrowness and niggardliness in the "accursed policy" of the Tariff, to which he represented the people of New England as wedded, he went on, for a full hour, with remarks, the whole scope of which was to exhibit the results of this policy, in feelings and in measures unfavorable to the West. I thought his opinions unfounded and erroneous, as to the general course of the Government, and ventured to reply to them.

The gentleman had remarked on the analogy of other cases, and quoted the conduct of European Governments, towards their own subjects, settling on this continent, as in point, to show, that we had been harsh and rigid in selling, when we should have given the public lands to settlers. I thought the honorable member had suffered his judgment to be betrayed by a false analogy; that he was struck with an appearance of resemblance, where there was no real similitude. I think so still. The first settlers of North America were enterprising spirits, engaged in private adventure, or fleeing from tyranny at home. When arrived here, they were forgotten by the mother country, or remembered only to be oppressed. Carried away again by the appearance of analogy, or struck with the eloquence of the passage, the honorable member yesterday observed that the conduct of Government towards the Western emigrants, or my representation of it, brought to his mind a celebrated speech in the British Parliament. It was, sir, the speech of Col. Barre. On the question of the stamp act, or tea tax, I forget which, Col. Barre had heard a member on the Treasury Bench argue, that the people of the United States, being British colonists, planted by the maternal care, nourished by the indulgence, and protected by the arms of England, would not grudge their mite to relieve the mother country from the heavy burden under which she groaned. The language of Col. Barre, in reply to this, was—They planted by your care? Your oppression planted them in America. They fled from your tyranny, and grew by your neglect of them. So soon as you began to care for them, you showed your care by sending persons to spy out their liberties, misrepresent their character, prey upon them and eat out their substance.

And now does the honorable gentleman mean to maintain, that language like this is applicable to the conduct of the Government of the United States towards the Western emigrants, or to any representation given by me of that conduct? Were the settlers in the West driven thither by our oppression? Have they flourished only by our neglect of them? Has the Government done nothing but to prey upon them, and eat out their substance? Sir, this fervid eloquence of the British speaker, just, when and where it was uttered, and fit to remain an exercise for the schools, is not a little out of place, when it is brought thence to be applied here, to the conduct of our own country towards her own citizens. From America to England, it may be true; from Americans to their own Government it would be strange language. Let us leave it, to be recited and declaimed by our boys, against a foreign nation; not introduce it here, to recite and declaim ourselves against our own.

But I come to the point of the alleged contradiction. In my remarks on Wednesday, I contended that we could not give away gratuitously all the public lands; that we held them in trust; that the Government had solemnly pledged itself to dispose of them as a common fund for the common benefit, and to sell and settle them as its discretion should dictate. Now, sir, what contradiction does the gentleman find to this sentiment, in the speech of 1825? He quotes me as having then said, that we ought not to hug these lands as a very great treasure. Very well, sir, supposing me to be accurately reported, in that expression, what is the contradiction? I have not now said, that we should hug these lands as a favorite source of pecuniary income. No such thing. It is not my view. What I have said, and what I do say, is, that they are a common fund—to be disposed of for the common benefit—to be sold at low prices for the accommodation of settlers, keeping the object of settling the lands as much in view, as that of raising money from them. This I say now, and this I have always said. Is this hugging them as a favorite treasure? Is there no difference between hugging and hoarding this fund, on the one hand, as a great treasure, and on the other, of disposing of it at low prices, placing the proceeds in the general treasury of the Union? My opinion is, that as much is to be made of the land, as fairly and reasonably may be, selling it all the while at such rates as to give the fullest effect to settlement. This is not giving it all away to the States, as the gentleman would propose; nor is it hugging the fund closely and tenaciously, as a favorite treasure; but it is, in my judgment, a just and wise policy, perfectly according with all the various duties which rest on Government. So much for my contradiction. And what is it? Where is the ground of the gentleman's triumph? What inconsistency, in word or doctrine, has he been able to detect? Sir, if this be a sample of that discomfiture, with which the honorable gentleman threatened me, commend me to the word *discomfiture* for the rest of my life.

But, after all, this is not the point of the debate; and I must now bring the gentleman back to that which is the point.

The real question between me and him is, where has the doctrine been advanced, at the South or the East, that the population of the West should be retarded, or at least need not be hastened, on account of its effect to drain off the people from the Atlantic States? Is this doctrine, as has been alleged, of Eastern origin? That is the question. Has the gentleman found any thing, by which he can make good his accusation? I submit to the Senate, that he has entirely failed; and as far as this debate has shown, the only person who has advanced such sentiments, is a gentleman from South Carolina, and a friend to the honorable member himself. The honorable gentleman has given no answer to this; there is none which can be given. The simple fact, while it requires no comment to enforce it, defies all argument to refute it. I could refer to the speeches of another southern gentleman, in years before, of the same general character, and to the same effect, as that which has been quoted; but I will not consume the time of the Senate by the reading of them.

So then, sir, New England is guiltless of the policy of retarding Western population, and of all envy and jealousy of the growth of the New States. Whatever there be of that policy in the country, no part of it is her's. If it has a local habitation, the honorable member has probably seen, by this time, where he is to look for it; and if it now has received a name, he has himself christened it.

We approach, at length, sir, to a more important part of the honorable gentleman's observations. Since it does not accord with my views of justice and policy to give away the public lands altogether, as mere matter of gratuity, I am asked by the honorable gentleman on what ground it is, that I consent to vote them away, in particular instances? How, he inquires, do I reconcile with these professed sentiments, my support of measures appropriating portions of the lands to particular roads, particular canals, particular rivers, and particular institutions of education in the West? This leads, sir, to the real and wide difference, in political opinion, between the honorable gentleman and myself. On my part, I look upon all these objects, as connected with the common good, fairly embraced in its object and its terms; he, on the contrary, deems them all, if good at all, only local good. This is our difference. The interrogatory which he proceeded to put, at once explains this difference. "What interest," asks he, "has South Carolina in a canal in Ohio?" Sir, this very question is full of significance. It develops the gentleman's whole political system; and its answer expounds mine. Here we differ, *toto coelo*. I look upon a road over the Allegany, a canal round the Falls of the Ohio, or a canal or rail-way from the Atlantic to the western waters, as being objects large and extensive enough to be fairly said to be for the common benefit. The gentleman thinks otherwise, and this is the key to open his construction of the powers of the Government. He may well ask, upon his system, what interest has South Carolina in a canal in Ohio? On that system, it is true, she has no interest. On that system, Ohio and Carolina are different Governments, and different countries, connected here, it is true, by some slight and ill-defined bond of union, but, in all main respects, separate and diverse. On that system, Carolina has no more interest in a canal in Ohio than in Mexico. The gentleman, therefore, only follows out his own principles; he does no more than arrive at the natural conclusions of his own doctrines; he only announces the true results of that creed, which he has adopted himself, and would persuade others to adopt, when he thus declares that South Carolina has no interest in a public work in Ohio. Sir, we narrow-minded people of New England do not reason thus. Our *notion* of things is entirely different. We look upon the States, not as separated, but as united. We love to dwell on that union, and on the mutual happiness which it has so much promoted, and the common renown which it has so greatly contributed to acquire. In our contemplation, Carolina and Ohio are parts of the same country; States, united under the same General Government, having interests, common, associated, intermingled. In whatever is within the proper sphere of the constitutional power of this Government, we look upon the States as one. We do not impose geographical limits to our patriotic feeling or regard; we do not follow rivers and mountains, and lines of latitude, to find boundaries, beyond which public improvements do not benefit us. We who come here, as agents and representatives of these narrow-minded and selfish men of New England, consider ourselves as bound to regard, with equal eye, the good of the whole, in whatever is within our power of legislation. Sir, if a rail road or a canal, beginning in South Carolina, and ending in South Carolina, appeared to me to be of national importance and national magnitude, believing, as I do, that the power of Government extends to the encouragement of works of that description, if I were to stand up here, and ask, what interest has Massachusetts in a rail road in South Carolina, I should not be willing to face my constituents. These same narrow-minded men would tell me, that they had sent me to act for the whole country, and that one who possessed too little comprehension, either of intellect or feeling; one who was not large enough, in mind and heart, to embrace the whole, was not fit to be entrusted with the interest of any part. Sir, I do not desire to enlarge the powers of the Government, by unjustifiable construction; nor to exercise any not within a fair interpretation. But when it is believed that a power does exist, then it is, in my judgment, to be exercised for the general benefit of the whole. So far as respects the exercise of such a power, the States are one. It was the very object of the constitution to create unity of interests, to the extent of the powers of the General Government. In war and peace, we are one; in commerce, one; because the authority of the General Government reaches to war and peace, and to the regulation of commerce. I have never seen any more difficulty, in erecting light houses on the lakes, than on the ocean; in improving the harbors of inland seas, than if they were within the ebb and flow of the tide; or of removing obstructions in the vast streams of the West, more than in any work to facilitate commerce on the Atlantic coast. If there be power for one, there is power also for the other; and they are all and equally for the country.

There are other objects, apparently more local, or the benefit of which is less general, towards which, nevertheless, I have concurred, with others, to give aid, by donations of land. It is proposed to construct a road, in or through one of the new States, in which this Government possesses large quantities of land. Have the United States no right, as a great and untaxed proprietor, are they under no obligation, to contribute to an object thus calculated to promote the common good of all the proprietors, themselves included? And even with respect to education, which is the extreme case, let the question be considered. In the first place, as we have seen, it was made matter of compact with these States, that they should do their part to promote education. In the next place, our whole system of land laws proceeds on the idea that education is for the common good; because, in every division, a certain portion is uniformly reserved and appropriated for the use of schools. And, finally, have not these new States singularly strong claims, founded on the ground already stated, that the Government is a great untaxed proprietor, in the ownership of the soil? It is a consideration of great importance, that, probably, there is in no part of the country, or of the world, so great call for the means of education, as in those new States; owing to the vast numbers of persons within those ages in which education and instruction are usually received, if received at all. This is the natural consequence of recency of settlement and rapid increase. The census of these States shows how great a proportion of the whole population occupies the classes between infancy and manhood. These are the wide fields, and here is the deep and quick soil, for the seeds of knowledge and virtue; and this is the favored season, the very spring-time for sowing them. Let them be disseminated without stint. Let them be scattered with a bountiful, broad cast. Whatever the Government can fairly do towards these objects, in my opinion, ought to be done.

These, sir, are the grounds, succinctly stated, on which my votes for grants of lands for particular objects rest; while I maintain, at the same time, that it is all a common fund, for the common benefit. And reasons like these, I presume, have influenced the votes of other gentlemen from New England. Those who have a different view of the powers of the Government, of course, come to different conclusions, on these, as on other questions. I observed, when speaking on this subject before, that, if we looked to any measure, whether for a road, a canal, or any thing else, intended for the improvement of the West, it would be found, that, if the New England *ayes* were struck out of the lists of votes, the Southern *noes* would always have rejected the measure. The truth of this has not been denied, and cannot be denied. In stating this, I thought it just to ascribe it to the constitutional scruples of the South, rather than to any other less favorable or less charitable cause. But no sooner had I done this, than the honorable gentleman asks if I reproach him and his friends with their constitutional scruples. Sir, I reproach nobody—I stated a fact, and gave the most respectful reason for it that occurred to me. The gentleman cannot deny the fact; he may, if he choose, disclaim the reason. It is not long since I had occasion, in presenting a petition from his own State, to account for its being entrusted to my hands, by saying, that the constitutional opinions of the gentleman and his worthy colleague, prevented them from supporting it. Sir, did I state this as matter of reproach? Far from it. Did I attempt to find any other cause than an honest one, for these scruples? Sir, I did not. It did not become me to doubt nor to insinuate that the gentleman had either changed his sentiments, or that he had made up a set of constitutional opinions, accommodated to any particular combination of political occurrences. Had I done so, I should have felt, that, while I was entitled to little credit in thus questioning other people's motives, I justified the whole world in suspecting my own. But how has the gentleman returned this respect for others' opinions? His own candor and justice, how have they been exhibited towards the motives of others, while he has been at so much pains to maintain, what nobody has disputed, the purity of his own? Why, sir, he has asked *when,* and *how,* and *why,* New England votes were found going for measures favorable to the West? He has demanded to be informed whether all this did not begin in 1825; *and while the election of President was still pending?* Sir, to these questions retort would be justified; and it is both cogent, and at hand. Nevertheless, I will answer the inquiry, not by retort, but by facts. I will tell the gentleman *when,* and *how,* and *why,* New England has supported measures favorable to the West. I have already referred to the early history of the Government—to the first acquisition of the lands—to the original laws for disposing of them, and for governing the territories where they lie; and have shown the influence of New England men and New England principles in all these leading measures. I should not be pardoned were I to go over that ground again. Coming to more recent times, and to measures of a less general character, I have endeavored to prove that every thing of this kind, designed for Western improvement, has depended on the votes of New England; all this is true beyond the power of contradiction.

And now, sir, there are two measures to which I will refer, not so ancient as to belong to the early history of the public lands, and not so recent as to be on this side of the period when the gentleman charitably imagines a new direction may have been given to New England feeling and New England votes. These measures, and the New England votes in support of them, may be taken as samples and specimens of all the rest.

In 1820, (observe, Mr. President, in 1820,) the People of the West besought Congress for a reduction in the price of lands. In favor of that reduction, New England, with a delegation of forty members in the other House, gave thirty-three votes, and one only against it. The four Southern States, with fifty members, gave thirty-two votes for it, and seven against it. Again, in 1821, (observe, again, Sir, the time,) the law passed for the relief of the purchasers of the public lands. This was a measure of vital importance to the West, and more especially to the Southwest. It authorized the relinquishment of contracts for lands, which had been entered into at high prices, and a reduction in the other cases of not less than $37\frac{1}{2}$ per cent on the purchase money. Many millions of dollars—six or seven I believe, at least, probably much more—were relinquished by this law. On this bill, New England, with her forty members, gave more affirmative votes than the four Southern States, with their fifty-two or three members.

These two are far the most important measures respecting the public lands, which have been adopted within the last twenty years. They took place in 1820 and 1821. That is the time *when*. And as to the manner *how*, the gentleman already sees that, it was by voting, in solid column, for the required relief: and lastly, as to the cause *why*, I tell the gentleman, it was because the members from New England thought the measures just and salutary; because they entertained towards the West, neither envy, hatred, or malice; because they deemed it becoming them, as just and enlightened public men, to meet the exigency which had arisen in the West, with the appropriate measure of relief; because they felt it due to their own characters, and the characters of their New England predecessors in this Government, to act towards the new States in the spirit of a liberal, patronizing, magnanimous policy. So much, sir, for the cause *why;* and I hope that by this time, sir, the honorable gentleman is satisfied; if not, I do not know *when,* or *how,* or *why,* he ever will be.

Having recurred to these two important measures, in answer to the gentleman's inquiries, I must now beg permission to go back to a period yet something earlier, for the purpose of still further showing how much, or rather how little, reason there is for the gentleman's insinuation, that political hopes or fears, or party associations, were the grounds of these New England votes. And after what has been said, I hope it may be forgiven me, if I allude to some political opinions and votes of my own, of very little public importance, certainly, but which, from the time at which they were given and expressed, may pass for good witnesses on this occasion.

This Government, Mr. President, from its origin to the peace of 1815, had been too much engrossed with various other important concerns, to be able to turn its thoughts inward, and look to the development of its vast internal resources. In the early part of President Washington's administration, it was fully occupied with organizing the Government, providing for the public debt, defending the frontiers, and maintaining domestic peace. Before the termination of that administration, the fires of the French Revolution blazed forth, as from a new-opened volcano, and the whole breadth of the ocean did not entirely secure us from its effects. The smoke and the cinders reached us, though not the burning lava. Difficult and agitating questions, embarrassing to Government, and dividing public opinion, sprung out of the new state of our foreign relations, and were succeeded by others, and yet again by others, equally embarrassing, and equally exciting division and discord, through the long series of twenty years; till they finally issued in the war with England. Down to the close of that war, no distinct, marked, and deliberate attention had been given, or could have been given, to the internal condition of the country, its capacities of improvement, or the constitutional power of the Government, in regard to objects connected with such improvement.

The peace, Mr. President, brought about an entirely new, and a most interesting state of things: it opened to us other prospects, and suggested other duties. We ourselves were changed, and the whole world was changed. The pacification of Europe, after June, 1815, assumed a firm and permanent aspect. The nations evidently manifested that they were disposed for peace. Some agitation of the waves might be expected, even after the storm had subsided, but the tendency was, strongly and rapidly, towards settled repose.

It so happened, sir, that I was, at that time, a member of Congress, and like others, naturally turned my attention to the contemplation of the newly altered condition of the country, and of the world. It appeared plainly enough to me, as well as to wiser and more experienced men, that the policy of the Government would necessarily take a start in a new direction: because, new directions would necessarily be given to the pursuits and occupations of the people. We had pushed our commerce far and fast, under the advantage of a neutral flag. But there were now no longer flags, either neutral or belligerent. The harvest of neutrality had been great, but we had gathered it all. With the peace of Europe, it was obvious there would spring up in her circle of nations, a revived and invigorated spirit of trade, and a new activity in all the business and objects of civilized life.

Hereafter, our commercial gains were to be earned only by success, in a close and intense competition. Other nations would produce for themselves, and carry for themselves, and manufacture for themselves, to the full extent of their abilities. The crops of our plains would no longer sustain European armies, nor our ships longer supply those whom war had rendered unable to supply themselves. It was obvious, that, under these circumstances, the country would begin to survey itself, and to estimate its own capacity of improvement. And this improvement—how was it to be accomplished, and who was to accomplish it? We were ten or twelve millions of people, spread over almost half a world. We were twenty-four States, some stretching along the same sea-board, some along the same line of inland frontier, and others on opposite banks of the same vast rivers. Two considerations at once presented themselves, in looking at this state of things, with great force. One was, that that great branch of improvement, which consisted in furnishing new facilities of intercourse, necessarily ran into different States, in every leading instance, and would benefit the citizens of all such States. No one State, therefore, in such cases, would assume the whole expense, nor was the co-operation of several States to be expected. Take the instance of the Delaware Breakwater. It will cost several millions of money. Would Pennsylvania alone have ever constructed it? Certainly never, while this Union lasts, because it is not for her sole benefit. Would Pennsylvania, New Jersey, and Delaware, have united to accomplish it, at their joint expense? Certainly not, for the same reason. It could not be done, therefore, but by the General Government. The same may be said of the large inland undertakings, except that, in them, Government, instead of bearing the whole expense, co-operates with others who bear a part. The other consideration is, that the United States have the means. They enjoy all the revenues derived from commerce, and the States have no abundant and easy sources of public income. The custom-houses fill the general treasury, while the States have scanty resources, except by resort to heavy direct taxes.

Under this view of things, I thought it necessary to settle, at least for myself, some definite notions, with respect to the powers of the Government, in regard to internal affairs. It may not savor too much of self-commendation to remark, that, with this object, I considered the Constitution, its judicial construction, its cotemporaneous exposition, and the whole history of the legislation of Congress under it; and I arrived at the conclusion that Government had power to accomplish sundry objects, or aid in their accomplishment, which are now commonly spoken of as INTERNAL

IMPROVEMENTS. That conclusion, sir, may have been right, or it may have been wrong. I am not about to argue the grounds of it at large. I say only, that it was adopted and acted on even so early as in 1816. Yes, Mr. President, I made up my opinion, and determined on my intended course of political conduct, on these subjects, in the Fourteenth Congress, in 1816. And now, Mr. President, I have further to say, that I made up these opinions, and entered on this course of political conduct, *Teucro duce.* Yes, sir, I pursued, in all this, a South Carolina track. On the doctrines of Internal Improvement, South Carolina, as she was then represented in the other House, set forth, in 1816, under a fresh and leading breeze, and I was among the followers. But if my leader sees new lights, and turns a sharp corner, unless I see new lights also, I keep straight on in the same path. I repeat, that leading gentlemen from South Carolina were first and foremost in behalf of the doctrines of Internal Improvements, when those doctrines first came to be considered and acted upon in Congress. The debate on the Bank question, on the Tariff of 1816, and on the Direct Tax, will show who was who, and what was what, at that time. The Tariff of 1816, one of the plain cases of oppression and usurpation, from which, if the Government does not recede, individual States may justly secede from the Government, is, sir, in truth, a South Carolina Tariff, supported by South Carolina votes. But for those votes, it could not have passed in the form in which it did pass; whereas, if it had depended on Massachusetts votes, it would have been lost. Does not the honorable gentleman well know all this? There are certainly those who do, full well, know it all. I do not say this to reproach South Carolina. I only state the fact; and I think it will appear to be true, that among the earliest and boldest advocates of the Tariff, as a measure of protection, and on the express ground of protection, were leading gentlemen of South Carolina in Congress. I did not then, and cannot now, understand their language in any other sense. While this Tariff of 1816 was under discussion, in the House of Representatives, an honorable gentleman from Georgia, now of this House, (Mr. Forsyth,) moved to reduce the proposed duty on cotton. He failed, by four votes, South Carolina giving three votes, (enough to have turned the scale) against his motion. The act, sir, then passed, and received on its passage the support of a majority of the Representatives of South Carolina present and voting. This act is the first, in the order of those now denounced as plain usurpations. We see it daily, in the list, by the side of those of 1824 and 1828, as a case of manifest oppression, justifying disunion. I put it home, to the honorable member from South Carolina, that his own State was not only 'art and part' in this measure, but the *causa causans*. Without her aid, this seminal principle of mischief, this root of Upas, could not have been planted. I have already said, and it is true, that this act proceeded on the ground of protection. It interfered, directly, with existing interests of great value and amount. It cut up the Calcutta cotton trade by the roots, but it passed, nevertheless, and it passed on the principle of protecting manufactures, on the principle against free trade, on the principle *opposed to that which lets us alone.*—NOTE 2.

Such, Mr. President, were the opinions of important and leading gentlemen from South Carolina, on the subject of Internal Improvement, in 1816. I went out of Congress the next year; and returning again in 1823—thought I found South Carolina where I had left her. I really supposed that all things remained as they were, and that the South Carolina doctrine of Internal Improvements would be defended by the same eloquent voices, and the same strong arms, as formerly. In the lapse of these six years, it is true, political associations had assumed a new aspect, and new divisions. A party had arisen in the South, hostile to the doctrine of Internal Improvements, and had vigorously attacked that doctrine. Anti-consolidation was the flag under which this party fought; and its supporters inveighed against Internal Improvements, much after the manner in which the honorable gentleman has now inveighed against them, as part and parcel of the system of consolidation. Whether this party arose in South Carolina herself, or in her neighborhood, is more than I know. I think the latter. However that may have been, there were those found in South Carolina ready to make war upon it, and who did make intrepid war upon it. Names being regarded as things, in such controversies, they bestowed on the anti-improvement gentlemen the appellation of Radicals. Yes, sir, the name of Radicals, as a term of distinction, applicable and applied to those who denied the liberal doctrines of Internal Improvements, originated, according to the best of my recollection, somewhere between North Carolina and Georgia. Well, sir, these mischievous Radicals were to be put down, and the strong arm of South Carolina was stretched out to put them down. About this time, sir, I returned to Congress. The battle with the Radicals had been fought, and our South Carolina champions of the doctrines of Internal Improvement had nobly maintained their ground, and were understood to have achieved a victory. They had driven back the enemy with discomfiture—a thing, by the way, sir, which is not always performed when it is promised. A gentleman, to whom I have already referred in this debate, had come into Congress, during my absence from it, from South Carolina, and had brought with him a high reputation for ability. He came from a school with which we had been acquainted, *et noscitur a sociis.* I hold in my hand, sir, a printed speech of this distinguished gentleman, (Mr. McDuffie,) "on Internal Improvements," delivered about the period to which I now refer, and printed with a few introductory remarks upon consolidation; in which, sir, I think he quite consolidated the arguments of his opponents, the Radicals, if to *crush* be to consolidate. I give you a short but substantive quotation from these remarks. He is speaking of a pamphlet, then recently published, entitled "Consolidation;" and having alluded to the question of renewing the charter of the former Bank of the United States, he says: "Moreover, in the early history of parties, and when Mr. Crawford advocated a renewal of the old charter, it was considered a federal measure; which Internal Improvements *never was,* as this author erroneously states. This latter measure originated in the administration of Mr. Jefferson, with the appropriation for the Cumberland Road; and was first proposed, *as a system,* by Mr. Calhoun, and carried through the House of Representatives by a large majority of the Republicans, including almost every one of the leading men who carried us through the late war."

So then, Internal Improvement is not one of the Federal heresies. One paragraph more, sir:

"The author in question, not content with denouncing as Federalists General Jackson, Mr. Adams, Mr. Calhoun, and the majority of the South Carolina delegation in Congress, modestly extends the denunciation to Mr. Monroe, and the whole Republican party." Here are his words: 'During the Administration of Mr. Monroe much has passed which the Republican party would be glad to approve if they could!! But the principal feature, and that which has chiefly elicited these observations, is the renewal of the System of Internal Improvements.' "Now this measure was adopted by a vote of 115 to 86, of a Republican Congress, and sanctioned by a Republican President. Who, then, is this author—who assumes the high prerogative of denouncing, in the name of the Republican party, the Republican Administration of the country? A denunciation including within its sweep *Calhoun, Lowndes, and Cheves*—men who will be regarded as the brightest ornaments of South Carolina, and the strongest pillars of the Republican party, as long as the late war shall be remembered, and talents and patriotism shall be regarded as the proper objects of the admiration and gratitude of a free People!!"

Such are the opinions, sir, which were maintained by South Carolina gentlemen, in the House of Representatives, on the subject of Internal Improvements, when I took my seat there as a member from Massachusetts, in 1823. But this is not all: We had a bill before us, and passed it in that House, entitled "An act to procure the necessary surveys, plans, and estimates upon the subject of Roads and Canals." *It authorized the President to cause surveys and estimates to be made of the routes of such Roads and Canals as he might deem of national importance, in a commercial or military point of view, or for the transportation of the mail,* and appropriated thirty thousand dollars, out of the Treasury, to defray the expense. This act, though preliminary in its nature, covered the whole ground. It took for granted the complete power of Internal Improvement, as far as any of its advocates had ever contended for it. Having passed the other House, the bill came up to the Senate, and was here considered and debated in April, 1824. The honorable member from South Carolina was a member of the Senate at that time. While the bill was under consideration here, a motion was made to add the following proviso:

"*Provided,* That nothing herein contained shall be construed to affirm *or admit* a power in Congress, on their own authority, to make Roads or Canals, within any of the States of the Union." The yeas and nays were taken on this proviso, and the honorable member voted *in the negative!* The proviso failed.

A motion was then made to add this proviso, viz:

"*Provided,* That the faith of the United States is hereby pledged, that no money shall ever be expended for Roads or Canals, except it shall be among the several States, and in the same proportion as direct taxes are laid and assessed by the provisions of the Constitution."

The honorable member voted *against this proviso,* also, and it failed. The bill was then put on its passage, and the honorable member voted *for it,* and it passed, and became a law.

Now, it strikes me, sir, that there is no maintaining these votes, but upon the power of Internal Improvement, in its broadest sense. In truth, these bills for surveys and estimates have always been considered as test questions—they show who is for and who against Internal Improvement. This law itself went the whole length, and assumed the full and complete power. The gentleman's votes sustained that power, in every form in which the various propositions to amend presented it. He went for the entire and unrestrained authority, without consulting the States, and without agreeing to any proportionate distribution. And now suffer me to remind you,

Mr. President, that it is this very same power, thus sanctioned, in every form, by the gentleman's own opinion, that is so plain and manifest a usurpation, that the State of South Carolina is supposed to be justified in refusing submission to any laws carrying the power into effect. Truly, sir, is not this a little too hard? May we not crave some mercy, under favor and protection of the gentleman's own authority? Admitting that a road, or a canal, must be written down flat usurpation as ever was committed, may we find no mitigation in our respect for his place, and his vote, as one that knows the law?

The Tariff, which South Carolina had an efficient hand in establishing, in 1816, and this asserted power of Internal Improvement, advanced by her in the same year, and, as we have seen, approved and sanctioned by her Representatives in 1824, these two measures are the great grounds on which she is now thought to be justified in breaking up the Union, if she sees fit to break it up!

I may now safely say, I think, that we have had the authority of leading and distinguished gentlemen from South Carolina, in support of the doctrine of Internal Improvement. I repeat, that, up to 1824, I, for one, followed South Carolina; but, when that star, in its ascension, veered off, in an unexpected direction, I relied on its light no longer. [Here the Vice President said: Does the Chair understand the gentleman from Massachusetts to say that the person now occupying the Chair of the Senate has changed his opinions on the subject of Internal Improvements?] From nothing ever said to me, Sir, have I had reason to know of any change in the opinions of the person filling the Chair of the Senate. If such change has taken place, I regret it. I speak generally of the State of Carolina. Individuals, we know there are, who hold opinions favorable to the power. An application for its exercise, in behalf of a public work in South Carolina itself, is now pending, I believe, in the other House, presented by members from that State.

I have thus, sir, perhaps, not without some tediousness of detail, shown that if I am in error, on the subjects of Internal Improvement, how, and in what company, I fell into that error. If I am wrong, it is apparent who misled me.

I go to other remarks of the honorable member, and I have to complain, of an entire misapprehension of what I said on the subject of the national debt, though I can hardly perceive how any one could misunderstand me. What I said was, not that I wished to put off the payment of the debt, but, on the contrary, that I had always voted for every measure for its reduction, as uniformly as the gentleman himself. He seems to claim the exclusive merit of a disposition to reduce the public charge. I do not allow it to him. As a debt, I was, I am for paying it, because it is a charge on our finances, and on the industry of the country. But I observed, that I thought I perceived a morbid fervor on that subject—an excessive anxiety to pay off the debt, not so much because it is a debt simply, as because, while it lasts, it furnishes one objection to disunion. It is a tie of common interest, while it lasts. I did not impute such motives to the honorable member himself, but that there is such a feeling in existence, I have not a particle of doubt. The most I said was, that if one effect of the debt was to strengthen our Union, that effect itself was not regretted by me, however much others might regret it. The gentleman has not seen how to reply to this, otherwise than by supposing me to have advanced the doctrine that a national debt is a national blessing. Others, I must hope, will find less difficulty in understanding me. I distinctly and pointedly cautioned the honorable member not to understand me as expressing an opinion favorable to the continuance of the debt. I repeated this caution, and repeated it more than once; but it was thrown away.

On yet another point, I was still more unaccountably misunderstood. The gentleman had harangued against "consolidation." I told him, in reply, that there was one kind of consolidation to which I was attached, and that was, the CONSOLIDATION OF OUR UNION; and that this was precisely that consolidation to which I feared others were not attached. That such consolidation was the very end of the constitution—the leading object, as they had informed us themselves, which its framers had kept in view. I turned to their communication, and read their very words—"the consolidation of the Union"—and expressed my devotion to this sort of consolidation. I said, in terms, that I wished not, in the slightest degree, to augment the powers of this Government; that my object was to preserve, not to enlarge; and that by consolidating the Union, I understood no more than the strengthening of the Union, and perpetuating it. Having been thus explicit; having thus read from the printed book, the precise words which I adopted, as expressing my own sentiments, it passes comprehension, how any man could understand me as contending for an extension of the powers of the Government, or for consolidation, in that odious sense, in which it means an accumulation in the Federal Government, of the powers properly belonging to the States.

I repeat, sir, that in adopting the sentiment of the framers of the Constitution, I read their language audibly, and word for word; and I pointed out the distinction, just as fully as I have now done, between the consolidation of the Union and that other obnoxious consolidation which I disclaimed. And yet the honorable member misunderstood me. The gentlemen had said that he wished for no fixed revenue—not a shilling. If, by a word, he could convert the Capitol into gold, he would not do it. Why all this fear of revenue? Why, sir, because, as the gentleman told us, it tends to consolidation. Now, this can mean neither more nor less than that a common revenue is a common interest, and that all common interests tend to hold the Union of the States together. I confess I like that tendency; if the gentleman dislikes it, he is right in deprecating a shilling's fixed revenue. So much, sir, for consolidation.

As well as I recollect the course of his remarks, the honorable gentlemen next recurred to the subject of the Tariff. He did not doubt the word must be of unpleasant sound to me, and proceeded, with an effort, neither new, nor attended with new success, to involve me and my votes in inconsistency and contradiction. I am happy the honorable gentleman has furnished me an opportunity of a timely remark or two on that subject. I was glad he approached it, for it is a question I enter upon without fear from any body. The strenuous toil of the gentleman has been to raise an inconsistency, between my dissent to the Tariff in 1824, and my vote in 1828. It is labor lost. He pays undeserved compliment to my speech in 1824; but this is to raise me high, that my fall, as he would have it, in 1828, may be more signal. Sir, there was no fall at all. Between the ground I stood on in 1824, and that I took in 1828, there was not only no precipice, but no declivity. It was a change of position, to meet new circumstances, but on the same level. A plain tale explains the whole matter. In 1816, I had not acquiesced in the Tariff, then supported by South Carolina. To some parts of it, especially, I felt and expressed great repugnance. I held the same opinions in 1821, at the meeting in Faneuil Hall, to which the gentleman has alluded. I said then, and say now, that, as an original question, the authority of Congress to exercise the revenue power, with direct reference to the protection of manufactures, is a questionable authority, far more questionable, in my judgment, than the power of Internal Improvements. I must confess, sir, that, in one respect, some impression has been made on my opinions lately. Mr. Madison's publication has put the power in a very strong light. He has placed it, I must acknowledge, upon grounds of construction and argument, which seem impregnable. But even if the power were doubtful, on the face of the Constitution itself, it had been assumed and asserted in the first revenue law ever passed under that same Constitution; and, on this ground, as a matter settled by cotemporaneous practice, I had refrained from expressing the opinion that the Tariff laws transcended constitutional limits, as the gentleman supposes. What I did say at Faneuil Hall, as far as I now remember, was, that this was originally matter of doubtful construction. The gentleman himself, I suppose, thinks there is no doubt about it, and that the laws are plainly against the Constitution. Mr. Madison's letters, already referred to, contain, in my judgment, by far the most able exposition extant of this part of the Constitution. He has satisfied me, so far as the practice of the Government had left it an open question.

With a great majority of the Representatives of Massachusetts, I voted against the Tariff of 1824. My reasons were then given, and I will not now repeat them. But, notwithstanding our dissent, the great States of New York, Pennsylvania, Ohio, and Kentucky, went for the bill, in almost unbroken column, and it passed. Congress and the President sanctioned it, and it became the law of the land. What, then, were we to do? Our only option was, either to fall in with this settled course of public policy, and accommodate ourselves to it as well as we could, or to embrace the South Carolina doctrine, and talk of nullifying the statute by State interference.

This last alternative did not suit our principles, and, of course, we adopted the former. In 1827, the subject came again before Congress, on a proposition favorable to wool and woollens. We looked upon the system of protection as being fixed and settled. The law of 1824 remained. It had gone into full operation, and, in regard to some objects intended by it, perhaps most of them, had produced all its expected effects. No man proposed to repeal it; no man attempted to renew the general contest on its principle. But, owing to subsequent and unforeseen occurrences, the benefit intended by it to wool and woollen fabrics had not been realized. Events, not known here when the law passed, had taken place, which defeated its object in that particular respect. A measure was accordingly brought forward to meet this precise deficiency, to remedy this particular defect. It was limited to wool and woollens. Was ever any thing more reasonable? If the policy of the Tariff laws had become established in principle, as the permanent policy of the Government, should they not be revised and amended, and made equal, like other laws, as exigencies should arise, or justice require? Because we had doubted about adopting the system, were we to refuse to cure its manifest defects, after it become adopted, and when no one attempted its repeal? And this, sir, is the inconsistency so much bruited. I had voted against the Tariff of 1824—but it passed; and in 1827 and 1828, I voted to amend it, in a point essential to the interest of my constituents. Where is the inconsistency? Could I do otherwise? Sir, does political consistency consist in always giving negative votes? Does it require of a public man to refuse to concur in amending laws, because they passed against his consent? Having voted against the Tariff originally, does consistency demand that I should do all in my power to maintain an unequal Tariff, burdensome to my own constituents, in many respects, favorable in none? To consistency of that sort, I lay no claim—and there is another sort to which I lay as little—and that is, a kind of consistency by which persons feel themselves as much bound to oppose a proposition after it has become a law of the land, as before.

The bill of 1827, limited, as I have said, to the single object in which the Tariff of 1824 had manifestly failed in its effect, passed the House of Representatives, but was lost here. We had then the act of 1828. I need not recur to the history of a measure so recent. Its enemies spiced it with whatsoever they thought would render it distasteful; its friends took it, drugged as it was. Vast amounts of property, many millions, had been invested in manufactures, under the inducements of the act of 1824. Events called loudly, as I thought, for further regulation to secure the degree of protection intended by that act. I was disposed to vote for such regulation, and desired nothing more; but certainly was not to be bantered out of my purpose by a threatened augmentation of duty on molasses put into the bill for the avowed purpose of making it obnoxious. The vote may have been right or wrong, wise or unwise; but it is little less than absurd to allege against it an inconsistency with opposition to the former law.

Sir, as to the general subject of the Tariff, I have little now to say. Another opportunity may be presented. I remarked the other day, that this policy did not begin with us in New England; and yet, sir, New England is charged, with vehemence, as being favorable, or charged with equal vehemence, as being unfavorable to the Tariff policy, just as best suits the time, place, and occasion for making some charge against her. The credulity of the public has been put to its extreme capacity of false impression, relative to her conduct, in this particular. Through all the South, during the late contest, it was New England policy, and a New England administration, that was afflicting the country with a Tariff policy beyond all endurance, while on the other side of the Alleghany, even the act of 1828 itself, the very sublimated essence of oppression, according to Southern opinions, was pronounced to be one of those blessings, for which the West was indebted to the "generous South."

With large investments in manufacturing establishments, and many and various interests connected with and dependent on them, it is not to be expected that New England, any more than other portions of the country, will now consent to any measure, destructive or highly dangerous. The duty of the Government, at the present moment, would seem to be to preserve, not to destroy; to maintain the position which it has assumed; and, for one, I shall feel it an indispensable obligation to hold it steady, as far as in my power, to that degree of protection which it has undertaken to bestow.—No more of the Tariff.

Professing to be provoked, by what he chose to consider a charge made by me against South Carolina, the honorable member, Mr. President, has taken up a new crusade against New England. Leaving altogether the subject of the public lands, in which his success, perhaps, had been neither distinguished or satisfactory, and letting go, also, of the topic of the Tariff, he sallied forth, in a general assault, on the opinions, politics, and parties of New England, as they have been exhibited in the last thirty years. This is natural. The "narrow policy" of the public lands had proved a legal settlement in South Carolina, and was not to be removed. The "accursed policy" of the Tariff, also, had established the fact of its birth and parentage, in the same State. No wonder, therefore, the gentleman wished to carry the war, as he expressed it, into the enemy's country. Prudently willing to quit these subjects, he was, doubtless, desirous of fastening on others, which could not be transferred South of Mason and Dixon's line. The politics of New England became his theme; and it was in this part of his speech, I think, that he menaced me with such sore discomfiture. Discomfiture! Why, sir, when he attacks any thing which I maintain, and overthrows it; when he turns the right or left of any position which I take up; when he drives me from any ground I choose to occupy; he may then talk of discomfiture, but not till that distant day. What has he done? Has he maintained his own charges? Has he proved what he alleged? Has he sustained himself in his attack on the Government, and on the history of the North, in the matter of the public lands? Has he disproved a fact, refuted a proposition, weakened an argument, maintained by me? Has he come within beat of drum of any position of mine? Oh, no, but he has "carried the war into the enemy's country!" Carried the war into the enemy's country! Yes, sir, and what sort of a war has he made of it? Why, sir, he has stretched a drag-net over the whole surface of perished pamphlets, indiscreet sermons, frothy paragraphs, and fuming popular addresses; over whatever the pulpit, in its moments of alarm, the press in its heats, and parties in their extravagance, have severally thrown off, in times of general excitement and violence. He has thus swept together a mass of such things as, but that they are now old, the public health would have required him rather to leave in their state of dispersion. For a good long hour or two, we had the unbroken pleasure of listening to the honorable member, while he recited, with his usual grace and spirit, and with evident high gusto, speeches, pamphlets, addresses, and all the *et caeteras* of the political press, such as warm heads produce in warm times; and such as it would be "discomfiture," indeed, for any one, whose taste did not delight in that sort of reading, to be obliged to peruse. This is his war. This it is to carry the war into the enemy's country. It is in an invasion of this sort, that he flatters himself with the expectation of gaining laurels fit to adorn a Senator's brow!

Mr. President, I shall not, it will, I trust, not be expected that I should, either now, or at any time, separate this farrago into parts, and answer and examine its components. I shall hardly bestow upon it all, a general remark or two. In the run of forty years, sir, under this Constitution, we have experienced sundry successive violent party contests. Party arose, indeed, with the Constitution itself, and, in some form or other, has attended it through the greater part of its history. Whether any other Constitution than the old articles of confederation, was desirable, was, itself, a question on which parties formed; if a new Constitution were framed, what powers should be given to it, was another question; and, when it had been formed, what was, in fact, the just extent of the powers actually conferred, was a third. Parties, as we know, existed, under the first Administration, as distinctly marked, as those which manifested themselves at any subsequent period. The contest immediately preceding the political change in 1801, and that, again, which existed at the commencement of the late war, are other instances of party excitement, of something more than usual strength and intensity. In all these conflicts, there was, no doubt, much of violence on both and all sides. It would be impossible, if one had a fancy for such employment, to adjust the relative *quantum* of violence between these contending parties. There was enough in each, as must always be expected in popular Governments. With a great deal of proper and decorous discussion, there was mingled a great deal, also, of declamation, virulence, crimination, and abuse. In regard to any party, probably, at one of the leading epochs in the history of parties, enough may be found to make out another equally inflamed exhibition, as that with which the honorable member has edified us. For myself, sir, I shall not rake among the rubbish of by-gone times, to see what I can find, or whether I cannot find some-thing, by which I can fix a blot on the escutcheon of any State, any party, or any part of the country. General Washington's administration was steadily and zealously maintained, as we all know, by New England. It was violently opposed elsewhere. We know in what quarter he had the most earnest, constant, and persevering support, in all his great and leading measures. We know where his private and personal character were held in the highest degree of attachment and veneration; and we know, too, where his measures were opposed, his services slighted, and his character vilified. We know, or we might know, if we turned to the Journals, who expressed respect, gratitude, and regret, when he retired from the Chief Magistracy; and who refused to express either respect, gratitude, or regret. I shall not open those Journals. Publications more abusive or scurrilous never saw the light, than were sent forth against Washington, and all his leading mea-sures, from presses South of New England. But I shall not look them up. I employ no scavengers—no one is in attendance on me, tendering such means of retaliation; and, if there were, with an ass's load of them, with a bulk as huge as that which the gentleman himself has produced, I would not touch one of them. I see enough of the violence of our own times, to be no way anxious to rescue from forgetfulness the extravagancies of times past. Besides, what is all this to the present purpose? It has nothing to do with the public lands, in regard to which the attack was begun; and it has nothing to do with those sentiments and opinions, which, I have thought, tend to disunion, and all of which the honorable member seems to have adopted himself, and undertaken to defend. New England has, at times, so argues the gentleman, held opinions as dangerous, as those which he now holds. Suppose this were so; why should *he*, therefore, abuse New England? If he finds himself countenanced by acts of hers, how is it that, while he relies on these acts, he covers, or seeks to cover, their authors with reproach? But, sir, if, in the course of forty years, there have been undue effervescences of party in New England, has the same thing happened no where else? Party animosity and party outrage, not in New England, but elsewhere, denounced President Washington, not only as a Federalist, but as a Tory, a British agent, a man, who, in his high office, sanctioned cor-ruption. But does the honorable member suppose, that, if I had a tender here, who should put such an effusion of wickedness and folly in my hand, that I would stand up and read it against the South? Parties ran into great heats, again, in 1799, and 1800. What was said, sir, or rather what was not said, in those years, against John Adams, one of the signers of the Declaration of Independence, and its admitted ablest defender on the floor of Congress? If the gentleman wishes to increase his stores of party abuse and frothy violence; if he has a determined proclivity to such pursuits, there are treasures of that sort South of the Potomac, much to his taste, yet untouched—I shall not touch them.

The parties which divided the country at the commencement of the late war, were violent. But, then, there was violence on both sides, and violence in every State. Minorities and majorities were equally violent. There was no more violence against the war in New England, than in other States; nor any more appearance of violence, except that, owing to a dense population, greater facility of assembling, and more presses, there may have been more in quantity, spoken and printed there, than in some other places. In the article of sermons, too, New England is somewhat more abundant than South Carolina; and, for that reason, the chance of finding here and there an exceptionable one, may be greater. I hope, too, there are more good ones. Opposition may have been more formidable in New England, as it embraced a larger portion of the whole population; but it was no more unrestrained in its principle, or violent in manner. The minorities dealt quite as harshly with their own State Governments, as the majorities dealt with the Administration here. There were presses on both sides, popular meetings on both sides, aye, and pulpits on both sides, also. The gentleman's purveyors have only catered for him among the productions of one side. I certainly shall not supply the deficiency by furnishing samples of the other. I leave to him, and to them, the whole concern.

It is enough for me to say, that if, in any part of this, their grateful occupation; if, in all their researches, they find any thing in the history of Massachusetts, or New England, or in the proceedings of any legislative, or other public body, disloyal to the Union, speaking slightly of its value, proposing to break it up, or recommending non-intercourse with neighboring States, on account of difference of political opinion, then, sir, I give them all up to the honorable gentleman's unrestrained rebuke; expecting, however, that he will extend his buffetings, in like manner, *to all similar proceedings, wherever else found.*

The gentleman, sir, has spoken, at large, of former parties, now no longer in being, by their received appellations, and has undertaken to instruct us, not only in the knowledge of their principles, but of their respective pedigrees, also. He has ascended to the origin, and run out their genealogies. With most exemplary modesty, he speaks of the party to which he professes to have belonged himself, as the true Pure, the only honest, patriotic party, derived by regular descent, from father to son, from the time of the virtuous Romans! Spreading before us the *family tree* of political parties, he takes especial care to shew himself, snugly perched on a popular bough! He is wakeful to the expediency of adopting such rules of descent, as shall bring him in, in exclusion of others, as an heir to the inheritance of all public virtue, and all true political principle. His party, and his opinions, are sure to be orthodox; heterodoxy is confined to his opponents. He spoke, sir, of the Federalists, and I thought I saw some eyes begin to open and stare a little, when he ventured on that ground. I expected he would draw his sketches rather lightly, when he looked on the circle round him, and, especially, if he should cast his thoughts to the high places, out of the Senate. Nevertheless, he went back to Rome, *ad annum urbe condita,* and found the fathers of the Federalists, in the primeval aristocrats of that renowned Empire! He traced the flow of federal blood down, through successive ages and centuries, till he brought it into the veins of the American Tories, (of whom, by the way, there were twenty in the Carolinas, for *one* in Massachusetts.) From the Tories, he followed it to the Federalists: and, as the Federal Party was broken up, and there was no possibility of transmitting it further on this side the Atlantic, he seems to have discovered that it has gone off, collaterally, though against all the canons of descent, into the Ultras of France, and finally become extinguished, like exploded gas, among the adherents of Don Miguel! This, sir, is an abstract of the gentleman's history of Federalism. I am not about to controvert it. It is not, at present, worth the pains of refutation; because, sir, if at this day, any one feels the sin of Federalism lying heavily on his conscience, he can easily obtain remission. He may even obtain an indulgence, if he be desirous of repeating the same transgression. It is an affair of no difficulty to get into this same right line of patriotic descent. A man, now-a-days, is at liberty to choose his political parentage. He may elect his own father. Federalist, or not, he may, if he choose, claim to belong to the favored stock, and his claim will be allowed. He may carry back his pretensions just as far as the honorable gentleman himself: nay, he may make himself out the honorable gentleman's cousin, and prove, satisfactorily, that he is descended from the same political great grandfather. All this is allowable. We all know a process, sir, by which the whole Essex Junto could, in one hour, be all washed white from their ancient Federalism, and come out, every one of them, an original Democrat, dyed in the wool! Some of them have actually undergone the operation, and they say it is quite easy. The only inconvenience it occasions, as they tell us, is a slight tendency of the blood to the face, a soft suffusion, which, however, is very transient, since nothing is said by those whom they join, calculated to deepen the red on the cheek, but a prudent silence observed, in regard to all the past. Indeed, sir, some smiles of approbation have been bestowed, and some crumbs of comfort have fallen, not a thousand miles from the door of the Hartford Convention itself. And if the author of the ordinance of 1787 possessed the other requisite qualifications, there is no knowing, notwithstanding his Federalism, to what heights of favor he might not yet attain.

Mr. President, in carrying his warfare, such as it was, into New England, the honorable gentleman all along professes to be acting on the defensive. He elects to consider me as having assailed South Carolina, and insists that he comes forth only as her champion, and in her defence. Sir, I do not admit that I made any attack whatever on South Carolina. Nothing like it. The honorable member, in his first speech, expressed opinions, in regard to revenue, and some other topics, which I heard both with pain and with surprise. I told the gentleman that I was aware that such sentiments were entertained *out* of the Government, but had not expected to find them advanced in it; that I knew there were persons in the South who speak of our Union with indifference, or doubt, taking pains to magnify its evils, and to say nothing of its benefits; that the honorable member himself, I was sure, could never be one of these; and I regretted the expression of such opinions as he had avowed, because I thought their obvious tendency was to encourage feelings of disrespect to the Union, and to weaken its connexion. This, sir, is the sum and substance of all I said on the subject. And this constitutes the attack, which called on the chivalry of the gentleman, in his opinion, to harry us with such a foray, among the party pamphlets and party proceedings of Massachusetts! If he means that I spoke with dissatisfaction or disrespect of the ebullitions of individuals in South Carolina, it is true. But, if he means that I had assailed the character of the State, her honor, or patriotism; that I had reflected on her history or her conduct, he had not the slightest ground for any such assumption. I did not even refer, I think, in my observations, to any collection of individuals. I said nothing of the recent Conventions. I spoke in the most guarded and careful manner, and only expressed my regret for the publication of opinions which I presumed the honorable member disapproved as much as myself. In this, it seems, I was mistaken. I do not remember that the gentleman has disclaimed any sentiment, or any opinion, of a supposed anti-union tendency, which on all, or any of the recent occasions has been expressed. The whole drift of his speech has been rather to prove, that, in divers times and manners, sentiments equally liable to my objection have been promulged in New England. And one would suppose that his object, in this reference to Massachusetts, was to find a precedent to justify proceedings in the South, were it not for the reproach and contumely with which he labors, all along, to load these, his own chosen precedents. By way of defending South Carolina from what he chooses to think an attack on her, he first quotes the example of Massachusetts, and then denounces that example, in good set terms. This two-fold purpose, not very consistent with itself, one would think, was exhibited more than once in the course of his speech. He referred, for instance, to the Hartford Convention. Did he do this for authority, or for a topic of reproach? Apparently for both: for he told us that he should find no fault with the mere fact of holding such a Convention, and considering and discussing such questions as he supposes were then and there discussed; but what rendered it obnoxious was the time it was holden, and the circumstances of the country, then existing. We were in a war, he said, and the country needed all our aid—the hand of Government required to be strengthened, not weakened—and patriotism should have postponed such proceedings to another day. The thing itself, then, is a precedent; the time and manner of it, only, a subject of censure. Now, sir, I go much further, on this point, than the honorable member. Supposing, as the gentleman seems to, that the Hartford Convention assembled for any such purpose as breaking up the Union, because they thought unconstitutional laws had been passed, or to consult on that subject, or *to calculate the value of the Union;* supposing this to be their purpose, or any part of it, then, I say the meeting itself was disloyal, and was obnoxious to censure, whether held in time of peace or time of war, or under whatever circumstances. The material question is the *object.* Is dissolution the *object?* If it be, external circumstances may make it a more or less aggravated case, but cannot affect the principle. I do not hold, therefore, sir, that the Hartford Convention was pardonable, even to the extent of the gentleman's admission, if its objects were really such as have been imputed to it. Sir, there never was a time, under any degree of excitement, in which the Hartford Convention, or any other Convention, could maintain itself one moment in New England, if assembled for any such purpose as the gentleman says would have been an allowable purpose. To hold conventions to decide questions of constitutional law!—to try the binding validity of statutes, by votes in a convention! Sir, the Hartford Convention, I presume, would not desire that the honorable gentleman should be their defender or advocate, if he puts their case upon such untenable and extravagant grounds.

Then, sir, the gentleman has no fault to find with these recently promulgated South Carolina opinions. And, certainly, he need have none; for his own sentiments, as now advanced, and advanced on reflection, as far as I have been able to comprehend them, go the full length of all these opinions. I propose, sir, to say something on these, and to consider how far they are just and constitutional. Before doing that, however, let me observe, that the eulogium pronounced on the character of the State of South Carolina, by the honorable gentleman, for her Revolutionary and other merits, meets my hearty concurrence. I shall not acknowledge that the honorable member goes before me in regard for whatever of distinguished talent, or distinguished character, South Carolina has produced. I claim part of the honor, I partake in the pride, of her great names. I claim them for countrymen, one and all. The Laurenses, the Rutledges, the Pinckneys, the Sumpters, the Marions—Americans, all—whose fame is no more to be hemmed in by State lines, than their talents and patriotism were capable of being circumscribed within the same narrow limits. In their day and generation, they served and honored the country, and the whole country; and their renown is of the treasures of the whole country. Him, whose honored name the gentleman himself bears—does he suppose me less capable of gratitude for his patriotism, or sympathy for his sufferings, than if his eyes had first opened upon the light in Massachusetts, instead of South Carolina? Sir, does he suppose it in his power to exhibit a Carolina name, so bright, as to produce envy in my bosom? No, sir, increased gratification and delight, rather. Sir, I thank God, that, if I am gifted with little of the spirit which is able to raise mortals to the skies, I have yet none, as I trust, of that other spirit, which would drag angels down. When I shall be found, sir, in my place here, in the Senate, or elsewhere, to sneer at public merit, because it happened to spring up beyond the little limits of my own State, or neighborhood; when I refuse, for any such cause, or for any cause, the homage due to American talent, to elevated patriotism, to sincere devotion to liberty and the country; or, if I see an uncommon endowment of heaven—if I see extraordinary capacity and virtue in any son of the South—and if, moved by local prejudice, or gangrened by State jealousy, I get up here to abate the tithe of a hair from his just character and just fame, may my tongue cleave to the roof of my mouth!

Sir, let me recur to pleasing recollections—let me indulge in refreshing remembrance of the past—let me remind you that in early times no States cherished greater harmony, both of principle and of feeling, than Massachusetts and South Carolina. Would to God, that harmony might again return! Shoulder to shoulder they went through the Revolution—hand in hand they stood round the Administration of Washington, and felt his own great arm lean on them for support. Unkind feeling, if it exist, alienation and distrust, are the growth, unnatural to such soils, of false principles since sown. They are weeds, the seeds of which that same great arm never scattered.

Mr. President, I shall enter on no encomium upon Massachusetts—she needs none. There she is—behold her, and judge for yourselves. There is her history—the world knows it by heart. The past, at least, is secure. There is Boston, and Concord, and Lexington, and Bunker Hill—and there they will remain forever. The bones of her sons, falling in the great struggle for Independence, now lie mingled with the soil of every State, from New England to Georgia; and there they will lie forever. And, sir, where American liberty raised its first voice; and where its youth was nurtured and sustained, there it still lives, in the strength of its manhood, and full of its original spirit. If discord and disunion shall wound it—if party strife and blind ambition shall hawk at and tear it—if folly and madness—if uneasiness, under salutary and necessary restraint—shall succeed to separate it from that Union, by which alone its existence is made sure, it will stand, in the end, by the side of that cradle in which its infancy was rocked; it will stretch forth its arm, with whatever of vigor it may still retain, over the friends who gather round it; and it will fall at last, if fall it must, amidst the proudest monuments of its own glory, and on the very spot of its origin.

There yet remains to be performed, Mr. President, by far the most grave and important duty, which I feel to be devolved on me, by this occasion. It is to state, and to defend, what I conceive to be the true principles of the Constitution under which we are here assembled. I might well have desired that so weighty a task should have fallen into other and abler hands. I could have wished that it should have been executed by those, whose character and experience give weight and influence to their opinions, such as cannot possibly belong to mine. But, sir, I have met the occasion, not sought it; and I shall proceed to state my own sentiments, without challenging for them any particular regard, with studied plainness, and as much precision as possible.

I understand the honorable gentleman from South Carolina to maintain, that it is a right of the State Legislatures to interfere, whenever, in their judgment, this Government transcends its constitutional limits, and to arrest the operation of its laws.

I understand him to maintain this right, as a right existing *under* the Constitution; not as a right to overthrow it, on the ground of extreme necessity, such as would justify violent revolution.

I understand him to maintain an authority, on the part of the States, thus to interfere, for the purpose of correcting the exercise of power by the General Government, of checking it, and of compelling it to conform to their opinion of the extent of its powers.

I understand him to maintain, that the ultimate power of judging of the constitutional extent of its own authority, is not lodged exclusively in the General Government, or any branch of it; but that, on the contrary, the States may lawfully decide for themselves, and each State for itself, whether, in a given case, the act of the General Government transcends its power.

I understand him to insist, that if the exigency of the case, in the opinion of any State Government, require it, such State Government may, by its own sovereign authority, annul an act of the General Government, which it deems plainly and palpably unconstitutional.

This is the sum of what I understand from him, to be the South Carolina doctrine; and the doctrine which he maintains. I propose to consider it, and to compare it with the Constitution. Allow me to say, as a preliminary remark, that I call this the South Carolina doctrine, only because the gentleman himself has so denominated it. I do not feel at liberty to say that South Carolina, as a State, has ever advanced these sentiments. I hope she has not, and never may. That a great majority of her people are opposed to the Tariff laws, is doubtless true. That a majority, somewhat less than that just mentioned, conscientiously believe these laws unconstitutional, may probably also be true. But, that any majority holds to the right of direct State interference, at State discretion, the right of nullifying acts of Congress, by acts of State legislation, is more than I know, and what I shall be slow to believe.

That there are individuals, besides the honorable gentleman, who do maintain these opinions, is quite certain. I recollect the recent expression of a sentiment, which circumstances attending its utterance and publication, justify us in supposing was not unpremeditated. "The sovereignty of the State—never to be controlled, construed, or decided on, but by her own feelings of honorable justice."

[Mr. HAYNE here rose, and said, that for the purpose of being clearly understood, he would state, that his proposition was in the words of the Virginia resolution, as follows:

"That this Assembly doth explicitly and peremptorily declare, that it views the powers of the Federal Government, as resulting from the compact, to which the States are parties, as limited by the plain sense and intention of the instrument constituting that compact, as no farther valid than they are authorized by the grants enumerated in that compact; and that, in case of a deliberate, palpable, and dangerous exercise of other powers, not granted by the said compact, the States who are parties thereto have the right, and are in duty bound to interpose, for arresting the progress of the evil, and for maintaining, within their respective limits, the authorities, rights, and liberties, appertaining to them."]

MR. WEBSTER resumed:

I am quite aware, Mr. President, of the existence of the resolution which the gentleman read, and has now repeated, and that he relies on it as his authority. I know the source, too, from which it is understood to have proceeded. I need not say that I have much respect, for the constitutional opinions of Mr. Madison; they would weigh greatly with me, always. But, before the authority of his opinion be vouched for the gentleman's proposition, it will be proper to consider what is the fair interpretation of that resolution, to which Mr. Madison is understood to have given his sanction. As the gentleman construes it, it is an authority for him. Possibly, he may not have adopted the right construction. That resolution declares, that, *in the case of the dangerous exercise of powers not granted, by the General Government, the States may interpose to arrest the progress of the evil.* But how interpose, and what does this declaration purport? Does it mean no more, than that there may be extreme cases, in which the People, in any mode of assembly, may resist usurpation, and relieve themselves from a tyrannical government? No one will deny this. Such resistance is not only acknowledged to be just in America, but in England also. Blackstone admits as much, in the theory, and practice, too, of the English Constitution. We, sir, who oppose the Carolina doctrine, do not deny that the People may, if they choose, throw off any government, when it become oppressive and intolerable, and erect a better in its stead. We all know that civil institutions are established for the public benefit, and that when they cease to answer the ends of their existence, they may be changed. But I do not understand the doctrine now contended for to be that which, for the sake of distinctness, we may call the right of revolution. I understand the gentleman to maintain, that, without revolution, without civil commotion, without rebellion, a remedy for supposed abuse and transgression of the powers of the General Government lies in a direct appeal to the interference of the State Governments. [Mr. Hayne here rose: He did not contend, he said, for the mere right of revolution, but for the right of constitutional resistance. What he maintained, was, that, in case of a plain, palpable violation of the Constitution, by the General Government, a State may interpose; and that this interposition is constitutional.] Mr. Webster resumed: So, Sir, I understood the gentleman, and am happy to find that I did not misunderstand him. What he contends for, is, that it is constitutional to interrupt the administration of the Constitution itself, in the hands of those who are chosen and sworn to administer it, by the direct interference, in form of law, of the States, in virtue of their sovereign capacity. The inherent right in the People to reform their government, I do not deny; and they have another right, and that is, to resist unconstitutional laws, without overturning the Government. It is no doctrine of mine, that unconstitutional laws bind the People. The great question is, *whose prerogative is it to decide on the constitutionality or unconstitutionality of the laws?* On that, the main debate hinges. The proposition, that, in case of a supposed violation of the Constitution by Congress, the States have a constitutional right to interfere, and annul the law of Congress, is the proposition of the gentleman: I do not admit it. If the gentleman had intended no more than to assert the right of revolution, for justifiable cause, he would have said only what all agree to. But I cannot conceive that there can be a middle course, between submission to the laws, when regularly pronounced constitutional, on the one hand, and open resistance, which is revolution, or rebellion, on the other. I say, the right of a State to annul a law of Congress, cannot be maintained, but on the ground of the unalienable right of man to resist oppression; that is to say, upon the ground of revolution. I admit that there is an ultimate violent remedy, above the Constitution, and in defiance of the Constitution, which may be resorted to, when a revolution is to be justified. But I do not admit that, under the Constitution, and in conformity with it, there is any mode in which a State Government, as a member of the Union, can interfere and stop the progress of the General Government, by force of her own laws, under any circumstances whatever.

This leads us to inquire into the origin of this Government, and the source of its power. Whose agent is it? Is it the creature of the State Legislatures, or the creature of the People? If the Government of the United States be the agent of the State Governments, then they may control it, provided they can agree in the manner of controlling it; if it be the agent of the People, then the People alone can control it, restrain it, modify, or reform it. It is observable enough, that the doctrine for which the honorable gentleman contends, leads him to the necessity of maintaining, not only that this General Government is the creature of the States, but that it is the creature of each of the States severally; so that each may assert the power, for itself, of determining whether it acts within the limits of its authority. It is the servant of four-and-twenty masters, of different wills and different purposes, and yet bound to obey all. This absurdity (for it seems no less) arises from a misconception as to the origin of this Government and its true character. It is, sir, the People's Constitution, the People's Government; made for the People; made by the People; and answerable to the People. The People of the United States have declared that this Constitution shall be the Supreme Law. We must either admit the proposition, or dispute their authority. The States are, unquestionably, sovereign, so far as their sovereignty is not affected by this supreme law. But the State Legislatures, as political bodies, however sovereign, are yet not sovereign over the People. So far as the People have given power to the General Government, so far the grant is unquestionably good, and the Government holds of the People, and not of the State Governments. We are all agents of the same supreme power, the People. The General Government and the State Governments derive their authority from the same source. Neither can, in relation to the other, be called primary, though one is definite and restricted, and the other general and residuary. The National Government possesses those powers which it can be shown the People have conferred on it, and no more. All the rest belongs to the State Governments or to the People themselves. So far as the People have restrained State sovereignty, by the expression of their will, in the Constitution of the United States, so far, it must be admitted, State sovereignty is effectually controlled. I do not contend that it is, or ought to be, controlled farther. The sentiment to which I have referred, propounds that State sovereignty is only to be controlled by its own "feeling of justice;" that is to say, it is not to be controlled at all: for one who is to follow his own feelings is under no legal control. Now, however men may think this ought to be, the fact is, that the People of the United States have chosen to impose control on State sovereignties. There are those, doubtless, who wish they had been left without restraint; but the Constitution has ordered the matter differently. To make war, for instance, is an exercise of sovereignty; but the Constitution declares that no State shall make war. To coin money is another exercise of sovereign power; but no State is at liberty to coin money. Again, the Constitution says that no sovereign State shall be so sovereign as to make a treaty. These prohibitions, it must be confessed, are a control on the State sovereignty of South Carolina, as well as of the other States, which does not arise "from her own feelings of honorable justice." Such an opinion, therefore, is in defiance of the plainest provisions of the Constitution.

There are other proceedings of public bodies which have already been alluded to, and to which I refer again for the purpose of ascertaining, more fully, what is the length and breadth of that doctrine, denominated the Carolina doctrine, which the honorable member has now stood up on this floor to maintain. In one of them I find it resolved, that "the Tariff of 1828, and every other Tariff designed to promote one branch of industry at the expense of others, is contrary to the meaning and intention of the Federal compact; and, as such, a dangerous, palpable, and deliberate usurpation of power, by a determined majority, wielding the General Government beyond the limits of its delegated powers, as calls upon the States which compose the suffering minority, in their sovereign capacity, to exercise the powers which, as sovereigns, necessarily devolve upon them, when their compact is violated."

Observe, sir, that this resolution holds the Tariff of 1828, and every other Tariff, designed to promote one branch of industry at the expense of another, to be such a dangerous, palpable, and deliberate usurpation of power, as calls upon the States, in their sovereign capacity, to interfere by their own authority. This denunciation, Mr. President, you will please to observe, includes our old Tariff of 1816, as well as all others; because that was established to promote the interest of the manufactures of cotton, to the manifest and admitted injury of the Calcutta cotton trade. Observe, again, that all the qualifications are here rehearsed and charged upon the Tariff, which are necessary to bring the case within the gentleman's proposition. The Tariff is a usurpation; it is a dangerous usurpation; it is a palpable usurpation; it is a deliberate usurpation. It is such a usurpation, therefore, as calls upon the States to exercise their right of interference. Here is a case, then, within the gentleman's principles, and all his qualifications of his principles. It is a case for action. The Constitution is plainly, dangerously, palpably, and deliberately violated; and the States must interpose their own authority to arrest the law. Let us suppose the State of South Carolina to express this same opinion, by the voice of her Legislature. That would be very imposing; but what then? Is the voice of one State conclusive? It so happens that at the very moment when South Carolina resolves that the Tariff laws are unconstitutional, Pennsylvania and Kentucky, resolve exactly the reverse. *They* hold those laws to be both highly proper and strictly constitutional. And now, sir, how does the honorable member propose to deal with this case? How does he relieve us from this difficulty, upon any principle of his? His construction gets us into it; how does he propose to get us out?

In Carolina, the Tariff is a palpable, deliberate usurpation; Carolina, therefore, may *nullify* it, and refuse to pay the duties. In Pennsylvania, it is both clearly constitutional, and highly expedient; and there, the duties are to be paid. And yet, we live under a Government of uniform laws, and under a Constitution, too, which contains an express provision, as it happens, that all duties shall be equal in all the States! Does not this approach absurdity?

If there be no power to settle such questions, independent of either of the States, is not the whole Union a rope of sand? Are we not thrown back again, precisely, upon the old Confederation?

It is too plain to be argued. Four-and-twenty interpreters of constitutional law, each with a power to decide for itself, and none with authority to bind any body else, and this constitutional law the only bond of their Union! What is such a state of things, but a mere connexion during pleasure, or, to use the phraseology of the times, *during feeling?* And that feeling, too, not the feeling of the People, who established the Constitution, but the feeling of the State Governments.

In another of the South Carolina Addresses, having premised that the crisis requires "all the concentrated energy of passion," an attitude of open resistance to the laws of the Union is advised. Open resistance to the laws, then, is the constitutional remedy, the conservative power of the State, which the South Carolina doctrines teach for the redress of political evils, real or imaginary. And its authors further say, that, appealing with confidence to the Constitution itself, to justify their opinions, they cannot consent to try their accuracy by the Courts of Justice. In one sense, indeed, sir, this is assuming an attitude of open resistance in favor of liberty. But what sort of liberty? The liberty of establishing their own opinions, in defiance of the opinions of all others; the liberty of judging and of deciding exclusively themselves, in a matter in which others have as much right to judge and decide as they; the liberty of placing their own opinions above the judgment of all others, above the laws, and above the Constitution. This is their liberty, and this is the fair result of the proposition contended for by the honorable gentleman. Or it may be more properly said, it is identical with it, rather than a result from it.

In the same publication, we find the following: "Previously to our Revolution, when the arm of oppression was stretched over New England, where did our northern brethren meet with a braver sympathy than that which sprung from the bosoms of Carolinians. *We had no extortion, no oppression, no collision with the King's ministers, no navigation interests springing up, in envious rivalry of England."*

This seems extraordinary language. South Carolina no collision with the King's ministers, in 1775! No extortion! No oppression! But, sir, it is also most significant language. Does any man doubt the purpose for which it was penned? Can any one fail to see that it was designed to raise in the reader's mind the question, whether, *at this time*—that is to say, in 1828— South Carolina has any collision with the King's ministers, any oppression, or extortion, to fear from England? Whether, in short, England is not as naturally the friend of South Carolina as New England, with her navigation interests springing up in envious rivalry of England?

Is it not strange, sir, that an intelligent man in South Carolina, in 1828, should thus labor to prove, that, in 1775, there was no hostility, no cause of war, between South Carolina and England? That she had no occasion, in reference to her own interest, or from a regard to her own welfare, to take up arms in the revolutionary contest? Can any one account for the expression of such strange sentiments, and their circulation through the State, otherwise than by supposing the object to be, what I have already intimated, to raise the question, if they had no *"collision"* (mark the expression) with the ministers of King George the Third, in 1775, what *collision* have they, in 1828, with the ministers of King George the Fourth? What is there now, in the existing state of things, to separate Carolina from *Old*, more, or rather, than from *New* England?

Resolutions, sir, have been recently passed by the Legislature of South Carolina. I need not refer to them: they go no farther than the honorable gentleman himself has gone—and, I hope, not so far. I content myself, therefore, with debating the matter with him.

And now, sir, what I have first to say on this subject is, that, at no time, and under no circumstances, has New England, or any State in New England, or any respectable body of persons in New England, or any public man of standing in New England, put forth such a doctrine as this Carolina doctrine.

The gentleman has found no case, he can find none, to support his own opinions by New England authority. New England has studied the Constitution in other schools, and under other teachers. She looks upon it with other regards, and deems more highly and reverently, both of its just authority, and its utility and excellence. The history of her legislative proceedings may be traced—the ephemeral effusions of temporary bodies, called together by the excitement of the occasion, may be hunted up—

they have been hunted up. The opinions and votes of her public men, in and out of Congress, may be explored—it will all be in vain. The Carolina doctrine can derive from her neither countenance nor support. She rejects it now; she always did reject it; and till she loses her senses, she always will reject it. The honorable member has referred to expressions, on the subject of the Embargo law, made in this place, by an honorable and venerable gentleman, (Mr. Hillhouse) now favoring us with his presence. He quotes that distinguished Senator as saying, that, in his judgment, the embargo law was unconstitutional, and that, therefore, in his opinion, the People were not bound to obey it. That, sir, is perfectly constitutional language. An unconstitutional law is not binding; *but then it does not rest with a resolution or a law of a State Legislature to decide whether an act of Congress be, or be not, constitutional.* An unconstitutional act of Congress would not bind the People of this District, although they have no legislature to interfere in their behalf; and, on the other hand, a constitutional law of Congress does bind the citizens of every State, although all their legislatures should undertake to annul it, by act or resolution. The venerable Connecticut Senator is a constitutional lawyer, of sound principles, and enlarged knowledge; a statesman practised and experienced, bred in the company of Washington, and holding just views upon the nature of our Governments. He believed the embargo unconstitutional, and so did others; but what then? Who, did he suppose, was to decide that question? The State Legislatures? Certainly not. No such sentiment ever escaped his lips. Let us follow up, sir, this New England opposition to the embargo laws; let us trace it, till we discern the principle, which controlled and governed New England, throughout the whole course of that opposition. We shall then see what similarity there is between the New England school of constitutional opinions, and this modern Carolina school. The gentleman, I think, read a petition from some single individual, addressed to the Legislature of Massachusetts, asserting the Carolina doctrine—that is, the right of State interference to arrest the laws of the Union. The fate of that petition shows the sentiment of the legislature. It met no favor. The opinions of Massachusetts were otherwise. They had been expressed, in 1798, in answer to the resolutions of Virginia, and she did not depart from them, nor bend them to the times. Misgoverned, wronged, oppressed, as she felt herself to be, she still held fast her integrity to the Union. The gentleman may find in her proceedings much evidence of dissatisfaction with the measures of Government, and great and deep dislike to the Embargo; all this makes the case so much the stronger for her; for, notwithstanding all this dissatisfaction and dislike, she claimed no right, still, to sever asunder the bonds of the Union. There was heat, and there was anger, in her political feeling—be it so—her heat or her anger did not, nevertheless, betray her into infidelity to the Government. The gentleman labors to prove that she disliked the Embargo, as much as South Carolina dislikes the Tariff, and expressed her dislike as strongly. Be it so; *but did she propose the Carolina remedy?—did she threaten to interfere, by State authority, to annul the laws of the Union?* That is the question for the gentleman's consideration.

No doubt, sir, a great majority of the People of New England conscientiously believed the Embargo law of 1807 unconstitutional; as conscientiously, certainly, as the People of South Carolina hold that opinion of the Tariff. They reasoned thus: Congress has power to regulate commerce; but here is a law, they said, stopping all commerce, and stopping it indefinitely. The law is perpetual; that is, it is not limited in point of time, and must, of course, continue, until it shall be repealed by some other law. It is as perpetual, therefore, as the law against treason or murder. Now, is this regulating commerce, or destroying it? Is it guiding, controlling, giving the rule to commerce, as a subsisting thing; or is it putting an end to it altogether? Nothing is more certain, than that a majority in New England, deemed this law a violation of the Constitution. The very case required by the gentleman, to justify State interference, had then arisen. Massachusetts believed this law to be *"a deliberate, palpable, and dangerous exercise of a power, not granted by the Constitution."* Deliberate it was, for it was long continued; palpable, she thought it, as no words in the Constitution gave the power, and only a construction, in her opinion most violent, raised it; dangerous it was, since it threatened utter ruin to her most important interests. Here, then, was a Carolina case. How did Massachusetts deal with it? It was, as she thought, a plain, manifest, palpable violation of the Constitution; and it brought ruin to her doors. Thousands of families, and hundreds of thousands of individuals, were beggared by it. While she saw and felt all this, she saw and felt, also, that, as a measure of national policy, it was perfectly futile; that the country was no way benefitted by that which caused so much individual distress; that it was efficient only for the production of evil, and all that evil inflicted on ourselves. In such a case, under such circumstances, how did Massachusetts demean herself? Sir, she remonstrated, she memorialized, she addressed herself to the General Government, not exactly "with the concentrated energy of passion," but with her own strong sense, and the energy of sober conviction. But she did not interpose the arm of her own power to arrest the law, and break the embargo. Far from it. Her principles bound her to two things; and she followed her principles, lead where they might. First, to submit to every constitutional law of Congress, and, secondly, if the constitutional validity of the law be doubted, to refer that question to the decision of the proper tribunals. The first principle is vain and ineffectual without the second. A majority of us in New England believed the embargo law unconstitutional; but the great question was, and always will be, in such cases, who is to decide this? Who is to judge between the People and the Government? And, sir, it is quite plain, that the Constitution of the United States confers on the Government itself, to be exercised by its appropriate Department, and under its own responsibility to the People, this power of deciding ultimately and conclusively, upon the just extent of its own authority. If this had not been done, we should not have advanced a single step beyond the Old Confederation.

Being fully of opinion that the Embargo law was unconstitutional, the people of New England were yet equally clear in the opinion—it was a matter they did doubt upon—that the question, after all, must be decided by the Judicial Tribunals of the United States. Before those tribunals, therefore, they brought the question. Under the provisions of the law, they had given bonds, to millions in amount, and which were alleged to be forfeited. They suffered the bonds to be sued, and thus raised the question. In the old-fashioned way of settling disputes, they went to law. The case came to hearing, and solemn argument; and he who espoused their cause, and stood up for them against the validity of the Embargo act, was none other than that great man, of whom the gentleman has made honorable mention, SAMUEL DEXTER. He was then, sir, in the fulness of his knowledge, and the maturity of his strength. He had retired from long and distinguished public service here, to the renewed pursuit of professional duties; carrying with him all that enlargement and expansion, all the new strength and force, which an acquaintance with the more general subjects discussed in the national councils, is capable of adding to professional attainment, in a mind of true greatness and comprehension. He was a lawyer, and he was also a statesman. He had studied the Constitution, when he filled public station, that he might defend it; he had examined its principles, that he might maintain them. More than all men, or at least as much as any man, he was attached to the General Government and to the union of the States. His feelings and opinions all ran in that direction. A question of constitutional law, too, was, of all subjects, that one which was best suited to his talents and learning. Aloof from technicality, and unfettered by artificial rule, such a question gave opportunity for that deep and clear analysis, that mighty grasp of principle, which so much distinguished his higher efforts. His very statement was argument; his inference seemed demonstration. The earnestness of his own conviction, wrought conviction in others. One was convinced, and believed, and assented, because it was gratifying, delightful to think, and feel, and believe, in unison with an intellect of such evident superiority.

Mr. Dexter, sir, such as I have described him, argued the New England cause. He put into his effort his whole heart, as well as all the powers of his understanding; for he had avowed, in the most public manner, his entire concurrence with his neighbors, on the point in dispute. He argued the cause, it was lost, and New England submitted. The established tribunals pronounced the law constitutional, and New England acquiesced. Now, sir, is not this the exact opposite of the doctrine of the gentleman from South Carolina? According to him, instead of referring to the Judicial tribunals, we should have broken up the Embargo, by laws of our own; we should have repealed it, *quoad* New England; for we had a strong, palpable, and oppressive case. Sir, we believed the embargo unconstitutional; but still, that was matter of opinion, and who was to decide it? We thought it a clear case; but, nevertheless, we did not take the law into our own hands, *because we did not wish to bring about a revolution, nor to break up the Union:* for, I maintain, that, between submission to the decision of the constituted tribunals, and revolution, or disunion, there is no middle ground—there is no ambiguous condition, half allegiance, and half rebellion. And, sir, how futile, how very futile, it is, to admit the right of State interference, and then attempt to save it from the character of unlawful resistance, by adding terms of qualification to the causes and occasions, leaving all these qualifications, like the case itself, in the discretion of the State Governments. It must be a clear case, it is said; a deliberate case; a palpable case; a dangerous case. But then the State is still left at liberty to decide for herself, what is clear, what is deliberate, what is palpable, what is dangerous. Do adjectives and epithets avail any thing? Sir, the human mind is so constituted, that the merits of both sides of a controversy appear very clear and very palpable, to those who respectively espouse them; and both sides usually grow clearer, as the controversy advances. South Carolina sees unconstitutionality in the Tariff; she sees oppression there, also; and she sees danger. Pennsylvania, with a vision not less sharp, looks at the same Tariff, and sees no such thing in it—she sees it all constitutional, all useful, all safe. The faith of South Carolina is strengthened by opposition, and she now not only sees, but *Resolves,* that the tariff *is* palpably uncon-stitutional, oppressive, and dangerous; but Pennsylvania, not to be behind her neighbors, and equally willing to strengthen her own faith by a confi-dent asseveration, *Resolves,* also, and gives to every warm affirmative of South Carolina, a plain, downright, Pennsylvania negative. South Car-olina, to shew the strength and unity of her opinion, brings her Assembly to a unanimity, within seven voices; Pennsylvania, not to be outdone in this respect more than others, reduces her dissentient fraction to a single vote. Now, sir, again, I ask the gentleman, what is to be done? Are these States both right? Is he bound to consider them both right? If not, which is in the wrong? or rather, which has the best right to decide? And if he, and if I, are not to know what the Constitution means, and what it is, till those two State Legislatures, and the twenty-two others, shall agree in its construction, what have we sworn to, when we have sworn to maintain it? I was forcibly struck, sir, with one reflection, as the gentleman went on in his speech. He quoted Mr. Madison's resolutions to prove that a State may interfere, in a case of deliberate, palpable, and dangerous exercise of a power not granted. The honorable member supposes the Tariff law to be such an exercise of power; and that, consequently, a case has arisen in which the State may, if it see fit, interfere by its own law. Now it so hap-pens, nevertheless, that Mr. Madison himself deems this same Tariff law quite constitutional. Instead of a clear and palpable violation, it is, in his judgment, no violation at all. So that, while they use his authority for a hy-pothetical case, they reject it in the very case before them. All this, sir, shows the inherent—futility—I had almost used a stronger word—of con-ceding this power of interference to the States, and then attempting to se-cure it from abuse by imposing qualifications, of which the States themselves are to judge. One of two things is true; either the laws of the Union are beyond the discretion, and beyond the control of the States; or else we have no Constitution of General Government, and are thrust back again to the days of the Confederacy.

Let me here say, sir, that if the gentleman's doctrine had been received and acted upon in New England, in the times of the embargo and non-in-tercourse, we should probably not now have been here. The Government would, very likely, have gone to pieces, and crumbled into dust. No stronger case can ever arise than existed under those laws; no States can ever entertain a clearer conviction than the New England States then en-tertained; and if they had been under the influence of that heresy of opin-ion, as I must call it, which the honorable member espouses, this Union would, in all probability, have been scattered to the four winds. I ask the gentleman, therefore, to apply his principles to that case; I ask him to come forth and declare, whether, in his opinion, the New England States would have been justified in interfering to break up the embargo system, under the conscientious opinions which they held upon it? Had they a right to annul that law? Does he admit or deny? If that which is thought palpably unconstitutional in South Carolina, justifies that State in arresting the progress of the law, tell me, whether that which was thought palpably unconstitutional also in Massachusetts, would have justified her in doing the same thing? Sir, I deny the whole doctrine. It has not a foot of ground in the Constitution to stand on. No public man of reputation ever advanced it in Massachusetts, in the warmest times, or could maintain himself upon it there at any time.

I wish now, sir, to make a remark upon the Virginia Resolutions of 1798. I cannot undertake to say how these resolutions were understood by those who passed them. Their language is not a little indefinite. In the case of the exercise, by Congress, of a dangerous power, not granted to them, the resolutions assert the right, on the part of the State, to interfere, and arrest the progress of the evil. This is susceptible of more than one interpretation. It may mean no more than that the States may interfere by complaint and remonstrance; or by proposing to the People an alteration of the Federal Constitution. This would all be quite unobjectionable; or, it may be, that no more is meant than to assert the general right of revolution, as against all Governments, in cases of intolerable oppression. This no one doubts; and this, in my opinion, is all that he who framed the resolutions could have meant by it: for I shall not readily believe, that he was ever of opinion that a State, under the Constitution, and in conformity with it, could, upon the ground of her own opinion of its unconstitutionality, however clear and palpable she might think the case, annul a law of Congress, so far as it should operate on herself, by her own legislative power.

I must now beg to ask, sir, whence is this supposed right of the States derived?—where do they find the power to interfere with the laws of the Union? Sir, the opinion which the honorable gentleman maintains, is a notion, founded in a total misapprehension, in my judgment, of the origin of this Government, and of the foundation on which it stands. I hold it to be a popular Government, erected by the People; those who administer it responsible to the People; and itself capable of being amended and modified, just as the People may choose it should be. It is as popular, just as truly emanating from the People, as the State Governments. It is created for one purpose; the State Governments for another. It has its own powers; they have theirs. There is no more authority with them to arrest the operation of a law of Congress, than with Congress to arrest the operation of their laws. We are here to administer a Constitution emanating immediately from the People, and trusted, by them, to our administration. It is not the creature of the State Governments. It is of no moment to the argument, that certain acts of the State Legislatures are necessary to fill our seats in this body. That is not one of their original State powers, a part of the sovereignty of the State. It is a duty which the People, by the Constitution itself, have imposed on the State Legislatures; and which they might have left to be performed elsewhere, if they had seen fit. So they have left the choice of President with electors; but all this does not affect the proposition, that this whole Government, President, Senate, and House of Representatives, is a popular Government. It leaves it still all its popular character. The Governor of a State, (in some of the States) is chosen, not directly by the People, but by those who are chosen by the People, for the purpose of performing, among other duties, that of electing a Governor. Is the Government of the State, on that account, not a popular Government? This Government, sir, is the independent offspring of the popular will. It is not the creature of State Legislatures; nay, more, if the whole truth must be told, the People brought it into existence, established it, and have hitherto supported it, for the very purpose, amongst others, of imposing certain salutary restraints on State sovereignties. The States cannot now make war; they cannot contract alliances; they cannot make, each for itself, separate regulations of commerce; they cannot lay imposts; they cannot coin money. If this Constitution, sir, be the creature of State Legislatures, it must be admitted that it has obtained a strange control over the volitions of its creators.

The People, then, sir, erected this Government. They gave it a Constitution, and in that Constitution they have enumerated the powers which they bestow on it. They have made it a limited Government. They have defined its authority. They have restrained it to the exercise of such powers as are granted; and all others, they declare, are reserved to the States or the People. But, sir, they have not stopped here. If they had, they would have accomplished but half their work. No definition can be so clear, as to avoid possibility of doubt; no limitation so precise, as to exclude all uncertainty. Who, then, shall construe this grant of the People? Who shall interpret their will, where it may be supposed they have left it doubtful? With whom do they repose this ultimate right of deciding on the powers of the

Government? Sir, they have settled all this in the fullest manner. They have left it, with the Government itself, in its appropriate branches. Sir, the very chief end, the main design, for which the whole Constitution was framed and adopted, was to establish a Government that should not be obliged to act through State agency, or depend on State opinion and State discretion. The People had had quite enough of that kind of Government, under the Confederacy. Under that system, the legal action—the application of law to individuals, belonged exclusively to the States. Congress could only recommend—their acts were not of binding force, till the States had adopted and sanctioned them. Are we in that condition still? Are we yet at the mercy of State discretion, and State construction? Sir, if we are, then vain will be our attempt to maintain the Constitution under which we sit.

But, sir, the People have wisely provided, in the Constitution itself, a proper, suitable mode and tribunal for settling questions of constitutional law. There are, in the Constitution, grants of powers to Congress; and restrictions on these powers. There are, also, prohibitions on the States. Some authority must, therefore, necessarily exist, having the ultimate jurisdiction to fix and ascertain the interpretation of these grants, restrictions, and prohibitions. The Constitution has itself pointed out, ordained, and established that authority. How has it accomplished this great and essential end? By declaring, sir, that *the Constitution and the laws of the United States, made in pursuance thereof, shall be the supreme law of the land, any thing in the Constitution or laws of any State to the contrary notwithstanding.*

This, sir, was the first great step. By this, the supremacy of the Constitution and laws of the United States is declared. The People so will it. No State law is to be valid, which comes in conflict with the Constitution, or any law of the United States. But who shall decide this question of interference? To whom lies the last appeal? This, sir, the Constitution itself decides, also by declaring, *"that the Judicial power shall extend to all cases arising under the Constitution and Laws of the United States."* These two provisions, sir, cover the whole ground. They are, in truth, the key-stone of the arch. With these, it is a Constitution; without them, it is a Confederacy. In pursuance of these clear and express provisions, Congress established, at its very first session, in the Judicial act, a mode for carrying them into full effect, and for bringing all questions of constitutional power to the final decision of the Supreme Court. It then, sir, became a Government. It then has the means of self-protection; and, but for this, it would, in all probability, have been now among things which are past. Having

constituted the Government, and declared its powers, the People have further said, that since somebody must decide on the extent of these powers,
the Government shall itself decide; subject, always, like other popular governments, to its responsibility to the People. And now, sir, I repeat, how is
it that a State Legislature acquires any power to interfere? Who, or what,
gives them the right to say to the People, "We, who are your agents and
servants for one purpose, will undertake to decide, that your other agents
and servants, appointed by you for another purpose, have transcended the
authority you gave them!"? The reply would be, I think, not impertinent—
"Who made you a judge over another's servants? To their own masters
they stand or fall."

Sir, I deny this power of State Legislatures altogether. It cannot stand
the test of examination. Gentlemen may say, that, in an extreme case, a
State Government might protect the People from intolerable oppression.
Sir, in such a case, the People might protect themselves, without the aid of
the State Governments. Such a case warrants revolution. It must make,
when it comes, a law for itself. A nullifying act of a State Legislature cannot alter the case, nor make resistance any more lawful. In maintaining
these sentiments, sir, I am but asserting the rights of the People. I state
what they have declared, and insist on their right to declare it. They have
chosen to repose this power in the General Government, and I think it my
duty to support it, like other constitutional powers.

For myself, sir, I do not admit the jurisdiction of South Carolina, or
any other State, to prescribe my constitutional duty, or to settle, between
me and the People, the validity of laws of Congress, for which I have
voted. I decline her umpirage. I have not sworn to support the Constitution according to her construction of its clauses. I have not stipulated, by
my oath of office, or otherwise, to come under any responsibility, except
to the People, and those whom they have appointed to pass upon the
question, whether laws, supported by my votes, conform to the Constitution of the country. And, sir, if we look to the general nature of the case,
could any thing have been more preposterous, than to make a Government for the whole Union, and yet leave its powers subject, not to one interpretation, but to thirteen, or twenty-four, interpretations? Instead of
one tribunal, established by all, responsible to all, with power to decide
for all—shall constitutional questions be left to four and twenty popular
bodies, each at liberty to decide for itself, and none bound to respect the
decisions of others; and each at liberty, too, to give a new construction on
every new election of its own members? Would any thing, with such a

principle in it, or rather with such a destitution of all principle, be fit to be called a Government? No, sir. It should not be denominated a Constitution. It should be called, rather, a collection of topics, for everlasting controversy; heads of debate for a disputatious People. It would not be a Government. It would not be adequate to any practical good, nor fit for any country to live under. To avoid all possibility of being misunderstood, allow me to repeat again, in the fullest manner, that I claim no powers for the Government by forced or unfair construction. I admit, that it is a Government of strictly limited powers; of enumerated, specified, and particularised powers; and that whatsoever is not granted, is withheld. But notwithstanding all this, and however the grant of powers may be expressed, its limit and extent may yet, in some cases, admit of doubt; and the General Government would be good for nothing, it would be incapable of long existing, if some mode had not been provided, in which those doubts, as they should arise, might be peaceably, but authoritatively, solved.

And now, Mr. President, let me run the honorable gentleman's doctrine a little into its practical application. Let us look at his probable *modus operandi*. If a thing can be done, an ingenious man can tell *how* it is to be done. Now, I wish to be informed *how* this State interference is to be put in practice, without violence, bloodshed, and rebellion. We will take the existing case of the Tariff law. South Carolina is said to have made up her opinion upon it. If we do not repeal it, (as we probably shall not,) she will then apply to the case the remedy of her doctrine. She will, we must suppose, pass a law of her Legislature, declaring the several acts of Congress, usually called the Tariff Laws, null and void, so far as they respect South Carolina, or the citizens thereof. So far, all is a paper transaction, and easy enough. But the collector at Charleston is collecting the duties imposed by these Tariff Laws—he, therefore, must be stopped. The Collector will seize the goods if the Tariff duties are not paid. The State authorities will undertake their rescue: the Marshal, with his posse, will come to the Collector's aid, and here the contest begins. The militia of the State will be called out to sustain the nullifying act. They will march, sir, under a very gallant leader: for I believe the honorable member himself commands the militia of that part of the State. He will raise the NULLIFYING ACT on his standard, and spread it out as his banner! It will have a preamble, bearing, that the Tariff Laws are palpable, deliberate, and dangerous violations of the Constitution! He will proceed, with this banner flying, to the Customhouse in Charleston:

"All the while,
Sonorous metal blowing martial sounds."

Arrived at the custom-house, he will tell the Collector that he must collect no more duties under any of the Tariff laws. This, he will be somewhat puzzled to say, by the way, with a grave countenance, considering what hand South Carolina herself had in that of 1816. But, sir, the Collector would, probably, not desist at his bidding—here would ensue a pause: for they say, that a certain stillness precedes the tempest. Before this military array should fall on the custom-house, collector, clerks, and all, it is very probable some of those composing it, would request of their gallant commander-in-chief, to be informed a little upon the point of law; for they have, doubtless, a just respect for his opinions as a lawyer, as well as for his bravery as a soldier. They know he has read Blackstone and the Constitution, as well as Turrene and Vauban. They would ask him, therefore, something concerning their rights in this matter. They would inquire, whether it was not somewhat dangerous to resist a law of the United States. What would be the nature of their offence, they would wish to learn, if they, by military force and array, resisted the execution in Carolina of a law of the United States, and it should turn out, after all, that the law *was constitutional?* He would answer, of course, treason. No lawyer could give any other answer. John Fries, he would tell them, had learned that, some years ago. How, then, they would ask, do you propose to defend us? We are not afraid of bullets, but treason has a way of taking people off, that we do not much relish. How do you propose to defend us? "Look at my floating banner," he would reply; "see there the *nullifying law!*" Is it your opinion, gallant commander, they would then say, that if we should be indicted for treason, that same floating banner of your's would make a good plea in bar? "South Carolina is a sovereign State," he would reply. That is true—but would the Judge admit our plea? "These tariff laws," he would repeat, "are unconstitutional, palpably, deliberately, dangerously." That all may be so; but if the tribunals should not happen to be of that opinion, shall we swing for it? We are ready to die for our country, but it is rather an awkward business, this dying without touching the ground! After all, that is a sort of *hemp-*tax, worse than any part of the Tariff.

Mr. President, the honorable gentleman would be in a dilemma, like that of another great General. He would have a knot before him, which he could not untie. He must cut it with his sword. He must say to his followers, defend yourselves with your bayonets; and this is war—civil war.

Direct collision, therefore, between force and force, is the unavoidable result of that remedy for the revision of unconstitutional laws which the gentleman contends for. It must happen in the very first case to which it is applied. Is not this the plain result? To resist, by force, the execution of a law, generally, is treason. Can the Courts of the United States take notice of the indulgences of a State to commit treason? The common saying, that a State cannot commit treason herself, is nothing to the purpose. Can she authorize others to do it? If John Fries had produced an act of Pennsylvania, annulling the law of Congress, would it have helped his case? Talk about it as we will, these doctrines go the length of revolution. They are incompatible with any peaceable administration of the Government. They lead directly to disunion and civil commotion; and, therefore, it is, that at their commencement, when they are first found to be maintained by respectable men, and in a tangible form, I enter my public protest against them all.

The honorable gentleman argues, that if this Government be the sole judge of the extent of its own powers, whether that right of judging be in Congress, or the Supreme Court, it equally subverts State sovereignty. This the gentleman sees, or thinks he sees, although he cannot perceive how the right of judging, in this matter, if left to the exercise of State Legislatures, has any tendency to subvert the Government of the Union. The gentleman's opinion may be, that the right *ought not* to have been lodged with the General Government; he may like better such a Constitution, as we should have under the right of State interference; but I ask him to meet me on the plain matter of fact—I ask him to meet me on the Constitution itself—I ask him if the power is not found there—clearly and visibly found there? — Note 3.

But, sir, what is this danger, and what the grounds of it? Let it be remembered, that the Constitution of the United States is not unalterable. It is to continue in its present form no longer than the People who established it shall choose to continue it. If they shall become convinced that they have made an injudicious or inexpedient partition and distribution of power, between the State Governments and the General Government, they can alter that distribution at will.

If any thing be found in the National Constitution, either by original provision, or subsequent interpretation, which ought not to be in it, the People know how to get rid of it. If any construction be established, unacceptable to them, so as to become, practically, a part of the Constitution, they will amend it, at their own sovereign pleasure. But while the people choose to maintain it, as it is; while they are satisfied with it, and refuse to change it; who has given, or who can give, to the State Legislatures a right to alter it, either by interference, construction, or otherwise? Gentlemen do not seem to recollect that the People have any power to do any thing for themselves; they imagine there is no safety for them, any longer than they are under the close guardianship of the State Legislatures. Sir, the People have not trusted their safety, in regard to the general Constitution, to these hands. They have required other security, and taken other bonds. They have chosen to trust themselves, first, to the plain words of the instrument, and to such construction as the Government itself, in doubtful cases, should put on its own powers, under their oaths of office, and subject to their responsibility to them; just as the People of a State trust their own State Governments with a similar power. Secondly, they have reposed their trust in the efficacy of frequent elections, and in their own power to remove their own servants and agents, whenever they see cause. Thirdly, they have reposed trust in the Judicial power, which, in order that it might be trust-worthy, they have made as respectable, as disinterested, and as independent as was practicable. Fourthly, they have seen fit to rely, in case of necessity, or high expediency, on their known and admitted power, to alter or amend the Constitution, peaceably and quietly, whenever experience shall point out defects or imperfections. And, finally, the People of the United States have, at no time, in no way, directly or indirectly, authorized any State Legislature to construe or interpret *their* high instrument of Government; much less to interfere, by their own power, to arrest its course and operation.

If, sir, the People, in these respects, had done otherwise than they have done, their Constitution could neither have been preserved, nor would it have been worth preserving. And, if its plain provisions shall now be disregarded, and these new doctrines interpolated in it, it will become as feeble and helpless a being as its enemies, whether early or more recent, could possibly desire. It will exist in every State, but as a poor dependent on State permission. It must borrow leave to be; and will be, no longer than State pleasure, or State discretion, sees fit to grant the indulgence, and to prolong its poor existence.

But, sir, although there are fears, there are hopes also. The People have preserved this, their own chosen Constitution, for forty years, and have seen their happiness, prosperity, and renown, grow with its growth, and strengthen with its strength. They are now, generally, strongly attached to it. Overthrown by direct assault, it cannot be; evaded, undermined, NULLI-FIED, it will not be, if we, and those who shall succeed us here, as agents and representatives of the People, shall conscientiously and vigilantly discharge the two great branches of our public trust—faithfully to preserve, and wisely to administer it.

Mr. President, I have thus stated the reasons of my dissent to the doctrines which have been advanced and maintained. I am conscious of having detained you and the Senate much too long. I was drawn into the debate, with no previous deliberation such as is suited to the discussion of so grave and important a subject. But it is a subject of which my heart is full, and I have not been willing to suppress the utterance of its spontaneous sentiments. I cannot, even now, persuade myself to relinquish it, without expressing, once more, my deep conviction, that, since it respects nothing less than the Union of the States, it is of most vital and essential importance to the public happiness. I profess, sir, in my career, hitherto, to have kept steadily in view the prosperity and honor of the whole country, and the preservation of our Federal Union. It is to that Union we owe our safety at home, and our consideration and dignity abroad. It is to that Union that we are chiefly indebted for whatever makes us most proud of our country. That Union we reached only by the discipline of our virtues in the severe school of adversity. It had its origin in the necessities of disordered finance, prostrate commerce, and ruined credit. Under its benign influences, these great interests immediately awoke, as from the dead, and sprang forth with newness of life. Every year of its duration has teemed with fresh proofs of its utility and its blessings; and, although our territory has stretched out wider and wider, and our population spread farther and farther, they have not outrun its protection or its benefits. It has been to us all a copious fountain of national, social, and personal happiness. I have not allowed myself, sir, to look beyond the Union, to see what might lie hidden in the dark recess behind. I have not coolly weighed the chances of preserving liberty, when the bonds that unite us together shall be broken asunder. I have not accustomed myself to hang over the precipice of disunion, to see whether, with my short sight, I can fathom the depth of the abyss below; nor could I regard him as a safe counsellor in the affairs of this Government, whose thoughts should be mainly bent on considering, not how the Union should be best preserved, but how tolerable might be the condition of the People when it shall be broken up and destroyed. While the Union lasts, we have high, exciting, gratifying prospects spread out before us, for us and our children. Beyond that I seek not to penetrate the veil. God grant that, in my day, at least, that curtain may not rise. God grant that on my vision never may be opened what lies behind. When my eyes shall be turned to behold, for the last time, the sun in Heaven, may I not see him shining on the broken and dishonored fragments of a once glorious Union; on States dissevered, discordant, belligerent; on a land rent with civil feuds, or drenched, it may be, in fraternal blood! Let their last feeble and lingering glance, rather behold the gorgeous Ensign of the Republic, now known and honored throughout the earth, still full high advanced, its arms and trophies streaming in their original lustre, not a stripe erased or polluted, nor a single star obscured—bearing for its motto, no such miserable interrogatory as, *What is all this worth?* Nor those other words of delusion and folly, *Liberty first, and Union afterwards*—but every where, spread all over in characters of living light, blazing on all its ample folds, as they float over the sea and over the land, and in every wind under the whole Heavens, that other sentiment, dear to every true American heart—Liberty *and* Union, now and forever, one and inseparable!

NOTES.

NOTE I.

Wednesday, February 21, 1787.

Congress assembled: Present, as before.

The report of a grand Committee, consisting of Mr. Dane, Mr. Varnum, Mr. S. M. Mitchell, Mr. Smith, Mr. Cadwallader, Mr. Irvine, Mr. N. Mitchell, Mr. Forrest, Mr. Grayson, Mr. Blount, Mr. Bull, and Mr. Few; to whom was referred a letter of 14th September, 1786, from J. Dickinson, written at the request of Commissioners from the States of Virginia, Delaware, Pennsylvania, New Jersey, and New York, assembled at the city of Annapolis, together with a copy of the report of said Commissioners to the Legislatures of the States by whom they were appointed, being an order of the day, was called up, and which is contained in the following resolution, viz.:—

"Congress having had under consideration the letter of John Dickinson, Esq., Chairman of the Commissioners, who assembled at Annapolis during the last year; also, the proceedings of the said Commissioners, and entirely coinciding with them, as to the inefficiency of the Federal Government, and the necessity of devising such further provisions as shall render the same adequate to the exigencies of the Union, do strongly recommend to the different Legislatures to send forward Delegates to meet the proposed Convention, on the second Monday in May next, at the city of Philadelphia."

NOTE 2.

Extracts from Mr. Calhoun's Speech, on Mr. Randolph's motion to strike out the minimum valuation on Cotton Goods, in the House of Representatives, April, 1816.

"The debate, heretofore, on this subject, has been on the degree of protection which ought to be afforded to our cotton and woollen manufactures; all professing to be friendly to those infant establishments, and to be willing to extend to them adequate encouragement. The present motion assumes a new aspect. It is introduced, professedly, on the ground that manufactures ought not to receive any encouragement; and will, in its operation, leave our cotton establishments exposed to the competition of the cotton goods of the East Indies, which, it is acknowledged on all sides, they are not capable of meeting with success, without the proviso proposed to be stricken out by the motion now under discussion. Till the debate assumed this new form, he determined to be silent; participating, as he largely did, in that general anxiety which is felt, after so long and laborious a session, to return to the bosom of our families. But on a subject of such vital importance, touching, as it does, the security and permanent prosperity of our country, he hoped that the House would indulge him in a few observations.

"To give perfection to this state of things, it will be necessary to add, as soon as possible, a system of Internal Improvements, and, at least, such an extension of our navy, as will prevent the cutting off our coasting trade. The advantage of each is so striking, as not to require illustration, especially after the experience of the late war.

"He firmly believed that the country is prepared, even to maturity, for the introduction of manufactures. We have abundance of resources, and things naturally tend, at this moment, in that direction. A prosperous commerce has poured an immense amount of commercial capital into this country. This capital has, till lately, found occupation in commerce; but that state of the world which transferred it to this country, and gave it active employment, has passed away, never to return. Where shall we now find full employment for our prodigious amount of tonnage? Where markets for the numerous and abundant products of our country! This great body of active capital, which, for *the moment*, has found sufficient employment in supplying our markets, exhausted by the war, and measures preceding it, must find a new direction: it will not be idle. What channel can it take, but that of manufactures? This, if things continue as they are, will be its direction. It will introduce an era in our affairs, in many respects highly advantageous, and ought to be countenanced by the Government. Besides, we have already surmounted the greatest difficulty that has ever been found in undertakings of this kind. The cotton and woollen manufactures are not to be *introduced*—they are *already* introduced to a great extent; freeing us entirely from the hazards, and, in a great measure, the sacrifices experienced in giving the capital of the country a new direction. The restrictive measures, and the war, though not intended for that purpose, have, by the necessary operation of things, turned a large amount of capital to this new branch of industry. He had often heard it said, both in and out of Congress, that this effect alone would indemnify the country for all its losses. So high was this tone of feeling, when the want of these establishments was practically felt, that he remembered, during the war, when some question was agitated respecting the introduction of foreign goods, that many then opposed it on the grounds of injuring our manufactures. He then said, that war alone furnished sufficient stimulus, and perhaps too much, as it would make their growth unnaturally rapid; but that, on the return of peace, it would then be time to show our affection for them. He, at that time, did not expect an apathy and aversion to the extent which is now seen. But it will no doubt be said, if they are so far established, and if the situation of the country is so favorable to their growth, where is the necessity of affording them protection? It is to put them beyond the reach of contingency.

"It has been further asserted that manufactures are the fruitful cause of pauperism; and England has been referred to, as furnishing conclusive evidence of its truth. For his part, he could perceive no such tendency in them, but the exact contrary, as they furnished new stimulus and means of subsistence to the laboring classes of the community. We ought not to look at the cotton and woollen establishments of Great Britain for the prodigious numbers of poor with which her population was disgraced; causes much more efficient exist. Her poor laws, and statutes regulating the prices of labor, with taxes, were the real causes. But if it must be so; if the mere fact that England manufactured more than any other country, explained the cause of her having more beggars, it is just as reasonable to refer her courage, spirit, and all her masculine virtues, in which she excels all other nations, with a single exception—he meant our own—in which we might, without vanity, challenge a pre-eminence. Another objection had been, which he must acknowledge was better founded, that capital employed in manufacturing produced a greater dependence on the part of the employed, than in commerce, navigation, or agriculture. It is certainly an evil, and to be regretted; but he did not think it a decisive objection to the system; especially when it had incidental political advantages which, in his opinion, more than counterpoised it. It produced an interest strictly American, as much so as agriculture, in which it had the decided advantage of commerce or navigation. The country will, from this, derive much advantage. Again: it is calculated to bind together more closely our widely spreaded Republic. It will greatly increase our mutual dependence and intercourse; and will, as a necessary consequence, excite an increased attention to Internal Improvements, a subject every way so intimately connected with the ultimate attainment of national strength, and the perfection of our political institutions."

Extracts from the Speech of Mr. Calhoun, April, 1816—On the Direct Tax.

"In regard to the question, how far manufactures ought to be fostered, Mr. C. said, it was the duty of this country, as a means of defence, to encourage the domestic industry of the country, more especially that part of it which provides the necessary materials for clothing and defence. Let us look to the nature of the war most likely to occur. England is in the possession of the ocean. No man, however sanguine, can believe that we can deprive her, soon, of her predominance there. That control deprives us of the means of maintaining our army and navy cheaply clad. The question relating to manufactures must not depend on the abstract principle, that industry left to pursue its own course, will find in its own interest all the encouragement that is necessary. I lay the claims of the manufactures entirely out of view, said Mr. C.; but, on general principles, without regard to their interest, a certain encouragement should be extended, at least to our woollen and cotton manufactures.

"This nation," Mr. C. said, "was rapidly changing the character of its industry. When a nation is agricultural, depending for supply on foreign markets; its people may be taxed through its imports, almost to the amount of its capacity. The nation was, however, rapidly becoming to a considerable extent a manufacturing nation."

To the quotations from the speeches and proceedings of the Representatives of South Carolina, in Congress, during Mr. Monroe's Administration, may be added the following extract from Mr. Calhoun's Report on Roads and Canals, submitted to Congress on 7th of January, 1819, from the Department of War:

"A judicious system of Roads and Canals, constructed for the convenience of commerce, and the transportation of the mail only, without any reference to military operations, is itself among the most efficient means for 'the more complete defence of the United States.' Without adverting to the fact that the roads and canals which such a system would require, are, with few exceptions, precisely those which would be required for the operations of war; such a system, by consolidating our Union, increasing our wealth and fiscal capacity, would add greatly to our resources in war. It is in a state of war when a nation is compelled to put all its resources, in men, money, skill, and devotion to country, into requisition, that its Government realizes, in its security, the beneficial effects from a People made prosperous and happy by a wise direction of its resources in peace.

"Should Congress think proper to commence a system of roads and canals for 'the more complete defence of the United States,' the disbursements of the sum appropriated for the purpose might be made by the Department of War, under the direction of the President. Where incorporate companies are already formed, or the road or canal commenced, under the superintendence of a State, it perhaps would be advisable to direct a subscription on the part of the United States, on such terms and conditions as might be thought proper."

NOTE 3.

The following resolutions of the Legislature of Virginia, bear so pertinently and so strongly on this point of the debate, that they are thought worthy of being inserted in a note, especially as other resolutions of the same body are referred to in the discussion. It will be observed that these resolutions were unanimously adopted in each House.

VIRGINIA LEGISLATURE.
Extract from the Message of Gov. Tyler, of Virginia, Dec. 4, 1809.

"A proposition from the State of Pennsylvania is herewith submitted, with Governor Snyder's letter accompanying the same, in which is suggested the propriety of amending the Constitution of the United States, so as to prevent collision between the Government of the Union and the State Governments."

HOUSE OF DELEGATES—*Friday, December 15, 1809.*

On motion, *Ordered,* That so much of the Governor's communication as relates to the communication from the Governor of Pennsylvania, on the subject of an amendment, proposed by the Legislature of that State, to the Constitution of the United States, be referred to Messrs. Peyton, Otey, Cabell, Walker, Madison, Holt, Newton, Parker, Stevenson, Randolph [of Amelia,] Cocke, Wyatt, and Ritchie.—*Page 25 of the Journal.*

Thursday, January 11, 1810.

Mr. Peyton, from the Committee to whom was referred that part of the Governor's communication which relates to the amendment proposed by the State of Pennsylvania, to the Constitution of the United States, made the following Report:

The Committee to whom was referred the communication of the Governor of Pennsylvania, covering certain resolutions of the Legislature of that State, proposing an amendment of the Constitution of the United States, by the appointment of an impartial tribunal to decide disputes between the States and Federal Judiciary, have had the same under their consideration, and are of opinion, that a tribunal is already provided by the Constitution of the United States, to wit: the Supreme Court, more eminently qualified, from their habits and duties, from the mode of their selection, and from the tenure of their offices, to decide the disputes aforesaid, in an enlightened and impartial manner, than any other tribunal which could be created.

The members of the Supreme Court are selected from those in the United States who are most celebrated for virtue and legal learning, not at the will of a single individual, but by the concurrent wishes of the President and Senate of the United States: they will, therefore, have no local prejudices and partialities. The duties they have to perform lead them, necessarily, to the most enlarged and accurate acquaintance with the jurisdiction of the Federal and State Courts together, and with the admirable symmetry of our Government. The tenure of their offices enables them to pronounce the sound and correct opinions they may have formed, without fear, favor, or partiality.

The amendment to the Constitution, proposed by Pennsylvania, seems to be founded upon the idea that the Federal Judiciary will, from a lust of power, enlarge their jurisdiction, to the total annihilation of the jurisdiction of the State Courts; that they will exercise their will, instead of the law and the Constitution.

This argument, if it proves any thing, would operate more strongly against the tribunal proposed to be created, which promised so little, than against the Supreme Court, which, for the reasons given before, have every thing connected with their appointment calculated to ensure confidence. What security have we, were the proposed amendment adopted, that this tribunal would not substitute their will and their pleasure in place of the law? The Judiciary are the weakest of the three Departments of Government, and least dangerous to the political rights of the Constitution; they hold neither the purse nor the sword; and, even to enforce their own judgments and decisions, must ultimately depend upon the Executive arm. Should the Federal Judiciary, however, unmindful of their weakness, unmindful of the duty which they owe to themselves and their country, become corrupt, and transcend the limits of their jurisdiction, would the proposed amendment oppose even a probable barrier in such an improbable state of things?

The creation of a tribunal, such as is proposed by Pennsylvania, so far as we are able to form an idea of it from the description given in the resolutions of the Legislature of that State, would, in the opinion of your Committee, tend rather to invite, than to prevent, collisions between the Federal and State Courts. It might also become, in process of time, a serious and dangerous embarrassment to the operations of the General Government.

Resolved, therefore, That the Legislature of this State do disapprove of the amendment to the Constitution of the United States, proposed by the Legislature of Pennsylvania.

Resolved, also, That his Excellency the Governor, be, and he is hereby, requested to transmit forthwith, a copy of the foregoing preamble and resolutions, to each of the Senators and Representatives of this State in Congress, and to the Executive of the several States in the Union, with a request that the same be laid before the Legislatures thereof.

The said resolutions being read a second time, were, on motion, ordered to be referred to a Committee of the Whole House on the state of the Commonwealth.

Tuesday, January 23, 1810.

The House, according to the order of the day, resolved itself into a Committee of the Whole House on the state of the Commonwealth, and after some time spent therein, Mr. Speaker resumed the Chair, and Mr. Stanard, of Spottsylvania, reported that the Committee had, according to order, had under consideration the preamble and resolutions of the Select Committee, to whom was referred that part of the Governor's communication which relates to the amendment proposed to the Constitution of the United States, by the Legislature of Pennsylvania, had gone through with the same, and directed him to report them to the House without amendment; which he handed in at the Clerk's table.

And the question being put on agreeing to the said preamble and resolutions, they were agreed to by the House unanimously.

Ordered, That the Clerk carry the said preamble and resolutions to the Senate, and desire their concurrence.

In Senate—Wednesday, January 24, 1810.

The preamble and resolutions on the amendment to the Constitution of the United States proposed by the Legislature of Pennsylvania, by the appointment of an impartial tribunal to decide disputes between the State and Federal Judiciary, being also delivered in and twice read, on motion, was ordered to be committed to Messrs. Nelson, Currie, Campbell, Upshur, and Wolfe.

Friday, January 26.

Mr. Nelson reported, from the committee to whom was committed the preamble and resolutions on the amendment proposed by the Legislature of Pennsylvania, &c. &c. that the Committee had, according to order, taken the said preamble, &c. under their consideration, and directed him to report them without any amendment.

And on the question being put thereupon, the same was agreed to unanimously.

MR. WEBSTER'S LAST REMARKS.

Mr. HAYNE having rejoined to Mr. WEBSTER, especially on the constitutional question—

Mr. WEBSTER arose, and, in conclusion, said:

A few words, Mr. President, on this constitutional argument, which the honorable gentleman has labored to reconstruct.

His argument consists of two propositions, and an inference. His propositions are—

1. That the Constitution is a compact between the States.

2. That a compact between two, with authority reserved to one to interpret its terms, would be a surrender to that one, of all power whatever.

3. Therefore, (such is his inference) the General Government does not possess the authority to construe its own powers.

Now, sir, who does not see, without the aid of exposition or detection, the utter confusion of ideas, involved in this, so elaborate and systematic argument.

The Constitution, it is said, is a compact *between States;* if so, the States, then, and the States only, *are parties to the compact.* How comes the General Government itself *a party?* Upon the honorable gentleman's hypothesis, the General Government is the result of the compact, the creature of the compact, not one of the parties to it. Yet the argument, as the gentleman has now stated it, makes the Government itself one of its own creators. It makes it a party to that compact, to which it owes its own existence.

For the purpose of erecting the Constitution on the basis of a compact, the gentleman considers the States as parties to that compact; but as soon as his compact is made, then he chooses to consider the General Government, which is the offspring of that compact, not its offspring, but one of its parties; and so, being a party, has not the power of judging on the terms of compact. Pray, sir, in what school is such reasoning as this taught?

If the whole of the gentleman's main proposition were conceded to him, that is to say—if I admit for the sake of the argument, that the Constitution is a compact between States, the inferences, which he draws from that proposition, are warranted by no just reason. Because, if the Constitution be a compact between States, still, that Constitution, or that compact, has established a Government, with certain powers; and whether it be one of those powers, that it shall construe and interpret for itself, the terms of the compact, in doubtful cases, is a question which can only be decided by looking to the compact, and inquiring what provisions it contains on this point. Without any inconsistency with natural reason, the Government, even thus created, might be trusted with this power of construction. The extent of its powers, therefore, must still be sought for in the instrument itself.

If the old Confederation had contained a clause, declaring that resolutions of the Congress should be the supreme law of the land, any State law or constitution to the contrary notwithstanding, and that a committee of Congress, or any other body created by it, should possess Judicial powers, extending to all cases arising under resolutions of Congress, then the power of ultimate decision would have been vested in Congress, under the Confederation, although that Confederation was a compact between States; and, for this plain reason: that it would have been competent to the States, who alone were parties to the compact, to agree, who should decide, in cases of dispute arising on the construction of the compact.

For the same reason, sir, if I were now to concede to the gentleman his principal propositions, viz. that the Constitution is a compact between States, the question would still be, what provision is made, in this compact, to settle points of disputed construction, or contested power, that shall come into controversy? and this question would still be answered, and conclusively answered, by the Constitution itself. While the gentleman is contending against construction, he himself is setting up the most loose and dangerous construction. The Constitution declares, that *the laws of Congress shall be the supreme law of the land.* No construction is necessary here. It declares, also, with equal plainness and precision, *that the Judicial power of the United States shall extend to every case arising under the laws of Congress.* This needs no construction. Here is a law, then, which is declared to be supreme; and here is a power established, which is to interpret that law. Now, sir, how has the gentleman met this? Suppose the Constitution to be a compact, yet here are its terms, and how does the gentleman get rid of them? He cannot argue the *seal off the bond,* nor the words out of the instrument. Here they are—what answer does he give to them? None in the world, sir, except, that the effect of this would be to place the States in a condition of inferiority; and because it results, from the very nature of things, there being no superior, that the parties must be their own judges! Thus closely and cogently does the honorable gentleman reason on the words of the Constitution. The gentleman says, if there be such a power of final decision in the General Government, he asks for the grant of that power. Well, sir, I show him the grant—I turn him to the very words—I show him that the laws of Congress are made supreme; and that the Judicial power extends, by express words, to the interpretation of these laws. Instead of answering this, he retreats into the general reflection, that it must result *from the nature of things,* that the States, being parties, must judge for themselves.

I have admitted, that, if the Constitution were to be considered as the creature of the State Governments, it might be modified, interpreted, or construed, according to their pleasure. But, even in that case, it would be necessary that they should *agree.* One, alone, could not construe it; one, alone, could not modify it. Yet the gentleman's doctrine is, that Carolina, alone, may construe and interpret that compact which equally binds all, and gives equal rights to all.

So then, sir, even supposing the Constitution to be a compact between the States, the gentleman's doctrine, nevertheless, is not maintainable; because, first, the General Government is not a party to that compact, but a *Government* established by it, and vested by it with the powers of trying and deciding doubtful questions; and, secondly, because, if the Constitution be regarded as a compact, not one State only, but all the States, are parties to that compact, and one can have no right to fix upon it her own peculiar construction.

So much, sir, for the argument, even if the premises of the gentleman were granted, or could be proved. But, sir, the gentleman has failed to maintain his leading proposition. He has not shown, it cannot be shown, that the Constitution is a compact between State Governments. The Constitution itself, in its very front, refutes that idea: it declares that it is ordained and established *by the People of the United States.* So far from saying that it is established by the Governments of the several States, it does not even say that it is established by the People *of the several States;* but it pronounces that it is established by the People of the United States, in the aggregate. The gentleman says, it must mean no more than the People of the several States. Doubtless, the People of the several States, taken collectively, constitute the People of the United States; but it is in this, their collective capacity, it is as all the People of the United States, that they establish the Constitution. So they declare; and words cannot be plainer than the words used.

When the gentleman says the Constitution is a compact between the States, he uses language exactly applicable to the old Confederation. He speaks as if he were in Congress before 1789. He describes fully that old state of things then existing. The Confederation was, in strictness, a compact; the States, as States, were parties to it. We had no other General Government. But that was found insufficient, and inadequate to the public exigencies. The People were not satisfied with it, and undertook to establish a better. They undertook to form a General Government, which should stand on a new basis—not a confederacy, not a league, not a compact between States, but a *Constitution;* a Popular Government, founded in popular election, directly responsible to the People themselves, and divided into branches, with prescribed limits of power, and prescribed duties. They ordained such a Government; they gave it the name of a *Constitution,* and therein they established a distribution of powers between this, their General Government, and their several State Governments. When they shall become dissatisfied with this distribution, they can alter it. Their own power over their own instrument remains. But until they shall alter it, it must stand as their will, and is equally binding on the General Government and on the States.

The gentleman, sir, finds analogy, where I see none. He likens it to the case of a treaty, in which, there being no common superior, each party must interpret for itself, under its own obligation of good faith. But this is not a treaty, but a Constitution of Government, with powers to execute itself, and fulfil its duties.

I admit, sir, that this Government is a Government of checks and balances; that is, the House of Representatives is a check on the Senate, and the Senate is a check on the House, and the President a check on both. But I cannot comprehend him, or, if I do, I totally differ from him, when he applies the notion of checks and balances to the interference of different Governments. He argues, that if we transgress, each State, as a State, has a right to check us. Does he admit the converse of the proposition, that we have a right to check the States? The gentleman's doctrines would give us a strange jumble of authorities and powers, instead of Governments of separate and defined powers. It is the part of wisdom, I think, to avoid this; and to keep the General Government and the State Governments, each in its proper sphere, avoiding, as carefully as possible, every kind of interference.

Finally, sir, the honorable gentleman says, that the States will only interfere, by their power, to preserve the Constitution. They will not destroy it, they will not impair it—they will only save, they will only preserve, they will only strengthen it! Ah! sir, this is but the old story. All regulated Governments, all free Governments, have been broken up by similar disinterested and well disposed interference! It is the common pretence. But I take leave of the subject.

Speech of Mr. Hayne,

of South Carolina

[January 27, 1830]

The resolution of Mr. Foot, of Connecticut, relative to the public lands, being under consideration, Mr. Hayne addressed the Chair as follows:

I DO NOT RISE AT THIS LATE HOUR,* Mr. President, to go at large into the controverted questions between the Senator from Massachusetts and myself, but merely to correct some very gross errors into which he has fallen, and to afford explanations on some points, which, after what has fallen from that gentleman, may perhaps be considered as requiring explanation. The gentleman has attempted, through the whole course of his argument, to throw upon me the blame of having provoked this discussion. Though standing himself at the very head and source of this angry controversy, which has flowed from him down to me, he insists that I have troubled the waters. In order to give color to this charge, (wholly unfounded, Sir, as every gentleman of this body will bear witness,) he alludes to my excitement when I first rose to answer the gentleman, after he had made his attack upon the South. He charges me with having then confessed that I had something rankling in my bosom which I desired to discharge. Sir, I have no recollection of having used that word. If it did escape me, however, in the excitement of the moment, it was not indicative of any personal hostility towards that Senator—for in truth, Sir, I felt none—but proceeded from a sensibility, which could not but be excited by what I had

---

*The lateness of the hour when Mr. W. resumed his seat, compelled Mr. H. to curtail his remarks in reply, especially those which related to the Constitutional question. In the Speech as here reported, the arguments omitted are supplied. The great importance of the question, makes it desirable, that nothing should be omitted necessary to its elucidation.

---

a right to consider as an unprovoked and most unwarrantable attack upon the South, through me.

The gentleman boasts that he has escaped unhurt in the conflict. The shaft, it seems, was shot by too feeble an arm to reach its destination. Sir, I am glad to hear this. Judging from the *actions* of the gentleman, I had feared that the arrow had penetrated even more deeply than I could have wished. From the beating of his breast, and the tone and manner of the gentleman, I should fear he *is* most sorely wounded. In a better spirit, however, I will say, I hope his wounds may heal kindly, and leave no scars behind; and let me assure the gentleman, that however deeply the arrow may have penetrated, its point was not envenomed. It was shot in fair and manly fight, and with the twang of the bow, have fled the feelings which impelled it. The gentleman indignantly repels the charge of having avoided the Senator from Missouri, (Mr. BENTON) and selected me as his adversary, from any apprehension of being overmatched. Sir, when I found the gentleman passing over in silence the arguments of the Senator from Missouri, which had charged the East with hostility towards the West, and directing his artillery against me, who had made no such charge, I had a right to inquire into the causes of so extraordinary a proceeding. I suggested some as probable, and among them, that to which the gentleman takes such strong exception. Sir, has he now given any sufficient reason for the extraordinary course of which I have complained? At one moment he tells us that "he did not hear the whole of the argument of the gentleman from Missouri," and again, "that having found a responsible indorser of the bill, he did not think proper to pursue the drawer." Well, Sir, if the gentleman answered the arguments which he did not hear, why attribute them to me, whom he did hear, and by whom they were certainly not urged? If he was determined to pursue the parties to the bill, why attempt to throw the responsibility on one who was neither the drawer nor the indorser? Let me once more, Sir, put this matter on its true footing. I will not be forced to assume a position in which I have not chosen to place myself. Sir, I disclaim any intention whatever in my original remarks on the public lands, to impute to the East hostility towards the West. I imputed none. I did not utter one word to that effect. I said nothing that could be tortured into an attack upon the East.

I did not mention the "accursed tariff"—a phrase which the gentleman has put into my mouth. I did not even impute the policy of Mr. Rush to New England. In alluding to that policy I noticed its source, and spoke of it as I thought it deserved. Sir, I am aware that a gentleman who rises without premeditation, to throw out his ideas on a question before the House, may use expressions of the force and extent of which he may, at the time, not be fully aware. I should not, therefore, rely so confidently on my own recollections, but for the circumstance, that I have not found one gentleman who heard my remarks, [except the Senator from Massachusetts himself,] who supposed that one word had fallen from my lips that called for a reply of the tone and character of that which the gentleman from Massachusetts thought proper to pronounce—not one, who supposed that I had thrown out any imputations against the East, or justly subjected myself or the South to rebuke, unless, indeed, the principles for which I contended were so monstrous, as to demand unmeasured reprobation. Now, Sir, what were those principles? I have already shown, that, whether sound or unsound, they are not separated by a "hair's breadth" from those contended for by the gentleman himself in 1825, and, therefore, that he, of all men, had the least right to take exception to them.

Sir, the gentleman charges me with having unnecessarily introduced the slave question; with what justice, let those determine who heard that gentleman pointing out the superiority of Ohio over Kentucky, and attributing it to that happy stroke of New England policy, by which slavery was forever excluded North of the Ohio river. Sir, I was wholly at a loss to conceive why that topic had been introduced here at all, until the gentleman followed it up by an attack upon the principles and policy of the South. When that was done, the object was apparent, and it became my duty to take up the gauntlet which the gentleman had thrown down, and to come out, without reserve, in defence of our institutions, and our principles. The gentleman charges us with a morbid sensibility on this subject. Sir, it is natural and proper that we should be sensitive on that topic, and we must continue so, just so long as those who do not live among us, shall be found meddling with a subject, with which they have nothing to do, and about which they know nothing. But, Sir, we will agree, now, henceforth, and forever, to avoid the subject altogether, never even to mention the word *slavery* on this floor, if gentlemen on the other side will only consent not to intrude it upon us, by forcing it unnecessarily into debate. When introduced, however, whether by a hint, or a sneer, by the imputation of weakness to slave holding States, or in any other way, we must be governed entirely by our own discretion, as to the manner in which the attack must be met. When the proposition was made here, to appropriate the public lands to emancipation, I met it with a protest. I have now met an attack of a different character by an argument.

The gentleman in alluding to the Hartford Convention, told us that he had nothing to do with it, and had nothing to say either for or against it, and yet he undertook, at the same time, to recommend that renowned assembly as a precedent to the South.

Sir, unkind as my allusion to the Hartford Convention has been considered by its supporters, I apprehend that this disclaimer of the gentleman's will be regarded as "the unkindest cut of all." When the gentleman spoke of the Carolina Conventions, of Colleton and Abbeville, let me tell him, that he spoke of that which never had existence, except in his own imagination. There have, indeed, been meetings of the people in those districts, composed Sir, of as high-minded and patriotic men as any country can boast of; but we have had no "convention" as yet; and when South Carolina shall resort to such a measure for the redress of her grievances, let me tell the gentleman that, of all the assemblies that have ever been convened in this country, the Hartford Convention is the very last we shall consent to take as an example; nor will it find more favor in our eyes, from being recommended to us by the Senator from Massachusetts. Sir, we would scorn to take advantage of difficulties created by a foreign war, to wring from the federal government a redress even of our grievances. We are standing up for our constitutional rights in a time of profound peace; but if the country should, unhappily be involved in a war tomorrow, we should be found flying to the standard of our country—first driving back the common enemy, and then insisting upon the restoration of our rights.

The gentleman, speaking of the tariff and internal improvements, said, that in supporting these measures, he had but followed "a Carolina lead." He also quoted, with high encomium, the opinion of the present Chairman of the Committee of Ways and Means, of the other House, in relation to the latter subject. Now, Sir, it is proper that the Senator from Massachusetts should be, once for all, informed, that South Carolina acknowledges no leaders, whom she is willing blindly to follow, in any course of policy. The "Carolina doctrines" in relation to the "American system," have been expounded to us by the resolutions of her legislature, and the remonstrances of her citizens, now upon your table; and when the gentleman shows us one of her distinguished sons expressing different sentiments, he neither changes her principles, nor subjects the State to a charge of inconsistency. Sir, no man can entertain a higher respect than I do, for the distinguished talents, high character, and manly independence of the gentleman alluded to, (Mr. McDuffie;) but if he now entertains the opinions attributed to him, in relation to internal improvements and the public lands, there can be no doubt that his sentiments, in these respects, differ widely from those of a large majority of the people of South Carolina; while in relation to the tariff, and other questions of vital importance, he not only goes heart and hand with us, but is himself a host.

The gentleman considers the tariff of 1816, and the bonus bill, as the foundations of the American system, and intimates, that the former would not have prevailed, but for South Carolina votes. Now, Sir, as to the Tariff of 1816, I think a great mistake prevails throughout the country, in regarding it as the commencement of the existing policy. That was not a bill for *increasing*, but for *reducing duties*. During the war, double duties had been resorted to, for raising the revenue necessary for its prosecution. Manufactures had sprung up under the protection incidentally afforded by the restrictive measures, and the war.—On the restoration of peace, a scale of duties was to be established, adapted to the situation in which the country was, by that event, placed. All agreed that the duties were to be reduced, and that this reduction must be gradual. We had a debt on our hands of $140 or $150,000,000. Admonished by recent experience, a Navy was to be built up, and an extensive system of fortifications to be commenced. The operation, too, of a sudden reduction of duties upon the manufactures which had been forced into existence by the war, and which then bore their full proportion of the direct taxes, was also to be taken into consideration; and under all of these circumstances, it was determined to reduce the duties gradually, until they should reach the lowest amount necessary for revenue in time of peace. Such, Sir, was the true character of the tariff law of 1816. By that bill (reported, Sir, by the lamented Lowndes, a steady opponent of the protecting system,) the duties on woollen and cotton goods were at once *reduced* to 25 per cent, with a provision, that they should, in the course of three years, *be further reduced* to twenty per cent., while, by the tariff of 1824, the duties on the same articles were at once *increased* to 30 per cent., and were to go on increasing to 37 1/2 per cent.; and by the tariff of 1828, have been carried much higher. And yet the tariff of 1816 is now quoted as an authority for the tariffs of 1824 and 1828; by which, duties admitted to be already high enough for all the purposes of revenue, are to go on increasing, year after year, for the avowed purpose of promoting domestic manufactures, by preventing importations. Suppose, Sir, the New England gentlemen were now to join the South in going back to a tariff for revenue, and were to propose to us gradually to reduce all the existing duties, so that they should come down, in two or three years, to fifteen or twenty per cent—would the gentleman consider us as sending in our adhesion to the American system, by voting for such a re-duction? And if not, how can he charge the supporters of the tariff of 1816 with being the fathers of that system? In this view of the subject, it is not at all material, whether the Representatives from South Carolina voted for that measure or not; or whether the passage of the bill depended on their votes. On looking into the journals, however, it will be found that the bill actually passed the House of Representatives, by a vote of 88 to 54; and would have succeeded, if every member from South Carolina had voted against it.

The gentleman next mentions the "Bonus Bill" as the first step in the system of Internal Improvement. That was a bill, Sir, not appropriating, but setting apart a fixed sum (the Bank Bonus) for Internal Improvements, to be distributed among the States, on principles of perfect equality, and to be applied "by consent of the States" themselves. Though Mr. Madison put his veto on that bill, it was supposed, at the time, to be in the spirit of his own message; and though I must express my dissent from the measure, no doubt can exist, that if the system of Internal Improvement had been pros-ecuted on the principles of that bill, much of the inequality and injustice that have since taken place would have been avoided. But, Sir, I am by no means disposed to deny, or to conceal the fact, that a considerable change has taken place in the Southern States, and in South Carolina in particular, in relation to Internal Improvements, since that measure was first broached, at the close of the last war. Sir, when we were restored to a state of peace, the attention of our prominent statesmen was directed to plans for the restoration of the country from the wounds of the war, and the public mind received a strong impulse towards Internal Improvements. The minds of the eminent men of the South had, by the events of that war, re-ceived for the time a direction rather favorable to the enlargement of the powers of the Government. They had seen the public arm paralyzed by the opposition to that war, and it was quite natural that they should at that time rather be disposed to strengthen than to weaken the powers of the Federal Government. Internal Improvements sprang up in that heated soil, and I have no doubt that as a new question, hardly examined, and very lit-tle understood, the people of the South, for a short period, took up the be-lief that, to a certain extent, and under certain guards, the system could be beneficially and constitutionally pursued. But, Sir, before time had been al-lowed for the formation of any fixed and settled opinions, the evils of the system were so fully developed, the injustice, the inequality, the corruption flowing from it, and the alarming extent of powers claimed for the Federal

Government by its supporters, became so manifest, as thoroughly to satisfy the South, that the system of Internal Improvement, on the principles on which it was to be administered, was not only unequal and unjust, but a most alarming innovation on the Constitution.

The gentleman has alluded to my own vote on the survey bill of 1824. Sir, I have to return him my thanks for having afforded me, by that allusion, an opportunity of explaining my conduct in relation to the system of Internal Improvements. At the time that I was called to a seat in this House, I had been for many years removed from political life, and engaged in the arduous pursuit of a profession, which abstracted me almost entirely from the examination of political questions. The gentleman tells us he had not made up his own mind on this subject as late as 1817. Sir, I had not even fully examined it in 1823. But even at that time, I entertained doubts, both as to the constitutionality and expediency of the system. I came here with these feelings, and before I was yet warm in my seat, the survey bill of 1824 was brought up. We were then expressly told by its advocates, that its object was not to establish a system of Internal Improvements, but merely to present to Congress and the country a full view of the whole ground, leaving it hereafter to be decided whether the system should be prosecuted, and if so, on what principles? Sir, I was induced to believe, that no great work would be undertaken until the objects of that survey bill should be accomplished—that is to say, until the President should submit the whole scheme in one connected view, so that we should have before us at once all the measures deemed to be of "national importance," to which the attention of Congress might be directed.

Sir, I did suppose that a few great works, in which all the States would have a common interest, and which might therefore be considered as of "national importance," were alone intended to be embraced in that bill, and that in one or two years, the whole of the surveys would be completed, when Congress would have it in their power to decide whether the system should be carried on at all, and if so, on what principles. Sir, I know that more than one gentleman who voted for the survey bill of 1824, expressly stated at the time, that they did not intend to commit themselves on the general question; and I was one of that number. And it was expressly because I did not consider that bill, as committing those who supported it, for or against any system of Internal Improvement, that I voted against every amendment, calculated to give any expression of opinion, one way or the other. I was unwilling to deprive it of the character which it bore on its face, as a measure intended merely to bring before the public in a single view, the entire scheme, so as to enable us to judge of its practicability and expediency. Sir, in all these views and expectations, I was deceived. By the year 1826, it came to be fully understood that these surveys were never to be finished, and that $50,000 per annum was to be appropriated, merely to give popularity to the system, by feeding the hopes of the people in all parts of the country. In the mean time, too, appropriations were made and new works commenced, just as if no surveys were going on. Sir, as soon as I discovered the true character of the survey bill, I opposed it openly on this floor, and have since constantly voted against all appropriations for surveys. Sir, as to the system of Internal Improvement, my first impressions against it were fully confirmed, very soon after I took my seat here, and (except in cases which I consider as exceptions from the general rule,) I have uniformly voted against all appropriations for Internal Improvements, against the Cumberland Road, the Chesapeake and Delaware Canal, and all other works of a similar character. But Sir, if the South, or the statesmen of the South, had committed themselves ever so deeply on this subject, does the gentleman from Massachusetts suppose it would afford any excuse for their continued support of a system conducted on principles which now manifestly appear to be as unconstitutional as they are unequal and unjust? Surely not.

The gentleman has made his defence for his conduct in relation to the tariff of 1828. He considers the country as being committed by the tariff of 1824 to go on with the system. Sir, we wholly deny that the country is in any way committed, or that Congress could commit it on such a subject, much less to the support of a ruinous, unjust, and unconstitutional policy. But how, if such a committal were possible, could the imposition of a duty of 20 or 30 per cent. commit us to the imposition of duties of 50 or 100? The gentleman is mistaken in supposing that I charged him with having, in 1820, denounced the tariff as "utterly unconstitutional;" I stated that he had called its constitutionality in question. I have now before me the proceedings of the Boston meeting, to which I referred, and will read them, that there may be no mistake on the subject. In the resolutions reported by a committee, (of which Mr. W. was a member,) it was, among other things,

1. "*Resolved*, That no objection ought ever to be made to any amount of taxes equally apportioned, and imposed for the purpose of raising revenue, necessary for the support of government, but that taxes imposed on the people, for the benefit of any one class of men, (the manufacturers,) are equally inconsistent with *the principles of the Constitution*, and with sound policy."

2. "*Resolved,* That, in our opinion, the proposed tariff, and the principles on which it is avowedly founded, would, if adopted, have a tendency, however different may be the motives of those who recommend them, to diminish the industry, impede the prosperity, and corrupt the morals of the people."

In support of these anti-tariff resolutions, (which were unanimously adopted,) Mr. Webster said:

"There is a power in names; and those who had pressed the tariff on Congress, and on the country, had represented it as immediately, and almost exclusively, connected with *domestic industry,* and national independence. In his opinion, no measure could prove more injurious to the industry of the country, and nothing was more fanciful than the opinion that national independence rendered such a measure necessary. He certainly thought it might be doubted, whether Congress would not be acting somewhat against *the spirit and intention of the Constitution,* in exercising the power to control essentially the pursuits and occupations of individuals, not as incidental to the exercise of any other power, but as a substantial and direct power. If such changes were wrought incidentally only, and were the necessary consequence of such impost as Congress, for the leading purpose of revenue, should enact, then they could not be complained of. But he doubted whether Congress fairly possessed the power of turning the incident into the principal; and instead of leaving manufactures to the protection of such laws as should be passed with a primary regard to revenue, of enacting laws, with the avowed object of giving a preference to particular manufactures, &c."

Sir, these are good sound "South Carolina doctrines," and if the gentleman finds reason to abandon them now, we cannot consent to go with him.

We have been often reproached, Sir, with lending our aid to some of the most obnoxious provisions of the Tariff of 1828. What was the fact? Not an amendment was put into that bill here, which did not go to reduce the duties. That bill came to the Senate in a form in which it was known that it could not pass. Gentlemen who would not vote for it, in that shape,—but who wished it to pass, called upon us to aid them in amending it, to suit their own purposes. Sir, if we had lent our aid to such an object, we would have deserved any fate that could have befallen us. We proceeded throughout on the open and avowed ground of hostility to the whole system, and acted accordingly.

To disprove my observations, that the New England members, generally, did not support *Internal Improvements* in the west, before that memorable era, the winter of 1825, the gentleman quoted two votes in 1820 and 1821, reducing the price, or extending the time of payment for the *Public Lands*. Now, Sir, the only objection to his authority, is, that it has no manner of relation to the point in dispute. I stated that New England did not support Internal Improvements, as a branch of the American system, before 1825. The gentleman proves, that on two occasions, they voted for certain measures in relation to the Public Lands—measures which I had always supposed had been forced upon Congress by motives of interest,— but which, whatever may have been their character, do not touch the point in dispute in the smallest degree. I think this mode of meeting my argument, however creditable to the gentleman's ingenuity, amounts to an acknowledgment that it is unanswerable.

The gentleman complains of his arguments having been misunderstood in relation to consolidation. He thinks my misapprehension almost miraculous in treating his as an argument in favor of the "consolidation of the government." Now, Sir, what was the point in dispute between us? I had deprecated the consolidation of the government. I said not one word against "the consolidation of the Union." I went further, and pointed out and deprecated some of the means, by which this consolidation was to be brought about. The gentleman gets up and attacks me and my argument at every point, ridicules our fears about "consolidation," and finally reads a passage from a letter of General Washington's, stating that one of the objects of the Constitution was, "the consolidation of the Union." Surely, Sir, under these circumstances, I was not mistaken in saying, that the authority quoted did not apply to the case, as the point in dispute was the "consolidation of the government," and not of "the Union." But, Sir, the gentleman has relieved me from all embarrassment on this point, by going fully into the examination of the Virginia doctrines of '98, and while he denounces them, giving us his own views of the powers of the Federal Government; views which, in my humble judgment, stop nothing short of the consolidation of all power in the hands of the Federal Government. Sir, when I last touched on this topic, I did little more than quote the high authorities on which our doctrines rest; but after the elaborate argument which we have just heard from the gentleman from Massachusetts, it cannot be supposed, that I can suffer them to go to the world unanswered. I entreat the Senate therefore to bear with me, while I go over as briefly as possible *the most prominent arguments of the gentleman*.

The proposition which I laid down and from which the gentleman dissents, is taken from the Virginia resolutions of '98, and is in these words, "that in case of a deliberate, palpable, and dangerous exercise by the Federal Government *of powers not granted* by the compact [the constitution] the States who are parties thereto, *have a right to interpose,* for arresting the progress of the evil, and for maintaining within their respective limits, the authorities, rights and liberties appertaining to them." The gentleman insists that the States have no right to decide whether the constitution has been violated by acts of Congress or not,—but *that the Federal Government is the exclusive judge of the extent of its own powers;* and that in case of a violation of the constitution, however "deliberate, palpable and dangerous," a State has no constitutional redress, except where the matter can be brought before the Supreme Court, whose decision must be final and conclusive on the subject. Having thus distinctly stated the points in dispute between the gentleman and myself, I proceed to examine them. And here it will be necessary to go back to the origin of the Federal Government. It cannot be doubted, and is not denied, that before the formation of the constitution, each State was an independent sovereignty, possessing all the rights and powers appertaining to independent nations; nor can it be denied that, after the constitution was formed, they remained equally sovereign and independent, as to all powers, not expressly delegated to the Federal Government. This would have been the case even if no positive provision to that effect had been inserted in that instrument. But to remove all doubt it is expressly declared, by the 10th article of the amendment of the constitution, "that the powers not delegated to the States, by the constitution, nor prohibited by it to the States, are reserved to the States respectively, or to the people." The true nature of the Federal constitution, therefore, is, (in the language of Mr. Madison,) "a compact to which the States are parties," a compact by which each State, acting in its sovereign capacity, has entered into an agreement with the other States, by which they have consented that certain designated powers shall be exercised by the United States, in the manner prescribed in the instrument. Nothing can be clearer, than that, under such a system, the Federal Government, exercising strictly delegated powers, can have no right to act beyond the pale of its authority; and that all such acts are void. A State, on the contrary, retaining all powers not expressly given away, may lawfully act in all cases where she has not voluntarily imposed restrictions on herself. Here then is a case of a compact between sovereigns, and the question arises—what is the remedy for a clear violation of its express terms by one of the parties? And here the plain obvious dictate of common sense, is in strict conformity with the understanding of mankind, and the practice of nations in all analogous cases—"that where resort can be had to no common superior, the parties to the compact must, themselves, be the rightful judges whether the bargain has been pursued or violated." (Madison's Report, p. 20.) When it is insisted by the gentleman that one of the parties "has the power of deciding ultimately and conclusively upon the extent of its own authority," I ask for the grant of such a power. I call upon the gentleman to shew it to me in the constitution. It is not to be found there. If it is to be inferred from the nature of the compact, I aver, that not a single argument can be urged in support of such an inference, in favor of the United States, which would not apply, with at least equal force, in favor of a State. All sovereigns are of necessity equal, and any one State, however small in population or territory, has the same rights as the rest, just as the most insignificant nation in Europe is as much sovereign as France, or Russia, or England.

The very idea of a division of power by compact, is destroyed by a right claimed and exercised by either to be the exclusive interpreter of the instrument. Power is not divided, where one of the parties can arbitrarily determine its limits. A compact between two, with a right reserved to one, to expound the instrument according to his own pleasure, is no compact at all, but an absolute surrender of the whole subject matter to the arbitrary discretion of the party who is constituted the judge. This is so obvious, that, in the conduct of human affairs between man and man, a common superior is always looked to as the expounder of contracts. But if there be no common superior, it results, from the very nature of things, that the parties *must be their own judges*. This is admitted to be the case where treaties are formed between independent nations, and if the same rule does not apply to the federal compact, it must be because the Federal is superior to the State Government, or because the States have surrendered their sovereignty. Neither branch of this proposition can be maintained for a moment. I have already shewn that all sovereigns must, as such, be equal. It only remains, therefore, to inquire whether the States have surrendered their sovereignty, and consented to reduce themselves to mere corporations. The whole form and structure of the Federal Government, the opinions of the framers of the Constitution, and the organization of the State Governments, demonstrate that though the States have surrendered certain specific powers, they have not surrendered their sovereignty. They have each an independent Legislature, Executive, and Judiciary, and exercise jurisdiction over the lives and property of their citizens. They have, it is true, voluntarily restrained themselves from doing certain acts, but, in all other respects, they are as omnipotent as any independent nation whatever. Here, however, we are met by the argument that the Constitution was not formed by *the States*, in their sovereign capacity, but by *the People*, and it is therefore inferred that the Federal Government, being created by all the People, must be supreme, and though it is not contended that the Constitution may be rightfully violated, yet it is insisted that from the decisions of the Federal Government there can be no appeal. It is obvious that this argument rests on the idea of State inferiority. Considering the Federal Government as one whole, and the States merely as component parts, it follows, of course, that the former is as much superior to the latter, as the whole is to the parts of which it is composed. Instead of deriving power by delegation from the States to the Union, this scheme seems to imply that the individual States derive their power from the United States, just as petty corporations may exercise so much power, and no more, as their superior may permit them to enjoy. This notion is entirely at variance with all our conceptions of State rights, as those rights were understood by Mr. Madison and others, at the time the Constitution was framed. I deny that the Constitution was framed by the People in the sense in which that word is used on the other side, and insist that it was framed by the States acting in their sovereign capacity. When, in the preamble of the Constitution, we find the words "we, the People of the United States," it is clear, they can only relate to the People as citizens of the several States, because the Federal Government was not then in existence.

We accordingly find, in every part of that instrument, that the people are always spoken of in that sense. Thus, in the 2d section of the 1st article, it is declared, "That the House of Representatives shall be composed of members chosen every second year, by the people of the several States." To show, that, in entering into this compact, the States acted in their sovereign capacity, and not merely as parts of one great community, what can be more conclusive than the historical fact, that, when every State had consented to it except one, she was not held to be bound. A majority of the people in any State bound that State, but nine-tenths of all the people of the United States could not bind the people of Rhode Island, until Rhode Island, as a State, had consented to the compact. It cannot be denied, that, at the time the Constitution was framed, the people of the United States were members of regularly organized governments, citizens of independent States; and, unless these State governments had been dissolved, it was impossible that the people could have entered into any compact but as citizens of these States. Suppose an assent to the Constitution had been given by all the people within a certain district of any State, but that the State, in its sovereign capacity, had refused its assent, would the people of that district have become citizens of the United States? Surely not. It is clear, then, that, in adopting the Constitution, the people did not act, and could not have acted in any other character than as citizens of their respective states. And if, on the adoption of the Constitution, they became citizens of the United States, it was only by virtue of that clause in the Constitution which declares "that the citizens of each State shall be entitled to all the privileges and immunities of citizens of the several States." In choosing members to the Convention, the States acted through their Legislatures, by whose authority the Constitution, when framed, was submitted for ratification to Conventions of the People, the usual and most appropriate organ of the sovereign will. I am not disposed to dwell longer on this point, which does appear to my mind to be too clear to admit of controversy. But I will quote from Mr. Madison's report, which goes the whole length in support of the doctrines for which I have contended:

"The other position involved in this branch of the resolution, namely, 'that the States are parties to the Constitution or compact,' is, in the judgment of the committee, equally free from objection." It is, indeed, true, that the term 'States' is sometimes used in a vague sense, and sometimes in different senses, according to the subject to which it is applied. Thus, it sometimes means the separate sections of territory occupied by the political societies within each; sometimes the particular governments established by those societies; sometimes those societies as organized into those particular governments; and, lastly, it means *the people composing those political societies, in their highest sovereign capacity.*" Although it might be wished that the perfection of language admitted less diversity in the signification of the same words, yet little inconvenience is produced by it, where the true sense can be collected with certainty from the different applications. In the present instance, whatever different constructions of the term 'States,' in the resolution, may have been entertained, all will at least concur in that last mentioned; because, in that sense the Constitution was submitted to the 'States;' in that sense the 'States' ratified it; and in that sense of the term 'States,' they are consequently parties to the compact, from which the powers of the Federal Government result."

Having now established the position that the Constitution was a compact between sovereign and independent States, having no common superior, "it follows of necessity," (to borrow the language of Mr. Madison,) "that there can be no tribunal above their authority to decide in the last resort, whether the compact made by them be violated, and consequently, that, as the parties to it, they must themselves decide, in the last resort, such questions as may be of sufficient magnitude to require their interposition."

But, the gentleman insists that the tribunal provided by the Constitution, for the decision of controversies between the States and the Federal Government, is the Supreme Court. And here again I call for the authority on which the gentleman rests the assertion, that the Supreme Court has any jurisdiction whatever over questions of sovereignty between the States and the United States. When we look into the Constitution, we do not find it there. I put entirely out of view any act of Congress on the subject. We are not looking into the laws, but the Constitution.

It is clear that questions of sovereignty are not the proper subjects of *judicial investigation.* They are much too large, and of too delicate a nature, to be brought within the jurisdiction of a Court of justice. Courts, whether supreme or subordinate, are the mere creatures of the sovereign power, designed to expound and carry into effect its sovereign will. No independent state ever yet submitted to a Judge on the bench the true construction of a compact between itself and another sovereign. All Courts may incidentally take cognizance of treaties, where rights are claimed under them, but who ever heard of a Court making an inquiry into the authority of the agents of the high contracting parties to make the treaty,—whether its terms had been fulfilled, or whether it had become void, on account of a breach of its condition on either side? All these are political, and not judicial questions. Some reliance has been placed on those provisions of the Constitution which constitute "one Supreme Court," which provide, "that the judicial power shall extend to all cases in law and equity arising under this Constitution, the laws of the United States and treaties," and which declare "that the Constitution, and the laws of the United States *which shall be made in pursuance thereof,* and all treaties, &c. shall be the supreme law of the land," &c. Now, as to the name of the *Supreme Court,* it is clear that the term has relation only to its supremacy over the inferior Courts provided for by the Constitution, and has no reference whatever to any supremacy over the sovereign States. The words are, "the judicial power of the United States shall be vested in one Supreme Court, and such inferior Courts as Congress may from time to time establish," &c. Though jurisdiction is given "in cases arising under the Constitution," yet it is expressly limited to "cases in law and equity," shewing conclusively that this jurisdiction was incidental merely to the ordinary administration of justice, and not intended to touch high questions of conflicting sovereignty. When it is declared that the Constitution and the laws of the United States "made in pursuance thereof, shall be the supreme law of the land," it is manifest that no indication is given either as to the power of the Supreme Court, to bind the States by its decisions, nor as to the *course to be pursued in the event of laws being passed not in pursuance of the Constitution.* And I beg leave to call gentlemen's attention to the striking fact, that the powers of the Supreme Court in relation to questions arising under "the laws and the Constitution," are co-extensive with those arising under treaties. In all of these cases the power is limited to questions arising "in law and equity," that is to say, to cases where jurisdiction is incidentally acquired in the ordinary administration of justice. But as with regard to treaties, the Supreme Court has never assumed jurisdiction over questions arising between the sovereigns who are parties to it; so under the Constitution, they cannot assume jurisdiction over questions arising between the individual States and the United States.

If they should do so, they would be acting entirely out of their sphere. *Umpires* are indeed sometimes appointed by special agreement; but in the case before us, there can be no pretence that the Supreme Court have been specially constituted umpires. But if the Judiciary are, from their character and the peculiar scope of their duties, unfit for the high office of deciding questions of sovereignty, much more strongly is the Supreme Court disqualified from assuming the umpirage between the States and the United States, because it is created by, and is indeed merely one of the departments of the Federal Government. The United States have a Supreme Court; each State has also a Supreme Court. Both of them, in the ordinary administration of justice, must, of necessity, decide on the constitutionality of laws; but when it becomes a question of sovereignty between these two independent Governments, the subject matter is equally removed from the jurisdiction of both. If the Supreme Court of the United States can take cognizance of such a question, so can the Supreme Courts of the States. But, Sir, can it be supposed for a moment, that when the States proceeded to enter into the compact, called the Constitution of the United States, they could have designed, nay, that they could, under any circumstances, have consented to leave to a court to be created by the Federal Government the power to decide, finally, on the extent of the powers of the latter, and the limitations on the powers of the former. If it had been designed to do so, it would have been so declared, and assuredly some provision would have been made to secure, as umpires, a tribunal somewhat differently constituted from that whose appropriate duty is the ordinary administration of justice. But to prove, as I think, conclusively, that the Judiciary were not designed to act as umpires, it is only necessary to observe that, in a great majority of cases, that court could manifestly not take jurisdiction of the matters in dispute. Whenever it may be designed by the Federal Government to commit a violation of the Constitution, it can be done, and always will be done in such a manner as to deprive the court of all jurisdiction over the subject. Take the case of the Tariff and Internal Improvements, whether constitutional or unconstitutional, it is admitted that the Supreme Court *have no jurisdiction*. Suppose Congress should, for the acknowledged purpose of making an equal distribution of the property of the country, among States or individuals, proceed to lay taxes to the amount of $50,000,000 a year. Could the Supreme Court take cognizance of the act laying the tax, or making the distribution? Certainly not.

Take another case which is very likely to occur. Congress have the *unlimited power of taxation*. Suppose them also to assume an *unlimited power of appropriation*. Appropriations of money are made to establish presses, promote education, build and support churches, create an order of nobility, or for any other unconstitutional object; it is manifest that, in none of these cases, could the constitutionality of the laws making those grants be tested before the Supreme Court. It would be in vain, that a State should come before the Judges with an act appropriating money to any of these objects, and ask of the Court to decide whether these grants were constitutional. They could not even be heard; the Court would say, they had nothing to do with it; and they would say rightly. It is idle, therefore, to talk of the Supreme Court affording any security to the States, in cases where their rights may be violated by the exercise of unconstitutional powers on the part of the Federal Government. On this subject Mr. Madison, in his report says: "But it is objected, that the judicial authority is to be regarded as the sole expositor of the Constitution in the last resort; and it may be asked, for what reason, the declaration by the General Assembly, supposing it to be theoretically true, could be required at the present day, and in so solemn a manner.

"On this objection it might be observed, first: that there may be instances of usurped power, which the forms of the Constitution would never draw within the control of the Judicial Department: Secondly, that if the decision of the Judiciary be raised above the authority of the sovereign parties to the Constitution, the decisions of the other Departments, not carried by the forms of the Constitution before the Judiciary, must be equally authoritative and final with the decisions of that Department. But the proper answer to the objection is, that the resolution of the General Assembly relates to those great and extraordinary cases in which all the forms of the Constitution may prove ineffectual against infractions dangerous to the essential rights of the parties to it. The resolution supposes that dangerous powers not delegated, may not only be usurped and executed by the other Departments, but that the Judicial Departments also, may exercise or sanction dangerous powers beyond the grant of the Constitution, and consequently, that the ultimate right of the parties to the Constitution to judge whether the compact has been dangerously violated, must extend to violations by one delegated authority, as well as by another—by the Judiciary, as well as by the Executive or Legislative.

"However true, therefore, it may be, that the Judicial Department is, in all questions submitted to it by the forms of the Constitution, to decide in the last resort, this resort must necessarily be deemed the last in relation to the authorities of the other Departments of the Government; not in relation *to the rights of the parties to the constitutional compact,* from which the judicial as well as the other Departments, hold their delegated trusts. On any other hypothesis, the delegation of Judicial power would annul the authority delegating it; and the concurrence of this Department with the others in usurped powers, might subvert forever, and beyond the possible reach *of any rightful remedy,* the very Constitution which all were instituted to preserve."

If, then, the Supreme Court are not, and from their organization, cannot be the umpires in questions of conflicting sovereignty, the next point to be considered is, whether Congress themselves possess the right of deciding conclusively on the extent of their own powers. This, I know, is a popular notion, and it is founded on the idea, that as all the States are represented here, nothing can prevail which is not in conformity with the will of the majority—and it is supposed to be a republican maxim "that the majority must govern." Now, Sir, I admit that much care has been taken to secure the States and the People from rash and unadvised legislation. The organization of two houses, the one the representatives of the States, and the other of the people, manifest an anxiety to secure equality and justice in the operation of the Federal System. But all this has done no more than to secure us against any laws, but such as should be assented to by a majority of the representatives in the two Houses of Congress.

Now will any one contend that it is the true spirit of this Government, that the *will of a majority of Congress* should, in all cases, be *the supreme law?* If no security was intended to be provided for the rights of the States, and the liberty of the citizen, beyond the mere organization of the Federal Government, we should have had no written Constitution, but Congress would have been authorized to legislate for us, in all cases whatsoever; and the acts of our State Legislatures, like those of the present legislative councils in the Territories, would have been subjected to the revision and control of Congress. If the will of a majority of Congress is to be the supreme law of the land, it is clear the Constitution is a dead letter, and has utterly failed of the very object for which it was designed—the protection of the rights of the minority. But when, by the very terms of the compact, strict limitations are imposed on every branch of the Federal Government, and it is, moreover, expressly declared, that all powers, not granted to them, "are reserved to the States or the People," with what show of reason can it be contended, that the Federal Government is to be the exclusive judge of the extent of its own powers? A *written Constitution* was resorted to in this country, as a great experiment, for the purpose of ascertaining how far the rights of a minority could be secured against the encroachments of majorities—often acting under party excitement, and not unfrequently under the influence of strong interests. The moment that Constitution was formed, the will of the majority ceased to be the law, except in cases that should be acknowledged by the parties to it to be *within the Constitution,* and to have been thereby submitted to their will. But when Congress, (exercising a delegated and strictly limited authority) pass beyond these limits, their acts become null and void; and must be declared to be so by the Courts, in cases within their jurisdiction; and may be pronounced to be so, by the States themselves, in cases not within the jurisdiction of the Courts, or of *sufficient importance to justify such an interference.* I will put the case strongly. Suppose, in the language of Mr. Jefferson, the Federal Government, in its three ruling branches, should, (at some future day,) be found "to be in combination to strip their colleagues, the State authorities, of the powers reserved by them, and to exercise themselves all powers, foreign and domestic," would there be no constitutional remedy against such an usurpation? If so, then Congress is supreme, and your Constitution is not worth the parchment on which it is written. What the gentleman calls the right of revolution would exist, and could be exerted as well without a Constitution as with it.

It is in vain to tell us, that all the States are represented here. Representation may, or may not, afford security to the people. The only practical security against oppression, in representative governments, is to be found in this, that *those who impose the burthens,* are compelled to *share them.* Where there are conflicting interests, however, and a *majority* are enabled to impose burthens on the *minority,* for their own advantage, it is obvious that representation, on the part of that minority, can have no other effect than to "furnish an apology for the injustice." What security would a representation of the American colonies, in the British Parliament, have afforded to our ancestors? What would be the value of a West India representation there now? Of what value is *our representation here,* on questions connected with the "American system;" where, (to use the strong language of a distinguished statesman) the "imposition is laid, not by the representatives of those who *pay the tax,* but by the representatives of those who are *to receive the bounty?*" Sir, representation will afford us ample security if the Federal Government shall be strictly confined within the limits prescribed by the constitution, and if, limiting its action to matters in which all have a common interest, the system shall be made to operate equally over the whole country. But it will afford us none, if the will of an interested majority shall be the supreme law, and Congress shall undertake to legislate for us, in all cases whatsoever. Before I leave this branch of the subject, I must remark, that, while gentlemen admit, as they do, that the Courts may nullify an act of Congress, by declaring it to be unconstitutional, it is impossible for them to contend, that *Congress are the final judges* of the extent of their own powers.

I think I have now shown, that the right of a State to judge of infractions of the constitution, on the part of the Federal Government, results from the very nature of the compact; and that, neither by the express provisions of that instrument, nor by any fair implication, is such a power exclusively reserved to the Federal Government, or any of its departments—executive, legislative, or judicial. But I go farther, and contend, that the power in question may be fairly considered as reserved to the States, by that clause of the constitution before referred to, which provides, "that all powers not delegated to the United States, are reserved to the States, respectively, or to the people."

No doubt can exist, that, before the States entered into the compact, they possessed the right to the fullest extent, of determining the limits of their own powers—it is incident to all sovereignty. Now, have they given away that right, or agreed to limit or restrict it in any respect? Assuredly not. They have agreed, that certain specific powers shall be exercised by the Federal Government; but the moment that Government steps beyond the limits of its charter, the right of the States "to interpose for arresting the progress of the evil, and for maintaining within their respective limits the authorities, rights, and liberties, appertaining to them," is as full and complete as it was before the Constitution was formed. It was plenary then, and never having been surrendered, must be plenary now. But what then? asks the gentleman. A State is brought into collision with the United States, in relation to the exercise of unconstitutional powers: who is to decide between them? Sir, it is the common case of difference of opinion between sovereigns, as to the true construction of a compact. Does such a difference of opinion necessarily produce war? No. And if not, among rival nations, why should it do so among friendly States? In all such cases, some mode must be devised by mutual agreement, for settling the difficulty; and most happily for us, that mode is clearly indicated in the Constitution itself, and results indeed from the very form and structure of the Government. The creating power is three fourths of the States. By their decision, the parties to the compact have agreed to be bound, even to the extent of changing the entire form of the Government itself; and it follows of necessity, that in case of a deliberate and settled difference of opinion between the parties to the compact, as to the extent of the powers of either, resort must be had to their common superior—(that power which may give any character to the Constitution they may think proper,) viz: three-fourths of the States. This is the view of the matter taken by Mr. Jefferson himself, who in 1821, expressed himself in this emphatic manner: "It is a fatal heresy to suppose, that either our State Governments are superior to the Federal, or the Federal to the State; neither is authorized literally to decide what belongs to itself, or its copartner in government, in differences of opinion between their different sets of public servants: the appeal is to neither, but to their employers, peaceably assembled by their representatives in convention."

But it has been asked, Why not compel a State, objecting to the constitutionality of a law, to appeal to her sister States, by a proposition to amend the constitution? I answer, because, such a course would, in the first instance, admit the exercise of an unconstitutional authority, which the States are not bound to submit to, even for a day, and because it would be absurd to suppose that any redress would ever be obtained by such an appeal, even if a State were at liberty to make it. If a majority of both Houses of Congress should, from any motive, be induced deliberately, to exercise "powers not granted," what prospect would there be of "arresting the progress of the evil," by a vote of three fourths? But the constitution does not permit a minority to submit to the people a proposition for an amendment of the constitution. Such a proposition can only come from "two-thirds of the two Houses of Congress, or the Legislatures of two-thirds of the States." It will be seen therefore, at once, that a minority, whose constitutional rights are violated, can have no redress by an amendment of the constitution. When any State is brought into direct collision with the Federal Government, in the case of an attempt, by the latter, to exercise unconstitutional powers, the appeal must be made by Congress, (the party proposing to exert the disputed power,) in order to have it expressly conferred, and, until so conferred, the exercise of such authority must be suspended. Even in cases of doubt, such an appeal is due to the peace and harmony of the Government. On this subject our present Chief Magistrate, in his opening message to Congress, says: "I regard *an appeal to the source of power*, in cases of real doubt, and where its exercise is deemed indispensable to the general welfare, as among *the most sacred of all our obligations*. Upon this country, more than any other, has, in the providence of God, been cast the special guardianship of the great principle of adherence to *written constitutions*. If it fail here all hope in regard to it will be extinguished. That this was intended to be a government of limited and specific, and not general powers, must be admitted by all; and it is our duty to preserve for it the character intended by its framers. The scheme has worked well. It has exceeded the hopes of those who devised it, and became an object of admiration to the world. Nothing is clearer, in my view, than that we are chiefly indebted for the success of the constitution under which we are now acting, to the watchful and auxiliary operation of the State authorities. This is not the reflection of a day, but belongs to the most deeply rooted convictions of my mind. I cannot, therefore, too strongly or too earnestly, for my own sense of its importance, warn you against all encroachments upon the legitimate sphere of State sovereignty. Sustained by its healthful and invigorating influence, the Federal system can never fail."

But the gentleman apprehends that this will "make the Union a rope of sand." Sir, I have shown that it is a power indispensably necessary to the preservation of the constitutional rights of the States, and of the people. I now proceed to show that it is perfectly safe, and will practically have no effect but to keep the Federal Government within the limits of the constitution, and prevent those unwarrantable assumptions of power, which cannot fail to impair the rights of the States, and finally destroy the Union itself. This is a government of checks and balances. All free governments must be so. The whole organization and regulation of every department of the Federal, as well as of the State Governments, establish, beyond a doubt, that it was the first object of the great fathers of our federal system to interpose effectual checks to prevent that over-action, which is the besetting sin of all governments, and which has been the great enemy to freedom over all the world. There is an obvious and wide distinction, between the power of acting, and of preventing action, a distinction running through the whole of our system. No one can question, that in all really doubtful cases, it would be extremely desirable to leave things as they are. And how happy would it be for mankind, and how greatly would it contribute to the peace and tranquillity of this country, and to that mutual harmony on which the preservation of the Union must depend, that the Federal Government (confining its operations to subjects clearly federal,) should only be felt in the blessings which it dispenses. Look, Sir, at our system of checks. The House of Representatives checks the Senate, the Senate checks the House, the Executive checks both, the Judiciary checks the whole; and it is in the true spirit of this system, that the States should check the Federal Government, at least so far as to preserve the constitution from "gross, palpable and deliberate violations," and to compel an appeal to the amending power, in cases of real doubt and difficulty. That the States possess this right, seems to be acknowledged by Alexander Hamilton himself. In the 51st No. of the Federalist, he says, "that in a single republic all the powers surrendered by the people, are submitted to the administration of a single government, and usurpations are guarded against by a division of the government into separate departments. In the compound republic of America, the power surrendered by the people is first divided between two distinct governments, and then the portion allotted to each sub-divided into separate departments; hence a double security arises to the rights of the people. The different governments *will control each other*, at the same time each will be controlled by itself."

I have already shown, that it has been fully recognized by the Virginia resolutions of '98, and by Mr. Madison's report on these resolutions, that it is not only "the right, but the duty of the States," to "judge of infractions of the constitution," and "to interpose for *maintaining within their limits the authorities, rights, and liberties, appertaining to them.*"

Mr. Jefferson, on various occasions, expressed himself in language equally strong. In the Kentucky resolutions of '98, prepared by him, it is declared that the federal government "was not made the exclusive and final judge of the extent of the powers delegated to itself since that would have made its discretion, and not the Constitution the measure of its powers, but that, as in all other cases of compact among parties having no common judge, each party has an equal right *to judge for itself, as well of infractions as the mode and measure of redress.*"

In the Kentucky resolutions of '99, it is even more explicitly declared, "that the several States which formed the Constitution, being sovereign and independent, have the unquestionable right *to judge of its infraction,* and that *a nullification* by those sovereignties of all unauthorized acts done under color of that instrument is *the rightful remedy.*"

But the gentleman says, this right will be dangerous. Sir, I insist, that of all the checks that have been provided by the Constitution, this is by far the safest, and the least liable to abuse. It is admitted by the gentleman, that the Supreme Court may declare a law to be unconstitutional, and check your further progress. The Supreme Court consists of only seven judges: four are a quorum, three of whom are a majority, and may exercise this mighty power. Now, the Judges of this Court are without any direct responsibility, in matters of opinion, and may certainly be governed by any of the motives, which it is supposed will influence a State in opposing the acts of the Federal Government. Sir, it is not my desire to excite prejudice against the Supreme Court. I not only entertain the highest respect for the individuals who compose that tribunal, but I believe they have rendered important services to the country; and that, confined within their appropriate sphere, (the decision of questions "of law and equity,") they will constitute a fountain from which will forever flow the streams of pure and undefiled justice, diffusing blessings throughout the land. I object only to the assumption of political power by the Supreme Court, a power which belongs not to them, and which they cannot safely exercise. But, surely, a power which the gentleman is willing to confide to *three Judges of the Supreme Court,* may safely be entrusted to *a sovereign State.* Sir, there are so many powerful motives to restrain a State from taking such high ground as to interpose her sovereign power to protect her citizens from unconstitutional laws, that the danger is not that this power will be wantonly exercised, but that she will fail to exert it, even on proper occasions.

A State will be restrained by a sincere love of the Union. The People of the United States cherish a devotion to the Union, so pure, so ardent, that nothing short of intolerable oppression, can ever tempt them to do any thing that may possibly endanger it. Sir, there exists, moreover, a deep and settled conviction of the benefits, which result from a close connexion of all the States, for purposes of mutual protection and defence. This will co-operate with the feelings of patriotism to induce a State to avoid any measures calculated to endanger that connexion. A State will always feel the necessity of consulting public opinion, both at home and abroad, before she resorts to any measures of such a character. She will know that if she acts rashly, she will be abandoned even by her own citizens, and will utterly fail in the object she has in view. If, as is asserted in the declaration of independence, all experience has proved that mankind are more disposed to suffer while evils are sufferable, than to resort to measures for redress, why should this case be an exception, where so many additional motives must always be found for forbearance? Look at our own experience on this subject. Virginia and Kentucky, so far back as '98, avowed the principles for which I have been contending—principles which have never since been abandoned; and no instance has yet occurred, in which it has been found necessary, practically to exert the power asserted in those resolutions.

If the alien and sedition laws had not been yielded to the force of public opinion, there can be no doubt, that the State of Virginia would have interposed to protect her citizens from its operation. And if the apprehension of such an interposition by a State, should have the effect of restraining the Federal Government from acting, except in cases clearly within the limits of their authority, surely no one can doubt the beneficial operation of such a restraining influence. Mr. Jefferson assures us, that the embargo was actually yielded up, rather than force New England into open opposition to it. And it was right to yield it, Sir, to honest convictions of its unconstitutionality, entertained by so large a portion of our fellow citizens. If the knowledge that the States possess the Constitutional right to interpose, in the event "of gross, deliberate, and palpable violations of the Constitution," should operate to prevent a perseverance in such violations, surely the effect would be greatly to be desired. But there is one point of view, in which this matter presents itself to my mind with irresistible force. The Supreme Court, it is admitted, may nullify an act of Congress, by declaring it to be unconstitutional. Can Congress, after such a nullification, proceed to enforce the law, even if they should differ in opinion from the Court? What then would be the effect of such a decision? And what would be the remedy in such a case? Congress would be *arrested in the exercise of the disputed power,* and the only remedy would be, *an appeal to the creating power,* three-fourths of the States, for an amendment of the Constitution. And by whom must such an appeal be made? It must be made by the party proposing to exercise the disputed power. Now I will ask, whether a sovereign State may not be safely entrusted with the exercise of a power, operating merely as a check, which is admitted to belong to the Supreme Court, and which may be exercised every day, by any three of its members? Sir, no ideas that can be formed of arbitrary power on the one hand, and abject dependence on the other, can be carried further, than to suppose, that three individuals, mere men, "subject to like passions with ourselves," may be safely entrusted with the power to nullify an act of Congress, because they conceive it to be unconstitutional; but that a sovereign and independent State, even the great State of New York, is bound, implicitly, to submit to its operation, even where it violates, in the grossest manner, her own rights, or the liberties of her citizens. But we do not contend that a common case would justify the interposition.

This is "the extreme medicine of the State," and cannot become our daily bread.

Mr. Madison, in his report, says, "It does not follow, however, that because the States, as sovereign parties to their constitutional compact, must ultimately decide whether it has been violated, that such a decision ought to be interposed, either in a hasty manner, or on doubtful and inferior occasions. Even in the case of ordinary conventions between different nations, where, by the strict rule of interpretation, a breach of a part may be deemed a breach of the whole, every part being deemed a condition of every other part, and of the whole, it is always laid down, that the breach must be both wilful and material to justify an application of the rule. But in the case of an intimate and Constitutional Union, like that of the United States, it is evident, that the interposition of the parties, in their sovereign capacity, can be called for by occasions only, deeply and essentially affecting the vital principles of their political system.

"The resolution has, accordingly, guarded against any misapprehension of its object, by expressly requiring, for such an interposition, 'the case of a deliberate, palpable, and dangerous breach of the Constitution, by the exercise of powers not granted by it.' 'It must be a case, not of a light and transient nature, but of a nature dangerous to the great purposes for which the Constitution was established.' It must be a case, moreover, not obscure or doubtful in its construction, but plain and palpable. Lastly, it must be a case, not resulting from a partial consideration, or hasty determination; but a case stamped with a final consideration, and deliberate adherence. It is not necessary, because the resolution does not require that the question should be discussed, how far the exercise of any particular power, ungranted by the Constitution, would justify the interposition of the parties to it. As cases might easily be stated, which none would contend ought to fall within that description; and cases, on the other hand, might, with equal ease, be stated, so flagrant and so fatal, as to unite every opinion in placing them within the description.

"But the resolution has done more than guard against misconstruction, by expressly referring to cases of a deliberate, palpable, and dangerous nature. It specifies *the object of the interposition* which it contemplates to be solely that of *arresting the progress of the evil of usurpation,* and of maintaining the authorities, rights, and liberties appertaining to the States, as parties to the Constitution."

No one can read this, without perceiving that Mr. Madison goes the whole length, in support of the principles for which I have been contending.

The gentleman has called upon us to carry out our scheme *practically.* Now, Sir, if I am correct in my view of this matter, then it follows, of course, that the right of a State being established, the Federal Government is *bound to acquiesce* in a solemn decision of a state, acting in its sovereign capacity, at least so far as to make an appeal to the People for an amendment of the Constitution. This solemn decision of a State, (made either through its Legislature or a Convention, as may be supposed to be the proper organ of its sovereign will—a point I do not propose now to discuss) binds the Federal Government under the highest constitutional obligation, not to resort to any means of coercion against the citizens of the dissenting State. How then can any collision ensue between the Federal and State Governments, unless indeed, the former should determine to enforce the law by unconstitutional means? What could the Federal Government do in such a case?—Resort, says the Gentleman, to the courts of justice. Now, can any man believe, that in the face of a solemn decision of a State, that an act of Congress is "a gross, palpable, and deliberate violation of the Constitution," and the interposition of its sovereign authority, to protect its citizens from the usurpation, that juries could be found ready, merely to register the decrees of the Congress, wholly regardless of the unconstitutional character of their acts? Will the gentleman contend that juries are to be coerced to find verdicts at the point of the bayonet? And, if not, how are the United States to enforce an act, solemnly pronounced to be unconstitutional? But if the attempt should be made to carry such a law into effect, by force, in what would the case differ, from an attempt to carry into effect an act nullified by the Courts, or to do any other unlawful and unwarrantable act? Suppose Congress should pass an agrarian law, or a law emancipating our slaves, or should commit any other gross violation of our constitutional rights, will any gentleman contend that the decision of every branch of the Federal

Government in favor of such laws could prevent the States from declaring them null and void, and protecting their citizens from their operation?

Sir, if Congress should ever attempt to enforce any such laws, they would put themselves so clearly in the wrong, that no one could doubt the right of the State to exert its protecting power.

Sir, the gentleman has alluded to that portion of the Militia of South Carolina with which I have the honor to be connected; and asked how they would act in the event of the nullification of the tariff law by the State of South Carolina? The tone of the gentleman on this subject did not seem to me as respectful as I could have desired. I hope, Sir, no imputation was intended.

[Mr. WEBSTER—"Not at all; just the reverse."]

Well, Sir, the gentleman asks what their leaders would be able to read to them out of Coke upon Littleton, or any other law book, to justify their enterprise? Sir, let me assure the gentleman, that when any attempt shall be made from any quarter, to enforce *unconstitutional laws,* clearly violating our essential rights, our leaders, (whoever they may be) will not be found reading black letter from the musty pages of old law books. They will look to the Constitution, and when called upon by the sovereign authority of the State to preserve and protect the rights secured to them by the charter of their liberties, they will succeed in defending them, or "perish in the last ditch." Sir, I will put the case home to the gentleman. Is there any violation of the constitutional rights of the States, and the liberties of the citizen, (sanctioned by Congress and the Supreme Court,) which he would believe it to be the right and duty of a State to resist? Does he contend for the doctrine "of passive obedience and non-resistance"? Would he justify an open resistance to an act of Congress sanctioned by the Courts, which should abolish the trial by jury, or destroy the freedom of religion, or the freedom of the press? Yes, Sir, he would advocate resistance in such cases; and so would I, and so would all of us. But such resistance would, according to his doctrine, be *revolution;* it would be *rebellion.* According to my opinion it would be just, legal, and *constitutional resistance.* The whole difference between us, then, consists in this: The gentleman would make force the only arbiter in all cases of collision between the States and the Federal Government. I would resort to a peaceful remedy—the interposition of the State to "arrest the progress of the evil," until such times as "a Convention, (assembled at the call of Congress or two-thirds of the States,) shall decide to which they mean to give an authority claimed by two of their organs." Sir, I say with Mr. Jefferson, (whose words I have here borrowed) that "it is the peculiar wisdom and felicity of our Constitution, to have provided this *peaceable appeal,* where that of other nations," (and I may add that of the gentleman) "is at once *to force.*"

The gentleman has made an eloquent appeal to our hearts in favor of union. Sir, I cordially respond to that appeal. I will yield to no gentleman here in sincere attachment to the Union,—but it is a Union *founded on the Constitution,* and not such a Union as that gentleman would give us, that is dear to my heart. If this is to become one great "consolidated government," swallowing up the rights of the States, and the liberties of the citizen, "riding and ruling over the plundered ploughman, and beggared yeomanry," the Union will not be worth preserving. Sir it is because South Carolina loves the Union, and would preserve it forever, that she is opposing now, while there is hope, those usurpations of the Federal Government, which, once established, will, sooner or later, tear this Union into fragments. The gentleman is for marching under a banner studded all over with stars, and bearing the inscription *Liberty* and *Union.* I had thought, sir, the gentleman would have borne a standard, displaying in its ample folds a brilliant sun, extending its golden rays from the centre to the extremities, in the brightness of whose beams, the "little stars hide their diminished heads." Our's, Sir, is the banner of the Constitution, the twenty-four stars are there in all their undiminished lustre, on it is inscribed, *Liberty—the Constitution—Union.* We offer up our fervent prayers to the Father of all mercies, that it may continue to wave for ages yet to come, over a free, a happy, and a united people.

Thomas Hart Benton

Thomas Hart Benton was born in North Carolina in 1782. He attended the University of North Carolina and the law department in the College of William and Mary, and was admitted to the bar in Tennessee in 1806. He was a member of the state Senate from 1809 to 1811. Benton was active in the War of 1812, serving as aide-de-camp to General Andrew Jackson and as colonel of an infantry regiment. Following the war, he moved to St. Louis, Missouri, where he practiced law, was a newspaper editor, and won election to the U.S. Senate as a Republican. He was reelected in 1827. Benton supported policies to promote western interests, including hard money, cheap land, internal improvements, and a protective tariff on selected goods. Although a supporter of Henry Clay in the election of 1824, thereafter he became an ardent Democrat and was a leading spokesman in the Senate for the Jackson administration. Benton opposed nullification in 1832 but thought Jackson's Proclamation on Nullification was too strong. He opposed the compromise tariff act of 1833 because he believed it too favorable to the protective system. Benton vigorously defended Jackson's veto of the Bank of the United States and his policy for removal of federal deposits from the Treasury. He opposed the annexation of Texas but supported the Mexican War. On slavery, Benton was a moderate who opposed both secessionists and abolitionists. In the debate over the Compromise of 1850, his opposition to Clay's omnibus bill cost him the support of proslavery forces and led to his defeat in 1850. He was elected to the House of Representatives in 1852, and in 1854 opposed the repeal of the Missouri Compromise. In the election of 1856, Benton supported Buchanan against Fremont, who was his son-in-law. Benton died in 1858.

Speech of Mr. Benton,

of Missouri

[January 20 and 29, February 1 and 2, 1830]

The resolution of Mr. Foot, of Connecticut, relative to the
public lands, being under consideration, Mr. Benton addressed
the Chair as follows:

MR. BENTON SAID HE COULD NOT PERMIT THE SENATE TO ADJOURN,
and the assembled audience of yesterday to separate, without seeing
an issue joined on the unexpected declaration then made by the Senator
from Massachusetts, [Mr. WEBSTER]—the declaration that the Northeast
section of the Union had, at all times, and under all circumstances, been
the uniform friend of the West, the South inimical to it, and that there
were no grounds for asserting the contrary. Taken by surprise, as I was,
said Mr. BENTON, by a declaration, so little expected, and so much in conflict with what I had considered established history, I felt it to be due to all
concerned to meet the declaration upon the instant—to enter my earnest
dissent to it, and to support my denial by a rapid review of some great historical epochs. This I did upon the instant, without a moment's prepara-
tion, or previous thought; but I checked myself in an effusion, in which
feeling was at least as predominant as judgment, with the reflection that issues of fact, between Senators, were not to be decided by bandying contra-
dictions across this floor; that it was due to the dignity of the occasion to
proceed more temperately, and with proof in hand for every thing that I
should urge. I then sat down with the view of recommencing coolly and
regularly as soon as I could refresh my memory with dates and references.
The warmth of the moment prevented me from observing what was most
obvious—namely, that the resolution under discussion was itself the most
pregnant illustration of my side of the issue. It is a resolution of direst import to the new States in the West, involving, in its four fold aspect, the
stoppage of emigration to that region, the limitation of its settlement, the

---

suspension of surveys, the abolition of the Surveyor's offices, and the surrender of large portions of Western territory to the use and dominion of wild beasts; and, in addition to all this, connecting itself, in time and spirit, with another resolution, in the other end of the Capitol, for delivering up the public lands, in the new States to the avarice of the old ones, to be coined in gold and silver for their benefit. This resolution, thus hostile in itself, and aggravated by an odious connexion, came upon us from the NORTHEAST, and was resisted by the SOUTH. Its origin, and its progress, was a complete exemplification of the relative affection which the two Atlantic sections of the Union bear to the West. Its termination was to put the seal upon the question of that affection. The Senator from Massachusetts, (Mr. WEBSTER) to whom I am now replying, was not present at the offering of that resolution. He arrived when the debate upon it was far advanced, and the temper of the *South* and *West* fully displayed. He saw the condition of his friends, and the consequences of the movement which they had made. Their condition was that of a certain army, which had been conducted, by two consuls, into the *Caudine Forks;* the consequences might be prejudicial to the Northeast—more accurately speaking, to a political party in the Northeast! His part was that of a prudent commander—to extricate his friends from a perilous position; his mode of doing it ingenious, that of starting a new subject, and moving the indefinite postponement of the impending one. His attack upon the South was a cannonade, to divert the attention of the assailants; his concluding motion for indefinite postponement, a signal of retreat and dispersion to his entangled friends. They may obey the signal. They may turn head upon their speeches, and vote for the postponement, and avoid a direct vote upon the resolution, and give up the pursuit after that information which was so indispensable to do justice and to avoid suspicion; but in doing so, they take my ground against the resolution; for indefinite postponement is REJECTION; and whether rejected or not, the indelible character of the resolution must remain. It was hostile to the West! It came from the Northeast! and was resisted by the South!

Before I proceed to the main object of this reply, I must be permitted, Mr. President, to tear away some ornamental work, and to remove some rubbish, which the Senator from Massachusetts, (Mr. W.) has placed in the way, either to decorate his own march, or to embarrass mine. He has brought before us a certain Nathan Dane, of Beverly, Massachusetts, and loaded him with such an exuberance of blushing honors, as no modern name has been known to merit, or to claim. Solon, Lycurgus, and Numa

Pompilius, are the renowned legislators of antiquity to whom he is compared, and, only compared, for the purpose of being placed at their head.
So much glory was earned by a single act, and that act, the supposed au-
thorship of the ordinance of 1787, for the Government of the North Western Territory, and especially of the clause in it which prohibits slavery and
involuntary servitude. Mr. Dane was assumed to be the author of this Ordinance, and especially of this clause, and upon that assumption was
founded, not only, the great superstructure of Mr. Dane's glory, but a claim
also upon the gratitude of Ohio, and all the North West, to the unrivalled
legislator, who was the author of their happiness, and to the quarter of the
Union which was the producer of the legislator. So much encomium, and
such grateful consequences, it seems a pity to spoil; but spoilt they must
be; for Mr. Dane was no more the author of that Ordinance, Mr. President, than you, or I, who, about that time were "mewling and puling in our
nurses' arms." That Ordinance, and especially the non-slavery clause, was
not the work of Nathan Dane, of Massachusetts, but of Thomas Jefferson,
of Virginia. It was reported by a Committee of three, Messrs. Jefferson, of
Virginia, Chase, of Maryland, and Howell, of R.I.—a majority from slave
States, in April 1784, nearly two years before Mr. Dane became a member
of Congress. The clause was not adopted at that time, there being but six
States in favor of it, and the articles of confederation, in questions of that
character, requiring seven. The next year, '85, the clause, with some modification, was moved by Mr. King, of New York, as a proposition to be sent
to a Committee, and was sent to the Committee accordingly; but, still did
not ripen into a law. A year afterwards, this clause, and the whole Ordinance was passed upon the report of a Committee of six members, of
whom, the name of Mr. Dane, stands No. 5 in the order of arrangement on
the Journal. There were but eight States present at the passing of this Ordinance, namely, Massachusetts, New York, New Jersey, Delaware, Virginia, North Carolina, South Carolina, and Georgia; and every one voted
for it. [Mr. B. read the parts of the Journal which verified these statements, and continued:] So passes away the glory of this world. But yesterday the name of Nathan Dane, of Beverly, Massachusetts, hung in
equipose against half the names of the sages of Greece and Rome. Poetry
and eloquence were at work to blazon his fame; marble and brass, and history and song, were waiting to perform their office. The celestial honors of
the apotheosis seemed to be only deferred for the melancholy event of the
sepulchre. To-day, all this superstructure of honors, human & divine, dis-
appears from the earth. The foundation of the edifice is sapped; and the

superhuman glories of him, who, twenty four hours ago, was taking his station among the demi-gods of antiquity, have dispersed and dissipated into thin air,—vanishing like the baseless fabric of a vision, which leaves not a wreck behind.

So much for the ornamental work; now for the rubbish.

The Senator from Massachusetts, (Mr. W.) has dwelt with much indignation upon certain supposed revilings of the New England character. He did not indicate the nature of the revilings, nor the name of the reviler. I, for one, disclaim a knowledge of the thing, and the doing of the thing itself. I deal in no general imputations upon communities. Such reflections are generally unjust, and always unwise. I am no defamer of New England. The man must be badly informed upon the history of these States who does not know the great points of the New England character. He must poorly appreciate national renown in arms and letters,—national greatness, resting on the solid foundations of religion, morality, and learning, who does not respect the people among whom these things are found in rich abundance. Yet, I must say, the speech of yesterday forces me to say it, that, in a political point of view, the population of New England does not stand undivided before me. A line of division is drawn through the mass, whether "horizontally," leaving the rich and well-born above, the poor and ill-born below; or, vertically, so as to present a section of each layer, is not for me to affirm. The division exists. On one side of it we see friends who have adhered to us in every diversity of fortune, who have been with us in six troubles, and will not desert us in the seventh; men who were with us in '98, and in the late war, whose grief and joy rose and sunk with ours in the struggle with England, who wept with us over the calamities of the north-west, and rejoiced in the splendid glories of the south-west! On the other side, we see those who were against us in all these trials; who thought it unbecoming a moral and religious people to celebrate the triumphs of their own country over its enemy, but quite becoming the same people, to be pleased at the victories of the enemy, over their country; who gave a dinner to him that surrendered Detroit. The line of division exists. On one side of it, stands the democracy of New England, to whom we give the right hand of fellowship at home and abroad; on the other side, all that stands opposed to that democracy, for whose personal welfare we have the best wishes, but with whom we must decline, as publicly as it was proffered, the honor of that alliance which was yesterday vouchsafed to the West, if not in direct terms, at least by an implication which no one misunderstood. When, then, the People of New England shall read of these revilings, in that well delivered speech of yesterday, let them remember that an issue of fact is joined upon the assertion, and that it is contained in the same speech which supposes Nathan Dane, of Beverly, Massachusetts, to have been the author of a certain production in the year 1786, which the Journals of Congress shew to have been the work of Thomas Jefferson, of Monticello, Vir., in the year 1784! The same speech which claims, for New England, the gratitude of the North-western States for passing that ordinance, when the Journals prove, that it had the votes of four States, from the south of the Potomac, and only one from New England! When it could have passed without the New England vote, but not without three of the Southern ones!

But I did say something which might be understood as a reproach upon some of the leading characters of New England; it was upon the subject of emigration to the West, and their opposition to it. I quoted high authority at the time, the authority of gentlemen who had served in Congress, and made their statements in the Virginia Convention, under the highest moral responsibilities. Their statement is denied. I will, therefore, produce authority from a different quarter, and of a more recent application; the letter of a son of New England, to another son of the same quarter of the Union.

THE LETTER.

"From the Boston Centinel, April 18th, 1827.

An extract from a letter written by the Hon. JOHN QUINCY ADAMS, while Minister at the Court of Russia, to Dr. BENJAMIN WATERHOUSE, in Cambridge, dated

St. PETERSBURGH, 24th Oct. 1813.

(The Dr. had mentioned the *vast emigration* from New England to the Western Territories, about, and previously to the time of his writing; to which portion of his letter, Mr. ADAMS replied as follows:—)

"I am not displeased to hear that *Ohio, Kentucky, Indiana, Louisiana,* are rapidly peopling with Yankees. I consider them as an excellent race of People, and as far as I am able to judge, I believe that their moral and political character, far from degenerating, improves by emigration. I have always felt on that account a sort of predilection for these rising Western States; *and have seen with no small astonishment, the prejudices harbored against them.* There is not upon this globe of Earth, a spectacle exhibited by man, so interesting to my mind, or so consolatory to my heart, as this metamorphosis of howling deserts into cultivated fields and populous villages, which is yearly, daily, hourly, going on by the hands chiefly of New England men, in our Western States and Territories.

"If New England loses her influence in the Councils of the Union, it will not be owing to any diminution of her population, occasioned by these emigrations: it will be from the *partial, sectarian,* or as Hamilton called it, *clannish* spirit, which makes so many of her *political leaders jealous and envious of the west and South.* This spirit is in its nature *narrow and contracted;* and it always works *by means like itself.* Its natural tendency is to *excite and provoke* a counteracting spirit of the same character; and it has actually produced that effect in our country. It has combined the Southern and Western parts of the United States, not in a league, but in a concert of political views adverse to those of New England. The fame of all the great Legislators of antiquity is founded upon their contrivances to strengthen and multiply the principles of attraction in civil society:— *Our legislators seem to delight in multiplying and fomenting the principles of repulsion.*"

Having read this letter of Mr. Adams, Mr. B. continued. I will make no comment on the language here used. It is sufficiently significant without that trouble.—"Partial—sectarian—clannish—jealous—envious—narrow—contracted—excite—provoke—multiplying—fomenting—principles of repulsion"—are phrases which need no aid from the dictionary to uncover their pregnant meaning. I will only ask for three or four concessions:

1. That the authority of the writer of the letter is canonical, and binding on the church.

2. That it goes the full length of charging the New England leaders of 1813, with opposition to Western emigration.

3. That nothing which I have said of the motives, or conduct of those who oppose this emigration, can compare in severity of expression with the language of Mr. Adams.

4. That the political leaders of whom he spoke as opposing emigration to the West, upon such motives, and by such means, are the same who are now denying it on this floor, and wooing the West into an alliance with them.

I gave yesterday, Mr. President, the brief history of the great attempt in '86, 7, 8, to surrender the navigation of the Mississippi—to surrender it in violation of the articles of confederation, by a majority of *seven* States, when the requisite majority of *nine* could not be obtained—the protracted resistance of these attempts by the Southern States—their final defeat by a movement from North Carolina—and the secrecy in which the whole was enveloped. The history of these things were given then; the proofs will be produced now; the epoch and the subject are entitled to the first degree of consideration in this inquiry into the relative affection of two great sections of the Union to a third; for on this question of a surrender of the navigation of the Mississippi, to the King of Spain, commenced that line of separation between the conduct of the Northeast, and of the South, towards the West, which has continued to this day.

The first movement upon this subject was in the winter of '79–80. It came through the French Ambassador, the Chevalier de la Luzerne, the United States having no diplomatic relations, at that time, with the King of Spain. The Chevalier, in a secret communication to Congress, informed them, by the command of the King of France, that the King of Spain would join the United States against England upon four conditions, namely:

1. That the settlements and boundary of the United States should not extend further West than to the heads of the rivers that flowed into the Atlantic ocean.

2. That the exclusive navigation of the Mississippi should belong to Spain.

3. That the Floridas should belong to her.

4. That the Southern States should be restrained from making settlements to the west of the Alleghanies, and that all the country beyond these mountains should be considered as British possessions, and proper objects for the arms, and permanent conquest of Spain. (Secret Journals, vol. 2, p. 310.)

The proffered alliance of Spain, upon these conditions, was rejected by Congress. But her alliance was an object of the first importance, and to obtain it if possible, without the worst of these conditions, Mr. Jay was despatched to Madrid. On the subject of the Mississippi, Mr. Jay was directed to make a *sine qua non* of the free navigation of that river, and the use of a port near its mouth; on the subject of the West, for I limit myself to these points, he was directed to say that the West being settled by citizens of the United States, friendly to the Revolution, Congress would not assign them over to any foreign power. These instructions were *unanimously* given. This was in the commencement of the year '80. One year afterwards, to wit—the 15th of Feb. '81, one month before the battle of *Guilford Court House,* the delegates of Virginia, in pursuance to instructions from their constituents, moved to recede from so much of the previous instruction of Mr. Jay, as made the free navigation of the Mississippi, *a sine qua non,* PROVIDED, that Spain should *"unalterably"* insist upon it, and not otherwise come into the alliance against England; and that the Minister be *"ordered to exert every possible effort"* to obtain the alliance *without* the surrender of the navigation of the river. On the question to agree to this modification of the instructions, the vote stood—Yeas, Pennsylvania, Virginia, South Carolina, Georgia, New Hampshire, Rhode Island, Delaware, Maryland, (the four latter having but one member each present.) Nays, Massachusetts, Connecticut, and North Carolina. New York divided and not counted.

This, Mr. President, is the case mentioned by Mr. Madison, in the Virginia Convention; the instance of willingness, on the part of the Southern States, to give up the navigation of the Mississippi, and its resistance by the Northern States, to which he alluded. The journals show the facts of the case. They control the recollections of Mr. Madison, and leave me not a word to say. But, the question of this navigation, and these instructions, did not stop here. On the 10th of August following, it was proposed to vest the Minister at Madrid with discretionary power over the navigation of the Mississippi, and unanimously rejected. The proposition stands thus, p. 468 of the 4th volume of the journal:

> "That the Minister be empowered to make such further cession of the right of these United States to the navigation of the Mississippi as he may think proper; and on such terms and conditions as he may think most for the honor and interest of these United States."

Upon the question of adopting this proposition, the votes were unanimously against it, not of States only, but of Members; every Member of every State present voting in the negative. This was a proud instance of unanimity. The result of it was, the acquisition of the alliance of Spain, without a surrender of the great right of navigation in the King of Floods.

The question of the navigation of this river, then slept for four years, until the summer of 1785, when Don Gardoqui, the Spanish *encargado de negocios,* arrived in the United States, with powers to negotiate a treaty. Mr. Jay, the Secretary of State for Foreign Affairs, was appointed to treat with him. The instructions to Mr. Jay limited his negotiation to two points, namely: *boundaries* and *navigation;* and on this latter point, the last clause of his instructions made the free navigation of the Mississippi and the use of a port near its mouth, an indispensable condition to the conclusion of a treaty. These instructions seem to have been given with entire unanimity. No division of sentiment appears on the journal, and nearly a whole year elapsed before any thing appears upon the subject of this negotiation, thus committed to Mr. Jay and Don Gardoqui. At the end of that time, it was brought before Congress, by a letter from Mr. Jay, in secret session, and gave rise to proceedings which I beg leave to read, not chusing to trust any thing to my memory, or to risk the possible substitution of my own language for that of the record, in a case of so much delicacy and moment.

> *The letter of Mr. Jay to the President of Congress.*
> "Office of Foreign Affairs, May 29, 1786.
>
> "SIR: In my negotiations with Mr. Gardoqui, I experience certain difficulties, which, in my opinion, should be so managed, as that even the existence of them should remain a secret for the present. I take the liberty, therefore, of submitting to the consideration of Congress, whether it might not be advisable to appoint a committee, with power to instruct and direct me on every point and subject relative to the proposed treaty with Spain. In case Congress should think proper to appoint such a committee, I really think it would be prudent to keep the appointment of it secret, and to forbear having any conversation on subjects connected with it, except in Congress, and in meetings on the business of it.
>
> Signed, &c.
> JOHN JAY."

This letter was referred to a committee of three, namely: Mr. King, of N.Y. Mr. Pettit, of Penn. and Mr. Monroe, of Vir. They reported, that the letter should be taken under consideration, in committee of the whole House. This committee resolved to hear the Secretary in person, fixed a day for his attendance, and ordered him to state the difficulties of which his letter had given intimation.

He did so in a written statement, which, including letters from Don Gardoqui, occupies some thirty pages of the Journal. The points of it, so far as they are material to the question now before the Senate, were, that the pending negotiation for *boundaries* and *navigation,* should also include *commerce;* that the U. States should abandon to the King of Spain the exclusive navigation of the Mississippi, for twenty-five or thirty years, and that Spain should purchase many articles from the United States, of which pickled salmon, train oil, and codfish, were particularly dwelt upon. (*Vol. 4, pages 45 to 63.*) From this instant, Mr. President, the division between the North and South, on the subject of the West, sprung into existence. A series of motions and votes ensued, and a struggle, which continued two years, in which Maryland and all South, voted one way, and New Jersey, and all North, voted the other. The most important of these motions were, 1. a motion by Mr. King, of N. York, to repeal the clause in the instructions to Mr. Jay which made the navigation of the Mississippi a *sine qua non*, which was carried by the seven Northern States against the others. 2. A motion by Mr. Pinckney, of S. Carolina, to revoke the whole instruction, and stop the negociation; lost by the same vote. 3. A motion by Mr. Pinckney, seconded by Mr. Monroe, to declare it a violation of the articles of the Confederation for *seven* States to alter the instructions for negotiating a treaty, those articles requiring the consent of *nine* States on questions of that kind; lost by the same vote. 4. A motion by the Delegates from Virginia to make it a *sine qua non*, that the citizens of the United States should have the privilege of taking their produce to New Orleans; the U. States to have a Consul, and the citizens Factors there; that the vessels be allowed to return empty, and the produce to be exported on paying a small export duty: lost by the same array of votes. 5. A motion made by Mr. St. Clair, seconded by Mr. King, to make the same proposition, to be obtained, if possible, but not a *sine qua non;* carried by the *ayes* of New Hampshire, Massachusetts, Rhode Island, Connecticut, New York, New Jersey, Pennsylvania, 7, against the *noes* of Maryland, Virginia, N. Carolina, South Carolina, Georgia, 5, Delaware not present.

I pause a moment, Mr. President, in the narrative of these occurrences to remark that the motion of the Virginia delegation above stated, has been misunderstood; that it has been supposed that that delegation and the South which voted with them, were then in favor of paying tribute to Spain, and abandoning for ever the upward, or ascending navigation of the Mississippi, and that the seven Northern States prevented that calamity to the West. Nothing can be more erroneous than this conception. The attempt of Virginia was to save at all events—to make sure, by a *sine qua non*, of this poor privilege, of exporting, paying an export duty of $2\frac{1}{2}$ per cent. and returning empty, and this, after seeing that the whole right to the navigation, descending as well as ascending, was to be surrendered for twenty-five or thirty years. The vote of the seven Northern States against the Virginia proposition was to have an opportunity of doing not better, but worse, for the West; to make this same proposition, not an indispensable condition to the conclusion of a treaty, but a mere proposal, to be obtained if it could, and if not, the whole right of navigation to be abandoned for 25 or 30 years. This is what they shewed to be their disposition in adopting Mr. King's motion immediately after rejecting that of the Virginia delegation. Mr. King's being a substantial copy of the other, except in the essential particulars of the *sine qua non;* and for this the seven Northern States voted; the six others opposed it.

I now resume my narrative.

The next motion and vote stands thus upon the Journal of the 28th Sept. '86.

"Moved by Mr. Pinckney, seconded by Mr. Carrington, That the injunction of secrecy be taken off, so far as to allow the delegates in Congress to communicate to the Legislatures and Executives of their several States, the acts which have passed, and the questions which have been taken in Congress respecting the negotiations between the U. States and his Catholic majesty.

The motion was lost by the following vote:

Massachusetts.—Mr. Gorham, no, Mr. King, no, Mr. Dane, no.

Rhode Island.—Mr. Manning, no, Mr. Miller, no.

Connecticut.—Mr. Johnson, no—Mr. Sturges, no.

New York.—Mr. Haring, no, Mr. Smith, no.

New Jersey.—Mr. Cadwallader, no, Mr. Symmes, ay, Mr. Hornblower, no.

Pennsylvania.—Mr. Pettit, no, Mr. St. Clair, no.

Maryland.—Mr. Ramsay, ay, (not counted.)

Virginia.—Mr. Monroe, ay, Mr. Carrington, ay, Mr. Lee, ay.

North Carolina.—Mr. Bloodworth, ay, Mr. White, ay.

South Carolina.—Mr. Pinckney, ay, Mr. Parker, ay.

Georgia.—Mr. Houston, no, Mr. Few, ay. (Divided.)

In April, 1787, Mr. Madison having become a member of Congress, moved two resolutions, one to transfer the negotiation with Spain from the United States to Madrid; the other to charge Mr. Jefferson, then in France, with the conduct of it. (Secret Journals, vol. 4, p. 339.) The object of these resolutions could not be mistaken. They were referred by

Congress to Mr. Jay, Secretary for Foreign Affairs, and still engaged in the negotiation with Don Gardoqui. He reported at large against the expediency of the transfer, treating it as a project to gain time, and complaining that the secret of the Spanish negotiations had leaked out of Congress. This report and the motion of Mr. Madison, seemed to have been undisposed of, when an incident in real life, and the firm stand of one of the States, brought the majority of Congress to a pause, and extricated the Mississippi from its imminent danger. This was the arrest of a citizen of North Carolina, and the confiscation of his vessel and cargo, by the Spanish Governor, Grandpré at Natchez, and the decisive character of the appeal made by the Legislature, the Governor, and the delegates in Congress from that State, for the redress of that outrage. Mr. Madison availed himself of the feeling produced by these incidents, to make another attempt to get rid of the subject, and, in September 1788, offered a resolution that no further progress be made in the negotiation with Spain, and that the whole subject be referred to the new Federal Government, which was to go into operation the ensuing year. This resolution was agreed to, and the Mississippi saved. Thus ended an arduous and eventful struggle. The termination was fortunate and happy; but the spirit which produced it has never gone to sleep. The idea that the Western rivers are a *fund* for the purchase of Atlantic advantages, in treaties with Foreign Powers, has been acted upon often since: The Mississippi, the Arkansas, the Red River, the Sabine and the Columbia, can bear witness of this. The idea that the growth of the West was incompatible with the supremacy of the northeast, has since crept into the legislation of the Federal Government, as will be fully developed in the course of this debate.

I have already given the proof of the fact, that the South is entitled to the honor of *originating* the clause against slavery in the Northwest Territory: the state of the votes upon its adoption also shows that she is entitled to the honor of *passing* it; there being but eight States present, four from each side of the Potomac, only one from New England, and all voting for it. This shows the great mistake which is committed in claiming the merit of that ordinance for the Northeast, and founding upon that claim a title to the gratitude of the Northwestern States. The ordinance of the same epoch, for the sale of the Western lands, has also been celebrated, and deservedly, for the beauty and science of its system of surveys. The honor of this ordinance is also assumed for the Northeast. Let it be so. I know nothing to the contrary, and what I do know, favors that idea. The ordinance came from a committee of twelve, of whom eight were from the

North, four from the South side of the Potomac. But, as it came from that committee, it would have left the whole Northwestern region a haunt for wild beasts and savages. The clause which required that every previous township should be sold out complete, before a subsequent one was offered for sale, would have produced this result, and was intended to produce it. Virginia, the South, and some Northern States, expunged that clause; Massachusetts and some others contended for it to the last. The Northwest is therefore indebted to the South for the sale of its lands: it is also indebted to it for an unsuccessful attempt to promote the settlement of the country by reducing the size of the tracts to be sold. The ordinance, as reported, fixed 640 acres as the smallest division that might be offered for sale. Mr. Grayson, of Virginia, seconded by Mr. Monroe, moved to reduce the quantity to 320 acres, but failed in the attempt. The Virginia delegation voted for it unanimously; South Carolina and Georgia both voted for it, but having but one member present, the vote did not count. Maryland voted for it; all the rest of the States against. Another attempt to benefit the settler, and promote the sale of the country, deserves a notice, though unsuccessful. It was the motion to reduce the price, fixed in the ordinance, from one dollar per acre to sixty-six and two-thirds cents. This motion was made by Mr. Beatty, of New Jersey, seconded by Mr. McHenry of Maryland, and was supported by the votes of four States, to wit: New York, New Jersey, Maryland, and South Carolina; Pennsylvania divided, and counted nothing; the rest of the States, Virginia inclusive, voted against it. The motion failed, though respectably supported; the price remained at one dollar, which is twenty-five cents less than the present minimum price of the same lands after forty-five years picking; and it is worthy of remark, that one-third of the States were then, when the lands were all fresh and unpicked, in favor of establishing a minimum price at sixty-six and two thirds cents per acre; a fraction only over one-half of the present minimum!

I now approach, Mr. President, the subject of most engrossing interest to the young West—its sufferings under Indian wars, and its vain appeals, for so many years, to the Federal Government for succor and relief. The history of twelve years' suffering in Tennessee, from 1780 to 1792, when the inhabitants succeeded in conquering peace without the aid of federal troops; and of sixteen years carnage in Kentucky, from 1774 to 1790, when the first effectual relief began to be extended—would require volumes of detail, for which we have no time, and powers of description, for which I have no talent. Then was witnessed the scenes of woe and death, of carnage and destruction, which no words of mine can ever paint: instances of heroism in men, of fortitude and devotedness in women, of instinctive courage in little children, which the annals of the most celebrated nations can never surpass. Then was seen the Indian warfare in all its horrors; that warfare which spares neither decrepit age, nor blooming youth, nor manly strength, nor infant weakness—in which the sleeping family awoke from their beds in the midst of flames and slaughter—when virgins were led off captive by savage monsters—when mothers were loaded with their children, and compelled to march; and when unable to keep up, were relieved of their burthen by seeing the brains of infants beat out on a tree—when the slow consuming fire of the stake devoured its victim in the presence of pitying friends and in the midst of exulting demons; when the corn was planted, the fields were ploughed, the crops were gathered, the cows were milked, water was brought from the spring, and God was worshipped, under the guard and protection of armed men; when the night was the season for travelling, the impervious forest the high-way, and the place of safety, most remote from the habitation of man; when every house was a fort, and every fort subject to siege and assault. Such was the warfare in the infant settlements of Kentucky and Tennessee, and which the aged men, actors in the dreadful scenes, have related to me so many times. Appeals to the Federal Government were incessant and vain, during the long progress of these disastrous wars; but as the revolutionary struggle was going on during a part of the time, and engrossed the resources of the Union, I will draw no example from that period. I will take a period posterior to the revolution. Three years after the peace with Great Britain, when the settlements in the West had taken a permanent form, when the Indian hostilities were most inveterate, when the Federal Government had a military peace establishment of seven hundred men; and when the acceptance of the cessions of the public lands in the West, made the duty of protection no less an object of interest to the Union, than of justice and humanity to the inhabitants. I will take the year 1786. What was the relative conduct of the North and South to the infant, suffering, bleeding, imploring West, in this season of calamity to her, and ability in them to give her relief? What was *then* the conduct of each? It was that of unrelenting severity on the part of the North—of generous and sympathising friendship on the part of the South! The evidence which cannot err will prove this, and will cover with confusion the bold declarations which have imposed upon me the duty of this reply. I speak of the Journals of the Old Congress, quotations from which I now proceed to read.

"Journals of Congress, vol. 4, p. 654."

Wednesday, June 21, 1786.

"The Secretary of War, to whom was referred a motion of Mr. Grayson, of Virginia, having reported the following resolution:

"That the Secretary of War direct the commanding officer of the troops to detach two companies to the Rapids of the Ohio, to protect the inhabitants from the depredations and incursions of the Indians."

Mark well, Mr. President, the terms of this resolution; to *detach* two companies then in service—not to *raise* them; for the purpose of *protecting* the inhabitants, not to *attack* the Indians. No expense in this; a mere change of position to a part of the military force then on foot. Observe the course of treatment the resolution received.

The first movement against it came from the North, in a motion to refer the resolution to a *peace* committee on Indian Affairs. The yeas and nays on that motion were:

Massachusetts—Aye.

New York—Aye.

Maryland—No.

Virginia—No.

North Carolina—No.

Pennsylvania—Divided.

New Jersey—Divided.

New Hampshire, Rhode Island, and Georgia—But one member—not counted.

Delaware and South Carolina—Absent.

The motion to refer was thus lost for want of seven ayes.

The second movement was from the South, Mr. Lee, of Virginia, seconded by Mr. Grayson, having moved to substitute *four* for *two,* so as to *double* the intended protection.

The vote upon this motion was—

Massachusetts—No.

New York—No.

New Jersey—No.

Pennsylvania—No.

Maryland—No.

North Carolina—No.

New Hampshire—No.

Virginia—Aye.

Georgia—Aye.

Delaware and South Carolina—Absent.

The third trial was on the adoption of the resolution, and exhibited the following vote:

New Hampshire—Mr. Long,* aye.

Massachusetts—Mr. Gorham, no, Mr. King, no, Mr. Sedgwick, no, Mr. Dane, no.

Rhode Island—Mr. Manning,* aye.

New York—Mr. Haring, aye, Mr. Smith, aye.

New Jersey—Mr. Symmes, aye, Mr. Hornblower, aye.

Pennsylvania—Mr. Pettit, aye, Mr. Wilson, aye.

Maryland—Mr. Henry, aye, Mr. Hindman, aye, Mr. Harrison, aye.

Virginia—Mr. Grayson, aye, Mr. Monroe aye, Mr. Lee, aye.

North Carolina—Mr. Bloodworth, aye, Mr. White, aye.

Georgia—Mr. Few, aye.*

Those marked with an asterisk, having but one number, were not counted. Six States only of those fully represented voted in favor of the resolution; it was consequently lost! Lost for want of the vote of one State, and that State was Massachusetts! The next day that vote was supplied, but not by Massachusetts. Mr. PINCKNEY and Mr. HUGER arrived from SOUTH CAROLINA. Mr. Pinckney, seconded by Mr. Carrington, of Virginia, immediately moved the rejected resolution over again, and SOUTH CAROLINA voting with the *ayes*, made *seven* affirmative States, and carried the resolution.

This, Mr. President, is the history of the first relief ever extended by the Federal Government to the inhabitants of Kentucky. Your State, sir, now painted as the enemy of the West, turned the scale in favor of that small but acceptable succor. It hung upon one vote; *Massachusetts* denied that vote! SOUTH CAROLINA came and gave it!

The instant this much was obtained, the generous delegates of the great and magnanimous Virginia commenced operations to procure the real and effectual protection which the case required, namely, an expedition into the Indian territory north of the Ohio river. The Governor of Virginia, on the 16th of May, '86, in a letter to Congress, had recommended this course, and offered the militia of his State to execute it. The letter was referred to a committee of three, Messrs. Grayson and Monroe, of Vir. and Mr. Dane, of Massachusetts. On the 29th of June, just seven days after the vote had passed for detaching two companies to the Falls of the Ohio, Mr. Grayson reported upon the recommendation of the Governor of Virginia. It was such a report as might be expected from a committee of which Virginia delegates constituted the majority. It recommended the expedition, and gave the most solid and convincing reasons for agreeing to it. The whole report is spread upon the Journal of that day, (vol. 4, p. 657.) Justice to the patriots who drew it, and justice also to those who supported, and opposed, it, would require it to be read, but time forbids. I can only repeat, in a condensed recital, its leading contents. It showed that the hostile Indians were bent on war; that they had treated with contempt the application which the United States had made to them, to meet commissioners at the mouth of the Great Miami, and conclude a peace; that, issuing from their vast forests beyond the Ohio, and returning to them for refuge, the war was to them a gratification of their savage thirst for blood and plunder, without danger of chastisement; that, while confined to defence on our side, and offence on their side, they had every motive which their savage policy required, to carry on the war, and no motive to stop it; that a march into their country was the only means of compelling them to accept peace; and, it concluded with a resolution that the two companies ordered to the Falls of Ohio, and one thousand Virginia militia, drawn from the district of Kentucky, under the command of a superior officer, be ordered to march into the hostile Indian territory, armed with the double authority of Commissioner and General, to treat as well as to fight.

We will now see the reception which this report and resolution met with.

The first movement upon it was in the way of a side blow, one of those operations in legislation which have the two fold advantage of doing most mischief, and doing it without appearing to be absolutely hostile to the measure. It was a motion to *postpone* the consideration of the resolution, for the purpose of considering a proposition which was the reverse of Mr. Grayson's report in all its material facts and conclusions. This new proposition recited, that Congress had received information that *small parties* of

Indians had crossed the Ohio, and committed depredations on the district of Kentucky; *but had not sufficient evidence of the aggression or hostile disposition* of any tribes of Indians to justify the United States in carrying the war into the Indian country; and proposed a *Resolve,* that Congress would proceed—*in the organization of the Indian Department!!!* and adopt such measures as would *secure peace to the Indians,* and safety to the inhabitants of the frontiers.

Let it be remembered, Mr. President, that this proposition was offered on the 29th of June, 1786, when the Indian war in Kentucky had raged for twelve years, when thousands of men, women, and children, had perished; that it was four years after the great battle of the Blue Licks, that disastrous battle in which the flower of western chivalry was cut down, and the whole land filled with grief and covered with mourning; that it was the very same year in which an offer to treat for peace, at the mouth of the Great Miami, had been contemptuously rejected; and, after recollecting these things, then judge of its statements and conclusions! To me it seems to class itself with the motions afterwards witnessed in the French national convention, to proceed to the order of the day when petitions were presented to save the lives of multitudes upon the point of assassination. The motion to postpone was made; the yeas and nays were called for by Mr. Grayson; the delegations of several States voted for it—and let the journal of the day announce their names.

New Hampshire.—Mr. Livermore, no, Mr. Long, aye.

Massachusetts.—Mr. Gorham, aye, Mr. King, aye, Mr. Sedgwick, aye, Mr. Dane, no.

Rhode Island.—Mr. Manning, no.

New York.—Mr. Haring, aye, Mr. Smith, aye.

New Jersey.—Mr. Symmes, no, Mr. Hornblower, aye.

Pennsylvania.—Mr. Pettit, aye, Mr. Bayard, aye.

Maryland.—Mr. Henry, aye, Mr. Hindman, no, Mr. Harrison, no, Mr. Ramsay, no.

Virginia.—Mr. Grayson, no, Mr. Monroe, no, Mr. Carrington, no, Mr. Lee, no.

North Carolina.—Mr. Bloodworth, no, Mr. White, no.

South Carolina.—Mr. Pinckney, no, Mr. Huger, no.

Georgia.—Mr. Few, no.

The motion to postpone was lost, only three States voting for it. Some amendments were agreed in, the resolution put on its passage, and *rejected!* New Hampshire, Massachusetts, New York, New Jersey, Pennsylvania, and Maryland, voting no. Virginia, North Carolina, and South Carolina, aye. Delaware, absent. Rhode Island, but one member present. The vote of Georgia lost by the refusal of a member to vote, [Mr. Houston] who seemed, upon all trial questions between the different sections of the Union, to occupy a false position.

Defeated, but not subdued—repulsed, but not vanquished—invincible in the work of justice and humanity, the Virginia delegation immediately commenced new operations, and devised new plans for the relief of the West. On the very next day, June 30th, a motion was made by Mr. Lee, seconded by Mr. Monroe, to have one thousand men, of the Virginia militia, *held in readiness,* and called out, *in case of necessity,* for the protection of the West. Even this was resisted! A motion was made by Mr. King, of Massachusetts, seconded by Mr. Long, of New Hampshire, to strike out the number "one thousand." It was struck out accordingly, there being but five states, to wit: Maryland, Virginia, North Carolina, South Carolina, and Georgia, in favor of retaining it. The resolution, eviscerated of this essential part, was allowed to pass; and thus, on the 30th day of June, in the year 1786, the Governor of Virginia obtained the privilege from the Continental Congress, to order some militia in Kentucky to hold themselves in readiness to protect the country, in case of necessity! Thus, at the end of twelve years from the commencement of the Indian wars, Kentucky obtained the assent of Congress to the defence of herself! Tennessee never obtained that much! She fought out the war from 1780 to 1792 upon her own bottom, without the assent, and against the commands of Congress. Expresses were often despatched to recall her expeditions going in pursuit of Indians who had invaded her settlements. The decisive expedition to the Cherokee town of Nicojac, which was framed upon the plan of Mr. Grayson, was, in legal acceptation, a lawless invasion of a friendly tribe. The brave and patriotic men who swam the Tennessee river, three quarters of a mile wide, in the dead of the night, shoving their arms before them on rafts, and stormed the town, and drove the Indians from the gap in the mountain—the Thermopylae of the country—and gave peace to the Cumberland settlements—did it with Federal halters round their necks: for the expedition was contrary to law. And now, in the face of history which proclaims, and journals which record, these facts—in contempt of all memory that retains, and tradition that recounts them, Massachusetts and the Northeast, which abandoned the infant west to the rifle, the hatchet, the knife, and the burning stake of the Indians, are to be put forth as the friends of the West! Virginia, and the South, which labored for them with a zeal and perseverance which eventually obtained the kind protection recommended in the report of Mr. Grayson—the expedition of Harmar, St. Clair, and Wayne—are to be set down as their enemies! And upon this settlement of the account, the West is now to be wooed into an alliance with the trainbands of New England federalism—the elite of the Hartford Convention—for the oppression of Virginia and the South, and the subjugation of New England Democracy! History and the journals are to be faced down with the assertion that the protecting arm of the Government was forever stretched over the infant settlements of the West, the North taking the lead of the South in its defence and protection!

Two more brief references to incidents of different characters, but highly pertinent and instructive, will complete my selection of examples from the history of the Old Congress. One was a refusal, on the 25th of July, 1787, to treat for a cession of Indian lands either on the North, or the South side of the Ohio; the other was a refusal, on the 2d of August of the same year, to let Virginia *"be credited"* with the expenses of an expedition which she had carried on in the Winter of '86–'87, against the Indians on *both* sides of the Ohio river, because that expedition was *"not authorized"* by the United States. The journals of the day will shew the particulars, and exhibit the delegation of Massachusetts that Nathan Dane included, who is now to be set up as the founder, legislator, and benefactor of the Northwest—as heading the opposition on both occasions. And here I submit, that, thus far, the assertion of the Senator from South Carolina, [Mr. HAYNE] that the West had received hard treatment from the Federal Government, is fully sustained. His remark was chiefly directed to the hard terms on which they get lands; but it holds good on the important point of long neglect, the effect of Northern jealousy, in giving protection against the Indians.

JANUARY 29, 1830.—*Second Day.*

I resume my Speech, said Mr. B. at the point at which it was suspended, when I gave way to the natural and laudable impatience of the Senator from South Carolina, who sits on my right (Mr. HAYNE) to vindicate himself, his

State, and the South, from what appeared to me to be a most gratuitous aggression. Well and nobly has he done it. Much as he had done before to establish his reputation as an orator, a statesman, a patriot, and a gallant son of the South, the efforts of these days eclipse and surpass the whole. They will be an era in his Senatorial career which his friends and his country will mark and remember, and look back upon with pride and exultation.

Before I go on with new matter, said Mr. B., I must be permitted to reach back, and bring up, in the way of recapitulation, and for the purpose of joining together the broken ends of my speech, the heads and substance of the great facts which I quoted and established at the commencement of this reply. They are:

1. The attempt of the seven Northern States in 1786, 87—88, to surrender the navigation of the Mississippi, to the King of Spain.

2. The attempt to effect that surrender, in violation of the articles of confederation, by the votes of seven States when nine could not be had.

3. The design of this surrender, to check the growth of the West.

4. The clause in the first Ordinance for the sale of the public lands, in the North Western Territory, which required the previous townships to be sold out complete before the subsequent ones could be offered for sale.

5. The refusal to sell a less quantity than 640 acres together.

6. The refusal to reduce the minimum price from one dollar, to sixty six and two thirds cents, per acre.

7. The opposition, in 1786, to the motion to detach two companies to the Falls of the Ohio, for the protection of Kentucky against the incursions and depredations of the Indians.

8. The opposition to Mr. Grayson's unanswerable report, in the same year, in favor of sending an expedition into the hostile Indian country.

9. The refusal, at the same time, to permit Virginia to hold "one thousand" of her own militia in readiness to protect Kentucky.

10. The refusal, in 1787, to treat for a cession of Indian lands on either side of the Ohio.

11. The refusal in the same year to let Virginia *be credited* with the expenses of an expedition, carried on in the winter of '86, '87, by her troops, on both sides of the Ohio river for the defence of the West.

12. The refusal for twelve years, from '74 to '86, to send any aid to Kentucky.

13. The refusal, throughout the entire war, to send any aid to the Cumberland settlements in Tennessee.

14. The opposition to western emigration, as proved by Mr. Adams's letter.

In all these instances, and I have omitted a thousand others, having confined myself to a single and brief period by way of example, and that period the one when the termination of the revolutionary war, peace with all the world, and a standing force of 700 men, made it easy to give protection to the West; and when the cession of the western lands to the federal government for the payment of the revolutionary debt, and the establishment of new States in the Northwest, devolved the business of Western protection upon the federal government, no less as an object of interest to themselves, than of duty to the settlers. In all these instances I have exhibited the States of Massachusetts and Virginia as antagonist powers, the one opposing, the other supporting, the measures favorable to the West, and each supported by more or less of its neighboring States.

The Senator from Massachusetts, (Mr. WEBSTER,) has since occupied the floor two days, and has taken no notice of facts so highly authenticated, drawn from sources so wholly unimpeachable, and so pointedly conflicting with the denials and assertions which he has made on this floor. It is not for me to account for this neglect, or forbearance. Rhetoricians lay down two cases in which silence upon the adversaries' arguments, is the better part of eloquence; first, where they are too insignificant to merit any notice; secondly, where they are too well fortified to be overthrown. In such cases it is recommended as the safest course, to pass them by without notice, and, as if they had not been heard. I do not intimate which, or if either of these rules governed the conduct of the Senator from Massachusetts. I can very well conceive of a third, and very different reason for this inattention—a reason which was seen in the fulness of the occupation which the Senator from South Carolina (Gen. HAYNE) had given him. True, the Senator from Massachusetts tells us that he felt nothing of all that—that the arrows did not pierce—and makes a question whether the arm of the Senator from South Carolina was strong enough to spring the bow? This he repeated so many times, and with looks so well adjusted to the declaration, that we all must have been reminded of what we have read in ancient books, of the brave gladiator who, receiving the fatal thrust which starts the cry of *"hoc habet"* from the whole amphitheatre, instead of displaying his wound, and beseeching pity, collects himself over his centre of gravity, assumes a graceful attitude, dresses his face in smiles, bows to the ladies, and acts the unhurt hero in the agonies of death.

But admitting that the arrows did not pierce: What then? Is it proof of the weakness of the arm that sprung the bow, or of the impenetrability of the substance that resisted the shaft? We read in many books of the polished brass that resists, not only arrows, but the iron-headed javelins, thrown by gigantic heroes. But, pierced or not pierced, we have all witnessed one thing; we have seen the Senator from Massachusetts occupy one whole day in picking these arrows out of his body; and to judge from the length and seriousness of this occupation, he might be supposed to have been stuck as full of them as the poor fellow whose transfixed effigy on the first leaf of our annual almanacs attracts the commiseration of so many children.

I pass by these inquiries, Mr. President, and come to the things which concern me most;—the renewed and repeated declarations of the Senator from Massachusetts, (Mr. W.) that from first to last, from the beginning to the ending of the chapter of this Government, all the measures favorable to the West, have been carried by northern votes, in opposition to southern votes; that this has always been the case; that there are no grounds for asserting the contrary; and that the West is ungrateful to desert these ancient friends in the North for a new alliance in the South. These, sir, are the things for me to attend to. They concern me somewhat, because I have asserted the contrary; they concern the Union much more, because upon the propagation and belief of these assertions depends a most unhallowed combination for the Government of this Confederacy, commencing in the oppression of one half of it, and ending in the ruin of the whole. These considerations impel me forward, and impose upon me the high obligation to make out my case; to shew the South to be the ever generous friend of the West,—the democracy of the North the same,— and the political adversaries of both, to have been the unrelenting enemies of the West, until new views, and recent events, have substituted the soft and sweet game of amorous seduction for the ancient and iron system of contempt and hostility. In discharging this duty, I shall confine myself to an elevated selection of historical facts,—to the great epochs, and great questions, which are cardinal in their nature, notorious in their existence, eventful in their consequences, and pertinent in their application, to the trial of the issue joined. On this plan, skipping over many minor measures, I come to the great epoch of the Louisiana purchase, and the resulting measures connected with that event.

The first point of view under which we must look at that great measure, Mr. President, is its incredible value, and the absolute necessity, then created by extraordinary events, for making the acquisition. The West at that period (1803,) was filling up with people, and covering over with wealth and population. It was no more the feeble settlement which the Congress of the Confederation had seen, and whose right, few as they were, to the free navigation of the Mississippi, had given birth to the most arduous struggle ever beheld in that Congress. *States* had superceded these infant settlements. Ohio, Kentucky, and Tennessee, had been admitted into the Union; the territories of Indiana, Illinois, and Mississippi were making their way to the same station. The Western settlements of Pennsylvania and Virginia lined the left bank of the Ohio for half the length of its course. All was animated with life, gay with hope, independent in the cultivation of a grateful soil, and rich in the prospect of sending their accumulated productions to all the markets of the world, through the great channel which conducted the King of Rivers to the bosom of the Ocean. The treaty with Spain in the year 1795 had guaranteed this right of passage; had stipulated, moreover, for a right of deposit in New Orleans; with the further stipulation that, if this place of deposit should ever be denied, another should immediately be assigned, equally convenient for storing produce and merchandize, and for the exchange of cargoes between the river and the sea vessels. This right of deposit, thus indispensable, and thus secured, was violated in the fall of 1802. New Orleans, at that time, was suddenly shut up, and locked against us, and no other place was assigned at which western produce could be landed, left, or sold. The news of this event stunned the West. I well recollect the effect upon the country, for I saw it, and felt it in my own person. I was a lad then, the eldest of a widow's sons—was living in Tennessee, and had come into Nashville to sell the summer's crop, and lay in the winter's supplies. We raised cotton, then, in that Southern part of Tennessee, and the price of fifteen cents a pound which had been paid for it, and three or four hundred pounds to the acre, and so many acres to the hand, had filled us all with golden hopes. I came into Nashville to sell the Summer's crop. I offered it to the merchant—a worthy man—with whom we dealt. His answer, and the reason, came together, and gave the first intelligence of my own loss and the calamity of the country. Not a cent could he give for the cotton, for he was not a griper to take it for a nominal price. Not an article could be advanced upon the faith of it—not even the indispensable item of one barrel of salt. The salt and the articles were indeed furnished, and upon indulgent terms, but not upon the faith of the cotton; that was recommended to be laid away, and to wait the course of events. This was the state of one and of all—of the entire country—Tennessee, Kentucky, Ohio, the western counties of Pennsylvania and Virginia; the territories of Indiana, Illinois and Mississippi. Every where, at every farm, the labor of the year was annihilated; the produce of the fields seemed to be changed into dust—struck by the wand of an enchanter which transformed cotton, tobacco, and hemp, into the useless leaves of the forests. The shock was incredible, the sensation universal, the resentment overwhelming, the cry for redress loud and incessant. Congress met. That great man was then President, whose memory it has been my grief and shame to see struck at, this day, on this floor. The energy of the People, and the blessing of God, had just made THOMAS JEFFERSON President of these United States. It was a blessed election, and a providential one, for the People of the West! *Upon that event depended the acquisition of Louisiana!* Congress met. The outrage at New Orleans was the main topic in the President's message. His public message to the House of Representatives, replete with the spirit which filled the West, is known to the Union. His confidential message in the Senate is not known. It has been locked up, until lately, in the sealed book of our secret proceedings. That seal is now broken, and I will read the part of this confidential message which developed the means of recovering, enlarging, and securing our violated rights, and asked the aid of the Senate in doing so. It is the message which nominated the Ministers to France who made the purchase of Louisiana.

The Message—Extract.

"While my confidence in our Minister Plenipotentiary at Paris is entire and undiminished, I still think that these objects might be promoted by joining with him a person sent from hence directly, carrying with him the feelings and sentiments of the nation excited on the late occurrence, impressed by full communications of all the views we entertain on this interesting subject, and thus prepared to meet and improve, to an useful result, the counter propositions of the other contracting party, whatsoever form their interest may give to them; and to secure to us the ultimate accomplishment of our object: I, therefore, nominate R. R. Livingston to be Minister Plenipotentiary, and James Monroe to be

Minister Extraordinary and Plenipotentiary, with full powers to both jointly, or to either, on the death of the other, to enter into a treaty or convention with the First Consul of France, for the purpose of enlarging, and more effectually securing, our rights and interests in the river Mississippi, and in the territories Eastward thereof."

The reason for sending an additional Minister is here stated, and stated with force and clearness. Mr. Livingston was in Paris, and, however faithful and able he might be, he was a stranger to the feelings excited by the occasion. The addition of Mr. Monroe would only make an embassy of two persons. Embassies of three, as in the mission to the French Republic in '98, and of five, as at Ghent, in 1815, have been seen in our country. An embassy of two, in such a case as the violation of our right of deposite at New Orleans, and only one of them fresh from the United States, could not be considered extraordinary, or extravagant. The selection of Mr. Monroe was, of all others, the most fit and acceptable. He was a citizen of Virginia—that great State, which had been the most early, stedfast, and powerful friend of the West; he was the champion of the Mississippi in that struggle of two years, under lock and key, when seven States undertook to surrender the navigation of that river; he was the Ambassador called for by the public voice of the South and West, and Mr. Randolph was the organ of that voice on the floor of the House of Representatives, when he declared that Mr. Jefferson could nominate no other person than Mr. Monroe. He was nominated. I have shewn the message that did it, and the reasons that influenced the President. Let us now continue our reading of the journal, and see how that nomination was received by the Senators from the *North* and from the *South*.

The Journal.
"Wednesday, January 12th, 1803.

"The Senate took into consideration the message of the President of the United States, of January 11th, nominating Robert R. Livingston to be Minister Plenipotentiary, and James Monroe to be Minister Extraordinary and Plenipotentiary, to enter into a treaty or convention with the First Consul of France, for the enlarging and more effectually securing our rights and interests on the river Mississippi; and

"*Resolved*, That they consent and advise to the appointment of R. R. Livingston, agreeably to the nomination.

"On the question, Will the Senate consent and advise to the nomination of James Monroe? the yeas were, Messrs. Anderson, Baldwin, Bradley,

Breckenridge, Clinton, Cocke, Ellery, T. Foster, Franklin, Jackson, Logan, Nicholas, Stone, Sumpter, and Wright—15. The nays, Messrs. Dayton, Dwight, Foster, Hillhouse, Howard, J. Mason, Morris, Ogden, Olcott, Plumer, Tracey, Wells, and White—12."

Fifteen for, twelve against, the nomination of Mr. Monroe. A majority of three votes in his favor; which is a difference of two voters; so that the nomination of Mr. Monroe, lacked but two of being rejected. Whence came these twelve? Every one from the North of the Potomac, nearly all from New England, and the whole from the ranks of that political party whose survivors, and residuary legatees, are now in hot pursuit of the alliance of the West! If any evidence is wanting to shew that the vote against Mr. Monroe was a vote against the object of his mission, it will be found, ten days afterwards, in the same journal upon the passage of a Bill appropriating two millions of dollars to accomplish the purposes of the mission. On this bill the vote stood:

YEAS.—"Messrs. Anderson, Baldwin, Bradley, Breckenridge, Clinton, Cocke, Ellery, T. Foster, Jackson, Logan, S.T. Mason, Nicholas, Sumpter, and Wright.—14."

NAYS.—"Messrs. Dayton, Dwight Foster, Hillhouse, Howard, J. Mason, Morris, Olcott, Plumer, Ross, Stone, Wells and White.—12."

Mr. Monroe went. Fortune was at work for the West while nearly one half of the American Senate, and a large proportion of the House of Representatives, were at work against her. War between France and England was impending; the loss of Louisiana in that war was among the most certain of its events; to get rid of the Province before the declaration of hostilities, was the policy of the First Consul; and the cession to the United States was determined on before our Minister could arrive. This was the work of Providence, or Fortune, which no one here could foresee; which few are lawyerlike enough to lay hold of to justify the previous opposition to Mr. Monroe, and the vote against the two millions. The treaty of cession was signed by the First Consul; was brought home, made known to the nation, and received in the South and West, with one universal acclaim of joy. Throughout the South and West it was hailed as a national benefaction, prepared by Fortune, seized by Jefferson, and entitled to the devout thanksgiving of the American people. Not so in the northeast. There a violent opposition broke out against it, upon the express ground that it would increase the power of the West; and when the treaty came up for ratification in the Senate, it received seven votes against it, being so many of the same party which had voted against the nomination of Mr. Monroe and the appropriation of two millions. In the House of Representatives the money bill for carrying the treaty into effect was voted against by twenty-five members, nearly the whole from the geographical quarter, and from the political party, that had opposed the treaty in the Senate.

The crisis was over; the great event was consummated. Louisiana was acquired; the navigation of the Mississippi secured; the prosperity of the West established forever. The glory of Jefferson was complete. He had found the Mississippi the boundary, and he made it the centre of the Republic. He re-united the two halves of the Great Valley, and laid the foundation for the largest empire of freemen that Time or Earth ever beheld. He planted the seed of imperishable gratitude in the hearts of myriads of generations who shall people the banks of the Father of Floods, and raise the votive altar, and erect the monumental statue, to the memory of *him* who was the instrument of GOD in the accomplishment of so great a work. And great is my grief and shame to have lived to see *his* name attacked in the American Senate! To have been myself the unconscious instrument of clearing the way for an impeachment of *his word!* and that upon the recollections of memories from whose tablets the stream of time may have washed away this small part of their accumulated treasures.

Let us pause, Mr. President, and reflect for a moment, upon the consequences to the West, and to the Union, if President Jefferson had not seized the opportunity of purchasing Louisiana; or, having purchased it, the Senate, or the House of Representatives, should have rejected the acquisition. In the first place, it is to be remembered, that France, emerging from the vortex of her revolution, overflowing with warriors, and governed by the Conqueror, who was catching at the sceptre of the world, was *then* the owner of Louisiana. The First Consul had extorted it from the King of Spain in the year 1800; and the violation of the right of deposit at New-Orleans, was his first act of ownership over the new possession, and the first significant intimation to us, of the new kind of neighbor that we had acquired. Cotemporaneously with this act of outrage upon us, was the concentration of twenty-five thousand men, under the general of division, afterwards Marshal Victor, in the ports of Holland, for the military occupation of Louisiana. So far advanced were the preparations for this expedition, that the troops were ready to sail; and commissaries to provide for their reception, were engaged in New-Orleans and St. Louis, when the transfer of the province was announced. Now, sir, put it on either foot:

Louisiana remains a French, or becomes a British, possession. In the first contingency, we must have become the ally, or the enemy, of France. The system of Bonaparte admitted of no neutrals; and our alternatives would have been, between falling into the train of his continental system, or maintaining a war against him upon our own soil. We can readily decide, that the latter would have been most honorable; but it is hard to say, which would have been most fatal to our prosperity, and most disastrous to our republican institutions. In the second contingency, and the almost certain one, we should have had England established on our western, as well as on our northern frontier; and I may add, our southern frontier also; for Florida, as the property of the ally of France, would have been a fair subject of British conquest in the war with France and Spain, and a desirable one, after the acquisition of Louisiana, and as easily taken as wished for; the vessel that brought home the news of the victory at Trafalgar, being sufficient to summon and reduce the places of Mobile, Pensacola, St. Marks, and St. Augustine. This nation, thus established upon three sides of our territory, the most powerful of maritime powers, jealous of our commerce, panting for the dominion of the seas, unscrupulous in the use of savage allies, and nine years afterwards to be engaged in a war with us! The results of such a position, would have been, the loss, for ages and centuries, of the navigation of the Mississippi; the permanent occupation of the Gulf of Mexico by the British fleet; the consequent control of the West Indies; and the ravage of our frontiers by savages in British pay. These would have been the permanent consequences, to say nothing of the fate of the late war, commenced with our enemy encompassing us on three sides with her land forces, and covering the ocean in front with her proud navy, victorious over the combined fleets of France and Spain, and swelled with the ships of all nations. From these calamitous results, the acquisition of Louisiana delivered us; and the heart must be but little turned to gratitude and devotion, which does not adore the Providence that made the great man President, who seized this gift of fortune, and overthrew the political party that would have rejected it.

The treaty was ratified, and not much to spare; one-third of the Senate would have defeated it, and the votes stood 7 to 24. But the ratification was only one half the business; many legislative enactments were necessary to make the new acquisition available and useful, and the whole of these measures received more or less of determined opposition from the same geographical quarter and political party which had opposed the purchase. I will specify a few of the leading measures to which this opposition extended.

1. The bill to enable the Senate to take possession of Louisiana: Nays in the Senate—Messrs. Adams, Hillhouse, Olcott, Pickering, Plumer, Tracy.

2. The bill to create a fund in stock for the Louisiana debt: Nays—Messrs. Hillhouse, Pickering, Tracy, Wells and White.

3. The bill for extending certain laws of the United States to Louisiana: Nays—Messrs. Adams, Plumer, and Wells.

Among the laws to be thus extended, were all those for the regulation of the Custom House, navigation and commerce. If it had been rejected, New Orleans could not have been used as an American port.

4. The bill to establish a separate territory in Upper Louisiana: Nays—Messrs. Adams, Olcott, Hillhouse, Plumer and Stone.

5. The bill to extend the powers of the Surveyors General to Louisiana: Nays—Messrs. Adair, Adams, Bayard, Bradley, Gilman, Hillhouse, Pickering, Plumer, Smith, of Md. Smith, of Vermont, Wright—all North of the Potomac except one.

This vote, Mr. President, is the connecting link between the nonsettlement clause, or the sell-out-complete clause, in the ordinance of 1785, and the non-survey, and non-emigration resolution now under debate. The three acts stand at twenty years apart—a wide distance in point of time—but they lie close together in spirit and intention, and announce a never-sleeping watchfulness over the prevention of Western settlement and Western improvement.

6. Various bills for the confirmation of private claims, generally opposed by the like number of votes and voters.

7. The bill for the admission of the State of Louisiana into the Union: Nays—Messrs. Bayard, Champlin, Dana, Gorman, Gilman, Goodrich, Horsey, Lloyd, Pickering and Reed.

8. The bill to authorize the State of Louisiana to accept an enlargement of its territory: Nays—Messrs. Bradley, Franklin, Gorman, Gilman, Lambert, Lloyd and Reed.

This bill was passed after West Florida was reduced to the possession of the United States. Its object was to permit the State of Louisiana, if she thought proper, to include within her limits all the territory East of the lakes Ponchartrain and Maurepas, the river Iberville, and East of the Mississippi, (above that river) to the line of the Mississippi Territory, and out to Pearl river. The importance of it will be seen by knowing that the State of Louisiana, at that time, included no territory East of the Mississippi, but the Isle of Orleans.

9. The resolutions of the Legislature of Massachusetts, in June, 1813, asserting the unconstitutionality of the act of Congress which admitted the State of Louisiana into the Union, and extended the laws of the United States thereto, and instructing the Massachusetts delegation in Congress to do their best to obtain its repeal. I will read them:

THE MASSACHUSETTS RESOLUTIONS.

"Resolutions of the Legislature of Massachusetts, reported by a committee composed of Messrs. Josiah Quincy, Ashman and Fuller, on the part of the Senate; and Messrs. Thatcher, Lloyd, Hall and Bates, on the part of the House, and recorded in the Boston Centinel, June 26th, 1813, appended to a long report, viz:

"*Resolved,* As the sense of this Legislature, that the admission into the Union of States created in countries not comprehended within the original limits of the United States, is not authorized by the letter or the spirit of the Federal Constitution.

"*Resolved,* That it is the *interest* and duty of the people of Massachusetts to oppose the admission of such States into the Union, as a measure tending to the *dissolution* of the confederacy.

"*Resolved,* That the act passed the eighth day of April, 1812, entitled an act for the admission of Louisiana into the Union, and to extend the laws of the United States to the said State, is a violation of the Constitution of the United States; and that the Senators of this State in Congress be instructed, and that the Representatives be requested to use the utmost of their endeavors to obtain a repeal of the same."

This was the solemn act of Massachusetts, governed by that political party, which now seeks the command of the West, under the name of an alliance! The Senator from Louisiana, who sits on my left, (Mr. JOHNSTON) adheres with a generous devotion—I call it generous, for it survives the downfall of its object—to that party which passed these resolutions, and would have kept his State out of the Union, and by consequence, himself out of this chamber. I do not reproach such generosity, but I contend for its limitation. The heart of that Senator belongs to his country, and I trust that his country will again possess him. He and I were once together. Our separation was from a point, and by slight degrees, though now so wide, like the travellers in the desert, parting from each other on two diverging lines; for a long time within hail—a long time in view—at last completely separated—but never way-layers nor destroyers of each other. I shall hope to see him return to the right line, and join his old companions. Nothing has happened to make him, or them, blush, at finding themselves again together. [Mr. B. here said something to Mr. Johnston (who sat near him) in an under tone, and in a playful mood—*en badinant*—the purport of which was, that he would wish to see him laid on the shelf, for a while, notwithstanding.]

The admission of the State of Mississippi into the Union furnishes me with the next example in support of my side of the issue joined. It was no part of the Territory of Louisiana, but a part of the original territory of the United States. Constitutional objections could not reach it, yet it met with the usual quantum of opposition. It was a Western measure, and what was worse, a Southwestern measure, and the Journals of the Senate exhibit eleven nays to its admission. They were Messrs. Ashmun, Dagget, Goldsborough, Hunter, King, Macon, Mason, of N. H., Smith, Thompson, Tichenor, and Varnum. The name of the venerable Macon, which appears in this list, may be seized upon to cover the motives of all the others; but to do that it should first be shewn that he and they voted upon the same motive. We know that votes may sometimes be alike and the motives be different. That the vote of Mr. Macon was unfriendly to the Southwest, is a supposition contradicted by the acts of half a century; that the vote of the others was unfriendly, may be decided by the same test, the tenor of all previous conduct. After all, the instance would go but a short distance towards proving, "that every measure, favorable to the West, had been carried by New England votes in opposition to Southern votes."

I come now to the admission of Missouri, but do not mean to dwell upon it. The event is too recent—the facts connected with it, too notorious—to require proof, or even to admit of recital, here. The struggle upon that question, divided itself into two parts; the first, to prevent the existence of slavery in Missouri; the second, to secure the entrance of free blacks and mulattoes into it. Each part of the struggle divided the Union into two parts, the Potomac and Ohio the dividing line, with slight exceptions; the South in favor of the rights of Missouri, the North against them. In the ranks of the latter were seen all the survivors of the ancient advocates for the surrender of the Mississippi—all the survivors of those who in the Congress of the confederation opposed the protection of the West; all the opponents to the acquisition of Louisiana; all the power of the federal party; and all the gentlemen of the Northeast who are now paying their addresses to the West. The contest, upon its face, was a question of slavery and the rights of free negroes and mulattoes; in its heart, it was a question of political power, and so declared upon this floor by Mr. King, of New York. It was a terrible agitation, and convulsed the country, and, in a certain quarter of the country, swept all before it. The gentleman who has moved this resolution—the resolution now under discussion—was the victim of that storm, (Mr. FOOT, of Conn.) He was then a member of the the House of Representatives. He would not join in this crusade against Missouri, and he fell under the dipleasure of his constituents. But he fell on the side of honor and patriotism, with his conscience and his integrity in his arms; and the consequence of such a fall is to rise again, and to ascend higher than ever. The gentleman will appreciate the spirit in which I speak. My encomiums, poor as they may be, here, or elsewhere, are neither profuse nor indiscriminate. I do justice to the motive which has made him the mover of the resolution to which I am so earnestly opposed. He believes it to be right, and that belief, erroneous as I hold it to be, is the effect of that unhappy part of our political system which makes the representatives of remote States judges of the local measures of another State, with the proprieties of which they have no means of personal information. I oppose his resolution to the uttermost, but I respect his motive; I thank him for his vote in favor of Missouri in the crisis of her struggle, and for his motion some days ago in favor of donations to actual settlers. We may contend upon points of policy; but here, and elsewhere, and above all in Missouri, if found there, I, and mine, will do honor to him and his.

Yes, sir, the Missouri struggle is too recent to admit of recitals, or to require proofs. It was but the other day that it all occurred; but the other day that the Representative and the Senators of that State, myself one of them, were repulsed from the doors of Congress, and *deforced,* for one entire session, of their legitimate seats among you. And, what is now incredibly strange, what surpasses imagination, and staggers credulity, is to see myself called upon to deny that scene; called upon to treat the whole as an optical illusion; to reverse it, in fact, and submit to the belief that those whose blows we felt kicking and shoving us out, were the ones that drew us in! and those whose helping hands we felt drawing and hauling us in, are the identical ones who kicked and shoved us out!

The State of Missouri, Mr. President, was kept out of the Union one whole year for the clause which prohibited the future entry and settlement of free people of color. And what have we seen since? The actual expulsion of a great body of free colored people from the State of Ohio, and not one word of objection, not one note of grief, from those who did all in their power to tear up the Constitution and break the Union to pieces, because, at some future day, it might happen that some free blacks would wish to emigrate to Missouri, and could not do it for this clause in her Constitution! The papers state the compulsory expatriation from Cincinnati at two thousand souls; the whole number that may be compelled to expatriate from the State of Ohio, at ten thousand! This is a remarkable event, sir, paralleled only by the expulsion of the Moors from Spain, and the Hugonots from France. Let me not be misunderstood: I am not complaining of Ohio, I admit her right to do what she did. We are informed that this severe measure was the consequence of enforcing an old law, made for the benefit of the slave holding States, and now found to be as necessary to Ohio as to them, and by which she has relieved herself, in thirty days, of the accumulated evil of thirty years. I complain not of this. My present business is with those who kept me out of my seat, kept my State out of the Union, and did all in their power to break up this Confederacy, because free people of color were prohibited from coming to live in Missouri!

My occupation, for the present, is with these characters—"*Les Amis des Noirs*"—the friends of the blacks—*then* so plenty, *now* so scarce! Where are they? Where gone? How shrunk up? Not even one friend, one voice here! Where are the crowds that *then* thronged the public meetings? Where are the tongues which were *then* so fluent? The sighs, then so piercing? The eyes, then so wet with tears? All gone; all silent; all hushed! The thronged crowd has disappeared; the fluent tongue has cleaved to the roof of the mouth, the piercing sigh has died away, and the streaming eye, exhausted of its fluid contents, has dried up to the innermost sources of the lachrymal duct, and hangs over the pitiable scene, with the arid composure of a rainless cloud in the midst of the sandy desert. The Senator from Massachusetts, [Mr. W.] so copious and encomiastic upon the subject of Ohio, so full and affecting upon the topic of freedom, and the rights of freemen in that State, was incomprehensibly silent, and fastidiously mute, upon the question of this wonderful expatriation; an expatriation which sent a generation of free people from a republican State to a monarchical province, to seek, in a strange land, and beyond the icy lakes, the hospitality and protection of a foreign king! For them he had nothing to say. Their condition attracted no part of his regards. They are gone; unwept and unsung, they have gone to experience the fate, and to renew the history, of the abducted slaves of the Revolution, who were taken from their homes and their masters, collected into a settlement in the British

province of Nova Scotia, became a pestilence there, and were exiled to
Sierra Leone, to perish under the climate and the savages. For these people, and the pitiable fate that awaits them, the eloquent declaimer upon
the blessings of liberty in Ohio, had nothing to say. I thought, indeed, at
one time, he was taking their track: it was when he was engaged in that
lively personification of the soil of Ohio, which would not hear the tread
of a slave's foot upon it; which rebelled, and revolted, against the servile
impression until it threw off and discharged, the base, incongruous load;
something like a kicking up horse, when a monkey is put upon his back. I
thought, at that time, that the metaphorical orator, pushing his tropes and
figures to that "bourne" from which some flights of eloquence have never
returned, was going to put the climax upon the regurgitative faculties of
this miraculous soil, and show us, in this great emigration of free blacks,
that it would not bear the tread of a foot that ever had been in slavery! But,
suddenly, and to me unexpectedly, his ideas took another turn. Instead of
crossing the Lakes to pity the blacks, he crossed the river to pity the
whites. He faced about to the South, crossed over into Kentucky, made a
domiciliary visit into the country—and fell, incontinently, to shingling the
ground, and blacking the inhabitants, until they all looked like ebonies,
and were mired, thirty layers deep, in conflicting land titles. When I saw
that, Mr. President, I smote my breast, and heaved a sigh, at the sad vicis-
situde of human affections. I felt, if I did not cry out, for Kentucky! Poor
Kentucky! But yesterday, the loved and cherished object of all affection!
the engrossing theme of every praise! Now scanned and criticised! Her
faults all told, and counted! Her value cast up! The sum found less! and the
late adored object, thrown "*as a worthless weed away!*"

FEBRUARY 1, 1830. *Third Day.*

I was on the subject of slavery, Mr. President, as connected with the
Missouri question, when last on the floor. The Senator from South Carolina, [Mr. HAYNE,] could see nothing in the question before the Senate,
nor in any previous part of the debate, to justify the introduction of that
topic: neither could I. He thought he saw the ghost of the Missouri question brought in among us: so did I. He was astonished at the apparition: I
was not; for a close observance of the signs in the West had prepared me for
this development from the East. I was well prepared for that invective
against slavery, and for that amplification of the blessings of exemption
from slavery, exemplified in the condition of Ohio, which the Senator from
Massachusetts indulged in, and which the object in view required to be

derived from the North East. I cut the root of that derivation by reading a passage from the Journals of the old Congress; but this will not prevent the invective and encomium from going forth to do their office; nor obliterate the line which was drawn between the free State of Ohio and the slave State of Kentucky. If the only results of this invective and encomium were to exalt still higher the oratorical fame of the speaker, I should spend not a moment in remarking upon them. But it is not to be forgotten that the terrible Missouri agitation took its rise from the "substance of two speeches" delivered on this floor; and, since that time, anti-slavery speeches, coming from the same political and geographical quarter, are not to be disregarded here. What was said upon that topic was certainly intended for the North side of the Potomac and Ohio; to the People, then, of that division of the Union, I wish to address myself, and to disabuse them of some erroneous impressions. To them I can truly say, that slavery, in the abstract, has but few advocates or defenders in the slave-holding States, and that slavery as it is, an hereditary institution descended upon us from our ancestors, would have fewer advocates among us than it has, if those who have nothing to do with the subject, would only let us alone. The sentiment in favor of slavery was much weaker before those intermeddlers began their operations than it is at present. The views of leading men in the North and the South were indisputably the same in the earlier periods of our Government. Of this our legislative history contains the highest proof. The foreign slave trade was prohibited in Virginia as soon as the Revolution began. It was one of her first acts of sovereignty. In the Convention of that State which adopted the Federal Constitution, it was an objection to that instrument that it tolerated the African slave trade for twenty years. Nothing that has appeared since has surpassed the indignant denunciations of this traffic by Patrick Henry, George Mason, and others in that Convention. The clause in the Ordinance of '86 against slavery in the North-West, as I have before shown, originated in a Committee of three members, of whom two were from slave-holding States. That clause, and the whole Ordinance, received the vote of every slave State present, at its final passage. There were but eight States present, four from the South of the Potomac, and only one from New England. It required seven States to pass the Ordinance; it could have been passed without the New England State, but not without three at least of the Southern ones. It had all four: Virginia, the two Carolinas, and Georgia. Compare this with the vote on the Missouri restriction, when intermeddlers and designing politicians had undertaken to regulate the South upon the subject of slavery! The Report in the House of Representatives, some twenty years ago, against the application from Indiana, for a limited admission of slaves, was drawn by Mr. Randolph; the same Mr. Randolph whose declaration in the House of Representatives only three years ago, that he would hang any man who would bring an African into Virginia—was falsified for the basest purposes, by substituting "Irishman" for African! Yes, sir, slavery as it is, and as it exists among us, would have fewer advocates, if those who have nothing to do with it would let it alone. But they will not let it alone. A geographical party, and chiefly a political *caste*, are incessantly at work upon this subject. Their operations pervade the States, intrude into this chamber, display themselves in innumerable forms, and the thickening of the signs announces the forthcoming of some extraordinary movement. Sir, I regard with admiration, that is to say with wonder, the sublime morality of those, who cannot bear the abstract contemplation of slavery, at the distance of five hundred or a thousand miles off. It is entirely above, that is to say, it affects a vast superiority over the morality of the primitive Christians, the Apostles of Christ, and Christ himself. Christ and the Apostles appeared in a province of the Roman empire, when that empire was called the Roman world, and that world was filled with slaves. Forty millions was the estimated number, being one-fourth of the whole population—single individuals held twenty thousand slaves. A freed-man, one who had himself been a slave, died the possessor of four thousand—such were the numbers. The rights of the owners over this multitude of human beings, was that of life and death, without protection from law, or mitigation from public sentiment. The scourge, the cross, the fish-pond, the den of the wild beast, and the arena of the gladiator, was the lot of the slave upon the slightest expression of the master's will. A law of incredible atrocity made all slaves responsible with their own lives, for the life of their master; it was the law that condemned the whole household of slaves to death, in case of the assassination of the master; a law under which as many as four hundred have been executed at a time. And these slaves were the white people of Europe, and of Asia Minor, the Greeks, and other nations, from whom the present inhabitants of the world derive the most valuable productions of the human mind. Christ saw all this—the number of the slaves—their hapless condition— and their white color, which was the same with his own; yet he said nothing against slavery; he preached no doctrines which led to insurrection and massacre; none which, in their application to the state of things in our country, would authorize an inferior race of blacks to exterminate that superior race of whites, in whose ranks he himself appeared upon earth. He preached no such doctrines; but those of a contrary tenor, which inculcated the duty of fidelity and obedience on the part of the slave; humanity and kindness on the part of the master. His Apostles did the same. St. Paul sent back a runaway slave to his owner, Onesimus, with a letter of apology and supplication. He was not the man to harbor a runaway, much less to entice him from his master; and least of all, to excite an insurrection.

Slavery, which once filled the Roman world, has disappeared from most of the countries which composed that great dominion. It has disappeared from nearly all Europe, and from half the States of this Union. There and here it has ceased upon the same principle—upon the principle of economy, and a calculation of interest; a calculation which, in a certain density of population, and difficulty of subsistence, makes it cheaper to hire a man than to own him; cheaper to pay for the work he does, and hear no more of him, than to be burthened with his support from the cradle to the grave. Slavery never ceased any where on a principle of religion; the religion of all nations consecrates it. Its abolition cannot be enforced among Christians, on that ground, without reproaching the founder of their religion. Many who think themselves Christians, are now engaged in preaching against slavery, but they had better ascertain whether they have fulfilled the precepts of Christ, before they assume a moral superiority over him, and undertake to do what he did not. To the politicians who are engaged in the same occupation, it is needless to give the like admonition. They have their views, and the success of these would be poorly promoted by following the precepts of the Gospel. Their kingdom *is* of this world, and to reach it, they will do the things they ought not, and leave undone the things which they ought to do. Slavery will cease, in the course of some generations, in several of the States where it now exists, and cease upon the same principle on which it has disappeared elsewhere. In some parts it is not sustainable now upon a calculation of interest. Habit and affection is the main bond. A great amelioration in the condition of the slave has taken place. In most of the States they are as members of the family, and in all the essential particulars of labor, food, and raiment, they fare as the rest of the laboring community. Some masters are cruel; but the laws condemn such cruelty, and, what is more effectual than the law, is the abhorrence of public sentiment. But cruelty is not confined to the black slave; it extends to the white apprentice, to the orphans that are bound out, and to the children of the poor that are hired to the rich. Many of these can, and often do, tell pitiable tales of stinted food, and excessive work—of merciless beatings, brutal indignities, and precocious debaucheries. The advance of the public mind has been great upon the subject of slavery. Let any one look back to the conferences at Utrecht in 1712, when England was ready to continue the greatest of her wars for the sake of the *asiento*—the contract for supplying Spanish America with slaves—and see the conduct of the Virginia Assembly in 1776, and England herself in 1780, denouncing and punishing that traffic as a crime against God and man. It has not advanced of late, but retrograded. I speak of these United States. Witness the two epochs of the ordinance of '86, and the admission of Missouri in 1820. Intrusive, and political intermeddling, produced this reverse. Such meddling can do no good to the objects of its real, or affected commiseration. It does harm to them. It prevents the enactment of some kind laws, and occasions the passage of some severe ones. It totally checks emancipation, and deprives the slave of instruction, as the most merciful way of saving him from the penalties of murder and insurrection, which the reading of incendiary pamphlets might lead him to incur.

I have been full, I am afraid tedious, Mr. President, on the subject of slavery. My apology must be found in the extraordinary introduction of this topic by the Senator from Massachusetts (Mr. WEBSTER.) I foresee that this subject is to act a great part in the future politics of this country; that it is to be made one of the instruments of a momentous movement— not for dividing the Union—something more practicable and more damnable than that. The prevention of a world of woe may depend upon the democracy of the non-slaveholding States. The preservation of their own republican liberties may depend upon it. Never was their stedfast adhesion to the principles they profess, and to their natural allies, more necessary than at present. To them I have been speaking; to them I continue to address myself. I beseech and implore them to suffer their feelings against slavery to have no effect upon their political conduct; to join in no combinations against the South for that cause; to leave this whole business to ourselves. I think they can well let it alone, upon every principle of morals or policy. Are they Christians? Then they can tolerate what Christ and the Apostles could bear. Are they Patriots? Then they can endure what the Constitution permits. Are they philosophers? Then they can bear the abstract contemplation of the ills which afflict others, not them. Are they friends and sympathisers? Then they must know that the wearer of the shoe knows best where it pinches, and is most concerned to get it off. Are they republicans? Then they must see the downfall of themselves and the elevation of their adversaries, in the success of a crusade, under federal banners, against their natural allies, in the South and West.

Let the democracy of the North remember, that it is the tendency of all confederacies to degenerate into a sub-confederacy among the powerful, for the government and oppression of the weaker members. Let them recollect that ambition is the root of these sub-confederacies; religion, avarice, and geographical antipathies, the instruments of their domination; oppression, civil wars, pillage, and tyranny, their end. So says the history of all confederacies. Look at them. The Amphictyonic league—a confederacy of thirty members—received the law and the lash from Sparta, Thebes, and Athens. The Germanic confederation, of three hundred States and free cities, was governed by the nine great electorates, which ruled and pillaged as they pleased; the Imperial Diet being to them something like what the Supreme Court is proposed to be here, a tribunal before which the States and free cities could be called, placed under the ban of the Empire, and delivered up to military execution. The seven United Provinces; the strong province of Holland alone deciding upon all questions of peace and war, loans and taxes, and dragooning the inferior provinces into acquiescence and compliance. The thirteen Swiss Cantons, in which the strong, aristocratic Cantons pillaged and ravaged the weak ones on account of their religion and democracy, often calling in the Dukes of Savoy to assist in the chastisement. Let the democracy of the North remember these things, and then eschew, as they would fly the incantations of the serpent, the syren songs of ancient foes who would enlist their feelings in a concert of action which is to end in arraying one-half of the States of this Union against the other. Have we no ambition in this Confederacy? no means of enabling it to work as in Greece, Germany, Holland, and the Swiss Cantons? Look at the fallen leaders, panting for the recovery of lost power. Look at the ten millions of surplus in the Treasury, after the extinction of the public debt—at the three hundred millions of acres of public land in the new States and Territories—at the forty millions of exports of the South, and see if there be not, in the modes of dividing these, among certain strong States, for internal improvement, education, and protection of domestic industry, ample means for acting on the feelings of avarice. Look at the excitements getting up about Indians, slaves, masonry, Sunday mails, &c. and see if there are no materials for working upon religion or fanaticism.

The Senator from Massachusetts, (Mr. W.) had a vision, Mr. President, in the after part of his second day's speaking. He saw an army with banners, commanded by the new Major General of South Carolina, the Senator who sits on my right, (General HAYNE) marching forward upon the Custom House in Charleston, sometimes expounding law as a civilian, sometimes fighting as a General. It was a pleasant vision, sir, but no more than a vision. Now, Mr. President, I can have a vision also, and of a banner, with inscriptions upon it, floating over the head of the Senator from Massachusetts, (Mr. W.) while he was speaking:—the words "MISSOURI QUESTION, COLONIZATION SOCIETY, ANTI-SLAVERY, GEORGIA INDIANS, WESTERN LANDS, MORE TARIFF, INTERNAL IMPROVEMENT, ANTI-SUNDAY MAILS, ANTI-MASONRY." A cavalcade under the banner,—a motley group,—a most miscellaneous concourse,—the speckled progeny of many conjunctions,—veteran Federalists, benevolent females, politicians who have lost their *caste*—National Republicans—all marching on to the next Presidential election, and chanting the words on the banner, and repeating, "under these signs we conquer." Did you see it, Mr. President? Your look says No. But I cannot be *looked* out of my vision. I did see something, the shade at least of a substance—the apparition of a real event—making its way from the womb of time, and casting its shadow before. I shall see it again—at Philippi—and that before the Greek kalends—about the ides of November, 1832.

I mean no disrespect, sir, to the benevolent females for whom I have found a place in this procession. Far from it. They have earned the place by the part they are acting in the public meetings for the instruction of Congress on the subject of these Georgia Indians. For the rest, I had rather take my chance, in such a cavalcade, among these benevolent females, than among the unbenevolent males; had rather appear in the feminine, than in the masculine gender; had rather march in bonnet, cloak, and petticoats, than in hat, coat, and pantaloons. With the aid of the famous corset-maker, Madame Cantalo, to draw me up a little, I had rather trip it along as a Miss, in frock and pantalets, than figure as a war chief of the Georgia Cherokees, bedecked and bedizzened in all the finery of paint and feathers. I had rather be on foot among the damsels than on horse among the leaders; white, black, and red. I apprehend these leaders will be on foot on the return march, dismounted and discomfited, unhorsed and unharnessed, better prepared for the flight than the fight, and *leading* the ladies out of danger after having *led* them into it. In that retreat I would recommend it to the benevolent females, to place no reliance upon the performances of their delicate little feet. Their unequal steps would vainly strive to keep up with the "*double quick time*" of their swift conductors. No helping hand then to be stretched back for the "*little Iulus.*" It would be a race that Virgil has described, a long interval between the great heroes ahead, and the little ones behind. I would recommend it to these ladies, not to douse their bonnets, and tuck up their coats, for such a race, but to sit down on the way side, and wait the coming of the conquerors. The new Major General of South Carolina will then be in the field in reality; his banner will then be seen, not advancing upon a custom house, but pursuing the flying host of the National Republicans, and from him the "*benevolent females*" will have nothing to fear.

I come now, Mr. President, to a momentous period in this Union, one well calculated to test other questions besides that of relative friendship to the West. I speak of the late war with Great Britain. We began it for wrongs on the ocean, but the West quickly became its principal theatre, and in the beginning encountered defeats and disasters, which called for the aid and sympathy of other parts of the Union. I say nothing about the declaration of war; that was a question of opinion, and might have two sides to it; but after the bloody conflict was began, there was but one side for Americans. The Senator from Massachusetts has laid down the law of duty to a citizen, (when the Government has adopted a line of policy) in accounting for his support of the tariff of 1828, after opposing that of 1824. The Government had adopted the tariff policy, he says, and thereupon it became his duty to support that policy. I will not stop to inquire how far future opposition was concluded in such a case. It is sufficient, for my present purpose, to shew that the Senator from Massachusetts has laid down this acquiescence in, and support of, the policy of the Government, in a case of common and ordinary legislation; after that, it cannot be denied, in the highest of all cases, to which it can apply, that of a foreign war, and that war calamitous to his own country. New England, more accurately speaking, the then dominant party in New England, opposed the declaration of war, and that after a leader of that party had declared upon the floor of the House of Representatives, that the Administration could not be kicked into war. She opposed the declaration; but I leave that out of the question. The war is declared, it is commenced, it is disastrous; and the heaviest disasters fall upon the West. Her armies are beaten; her frontier posts taken; her territory invaded. Her soil is red with the blood, and white with the bones of her sons. Her daughters are in mourning: the land is filled with grief; and cries for succor pervade the Union. Where was then relief for the West? What was then the conduct of the North-east? What the conduct of the South?   *   *   *   *
The Senator from South Carolina, (Gen. HAYNE,) has shewn you what was the conduct of the North-east. He has read the acts which history, and his eloquence will deliver down to posterity, shewing that the then dominant

party in New England, was as well disposed to aid the enemy as to aid the West. He shewed that it was a main object of the Hartford Convention to exclude the West from the Union. The Senator from Massachusetts made light of these readings; he called them uncanonical collects. In one respect a part of them were like a collect; they came from the pulpit; but instead of being prayers, unless the prayers of the devil and his black angels be understood, they were curses, execrations, and damnation to the West. The Senator from Massachusetts denied their authority, and washed his hands of them. I will, therefore, read him something else; the authority of which will not be so readily denied, nor the hands so easily washed of. I speak of a speech delivered on the floor of the House of Representatives about the middle of the late war, when things were at their worst, and of certain votes upon the army bill, the militia bill, the load bill, the tax bill, and the Treasury note bill. And first of the speech. It purports to have been delivered by the Senator, to whom I am now replying, in the session of 1813–14, on the discussion of the bill to fill the ranks of the regular army.

The Speech—*An Extract.*

"It is certain that the real object of this proposition to increase the military force to an extraordinary degree, by extraordinary means, is to act over again the scenes of the two last campaigns. To that object I cannot lend my support. I am already satisfied with the exhibition.

"Give me leave to say, sir, that the tone on the subject of the conquest of Canada seems to be not a little changed. Before the war, that conquest was represented to be quite an easy affair. The valiant spirits who mediated it, were only fearful lest it should be too easy to be glorious. They had no apprehension, except that resistance would be so powerful as to render the victory splendid.   *   *   *   How happens it, sir, that this country, so easy of acquisition, and over which, according to the prophecies, we were to have been, by this time, legislating, dividing it into States and Territories, is not yet ours? Nay, sir, how happens it, that we are not even free of invasion ourselves; that gentlemen here call on us by all the motives of patriotism, to assist in the defence of our own soil, and pourtray before us the state of the frontiers, by frequent and animated allusion to all those topics which the modes of Indian warfare usually suggest?

"This, sir, is not what we were promised. This is not the entertainment to which we were invited. This is no fulfillment of those predictions, which it was deemed obstinacy itself not to believe. This is not the harvest of greatness and glory, the seeds of which were supposed to be sown, with the declaration of war.

"When we ask, sir, for the causes of these disappointments, we are told that they are owing to the opposition which the war encounters, in this House and among the people. All the evils which afflict the country are imputed to the opposition. This is the fashionable doctrine, both here and elsewhere. It is said to be owing to opposition that the war became necessary; and owing to opposition also that it has been prosecuted with no better success.

"This, sir, is no new strain. It has been sung a thousand times. It is the constant tune of every weak or wicked administration. What Minister ever yet acknowledged, that the evils which fell on his country, were the necessary consequences of his own incapacity, his own folly, or his own corruption? What possessor of political power ever yet failed to charge the mischiefs resulting from his own measures, upon those who had uniformly opposed those measures?

$$* \quad * \quad * \quad * \quad * \quad * \quad * \quad * \quad *$$

"You are, you say, at war for maritime rights and free trade. But they see you lock up your commerce, and abandon the ocean. They see you invade an interior province of the enemy. They see you involve yourselves in a bloody war with the native savages: and they ask you if you have in truth, a maritime controversy with the Western Indians, and are really contending for sailors' rights with the tribes of the Prophet."

This speech requires no comment, and will admit of none. Its own words go beyond any that could be substituted. "Valiant spirits—too easy to be glorious—tone changed—prophecies unfulfilled—frontiers invaded—assistance called for—entertainment—animated allusions to the modes of Indian warfare—bloody war with the Savages—contending with tribes of the Prophet for sailors rights—weak and wicked—folly and corruption—lend no support—satisfied with the exhibition."

These phrases of cutting sarcasm, of cool contempt, of bitter reproach, and stern denial of succor, deserve to be placed in a parallel column with what we have just heard of love to the West, and of the protecting arm extended over her. I will not dwell upon them; but there are two phrases which extort a brief remark: "Satisfied with the exhibition"—"lend no support." What was the exhibition of these two campaigns, the first and second of the war, to which this expression of satisfaction, and denial of support, extends? It was this: In the Southwest, the massacre at Fort Mimms; the Creek nation in arms; British incendiaries in Pensacola and St. Marks, exciting Savages to war and slaves to rebellion; the present

President of the United States at the Ten Islands of the Coosa river, in a stockade of twenty yards square, with forty young men of Nashville, holding the Creek nation in check, and calling for support. In the Northwest, all the forts which covered the frontiers, captured and garrisoned by the enemy; Michigan Territory reduced to the condition of a British province; Ohio invaded; the enemy encamped, and entrenched, upon her soil; the British flag flying over it—over that soil of Ohio which, according to what we have just heard, could not bear the tread of a slave, now trod in triumph by the cruel Proctor and his ferocious myrmidons. This is the exhibition which the first and second campaigns presented in the West—for I limit myself to that quarter of the Union, the present question being one of relative friendship to the West. This is the exhibition which the West presented—these the scenes which called for succor, and to relieve which the extract that I have read declares that none would be lent. The author of that speech was satisfied with this exhibition, he would do nothing to change it. The political and geographical party with which he acted, were equally well satisfied, and equally determined to let things remain as they were. They voted accordingly against every measure for the relief of the bleeding and invaded West; against the bill to fill the ranks of the regular army—against the bill to call out the militia—against the bill to borrow money—against the bill to lay taxes—against the bill to issue Treasury notes! The Journals of Congress will shew the recorded votes of those who now set up for the exclusive friends of the West, in opposition to all these bills. The reading of the yeas and nays, on the whole of these measures, would be tedious and unnecessary; a single set will shew how they stood in every instance. I select, for my example, the vote in the House of Representatives on the passage of the bill the discussion of which called forth the speech from which an extract has been made.

THE VOTE.

Yeas.	Nays.
	NEW HAMPSHIRE.
	Messrs. Cilley, Hale, Vose, Webster, Wilcox.
	MASSACHUSETTS.
Messrs. Hubbard, Parker.	Baylies, Bigelow, Bradbury, Brigham, Davis, Dewey, Ely, King, Pickering, John Reed, Wm. Reed, Ruggles, Ward, Wheaton, Wilson.

Yeas.	Nays.

CONNECTICUT.

| | Champion, Davenport, Law, Moseby, Pitkin, Sturges, Taggart. |

NEW YORK.

| Avery, Fisk, Lefferts, Sage, Taylor. | Geddes, Grosvenor, Kent, Lovett, Miller, Moffitt, Oakley, Post, Shepperd, Smith, Winter. |

VERMONT.

| Bradley, Fisk, Skinner. | |

RHODE ISLAND.

| | Jackson, Potter. |

NEW JERSEY.

| Hasbrouck, Ward. | Boyd, Cox, Hafey, Schureman, Stockton. |

PENNSYLVANIA.

| Anderson, Bard, Brown, Conard, Crawford, Crouch, Findlay, Glasgow, Griffith, Ingersoll, Ingham, Lyle, Piper, Rea, Roberts, Seybert, Smith, Tannehill, Udree, Whitehill, Wilson. | Markell. |

DELAWARE.

| | Cooper, Ridgely. |

MARYLAND.

| Archer, Kent, McKim, Moore, Nelson, Ringgold, Wright. | |

VIRGINIA.

| Burwell, Clopton, Dawson, Eppes, Gholston, Hawes, Hungerford, Jackson, Johnson, Kerr, McCoy, Newton, Pleasants, Rich, Roane, Smith. | Bayly, Caperton, Lewis, Sheffey. |

NORTH CAROLINA.

| Alston, Forney, Franklin, Kennedy, Macon, Murfree, Yancey. | Culpeper, Gaston, Pierson, Stanford, Sherwood, and Thompson.—58. |

SOUTH CAROLINA.

| Calhoun, Chappell, Cheves, Earle, Evans, Gordon, Kershaw, Lowndes. | |

Yeas.	Nays.

GEORGIA.

Barnet, Forsyth, Hall, Telfair, Troup.

KENTUCKY.

Clark, Desha, Duvall, McKee,
Montgomery, Ormsby, Sharp.

TENNESSEE.

Bowen, Grundy, Harris, Humphreys,
Rhea, Sevier.

OHIO.

Alexander, Beale, Caldwell, Creighton,
Kilbourn, McLean.

LOUISIANA.

Robertson.—97.

Such were the votes of the NORTH and SOUTH on the passage of this bill. Such were the votes of the then dominant party, of the North East, in that dark hour of calamity, and trial, to the West. Such was their answer in reply to our calls for help,—even the calls of that Ohio, which is now the cherished object of all affection, the chosen theme of highest eulogy, the worshipped star in that new constellation of superior planets, which are to shed, not, their "selectest influences," but, "disastrous twilight, on half the States." It is not for me, Mr. President, to trace a parallel between these votes, and the words, and acts of the same political party, in the States, from which the voters came. It is not for me to measure the difference between the conduct which gives aid to the enemy, and that which denies aid to your own country. The question is a close one, and may exercise the ingenuity of those who can detect the difference between the "West side, and the North West side of a hair." It is not for me to confound these votes, and the extract of the speech, with the words and acts of those who received the successes of their own country with grief, & its defeats with joy; who held "soft intercourse" with the enemy when he had established himself upon the soil, and upon the calamities, of this Union; who saw with savage exultation the cruel massacre, and dreadful burning, of the wounded prisoners at the river Raisin, and gave vent to their hellish joy, from the holy pulpit, in the impious declaration that, "God had given them blood to drink." It is not for me to confound these things; it may be for others to unmix them. I turn to a more grateful task,—to the contemplation of the conduct of the South, in the same season of woe and calamity. What was then their conduct? What their speeches, and their votes, in Congress? Their efforts at home? Their prayers in the temple of God? Time and ability would fail in any attempt to perform this task; to enumerate the names and acts of those generous friends, in the South, who then stood forth our defenders and protectors, and gave us men and money, and beat the domestic foe in the Capitol, while we beat the foreign one in the field. Time, and my ability, would fail to do them justice; but there is one State in the South, the name and praise of which, the events of this debate would drag from the stones of the West, if they could rise up in this place and speak! It is the name of that State upon which the vials, filled with the accumulated wrath of years, have been suddenly and unexpectedly emptied before us, on a motion to postpone a land debate. That State whose microscopic offence in the obscure parish of Colleton, is to be hung in equipose, with the organized treason, and deep damnation, of the Hartford Convention: That State, whose present dislike to a Tariff which is tearing out her vitals, is to be made the means of exciting the West against the whole South: That State, whose dislike to the tariff laws, is to be made the pretext for setting up a despotic authority in the Supreme Court: That State, which, in the old Congress in 1785, voted for the reduction of the price of Public Lands, to about one half of the present minimum; which, in 1786 redeemed, after it was lost, and carried by its single vote, the first measure that ever was adopted for the protection of Kentucky, that of the two companies sent to the Falls of Ohio: That State, which in the period of the late war, sent us a Lowndes, a Cheves, and a Calhoun, to fight the battles of the West in the Capitol, and to slay the Goliaths of the North: That State which, at this day, has sent to this chamber, the Senator (Genl. Hayne,) whose liberal and enlightened speech on the subject of the Public Lands, has been seized upon, and made the pretext, for that premeditated aggression upon South Carolina, and the whole South, which we have seen met with a promptitude, energy, gallantry, and effect, that has forced the assailant to cry out, an hundred times, that he was still alive, though we all could see that he was most cruelly pounded.

Memory, Mr. President, is the lowest faculty of the human mind—the irrational animals possess it in common with man—the poor beasts of the field have memory. They can recollect the hand that feeds, and the foot that kicks them; and the instinct of self preservation, tells them to follow one, and to avoid the other. Without any knowledge of Greek or Latin, these mute, irrational creatures "fear the Greek offering presents;" they shun the food, offered by the hand that has been lifted to take their life. This is their instinct; and shall man, the possessor of so many noble faculties, with all the benefits of learning and experience, have less memory, less gratitude, less sensibility to danger, than these poor beasts? And shall he stand less upon his guard, when the hand, that smote, is stretched out to entice? shall man, bearing the image of his Creator, sink thus low? shall the generous son of the west fall below his own dumb and reasonless cattle, in all the attributes of memory, gratitude, and sense of danger? shall his *"Timeo Danaos"* have been taught to him in vain? shall he forget the things which he saw, and part of which he was—the events of the late war—the memorable scenes of fifteen years ago? The events of former times, of forty years ago, may be unknown to those who are born since. The attempt to surrender the navigation of the Mississippi; to prevent the settlement of the West; the refusal to protect the early settlers of Kentucky and Tennessee, or to procure for them a cession of Indian lands; all these trials, in which the South was the saviour of the West, may be unknown to the young generation, that has come forward since; and with respect to these events, being uninformed, they may be unmindful and ungrateful. They did not see them; and, like the second generation of the Israelites, in the Land of Promise, who knew not the wonders which God had done for their forefathers in Egypt, they may plead ignorance, and go astray after strange gods—after the Baals and the Astaroths of the Heathen; but not so of the events of the last war. These they saw! the aid of the South they felt! the deeds of a party in the north-east, they felt also! Memory will do its office for both; and base and recreant is the son of the West, that can ever turn his back upon the friends that saved, to go into the arms of the enemy, that mocked and scorned him in that season of dire calamity.

I proceed to a different theme. Among the novelties of this debate, Mr. President, is that part of the speech of the Senator from Massachusetts which dwells, with such elaboration of argument and ornament, upon the love and blessings of Union, the hatred and horror of disunion. It was a part of the Senator's speech which brought into full play, the favorite, Ciceronian figure, of amplification. It was up to the rule in that particular. But, it seemed to me, that there was another rule, and a higher, and a precedent one, which it violated. It was the rule of *Propriety;* that rule which requires the fitness of things to be considered; which requires the time, the place, the subject, and the audience, to be considered; and condemns the delivery of the argument, and all its flowers, if it fails in congrument to these particulars. I thought the essay upon union, and disunion, had so failed. It came to us when we were not prepared for it, when there was nothing in the Senate, nor in the country, to grace its introduction; nothing to give or to receive, effect to, or from, the impassioned scene that we witnessed. It may be, it was the prophetic cry of the distracted daughter of Priam, breaking into the Council, and alarming its tranquil members with vaticinations of the fall of Troy: But to me, it all sounded like the sudden proclamation for an earthquake, when the sun, the earth, the air, announced no such prodigy; when all the elements of Nature were at rest, and sweet repose pervading the world. There was a time, Mr. President, and you, and I, and all of us, did see it, when such a speech would have found, in its delivery, every attribute of a just and rigorous *Propriety!* It was at the time when the Five-striped-banner was waving over the land of the North! when the Hartford Convention was in session! when the language in the Capitol was, "Peaceably if we can, forcibly, if we must!" when the cry, out of doors, was, "the Potomac the boundary; the negro States by themselves! The Alleganies the boundary, the western savages by themselves! The Mississippi the boundary, let Missouri be governed by a Prefect, or given up as a haunt for wild beasts!" That time was the fit occasion for this speech: and if it had been delivered then, either in the Hall of the House of Representatives, or in the Den of the Convention, or in the high way, among the bearers and followers of the Five-striped-banner, what effects must it not have produced? What terror and consternation among the plotters of disunion! But, here, in this loyal and quiet assemblage, in this season of general tranquillity and universal allegiance, the whole performance has lost its effect for want of affinity, connexion, or relation, to any subject depending, or sentiment expressed in the Senate; for want of any application, or reference, to any event impending in the country.

I now take leave, Mr. President, of this part of my subject, with one expression of unmixed satisfaction, at a part, a very small part, of the speech of the Senator from Massachusetts; it is the part in which he disclaimed, in reply to an inquiry from you, sir, the imputation of a change of policy on the Tariff and Internal Improvement questions. Before that disclaimer was heard, a thousand voices would have sworn to the imputation; since, no one will swear it. And the reason given for not referring to you, for not speaking *at* you, was decent and becoming. You have no right of reply, and manhood disdains to attack you. This I comprehend to have been the answer, and the reason, so promptly given by the Senator from Massachusetts, in reply to your inquiry. I am pleased at it. It gives me an opportunity of saying there was something in that speech which commands my commendation, and, at the same time, relieves me from the duty of stating to the Senate a reason why the presiding officer, being Vice President of the United States, should not be struck at from this floor. He cannot reply!—and that disability is his shield in the eyes of all honorable men.

FEBRUARY 2, 1830.—*Fourth Day.*

I touched incidentally, Mr. President, towards the conclusion of my speech of yesterday, on the large—I think I may say despotic—power, claimed by the Senator from Massachusetts [Mr. WEBSTER] for the Federal Supreme Court, over the independent States, whose voluntary union has established this Confederacy. I touched incidentally upon it, and now recur to it for the purpose of making a single remark, and presenting a single illustration of the consequences of that doctrine. That Court is called Supreme; but this character of supremacy, which the Federal Constitution bestows upon it, has reference to inferior courts—the District and Circuit Courts—and not to the States of this Union. A power to decide on the Federal Constitutionality of State laws, *and to bind the State by the decision, in the manner asserted by the Senator from Massachusetts,* is a power to govern the States. It is power over the *sovereignty* of the States; and that power includes, in its practical effects, authority over every minor act and proceeding of the States. The range of Federal authority was large under the words of the Constitution; it is becoming unlimited under the assumption of implied powers. The room for conflict between Federal, and State laws, was sufficiently ample, in cultivating the clear and open field of the expressed powers; but, when the exploration of the wilderness of implications is to be added to it, the recurrence of these conflicts becomes incessant and universal, covering all time, and meeting at every point of State or Federal policy. The annihilation of the States, under a doctrine which would draw all these conflicts to the Federal Judiciary, and make its decisions binding upon the States, and subjected to the penalties of treason all who resisted the execution of these decrees, would produce that consequence. It would annihilate the States! It would reduce them to the abject condition of provinces of the FEDERAL EMPIRE! It would enable the dominant party in Congress, at any moment, to execute the most frightful designs. Let us suppose a case—one by no means improbable—on the contrary, almost absolutely certain, in the event of the success of certain measures, now on foot: The late Mr. King, of New York, when a member of the American Senate, declared upon this floor, that slavery in these

United States, in point of law and right, did not exist, and could not exist, under the nature of our free form of Government; and that the Supreme Court of the United States would so declare it. This declaration was made about ten years ago, in the crisis, and highest paroxysm, of the Missouri agitation. Since then we have seen this declaration repeated and enforced, in every variety of form and shape, by an organized party in all the non-slaveholding States. Since then, we have seen the principles of the same declaration developed in legislative proceedings in the shape of committee reports and public debate, in the halls of Congress. Since then we have had the *D'Auterive* case, and seen a petition presented from the Chair of the House of Representatives, Mr. JOHN W. TAYLOR being Speaker, in which the *total destruction* of all the States that would not abandon slavery was expressly represented as a *sublime* act. With these facts before us, and myriads of others, which I cannot repeat, but which are seen by all, the probability of a federal legislative act against slavery, rises in the scale, and assumes the character of moral certainty, in the event of the success of certain designs, now on foot. So much for what may happen in Congress. Now for the Judiciary. I have just referred to the declaration of an Ex-Senator [Mr. KING of New York] of all others the best acquainted with the *arcana* of his party—who was to that party for a full quarter of a century, the law and the prophets—for a bold assertion of what the Supreme Court would do in a question of existence, or non-existence of slavery in the United States. He openly asserted that the Supreme Court would declare that no such thing could exist! It is not to be presumed that that aged, experienced, informed and responsible Senator would have hazarded an assertion of such dire and dreadful import—an assertion so delicately affecting the Judges then on the Bench of that Court—a majority of them his personal and political friends—and looking to such disastrous consequences to the Union, without probable, if not certain grounds, for the basis of his assertion. That he had such grounds, so far at least as one of the Judges was concerned, seems to be incontestable. A charge delivered to a Grand Jury by Mr. Justice Story, at Portsmouth, New Hampshire, in the month of May, 1820—(for the date is material—it tallies, in point of time, with the assertion in the Senate, and was classed for Review, as an article of politics, in the North American Review, with the substance of Mr. King's two speeches, on the floor of the Senate, which were the signal for the Missouri strife—a signal as well understood, and as implicitly obeyed, as the signal for battle in the Roman Camp, when the Red Mantle of the Consul was hung on the outside of the tent:) this charge, to a

Grand Jury, establishes the fact of authority for the assertion of Mr. King, so far at least, as one of the Judges is concerned. But as every man should be judged by his own words, and not upon the recital of another, let the charge itself be read; let the Judge announce his own sentiments, in his own language.

The Charge—Extract.

"The existence of slavery under any shape is so repugnant to the natural rights of man and the dictates of justice, that it seems difficult to find for it any adequate justification. It undoubtedly had its origin in times of barbarism, and was the ordinary lot of those who were conquered in war. It was supposed that the conqueror had a right to take the life of his captive, and by consequence might well bind him to perpetual servitude. But the position itself on which this supposed right is founded is not true. No man has a right to kill his enemy, except in cases of absolute necessity; and this absolute necessity ceases to exist, even in the estimation of the conqueror himself, when he has spared the life of his prisoner. And even if in such cases it were possible to contend for the right of slavery, as to the prisoner himself, it is impossible that it can justly extend to his *innocent* offspring through the whole line of descent. I forbear, however, to touch on this *delicate* topic, not because it is not worthy of the most deliberate attention of all of us: but it does not *properly fall* in my province on the present occasion."

*　*　*　*　*　*　*　*　*

"And, gentlemen, how can we justify ourselves, or apologise, for an *indifference* to this subject? Our constitutions of government have declared that all *men* are born free and *equal,* and have certain unalienable rights, among which are the right of enjoying their lives, *liberty,* and property, and seeking and obtaining their own safety and happiness. May not the miserable African ask, 'Am I not a man and a brother?' We boast of our noble strength against the encroachments of tyranny, but do we forget that it assumed the mildest form in which authority ever assailed the rights; and yet there are men amongst us who think it no wrong to condemn the shivering negro to perpetual slavery."

*　*　*　*　*　*　*　*　*

"We believe in the *Christian* religion. It commands us to have good will to all men; to love our neighbors as ourselves, and to do unto all men as we would they should do unto us. It declares our accountability to the

Supreme God for all our actions, and holds out to us a state of future rewards and punishments, as the sanction by which our conduct is to be regarded. And yet there are men calling themselves Christians, who degrade the negro by ignorance to a level with the brutes, and deprive him of all the consolations of religion. He alone, of all the rational creation, they seem to think is to be at once accountable for his actions, and yet his actions are not to be at his own disposal; but his mind, his body, and his feelings are to be sold to perpetual bondage."

We will take the case of slavery then as the probable, and in the event of the success of certain designs now on foot, as the certain one, on which the new doctrine of judicial supremacy over the States, may be tried. The case of the Georgia Cherokees is a more proximate, and may be a precedent one; but, as no intimation of the possible decision of the court in that case, has been given, I shall pretermit it, and limit myself to the slavery case, in which the declaration of Mr. King, and the charge of one of the Judges leaves me at liberty to enter, without guilt of intrusion, into that *sanctum sanctorum* of the Judiciary—the privy chamber of the Judges—the door of which has been flung wide open. Let us suppose then that a law of Congress passes, declaring that slavery does not exist in the United States—that the States South of the Potomac and Ohio, with Missouri from the West of the Mississippi, deny the constitutionality of the law—that the Supreme Court takes cognizance of the denial—commands the refractory States to appear at its Bar—decides in favor of the law of Congress, and puts forth the decree which, according to the new doctrine, it is TREASON to resist! What next? Either, acquiescence or resistance, on the part of the slave States. Acquiescence involves, on the part of the States towards this Court, a practical exemplification of the old slavish doctrines of passive obedience and non-resistance which the Sacheverells of Queen Anne's time preached and promulgated in favor of the King against the subject; with all the mischief, superadded, of turning loose two millions of slaves here, as the French national convention and their agents, Santhonax and La Croix, had turned loose the slaves of the West India Islands. Resistance incurs all the guilt of treason and rebellion; draws down upon the devoted States the troops and fanatics of the Federal Government, arms all the negroes according to the principle declared in D'Auterive's case, and calls in, by way of attending to the women and children, the knife and the hatchet of those Georgia Cherokees which it is now the organized policy of a political party, to retain, and maintain, in the bosom of the SOUTH.

We have read, and heard, much, Mr. President, of late years of the madness and violence of the people—the tyranny and oppression of military leaders: but we have heard nothing of judicial tyranny, judicial oppression, and judicial subserviency, to the will, and ambition, of the King or President of a country. Nothing has been said on this branch of the subject, and, yet, nothing that I have ever seen, or read of, has sunk so deep upon my mind as the history of judicial tyranny, exemplified in the submission of the Judges to the will of those who made them. My very early reading led me to the contemplation of the most impressive scenes of this character, which the history of any country affords: I speak of the British State Trials, which I read at seven or eight years old under the direction of a mother, then a very young, now an aged widow. It was *her* wish to form her children to a love of Liberty, and a hatred of Tyranny, and, with her, I had wept over the fate of Raleigh, and Russell, and Sydney, and I will add, the Lady Alice Lyle, before I could realize the conception that they belonged to a different country, and a different age, from my own. I drank deep at that fountain! I drew up repeated, copious and overflowing draughts of grief and sorrow, for suffering victims—of resentment, fear, and terror, for their cruel oppressors. Nothing which I have read in history since, not even the massacres of Marius and Sylla, nor the slaughters of the French Revolution, have sunk so deep upon my mind as the scenes which the British State Trials disclosed to me; the view of the illustrious of the land seized upon the hint of the King, carried to the dungeon, from the dungeon to the court, from the court to the scaffold; there, the body half-hung, cut down half-alive, the belly ript open, and the bowels torn out, the limbs divided and stuck over gates, the property confiscated to the King, the blood of the family attainted, and widows and orphans turned out to scorn and want. Nothing which I have ever read equals the deep impression of these scenes; partly because they came upon my infant mind, more, because it was a cold-blooded business, a heartless tyranny, in which the judges acted for the King, without passions of their own, and are stript of all the extenuations which contending parties claim for their excesses when either gets the upper hand in the crisis of great struggles. True, these scenes of judicial tyranny and oppression existed long since; but where is the modern instance of judicial opposition to the will of the King, or President, of the country for the time being? Are there five instances in five centuries? Are there four? three? two? one? No, not one! The nearest approach to such opposition, in the history of the British Judiciary, is the famous case of the ship money, when four Judges, out of twelve, ventured an opinion against the Crown. In our own country no opposition from the Bench has gone that length. The odious, and notorious, sedition law was enforced throughout the land by Federal Judges. Not one declared against it; and if a civil war, in that disastrous period between the Presidents Washington and Jefferson, had depended upon the judicial enforcement of that act, we should have had civil war. We have heard much, Mr. President, of the independence of the Judges, but since, about eight hundred years ago, when the old King Alfred hung four and forty of them in one year, for false judgments, there have been but few manifestations of judicial independence in reference to the power from which they derive their appointment. Since that time, the judges and the appointing power have usually thought alike in all the cardinal questions which affect that power. This may be accounted for without drawing an inference to the dishonor of the Judge, and as it will answer my purpose just as well to place the account upon that foot, I will cheerfully do it. I will say, then, that Kings and Presidents, having the nomination of judges, forever have chosen, and upon all the principles of human action with which I am acquainted, forever will chuse these high judicial officers from the class of men whose political creed corresponds with their own. This is enough for me; it is enough for the illustration of the subject which we have in hand. Supposing, then, a certain design, now on foot, to succeed; supposing, some four or eight years hence, a new creation of judges to come forth, either under a new law for the extension of the Judiciary, or to fill up vacancies; supposing the doctrine to be established which is now announced by the Senator from Massachusetts, [Mr. WEBSTER,] and that Court has to pass upon a slavery law, or an Indian law, which the States hold to be void, and the Court decree it to be binding, where is then the legitimate conclusion of the gentleman's doctrine? Passive obedience and non-resistance to the Supreme Court, and the President that made it, or civil war, with Indians and Negroes for the allies of the Federal Government. Sir, I do not argue this point of the debate; I have a task before me—the rectification of the assertions of the Senator from Massachusetts—which I mean to execute. I have turned aside from that task to make a remark upon the doctrine, and to illustrate it by an example, which would make the Supreme Federal Court despotic over the States. I return to my task, with repeating the words of him, [Mr. Randolph,] whose words will be the rallying cry of liberty and patriotism in ages yet to come: I repeat then, but without the magical effect of that celestial infusion which God vouchsafed to him,—

divine elocution—the words which, three months ago, electrified the Virginia Convention: "*The chapter of Kings, in the Holy Bible, follows next after the chapter of Judges.*"

I will now, Mr. President, take up the instances, I belive there are but few of them, and that I can make short work of them, quoted by the Senator from Massachusetts (Mr. W.) in support of his assertion, that all the measures favorable to the West, have been carried by Northern votes in opposition to Southern ones. He asserted this to be the case from the beginning to the ending, from the first to the last, of the chapter of this Government; but he did not go back to the beginning of the chapter, nor even to the middle of it, nor in fact, further than some ten leaves of it. He got back to the year 1820,—just to the edge of the Missouri question, but not a word of that,—and began with the reduction of the price of Public Land from $2, to $1.25 per acre. That he proclaims as a Western measure, and dwells upon it, that New England gave thirty-three votes in favor of that reduction, and the four Southern States but thirty-two! Verily, this is carrying the measure in opposition to the votes of the South, in a new and unprecedented sense of the word. But was it a western measure? The history of the day tells us no; that the Western members were generally against it, because it combined a change of terms from the credit, to the ready money system, with the reduction. This made it unacceptable to the Western members, and they voted against it almost in a body. The leading men of the West opposed it; Mr. Clay in a speech, with great earnestness. Mr. Trimble, and Mr. Metcalfe, of Kentucky, voted against it; both the Kentucky Senators did the same; both the present Senators from Indiana; the Representative from Illinois, and many others. The opposition, though not universal, was general from the West; and no member lost the favor of his constituents on that account. The Senator's first instance, then, of New England favor to the West, happens to be badly selected. It fails at both points of the argument; at the alleged victory over the South, in behalf of the West, and at the essential feature of favor to the West itself. This is a pity. It knocks one leg off of the stool which had but two legs to it from the beginning. The Senator had but two instances, of New England favor to the West, prior to the cooing and billing of the Presidential Election in the House of Representatives in 1825. One of these is gone; now for the next. This next one, sole survivor of a stinted race, is the extension of credit to the land debtors in the year 1821. This I admit to be a measure of cherished importance to the West. Let us see how the rival parties divided upon it.

The Senator from Massachusetts stated the division loosely, and without precision as to the numbers. He said that New England, with 40 members in the House of Representatives, gave more affirmative votes than the four Southern States with their 52 members. How many more he did not say; and that want of precision, induced me to cause the matter to be looked into, and the result appears to be that in the list of yeas, New England, on that occasion, beat the South two votes, and in the list of nays, she beat three votes; that is to say, she gave two votes more than the South did for the passage of the bill, and three votes more than the South against the passage of it! This leaves a majority of one in favor of the South, and so, off goes the other leg of the two legged stool; and the Senator from Massachusetts, according to my arithmetic, is flat upon the ground.

I think, Mr. President, it was in the triumph of his soul at having two instances, and those the ones I have dissected, in which New England gave favorable votes to the West, prior to the honey-moon of the Presidential election of 1825, that the Senator from Massachusetts, broke out into his *"time* WHEN,"—*"manner* HOW," and *"cause* WHY,"—which seemed to have been received as attic wit "by some quantity of barren spectators," that chanced to be then present. I think it was in reference to these two instances that the Senator from Massachusetts made his address to the Senator from S. C. (Genl. HAYNE) and still ringing the changes upon the *when,* the *how,* and the *why,* said to the Senator from S. C. that if this did not satisfy him of the disinterested affection of the North East, to the West, prior to the scenes of soft dalliance, which accompanied the Presidential election of 1825, that he did not know *how* he ever would be satisfied. Good, sir, let us close a bargain,—pardon the phrase,—on that word. The Senator from Massachusetts knows of nothing to prove affection in the North East to the West, prior to the sweet conjunction and full consummation of 1825, except these two instances. They seemed to be but a poor dependence,—a small plaster for a large sore,—when he brought them forward: What are they now? Reduced to nothing,—literally nothing,—worse than nothing,—an admitted acknowledgment that the case wanted proof, and that none can possibly be found!

But the tariff! the tariff! That is a blessing, at least, which the West must admit it received from the Northeast! Not the tariff of 1824; for against that, it is avowed by the Senator from Massachusetts that the New England delegation voted in solid column. It is the tariff of 1828 to which he alludes, and for the blessings of which to the West, he now claims its gratitude to the Northeast. Upon this claim I have two answers to make: first, that this instance of affection to the West, is posterior to the election of 1825, and falls under the qualification of the entire system of changes which followed, consequentially, upon the approximation, and conjunction, of the planets which produced that event. Secondly, that almost the only item in that tariff of any real value to the West—the increased duty on hemp—was struck at from the Northeast, and defended from the South. The Senator from Massachusetts, to whom I am now replying, himself moved to expunge the clause which proposed to grant us that increase of duty. True, he proposed to substitute a nominal and illusory bounty on the insignificant quantity of hemp used on the ships of war of the United States, being the one twentieth part of what is used on the merchant vessels, and undertook to make us believe that the one twentieth part of a thing was more than the whole. He could not make us believe it. We refused his bounty; we voted 18 against him, being every Senator from the West; New England voted ten out of twelve against us; the South voted eight out of eight for us; and the increased duty on hemp was saved; saved by that South, in opposition to that New England, which the Senator from Massachusetts has so often declared to be the friend of the West, and to have carried every measure favorable to it in opposition to the votes of the South!

Internal improvement was the last resort of the Senator's ingenuity, for showing the affection of the Northeast to the West. It was on this point that his appeal to the West, and calls for an answer, were particularly addressed. The West will answer; and, in the first place will show the amount, in value, in money, of the favors thus rendered, in order to ascertain the quantity of gratitude due, and demandable, for it. On this point we have authentic data to go upon. A resolution of the Senate, of which I was myself the mover, addressed to the ex-administration in the last year of its existence, called upon the then President to exhibit to the Congress a full statement of all the money expended by the Federal Government, from 1789 to 1828, in each of the States, upon works of internal improvement. The report was made, authenticated by the signatures of the President, Mr. Adams, the Secretary of the Treasury, Mr. Rush, and several heads of bureaus. It is No. 69, of the Senate Documents for the session 1828–1829, and at page 13 of the Document, the table of recapitulation is found, which shows the amount expended in each State. Let us read some items from it.

THE TABLE.

1. Kentucky $90,000
2. Tennessee 4,200
3. Indiana .... nothing.
4. Illinois 8,000
5. Mississippi 23,000
6. Missouri ...... nothing.
7. Louisiana ..... do.

A most beggarly account, Mr. President! About $125,000 in seven Western States, up to the end of that Administration, which assumed to be the exclusive champion of internal improvement. A small sum truly, for the young and blooming West to take, for the surrender of all her charms, to the ancient and iron-hearted enemy of her name. Ohio, it is not to be dissembled, has received something more; but that depends upon another principle, the principle of governing the West through her.

But the Cumberland road; that great road, the construction of which, as far as the Ohio river, cost near two millions of dollars. Sir, the man must have a poor conception of the West, who considers the road to Wheeling as a Western object, to be charged upon the funds and the gratitude of the West. To the Eastern parts of Ohio it may be serviceable; but to all beyond that State, it is little known except by name. A thousand Eastern people travel it for one farmer or mechanic of Indiana, Illinois, Missouri, Kentucky, or Tennessee. It is, in reality, more an Eastern than a Western measure, built in good part with Western money, taken from the Western States, as I humbly apprehend, in violation of their compacts with the Federal Government. These compacts stipulate that two per cent. of the net proceeds of the sales of the public lands shall be laid out by Congress in making roads, or canals "*to*" the States, not *towards* them. The laws for building the Cumberland road have seized upon all this fund, already amounting in the four Northwestern States to $326,000, and applied it all to the Cumberland road. The same laws contain a curious stipulation, not to be found in any other law for making a road, which stipulates for the future reimbursement, out of the two per cent. fund, of all the money expended upon it. This truly is a new way of conferring a favor, and establishing a debt of gratitude! But when did the New England votes in favor of this road, and other Western objects, commence? How do they compare before, and since the Presidential election of 1825? Let the journals tell. Let confronting columns display the contrast of New England votes, upon this point, before and after that election.

THE CONTRAST.

BEFORE '25.	SINCE '25.
1. April 8th, 1816. To postpone bill to construct roads and canals—yeas, 7 out of 10.	1. February 24th, 1825. Motion to postpone appropriation for Cumberland road—yeas, 5 out of 12.
2. March 6th, 1816. Bill to relieve settlers on public lands by allowing them to enter the lands, &c.—nays, 8 out of 10.	2. March 1st, 1826. Bill to repair Cumberland road.—nays, 2 out of 12.
3. January 29th, 1817. Bill to admit Mississippi as a State into the Union—nays, 7 out of 10.	3. January 24th, 1827. Bill extending Cumberland road—nays, 5 out of 12.
4. May 19th, 1824. Bill to improve the navigation of the Ohio river—nays, 7 out of 12.	4. March 28th, 1828. Bill to give land to Kenyon College—3 out of 12.
5. April 24th, 1824. Bill for surveys of roads, &c.—nays, 9 out of 12.	5. December, 1828. Bill for making compensation for Indian depredations in Missouri—yeas, 4 out of 12.

Yes, Mr. President, the Presidential election of 1825 was followed by a system of changes. There seems to have been a surrender and sacrifice of principles, on that occasion, somewhat analogous to the surrender, and murder, of friends which followed the conjunction of Anthony, Lepidus and Cesar. It would seem that some guardian genius had whispered, the "Tariff, Internal Improvement, and Slavery, are the questions to govern this Union: Now let us all agree, and throw up old scruples, and work together upon Slavery, Tariff, and Internal Improvement." They did throw up! Old scruples flew off like old garments. Leading politicians came "to the right about:" the rank and file followed; and the consequence was the confronting votes, and conduct, which five years of explanations and justifications leave at the exact point at which they began.

The canal across the Alleghanies is mentioned. I utterly disclaim and repudiate that canal as a Western object. And here, Mr. President, I take up a position which I shall fortify and establish on some future occasion. It is this: That every canal, and every road, tending to draw the commerce of the Western States across the Alleghany mountains, is an injury to the people of the West. My idea is this: That the great and bulky productions of the West will follow the course of the waters, and float down the rivers to New Orleans; that our export trade must, and will, go there; that this city cannot buy all, and sell nothing; that she must have the benefit of the import trade with us; that the people of the West must buy from *her* as well as she from them; that the system of exchange and barter must take effect there; that if it does not, and the West continues to sell its world of productions to New Orleans for ready money, and carries off that money to be laid out in the purchase of goods in Atlantic cities, the people of the West are themselves ruined; for New Orleans cannot stand such a course of business; she will fail in supplying the world of money which the world of produce requires; and the consequence will be the downfall of prices in every article. This is somewhat the case now. New Orleans is called an uncertain market; her prices for beef, pork, flour, bacon, whiskey, tobacco, hemp, cotton, and an hundred other articles, are compared with the prices of like articles in the Atlantic cities, and found to be less; and then she is railed against as a bad market; as if these low prices was not the natural and inevitable effect of selling every thing, and buying nothing, there. As to the idea of sending the products of the West across the Alleganies, it is the conception of insanity itself! No rail roads or canals will ever carry them, not even if they do it gratis! One trans-shipment, and there would have to be several, would exceed the expense of transportation to New Orleans, to say nothing of the up-stream work of getting to the canal, or rail way; itself far exceeding the whole expense, trouble, and delay of getting to New Orleans. Besides, such an unnatural reversal of the course of trade would be injurious to the Western cities—to Cincinnati, Louisville, St. Louis, and to many others. It would be injurious and fatal to our inland navigation—the steamboats of the West. They are our ships; their tonnage is already great, say 300,000 tons; the building of them gives employment to many valuable trades, and creates a demand for many articles which the country produces. To say nothing of their obvious and incredible utility in the transportation of persons, produce, and merchandize, each steam boat has itself become a market, a moving market, that comes to the door of every house on the rivers, taking off all its surplus fowls, and vegetables; all its surplus wood; the expenditure for this single object, wood, in the past year, in two calculations made for me, ranged between nine hundred thousand, and one million of dollars. No, sir, the West is not going to give up their steam boats,—their ships, not of the desert, but of noble rivers. They are not going to abandon the Mississippi, *mare nostrum,*—our sea,—for

the comfort of scaling the Alleghany mountains with hogsheads of tobacco, barrels of whiskey, pork, and flour, bales of hemp, and coops of
chickens and turkeys, on their backs! We are not going to impoverish New
Orleans, by selling our produce to her, and buying our merchandize elsewhere, and in that impoverishment committing suicide upon ourselves.
Nor am I going to pursue this subject, and explore it in all its important
bearings at this time; I have that task to perform; but it will be reserved for
another occasion.

I resume the subject of Internal Improvement. I say, and I say it with
the proof in hand, that this whole business has been a fraud upon the
West. Look at its promise and performance. Its promise was, to equalize
the expenditure of public money, and to counterbalance, upon roads and
canals in the West, the enormous appropriations for fortifications, navy
yards, light houses, and ships, on the Atlantic board; its performance has
been, to increase the inequality of the expenditure; to fix nearly the whole
business of Internal Improvement on the east of the Alleghany mountains; to add this item, in fact, to all the other items of expenditure in the
East! Such was the promise; such has been the performance. Facts attest
it; and let the facts speak for themselves.

THE FACTS.

1. Cumberland road to Wheeling.	$2,000,000
2. Delaware Breakwater, (required)	2,500,000
3. Canal over the Allegany, (subscribed)	1,000,000
4. Baltimore Rail Road, (demanded)	1,000,000
5. Delaware and Chesapeake Canal,	450,000
6. Nantucket harbor, (demanded)	900,000

Here we go by the million, Mr. President, while the West, to whom all
the benefits of this system were promised, obtains with difficulty, and
somewhat as a beggar would get a penny, a few miserable thousands. But,
sir, it is not only in the great way, but in the small way also, that the West
has been made the dupe of this delusive policy. She has lost not only by the
gross, but by retail. Look at the facts again. See what her partner in this
work of Internal Improvement—the Northeast—which commenced business with her in 1825, has since received, in the small way, and upon items
that the West never heard of, under this head of Internal Improvement.

THE FACTS AGAIN.

1.	Preservation of Little Gull Island,	$30,000
2.	Preservation of Smutty Nose Island	15,000
3.	Preservation of Plymouth beach,	49,000
4.	Preservation of Islands in Boston harbor,	63,000
5.	Improvement of the Hyannis harbor,	10,000
6.	Improvement of Squam and Gloucester,	6,000
7.	Preservation of Deer Island,	87,000
8.	Removing a Sand bar in Merrimac river,	32,000
9.	Building a pier at Stonington,	20,000
10.	Making a road to Mars' hill,	57,000

Near $400,000, Mr. President, actually paid out in this small way, and upon these small items, in New England, while seven States in the West, up to the last day of the Coalition administration, had had expended within their limits, for all objects, great and small—Indian roads, and the light-house at Natchez included—but $125,000. And this, sir, is the New England help for which the Senator from Mass. (Mr. W.) stood up here, challenging the gratitude of the West! But this is not all; the future is still to come; a goodly prospect is ahead; and let us take a view of it. The late administration, in one of its communications to Congress, gave in a list of projects selected for future execution. I will recite a few of them.

THE PROJECTS.

1.	Improvement	at Saugatuck.
2.	do.	at Amounisuck.
3.	do.	at Pasumsic.
4.	do.	at Winnispisseogee.
5.	do.	at Piscataqua.
6.	do.	at the Ticonic Falls.
7.	do.	at Lake Memphramagog.
8.	do.	at Conneaut creek.
9.	do.	at Holmes' hole.
10.	do.	at Lovejoy's narrows.
11.	do.	at Steele's ledge.
12.	do.	at Cowhegan.
13.	do.	at Androscoggin.
14.	do.	at Cobbiesconte.
15.	do.	at Ponceaupechaux, *alias,* Soapy-Joe.

Such, Mr. President, are a sample of the projects held in abeyance by the late administration, and to be executed in future. They were selected as *national* objects!—national!—and not a man in the two Americas, outside of the *nation* of New-England, who can take up the list, and tell where they are, without a prompter or a gazetteer. And now, sir, what are the results of this partnership, of five years standing, between the West and North-East, in the business of internal improvement?—First Nothing, or next to nothing, for Kentucky, Tennessee, Alabama, Mississippi, Louisiana, Illinois, Indiana, and Missouri.—Secondly: Eight or nine millions of dollars for large objects, east of the Allegany mountains.—Thirdly: Near $400,000 for small neighborhood objects, in New-England.—Fourthly: A selection of objects in the north east, for future national improvement, the very names of which are unknown in the neighboring States. These are the results. Let any one weigh and consider them, and say whether this business of internal improvement, has not been a delusion upon the West; if our partners in the East have not kept the loaf under their own arm, and cut off two or three huge huncks for themselves for every thin and narrow slice which they threw to us? What is worse, that is to say, what is truly mortifying to our pride, is, that we are not allowed to chuse for ourselves. It is in vain that we contend, that western objects should be somewhere in the valley of the Mississippi; our partners, assuming the office of guardians, tell us it is a mistake; that every true, genuine, native-born, full-blooded western improvement, must begin upon the Atlantic coast, and if one end of it points towards the setting sun, that is enough. It is now six years, Mr. President, since I made a movement upon an object actually western; one which, being completed, will produce more good for less money, according to my belief, than any other of which the wide extent of this confederacy is susceptible. It is the series of short canals, sir, amounting in the aggregate to twenty-seven miles, which would unite New-Orleans and Georgia—which would connect, by an inland steam-boat navigation, safe from storms, pirates, privateers, and enemies fleets, the Chatahooche and the Mississippi, the bays of Mobile, Pensacola, and St. Marks; and enable the provisions of the western country to go where they are exceedingly wanted, to the cotton plantations on the rivers Amite, the Pearl, and Pascagoula, in the State of Mississippi; the Tombigbee and Alabama rivers, in the State of Alabama; the Conecuh and Escambia, in West Florida; the Chatahoochee, for five hundred miles up it, on the dividing line of Georgia and Alabama. The Senator from Louisiana, who sits on my left, (Mr. JOHNSTON,) moved the bill that obtained the appropriation for surveying this route, four years ago; the Senator from the same State, who sits on my right, (Mr. LIVINGSTON) has sent a resolution to the Road and Canal Committee, to have the work began; and the fate of this undertaking may illustrate the extent to which the voice of the West can go, in selecting objects of improvement within its own limits, and for itself.

Such are the results of the Western attempts to equalize expenditures, to improve their roads and enrich themselves upon public money by means of the Internal Improvement power exercised by the Federal Government. The South, we are told, and told truly, has voted no part of these fine allowances to the West. And thence it is argued, and argued incorrectly, that she is an enemy to the West. Sir, the brief answer to that charge of enmity, is, that she has voted nothing on this account for herself; she has voted for us as she did for herself; the argument should be, that she loved us as well as she did herself; and this is all that conscionable people can require. But another view remains to be taken of this affection, which is to be tried by the money standard. It is this: That, if the South has voted us no public money for roads and canals, they have paid the West a great deal of their own private money for its surplus productions. The South takes the provisions of the West, its horses and mules besides, and many other items. The States south of the Potomac, south of the Tennessee river, and upon the lower Mississippi, is the gold and silver region of the West. Leave out the supplies which come from this quarter, and the stream that Missouri is drawing from Mexico, also to the South of us, and all the gold and silver that is derived from other places,—from any places north of Mason's and Dixon's line—would not suffice to pay the postage of our letters, and the ferriage of our rivers. This Southern trade is the true and valuable trade of the West; the trade which they cannot do without; and with these States it is proposed that we shall have a falling out, turn our backs upon them, and go into close connexion with a political *caste* in a quarter of the Union from which the West never did, and never can, find a cash market for her surplus products. I know that the West, Mr. President, is not credited for much sagacity, and the result of her Internal Improvement partnership, goes to justify the *Beotian* imputation to which we have been subject; but there are some things which do not require much sagacity, nor any book learning, to discover how they lie. Little children, for example, can readily find out on which side their bread is buttered, and the grown men of the West can as quickly discover from which side of Mason and Dixon's line, their gold and silver comes. We hear much about binding the different sections of the Union together; every road and every canal is to be a chain for that purpose. Granted. But why break the chains which we have already? Commerce is the strongest of all chains. It is the chain of interest. It binds together the most distant nations; aliens, in color, language, religion and laws. It unites the antipodes,—men whose feet are opposite, whose countries are separated by the entire diameter of the solid globe. We have a chain of this kind with the South, and, wo to the politician that shall attempt to cut it, or break it.

The late Presidential election was an affair of some interest to the West. The undivided front of the western electoral vote attested the unity, and the intensity, of her wishes on that point. Was that election carried by northern votes in opposition to southern ones? Was the West helped out by the North, in that hard struggle of four years duration? Yes, to the extent of one electoral vote from the republican district of Maine; to the extent of many thousand individual votes; but these came from the democracy, some few exceptions; but nothing from that party which now assumes to be the friend of the West, and so boldly asserts that every western measure has been carried by northern, in opposition to southern votes.

The graduation bill, Mr. President, is a western measure: there is no longer any dispute about that. It came from the West, and is supported by the West. Memorials from eight legislatures have demanded it; seventeen, out of eighteen, western Senators have voted for it. Has the northeast carried that bill in opposition to the South? It has repeatedly been before both Houses—was once on its final passage in this chamber, and wanted four votes, which was only a change of position in two voters, to carry it. Did the northeast, out of her twelve voters present, give us these two? She did not. Did she give us one? No, not one. There was but one from the North of Mason and Dixon's line, and that of an honorable Senator—I do not call him honorable by virtue of a rule—who is no longer a member of this body; I speak of Mr. Ridgely, of Delaware; that little State whose moral and intellectual strength on this floor has often kept her in the first rank of importance. How was it to the South? A brilliant and powerful support from the Senator of Virginia, not yet in his seat, [Mr. Tazewell,] whose name, for that support, is borne with honor upon the legislative page of Missouri and Illinois; a firm support from the two Senators from Georgia, [Messrs. Cobb and Berrien,] since ceased to be members. A motion for reconsideration from the venerable Macon—the friend of me and mine through four generations in a straight line—to reconsider the vote of rejection with a view of passing the main part, the first section, which contained the whole graduation clause. Several other Senators from the South, who then voted against the bill, expressed a determination to examine it further, and intimated the pleasure it would give them to vote for it at another time if found, upon further examination, to be as beneficial as I supposed. Thus stood the South and West upon that greatest and truest of all western measures; and we shall quickly see how they stand again; for the graduation bill is again before the Senate, and next in order after the subject now in hand.

How stand the North and South on another point of incalculable interest to the West; the motion now under discussion—no, not now under discussion—the motion now depending, to stop the surveys, to limit the sales of public lands, and to abolish the offices of the Surveyors General? How stand the parties on that point? Why, as far as we can discover, without the report of yeas and nays, the Northeast, with the exception of the Senator from New Hampshire on my right [Mr. Woodbury] against us; the South unanimous for us. And thus, the very question which has furnished a peg to hang the debate on which has brought out the assertion, that every measure friendly to the West, has been carried by New England votes in opposition to Southern votes, is itself evidence of the contrary, and would have placed that evidence before the West in the most authentic form, if the ingenious Senator from Massachusetts [Mr. Webster] had not evaded that consequence by moving an indefinite postponement, and thereby getting rid of a direct vote on the resolution which has become current under the name of the Senator who introduced it. [Mr. Foot of Connecticut.]

How stand the South and North upon another point, also of overwhelming concern to the West: the scheme for partitioning out the new States of the West among the old ones? Whence comes that scheme? Who supports it? What its real object? The West will be glad to know the *when,* the *why,* and the *how,* of that new and portentous scheme. But, first, what is it? Sir, it is a scheme to keep the new States in leading strings, and to send the proceeds of the sales of the public lands to the States from which the public lands never came. It is a scheme to divide the property of the weak among the strong. It is a scheme which has its root in the principle which partitioned Poland between the Emperors of Russia and Germany, and the King of Prussia. Whence comes it? From the Northeast. How comes it? By an innocent and harmless resolution of inquiry! When comes it? Cotemporaneously with this other resolution of innocent and harmless inquiry into the expediency of limiting the settlement, checking emigration to the West, and delivering up large portions of the new States to the dominion of wild beasts. These two resolutions come together and of them it may be said, *"These two make a pair."* A newspaper in the North East contained a letter written from this place, giving information that the resolution of the Senator from Connecticut, (Mr. FOOT) was brought in to anticipate and forestall the graduation bill. I saw the resolution in that light, Mr. President, before I saw the letter. I had announced it in that character long before I received the letter, and read it to the Senate. This resolution then was to check-mate my graduation bill! It was an offer of battle to the West! I accepted the offer; I am fighting the battle: some are crying out, and hauling off, but I am standing to it, and mean to stand to it. I call upon the adversary to come on and lay on, and I tell him—

"Damned be he that first cries out, ENOUGH."

Fair play and hard play, is the game I am willing to play at. War to the knife, and the knife to the hilt; but let the play be fair. Nothing foul; no blackguardism. This resolution then from the other end of the Capitol, twin brother to the one here, comes from the North East; is resisted by the South, and is ruinous to the West. New Hampshire, Rhode Island, Connecticut, Vermont, New Jersey, and Delaware, were unanimous for it; Massachusetts 9 to 1 for it; South Carolina and Georgia were unanimously against it; Virginia 10 to 1 against it; North Carolina 8 to 4 against it. This scene presents itself to my mind, Mr. President, as a picture with three figures upon it. First, the young West, a victim to be devoured. Secondly, the old North, attempting to devour her. Thirdly, the generous South, ancient defender and saviour of the West, stretching out an arm to save her.

Let these two resolutions pass, and ripen into the measures which their tenor implies to be necessary; and the seal is fixed, for a long period, on the growth and prosperity of the West. Under one of them the sales of the lands will be held back; under the other, every possible inducement will arise to screw up the price of all that is sold. From that moment, the West must bid adieu to all prospect of any liberal change in the policy of the United States in the sale and disposition of the Public Lands; no more favor to the settler; no justice to the States; no sales on fair and equitable terms. Grinding avarice will take its course, and feed full its deep and hungry maw. Laws will be passed to fix the minimum price at the highest rate; agents will be sent to attend the sales, & bid high against the farmer, the settler and the cultivator. Dreadful will be the prices then run up. The agents will act as attorneys for the plaintiffs, in the execution. The money is coming to the States they represent; they can bid what they please. They can bid off the whole country, make it the property of other States, and lease, or rent, small tracts to the inhabitants. The preservation of the timber will become an object of high consideration with these new Lords Proprietors; and hosts of spies, informers, prosecutors, and witnesses, will be sent into the new States, to waylay the inhabitants, and dog the farmers round their fields, to detect, and prosecute, the man who cuts a stick, or lifts a stone, or breaks the soil of these new masters and receivers. While the land is public property, and the proceeds go into the Treasury, like other public money, there is less interest felt in the sales by the individual States; but from the moment that the proceeds of the sales are to be divided out by a rule of proportion which would give nearly all to the populous States, from that moment, it would be viewed as *State property,* and every engine would be set to work to make the lands produce the utmost possible farthing for the individual States. Each member of Congress would calculate, in every question of sale or gift, how much his State, and how much he himself as a unit in that State, was to gain or lose by the operation. And, who are to be the foremost and most insatiable of these new Lords Proprietors? Let the vote, on the reference of the resolution, answer the question; let it tell. They are the States which never gave any land to the Federal Government! Massachusetts and Maine, which retained their thirty thousand square miles of vacant territory, and are now selling it at 25, at 20, at 10, and at 5 cents per acre. Connecticut, which seized upon two millions of acres of the land, which Virginia had ceded to the Federal Government, and held fast to the jurisdiction as well as the soil, until the Congress agreed to give her a deed "to all the right, title, interest and estate of the U. S." to the soil itself. Who are our defenders? They are the States south of the Potomac, which were themselves the great donors of land to the Federal Government. Virginia, the Carolinas, Georgia; these are our defenders! And without their defence, the West would fare now, as she would have fared without it, forty years ago, in the times of the Old Confederation.

I have now, Mr. President, gone through the *"chapter"* of the conduct of the Federal Government, and the relative affection of the NORTH and SOUTH to the West. I commenced without exordium, and shall finish without peroration. On two points more, and only two, I wish to be understood.

First, as to the reason which has induced me to enter, with this minuteness and precision of detail, into the question of relative affection from the North and South towards the West. That reason is this: that having been accustomed, for the last five years, to see and hear the South represented as the enemy of the West, and the Northeast as its friends, and in the very words used by the Senator from Massachusetts, (Mr. W.) on this floor, and having always maintained the contrary in the West, I could not, without suffering myself to be gagged hereafter with an unanswerable question, sit still and hear the same things repeated on this floor, without entering my solemn dissent, supported by authentic references, to their truth; especially, when I labor under the thorough conviction, that the object of these statements, both in the West, and in this chamber, is to produce a state of things hostile to the well-being of this Confederacy. *Secondly*, That in repeated references, in the course of my speech, to the Federal Party in the United States, I mean no proscription of that party in mass. I have a test to apply to each of them, and according to the proof of that test does the individual appear fair, or otherwise, before me. The test is this: *Is he faithful to his country in the hours of her trial?* As this question can be answered, so does he stand before me, a fair candidate, or otherwise, for a rateable proportion of the offices, subordinate to the highest, which this country affords. This declaration, I trust, Mr. President, will not be received as arrogant, but taken in its true spirit, as a qualification due to myself, of things said in debate, and which might be misunderstood. I am a Senator—have a voice upon nominations to office—and the country has a right to be informed of my principles of action, in the discharge of that important function.

JOHN ROWAN

John Rowan was born in Pennsylvania in 1773. His family moved to Louisville, Kentucky, and he received a classical education in the school of James Priestly in Bardstown. He studied law in Lexington, was admitted to the bar in 1795, and became a successful criminal lawyer and well-known orator. A member of the Kentucky constitutional convention in 1799, he was Kentucky secretary of state from 1804 to 1806, when he was elected as a Republican to the United States House of Representatives for one term. On the grounds that he was a congressman-elect, he turned down a request for legal assistance from Aaron Burr in 1806. Rowan was a member of the Kentucky House of Representatives from 1813 to 1817, in 1822 and 1824, and was a judge on the state court of appeals from 1819 to 1821. In Kentucky politics, he was a supporter of debtor relief measures and a critic of judicial conservatism. He was appointed by the legislature to adjust a boundary dispute with Tennessee in 1820, and a land claims dispute with Virginia in 1823. Rowan was elected as a states' rights Republican to the United States Senate in 1825. He served one term and was involved in efforts to reform the federal judicial system and abolish imprisonment for debt. In 1839 he was appointed commissioner for carrying out a treaty with Mexico. He was president of the Kentucky Historical Society from 1838 until his death in 1843.

Speech of Mr. Rowan,

of Kentucky

[February 4, 1830]

The resolution of Mr. Foot, of Connecticut, relative
to the public lands, being under consideration, Mr. Rowan
addressed the Chair as follows:

M R. R. SAID THAT, IN THE SHARE which he proposed to take in the
debate, he should enter into no sectional comparisons. He should
not attempt to detract from the just claims of any one of the States, nor
would he disparage his own by any attempt to eulogize it. A State should
be alike uninfluenced by eulogy and detraction. In his opinion, she could
not be justly the subject of either. There existed, necessarily, among the
States of the Union, very great diversities. It would be strange if there did
not. The habits, manners, customs, and pursuits of people would be different, as they should be found to be differently situated, in reference to climate, soil, and various other causes, which exerted a powerful influence
over their condition: for he held that we were more influenced by pride,
than reason or philosophy, when we asserted that it was competent to any
people to shape their condition according to their will. We were all more
or less affected by the force of circumstances; and while we seemed to be
under the direction of our will, were under the influence of the causes
which, though they were imperceptible, were unceasing in their operation
upon our inclinations. The fluids which sustain the life of man [said Mr.
R.] are not less of atmospheric or solar concoction, than those which sustain life in other animals, and even in vegetables. Can any man say, upon
any other hypothesis, why the tropical fruits do not grow in the New England States; why certain animal and vegetable growths are peculiar to certain climates, and found in no other; and why the stature and complexion
of man is different in different climates; and why there is a corresponding
difference in his temper and appetencies?

Now, would it not be as reasonable for men to taunt each other with these differences, which are obviously the effect of physical causes, as to indulge in the jeers and taunts which have characterized this debate? I would not ascribe to physical causes all the differences which are found to exist in the political, moral, and religious sentiments of people situated in different climates; but I would not deny to the heavens their legitimate influence upon people differently situated in reference to that influence. I suppose that an infinity of causes combine to diversify the human condition. The pursuits of a people possessing commercial facilities, will be very different from those of a people remote from the ocean, or any navigable stream. Their manners will take their hue from their pursuits; nor will their sentiments escape a tincture from the same cause. The truth is, that, with every people, their first and great object is their own happiness. To that object all their thoughts and all their exertions are directed. For those who inhabit a fertile country and a temperate or warm climate, nature has more than half accomplished this great object. The manners, habits, and notions, (to use a phrase of our Eastern brethren) of such a people will be very different from those of a people who have to win, by strenuous and unintermitted industry, a meagre subsistence from a sterile soil, in a rigorous climate. We all know that the soil of a southern is more prolific than that of a northern climate; that in the first the people are almost literally fed by the bounty of nature; while in the latter, a subsistence has to be conquered from her parsimony, by the most unceasing toil. The climate of the North imposes upon those who inhabit it the duty of obtaining, by much labor, a competent subsistence. It invigorates, by its rigors, the power of the muscular exertion, which it requires. That of the South inflicts languor, and with it an aversion from that labor which its prolific influence has rendered almost unnecessary. Frugality and economy, as the consequence of their necessary industry, characterize the Northern people: Those of the South are almost as profuse as their soil is prolific. In a Northern climate the labor of all is necessary to their sustenance and comfort. In the Southern the labor of a few will sustain all comfortably; and hence the labor of the South has fallen to the lot of slaves. Yes, sir, that slavery which the gentleman from Boston [Mr. Webster] has, in a spirit of implied rebuke, ascribed to Kentucky, in the contrasted view which he took of that State and the State of Ohio, has, if it be an evil, been thrown upon Kentucky by the destinies. That Kentucky has been somewhat retarded in its advances by the perplexity of its land titles, and its toleration of slavery, is, in his estimation, the misfortune of that State; and the exemption of Ohio from those evils has accelerated her march to the high destiny which awaits her. That she may be prosperous, great, and happy, is, I am sure, the wish of the people of Kentucky. They do not repine at their own condition, nor envy that of Ohio. The two States are neighbors, and have much intercourse, social and commercial. Nothing that can be said in relation to either of the States, by that or any other gentleman on this floor, can in the least effect the subsisting relations between them, or the internal police of either. The Senators from Ohio may have been gratified with the eulogy which he bestowed upon their State. Those of Kentucky were not in the least chagrined by his animadversions upon the condition of their State. They make no complaint that they were not assisted by the East in their wars with the savages. They feel a just pride in having triumphed over their savage enemies, without much assistance from that or any other quarter. Notwithstanding the imputed weakness of slavery, they were strong enough for their foes. Kentuckians never complain: complaint is the language of weakness—a language in which they never indulge. The Kentucky Senators perceived that the object of the Senator from Massachusetts, in complimenting Ohio so profusely, was really to compliment his own State: for, in the sequel, he ascribed all the fine attributes of character possessed by Ohio, and all their blissful effects, to the wisdom of New England statesmen.

It is true, that the people of Kentucky have been a good deal harassed by an unhappy perplexity in the titles to land in that State. The titles were derived mainly from Virginia, and the perplexity in them, to which allusion has been made, could not, at that time, and under the circumstances which then existed, have been avoided by any wisdom or foresight whatever. No blame attaches to Virginia or Kentucky on that account. A few years more and that perplexity will yield to the sacred force of proscription, the condition to which all titles to land must ultimately be reduced.

Yes, sir, perplexity of land titles and slavery have both existed in Kentucky; they both still exist. The former will, with the permission of the Supreme Court, soon cease to exist. But will those evils be at all mitigated by their introduction into this debate? Will the gratuitous mention made of them by the honorable Senator even alleviate them? Slavery must continue to exist in that State, whether for good or for evil, for years yet to come, notwithstanding his kind solicitude on the subject. And I have only to tell him that it is a subject which, so far as that State is concerned, belongs exclusively to herself, as a sovereign State. But, as the gentleman has mentioned that subject, (and it is one about which no gentleman from a non-slaveholding State can ever speak with any good effect, or for any good purpose) I must be permitted to talk a little about it. Sir, while I do not approve of slavery in the abstract, I cannot admire the morbid sensibility which seems to animate some gentlemen upon that subject.

It would appear, from the agony which the very mention of slavery seems to inflict upon the feelings of the two Senators who have discoursed about it, that it was a new thing in our land; that it had never been noticed or discussed before; or that those who had noticed and discussed it, were remarkable for the callosity of their feelings, or the obtuseness of their intellect. They seem not to be aware, that slavery has been not only tolerated, but advocated by the wisest and ablest jurists that ever lived; and that too upon first principles; upon the principles of natural justice.

The jurists deduce its justification from *war;* as a right which the captor has over the captive, whom he might have slain. From *crime;* that a life forfeited by crime may be justly commuted for, or rather transmuted into, slavery. From *debt;* that the debtor may justly enslave himself, in payment of a debt, which he cannot otherwise pay. From *subsistence;* that, in a state of population so dense as to reduce labor to its minimum price, that of *mere subsistence,* those individuals who cannot otherwise live, may justly enslave themselves for subsistence. In that state of things, the female who has thus enslaved herself becomes pregnant; during a portion of the period of gestation, she is unable, by reason of her pregnancy, to earn her subsistence by her labor; for subsistence during that period, both she and her offspring are hopeless debtors—the child, on account of the incapacity of the mother, during that time of gestation and parturition, of which it was the occasion—the mother on her own account; so that the infant was indebted before it was born, and becomes further indebted for its support during that period of its infancy in which it was incapable to earn its subsistence by its labor: and that thus, after laboring its whole life for its subsistence, it dies indebted for the support of itself and mother, during their respective incapacities.

Whether this reasoning be sound or fallacious, it is needless to inquire. It has the sanction of very high names. Without being able to refute it, my feelings have always been opposed to the conclusion to which it conducts my mind. But I have not been able, while I deprecated slavery, to perceive any practicable mode of weeding it out from among us. The condition of free people of color is infinitely worse than that of the slaves. Shunned by the whites, and not permitted to associate with the slaves, they are in a state of exile in the midst of society, and hasten through immorality and crime to extinction. I would ask the gentlemen if the States of New England would agree to receive into their society the emancipated slaves of the South and West? Sir, slavery has been reprobated throughout all time, but has never ceased to exist. It has prevailed through all time, and been tolerated by philosophers and Christians, of every sect and denomination, Jews, Gentiles, and Heathens. But if slavery be an evil, is there not some consolation in the reflection that it is not unmixed—that with a large portion of mankind it is connected with the very greatest good which they enjoy. It is a fact, verified by observation, that those who tolerate slavery are uniformly the most enthusiastic in their devotion to liberty. Montesquieu, whose name is, upon all subjects of this kind, very high authority, tells us that slavery is the natural state of man in warm, and liberty his natural state in cold climates. This sentiment is unhappily but too well supported by history.

The barrenness of the soil in high latitudes, the quantity of labor required *of all*, to produce a comfortable subsistence *for all*, and the rigors of the climate in which they live and toil, impress upon the people great vigor and hardihood of character, and qualify them to maintain and vindicate their liberty, whenever, and under whatever circumstances it may be assailed. Amid the severity and gloom of the climate, and the penury of nature, they find nothing so valuable, nothing which they estimate so highly, as their liberty. It is to them the greatest good, and compensates for the absence of all those bounties, which Nature has lavished upon the people of a warmer climate. They are necessarily free, and necessarily impressed with the value of their freedom, and possess the inclination, as well as the power to maintain it.

In Southern climates, nothing is so much dreaded as exposure to the fervid rays of the sun—and scarcely any thing is more enfeebling, and oppressive, than that exposure is to those who are not habituated to it. The special kindness of Heaven to man, is illustrated by holy writ, by reference to the refreshing influence of "the shadow of a great rock in a weary land." In such a climate, none will labor constantly; but those who are forced to do so, and those who are constrained by the force of circumstances to labor, soon become reconciled to their condition. The languor inflicted by the climate, disqualifies them to conquer their condition, and fits them for it—and, owing to the bounty of nature, the labor of a comparatively small portion of the people, will support *them all*. Those who do not labor, while they enjoy the refreshing influence of the shade, are left in the possession of liberty, with leisure to cultivate its theory, and contemplate its charms, until they become enamored with it. Liberty is the *beau ideal* of the Southern and Western Slave holders—and indeed is more or less so, with all the white population.—Their devotion to it, partakes of the spirit of idolatry—and this sentiment is heightened by the constant presence of slavery, and is more and more strengthened by the contrast which every day exhibits, between their own condition and that of the slaves. So that if this reasoning be correct, the cause of civil liberty is gainer by the numerical amount of her votaries, thus rescued from the fervors of a Southern climate. But a *few,* instead of *all* the people in such a climate, are slaves; and our Northern brethren, if this theory be correct, have only to lament, in common with all the disciples of liberty, that nature exacts from the people of the South, the toleration of slavery, as the only condition upon which they can themselves be free.

Then, Sir, the toleration of slavery ought not to be imputed by our Northern, to their Southern brethren, as matter of reproach; for if, according to the jurists, it be justifiable upon the principles of natural justice, the people of each State are at liberty to tolerate it or not, as they may choose. It is, in the case, a mere question of policy. But if the writers on public law should, in this case, have erred, and slavery is not in accordance with the laws of nature, the slave-holders of the South are excusable, because they have been reduced by the climate which they occupy, to the necessity of submitting to it, as the *least evil,* and that at last is the alternative presented to man, in his progress through life, whether in his individual or aggregate capacity. His choice is, in no instance, perfect good. It is between a greater, and a less evil.

But is not the theory which I have been urging, affirmed and illustrated by the history of the condition of mankind in all ages? Of what instance to the contrary, does history furnish an account? Of what Southern country were the people ever free, who did not tolerate slavery? There are many instances of Southern people, who tolerated slavery without being free themselves. But I believe there is no instance on record, of a Southern people being, and continuing to be free, who did not tolerate slavery. The Jews—the Greeks—the Romans, were respectively the freest people of the periods in which they lived, and they each tolerated slavery in its most repulsive form. They, too, were greatly in advance of other nations, in civilization and all the arts which embellish life. They gave important lessons on the science of free government, to their cotemporaries, and to succeeding generations. They, who but for the slavery which they tolerated, would have been slaves themselves, taught mankind how to live free, and what was greatly more important, how to die for the maintenance of their liberty. I do not mean that the science of free government was thoroughly understood by either of them. They were greatly in advance of their compeers, in that science, perhaps as much so, as we are in advance of them. And we, I regret to believe, are yet far short of perfection in it.

Whether the *principles* of free government will ever be so simplified, as to be comprehended and understood by the people generally, and whether it will be possible, even if such should be the fact, for them to resist successfully, the unceasing and almost imperceptible encroachments of aristocracy upon their rights, is a problem of the very deepest interest, and remains to be solved.

But I have been led away by this subject. It is one of great delicacy, and deep interest. It must not be meddled with from abroad. The Southern and Western States cannot agree that it shall be discussed by those, who can have no motives of even a philanthropic cast, to meddle with it at all. It is exclusively *their own subject,* and must be left to them, and the destinies.

The gentleman seemed to think that the Senator from South Carolina, (Mr. HAYNE,) was looking out for Western allies—that his object was to conciliate the West. The sentiments uttered by the Senator from the South, (Mr. HAYNE,) in relation to the public lands in some of the Western States, were elevated and just, and such as in my opinion might be expected from an enlightened statesman. There are no lands belonging to the United States in the State of Kentucky, and I thank heaven that such is the case. The slavery and perplexity of land titles, which have been imputed to Kentucky, may be very great evils, and the first of them has been felt as such by the people, to an afflicting extent. But in my judgment, both together are a very little matter, compared with the evil experienced by a State, whose territory belongs to the United States. In Kentucky, however perplexed the titles of her citizens to their lands were, the title of the State to all the territory within her limits, is unperplexed, simple, and sovereign. The Senator from South Carolina, therefore, could not, in all that he said in reference to the public lands, have expected to operate upon Kentucky, nor could he justly be suspected of an intention to propitiate the States in the valley of the Mississippi, because it was what they had a right to expect from him, and every other member of this body. And they ought not to be supposed to take as a favor, what they have just cause to demand as a right. No, Sir, if there was any indication given of illicit love, it was most obviously on the part of the Senator from Massachusetts, towards the State of Ohio. That he had no love towards

Kentucky, was very obvious, and that his regards for Ohio were of the ten-
derest sort, was most obvious. Whether she will reciprocate his love, is, I
think, somewhat problematical, but about that matter I have no concern. I
can only say that whatever may be the inclination of the East, or the
South, towards Kentucky, in regard to alliances, it may be abandoned. She
is not in a wooable condition; she is wedded to the Union, and will not
hear of any other alliance.

The Senator from Maine, too, [Mr. SPRAGUE,] has given us a most
glowing description, or rather depiction of New England. He does not, as
the gentleman from Massachusetts did, speak *of* New England *through*
Ohio. He speaks right *at her,* and directly *of* her. He has told us of the first
colonists, of the manner of their landing, and of the place at which they
landed. He has described them, not as hardy puritans, but as venerable pilgrims, landing upon the rock at Plymouth, with the bible in their hands—
yes, sir, the holy bible in their pious hands!! He has told us too, that they
extracted the model of their free and happy governments, from that sacred
volume, and that they got from that same holy book, those pure principles
of morality, and piety, and that love of order, which so signally characterize them at this day. And he has taken special care to inform us, that they
were inspired with an emphatic *abhorrence of slavery,* by the divine injunction of that same sacred volume, "to do unto others as they would that
others should do unto them."

While the Bible furnishes the very best rules by which to regulate the
conduct of individuals towards each other and their Maker, I must be allowed to say, that the pilgrims of Plymouth must have been very ingenious
to have discovered in it either the model of a free Government, or the political principles upon which a free Government can be predicated—with
the exception of what is called a theocracy—in which the priests ruled; all
the Governments of which it treats, were those of Kings and Judges. At
present, the representatives of the people of New England seem to have a
very decided preference for the *judges.* No man can read in the Bible of a
republic. Those pilgrims only took their government from the Bible, "until
they found leisure to make a better," and they did make, and do now enjoy,
a much better government, than any of which that good book speaks.

Sir, I was so charmed with the eloquence of the gentleman, that I fancied for the while that New England was a very elysium—that its surface
was gently undulating, carpeted with verdure of the deepest hue, inter-
spersed with flowers of every tint and flavor: that the forests were composed of sacred growths—the palm, the cedar, the fir tree, and the

olive—tenanted by birds of the most varied and vivid plumage, and of exquisite notes. That the music of the grove was rendered somewhat more solemn by the plaintive cooing of the dove, perched, not upon the withered limb of a thunder-scathed oak, but upon the verdant bough of its own olive—the tree from which it plucked the emblematic sprig, which it bore in its beak to the patriarchal voyager. That the venerable pilgrims sauntered upon the surface, or reclined in stately recumbency, upon the green banks of the pellucid streams, which meandered in every variety of curve, through the tall groves, and discoursed sweet music with the pebbles, except perhaps on Sundays. That in this posture of graceful recumbency, they inhaled the odoriferous breezes, which gently agitated the balmy air, and occasionally quaffed Nectar from the hand of the obsequious Ganymedes. But when the gentleman had closed his description, and the illusion produced on my fancy by his eloquence had subsided—or, in other words, Mr. President, when the poetry of his description was reduced to plain prose—I found it was all a *notion.* That he had been talking about the hardy New Englanders, and about the poor broken scrubby lands of New England, out of which the virtuous yeomanry of that country extract not only comfort, but wealth. That the fancied Nectar was neither more nor less, than plain New England rum; and that, in the generous use of it, each man was his own Ganymede, and helped himself with an alacrity proportioned to his thirst.

Now, Sir, I am willing to admit that the people of New England have many virtues; they are honest, industrious, enlightened, enterprising, and *moderately pious.* I admire their free school system, and have no doubt that it conduces greatly to the diffusion of much useful knowledge among the mass of the people. But, after all, they are no better than they should be— no better than their Southern or Western neighbors. The people of every State have their respective advantages and inconveniences; and are all of them more or less under the control of circumstances, over which they themselves have *no control.* They are all aiming at the same object, and all employ such means to promote it as their condition permits. To be happy is not less the aim of the other States, than of New England; and they perhaps have not been less successful than she. Let her not be so weak as to suppose, that none can enjoy it who do not conform to her standard. Let all the States unite in maintaining the freedom of each, and let each be free to pursue its own happiness in its own way. Comparisons, taunts, and reproaches, can produce no good effect, and may tend to disturb those good relations which ought to subsist among the people of our Union.

Let me not be understood as disparaging New England in any, the slightest degree. I rank her with her Sisters of the Union, neither more nor less fair or accomplished than either of them—they are all virtuous. The only freckle which I can discern of the face of New England, is, that she is sometimes a little too vain of her beauty, and too much disposed to trumpet it. I have never been in that region; but if I were to take their late representative in this body (Senator LLOYD,) as the criterion by which I should judge of them, I would certainly rate them very high. He would have filled the character of Senator in the proudest day of the Roman Republic—no man ever occupied a seat in the Senate of the United States, who was his superior, in all that constitutes excellence of character, in the Senator and the gentleman. I have no prejudices against, but rather partialities for, New England. Of one thing I am satisfied, and that is, that New England can, and will, *take care of herself.* My inclination is, that the other States should do the same; and that neither should unnecessarily, or wantonly, intermeddle with the concerns of the others.

But I did not rise, let me assure you, to discuss the subjects which I have cursorily noticed. I could not have been tempted by them, to encounter the embarrassment which speaking in this body has always inflicted upon me. I rose mainly to enter my solemn protest against some of the political doctrines advanced by the honorable gentleman from Massachusetts (Mr. WEBSTER.) He has asserted, in the course of this debate, that the constitution of the United States was not formed by the States; that it is not a compact formed by the States, but a government formed by the people; that it is a popular government, formed by the people at large; and he adds, "that if the whole truth must be told, they brought it into existence, established it, and have hitherto supported it, for the very purpose, among others, of imposing certain *salutary restraints* on *State sovereignties.*"

He asserts further, that in forming the General Government, the people conferred upon the Supreme Court of the United States, the power of imposing these certain salutary restraints upon the sovereignty of the States. Now, Sir, believing as I do, most solemnly, that these doctrines strike at the root of all our free institutions, and lead directly to a consolidation of the Government, I cannot refrain from attempting, however feeble the attempt may be, to expose their fallacy, and their dangerous tendency. It is the first time they have been openly avowed, (so far as I have been informed,) in either House of Congress. They were thought to be fairly inferrible, from the tenor and import of the first message of the late President ADAMS, to the Congress; but they were left to inference, and were not explicitly avowed. The recommendation of Secretary Rush, that the industry of the people should be regulated by Congress, must have been predicated upon his belief, and that of Mr. Adams, in these doctrines. But still the friends of Mr. Adams, when these doctrines were imputed to him, and his message quoted in support of the imputation, resisted it with warmth, and ascribed the inferences from the message, and from the report of Secretary Rush, to unkind or party feelings. Now, the explicit avowal of the honorable Senator, (Mr. W.) removes all doubt from the subject. We can no longer doubt as to what was the political faith of Mr. Adams. His most zealous and most distinguished apostle has avowed it. The two parties are now clearly distinguishable, by their opposite political tenets; the one headed by our illustrious Chief Magistrate, who is the friend and advocate of the rights of the States; the other party is *now* headed by the honorable Senator from Massachusetts, (Mr. Webster,) and is, as I shall contend, and attempt to prove, in favor of a consolidation of the Government—of a splendid Empire. The doctrine avowed is neither more nor less than that the State sovereignties are merely nominal, and that the Government was consolidated in its formation. How it has happened, that this essential characteristic of the Government was so long kept a secret from the people of the States, is a matter of some mystery. Why was it not avowed at the time the Constitution was formed? Why was this disclosure reserved until this time, and for this occasion? Is there any thing in the message of the President, or in the political condition of the people of the States, which demands its promulgation at this time? Are the people prepared, think you, to receive an entire new version of their Constitution? Will they give up their dependence upon their States respectively, and rely upon the great Central Government for the protection of their lives, liberty, and property? Sir, I think not; they are not yet sufficiently tamed and subdued, by the aristocracy of the land, and the encroachments of the General Government upon the rights of the States, to submit just at once.

Mr. President, I would ask the honorable Senator how his doctrine can be correct, consistently with the known state of facts, at the time the Constitution was formed. What was the condition of the people at that time? Were they at large, and unconnected by any political ties whatever? Or were they in a state of self government under distinct political associations? It is known to every body, that the people consisted of, and constituted thirteen distinct, independent, and sovereign States. That those States were connected together by a compact of Union, and that the great object of the people of the States, informing the Constitution, was that declared in its preamble, *to make the Union more perfect.* What union, I would ask, or union of what? Most certainly of the States, already united, whose union was thought to be imperfect. To give more compaction, and render more perfect, the Union of the States, was the great desideratum. To consolidate the union of the States was the object of the constitutional compact.

But I desire to be informed, how the people could absolve themselves from their allegiance, to their respective States, so as to be in a condition to form a National Government? And what need could they have for a National Government, before they had formed themselves into a nation; and how they could form themselves into a nation, one nation, without abandoning, or throwing off their State costume, and even dissolving the compacts, by which they were formed into States?

We all know, that there are but two conditions of mankind. The one natural, the other artificial. And we know that in a state of nature, there is no government. That all are equal in that condition, and when all are equal, there can be no government. The laws of nature are the only rules of human conduct in that condition, and each individual is his own expounder of those laws. He is the arbiter of his own rights and the avenger of his own wrongs. Such was not the condition of the people when the Constitution was formed: They were not at large and at liberty to improve their condition, by their confluent voice or agency. And if they had been so situated, they would not have formed such a Constitution as they did, as I shall attempt hereafter to shew. The Constitution is not adapted to the People, in any condition, which as one People they could occupy, while it is admirably adapted for their use, in their State capacities—the purpose for which it was formed.

I desire further to know, in what sense the words, *State* and *People* are used by him, when he says, "The People brought it (the constitution) into existence, for the purpose, amongst others, of *imposing certain salutary restraints upon State Sovereignties.*" Indeed, I should like to know in what sense he uses the word sovereignties, in that connexion. Now, sir, I understand *State* to mean the people who compose it,—that it is but a name by which they, in their collective capacity, are designated. By the people of the United States, I understand, the distinct collective bodies of people, who compose the States that are united by the Federal Constitution. And by the United States, I understand, the distinct collective bodies of people of which the States are composed. But I shall make myself better understood by a short analysis of the process by which a State is formed.

The power which is exerted in governments, must either have been willingly conceded by the people, or taken from them against their will. If it could only be obtained in the latter mode, there could be no free governments. In a state of nature, there is no power, (I mean moral power,) in one man, to direct, control, or govern another; all are free. The evils inseparable from this condition need not be enumerated by me: they have been portrayed by all elementary writers on the science of politics. It suffices to say, that they are such as to induce those in that condition to hasten to escape from it. All political doctors agree in telling us, that the transition from a state of nature to a state of civil society, is effected by an agreement among all who are to compose the society—of each with all, and all with each, that each, and his concerns, shall be directed by the understanding, and protected by the force or power of all. The agreement is reciprocal of each with all, and of all with each. The right which each man possessed in a state of nature, to direct himself and his own concerns, by his own will, is voluntarily surrendered by him to the society; and he agrees that he and his concerns shall thereafter be subject to the direction and control of the understanding or will of the society. This contract is either express or implied—but most frequently implied, and is necessarily supposed to have been formed by every people, among whom laws and government are found to exist. I say *necessarily:* for the power to make a law, or to govern, can be obtained upon no other supposition. It is denominated the social compact. It is the charter by which civil society is incorporated—by which it acquires personality and unity—by which the action of all the people, by a majority, or in any other mode which they may designate in their constitutional compact, is considered as the action of a moral agent—of a single person. This moral agent is, in reference to its own condition and concerns, called a State—probably from the fixed and stable condition of the people, compared with the invariable and fluctuating condition in a state of nature. In reference to other States it is called a nation, and acts and holds intercourse with them, as an individual person. Much confusion has arisen from the indiscriminate application of the word State to different and distinct subjects. Sometimes it is used to mean the government of the State, instead of the people in their political capacity.

There is nothing more common than to hear men, who are even distinguished for their political knowledge, say that in forming government, men surrender *a portion* of their natural rights to secure the protection of the balance. Yet there is no error more palpable. If that notion were correct, the legitimate power of the *State,* (and throughout this argument I shall use that word to mean the people of the State) would be too limited for any beneficial purpose. Then, indeed, a State would not possess sovereign power. The State, in that case, could not protect either the citizen or his property. He would not even be a citizen: for it is in consequence of his having surrendered not a part, but the whole of his self-control, that he is a citizen—and it is only as a citizen, that a State can demand any public service from him, or control him in any way. Neither could his property be subject to the control of the State, even in reference to its protection, if the control of it all had not been surrendered in the social compact. Now this individuality of the people produced by the social compact, subsists while that compact lasts, and it confers upon the State which it has formed, the self-preserving power to the extent of the moral and physical energy of all. The motives which lead to the formation of a State can never cease to exist; a state of nature, is at all times equally infested with insecurity and wretchedness, and of course there will always be the same motives for shunning it, and it can only be avoided by remaining in a state of civil society. Hence we have no account in history of the voluntary dissolution of the social compact. Civil societies have been destroyed by earthquakes, by deluge, and by the exterminating ravages of war, but never by a voluntary dissolution of their social compact. They have, to be sure, been often subdued into vassalage, or reduced to the condition of provinces. Indeed, it is difficult to conceive how they could be dissolved by the will or agency of the people who compose them. The will of the whole is the will of one political body—of one corporate agent; and a self-destroying will, or purpose, would be as unnatural in a body corporate, as in a body natural.

Again, any attempt by any of the members of the society, to thwart or counteract the self-preserving will of the whole, would be highly criminal, would be treason, and subject those who made the attempt to the fate, which they meditated against the body politic.

The States, therefore, remained in full vigor, while the Constitution of the United States was forming. They were not even shorn of any of their sovereign power by that process, for the gentleman says, that that instrument was brought into existence, among other reasons, for the purpose of imposing certain salutary restraints upon State sovereignties.

Now that which does not exist, cannot be restrained. He, therefore, admits the existence of the sovereignties of the States, not only at the time, but ever since the formation of the Constitution. If the sovereignty of each State was separate and distinct, and consisted in the concentrated will of the people of each, by what authority could the people of the State of

Georgia interfere in the reduction or modification of the sovereign power of the State of Virginia, and if they could not interfere in the regulation of the power of the State of Virginia, by what mode could the people of Virginia itself, other than their collective, their State capacity, diminish or modify the sovereign power of that State! The people of no one State could interfere with the rights of another, nor with its own, in any other capacity, than as the collective body which composed the State. But, upon the supposition, that the People of all the States, not in their State capacities, but at large, and by their confluent voice or agency, formed the Constitution. The difficulty still presents itself. By what authority did all unite in modifying the Constitution of each. They had not entered all into one general compact, and thereby conferred power upon the majority, to form the Constitution, by the adoption of the State machinery, which they had thrown off. This Government is not formed by the people at large, out of the *exuviae* of the States. But will the gentleman have the goodness to tell us, what is the power, and where does it reside, which is employed in altering the Constitution of a State? Does it not reside *exclusively* in the People of the State, and in their collective capacity, and must it not be exerted in that capacity, to produce any alteration in their Constitution? And must it not be exerted according to the mode prescribed in the Constitution? Can the People, pursuing that mode, be viewed in any other than their State capacities? The gentleman, I am sure, will answer these questions in the affirmative. Well, the State Constitutions were all affected, and seriously too, by the Constitution of the United States.

Now, if none but the people of a State, in their distinct State capacity, could affect its Constitution, then their action in forming the Constitution of the United States, must have been exerted in their State capacity. The States, whereby I mean the people of each, as a distinct political body, then must have formed the Constitution, and not the People at large. If these views are correct, how can the gentleman reconcile his idea, that the Constitution was formed by the People, and not by the States, with his other idea, that it was formed by the *People* to impose certain *restraints* upon State sovereignty. If the People acted in their distinct State capacities, then they could consistently impose restraints upon the exercise by the States of their sovereign power—but then they acted as States—and imposed the restraints by *compact;* and in no other capacity could they act, nor by any other mode than by compact, could they achieve that object. The social compact gives, as I have urged, unity and compaction to the People. It gives the power to the State, which it forms, of expressing its will by a majority. And thus it acts in forming its Constitutional compact, and in the exercise of its legislative power. This power of acting by majority, would be tyranny over the minority, if it had not been conceded by the social compact. Upon this ground it must be obvious, that the social, must precede the Constitutional compact, and that the power to form the latter must be derived from the former. But until there be a State, there can be neither need for a government, or the power to form it. So that, if the People had not, at the time the Constitution was formed, existed in distinct political bodies, they must all have existed in one political body, before they could either need a government, or possess the power to form one.

Sir, I know that the discussion of the elementary principles of government is dry and uninteresting—indeed all abstract discussion is so—but the Senator from Massachusetts has led the way. He has made it necessary for me, either to acquiesce in doctrines, which I consider dangerous to the liberties of the People, or to attempt to refute them. Indeed, I think it is greatly to be regretted, that the true principles of our free institutions have not been more frequently the subject of discussion. The clear comprehension and maintenance of them, is essential to the liberty of the People. To obliterate or obscure them, will always be, as it always has been, the purpose of those who would misrule, and oppress the People.

That the Constitution must, of necessity, have been formed by the States, and not by the people at large, I have attempted to prove by referring to natural principles, and to the existing state of things, at the time it was formed: I will refer you to that instrument itself for further proof of that fact. I have already called your attention to the preamble: It is in these words: "We, the People of the *United States,* in order *to form a more perfect Union,*" &c. Let me ask again, if the words *"we, the People of the United States,"* meant we the People *not* of the United States? Why were they termed People of the United States, if they considered themselves as absolved from their State relations, and at large? Can we construe the words *"United States"* in this connexion, to mean the People within the outer boundaries of the exterior States, without reference to the States and State institutions in any other sense? Are we not forbidden to give them this meaning by the words which follow, viz: *"to form a more perfect Union?"* The word Union can relate to nothing but the States. The object, as I have before stated, was to unite *them,* not the *People,* more perfectly: Besides, a more perfect union of the People cannot be produced by a constitutional, than by the social compact. It is not the object of a Constitution to unite the people. It pre-supposes their most perfect union under the social compact. It is owing alone to that pre-existing Union, that they can form a Constitution, or have any need for it. It would have been inappropriate, therefore, in the preamble to the Constitution, to have said, "in order to form *a more perfect Union,*" in reference to the People; besides, there was not then, nor had there existed, any political Union among the People— *merely as People.* The Union which existed under the articles of Confederation, was a Union of the States: To form a Union of the States more perfect than the one which then existed, was the object, I repeat, of the present Constitution.

That such was the intention of those who framed the Constitution, is obvious from the structure and phraseology of that instrument. In the 2d section of the 1st article, we find this provision: "The House of Representatives shall be composed of members chosen every second year by the people of the several States." And again, "Representatives and direct taxes shall be apportioned among the several States which may be included within this Union." We see, from what I have read, that the members were to be chosen, not by the people at large, but by the people of the several States—and this shows what was meant in the preamble, by the words, "we, the people of the United States." It shows that these words meant "the people of the several States." The people who formed the Constitution were to elect their members in the same character in which they formed that instrument—as the people of the several States. This idea is confirmed by the provision "that representation and direct taxes, shall be apportioned *among the several States.*" What several States? The answer is given in the same sentence—those "which may be included within this Union." Then the Union was of States: They were to be represented as States, and taxed as States; and only the States which might be included within the Union, were to pay tax and be entitled to be represented. Here, too, the word State most evidently means the people who compose it. They are to choose representatives and they are to be taxed as the collective bodies who constitute the State. Again, the same provision, farther on, reads thus: "The number of representatives shall not exceed one for thirty thousand: but each State shall have at least one representative, &c; and, until such enumeration shall be made, New Hampshire shall be entitled to choose three, Rhode Island one," &c. Here it is very evident, that the word "State," as used to mean the people of the State—population is made the basis of representation—the ratio is fixed at thirty thousand, but whether thirty thousand, or a smaller number of people, composed a State, it should have one Representative.

So, too, the provision that the State of New Hampshire should, until the next enumeration, be entitled to choose three representatives, means, that the people who composed that State should choose, and implies that their number was at least ninety thousand, and so of the other States. But hear this provision of the Constitution still further to the same effect: "When a vacancy happens in the representation from any State, the Executive authority *thereof* shall issue writs of election," &c. Who can misunderstand this language? Who does not see, from the clauses of the Constitution which I have read, that that instrument was made by the people of the States, in their State capacity; that the States made it. In the last clause there is an evident distinction between the State and the government of the State, "to fill a vacancy happening in any of the States; the Executive authority thereof should issue writs of election," &c. The States were to have the representatives one for every 30,000 composing it, and the Executive authority of the State was to issue writs to fill vacancies happening in the State. Now, the State is formed by the social compact; the Executive authority was formed by the constitutional compact; the Constitution, in all its references to the people, and in all its requisitions on them refers to them either by the term 'State,' or by the terms people of the State, as is evident from the clauses which I have read. But this distinction between the State and the Government thereof is obviously displayed in the third section of the first article: It relates to the creation of the Senate, the body which we now compose, and reads thus: "The Senate of the United States shall be composed of two Senators from each State, chosen by the Legislature thereof." Here the word State, as in the other instances which I have read, means the people incorporated by the social compact, and the Legislature which was created by the constitutional compact, must be referred to the Constitution, by which it was created.

The social compact created the State; the State created, by its constitutional compact, its government; and hence we say, the Government of the State, the Legislative, Executive, and Judicial authority of the State; the People of the State can speak or act only through their constitutional functionaries, or by convention.

The prevailing idea that, when the Constitution of a State is abolished, the people are thrown back into a state of nature, is erroneous, and one which, as used by aristocrats and office holders, does much harm. It is urged to deter the people, who are often duped by it, from that seasonable resort to first principles which is essential to the preservation of their liberty. Now, we all know, that the abolition by a State of its Constitution, no more affects the social compact, or the existence of the State, than the repeal of a statute affects it. The State made its Constitution, and enacted the statute. The same sovereign power was exerted in both instances, alike in the creation and the abolition of both, and exists in the unimpaired efficacy of the social compact.

Every State has its fixed and its variable attributes of character. The former is political, and identified with the social compact; the latter exists on the changeable qualities or habits of the people. Thus a nation is said to be brave or cowardly, sincere or faithless. The people of Spain were at one time remarkable for their fine chivalric spirit. Not so now. Punic faith is a lasting stigma upon Carthage. But that the compression of the people, by the social compact, into the unit called a State, remains, under all the changes of character which the people undergo, and all the changes of its government, which choice or accident may produce; or war or convulsion inflict, itself unchanged. If a republic becomes a monarchy, or if a monarchy becomes a republic, these are but changes of government; the civil society, or State, remains unaltered, and is sovereign, while ever it manages its own affairs by its own will. It is upon this principle that States are not absolved from their debts by revolution. The State, and not "the Government," is the contracting party, and nothing but the dissolution of the social compact, and consequent extinction of the State, can absolve from its payment.

Now, Sir, unless I am wrong as to the formation and character of States, and unless I have read the Constitution wrong, that instrument not only was not formed by the people at large, but could not, as I have before said, have been formed by them. It could not have been formed by the people in any other capacity than as States. It was, we know, formed by representatives from the States, and it was adopted by the representatives of the States, severally: for the members of the conventions in the several States, were not less representatives of the States severally, than their legislative representatives.

I contend, therefore, that the States made the Constitution, and thereby rendered the Union greatly more perfect, than it was under the articles of confederation. I contend, also, that the individuality, and sovereign personality of the States, were not at all impaired by that instrument. That the States remain plenary sovereigns, as much so as they were before the formation of the Constitution. That they have not by that instrument parted with one jot of their sovereign power. You seem to startle; but hear me. I contend that the States, as plenary sovereigns, agreed by the

Constitution, (which is but the compact of Union,)—that they would unite in exerting the powers therein specified and defined, for the purposes and objects therein designated, and through the agency of the machinery therein created. The power exercised by the functionaries of the General Government, is not inherent in them, but in the States, whose agents they are. The Constitution is their power of attorney, to do certain acts, and contains, connected with their authority to act, their letter of instructions, as to the manner on which they shall act. They are the servants. The power which gives validity to their acts, is in their masters, the States. Where, let me ask you, is the power of Congress during the recess of that body? Certainly not in the individual members—they do not carry it about with them. Suppose the Judges of the Supreme Court were by some fatality thrown out of existence, where would be the judicial power which they exercised, until others were appointed? Upon the death of the President, where is the supreme executive power of the Union? You may tell me in the Vice-President. But between the death of the President, and the induction of the Vice-President, where is it? The answer to these questions is most obvious. It is, that they possessed no sovereign power, that they were but the agents of the sovereign States—that the States retained all their sovereign power, and still retain it. That it is inherent in them—not in three-fourths of the States, but in all of them. In amending, or altering the Constitution they have agreed, that the voice of all, shall be expressed by three-fourths.

The sentiment that the States, by the formation of the Constitution, divested themselves of a large portion of their sovereign power, is in my humble opinion, as erroneous as it is unhappily prevalent. And this error will be advocated by all who are hostile to State sovereignty, and friendly to a consolidated government.

I have attempted to prove in a previous part of my argument, that a State could not, without dissolving its social compact, divest itself of its sovereign powers. To suppose that a State could be dependant, and sovereign, at the same time, would be to suppose it destitute of that unity, which is of the essence of its nature. It would be not only to misconceive the character of a State, but to ascribe to it two inconsistent modes of existence. Nor is it more admissable to suppose that a State is sovereign, and at the same time subject to certain salutary restraints upon the exercise of its sovereignty by any other power. For I lay it down as a truism in political science, that whenever a State is subject to the control of the will of any other power, it has ceased to be sovereign, and is the province of the power that may control it. I say, may control it, for its subjection does not consist in the actual exertion upon it, of the controlling power, but in its subjection to that control. Slaves are not always under the controlling action of their masters' will. Indeed they are but seldom so. Yet they are not the less slaves when they are not, than when they are under his actual control, because their slavery consists in their subjection to his will, and not in their actual continuous conformity to it.

It is for that reason, that slaves cannot form, or enter into, a social compact. They lack that exemption from control, that freedom of will, of which the sovereign power of the State is created by the social compact. Then if it is essential that the component parts of sovereignty—that the will of each member of the social compact shall be free from subjection, does it not follow that the sovereignty *itself* should be alike free from subjection? The sovereign power of the State, (as I have before urged) consists in the *free* will of all the members of civil society, compacted by the social compact, into a corporate person. The elements of this power being free, the aggregate must be so. There is, therefore, no *law* obligatory upon a sovereign State, but that which was obligatory upon its constituent parts. The laws of nature were alone obligatory upon man in a state of nature, and no other laws are obligatory upon a sovereign State: for all the rights, powers, and privileges which were possessed in a state of nature, by the individuals who compose the State, are concentrated, by the social compact, in the State, and constitute its sovereignty. Control implies superiority on the part of the controlling, and inferiority on the part of the controlled. But sovereigns are equal; and it is of the essence of sovereignty that it cannot admit of salutary restraints *aliunde*. It is a governing and self-governed power. Besides, a State would be unfit, indeed disqualified, to protect its citizens according to its stipulation in the social compact, if it were, as the Senator supposes, subject to those salutary restraints, by the judicial functionaries of the General Government. It would indicate by its weakness, that instead of protecting, it needed protection. The reciprocal duties and obligations which now exist between the States, and their citizens, would vanish. But the gentleman is kind in subjecting the States to none but *salutary* restraints. The Supreme Court are to judge whether the restraints are or are not *salutary*, which they *will*, no doubt, *seasonably* impose upon State sovereignties. The sovereign State is not to form any opinion on this subject, and therein, and by its passive acquiescence display, according to his opinion, its *sovereignty*. I can form no idea of a sovereignty subject to such restraints. It is illusive, and but the precursor, as I fear of a declaration hereafter to be made, that the States are not sovereign. Indeed it is to my mind nothing short of a virtual declaration to that effect *now:* for there is no such thing as half, or three quarters, or seven-eighths sovereign. Every State being a unit, must be entirely of one character—must be either sovereign or vassal; and I repeat that a State, subject to be controlled by any other power, is the vassal of that power.

I admit that a sovereign State may forbear to exercise her sovereign power, in relation to given objects, or classes of objects. She may stipulate thus to forbear the exertion of her sovereign powers, or she may stipulate to exercise her sovereign powers in conjunction with other States, in relation to a certain class of subjects, and to forbear to exert them individually upon any of those subjects. But the very stipulation, instead of renouncing the powers which are to be jointly exercised, implies their retention. Such a stipulation I consider the Constitution to be. I view it as an agreement between the sovereign States to *exert jointly* their respective powers, through the agency of the General Government, for the purposes, and in the manner delineated in that instrument of compact. Each State exerts its plenary sovereign power jointly, for all the legitimate purposes of the Union; and separately, for all the purposes of domiciliary or State concerns. An individual citizen may stipulate to transact a portion of his business by agent, and the balance by himself; and that he will forbear to exert his moral faculties or physical energies upon that class of subjects, which, by his stipulation, are to be acted upon by his agent; has he, by his stipulation, lessened, impaired, or diminished his moral or physical powers? Certainly not. The validity of the agency depends upon his retaining those faculties: for if he shall become insane, or die, the agent cannot act, because the power of his principal has become extinct. So it is the power, the full *subsisting* sovereign power of the States, which gives validity to the acts of the General Government. The validity of those acts does not result from the exercise of a *portion* of the sovereign power of each State.

Sir, we cannot conceive of a sovereign act, without the consciousness that it must have been performed by a sovereign power. An atom is a very small part of a globe, and yet the creation of that, implies the exertion of as plenary sovereign power as the creation of the globe. The creation of the latter, may require a greater, or more protracted exertion of power, than the former; but the odds is in the degree, and not in the character of the power. It is alike sovereign in both instances. The power in the State, which is exerted in taking from a citizen an acre of his land for a public high-way, is not less sovereign, than that which is exerted in taking his life for a crime—nothing less than plenary sovereign power can effect either; and there are no degrees of comparison in sovereign power; there is not sovereign, more sovereign, and most sovereign power. The States were, before the formation of the constitution, equal, for they were sovereign; since that instrument was formed, they are not less equal; because they are still sovereign, as much so *now* as *then;* and because the powers which they stipulated in that compact to forbear to exercise separately, and to exercise jointly, were equal. So that, if the powers which they exercise jointly, under the constitution, be considered, they are equal, and equally exerted, by the joint action of all the States, through their agents; and the powers which each may, consistently with their constitutional compact, exert separately, are equal; and whether viewed in their joint or separate action, they are equal. And when a new State is admitted into the Union, it enjoys by constitutional stipulation, an equality with the other States of the Union.

And here, Mr. President, I would ask the honorable Senator, if the constitution was formed by the People, as he alleges, and not by the States, how it happened to be provided in that instrument, that the enlargement of the Union should be by the admission of the States, and not of People, as such; and why the stipulation as to equality, should have related to the States, and not to the People? And while on this point, I would ask him, why the provision in that instrument for its adoption, referred it to the States, and not to the People; and why, under that provision, the little State of Delaware had as much weight in its adoption as the great State of Virginia?

But, Sir, I fear that I am fatiguing you and this honorable Body; my object has been, to show that the constitution was not, could not, have been formed by the People; that it must have been formed by the States; that the States acted as plenary sovereigns in forming it; that their sovereign character and individuality, was not impaired by that instrument; that it is now administered by them, in the character in which they made it, that of full and perfect sovereigns; that the constitution is nothing more, nor less, than a compact between sovereign States, who are parties to it; that the union of the States produced by it, is more perfect than that which existed under the articles of confederation; and that its increased perfection consists mainly in the stipulation, that the States may exert their joint legislative, executive, and judicial power, upon the People of each. This is a stipulation of each with all the others, and of all the others with each; and this is the stipulation to which the illustrious Washington alluded, when he spoke of the consolidation of the Union. But still, in this stipulation, the People are regarded as citizens, as collective bodies, constituting the States respectively. The States, in the joint exercise of power, through the agency of the General Government, must confine themselves to the powers stipulated in the bond of union—to the constitution; and in doing that, they must consider the People as citizens of their respective States. Thus, the constitution provides, that all trials for crime shall be in the State where the crime is alleged to have been committed; and so in the exercise of the power which allowed to Congress, to provide for organizing, arming, and disciplining the militia, and for governing such part of them as shall be employed in the service of the United States, they are regarded as the militia of the States severally; and each State has the right to appoint the officers for its own militia. So also it is stipulated, that "the citizens of each State shall be entitled to all the privileges and immunities of citizens in the several States."

Now, Mr. President, if I have been correct in my sentiments as to the process of forming a State, and as to the relation which the people of a State bear to each other and their duties resulting from that relation to the State, and the obligation of the State to them, and as to the origin, extent, and character of the sovereign power of a State, I think it will follow, that the sovereign power of a State is an unfit subject to be disposed of by judicial decision; and that the Supreme Court is an unfit tribunal to dispose of the sovereignty of the States, or in the language of the Senator from Massachusetts, (Mr. WEBSTER) "to impose certain salutary restraints upon State sovereignties." It will follow too, that his views and mine are *toto coelo* apart. He thinks that this is a consolidated Government. His denial that it was formed by the States, and assertion that it was formed by the people at large, cannot, whatever he may say upon that subject be construed into any thing else, than that this was a consolidated Government in its very formation. And the assertion of power which he has made for the Supreme Court, if it be sustained, must lead to the consolidation of the Government, if it were not before consolidated—so that, according to his notions, if we have not *now*, we must have, a consolidated Government. If it was formed by people, it is so, if they did not make it so, the Judges will; and therefore, according to his propositions and arguments, there is no mode of escaping from a consolidation of the Government.

Mr. President, my hope is in the intelligence of the people of the States. I consider that they will never submit, that the sovereign power of the States shall be narrowed down, controlled, or disposed of, by a quorum of the Judges of the Supreme Court. They will discern the intrinsic unfitness of the sovereignty of their States, for either forensic discussion or judicial decision, and oppose it with their suffrages, with the force of public opinion, and in whatever other way they may—we would deride with scorn and indignation, any sovereign of Europe, who would agree to submit the sovereignty of his State to the arbitrament of even neighboring sovereigns. How infinitely more exalted is the sovereignty of a State composed of free citizens? And how degrading is the idea that sovereignty, the sovereignty of free States, must be subjected to certain salutary restraints? Sir, the history of the world does not furnish an instance in which the sovereignty of a State was ever subjected to judicial decision; or to any other power than the God of Battles, and the Lord of Hosts!

But allow me, Sir, to inquire into the fitness of this tribunal, for the exercise of the power asserted for it by the honorable Senator; and allow me to preface the inquiry by a few observations upon the nature of our Governments. I have thus far, spoken much more about the States than about their Governments. In the Republics of our country, the great, the leading principle is, that the responsibility of the rulers, or public agents, shall be commensurate with the character and extent of the power confined to them. Our Governments are contrivances, or devices, by which the people govern themselves—by which the governed govern; ours are Governments of law. Indeed all free governments are of that character; and the great difficulty has always been to guard against, and check efficiently the influence of the selfish principle (which is so deeply rooted in human nature,) over those, who are entrusted with making and administering the laws. Now when we regard the zeal and vigilance with which the States, in the formation of their respective constitutions, and in the formation of the General Government too, endeavored to check this selfish principle in their political agents, and render them responsible, we shall be slow to believe that it was their intention, when they formed the Constitution of the United States, to confer upon the Judicial Department, this transcendent and all absorbing power.

It is to secure against the influence of this selfish principle of our nature, that in almost all the Governments of the States, the members of the Legislative Department are elected for short periods—those of the Representative branch generally for one year, and those of the Senate for from two to four years, and the Governors for a like period. The election of the Representatives is annual, that they may be under the control of the People. The longer period allowed to the members of the Senate is that they may not be deterred from checking any popular ebullitions, which might be displayed on the part of the House of Representatives; while, in turn, the members of the latter, might check any aristocratic tendency on the part of the Senate. The Governor is invested with a qualified checking veto upon both branches, and is himself checked by allowing a defined concurrent power in both to overrule his veto; and he is further checked, and the better qualified to exercise his checking power, by being rendered ineligible after a given period, to the gubernatorial chair. I speak, Mr. President, of the checks provided by a majority of the States in their Constitutions. I do not pretend to accuracy or precision, as to the detailed provisions of any.

So, too, in the General Government, biennial elections were intended to secure the responsibility of the members of the House of Representatives, and thereby to check the influence of the selfish principle in the members. The members of the Senate are elected for six years, and by the Legislatures of the States, to check the tendency to consolidation which the gentleman advocates. The two Houses were so constituted as to check each other, and the President was to check and be checked by both. The States were reduced to the condition of perfect equipollence in the Senate, and thus the small were enabled to check the large States, in any attempts they might make to oppress the small.

Sir, on this part of the subject I do not pretend to minute exactness. It would be tedious and is not required for my object, which is only to exhibit an outline of the vigilance and solicitude displayed by the States, in their respective Governments, and in the General Government too, to guard against the influence of this selfish principle in those to whom political agency might be assigned. But I need but have referred you to the State and General Governments, without referring specially to any of their provisions on this subject. They exhibit abundant, almost redundant solicitude to guard the liberty of the People against misrule on the part of the Government. And think you, sir, that after all this elaborate provision against misrule, the States could have intended to subject their Governments, and *their self governing power*, together with the liberties of the people, to the discretion of an irresponsible & unchecked Judiciary. Who does not see that the only security the people have for their liberty, their lives, and their property, is in the protecting power of the sovereignty of their respective States? and that when that sovereignty is subjected to the will of the Supreme Court, the people are subjected to the same tribunal, and that, after all their vigilance and caution, in guarding by every conceivable check, against oppression from their rulers, they are, by this doctrine, to be subjected to the rule of a judicial aristocracy? to the rule of four men—a majority of that tribunal—who are unknown to them, except by the fame or the feeling of their encroachments upon State rights—whose tenure of power is for life, and irresponsible? And yet the Senator modestly tells us "that if the *truth must be told*," such was the intention of the people who framed the Constitution.

Sir, if it be a truth, it had better not have been told. It is a truth worse than falsehood; or if told, it should have been told many years ago. The gentleman, by the manner of telling it, seems to admit that it had been concealed. He treats it as one of those precious truths, which nothing but necessity could drag from its concealment—"If the truth *must* be told;" *must* is a word which imports necessity. The necessity which produced this long concealed truth, will, no doubt, in due course of time, come out, as a truth that must be told. The sentiment, whether it be *a truth* or not, lurked in every part of the first message of Mr. Adams. He did not *feel* that he *must* tell it in the message, and yet he could not conceal it. Perhaps the design was only to make such an implied presentation of it, as might operate as an experiment upon the public feeling. If such was the design, they have mistaken the indications of public sentiment, unless I am greatly deceived; and yet it is announced with great confidence. The gentleman tells us, that the States must submit to the judicial restraints upon their sovereignty, or incur by resistance, the guilt of rebellion. That the decision of the Supreme Court, affirming a *palpably unconstitutional* law, which invades the sovereignty of a State, must be submitted to by the State, or it must incur the guilt of rebellion.

Mr. President, could the doctrine of passive obedience, and non-resistance, have been more explicitly urged; has it ever been more zealously advocated in any country? It is premature; the people of the States are not prepared for it yet. They are too well informed of their rights, and the principles upon which they depend, to be the dupes of that doctrine. There is scarcely a man in the community, who has participated at all in political discussion, that does not know, that rebellion consists in the resistance of *lawful* authority; that the resistance of *lawless* authority is not a crime, but a virtue. That the only mode of escaping from oppression, is by resisting the exercise of unlawful power. That patriotism requires such resistance. The citizens must, at their peril, distinguish between lawful and lawless power; and while they determine to retain their freedom, conform to the one, and oppose the other. It is a high duty, and *full of peril*, but, I repeat, it is the only condition on which liberty, the most precious gift of heaven to man, can be enjoyed and maintained. The alternative is a hard one. It presents *slavery,* to which passive obedience and non-resistance lead, and *liberty,* which requires from its votaries a prompt obedience to all lawful requirements, and a bold, and unfaltering resistance to lawless encroachments.

Sir, it is, I must repeat, too soon for those who rule, or hope to rule, to address their arguments to our *credulity* and our *fears;* to deny us the intelligence to discern our rights, and the right to maintain them. Will the gentleman say, that the States of Virginia and Kentucky, in the steps which they took to nullify the alien & sedition laws, were guilty of rebellion? Were their acts treasonable? If they were, then all the States were guilty of treason, at least, as accessaries after the fact, for they all sanctioned, by the moral force of their opinion, the proceedings of the resisting States. But against whom did those States, or can any State rebel? Rebellion means the resistance by an inferior of the lawful authority of a superior. It implies the violation of allegiance. To what power does a State owe allegiance! To what power is it subordinate? No one State owes allegiance to another, for if it did, that other would owe protection to it. Will the gentleman say, that any such relation exists between the States? Or, will he say, that a sovereign State can owe allegiance to any earthly power? I have attempted to prove that the States of this Union are equal, and have always been so, as well before, as since the formation of the Constitution. That the duties which they owe to each other under the Constitution, are *pactional;* and if I have succeeded, then it is impossible that they can commit rebellion, or incur the guilt of treason, by any violation of their covenant relations with each other. But, Sir, the idea that a *sovereign State* can commit treason, rebellion, or any crime whatever, is utterly inadmissible in the science of politics. The idea of crime cannot exist, where there is no conceivable or possible tribunal before which the culprit could be arraigned, and convicted.

Still less, Mr. President, can any State be supposed to incur the guilt of rebellion of treason, by resisting an unconstitutional law of the General Government, or an unconstitutional decision of the Supreme Court, upon a valid law of Congress. The General Government is the creature of the States; the offspring of their sovereign power; and will the gentleman say that the creator shall be governed by the lawless authority of the creature? Will he invert the rule of reason and of law upon that subject, and say that it is the superior that incurs guilt, by resisting the inferior, and not the inferior by resisting the superior?

But the threats which are brandished against States, or even individuals, who shall oppose the encroachment of the General Government upon the States, are uncalled for, and can only have the effect to provoke illegal resistance, or to awe into a degrading submission. If the States are true to themselves and faithful in the discharge of their high duties, they will move on in the majesty of their sovereign power, and maintain with a steady and equal hand both their governments, by restraining each, in the exercise of its legitimate powers, within its appropriate sphere. They will not encumber the Supreme Court with the exercise of this restraining power. In their hands it would not be a *restraining*, it would be an absorbing power.

Mr. President, this epithet of supremacy, which is so unceasingly applied to that Court, is calculated to swell the volume of their power in the minds of the unthinking. Its supremacy is entirely relative, and imports only that appellate and corrective jurisdiction, which it may exercise over the *subordinate Courts of the General Government*. The appellate court of every State is just as supreme as it is, and in the same way, and for the same reasons. It is not supreme in reference to the other departments of the Government, nor has it any supremacy in reference to the States; and yet the gentleman will have it that this Supreme Court, which derives its title of supremacy from its control over the proceedings of inferior judicial tribunals, shall control and restrain the Supreme Courts of the States, and the States themselves. That the *mere modicum* of judicial power which they are permitted by the States to exercise, shall be exerted to control them in the exercise of their sovereign power.

Sir, I deny that it was the intention of the States, in the formation of the Constitution, to invest that tribunal with the power of doing any political act whatever. The power accorded to that Court was *purely judicial,* and was intended to be so. If it had been intended that they should exercise the political power, which is now asserted for them, its exercise would have been subjected to some checks, to some responsibility. It cannot be reasonably supposed, that, after subjecting the exercise of political power by the other functionaries of the Government, to judicious and well devised checks, it was intended to subject all to the unchecked and irresponsible power of this Court; but, upon this point, I have given my opinions, in a previous part of my argument. I must, however, be permitted to say that the judges in the States, as well as in the General Government, even in reference to the exercise of their mere judicial powers, are left by the constitutions *dangerously* irresponsible. The independence of the Judiciary has, in my opinion, been greatly misconceived. Sir, the true independence of the Judges, consists in their *dependence* upon, and responsibility to the people. The surest exemption from dependence upon *any,* is dependence upon *all.* In free Governments we have nothing more *stable* than the will of the people. To be independent of that, is to rebel against the principles of free government. It is a dependence upon, and a conscious responsibility to, the will of the people, that will best secure the Judge from local, partial, and personal influences. But on what principle should those who *administer* the laws, be less responsible to the people, than those who *make* them? The laws operate as they are expounded, not as they are made. It is in the exposition of them, that they operate oppressively, and all responsibility is to secure against oppression; but there can be no oppression, or scarcely any, without the consent of the Judges. The Judges are irresponsible, and the people are every where oppressed. But I hold it to be universally true, that all power which may be *irresponsibly* exercised, will be exercised *oppressively.* It has always been so; it always will be so: for the Judges are but men.

But to return to the Judges of the Supreme Court. They are authorized to take jurisdiction of all causes in law and equity, arising under the Constitution, laws of Congress, and treaties; and that Constitution, together with the treaties, and the laws of Congress, made pursuant to it, are to be the supreme law of the land. This is their power, and this the character and force of the Constitution, laws of Congress, and treaties. Now, suppose there shall exist between two States, a dispute as to territorial boundary, and the Congress shall pass a law giving the disputed territory to one of the contending States; and suppose the Judges shall affirm the validity of this law. Must the State, whose territory has been thus invaded and taken from it by Congress, submit to the decision, or incur the guilt of rebellion? Is that to be the practical operation of the gentleman's doctrine? Or suppose the territorial boundary of any one of the States shall be altered by treaty, and a portion of its territory transferred to a foreign power, and the Supreme Court were to decide that the treaty was constitutional, must the State, thus dismembered, acquiesce, or, by resisting, be denounced as a rebel; and would the gentleman assert, that this operation was merely imposing a salutary restraint upon State sovereignty?

Now, Sir, I deny that the power to declare a law of Congress, or of any of the States, unconstitutional, was ever conferred, or intended to be conferred, upon the Judiciary of any of the States, or of the General Government, as a *direct substantive power.* The exercise of this power is incidental to the exercise of the mere judicial power, which was conferred. The validity of a law involved by a case, may be incidentally decided, in deciding the law and justice of *the case*. But the decision must be made with an eye to the law and justice of *the case*, and not in reference to the just, or unjust, exercise of the legislative power which was exerted in making the law. Not in the view to check, control, or restrain the legislative power. It must be given in the exercise of merely *judicial*, and not of *political* power.

Thus exercising its jurisdiction, the Court would command the respect and confidence of the People, as a judicial tribunal. But when it merges its appropriate judicial, in an assumed political character—when it exchanges its ermine for the woolsack and the mace, and asserts its right to impose restraints upon the sovereignty of States, it should be treated as an usurper, and driven back by the States within its appropriate judicial sphere. It is due from the States to their own self-respect, and the just rights of their citizens, to assert that they are competent to decide upon every question involving their own sovereignty; and that to neglect to maintain it, would be to renounce the character in which they formed the constitutional compact of Union. That the maintenance of its own sovereignty unimpaired, by each of the States, is essential to the liberty of the people, and to the preservation of the Union. And that to submit their sovereignty to the control of the Judiciary, would be to substitute a judicial oligarchy for the free institutions employed for self government by the People.

All the purposes for which civil society were instituted would be defeated in the control of the States by the Judiciary. Nothing less than sovereign power is competent to the management of the concerns of a State, and nothing less was pledged by the States, in the social compact, for the protection of the people. The State cannot redeem this pledge if it shall be controlled by the Judiciary. The Judiciary will govern, and not the State: for that power that governs those who govern, governs those who are governed; and how can a State protect its citizens from oppression if it is itself liable to be oppressed by their oppressor? So that a State is under a political necessity to vindicate its sovereignty from any *salutary restraints* which the Supreme Court may attempt to inflict upon it by resistance, or whatever means it may.

Mr. President, for security against oppression from abroad, we look to the sovereign power of the United States, to be exerted according to the compact of union; for security against oppression from within, or domestic oppression, we look to the sovereign power of the State. Now, all sovereigns are equal: the sovereignty of the State is equal to that of the Union: for the sovereignty of each is but a *moral person*. That of the State and that of the Union are each a moral person, and in that respect precisely equal. In physical force, the latter greatly transcends the former, but in essential sovereignty, they are not only naturally but necessarily equal: just as the sovereignty of the State of Delaware is equal to that of New York, or of Russia, though the physical power of those sovereignties are vastly different.

The unrestrained exercise of the sovereign power of the Union is necessary to all the purposes of the Union; and is it not as necessary that the sovereign power of the State should be unrestrained, as to all domestic purposes; and can any reason be assigned why the latter, more than the former, should be restrained by the Supreme Court? No reason can exist for the restraint of the one that does not equally apply to the other. But, in truth, the idea of controlling a sovereign State is so inconceivable, that I do not know in what terms to combat it.

Mr. President, I must be indulged in some further inquiries in relation to the unfitness of the Judges of the Supreme Court for the exercise of this controlling power over the sovereignty of the States, which the Senator from Massachusetts has asserted for them. What is there belonging to that Court which can, in the contemplation of sober reason, entitle it to the exercise of that transcendent and all absorbing power! Are the Judges peculiarly gifted, and exempt from the frailties incident to human nature? Are they, and will they always be, pure and infallible? Will they always be free from the influence of the selfish principle against which all free States have so sedulously endeavored to guard in their constitutions? On the contrary, are they not, will they not always be, subject to those impulses of ambition, those prejudices, and partialities, which are uniformly displayed by those who are at all concerned in the discussion or decision of political questions? I have no reference to the present incumbents; they are, some of them, talented, and all respectable men. They have my respect, and if they possessed the power of controlling sovereigns, they ought to be worshipped, because their likeness has never existed beneath the sun. But I would ask again, if any reasonable man can suppose that there is more safety to the rights of the Union, or of the States, in the wisdom and patriotism of the seven men who compose that Court, than in the wisdom and patriotism of the million and a half of people who compose the State of New York, or of even the fifty or sixty thousand who compose the little State of Delaware? Must the saying of the wise man be reversed in favor of that Court? Is it no longer true "that there is safety in a multitude of counsel?"

Does the gentleman pretend to have discovered that the converse of the proposition is true? I am sure that he will prefer no such pretensions: for it has been long the known belief of aristocrats, of monarchs, and of despots. With them it has been, and always will be a cherished truth, a truth sustained by their votaries, and enforced by themselves, at all times, and every where. The monarch who proclaimed "that there was safety in a multitude of counsel" did not himself act upon the principle which he avowed. This principle, so dear to the Republic, was asserted under the inspiration of that wisdom which distinguished the monarch of Judea from all other men—of that wisdom which is from above. May I not conclude, then, that no argument in favor of the power asserted for that court can justly be drawn from the paucity of its numbers? and that every argument which can be drawn from the number of the Judges, is against confiding to them a control over the State? Sir, if we refer to what may always be supposed to be the wisdom, purity, and patriotism, of the Judges of that Court, we cannot suppose that there ever will be a time when even the smallest State in the Union will not have engaged in administering its government a much greater number of men, any of whom will, in these respects, be the equals of the Judges. They will not only be their equals in patriotism, intelligence, and integrity, but greatly their superiors in an intimate practical acquaintance with the condition of the people, their habits, manners, customs, wants, and enjoyments. And, in addition to these, there will always be in the State a great many citizens as enlightened and as pure as either of the Judges or the State functionaries, whose vigilance will be employed in checking the officials, and restraining them within the sphere of their duty.

And, let me ask, if the enlightened functionaries of the State, and its enlightened citizens, will not always be as much interested in the correct administration of the Governments, General and State, in the happiness of the People, and in the perpetuity and prosperity of the Union, as those same Judges can be supposed to be? By what reason then can it be supposed that the framers of the Constitution were influenced to have accorded such power to the Judges? It is not expressly given in the Constitution: It is presumed to have been given by implication. But how can we obtain the power by implication from that instrument, unless we can reasonably suppose that those who framed it, meant to confer it. But, when we consider that this Court forms one Department of the Government, which Government is supposed to have encroached upon the sovereignty of a State, can we believe that the States, in forming the Constitution, intended to arm the Court with the power of deciding upon the legitimacy of its own encroachments? With the power of consecrating its own usurpations by its own decisions? A law of Congress, made in pursuance of the Constitution, is admitted on all sides to be supreme, and will be acquiesced in, and conformed to, by the States. The question is, whether a law in violation of the Constitution is supreme, or can be made so by the Court? Whether a State cannot form an opinion as to its invalidity, and interpose its veto, where its operation goes to deprive the State of its sovereign power? I contend that neither weakness or idiocy can be ascribed to a sovereign State, and, therefore, that a State may both think and act in the maintenance of its sovereignty.

Who ever before thought that one of the parties to a contest, was a competent judge of the matters in dispute? For, although the General Government was no party to the constitutional compact of Union—that having been formed by the States, who are the only parties to it—yet the Government which was created by that compact, when it encroaches upon the sovereign power of a State, may justly be considered, *quoad* the dispute, as a party to the contest, with the State, and, therefore, unfit to decide the matter in controversy. The case, it would seem to me, need but be stated to secure, with all intelligent men, the reprobation of the doctrine contended for on the part of the Court. Even in a contest between school children about their toys, or their amusements, neither will agree to let the other decide the matter in dispute. Sir, who does not perceive that the specification of the powers to be exercised by the General Government was entirely useless, if it was intended that those who were to exercise them, were to be the exclusive and final judges of the extent and legitimacy of their exercise?

But the power asserted for the Court, by the Honorable Senator, is unreasonable in other views. If those who formed the Constitution had intended to invest this tribunal with the political power of checking and regulating the Legislative and Executive Departments of the General Government, and of imposing certain salutary restraints upon the sovereignties of the States, they would not only have expressed that intention, but would have adapted and suited the forms of the Constitution to the full and efficient exercise of that power. Have they done so? This question must be answered in the negative by all who have paid the slightest attention to the specification of the powers allowed to be exercised by the General Government, and to the powers reserved to be exercised by the States. Let us suppose that the House of Representatives were to refuse to permit the members, or a portion of them, from a particular State, to take their seats in the legislative Hall of Congress: and that the Senate were to do the like, in relation to the Senators from any one of the States; or that any one of the States, or even a majority of them, were to refuse to elect Senators to Congress, or that a State were to make a Treaty with a foreign Power, or were to coin money; or let us suppose, further, that a person charged in any one of the States with treason, felony, or other crime, were to flee to another, and that other were to refuse, upon the demand of the Executive authority of the State from which he fled, to deliver him up, to be removed for trial to the State having jurisdiction of the crime. By what forms of the Constitution can the judicial power of the United States interfere in any of these cases, or in a hundred others which might be named? Sir, this mighty State-conserving power will be found, when subjected to the scrutiny of reason, to consist more in the fancy of those, who are desirous to see one splendid central government supply the place of the sovereign States, than in the nature and genius of our Governments, or in the intention of the States in forming the constitutional compact of union. And the great error which lies at the root of this monstrous doctrine, is in the erroneous supposition that the States, when they formed the Constitution divested themselves of, and delegated to the General Government, all the sovereign power which may be rightly exercised by the latter, and that they are less sovereign by so much power as may be thus exercised. That this sovereign power so delegated by the Constitution, is mysteriously lodged in that instrument, and exercised by the General Government in virtue of that lodgement.—(Sir, let me just say that sovereign power is an article that will not *keep cold*)—others think that this power abides in the functionaries of the Government, and almost all believe, that, let it be lodged where it may, it is out of the States and belongs to the General Government: that those who formed the Constitution, cut the sovereignty of each State into two parts, and gave much the largest portion to the General Government. I hope that I have, in a previous part of my argument, sufficiently refuted these erroneous, and, as I think, mischievous notions; and proved that sovereignty cannot exist in a divided State; that its unity and its life are inseparable; and, let me here add, that you might as well divide the human will—we can conceive of ten thousand diversities of its operation, but we cannot conceive of its separation into parts, neither can we conceive of the separation of sovereignty. It is the will of civil society—which society is a person whose will, in all its modes of operation, like the will of a human being, cannot, without destroying the person, be divided or separated into parcels, and when separated, it will be extinguished.

But, I may be asked, to what tribunal I would refer a question, involving the sovereign power of the State? I answer, most certainly not to the assailant of that power—not to the General Government, which shall have usurped it, and still less to the judicial department of that Government; and in my turn, I would ask to what tribunal should be referred an encroachment by the Supreme Court upon the sovereign power of a State: for that Court can, not only affirm an unconstitutional law, which assails the sovereignty of a State, but it can by construction (as we have in too many instances seen) give an unconstitutional efficacy to a perfectly constitutional law. It can, as we have seen, usurp the exercise of legislative power, and under the denomination of rules of Court, make laws under which the citizens of a State may be imprisoned contrary to law. Sir, the Congress have been obliged to interpose to prevent the exercise of this usurped power of the Judges, over the citizens of at least one of the States—I mean the State of Kentucky. And now, sir, the power of the State to legislate over its own soil, awaits upon the docket the decision of that tribunal.

But suppose the Congress, instead of restraining, as it did, the Judges of that Court, from incarcerating the citizens under color of their rules of Court, and contrary to the laws of the State, had refused to interfere. To what tribunal must the State have appealed for the protection of her citizens against lawless incarceration? The honorable Senator would say to the Supreme Court—to that very tribunal which had committed the outrage, I answer, emphatically, no. The sovereign power of the State should have been exerted for the protection of its own citizens. It can and ought to refuse to the court the use of its prisons, for purposes so oppressive of its citizens, and subversive of its sovereign power. It ought to exert its own governmental machinery to the extent of all their aptitudes, and of its own power, to protect its own citizens against aggressions so lawless and so enormous.

In such a case, the State should appeal to its own sovereign power, and decide for itself. Indeed, in every case involving its sovereignty, it must do so, or renounce its sovereign character—whether, it shall exert its self-protecting power, through the organs of its government, or through a convention, or by what other means it may, will depend upon the character of the aggression. Every State must speak its will through one or the other of those mediums. It may use the former, or employ the latter, according to its own opinion of their respective fitness, for the urgency.

And what, you will ask me, will be the result of this resistance by a State of an unconstitutional law of Congress, or an unconstitutional decision of the Supreme Court? I answer that the first result will be the preservation of the sovereignty of the State, and of the liberty of its citizens, at least for a time. The next result will be, that the attention of the people of the other States will be awakened to the aggression, and the Congress or the Supreme Court, whichever shall have been the aggressor, will be driven back, into the sphere of its legitimacy, by the rebuking force of public opinion. Such was the result of the nullifying resolutions of the States of Virginia and Kentucky, in relation to the alien and sedition laws. And such was the rebuking effect of public opinion in relation to the famous compensation law.

But if these results should not follow, you ask me what next? Must the State forbear to resist the aggression upon her sovereignty, and submit to be shorn of it altogether? I answer, no Sir, no; that she must maintain her sovereignty by every means within her power. She is good for nothing, even worse than good for nothing, without it. This, you will tell me, must lead to civil war. To war between the General Government and the resisting State. I answer, not at all, unless the General Government shall choose to consecrate its usurpations, by the blood of those it shall have attempted to oppress. And if the States shall be led by apprehensions of that kind, to submit to encroachments upon their sovereignties, they will most certainly not remain sovereigns long. Fear is a bad counsellor, of even an individual; it should never be consulted by a sovereign State.

No, Sir, it is in the power of Congress, instead of shedding the blood of the citizens, who assert the sovereignty of their State and resist its prostration, to refer the question to an infinitely more exalted tribunal than the Supreme Court. I mean to the States of this Union. They formed the Constitution—they are fit judges of questions involving sovereignty, being themselves sovereigns. The fifth article of the Constitution provides for the case. It reads thus: "The Congress, whenever two-thirds of both Houses shall deem it necessary to propose amendments to this Constitution, &c. &c. which when ratified by the Legislatures of three-fourths of the several States, or by conventions in three-fourths thereof, (not of the people at large, Mr. President, but of the States,) shall be valid to all intents and purposes as a part of this Constitution." Three-fourths of the States constitute the august tribunal to which Congress can refer the question. To this tribunal, the State can have no objection, because it was created by the Constitutional compact—because the power of amending the Constitution was accorded to it in that compact.

Mr. President, I state the case thus: The powers which the States, in their Constitutional compact, have allowed the General Government to exercise are special. The agents of the United States, in the exercise of those special powers, have, as one of the States alleges, transcended their specific limits, and infringed upon its sovereignty. The State resists the exercise of the power of which it complains, as unauthorized by any stipulation in the compact, and as incompatible with its own rights and duties as a sovereign. The agents, as functionaries of the General Government, say that the exercise of the obnoxious power is within their legitimate competency. But rather than be thought fastidiously nice, or perversely obstinate, modestly propose that the Supreme Court shall decide the matter. The State replies that it cannot, without violating every principle of congruity and self respect, submit any question in relation to its own sovereignty, to any portion of the subalterns of the States. That it is itself, in virtue of its sovereignty, the judge of its own rights, and bound as a sovereign to maintain them. That while a sovereign State cannot decently be supposed to violate the clear rights of the General Government, it cannot reasonably be required to surrender its own obvious rights, to the assertion of dubious powers on the part of that Government. That the right of sovereignty in the State is clear and unquestionable. That the right, under the alleged authority of which its sovereignty has been assailed, if it exist at all, must exist in specific grant. That the denial of its legitimate existence by a sovereign State, ought to induce the General Government either to abstain from exercising it, or to call upon the States to remove all doubt about its legitimacy, in an amendment to the Constitution, by the concurrent vote of three fourths of their number.

Mr. President, let me urge that this reply of the State is very reasonable, infinitely more so than the proposition on the part of the General Government, to which it is made. For if the power in question does not exist in the constitution, and is believed to be necessary for any of the great objects of the Union, the States will, by an amendment of the Constitution, accord its exercise to the General Government. Or if its existence in the Constitution is dubious, they will by an amendment, couched in explicit terms, remove all doubt; and thus, sir, the Government will avoid the tumult, confusion, and, perhaps, bloodshed, which might be connected with any attempt on the part of the General Government to divest a State of its sovereignty, and subdue it by force into vassalage. This is the course which the General Government *ought* to take in a question between itself and a sovereign State, in relation to the sovereignty of the latter, and the legitimacy of the power exerted by itself, in derogation of that sovereignty.

I say that Congress *should* take this course—that Congress should make the appeal to the tribunal of the States, because it claims to exercise a *special power,* and reason requires that when the existence of the power, or the legitimacy of its exercise, is questioned by a sovereign State, it should be able to show its authority free from all doubt. It is upon rational principles that in all Governments, courts of special and limited jurisdiction are required to accompany their acts, with the authority by which they were done; and their doings, unless their power to act is clearly shown, are considered as lawless and void. Sir, this principle limits the exercise of all special powers, whether legislative, executive, or judicial. A common corporation, chartered by a State, must be able to show in its charter an explicit authority for whatever power it claims to exercise, and its acts are void, unless its power to do them is explicitly granted in its charter. If the power under which it claims to act be dubious, instead of persisting to act, it must obtain from the Legislature an amendment of its charter, or abandon its claim to the power of acting, *quoad.* Now all the reasons which apply to the smallest corporation in relation to its chartered powers, apply with equal, with increased force to the Government of the United States, and to the Constitution, its charter.

It is a stupendous corporation, and becomes fearful in powers, when it claims for its judicial departments the exclusive right of legalizing by its decisions, the encroachments made by itself, upon the sovereignty of the States. The Constitution is its charter. Its powers are special and limited. To be safely exercised, they must be confined within the clear limits of the charter. If these limits may be transcended, all limitation was *useless.* If dubious powers may be exercised and enforced, then specification was useless.

It is upon this principle that officers of Government, before they can do any official act, must exhibit their commissions—their authority. No man occupies a seat in this body without having exhibited a clear title to it; and it might as reasonably be urged, that he could take his seat by force, without exhibiting title, or upon a doubtful title, as that the General Government shall exert by force a non-existing, or dubious power.

If a doubt had existed in the title of the Honorable Senator to a seat in this body, he would have had to go back and get his title so amended as to remove all doubt, before he could have occupied his seat. So the Congress, in relation to the exercise of even a doubtful power, should go back to the States, and obtain, by an amendment of their title, a removal of all doubt as to its legitimacy.

But another reason why Congress, and not the injured and resisting State, should make the appeal to the tribunal of the States, is, that an appeal by the State would be as unavailing as it would be unwise. A majority of the States have passed the obnoxious and questionable law complained of by the State. The State therefore *cannot* make the appeal *efficiently*, the Congress *can*. The State cannot do more than she has done. She must only poise herself upon her sovereignty, and resist its prostration. The Congress can do more. It can appeal *to* and obtain *from* the States an explicit decision of the question. And if it shall fail to make the appeal, and obtain the decision of that tribunal affirming its power, it should decline all further attempts to exert it. But again, the State is acknowledged to be a sovereign, and its sovereignty is acknowledged to be necessary, to the liberty of its citizens, and its own existence as a State. Its power is primitive, clear, and certain. That of the Government by which it is assailed, is derivative and doubtful; can any reasonable man say, that the former should yield to the latter, upon any other principle than that the latter is as abundant in force, as it is deficient in right? Reason itself would say, that the natural state of things should remain unaltered, unless the authority for removing or altering them, shall be full, clear, and legitimate.

Mr. President, throughout this debate the States have been treated as restless, querulous, impatient, disorganizing beings. It seems to have been taken for granted, that they are either too dull to comprehend the provisions of the Constitution, or too unprincipled to observe and maintain them. That the zeal to maintain the Union, and support the Constitution, by which it was formed, is exclusively with the functionaries of the General Government, that the States feel none of it. Now let us examine into this matter a little. All intelligent men act from motives. The States that formed the Union were composed of intelligent men. The motives which led to the formation of the Constitution, were to promote the happiness, tranquillity, liberty, and security of the people of the States. In furtherance of these great objects, the States agreed, in that instrument, to exert their sovereign power *jointly*, in making war, peace, and treaties, and levying money, and regulating commerce, &c. Their powers were to be exerted through the agency of the General Government. Now, can it be supposed that the motives which led to the formation of the Union have ceased to exist—have evaporated? That the people of the States are less inclined to be happy, tranquil, prosperous, secure, and free, *now*, than they were when the Union was formed? Or that their perceptions of its utility are less distinct and strong *now*, that its beneficial effects have been experienced, than they were *then*, when its beneficial effects were only anticipated? The States made the Constitution; and formed a more perfect Union, under the conviction that it was needed. Have occurrences, since that time, been calculated to prove that their convictions of its utility and necessity were erroneous? Have they given any indications to that effect? I believe not. On the contrary, they have evinced, from the period of its formation, up till this very moment, in which I am speaking, no sentiment in relation to any subject, so strongly as that of an affectionate regard for, and devotion to the Union. Why then this inquietude about the Union? Why is the gentleman inspired, *at this time*, with such a devotion to its consolidation? There was a time during the late war, when some zeal on that subject was felt; but at that time the reasons for it were apparent to all. For myself, I regard it as the Union of twenty-four sovereign States, and rely more upon their intelligence and zeal for its support, and continuance, than I do upon the power of the Supreme Court, or the inordinate zeal of any given number of *politicians*. It is upon the *people of the States,* and not upon the *politicians,* that solid reliance is to be placed, for the continuance, and just operation of all our institutions. They will maintain and vindicate the union, not for the purpose of imposing certain salutary restraints upon the sovereignty of the States; but for the high purposes and objects for which it was formed. Utility, Mr. President, was the object for which it was formed—and while it subserves that purpose, it will be maintained. But when purposes of splendor, and magnificence, of pageantry and parade, shall supersede those for which it was formed, whenever it shall be supposed that the sovereign States of which it is composed, must be whipped by the *patriotic functionaries* of the General Government, into the support of it—whenever its continuance shall be made to depend upon the power of the Supreme Court, exerted in subduing to its support the sovereign States; whenever the compact of union shall be so construed, as to give to the General Government the right of deciding upon the validity of its own encroachments, upon the sovereignties of the States; and let me add—whenever the States cease to maintain their sovereignty, and their own competency to maintain it against the encroachments of the General Government, then, indeed, will the duration of this Union become problematical.

We should never forget that the greatest good, when perverted, becomes the greatest evil. The Union, while it continues to be what it was, when it was formed, and what it was intended it should continue to be, an Union of *free, sovereign and independent States,* it will be considered by the States as the greatest conceivable political good—and for the maintenance and support of which, the people of the States would, when the occasion should demand it, pour out their blood like water. But even in their high estimation of it, they do not hold it as the greatest good. There is *one* still better, still more precious, which they rate infinitely higher. It is their liberty—and for the people to be free, the States must be free—and no State can be free, the sovereignty of which, is *subject* to the control of another—is subject to certain *restraints,* however salutary, imposed by the judicial department of *another* Government. But I feel confident, that while ever the Union conduces to the maintenance of the freedom of the States, the people of the States will maintain it, and whenever it shall be made the instrument of tyranny, and oppression, they will cast it off and form one more perfect. That is, if they retain the spirit of freedom—if they do not, it matters but little, what kind of Government they have.

And, indeed, upon the doctrine of the honorable Senator, relative to the power of the Supreme Court over the sovereignty of the States, I cannot see what is to prevent a perfect consolidation of the Government, and consequent monarchy or despotism. We have now, if he is right, a fearful oligarchy. Nothing but the forbearance of that tribunal can save us—we are denied the right of saving ourselves. The States must yield obedience to *their* sovereign mandate—must doff their sovereignty at the nod of the Judges. They cannot interpose their *veto,* but must submit to any salutary restraints which the Judges may choose to inflict upon their sovereignties. Sir, the power of imperial Rome, in her proudest days, were not superior to that asserted by the gentleman for the Supreme Court, nor were the humblest of her provinces in a condition more abject than that of these States, according to his doctrine.

The conquests of Rome were achieved at an incalculable expense of blood and treasure. But this tribunal may vassal twenty-four sovereign States without shedding one drop of blood, or expending one dollar of money. A single *curia advisore vult* will do the business.

Now, Sir, what is the condition of the States? They are not to resist encroachments upon their own sovereignty—resistance with them is crime. The Congress will not resist encroachments made by the Judiciary upon State sovereignty, because that encroachment is but a *salutary restraint,* and because the decision of the Court may, and no doubt often will be, but an affirmance of encroachment by the Legislative Department of the General Government; so that, sooner or later, State rights will be named only to point a sarcasm, or excite a smile of derision. Indeed a smile of that kind may even now be seen mantling upon the face of some gentlemen when that subject is named. Sir, these rights are exercised by the States in relation to subjects within their own territorial limits, and in a manner so little imposing as to attract but little attention from without.

The exercise of them is as obscure as it is beneficial. A State, in regulating its domiciliary concerns, exerts its sovereign power without its exterior trappings, without the usual lustre and imposing glare of national sovereignty. It never appears in *court dress*. It has no navy, no army, no diplomacy, no boundless revenue. In relation to all these subjects, the sovereign power of each is exercised jointly with that of the others. The General Government through whose agency the sovereign power of the States jointly is exerted, in relation to all these subjects, without having any national characteristic, without being more than a mere fiduciary for the States, is surrounded with the spendors and the patronage of a nation. And there is reason to apprehend that there are many, influenced by appearances, not less disposed to ascribe to it unqualified power, than some of its functionaries are to assume and exercise it.

But the whole argument of the gentleman has gone upon the predication that the States are to be kept in order by coercion only. That, but for the controlling power of the Supreme Court, they would transcend their appropriate spheres, and usurp the powers assigned by the Constitution to the General Government. Now, Sir, in what instance, I would ask, has any State displayed such a disposition? What exertion of power, by any one of them, since the formation of the Constitution, has been of that character? When did any one of the States attempt to make a treaty with a foreign power, or with any of the other States? Has any one of them attempted to make war—to coin money—to regulate commerce—to grant letters of marque and reprisal—to erect a navy—or raise and support armies—or to do any other act, or exercise any of the great powers separately, which they had agreed in the Constitution to exercise jointly? Has any State failed to send its proportion of members to the House of Representatives, or its two members to the Senate of the United States, or denied full faith and credit to the public acts, records, and judicial proceedings, of the other States? No State has violated, or attempted to violate the Constitution, in any of these particulars. I mention them, because in no one of them could the judiciary have interposed its restraining power, even if it were possessed by that department to the extent contended for. It could not, by the forms of the Constitution, have reached any one of the cases, by any conceivable exertion of its power. What, then, restrained the States from violating the Constitution, in any of the particulars which I have enumerated? If they are as prone to transcend the limits of their power as they are represented to be, one would think that in the course of fifty years, some instance of violation must have occurred. No, Sir, the security of the

Constitution from inroads upon it by the States, is to be found in that wisdom, which is always associated with sovereignty. If the concurrent will, and the concentrated wisdom of the people who compose a State, is not to be confided in, on what else under Heaven, I ask, can confidence be placed? That will is necessarily pure, because it is the will of the people; not as people, but as citizens. It is the will of all in relation to each, and of no one in relation to himself specially; and there is not a man, or set of men, on earth who, if they can be freed from selfish influences, will not act justly. Sir, that is the condition of the citizens of the States; their sentiments are all of that character; they are discolored in their operation, by the selfish influences of the political fiduciaries, through whose agency they take effect; and this discoloration, which is produced by the functionaries, is charged upon the citizens. It is the functionaries then, and not the citizens, who are to be feared; and those of the General Government not less than those of the States; and with both, those are most to be feared who are least responsible to the citizens; and, therefore, the judiciary is more to be dreaded than any other department. What motives, let me repeat, can the State have, to weaken or destroy the Union? They formed it, and after all, they have the power of maintaining or destroying it. It lives in the breath of their nostrils—in their intelligence—in their affections—and their conscious need of it. It was not formed by them under the coercive influence of the Supreme Court; it was the offspring of the unrestrained and unconstrained sovereignties of the States. Sir, the doctrine contended for, is parricidal; it is for the destruction of the parent, by its offspring; it is not the doctrine of Jefferson, or Madison, or Hamilton. But I am averse from quotation; a doctrine should be approved or reprobated; not because it has, or has not, had the sanction of this or that distinguished man, but because it is intrinsically right or wrong. I am opposed to the government of *living men*, still more of the *dead*. Our government should be that of *laws*, through the agency only of men. Every civil society, large enough to constitute and maintain itself as a state, should govern itself by its own will, through the medium of such devices as its wisdom shall select. It should act jointly with its associates, in reference to foreign objects, and separately in reference to its interior concerns; but it should maintain its sovereignty by all means and at all hazards; for there is not in the catalogue of evils, a single one so much to be deprecated by a State, as the prostration of its sovereignty—it is the loss of their liberty, to the people who compose it.

Mr. President, I fear I have fatigued you and the Senate; the only apology I can offer, is the importance of the subject which I have endeavored to discuss. I view the State sovereignties as the sheet anchor of the Union. I look to the States, and not to the Supreme Court, for its strength and perpetuity. I view the doctrine asserted by the gentleman as greatly more dangerous to this Union, than the Hartford Convention, or the war, through which it has so gloriously passed.

Sir, there is no danger of the States flying off from the Union; you may possibly drive them off, by attempting to prostrate their sovereignty, and make them vassals of the Supreme Court, or provinces of the General Government; but left in the undisturbed enjoyment of their own sovereign rights, they will cling to the Union, to the rock of their safety, and adhere to it, until time itself shall have grown old.

Mr. President, I cannot close without expressing my concurrence in the sentiments so eloquently and forcibly expressed by the honorable Senator from South Carolina, (Mr. Hayne,) in relation to the public lands. The Union would not, in my opinion, be weakened, but strengthened, by his mode of disposing of them; upon his plan, you would have farm where you have now a wilderness, freeholders where you have now day-laborers, and the abjection of poverty would be exchanged for the pride and patriotism of proprietorship. Sir, the strength of the Union is in the number and patriotism of the people of the sovereign States which compose it, and the wealth of the States consists in the *productive industry* of their citizens. Now, the strongest incentive to agricultural industry consists in the consciousness of each citizen that he is the proprietor of the soil which he cultivates. Let the public lands then be sold, not given, at a price, which aims rather at multiplying freeholders, than at increasing the revenue, as the primary object of selling them.

Another motive with the United States to sell the public lands at a very moderate price, should be to strengthen the weak and more exposed parts of the country. Emigrants should find in the reduced price of the lands, strong motives to settle, and thereby strengthen those weak and exposed parts. But the great, the paramount motive with me, to sell the public lands at the very lowest price, would be to release the States in which they lie, from their dependence upon the General Government; and the other States from the degradation of soliciting, of supplicating, Congress, for donations of them. The States should have the eventual or transcendental right of sovereigns to the soil within their limits.

Every policy, which has a tendency to humiliate the States, either by force or seduction, should, in my opinion, be deprecated. It is a tendency towards the consolidation of the Government, and the slavery of the people.

Revenue, for the same reasons, should not be unnecessarily accumulated in the public Treasury. The money, not needed by the Government, should not be exacted from the people. It should be left in their pockets; there it increases the incentives to industry, and the facilities to reward it. When the treasury of a monarch overflows, his subjects bleed: for war is the game at which monarchs delight to play, when they have money to sustain it. When the revenues of a republic are redundant, peculation, fraud, and corruption, nestle about the Treasury. Among free governments, that is the best which promotes the happiness, and protects the rights of the people, at the *least expense.* The people get their money by labor; whatever the government takes of it, more than is necessary to pay the just expenses of its administration, is to the extent of the excess, an infliction of slavery upon them. Revenue, beyond the necessary expenses of this government, can only be necessary for purposes of consolidation, not of the Union, but of the Government.

Mr. President, a word upon the road making power of the Government, or rather upon the expediency of the exercise of that power, by this Government: for the State of Kentucky has, for *the present,* silenced the question *with me,* as to the power. I am an instruction man, and will speak the sentiment of my State, according to its instructions, without inquiring into the reasons by which it was influenced in giving those instructions.

I cannot, however, repress the expression of my fears, that there is more of seduction in the captivating terms by which this system is designated, than there will be of solid, practical utility, in its process and results, "The American System." These are words of magic potency, with those who do not examine into their import, into the operation and effect of what they mean. If they are construed to mean the exercise of any power, not expressly allowed by the States, to be exercised by the General Government, then their import sanctions usurpation—then the Constitution ceases to be alone the bond of union. If they mean that the powers of the Union, instead of being exerted *for* the States, and *for* the great objects contemplated *by* the States, shall be exerted *within each State,* then, it behooves the States to inquire into the *cui bono*—into the policy of it. It behooves them to inquire, whether the money expended in making roads in each State, is the money of that State, collected from the people of it, or is the money of, and collected from, the people of another, to make roads in that State. Each

State should then inquire of itself, whether it would be willing to be taxed, for the purpose of making roads in another State. The people of Massachusetts would not be so much enamoured with the American System as they are, if they understood it to mean, that they should be taxed to make roads in Kentucky; nor would the people of Kentucky admire it greatly, when, by its operation, they were taxed to make roads in the State of Massachusetts, and so with the other States. Each would refuse to surrender the surplus produce of its labor, to embellish with fine roads and canals the surface of another State. Well, when they understand it to be nothing more than the exercise of a power by the General Government, in taxing the people of each State, and collecting the money *from them*, to make roads *for them*, in their own State, they will say, that the power of the State is competent to collect this money, and to make its own roads. That each State has discernment enough to lay out and superintend the making of its own roads, upon its own land. The General Government has no land in most of the States, and no sovereign jurisdiction over any of them. The only result of the exercise of this power by the Government, within the States, is to diminish the power and patronage of the State, and swell unnecessarily that of the General Government. If the State makes the road, it employs all whose agency shall be needed in the operation—engineers, superintendents, overseers, laborers, &c.; and it, instead of the tax gatherers of the General Government, collects, by the operation of *its own* revenue laws, from its own citizens, the money required for the object. It retains, as it ought, jurisdiction over the road, as a part of its own soil. It erects the gates, and regulates and collects the toll, by the agency of its own officers. All this is natural and appropriate: it is the just and natural operation of the sovereign power of the State, within its own limits, and with its own means. But, is the operation of the American system of this character? Is it natural, just, expedient, or legitimate, in this view of it? What, let me ask you, are the States for, if they are incompetent to make their own roads? You reply, to protect their citizens, and their property. But will they not, in this instance, surrender them over to be taxed by the General Government, and will they not subject their citizens to the jurisdiction of the Federal Courts, in all disputes which may arise, relative to the collection of the tolls, and relative to the lands over which the roads pass? The road is to be made, the gates erected, and tolls fixed, under a law of Congress, and then those laws are to be supreme, and cognizable by the Federal Judiciary alone. Sir, we have heard the power of the Supreme Court discoursed of, by the honorable Senator from Massachusetts, in relation to its control over State sovereignty; and ought the States to swell the power of this tribunal, by a voluntary surrender of their jurisdiction over their soil, their citizens, and the road-making power? Does any man, even the most devoted to the American system, believe that the people of the States would agree to a direct tax for the purpose of making roads in the States! And would the people of any one State agree to pay a direct tax for the purpose of making roads in another State?

Mr. President, the true American system is the sovereignty of the States, the freedom of citizens, and the constitutional strength and compaction of the Union. We hear nothing *now* scarcely, about any thing but the beneficent operation of the American system, and the beneficence of the General Government. We should take care that it may not turn out as it is with the prophet who swallowed the hook—"sweet to the palate, but bitter to the stomach." Would the people of Tennessee agree to be compelled by the General Government, to labor upon the roads of Kentucky, or the people of the latter to labor on the roads of the former? I think they would not. Well, is not the money of the people of each State their labor? Is it not the earnings of their labor? and where is the odds in reason, between making the people of Tennessee labor upon the roads in Kentucky, and taking the money which they have earned by their labor, and expending it upon making roads in the latter State?

But if the power of levying money in one State, and expending it in making roads in another, be conceded to Congress, what is to prevent that body from regulating and equalizing the labor of the people of the States? and, under that power, to equalize the crops of the different States? Is not that in fact the result of the principle? for the most productive States pay the most money into the Treasury. They make their money from their crops, and if it is to be expended in the least productive States, is not that equalizing the crops? But upon this principle might it not happen, that some of the small States would not have any of the money of other States expended within their limits, and even their own expended within the limits of another State? Might not the large, and as many of the small States, as would form a majority in both Houses of Congress, combine to expend the surplus revenue, in making of roads and of encouraging manufactures, within the limits of their own States respectively, to the entire exclusion of the minority. Eleven States in that case might be sacrificed to the encouragement of manufactures, and the making of roads in the other thirteen, and that, too, forever, according to the doctrine of the Hon. Senator from Massachusetts, (Mr. Webster) & the beneficent operation of the American system. None of the excluded States could, according to his doctrine, interpose its veto. If they did, they would incur the guilt of rebellion or treason. Sir, I am for the system of the Union, according to the constitutional compact of the States in the Constitution of the U. States.

Mr. President, every institution of man is purer at its commencement than at any after period of its history. There is in all human institutions, a fatal proclivity to degeneracy—even the institutions of our holy religion degenerate. Hence the people of every Government have their choice between reform and revolution. They must do the one, experience the other, or submit to vassalage. But even reform is derided now. No doctrines are well received that do not tend to centre all power in the General Government, and conduce to the annihilation of the sovereignty of the States, and the erection upon their ruins of a magnificent empire.

I am, with my whole heart, and in all its feelings, in favor of the Union; but it is the union of the *States*, and not an indiscriminate union of the people. I would not, by construction, or otherwise, reduce the States to *mere petty corporations*, and make them subservient to a judicial oligarchy—to a great central power of any kind. I would have the Union to consist of the free, sovereign, and independent States, of which it was intended by the Constitution to be composed; I would have the *citizens* of each to look to their State for the security and enjoyment of their rights and their liberty. The Union which I advocate is also represented by the stripes and the stars. Each stripe a State, and each star its sovereignty. I would not mingle the stripes, or blot out a star, for any earthly consideration; and I would have each star to brighten with its benign and unclouded light, the whole sphere of State sovereignty; I would have them all to shine with confluent lustre throughout the legitimate sphere of the Union. The stripes should thus wave, and the stars thus shine, if my wishes were consulted, until even Time himself should be enfeebled with age. But I am done, and I fear the Senate are glad of it.

WILLIAM SMITH

William Smith was born in South Carolina in 1762. He attended Mt. Zion College, studied law, and was admitted to the bar in 1784. He was elected as a Republican to the state senate from 1803 to 1808, and was elected judge of the South Carolina circuit court from 1808 to 1816. Smith was elected to the United States Senate in 1816, serving one term. He was an ardent defender of states' rights and an opponent of banks, capitalism, internal improvements, and the protective tariff. In national politics he aligned himself with William H. Crawford and in South Carolina politics was a political enemy of the nationalist views of John C. Calhoun. In 1823 he lost his Senate seat to Hayne, the candidate of the Calhoun faction in the South Carolina Republican party. Smith served in the South Carolina House of Representatives from 1823 to 1825, leading the attack on Republican policies of internal improvements and a protective tariff. He was elected to fill a vacancy in the U.S. Senate in 1826 and served until 1831. An ultrastrict constructionist, he played a leading role in the South Carolina protest against the tariff, but he opposed nullification and the plan to call a state convention. The Calhounite faction regarded him as too moderate and nationalistic, and he was defeated by the nullification candidate in 1830. His South Carolina political career ended in the state senate in 1832. Smith moved to Mississippi and then Alabama, where he served in the state House of Representatives from 1836 to 1840. In 1829 and in 1836, Smith declined nomination to the United States Supreme Court by President Andrew Jackson. He died in 1840.

Speech of Mr. Smith,

of South Carolina

[February 25, 1830]

The resolution of Mr. Foot, of Connecticut, relative to the
public lands, being under consideration, Mr. Smith addressed
the Chair as follows:

Mr. Smith said, this debate had assumed a wide range, and
encircled almost every political subject that had agitated this Government for the last forty years, and more. Although about to give my own
views to the Senate, said Mr. S., I do not aspire to ornament, but to illustrate what I may say. This debate has been one of feeling; and especially as
it related to the disposition, by the General Government, of the public
lands. And if I am to judge from the manner in which it has been treated
by gentlemen who have said a great deal concerning it, I should suppose
they had examined but superficially its extent and importance to the People of the United States. If your treasure is worth preserving for the use of
the Government, why should you sport away your public lands more than
your public monies? For the manner in which it is proposed to get rid of it,
if not sporting it away, it is probably as bad.

I do not intend to limit my remarks to the subject of the public lands,
entirely, but, after I shall have done with that, will take a cursory view of
several other topics that have excited much interest; which, perhaps, I may
not treat precisely as other gentlemen have done, yet, I will endeavor to
treat them fairly. I have always found that matters of fact give a fairer view
of party subjects than your abstract speeches. A gentleman who speaks abstractedly, generally, does little more than give you what is best suited to
his purpose. But if these topics are discussed for public use, the public are
entitled to hear all; otherwise the public are imposed upon; they are misguided by seeing but one side of the question. The public are always prepared to judge rightly, and, if correctly informed, will always do so. On the

subject of party politics—a subject from which there is more to fear than from any other that agitates your Government—the truth has not been half told; and when I reach it, I may perhaps differ from other gentlemen in the view that I may take of it.

On the subject of the public lands, their importance, which seems to be overlooked, and the manner in which the gentleman from New Hampshire, (Mr. Woodbury,) and my colleague, (Mr. Hayne,) propose to dispose of them, are so totally different from my own, as to require my first attention. And believing, as I do, that they have not treated that subject as its importance requires, I will first notice what they have respectively said on that question, and then give my reasons, founded on facts, why I differ from them.

The gentleman from New Hampshire says, in addition to doing justice to the People of the Western States, it is necessary to accelerate the sales of your public lands, as fast as possible, lest you drive your citizens to foreign countries, to seek for lands and comfortable homes. In support of this opinion, that gentleman informs us, that the British Government is now selling lands at reduced prices, not only in their Colonies in New Holland, but in the Canadas, and are, thereby, holding out inducements to your citizens to emigrate thither. That other European nations have adopted the same seductive policy. Even Persia holds out inducements to emigrants, by selling her lands at reduced prices. In consequence of your own delays, and this liberal policy of other nations, your citizens, we are told, are actually departing from the United States; by which we are to understand your States are to be depopulated, and your physical strength transferred to other countries, and to foreign enemies. This would be an injudicious policy, indeed, on the part of our Government, could we assent to the premises. But what possible inducement could an American citizen have to break up his household, sell off every thing, and transport himself to New Holland, a country that not one American in twenty thousand ever heard of, there to speculate upon a quarter section of land, when there are millions of acres lying at his own door, at $1.25 per acre? Or can we imagine that any motive whatever could induce an American to forego all the comforts held out at home, to look for better times in Persia? What is the fact as regards the Canadas? In 1825, I visited that country, and whilst at Quebec, and elsewhere, was informed, from high authority, that their Government imported from Ireland, annually, ten thousand people, and that another ten thousand, at least, come of their own accord, or were brought from that country by their wealthy friends. That most of these people went to Upper Canada, being esteemed the best portion of the British possessions in America, and there received a bounty in lands, farming utensils, and provisions, by the Government, and were there kept under some kind of guard, to prevent them from emigrating. Notwithstanding all those attentions, and all this vigilance on the part of Government, one half of them, at least, made their escape to the United States. The reasons why they should do so are obvious. Whilst this country, sir, continues to present so many, and such strong inducements to the enterprising, as well as the oppressed of other nations, we have none of the perils which that gentleman has brought to our view, to fear.

My colleague (Mr. HAYNE) had been still more importunate; and would induce a belief that this Government would be overwhelmed, if you do not forthwith dispose of your public lands, and that to the Western States; and reproaches the General Government for selling, instead of giving them to the Western People. Before I offer my own opinion, I will give his, in his own words, as far as he has published what he expressed. He says:

"No gentleman can fail to perceive that this is a question no longer to be evaded: it must be met—fairly and fearlessly met. A question that is pressed upon us in so many ways, that intrudes in such a variety of shapes, involving so deeply the feelings and interests of a large portion of the Union, cannot be put aside, or laid to sleep. We cannot long avoid it—we must meet and overcome it, or it will overcome us. Let us, then, Mr. President, be prepared to encounter it in a spirit of wisdom and justice." He further says:

"I believe that out of the Western country there is no subject in the whole range of our legislation, less understood, and in relation to which there exists so many errors, and such unhappy prejudices and misconceptions. There is a marked difference observable between our policy and that of every other nation that has attempted to establish colonies or create new States. The English, the French, and the Spaniards, have, successively, planted Colonies here, and have all adopted the same policy, which, from the very beginning of the world, had always been found necessary in the settlement of new countries, viz., a free grant of lands, *without money and without price.* The payment of *a penny, or a peppercorn,* was the stipulated price."

Here he contrasts the policy of these foreign Governments with the policy of our own Government, it being their policy to give away their lands, and ours to sell them for a fair price. And says of our policy:

"It would seem the cardinal point of our policy was not to settle the country, and facilitate the formation of new States, but to fill our coffers by coining our lands into gold. Let us consider for a moment, Mr. President, the effect of these two opposite systems on the condition of a new State. I will take the State of Missouri, by way of example. The inhabitants of this new State, under such a system, it is most obvious, must have commenced their operations under a load of debt, the annual payment of which must necessarily drain their country of the whole profits of their labor, just so long as this system shall last. Sir, the amount of this debt has, in every one of the new States, actually constantly exceeded the ability of the People to pay. What has been the consequence, sir? Almost universal poverty. Sir, under a system by which a drain like this is constantly operating upon the wealth of the whole community, the country may be truly said to be afflicted with a curse."[*]

My colleague, Mr. President, after passing a high eulogium on the English, French, and Spanish monarchies, for giving away their public lands "without money and without price, for a penny or a peppercorn," and a censure upon our own Government, for its oppression upon the People of the West, for selling, instead of giving them all the lands, has declared, *that after the public debt shall have been paid, if he should not give them away, he would, at least, sell them to the States in which they lie, for a mere nominal sum, and of that nominal sum he would not put one cent into the public treasury; and that he would now begin with the State of Ohio, as he considered that State ready for such a change in our policy.*[†]

Mr. President, in discussing subjects of public concern, I will always go with my colleague, whensoever good reasons exist to justify me in doing so. But, upon this occasion, my views are essentially different from his. He thinks the People of the Western States are excessively oppressed and borne down by the exactions of the General Government. I entertain a contrary opinion. I think the Government has been more than lenient to the People of the West. He has given his reasons for the opinions he entertains; I beg leave to give mine, why I am opposed to his propositions. He says the People of the West are hardly dealt with; the profits of their labor were annually drawn off to fill the coffers of the Treasury, and to be expended elsewhere; that the amount of their debts exceeded their ability

---

[*]The part marked with double commas contains verbatim what he said in his printed speech, as corrected by himself, and published in the Daily National Intelligencer, of January 29th.

[†]The part in italics is what Mr. Hayne expressed, verbatim, in his first speech, but which has been omitted in his speech as printed.

to pay; that under a system by which a drain like this is constantly operating upon the wealth of the whole community, the country may be truly said to be afflicted with a curse, &c.

Mr. President, it is not from any unkind feelings towards the People of the West that I am induced to differ with my colleague. On the contrary, I shall always rejoice in their prosperity. An overgrown prosperity, however, was not to be cherished, at the entire expense of the rest of the Union. I will endeavor to ascertain if these complaints, which seem to grate with such severity upon our feelings, were well founded, or imaginary, only. The Western States are compared to the colonies of the monarchical Governments of Europe; and their policy had been urged by my colleague as worthy our imitation. The colonies of monarchical Governments and the new States adopted into this Union, are totally different in their character. A colony founded by a monarch is never with a view to promote human happiness, or the private interest of the subject, but for the aggrandizement of the monarch himself. He does it to augment his power. He gives his domain to his subjects, "without money and without price"—"for a penny or a pepper corn." But he can strip them of every vestige of civil and religious liberty, if he chooses to do so. The lands composing the Western States do not belong to Congress; they belong to the People of the United States; not obtained by conquest, but purchased with their money. Congress is nothing more than their agent to dispose of them upon fair terms, and for a price; and that price to be placed in the public Treasury; not for the benefit of any particular portion of the States, but for the benefit of the Union; in which the Western States enjoy a full participation. These lands are not sold to, or forced upon, any portion of your citizens who had no alternative. They were the common property of the People. They were sold at auction to the highest bidder. Those who chose to buy, and every one had his option, bought with a view of going there to better his condition. They did not buy until the country was conquered and at peace. They were at no expense in conquering the country. It was conquered by the Government, and the lands surveyed, ready for the highest bidder to take possession immediately. Is it, sir, because a small portion of the People have, as a matter of free choice, bid off a small portion of your public lands, that you should surrender to them four or five hundred millions of acres for a mere nominal sum—for no other reason than because it is said they cannot pay their debts?

Sir, there are other insuperable objections to disposing of your lands in this way: for, suppose you were to sell to the State of Ohio all the public lands that lie within its chartered limits, for a mere nominal sum, could you expect thereby to purify the political morals of the community, or stay the importunities of the People of the West? Will not every other Western State demand the same indulgence? Then, sir, instead of being "lashed round the miserable circle of occasional argument," by a few individual debtors, you will be doubly "lashed" by the whole People of the West. They will at once ask you to remit that nominal sum; and, if there be not virtue and firmness enough in Congress to resist the "lashings" and importunities of a few public debtors, how are you to calculate upon such delicate statesmen, as this argument would imply Congress to consist of, to resist the pressure of the whole Western States, united in one common cause, and propelled by the same common interest? If we have not firmness enough to listen to the arguments of two or three gentlemen from the West, without being subdued, against the convictions of our own minds, we ought to say so at once, and tell the People of the West we know you ought not to have these lands, because they are the common property of us all; but we have no firmness to resist your importunities; therefore, take them, and save Congress from corruption.* Can any thing be more degrading? What can be more humiliating to a public assembly than to be informed it must prepare to get rid of an important public question, "or it will overcome us?" Such a prostration of your independence will put an end to your powers, and fit you solely for ministering to the vices and intrigues of all who may discover your imbecility. Sir, this is the argument with which Congress has more than once been assailed upon this question—the corruption it tended to introduce into Congress. Nothing can lead so directly to corruption as too great an imbecility in Congress to resist its approaches. If corruption cannot be met and resisted here, how is it to be resisted in the States, suppose you sell them the lands, where the State Legislatures can more easily be approached, and where there would be a more immediate access for the whole community? It is by no means my intention to impute corruption to the People of the West, or, in the least degree, to diminish their standing in this Union. I am proud to say I believe there does not exist a finer population in any State, in this or any other country than the population of the Western States. The reasons

---

*It is this easy yielding, which is so often submitted to, that has subjected us to the almost total annihilation of Southern influence in the councils of our country. To be called magnanimous, is but a poor compensation for the sacrifice of our dearest rights. This is about the amount of our portion in the benefit of the General Government. We have shared this largely. For it we gave our control over the tariff and internal improvement.

were obvious, and which I will not stop here to render. It has been those who have been yielding to their importunities that have given rise to this imputation. I have found no difficulty in resisting those importunities myself; nor do I fear the influence of corruption from that source.

Sir, as I believe all the declamation that we have heard uttered against the General Government, for its unrelenting rigor in its exactions from the Western States, and the oppression and distress which they have fallen under, by the misguided policy of Congress, to be totally unfounded, I will here inquire what had been the policy towards the new States, and if not distinguished by its favors conferred on the Western People. Among the favors gratuitously bestowed, was the setting apart every sixteenth section of the public lands for the use of public schools, which amounts to the thirty-sixth part of all the public lands owned by the Government. They have, also, five per cent. of all the public moneys arising from the sales of all public lands sold within their respective States, to be paid out of the public Treasury of the United States, and to be applied in the States, respectively, to make roads; lands for colleges, lands for every other public institution for which they have asked it; lands in great abundance for making roads and canals—half a million, and a million of acres at a time, have been given. When times grew hard, and they could not pay without great inconvenience for these over purchases, Congress enacted laws, authorizing every purchaser to relinquish to the Government any portion of the lands he had purchased, and transfer the moneys paid therefor, to the payment of such lands as he thought fit to retain. These laws had been reenacted whenever asked for. All moneys that had been forfeited for not complying with the stipulated conditions of sales of lands, were returned. Sir, Missouri, which my colleague had selected as a State on which the oppression of the General Government had fallen with an heavy hand, had received all those indulgences, privileges, and donations, with the other Western States. They had, moreover, been peculiarly cherished by the General Government. The public laws, under which the trial of title to lands claimed by the citizens of that State, and also claimed by the United States, had been modelled and remodelled to suit the wishes of her citizens, whenever her Senators have said to Congress that a change of the law was desired by their constituents. An army had been sent there, expressly, to guard her frontier. A school of army discipline had been established at St. Louis, for no obvious reason but to scatter the public moneys for the benefit of her citizens. A military force is kept up for the express purpose of escorting her Mexican traders through a wide wilderness, and kept up at a great expense to this Government. And at this time, it is about to be augmented by adding a corps of United States' cavalry of 500, that will cost this Government $100,000 per annum. Yet it is urged by the Senator from that State, [Mr. Benton,] and my colleague, that she is borne down and stript of her hard earnings, for no other reason than because the General Government will not surrender to her the vast domains, as a prey to inordinate speculation. The other Western States do not complain. They ask indulgences, and receive them; but they, with very few exceptions, believe that such a surrender would be destructive to their morals and harmony. Besides, sir, there were other considerations to be regarded. The United States had purchased those lands at a great expense. The original cost paid to France, Spain, to Georgia, and to the Indian tribes, amounts to more than $30,000,000. There are also a vast number of Indian annuities arising from Indian purchases, as a part of the price. Some of them to terminate at a given period. More than fifty of them, however, are permanent annuities, and must endure as long as the tribes to which they are payable, shall endure.* This perpetual yearly drain upon your Treasury will be felt, if your public lands are to be sold to the Western States for a mere nominal sum, and not a cent of that sum put into the Treasury. There are a vast many other incidental expenses, for removing Indians, for Indian treaties, and Indian agents. This is all to be left for the General Government to pay.

Sir, amidst all the ardor to relieve the Western States from the oppression of the General Government, neither my colleague [Mr. Hayne] nor the Senator from Missouri [Mr. Benton] had taken any notice of the interest which the United States have in this question. They have not referred to the vast quantity of lands which have been purchased by the General Government, nor to the condition of those lands. It would seem, from the views they have taken of the public lands, that they consider them of very little consequence, further than as a peace-offering from the General Government to the Western States. But those who have examined the question more at large, consider the sacrifice too great. The General Government, in order to ascertain the precise state of the public lands, that is, what quantity of acres had been purchased from the Indians by the Government; what portion of that had been surveyed by your public surveyors; what portion of it had been sold; what portion of the lands surveyed still remained to be sold; and what was the quantity of unsold lands, including what was unsur-

*See Senate Documents, 2d session, 16th Congress, vol. 1, No. 14.

veyed as well as what was surveyed. Also, the amount of moneys for the lands sold; the amount paid, and the amount then due from purchasers; a return of which had been made by the Treasury Department, as found recorded in the Senate Documents, 2d session, 19th Congress, vol. 3d, No. 63, where there will be seen the following statement:

"*A Statement of the Public Lands, 1st January,* 1826."

	ACRES.
The quantity then purchased	260,000,000
The quantity then surveyed	138,000,000
The quantity then sold, only	20,000,000
The quantity surveyed, and then unsold	118,000,000
The quantity surveyed and unsurveyed, and unsold	213,000,000

Amount of sales of public lands 1st of January, 1826 ....$	39,301,794
Amount of moneys paid by purchasers	31,345,963
Amount due by individuals	7,955,831

	ACRES.
Quantity of lands unsold	213,000,000
Deduct for barren lands one half	107,000,000
Will remain of good lands yet to sell	106,000,000
*This sold at the minimum price, $1.25, will give for revenue ..$	132,500,000

	ACRES.
There yet remain, upon a moderate calculation of lands yet in possession of the Indians, the titles to which you are constantly extinguishing. Then deduct half for barren lands	200,000,000
	100,000,000
Leaves of good lands for sale	100,000,000
Which sold at minimum price, $1.25, will give for revenue .....$	125,000,000
*Add to this the above $132,500,000	132,500,000
Will give a revenue of .....$	257,500,000

This, Mr. President, is not a supposed case, gotten up for the purpose of argument, that may be true, or may not be true, but is as certain as a mathematical axiom—a conclusion drawn from established premises, and cannot be controverted. And I would beg leave to ask the Senate, if they were prepared to sacrifice 257,500,000 dollars of revenue, to appease the importunities of two or three members of Congress from the Western States, because this revenue could not be grasped in a moment? Or because it is said "if we do not overcome the Western importunities, they will overcome us?" Or why, sir, should Missouri, already gorged with the bounties and privileges of this Government, be selected by the gentleman (Mr. H.) as an example by which to illustrate the oppression of the General Government upon the Western States? The General Government has "drained" from Missouri but very little of the profits of her labor, as yet, sir.

How stands the account between Missouri and the General Government?

	ACRES.
In Missouri, there had been sold only	980,282
There yet remains to be sold in that State	34,000,000
Of this, there have been surveyed and ready to sell	21,000,000

Before one thirty-fifth part of the public lands within her limits are sold, we are asked to withdraw the oppressive hand we are imposing upon Missouri, and forbear to draw from her people the whole profits of their labor.

We have come now, Mr. President, to the last view of this land question—one of much magnitude, and one that seems to have entirely escaped the observation of those gentlemen. During the Revolutionary war, in which all the States were engaged, it was suggested by some of them, that the wild lands to the West, although within the chartered limits of some of the States, yet lying beyond the limits of the population, and unappropriated, ought of right to belong to the Union. And whether this was a correct or an incorrect principle, so it was, that when that immense tract of country lying North-west of the Ohio river was ceded to the United States, by the State of Virginia, a provision was made in the act of cession:

"That all the lands within the territory so ceded to the United States, and not reserved for, or appropriated to, any of the before mentioned purposes, or disposed of in bounties to the officers and soldiers of the American army, shall be considered as a common fund for the use and benefit of such of the United States, as have become, or shall become, members of the confederation, or federal alliance of the said States, Virginia inclusive, according to their usual respective proportions in the general charge and expenditure, and shall be faithfully and bona fide disposed of for that purpose, and for no other use or purpose whatsoever."*

The public debt of the United States is now nearly extinguished, and will probably be quite so, without drawing much more from the public land fund, which has produced a long and ardent discussion in the House of Representatives, concerning a division of these lands among the several States of the Union, upon the provision in the act of cession. The proposition by those who are advocates for a division is, that the lands shall be divided among the several States, in proportion to representation. This principle, sir, is erroneous. If a division is to take place, the principle upon which it shall be made, is laid down in the act of cession itself, and can admit of no alteration or modification to suit present circumstances. To divide, according to the ratio of representation, would give to the State of New York 34-213, but would give to South Carolina, only 9-213, making a difference in favor of New York, with her present overgrown population, of nearly four times as much as that of South Carolina. But if you take the rule as laid down in the act of cession itself, it will give a very different result in favor of South Carolina. The plain and obvious meaning of the act cannot be mistaken. The words which bear upon this question are—

"Shall be considered a common fund for the use and benefit of such States, &c. according to their usual respective proportion in the general charge and expenditure."

These words are altogether retrospective; and evidently refer to "their usual respective proportions in the general charge and expenditure," incurred during the Revolutionary war. To arrive at that conclusion, it is only necessary to ascertain why this cession was made by Virginia to the United States; and at what time it was made, and what purposes it was to accomplish. It was entered into whilst the Union was under the articles of the Confederation. And the purposes it was intended to accomplish were, to indemnify the several States for what they had respectively expended in support of that war. It is as plain as the English language can convey it to our senses, that the "respective proportions of the general charge and expenditure," expressed in that cession, can attach to no other "charge and expenditure," but the charges

*See Laws of the United States, vol. 1, page 474.

and expenditures of that war. They point to that object alone—no other existed. And the "respective proportions of the general charge and expenditure," incurred in effecting the objects of the war, were settled upon as the equitable standard by which "the respective proportions" of each State should be measured.

Now, Mr. President, having laid down the premises so obviously deducible from the act of cession, we shall arrive at that conclusion which I anticipated would give a very different result in favor of South Carolina. To accomplish this, sir, it would be necessary to show what "the respective proportions in the general charge and expenditure" were. This I shall be enabled to do from the "Reports on the Finances."* In this report, the balances that appeared, after the war, to be due to the creditor States, are specifically stated. Of the creditor States there were but five—Massachusetts, Connecticut, New York, Virginia, and South Carolina.

> S. Carolina is a creditor State to the amount of $5,386,232
> Massachusetts stands next in amount, ... 5,226,801
> N. York is a creditor State only to the amount of 1,167,575

I will not pursue the statement any further. My object was to exhibit South Carolina the highest creditor State, and to contrast the claims of that State with the claims of New York, upon the principle laid down in the act of cession. Upon this principle, South Carolina will receive, in the division of these lands, nearly five times as much as the State of New York, if they are to be divided among the States. To divide on the ratio of representation, which appeared to be the principle agreed upon in the House of Representatives, a few days since, the State of New York would obtain nearly four times as much of the public lands as South Carolina would. This, sir, is a matter worth looking into, as regards South Carolina. To divide on the representative basis, will give New York four for one over South Carolina. To divide on the cession basis will give South Carolina five for one over New York. This will make a difference of nine to one in favor of South Carolina over New York.

Mr. President, I have endeavored to demonstrate that, in dividing among the several States the public lands, or the proceeds that shall arise from the sales thereof, the division must proceed upon the principle laid down in the act of cession, according to their respective proportions in the

*Reports on the Finances, vol. 1, pages 35, 36.

general charge and expenditure. How far I have succeeded, the Senate will determine. One thing is certain, that it never was intended by the cession to make the division upon the principle of representation. And this for the plainest reason imaginable. At the time this cession was made, the General Government was administered under the articles of Confederation; and under that system the representative principle was not known. The representation of each State was the same, and each State had but one vote: so that the division upon the representative principle could not have been thought of. It would have been nugatory, as every State had an equal representation. The negative of the representative principle is also sustained by the eighth article of the Confederation. This shows that the operations of the Government were not carried on upon that principle. That principle has grown up under the present Constitution of 1787, which being after the cession, cannot control such rights of the States as existed before that Constitution was ratified.

Sir, it appearing to me perfectly evident that the public lands are the property of the People of the several States, and not of the Western States, exclusively, and committed to the Government only to dispose of for their benefit; and if not necessary for revenue, then to be divided upon some given and settled principle, among them all, I have endeavored to prove that the settled standard by which the division shall be made, is, "according to the respective proportions of the charge and expenditure" of each State, in the prosecution of the Revolutionary war. And if, Mr. President, at a time when the public funds are sought for with an avidity heretofore unknown; when all are looking to the extinguishment of the public debt, and consider all beyond as public spoil, either to be given as bounties to purchase the patronage of the Western States, or divided out upon some new principle, most favorable to the large States, I have been fortunate enough, in the view I have taken, to show that the principle is already established, it will secure to the State of South Carolina the largest dividend; but a dividend proportioned only to the "charges and expenditures" she bore in that Revolutionary war, which gave you the sovereignty over those public lands. Notwithstanding it is a new view, and may essentially interfere with the propositions of other gentlemen, nevertheless, if it be a correct view, it is to be hoped, whensoever the partition shall take place, if a partition must be made, it will be made in pursuance of that principle, and not the principle of representation.

I will not propose a system for disposing of your public lands; I will leave that, sir, to some other hand. If, however, the sales were to go on, as heretofore, I think the Government would profit by it. I would permit the surveys to progress. I would not lower the minimum price. There will be time enough to do that, after the best lands are disposed of. However, I would do one thing, which heretofore has been rejected by Congress. It is this: I would give a fair commutation, in lands, to every pensioner, both of the Revolutionary war, and of the late war, in complete extinguishment of their pensions. If the pension system is to be kept up, the commutation would save the Government many millions of dollars; and would afford a home to the disabled or indigent soldier, and an inheritance to his family. I would go further, sir: I would give to every man who would settle on the public lands, and reside there one year, a half section, a quarter section, or a half quarter section, at the minimum price. I would not give this, or any other quantity, to any man, unless he should make certain improvements thereon, and cultivate a certain reasonable portion of the lands for one year. This would be filling the Western States with that description of population which constitutes the strength of a Government. Such a system as this will enable the poor and the enterprising man to procure a home. This privilege I would give to the occupant or cultivator only. The small quantity thus disposed of cannot lead to speculation. Let him who would speculate, buy at the sales, as heretofore, as the highest bidder. I clearly see, unless you hold out some such inducement as this, to keep the disposal of your lands going on, it is to become a source of bargain and sale, as the occasions of political speculations shall arise, and produce a scene of corruption that may overwhelm this Government; a scene more terrible than that produced by the Tariff and Internal Improvement, heretofore brought on you by degrees, and by a liberal policy, as it was called.

After closing his remarks relating to the subject of the public lands, Mr. Smith said:

And here, sir, I might close; but this discussion has gone so far, and spread so widely, and public expectation had become so excited on particular topics, on which I am not willing to be wholly silent, that I will pursue it a little further.

In the first speech with which the gentleman from Massachusetts (Mr. Webster) favored the Senate, he introduced the subject of slavery. I was sorry to find it brought into a debate of this peculiar character, and was not satisfied with that gentleman's remarks. However, I was pleased to find, when he addressed the Senate a second time, he gave such an explanation as to do away the odious impressions which had been received from his first remarks; and, in addition to his explanation, has very frankly acknowledged that slavery, as it exists in the United States, is protected by the Constitution. I am willing to receive these admissions from the gentleman; and am equally willing to admit them to be sincere. Whilst I have ever been sorry to hear this subject brought into debate, I have been disposed to admit any concessions of its constitutionality. Whatever may be the present opinion of the gentleman from Maine (Mr. HOLMES,) who also touched upon this subject, I well recollect when he struggled with us, side by side, at the most important and gloomy period of this subject, that has ever agitated this Government. We know the sacrifices he made on that occasion. We know there were other New England gentlemen who supported us with independence and manly zeal, on that occasion. We know another gentleman from Massachusetts, a member of the other House, who, if we believe his own declarations, is willing to go further with us, than merely acknowledging the right we have to hold slaves—he is ready to arm in our defence, in case of a servile war. Shall I reject such overtures as these, and pronounce them insincere? No, sir: I would rather thank him for his independence than challenge his motives. I have had, sir, as little reason to fear an improper interference with our slaves, from the New England States, as from any other States. There are, doubtless, some restless spirits in New-England, as well as elsewhere, who, borne away by fanaticism, or something worse, are sending their seditious pamphlets and speeches among our slaves, and taking other improper steps to excite insurrections; but those who are most devoted to this unholy service are nearer to us.*

The gentleman from Massachusetts (Mr. WEBSTER) has compared the comforts and advantages of the people of the free and slave States, and given a decided preference to the former. I believe, without arrogance or ostentation, there is, to say no more, as much comfort to be found in the slaveholding States as in any other portion of the Union. There is as much industry, as much kind feeling, as much charity, as much benevolence, as much hospitality, and as much morality; and all the social virtues are as much cherished, as they are any where, either in this or any other country.

I am not disposed, sir, in this desultory manner, to examine this subject in all its bearings. The occasion is not a suitable one. Nor will I go into the origin of slavery in this country. If I were to do so, I might, without fear of contradiction, say, that "Plymouth, the place where the pilgrims

---

*A paper published at Greenville, Tennessee, and a pamphlet published in Baltimore, were against slavery, and both sent to South Carolina, and were as poisonous as a viper.

landed," was the second port at which African slaves were bought and sold on our shores. I once examined this subject fully, but, at the same time, fairly and fearlessly. I say, sir, I will not enquire how slavery was first introduced here, but seeing they are here, and have been crowded from all the other States upon us to the South, I will address my arguments, or present my reasons, to the sober understanding of those that hear me, why they ought, and why they must be, left to time, and to the discretion of those who own them, to effect a change, if one can be effected, to alter (I cannot say to better) their condition. All the schemes of colonization, and returning them to their primitive country, are wholly visionary. These things do well enough to talk about; and sometimes have a political effect, or give pecuniary employment to those who have nothing else to do. But, sir, if they were now all free, and the Government had nothing farther to do than merely to transport them to Africa, you might take every cent from your treasury, your whole annual revenue, and it would not pay one-fourth part of the expense of their transportation—no, not one-fourth part.

Then, sir, what are we to do? Are we to turn them loose upon society; to shift places with their masters; they to become masters, and their masters to become slaves?—for, be assured, the two cannot live together as equals. What other effect is such a state of things to produce upon this community?

When the subject of slavery was once before the Senate, on a former occasion, I recollect it was stated by a very distinguished gentleman, then a Senator from Connecticut, (Mr. Daggett,) that in the town where he resided, there were an hundred and fifty white persons for one black person; and that there were at least three black persons for one white person, convicted of public crimes. To what extent would be the pillage and depredations of these people, were they all let loose upon society? What could check their rapacity? Its limits cannot be imagined. Some mad missionaries, and self-created philanthropists, with some of your raving politicians, affect to believe that the salvation of this Union depends upon the question of a general emancipation. But I will ask, if there be an orderly, honest, and peaceable citizen, either in the Northern, Southern, Eastern, or Western portion of this Union, who would calmly and deliberately give his assent to such a state of things. I will not believe, for a moment, there is such a one to be found. Therefore, I can scarcely believe that I ought here to make this a serious question. Whenever it shall happen, that any State shall bring this subject, in any serious form, before the public, I shall then be ready and willing to meet it, in any shape in which it may present itself, be that shape what it may.

We have been egregiously misrepresented, sir, by visionary theorists, speculating travellers, and ranting politicians, who would impose upon the world a belief that the slaves of the Southern States are starved, and miserable, and tortured, and treated like brutes. It is utterly false. They may travel from pole to pole, and traverse every region of the civilized world, and they will find that there is not a peasantry on the face of the earth, that enjoys so much civil liberty, and, at the same time, lives so comfortably, and so bountifully, as the slaves of the Southern States. The idea which has gone abroad, to the contrary, is visionary and fabulous. We are told, and the world is told, in the pamphlets and public speeches, written and uttered by blockheads that know nothing about it, that we never lie down to sleep in safety; that we are continually in fear of having our throats cut before we awake. In some of the cities, where these pretended philanthropists are daily tampering with, and exciting the slaves to insurrections, they have occasionally had some alarms; but on the plantations, and in the interior of the State, such a thing has never been heard of. Did it become necessary for me to arm against an enemy, either foreign or domestic, and the laws of my country would permit me, I would select my troops from my own slaves; I would put arms into their hands, and tell them to defend me—and they would do it; not from the timid fears of abject slaves, but from their devotion and attachment to me, as their benefactor and protector. I will not deny, that there are hard masters among the slaveholders, but that evil is doing away; public opinion, and that attachment that is constantly growing up between the master and his slaves, have nearly put it down. There is not to be found, sir, more cheerfulness, and more native gaiety, among the population, in any condition in life, than on a plantation of slaves, where they are treated well. Moreover, the slaves themselves know all this; and what is more, they feel it. They have none of that sickly longing for freedom, with distress, poverty, and starvation. I repeat it, sir, that there is no portion, I do not say of black population, but of the peasantry of Europe, or any where else, among whom there is more enjoyment, more hilarity, and more practical civil liberty—yes, civil liberty, in its true practical sense—than constantly exists among Southern slaves. As to crimes, they are so rare among them, as to be almost unknown. In proportion to their numbers, there are fewer public crimes committed than among any other people, of any other condition living.

This is not an exaggerated picture of their condition. Why, then, have we all this slang about emancipation and colonization? Were the Government able to pay for them, and transport them to Africa, it would be a sacrifice of their rights and their happiness. It would be sending them from a state of peace, protection, and plenty, to the miserable condition of starvation and butchery. I, sir, will never be the instrument of setting a negro free, or permitting the Government to do so, that he may be consigned to poverty and misery, when I am conscious I can make him comfortable the rest of his days.

Sir, one word more: In the State of Ohio, where slavery is not tolerated, there was at a time, a great deal of this kind feeling, as regarded the emancipation of slaves; many took sanctuary there, who had escaped from their masters. So strong was this feeling, at the crisis which brought about the admission of Missouri into the Union, that all the members of Congress from that State opposed her admission, unless under an express prohibition of slavery.* Since that period, however, they have found, from experience, that a free black population cannot be tolerated in that State, but under peculiar restrictions, imposed by law. In consequence whereof, the laws of that State have recently been enforced, and the free people of color, being unable to conform to its rigid exactions, have been led to seek an asylum in the British province of Upper Canada; where, we learn through the medium of the public prints, they have made a settlement, and expect to augment it by applying to the British Government for a large donation of lands. Should this colony succeed, and grow to any extent, if I might hazard an opinion, I would say, this might become a more formidable annoyance to the peace and safety of that State, than their former Indian neighbors. It is not for me to arraign the conduct of the good People of Ohio, for any municipal regulations their Legislature may have thought fit to adopt. If they be satisfied with that policy which has driven from that State the black people, whom they call free people of color, but many of whom are the slaves of American citizens, residing in other States, to the British possessions, it is not for me to complain. But suppose, by what has been called the humanity of their laws, slaves from other States should be still tolerated to take sanctuary there, and make that State a medium through which to pass from their rightful owners in the other States, to this

---

*General Harrison was an exception. He had thought well on the subject, and was decidedly opposed to the restriction. He put every thing to hazard, that he might discharge his duty.

---

new colony in Upper Canada, and that colony should be fostered by the British Government, may not the people of color, in case of a rupture between the two countries, become a thorn in the side of our fellow-citizens of Ohio? Perhaps there is no description of people in existence who so completely fill the character of marauding warriors and freebooters, as a colony of free blacks brought together under such circumstances.

With these remarks upon a subject of deep concern to the Southern States, and which ought to be of little concern to any body else, I shall pass on to the subject of Internal Improvement, of much concern to us all, and which has occupied more or less of the attention of every gentleman who hath participated in this debate.

In pursuing this theme, although of great magnitude, and of much importance to this Government, it will be my course, as well as it hath been of those gentlemen who have preceded me, not to give it a thorough investigation.

The debate upon this question has thrown but little light on it. It has been a debate more of censure than of illustration. Each gentleman has at least justified his own political course, whilst he reproached that of others. And some warmth has arisen, as regarded the origin of this measure. One asserting it originated in the South, another denying that fact, and imputing the origin to the North. Claiming no share of that honor myself, I am perfectly willing to leave that part of the controversy to those whom it may concern. But it is certainly worth remarking, that in all the warmth of discussion, they have confined themselves to expedience alone, without touching the constitutional question.

The gentleman from Massachusetts (Mr. Webster) has come out with his opinions very decidedly in favor of the power of Congress over the subject of Internal Improvement. His opinions and my opinions do not accord. However, whether they accord with mine or not, I like decided opinions upon political questions, because they can be met and combated. This gentleman assures us his mind is settled; that he has satisfied himself that the power exercised by the General Government, in constructing roads and excavating canals, is within that class of powers delegated to Congress by the Constitution; and that the exercise of that power is for the great interest of the Union. However I may be pleased with the frankness which that gentleman has displayed in avowing what his opinions are, I am, nevertheless, by no means satisfied with opinions only. They illustrate nothing, settle no point; nor is it by any means satisfactory that that gentleman should inform us that he had been associated with other gentlemen from South Carolina, in promoting the objects of Internal Improvement, or that it had its origin in South Carolina. It is enough that the people of South Carolina think for themselves upon this great question, and feel themselves bound by the opinions of no politicians. Without any compliments from me to place that gentleman conspicuously before the public, we know very well that he is well versed in the laws of his country, in the laws of nations, highly distinguished for his legal attainments, and long accustomed to the construction of legal instruments. I should have liked, therefore, to have heard from him, on this occasion, not only his opinions, but likewise his constitutional reasons, for his very decided opinions that Congress possessed this constitutional power.

The Senator from Kentucky (Mr. ROWAN) has dwelt a good deal upon this subject, but has arrived at no explicit opinion upon the constitutionality of the measure. He is equally learned and equally experienced in law and legal construction with most gentlemen. It would have been desirable to have heard his constitutional views, but he has not favored the Senate with them. He has assigned, as a justification of the course he has pursued himself, not that it was constitutional, but that his constituents believe the General Government has this power, and that it is for their convenience that the General Government should exercise it; and, as their representative, he felt himself bound to support it. He acknowledges the inexpedience of the exercise of this power by Congress; yet he has uniformly voted for every appropriation for the Louisville canal, especially, as well as for every other road and canal for which an appropriation has been asked.

I do not see the Senator from Missouri (Mr. BENTON) in his seat. I am sorry he is not there; but not intending to say any thing, as regards his opinions, in his absence, which I would not say were he present, it is not material. He has not been altogether uniform on this question. He has voted according to circumstances. Of the Cumberland road he has been a uniform supporter, always voting for appropriations, for its continuance, whenever asked for. He has uniformly, also, supported the appropriations for the Louisville canal, or for subscriptions by the General Government for stock in that Company, which are appropriations of the most exceptionable character. He is, however, opposed to appropriations for roads and canals that lead from the Western States to the Atlantic States, because, as he alleges, they divert the commerce of the Western States from its appropriate channel, the Mississippi, and appropriate market, New Orleans.

To what purpose, Mr. President, has this subject been brought into this debate? It has undergone an elaborate discussion by those gentlemen, but neither of whom have so much as attempted to give an exposition of the constitutional principle that confers this power upon Congress. It is not satisfactory to exercise the power without showing how the power is obtained. The exercise of this power produces a continued drain upon your treasury. It is much to be regretted that, whilst both the gentleman from Kentucky and the gentleman from Missouri, have given such a display upon constitutional principles, and State-right principles, this constitutional principle should not have been illustrated. In support of State rights, they have bestowed much consideration. But there is something irreconcilable to my mind that gentlemen can raise the State-right standard, and yet vote large appropriations for roads and canals, to be applied under the power of the General Government in the States. The State-right party cannot admit that doctrine. They consider the appropriations by Congress for Internal Improvement as the source of the evil. It is Internal Improvement that keeps alive your tariff. It is fed by your tariff. Without the former the latter would perish. How a statesman can support Internal Improvement and oppose the Tariff, is a paradox which I cannot solve. But how he can vote for both, and still advocate State rights, is a paradox that nobody can solve.

Another gentleman (Mr. HAYNE) has said, the law of 1824, which appropriated $30,000 to enable the President to obtain plans and surveys of roads and canals, was an experiment—that the subject was not well understood. This was a woful experiment, sir; an experiment that has rendered the Southern States completely tributary to the other States of the Union. The enactment of that law was hailed by the advocates of Internal Improvement, which had been balancing for eight years, between victory and defeat, as a confirmation of the power of Congress over Internal Improvement. The subject was as well understood by the members of Congress then, as it is now. The People at large did not understand it; nor never would, had the discussions been confined to Congress. That Congress understood it, cannot be questioned. It had been debated warmly in Congress, from 1816, till that law passed in 1824. The great bonus bill of 1817 underwent a thorough discussion in both branches of Congress, and passed both Houses, and was negatived by Mr. Madison. The next year it was resumed, and then underwent another very long and very animated discussion. And so it did every year, in some shape or other, until the act of 1824, which act, alone, has taken from your Treasury $30,000 every year since, except one, for plans and surveys, independent of millions for the making of roads and canals. On the bonus bill, sir, in 1817, only one fortnight after I first took my seat in the Senate, I made my stand. I voted against that bill in all its modifications. And I think, sir, I understood it as well then as I do now. I understood it then to be a political speculation, and a speculation in violation of the Constitution of my country. In 1820, or 1821, when it was contemplated to extend the Cumberland road, a resolution was submitted to the Senate, by General Lacock, then a Senator from Pennsylvania, to appropriate $10,000 for a survey. I opposed it. On that occasion I stood alone, except my worthy friend Mr. Macon, whom I regret is not here, voted with me. I was then told that nothing would be asked of the Government but to survey. I replied, if you make the survey, you must make the road. My prediction has been fully verified; the road has been extended every year. And you have appropriated more than $1,000,000 since that time, to continue that road. In this way, sir, we have suffered this system to grow up in our Government, by gradual encroachments.

On this subject, I have, on a former discussion, when it was properly before the Senate, in a shape upon which a vote could be directly taken, had the honor of giving my constitutional objections at full length. I shall forbear to do so here, and leave this subject precisely where I found it, a subject of debate without a conclusion.

I come now, Mr. President, to the subject of the Tariff, concerning which, there exists so much anxiety, and upon which there depends so much interest. It has occupied a conspicuous place in this discussion. And I have, from the commencement of the debate, felt an invincible reluctance to approach it here. I should have no reluctance, but, on the contrary, a great deal of pleasure, were this the time and place suitable for that occasion. The question is one of vital importance, not only to the State from which I come, but is of vital importance to the whole Union. In discussing it here, and at this time, who am I to address? I have the honor, it is true, to be surrounded by the Senate of the United States, who will, perhaps do me the favor to hear me. Also, the galleries are full of respectable citizens, who will probably give me their ordinary attention, likewise. To which of these bodies shall I appeal for a decision, whether I am right or wrong? If I appeal to the Senate, they have no such question before them. If to the galleries, they have no jurisdiction to decide upon any question here. And although we are in the Senate chamber, the Senate can no more decide upon this question, than the merest stranger in the galleries. It is a subject, sir, that ought not to be impaired by any common-place familiarity, in debate, where a complete investigation of all its bearings cannot be attained, and where no decision is sought for. It is lessening its consequence, and giving up more than half its importance. The time is approaching, when we shall be able to bring it before the Senate in a different form, where it can be discussed upon its merits, and the vote of the Senate passed upon it, to a useful purpose. But, seeing the subject has been brought before the Senate, although I do not intend to go into any thing like a general view of the question, I will, nevertheless, not pass it entirely unnoticed.

This discussion, sir, has involved the consideration of two great political questions: whether, if a State be borne down by the oppressive operation of a law of the United States, the proper appeal from that oppression, is not to the Judiciary: or whether, in such a case, the State aggrieved, has not a right to withdraw, and say to the rest of the Union, we no longer belong to you, because you have violated the compact with us; we have decided for ourselves that you have oppressed us; your laws are unconstitutional, and we will no longer continue a member of the Union.

On the first portion of this subject, if it could be heard before the Senate as a distinct proposition, and the Senate had the power to decide upon it, I would give it, as far as I should be able, the best consideration its importance would demand; but it is utterly out of the question for a speaker to investigate and descant upon a mere speculative political question, where no results are to be expected, as he would feel himself bound to do, were the question a real one, from which some solid and permanent good was to flow, instead of one that should yield little more than an opportunity of making a speech to raise his own fame. But as it has been the course, in this erratic flight of the Senate, that has drawn into its vortex any thing, and every thing, civil, religious and political, as the speaker may have thought fit to select, and this has been selected as one choice subject, by those who have gone before me, I will offer a few unpremeditated remarks.

For the Judges of the United States, I entertain the highest respect, both in their judicial character, as well as in their individual character: And am willing to attribute to them as much integrity, and as much talent, as falls to the share of any Judges, in this or any other country. But it seems to me that their province is limited to decisions between citizen and citizen, and between the United States and citizens, the individual States, &c. and in all cases of *meum et tuum*, their decisions are conclusive. But may not a distinction be taken, where a law is notoriously unconstitutional, and oppressive upon the whole community of a State; where the ground of complaint would be, that Congress had enacted a law, not only against the letter, but likewise against the spirit and meaning of the Constitution;

which law was undermining all the private rights of individuals, as well as rights appertaining to them as the community of a State?

Then, sir, suppose the Court of the United States always to consist of seven Judges, as it now does; and suppose a question upon the constitutionality of a law of the United States, that had vitally affected the people of a State, in their private and municipal rights, should come before these seven Judges, for their decision, and three of the seven should pronounce the law constitutional, and three others of the seven should pronounce it unconstitutional. Here the opinions of six of the seven are completely neutralized, and the whole weight of the question, be it of what moment it may, must devolve upon a single Judge. This single Judge would hold the balance, and have it in his power to decide the fate of the Union, by his single dictum. The entire operations of the law must cease, if he should say no: or its operation must go on, if he should say, aye; be the consequences what they may. The peace and happiness of the Union must be destroyed, or preserved, as he should be guided by prudence and honesty on the one hand, or by caprice and ambition on the other; because Judges are not always exempt from these passions. Or let us suppose a law affecting in a special manner, the private or municipal rights of the people of a whole State, should be enacted by Congress, to compel vessels going from one port to another, in the same State, or to a port in a different State, to clear out at the port of departure, and the master should refuse to do so, because the law was unconstitutional, as the Constitution expressly forbids it— should your Judges ever be misled to declare such a law constitutional, and the collector of the revenue should be resisted, could he who made the resistance be convicted of an offence against the Constitution of his country? If the opinions of the Judges are to be considered the Constitution; or if the Judges are clothed with this tremendous power; a power that gives to a single man the control of the destiny of this Union, is it not time to enquire, whether it be not fit to place it in some more responsible repository?

The other great question, whether a State has a right to secede from the Union, if Congress should pass an unconstitutional law, that should prove oppressive, is a question of still greater moment.

Were I to be asked what opinion I entertained of the power of a State to dissolve its political connexion with the Union, I would respond, Go ask my constituents. This is not the time, and place, and circumstances, that will justify a discussion of that question between the United States and the State of South Carolina. If South Carolina is aggrieved by the Tariff, and she most assuredly is, to an extent of great oppression, and the remedy is only to be found in a separation from the Union, it belongs exclusively to the people of that State to meet in convention, examine the subject, weigh the consequences, and settle the mode of operation. That is the course, and the only course, by which this question can be determined, and not by any flight of fancy that may exist in my imagination, or that of any other member of Congress. I unfeignedly believe, there is at this time in the Legislature of South Carolina, much talent, much patriotism, much devotion to the Union, and as much independence and firmness as could possibly be wanting to adopt any plan of operation that wisdom, patriotism, justice, interest, or the love of union, may dictate, for the relief of their burthens. I do not withhold my opinion here from fear of responsibility.—I shrink, Mr. President, from no responsibility imposed upon me as a member of this Senate. If the wisdom of my Legislature, whose province it is to determine upon that measure, and act upon that great occasion, should think proper to call a convention, and my country should honor me with a seat there, I will assume any responsibility which the wisdom of the occasion, or the interest of my country may require at my hands.

Sir, I will go further, and should the cupidity or the madness of the majority in Congress, push them on to impose one unconstitutional burthen after another, until it can be no longer borne, and no other alternative remains, I will then take upon myself the last responsibility of an oppressed People, and adopt the exclamation of the poet, *dulce et decorum est pro patria mori*; and if the exigencies of my country should ever demand it, I will be ready to shed my blood upon the altars of that country. I am attached to the Union; I wish to see it perpetuated; I wish it may endure through all time. But if the same causes exist in our Government, which have overturned other Governments, what right have we to expect an exemption from the fatality of other nations? We need not go abroad, or into ancient history, for instances to warn us. If we only go back to 1774 and 1775, we shall see a much less cause, producing that revolution which separated these United States from Great Britain, than now exists between the United States and the State of South Carolina. What was the exciting cause of that revolution? A three penny tax on tea, which was then merely the beverage of the rich, and a small tax upon stamps. It was these small duties that set the whole United States in a flame: and that flame spread with the velocity of the winds, from one end of the United States to the other. Massachusetts, Virginia, and South Carolina, were united then in the same cause, the defence of their civil liberty, which was threatened by the small duty on tea. Memorials and remonstrances were resorted to, but for a short time, until a company, in Boston, disguised in the habiliments of Indians, counselled, if not led, by the immortal HANCOCK, boarded the ships, and threw all the tea in the harbor overboard. May we not look for the same effects from the same causes, at all times, and in all places?

Whilst, Mr. President, I regret that, under existing circumstances, this picture is not too highly colored, yet I believe there is a redeeming spirit at hand. The Constitution itself, which has been made to bend, to suit the interests of majorities, is undergoing a new version. Investigations of its true and plain common-sense construction is going on in more hands than one.

Among the distinguished writers engaged in this investigation is Doctor COOPER, who has been alluded by gentlemen in this discussion; whose name is identified with every science; whose life has been devoted to the cause of civil liberty and human happiness. In his Political Economy, Consolidation, and other recent political pieces, has torn the mask from the delusion of constructive powers and party intrigue.

A writer under the signature of "Brutus," in his "Crisis," has, with a master hand, given an exposition to the great agitated points of the Constitution, on the subjects of the Tariff and Internal Improvement, that will remain a treasure to his country while talents shall be regarded.

The lectures of Mr. DEW, of Virginia, on the Restrictive System, are more like a mathematical analysis than the lectures of a Professor on Political Economy. His illustrations are so plain, so strong, and so conclusive, that they are perfect demonstrations of the errors and absurdity of the American System.

None of these writers have ever been answered by the advocates of Internal Improvement and the Tariff system. To these may be added, a paper recently published, by order of the House of Representatives, which will be read with much interest. It is the report of the Committee on Commerce, written, as we understand, by Mr. CAMBRELENG, the chairman of that committee. It gives a more expanded view, and furnishes more evidences, drawn from facts, of the great impolicy, and ruinous effects of the Tariff, than have appeared in any State paper, heretofore published by the Government. The disastrous effects which it has already, and will continue to produce upon our foreign commerce, are so fully and clearly established, that it must command admiration, and will be extensively read.

The flood of light, Mr. President, which those distinguished writers have shed upon this subject, to which may be added this report, cannot fail to enlighten the benighted minds of an honest, industrious community; and bring them to reflect, seriously, whether it be just to tax the many for the benefit of the few. The manufacturers themselves regret that this system has been introduced. And well they may, for it is now fully ascertained, that at least one half of the monied capital of the New England States, has been sacrificed by this *mania*; and a large proportion of the proprietors of manufacturing establishments bankrupted. Fortunes, that have been accumulating for half a century, have been swept away in an instant. There can be no probability that men of business, raised to active pursuits, and accustomed to employ their capital in some productive and advantageous manner, can remain devoted to a system that must produce their certain destruction. In addition to so many reasons that exist, why we may hope for an early dissolution of this oppressive system, another reason, as strong at least, if not stronger, than any other, is the certainty that the public debt of the United States will shortly be extinguished. When that period shall arrive, there will not be even a pretext for the continuation of the Tariff, except it be for the explicit and avowed purpose of protecting the manufacturers. And I beg leave, Mr. President, to ask, if there be even one man, who can for a moment suppose, that twelve millions of the free People of the United States will calmly submit to have the direction of the whole of their labor taken out of their own hands, and placed under the management of the General Government; not to secure a revenue for governmental purposes, but that the Government may, at its discretion, parcel out the profits of the labor of one portion of the Union, to bestow on those of another portion of the Union? Sir, it is morally certain that they will submit to no such tyranny. Nor will it be necessary for the People to rise in their might to put it down, either by one portion seceding from the rest, or by the more direful alternative, a civil war, that must drench the States with the blood of their own citizens. Public opinion must, and will correct this mighty evil, and in its own way, and leave the States still further to cultivate their Union, upon those pure principles that first brought them together. If I am mistaken, however, and these hopes should prove illusive, it will then be time for the States to determine what are their rights, and whether they have constitutional powers to secede from the Union.

But, sir, whilst I hope that a happy revolution in our political affairs awaits us at no distant period, resulting from this powerful combination of circumstances, I entertain not the least hope of relief from the justice or magnanimity of either the Eastern or Western States. They have got the Tariff, however, fixed upon us, and will no doubt hold on, until it becomes their interest to abandon it; and then, and not till then, can we hope for their concurrence in its repeal. The gentleman from Missouri (Mr. BEN-TON) appeared, at the beginning of this debate, to feel great sympathy for the oppressed planters of the Southern States; and some gentlemen hoped, that he might probably join the South, and lend his aid to repeal at once the oppressive Tariff. But, sir, that hope is gone. Instead of giving his aid to repeal the Tariff law entirely, and especially such parts of it as bear most oppressively upon the Southern States, he has introduced a bill, purporting to be—

> "A bill to provide for the abolition of unnecessary duties, to relieve the People from sixteen millions of taxes, and to improve the condition of the agriculture, manufactures, commerce and navigation, of the United States."

This is the title of the bill, sir, which is very specious, and would seem to indicate that the Tariff system was to be totally abolished, and that, as soon as this specious bill should be acted on. When you leave the preamble, and look into the provisions of the bill itself, it gives you a very different view. You will there find the duties to be reduced, are, for the most part, duties on articles of luxury; such duties as affect the rich classes of society only, and for which the laboring class of the community care nothing. Not a few of them are articles of extreme luxury. Amongst them are, "cocoa, olives, figs, raisins, prunes, almonds, currants, cambrics, lawns, cashmere shawls, gauze, thread and silk lace, essence of bergamot, and other essences used as perfumery, porcelain, Brussels carpeting, velvet cords," &c.

These are articles mostly used by the rich, the gay, and splendid. They are rarely used by that substantial class of citizens who move in the middle sphere of life. Indeed, there is not a single article in the whole catalogue, that the removal of the duties on which will materially affect the Southern States, but would prove as favorable to the Western States, and more so, than to any other portion of the Union. All spirits, woollens, and cotton goods, that come in competition with spirits, woollens, and cotton goods manufactured in the United States, are not included in this exemption from duties. Besides, even this supposed relief is, by the provisions of the bill itself, postponed for ten years. In ten years, if the present Tariff should continue, it will be perfectly immaterial whether they ever are taken off. If they are to be taken off, why not now? As well might it be postponed till another generation, as to postpone it ten years. The articles of iron and steel, in all their forms, and cotton and woollen goods, cotton bagging and cordage, and many other articles, are passed by, unnoticed, in this bill. These are the articles we wish to see duty free. They would restore your commerce and navigation, and give real relief. But, sir, what is of still greater importance to the Southern States, the gentleman has concluded this relief bill, by laying a heavy duty of $33\frac{1}{3}$ per cent. on all foreign furs and raw hides; a duty heretofore unknown, in any of our Tariff laws; a duty perfectly suited to Missouri, as that State is a grazing, as well as a fur State. Such a Tariff is precisely what she wants. These duties, added to the duties laid on lead, in all its forms, in the Tariff of 1828, which that gentleman (Mr. BENTON) voted for, with the express purpose of securing this duty on lead, will, for the present, complete her wishes. Furs and raw hides are articles of prime necessity in this great community; and, unless the People will consent to go without hats and shoes, or, in plain terms, go bareheaded and barefooted, the rest of the States must pay a very heavy tribute to enrich the people of Missouri. This may be a relief bill for Missouri, but for no other State. Besides, Mr. President, there is a bill reported more than a month, before this bill, by the Committee of Finance, which embraces the whole Tariff, without imposing any new burthens, and which, I hope, may be taken up in due time, and acted on.

Sir, I have pursued this subject much further than I originally intended. I will here abandon it, and reserve what I may wish to say further, until the question on the Tariff shall be fairly before the Senate, and will now advert to another leading topic in this debate, as there are many to choose from.

The topic, sir, I have alluded, is that which relates to the party politics of other times. A contest had arisen, of a singular character; which was, whether the Eastern States, or the Southern States, had been most friendly and magnanimous in promoting the growth, and advancing the interests of the States in the West. And in solving that question, the controversy had assumed a new aspect, and had been converted into one upon parties and party politics, of the most violent and personal character, between the gentleman from South Carolina, (Mr. HAYNE) and the gentleman from Massachusetts, (Mr. WEBSTER.) The gentleman from South Carolina had brought before the Senate a full view of the old Federal party of 1798. He had carried it back to the Whig and Tory parties of England, and derived the Federal party from the Tory party of that country. He had brought before the Senate the Hartford Convention, and read its Journals, to prove that a settled purpose had existed in the New England States to dissolve the Union. He had brought before the Senate the Olive Branch, and read many of its choice paragraphs, to illustrate the violent opposition in New England, to the late war between the United States and Great Britain: and concluded with the "Coalition," the ghost of which he supposed, had haunted the gentleman's (Mr. Webster's) imagination, and, like the ghost of "Banquo, would never down."

The gentleman from Massachusetts, (Mr. Webster), in reply to these charges of political heresy, says he had nothing to do with the Hartford Convention; that he had never read its journals; and if its ghost, like the ghost of Banquo, had risen to haunt the imagination of any body, "it could not shake its gory locks at him." And, in his turn, brings charges against South Carolina, and says, "other Conventions, of more recent existence, had gone further than the Hartford Convention;" and named what he called "the Colleton and Edgefield Conventions;" and read the proceedings of the Colleton meeting of 1828, after the enactment of the Tariff law of that year. These proceedings, he argued, were more inflammatory, and tended more to disunion than the proceedings of the Hartford Convention could possibly do.

If these Conventions, Mr. President, as they have been called, have existed, either in New England, or South Carolina, they are not chargeable to me. And should the ghosts of either, or all of them, arise, to haunt the imaginations of any concerned, I can exclaim, with the gentleman from Massachusetts, "They cannot shake their gory locks at me."

There has been much crimination and recrimination between those two gentlemen. One reproaches the other with political tergiversation, and it is reciprocated. The gentleman from South Carolina says the gentleman from Massachusetts had distinguished himself, whilst a member of the House of Representatives, in 1824, in opposition to the Tariff; but in 1828, took a different course in the Senate, and supported the Tariff. The gentleman from Massachusetts, on his part, says the gentleman from South Carolina, in 1824, while the act to procure the necessary plans and surveys of roads and canals, "which covered the whole subject of internal improvement," opposed every modification of the law that tended to diminish the power of Congress over that subject; but that he had since shifted his ground, and had become opposed to Internal Improvements. The speeches, the yeas and nays, and the Senate journals, have all been produced and read in the Senate, to substantiate those mutual accusations. Other members of the Senate, who have shared in this debate, have pursued the same course of crimination and recrimination; charging and proving on their opponents, whomsoever they may happen to be, that they had held and maintained, at different times, different opinions upon the same political subjects; and had voted on the one side at one time, and on the other side another time, as party interest or party feelings might dictate. These reciprocal vituperations have not been the result of a sudden gust of ardent feelings, or unguarded expressions, to pass off with the moment and be forgotten; but the records and journals of Congress, as far back as the Revolutionary war, have been ransacked and hunted up, and brought into the Senate—the speeches, and the yeas and nays read, to establish the inconsistency of each other; and, moreover, all this has gone abroad to adorn the public prints, and mingle in the party strifes of the day.

When such scenes as these are playing off in the Senate chamber, with open doors, and a crowded audience, if it be not a duty, it is, at least, justifiable for those who are conscious of having pursued a different course, to avow it in self-defence. In those accusings and defendings, in the course of this debate, a great deal of that kind of egotism which they necessarily involved, had been indulged. I will beg leave to indulge a little in this egotistic style, also. If any occasion will palliate this request, it must be such as the present.

Mr. President, I have had the honor of acting an humble part in public stations from an early period of my life; I have been eleven years in this Senate, and if it were not too ostentatious, I would invoke a scrutiny of my own votes and political opinions. I fear no challenges for inconsistent votes; I fear no journals, no yeas and nays. I claim no exemption from human fallibility. I may have given many erroneous votes, but am conscious I have never given an inconsistent vote, or held, at any time, inconsistent political opinions. If I have, I ask them to be proclaimed.

The origin of parties is as old as the Government itself. When the division between the Federalists and Republicans first took place, the parties were nearly balanced, as regarded numbers, and as regarded talents; and were, moreover, pretty equally dispersed throughout the United States. But all parties unanimously concurred in the election of Gen. Washington to the Presidency. At the close of his Administration, the distinction of parties was fully developed, and the contest for supremacy, between the two parties, commenced. The Federal party succeeded in the election of Mr. Adams, the elder. He had been a Revolutionary man, of distinguished fame, and his party, a little the strongest, placed him in the Presidency, as the successor of General Washington. And Mr. Jefferson, who then stood at the head of the Republican party, was elected Vice-President. The Federal party, considering themselves firmly fixed at the head of Government, for the next eight years at least, the better to secure the acquisition, and perpetuate their power, enacted the alien and sedition laws. The country became alarmed at this high-handed measure, and the Republican party, very justly, laid hold of it to show the dangerous tendency of augmenting the strength of the General Government, by the constructive powers of the Constitution, "to provide for the public good and general welfare." The consequences were, that the Republican party gained strength from this, and other circumstances, and at the next Presidential election, elected Mr. Jefferson over Mr. Adams. They held the power until the late war commenced; and through that war, until its termination, and the restoration of peace. The Federal party were universally opposed to the war, at its commencement. The Federalists of the Northern States, and many others, elsewhere, continued their opposition throughout the war. But the war having terminated triumphantly for the United States, the Federalists soon became too enfeebled to act any longer as a party. And having no fixed object, some turned Republicans, and being new converts, like all other new converts, became exceeding devout. Many respectable men amongst them, not disposed to abandon principles which they had honestly adopted, retired to private life. One portion, however, in the State of New York, about forty in number, the better to provide for themselves, made a formal renunciation of their principles, in a public address, in which they alleged there was no longer any Federal party to which they could hold on, therefore, they avowed their adhesion, for the future, to the strongest Republican party. Some humorous wag of the Federal party, upon seeing this formal renunciation, drew up a regular deed of conveyance; in which, *for divers good causes and valuable considerations him thereunto moving, did bargain, sell, release, and set over, in market overt, forty thousand Federalists, who had left their ranks, to the Republican party, in fee simple forever.*

It was now supposed that the Federal party had fallen, to rise no more, and they were much sought after, and greeted as brothers of the Republican family, by the leading politicians of the day. They were told there was but one party; that no such thing as a distinct Federal party, or a distinct Republican party, existed. But the phraseology was, "We are all Federalists, all Republicans." It became an invidious thing to denounce a gentleman as a Federalist. In the State of South Carolina, it was so taken, and generally understood by all: and so acted on. The community were said to be satisfied with it. Good feelings were said to be generated by it. It was pronounced as the great desideratum to strengthen the Union. In fine, there was nothing great or good which it was not to effect.

As an evidence of the temper and understanding of the citizens of South Carolina, upon the happy results of the amalgamation of the Federal and Republican parties, among many other instances, I will beg leave to read a few short passages from an eloquent oration, delivered in Charleston, on the 4th July, 1821, before the Cincinnati and Revolution Societies, by a distinguished gentleman of that place, who was a member of the Cincinnati Society. After speaking on other interesting relations between Great Britain and America, and the effects of the late war between them, he says:

"These are not the only reflections of an exhilarating character, which the late war is calculated to excite. It has led to the extinction of those parties, the collisions of which once weakened our country, and disturbed the harmony of its society.

"I come not here to burn the torch of Alecto—to me there is no lustre in its fires, nor cheering warmth in its blaze. Let us rather offer and mingle our congratulations, that those unhappy differences which alienated one portion of our community from the rest, are at an end, and that a vast fund of the genius and worth of our country has been restored to its service, to give new vigor to its career of power and prosperity.

"To this blessed consummation the administration of our venerable Monroe has been a powerful auxiliary.

"The delusions of past years have rolled away, and the mists that once hovered over forms of now unshaded brightness, are dissipated forever. We can now all meet and exchange our admiration and love, in generous confraternity of feeling, whether we speak of our Jefferson or our Adams, our Madison or our Hamilton, our Pinckney or our Monroe; the associations of patriotism are awakened, and we forget the distance in the political zodiac, which once separated these illustrious luminaries, in the full tide of glory they are pouring on the brightest pages of our history. This unanimity of sentiment is not a sickly calm, in which the high energies of the nation are sunk into a debilitating paralysis.

"This union can only annoy the demagogue, who lives by the proscription of one-half of his fellow-citizens, and in the delusions of a distempered state of public opinion. But to him who loves his country as a beautiful whole, not scarred and cut into compartments of sects and schisms, such a picture is one of unmixed triumph and gratulation. The necessity for the existence of parties in a free State, in the sense in which we have unfortunately understood them, is one of those paradoxes which the world has rather received than examined, and seems allied to the sophistry which would lead us to believe that the pleasures of domestic life are promoted by its dissensions, or that the jarring of the elements is essential to the harmony of the universe. No! an united is a happy, as well as an invincible People."*

Mr. President: I have never acted with that portion of politicians who were denominated Federalists. I formed my political creed at the eventful period of 1796. I then took my stand as a Republican of the Jefferson school; and I have never departed from it. And if the politicians of that, or any other school, say I have, they slander me. I have been uniformly opposed to the Federal principles; and am opposed to them now. I have been opposed to them because I thought them wrong. But whilst I have uniformly been opposed to Federal principles and Federal measures, I have as uniformly treated the persons and reputations of the Federal party, with every possible respect. I am aware that I have never been a favorite with that party. I have never sought to be so. I am, nevertheless, willing to attribute to them all the integrity and honesty of purpose, of any other party; but I am not willing to adopt their creed. There are gentlemen of that party with whom I am upon intimate terms, and whose friendship and society I esteem as a treasure; but we never converse on party politics.

I cannot, sir, be annoyed by any condition of my fellow-citizens that contributes to their social happiness. Party dissensions hold out no charms for my gratification. There is no faculty of my nature that could take sides in a contest for the proscription of any portion of the community to which I belong, upon party principles. But when I consider the destruction of the Federal, and its amalgamation with the Republican party, and look at the consequences that have resulted from that union, I cannot but believe that it has been a misfortune, instead of a blessing to this Government. It has defeated all the great purposes for which the Republican party was originally instituted. The Federal party was characterized by its constant tendency to extravagance; by its efforts to increase the powers of the General Government; by a free construction of the constitution; by the creation of new offices; profuse expenditure of public moneys; the establishment of banks, and the establishment of a standing army in time of peace. The Republican party were opposed to all these operations. It was decidedly by their opposition to these political errors, that they broke down the Federal party, and obtained the possession of the Government. Economy was the

---

*This oration was delivered by Major James Hamilton, Jr. late a member of Congress, on the 4th July, 1821.

---

watch-word of the Republican party; the purity of the constitution was their rallying point. They put down the constructive powers of the Government; the alien and sedition laws, based upon "the public good and general welfare," construction withered and died at their bidding, and never revived. They operated as a complete check upon every abuse of power in the hands of the Federal party, and particularly whilst that party held the Government.

By the operation of this powerful check, not a constitutional check, but of the vigilance of a strong opposition party, the Constitution itself was brought back to its common sense construction, and the extravagancies of the Government were levelled down to the proper exigencies of the Government.

When the Republican party got possession of the Government, and Mr. Jefferson came to the Presidency, they enacted the embargo law which he recommended, and which the Federal party opposed, upon the ground of its unconstitutionality; it being a creature of "the public good and general welfare" construction; which construction the Federal party, although in the minority, yet a very strong minority, denied to be the legitimate construction; and, by their opposition, that law could not be enforced to any valuable purpose, even under the Administration of Mr. Jefferson. The legitimacy of the war they could not deny; and whilst contending against the expediency of the war, with a large majority opposed to it, the war terminated successfully, and the Federal party terminated with it, as to all efficient purposes of a party. And thence, this "happy union" of the two great leading political parties was consummated. And no party was henceforth known but the Republican party, who have had the entire administration of the Government ever since; and whom it was expected would have administered the Government upon the pure Democratic principles, and a strict regard to the fair construction of the Constitution. And now the inquiry is, not what have they done, but what have they not done? They have given you an American System; they have given protection to that system with all its train of evils; they have given away your public lands, with an unsparing hand, to the Western States, to private corporations, and to other associations; they have appropriated large sums of money to make roads, canals, clear out rivers and creeks; they have appropriated large sums of money for a joint stock co-partnership with private corporations; and they have now a proposition to divide the surplus revenue amongst the several States, like the spoils of war amongst a successful clan.

All these measures have been effected within the last fifteen years, and since the fall of the Federal party. They have been effected by the Republican party, many of whom are supporting, and voting for most of those measures at this time. These are the blessed fruits of that union of parties, which never existed until the Federal party was extinct.

I would ask, sir, for what purpose Federalism has been raked from its embers at this time? Why has this new impulse been given to a subject that we have been taught to believe had gone down to oblivion? A subject that had been put to rest, long since, by the Republican party itself. What evidences have we that ought to alarm us at this period? There is no Presidential election pending; General Jackson has possession of the Presidential chair for the next three years; the Government is solely in the possession, and under the control of the Republican party. The Federalists never can be formidable if left to themselves; they are only so when associated with the Republicans.

It is not my intention to palliate the Federal policy. But to denounce them, when crumbled into dust, appears to me like the lion in the fable. Indeed we know of no party existing by that name. Nor has any existed by that name since the grand union. We know of individuals who still retain that name, and are proud of it; and who still retain a devotion to Federal principles. But as a body they are impotent: at least we think so in the Southern States; and they think so themselves. But they become an host when united with the Republicans; Republicans who call in Federal aid, when necessary to do so, to put down a rival and secure their own triumph; and who often throw themselves into the Federal ranks to help out a Federal candidate, in return, to put down a Republican, whom some Republican leader wishes to see displaced. They are often associated together under the Republican banner; contending in concert against other Republican candidates, for the same honors. And if a Federalist did not belong to the Hartford Convention, and approved of the war, no matter how late he came to that conclusion; they are, by public opinion, and the sanction of constant usage, entitled to participate in all the honors and offices of the Government. This toleration I am not disposed to complain off; but why are they alternately denounced and caressed? If the denunciation was only against the Hartford Convention, and Federalists opposed to the war, they can excite no terror; if against them, in mass, why are they cherished by the leading Republicans, or such as assume to be leaders?

The great misfortune to our country is, the Republican party, since its union with the Federal party, have separated and formed themselves into three or four parties; all calling themselves Republicans, each setting up for itself, and each striving to put down the others. And some politicians are not very fastidious about the means to be employed against a rival party. And when the repudiated Federalist is to be used to aid in a project of destruction, he is used in either character, as a Federalist or Republican, as the occasion may require.

After the election of President Monroe, three or four Republican parties rose upon the ruins of the Federalists. Amongst them was the Crawford party. Mr. Crawford being a man of distinguished talents, excellent morals, and greatly esteemed, more than ordinary means were employed to put him down. The presses were employed for that purpose. The *Washington Republican* was established in this city for that express purpose. Its papers were sent gratis throughout the Union. It denominated Mr. Crawford the *Radical Chief,* and those who supported him, *Radicals.* This being a new term in the political vocabulary, its definition was not understood. It was defined to mean—

> *"An old Federalist in a new form, holding the people to be too ignorant to choose a President, and that it is lawful to cheat and defraud them for their own good, upon the ground that they are their own worst enemies."*

To aid in this good cause, Mr. Adams, the *Coalition Chief,* was brought into the Republican ranks, and obtained, at least, the second place in the Republican family—and especially in the two Carolinas.

In North Carolina, where the Electors are elected by general ticket, there were two tickets run—one called the Crawford ticket, the other the People's ticket. In some of the counties, it was agreed, the better to prevent Mr. Crawford's success, that those who voted for the People's ticket, should endorse upon the ticket, "for General Jackson," or "for Mr. Adams," as the voter might choose, and when the election should close, and the tickets be counted, if the People's ticket succeeded, then the endorsements should be counted also, and whosoever had the greatest number—General Jackson or Mr. Adams—should be the People's candidate, and be supported by the People's Electors. The People's electors were elected, and they unanimously voted for General Jackson. But I suppose if Mr. Adams had had the greatest number of endorsements, he would have gotten the vote according to compact. This compact was not universal.

*This was the definition of a Radical, given by Mr. McDuffie, in a pamphlet which he published at Columbia, S. C. in November, 1824, immediately preceding the Presidential Election. In that pamphlet, he ranks General Jackson and Mr. Adams together, as the two most prominent Republican candidates, in South Carolina, for the Presidency. Since that period, the People of South Carolina have obtained the true definition of the term *Radical,* and are now fighting under its banner.

In South Carolina, Mr. Adams was equally beloved by many of the leading Republicans. In September of 1824, in the District of Edgefield, a very large and respectable assemblage of the people convened for the purpose of determining on the most suitable person as their Presidential candidate. They went into a formal election, and General Jackson was elected. But lest they should find that General Jackson would not be sustained in other States, they proceeded to a second choice, to be brought forward, in case General Jackson was not likely to succeed; and Mr. Adams was elected, as their second choice, to be kept in reserve. Their proceedings were published in the newspapers, and sent abroad to the world: recognizing Mr. Adams as a Republican, and second to none but General Jackson.

In the city of Charleston, October, 1824, on the day of the election for Representatives to Congress and to the State Legislature, who were to elect the Presidential electors, a full ticket of candidates published their names, and for that purpose addressed the following note to the editor of the Southern Patriot, in this form:

"Jackson and Adams Ticket."

"To the Editor of the Southern Patriot:"

"Sir: You are authorized to say that the following gentlemen will in no event vote for electors favorable to William H. Crawford, as President."*

To this declaration they annexed their names, eighteen of them in number. Among those names I recognise gentlemen of the first respectability, of the old Federal school. Also Republicans of the first respectability; all uniting in "confraternity," to support Mr. Adams as the Republican candidate, in case any thing should render the success of General Jackson doubtful; but in no event to support Mr. Crawford.

In February, 1824, a committee of the Republican members of Congress, consisting of twenty-four, three of them from South Carolina, were nominated to take the sense of Congress, whether it were expedient to meet in *caucus*, to fix upon a suitable candidate for the Presidency.† The committee reported it was inexpedient to meet in *caucus* at that time. The reasons were, because all the candidates were Republicans, and a *caucus* was only necessary in Federal times. Mr. Adams was one of these Republican candidates, and was elected.

Accompanying this report of the *anti-caucus* committee, was the following statement:

*See the Southern Patriot, 11th October, 1824.

†See Niles' Register, vol. 25, page 276.

"1. That of the 261 members of Congress, somewhere about 45 are Federalists—so that the *democratic members*, that might go into *caucus*, are 216."*

I will give one instance more of the facility and dexterity with which some of our Republicans can metamorphose a Federalist, to suit any occasion that may occur. The instance alludes to myself, and I hope I may be pardoned for mentioning it, as I was not an actor, but merely the subject of the stratagem. In less than two years after the leading party in Charleston, South Carolina, in October, 1824, had exhibited to their constituents and to the world, in their "Jackson and Adams ticket," exhibiting them as

---

*The proceedings of this *Anti-Caucus* committee demonstrably prove what I have elsewhere said, that the destruction of the Federal party, and its amalgamation with the Republican, instead of a blessing to this Union, may yet prove its overthrow. The evidence of the abuse of power in the hands of the Republicans, when the check of the Federal party was destroyed, is to be drawn from the following dates and facts:

On the 14th of February, 1824, this *Anti-Caucus* committee of 24 made their report, that it was inexpedient to meet in *Caucus*. They shewed, at that date, there were 216 Republicans, and only 45 Federalists. This put it beyond all doubt, that the Republicans, 216 to 45 Federalists, had the whole power and control of legislation in their own hands.

On the 30th of April, 1824, only two months and a half after the *Anti-Caucus* report, and during the same session, Congress enacted a law—

"To procure the necessary surveys, plans, and estimates upon the subject of roads and canals."—[See 7 vol. Laws U. S. page 239.]

This law is without limitation in its duration, and gives to the President unlimited powers over the whole subject, and the unlimited power "to appoint as many officers of the Engineer corps as he may think proper." And these Engineers have swarmed in every part of the Union ever since. Five Republican members from South Carolina, all of whom were opposed to a caucus, voted for that law.

On the 22d May, 1824, a little better than three months after the *anti-caucus* report, and during the same session, Congress enacted a law to amend the several acts, "imposing duties on imports."—[See 7 vol. Laws U. S. page 268.]

This law fixed upon us the most grievous burthen that any portion of the people of this Union ever endured. No member from South Carolina voted for this law. But what is the difference? Without the Tariff, Internal Improvement would expire: and vice versa.

Of the 216 Republican members, the Report of the *anti-caucus* committee says, 181 were opposed to a *caucus*. If 181 Republicans were associated to oppose the caucus, could not the same 181 Republicans have prevented the enactment of these ruinous laws? If they were Republican for one purpose, they were certainly Republican for every other purpose.

brother Republicans of the same school, and equally worthy of being supported for the Presidency, I had the honor of presenting my humble pretensions for public favor, and, although less than two years after the display of that ticket, I was denounced in a public newspaper as *the supporter and ally of John Q. Adams, who was himself a Federalist, and a friend to the Hartford Convention; and that I was opposed to General Jackson.** And this was enlarged upon and reiterated in the same paper; and this, too, when it was known, as far as I was known, that the reverse of all this, as related to myself, was literally true.

Sir, I never was the advocate of Mr. Adams. I am opposed, and have always been opposed, to his political principles. I erred in one thing: I did not abuse him in the streets and highways. Had I done so, it might have saved me from this reproach.

When General Jackson was first a candidate, although I was not one of his supporters, I was, nevertheless, one of his admirers, but not one of his traducers. Before he became a candidate, I had made up my mind in favor of Mr. Crawford, who had high claims, and General Jackson has too much regard for good faith to suppose I ought to have abandoned him. But, in the second canvass, I supported General Jackson throughout; and I will support him again, if he should consent to serve his country a second time. But, when I make this avowal, I am not pledged to follow General Jackson, or any other President, implicitly. I was not sent here to enlist under party banners, but to serve my country upon the principles of the Constitution, from which I hope General Jackson will never depart. Much has been said by the politicians, of their support of General Jackson for the Presidency. He was not placed in office by that portion of the community denominated politicians, who make Presidents for their own convenience, and to answer their own interest. They only followed in the train. They were forced into the ranks by public opinion. His party was his country, and his supporters were the sovereign People, who, not yet contaminated with the sickly and corrupt intrigues that will one day prostrate your country, bestowed the Presidency on him, for his long, his meritorious, and his well-tried services.

Sir, the great mass of the People of the United States are Republican, and seek after truth; and when correctly informed, will always decide justly. They love their country, and they love the Constitution; and would

*See the Charleston Mercury, in all July, August, and September, 1826, in which it was published. This essay was not editorial. The writer is neither known nor sought for. I shall always submit to a public scrutiny, but hope I may be permitted to contradict falsehoods. I ask no more.

always serve the one, and be guided by the other, were they freed from the polluted intrigues that daily surround them: generated in the party feuds of scheming politicians, who, without any fixed party principles, are everlastingly engaged in party intrigues, regardless of the Constitution, and regardless of the public good. This is a deplorable picture, but it is, nevertheless, true. You have at this moment four distinct parties: not well poised parties, of different political principles, calculated to operate as a salutary check on all sides, but all claiming to be of the true Republican school, and each party having a distinct candidate for the Presidency. The patriot may deplore, and the orator may denounce, the effects of rival political parties; but, sir, as well may you hope to stay the billows, or lull the tempest, by your single *fiat*, as to stay the existence of parties in this Government, whilst politicians have ambition to gratify, and distinctions to hope for.

Mr. President, I have as ardent love for the preservation of the Union of these States, as can inspire the heart of any gentleman whose voice has been heard in the Senate. I am sensible of its worth—I know its price was the blood of our ancestors—I know it swells our importance abroad, as a member of the family of nations—and I know the lustre it will shed upon the character of Republics. And as a testimony of my fervent desire for its long duration, I will beg leave to borrow the brilliant apostrophe of the gentleman from Massachusetts, if he will permit me; and "when my eyes shall be turned to behold, for the last time, the sun in Heaven, may I not see him shining on the broken and dishonored fragments of" the Constitution of my country, once the aegis of our rights and the palladium of our liberty; but let them rather behold that Constitution, regulating the enactments of Congress, according to its delegated and limited powers, dispensing equal laws, and equal rights, according to its well-defined and well-digested provisions, to every portion of the People of these States. I shall then die content, under a full belief that this Union may be as durable as time; and that the Union can only be broken up by the violation of the sacred principles of that Constitution.

John M. Clayton

John M. Clayton was born in Delaware in 1796 and was educated at Yale College and the Litchfield Law School. He was admitted to the bar in 1819. He was elected as a Federalist to the Delaware House of Representatives in 1824, and served as secretary of state of Delaware from 1826 to 1828. Clayton supported John Quincy Adams in the election of 1824 and was elected as a National Republican to the United States Senate in 1828. His first notable speech in the Senate was on the Foot resolution. He supported Jackson against nullification and assisted in the passage of the compromise tariff of 1833. He joined the Whig party and was an opponent of Jackson's policy on the Bank of the United States. Resigning from the Senate, he was chief justice of Delaware from 1836 to 1838. He was elected to the U.S. Senate in 1845, serving until 1849, when President Zachary Taylor appointed him Secretary of State. In 1852 he was reelected to the Senate and served until his death in 1856.

Speech of Mr. Clayton,

of Delaware

[March 4, 1830]

The resolution of Mr. Foot, of Connecticut, relative to the
public lands, being under consideration, Mr. Clayton
addressed the Chair as follows:

M R. PRESIDENT: IF I NEED AN APOLOGY FOR DISCUSSING TOPICS extrinsic or not strictly relevant to the subject of the resolution before
us, I shall find it in the example of honorable gentlemen, who, in going before me, have availed themselves, by general consent, of an opportunity to
debate on this motion, the full merits of other questions of momentous interest to our country. While the argument was of a sectional character, and
chiefly calculated to excite personal and local feeling, I desired no participation in it. But, although generally averse to any deviation from the ordinary rules of Parliamentary proceeding, and unwilling to originate any
new subject of controversy even in the boundless latitude given to this discussion, I cannot be silent while principles are boldly advanced and
pressed upon us, (no matter how inapplicable or inappropriate they may
appear,) which in my judgment are subversive of the interests of this nation, or hostile to the spirit of the Federal Constitution.

The resolution of the honorable Senator from Connecticut has nothing imperative in its character. It lays down no new principle, and proposes no new course of legislation; but simply asks an inquiry into the
expediency of either hastening the sales of the public domain, or of stopping the surveys for a limited period. The committee to whom the inquiry
is proposed to be entrusted, is composed of five members,* all of whom are
Representatives of States within whose limits are contained large portions

*Messrs. Barton of Missouri, Chairman, Livingston of Louisiana, Kane of Illinois, Ellis of Mississippi, and McKinley of Alabama.

---

of the public lands. Seeing in this fact a sufficient refutation of the objection that this inquiry may create unnecessary alarm in the West—entertaining the same confidence in the honorable members of that Committee which others have professed—believing that the subject proposed to be referred to them is important to the country, and that by the adoption of the resolution we may be furnished with an interesting document in their report, my own vote will be given against the motion for indefinite postponement. I agree with my honorable friend from Massachusetts (Mr. Webster) that the committee may investigate the whole subject without any express instructions. By the rules of the Senate, they already have full jurisdiction over the matter. But after all the discussion which has been elicited by the mere proposition to instruct them to inquire, it is not probable that the committee will do so without some further intimation from the Senate that a report on this subject would be acceptable. I cannot agree with the honorable Senator from New Hampshire, (Mr. Woodbury,) that the motion to postpone is calculated or intended to prevent a distinct expression of opinion on the subject: on the contrary, the postponement of the resolution, after discussion, would announce to the committee our indisposition to have the inquiry made during the present session. The Senator from Connecticut, (Mr. Foot,) who desires this information, and whose deportment here is distinguished for urbanity and courtesy to others, may be indulged without any apprehension of exciting unnecessary alarm in the West, while our refusal to adopt any measure to throw light on the subject may, possibly, create suspicion in other parts of our country, that we are wasting this portion of the nation's treasure, and are afraid that our profligacy may be exposed by this investigation.

I proceed now, sir, to a brief examination of what I conceive to have been the origin of this protracted and discursive debate. We have a bill on our files entitled, a bill "to graduate the price of the public lands, to make provision for actual settlers, and to cede the refuse upon equitable terms, and for meritorious objects, to the States in which they lie"—the same, sir, which has been alluded to by the Senator from Missouri (Mr. Benton) under the designation of "my graduation bill." When the gentleman from South Carolina (Mr. Hayne) first addressed the Senate on the resolution before us, I understood him to have pressed it as a measure of expediency, that the public lands should be sold to the States within whose limits they are situated, for a nominal consideration. The gentleman afterwards corrected this impression when his colleague (Mr. Smith of S. C.) declared that he also so understood him. Sir, the gentleman has the right to claim of us all that his statements should be properly represented. I now understand him to say that his proposition is not to cede away these lands for a nominal consideration, but to sell them on such liberal terms that revenue should not be even a secondary object in the sale. He urged with all his usual ability the impolicy of even considering them as a source of revenue. Sir, if I now comprehend all this doctrine, it has for its objects to make impressions which shall secure a favorable vote on this same graduation bill; and, if so, I dissent from the doctrine *toto coelo*. Whether this were or were not the great object of the debate, with the gentleman from South Carolina, it was plainly avowed to have been a motive for it by the Senator from Missouri, (Mr. Benton,) in the view which he took of the subject. The bill referred to proposes to limit the prices of these lands at once, to one dollar per acre, and then gradually to reduce those prices at the rate of twenty-five per cent. per annum, until the lands shall be offered, after the expiration of the third year, at twenty-five cents per acre. It further proposes to sell lands to actual settlers, whether trespassers or not, at gradually reduced prices, until, after the expiration of the third year, they are to receive them at five cents per acre. If that miserable pittance be not then paid, it proposes to cede eighty acres to every such settler, "without the payment of any consideration, and as a donation"—and finally, by the terms of it all the lands which shall remain not disposed of by these means at the end of five years, are to be given to the States in which they lie upon these conditions merely—that they shall apply them to the promotion of education and internal improvement at home, and refund to the Government the expenses of the surveys of the lands so ceded, at the rate of two hundred and sixteen dollars for each township of twenty-three thousand acres. In consequence of the enactment of such a law, probably very little would be bought until the expiration of the third year, when, if the interference of these States with a view to secure the whole to themselves for nothing, should not prevent the sales altogether, the lands would be purchased at a nominal price. Such a measure, sir, would not only be unjust to the citizens of the old States, but highly injurious to the Western settlers who have heretofore bought lands at a full and fair consideration. The value of property is merely relative, and is either enhanced or diminished by the estimate placed upon other property of the same kind. If a hundred millions of acres be thrown into market at twenty-five cents per acre, and a large quantity of land be offered to actual settlers at the same time at five cents per acre, the value of that which has been bought by fair purchasers at two dollars, or at one dollar and twenty-five cents per acre, is at once, other circumstances being equal, sunk to a level with the selling price of all the lands around it. We well know the operation upon our real property, in all parts of the Union, of the exposure at public sale of any very considerable portion of real property adjoining it. We know that if a great landed proprietor sells me a tract in the midst of his possessions at fifty dollars per acre, and then, from pecuniary embarrassment or from any other cause, exposes the residue to sale, by which he realizes only five dollars per acre for lands of equal fertility and advantages, my land, as an effect of this, is reduced to his last selling price. When he puts a million of acres around mine into market at a *nominal* sum, he equally diminishes the selling value of mine by the act, whether his motive for doing so be to augment population, and improve the country, or wantonly to effect my ruin. And should this bill become a law, the former purchasers who have paid full value would, in consequence of the depreciation of the property occasioned by the enactment, have a better equitable right to remuneration for losses by the Government, than many claimants whose demands are annually liquidated here without our hearing a note of remonstrance against them. This bill has been pending here for the last four years; and the disposition evinced to entertain it as a subject for future decision, has cherished expectations which are sedulously encouraged by rumors in the West, that its provisions will eventually be adopted. If my information be correct, and Western gentlemen near me can bear witness that it is so, anticipations have been too generally indulged that these lands will, before long, be offered for nothing. This must tend to impede our sales, and perhaps to some extent to suspend the settlement of our Western frontier—a result I suppose to be deprecated by none more deeply than by the gentleman from Missouri (Mr. Benton) himself. In the meantime, without the final action of Congress on the subject, the illusion is every year increasing; and, to add to the evil, we have now a new doctrine which has been already adverted to in this debate—that these lands of right belong to the new States within which they are situated. The gentleman from Missouri, in reference to the charge of hostility to the West, to prove or disprove which I would not myself now offer a single remark, has chosen to inform us that he has never obtained here more than a single vote for his graduation bill from the representatives of all the States northeast of the Potomac—and he adds, that vote was given in 1828 by a former Senator from the State which I have the honor in part to represent here. For this good deed, the gentleman from Missouri proceeded to pronounce a panegyric on that Senator, which was merited on stronger grounds. Though readily according in the justice which imputes the most correct motives to that gentleman, who is my neighbor, and with whom I live on terms of friendly intercourse, exercising as he doubtless did his conscientious judgment on the case, yet with my views, thus briefly explained, I am constrained to say that I cannot vote for this bill. According to my mode of considering it, it is a proposition to give away the birthright of our people for a nominal sum; and I am yet to learn that the citizens of the Middle States have indicated any feeling in regard to it differing from that expressed in the vote referred to, when, with a single exception, all the Senators representing States north of Mason's and Dixon's line, opposed the measure. They do not look to these lands, as has been unjustly stated, with the eye of an unfeeling landholder who parts with his acres as a miser parts with his gold. They view the new States as younger sisters in the same family, upon an equal footing with themselves, and entitled to an equal *share* of their patrimony; but having children to educate, and numerous wants to be supplied, they will think it ungenerous, unjust, and oppressive, should these younger sisters take away the *whole*. Sir, it is the inheritance which descended from our forefathers who wrested a part of it from the British crown at the expense of their blood and treasure, and paid for the rest of it by the earnings of their labour. It is not for me to say what are the feelings of the people of the Middle States on this subject. It is their privilege to speak for themselves, and they will doubtless, when they think it necessary, exercise that privilege. But I will say, that if they entertain the sentiments of their fathers, they will never consent to cede away hundreds of millions of acres of land for a nominal consideration, or gratuitously relinquish them to any new State, however loudly she may insist on the measure as due to *her* rights and *her* sovereignty, or however boldly she may threaten to defy the Federal Judiciary, and decide the controversy by her own tribunals, in her own favor. Those who are conversant with our revolutionary history, will remember that the exclusive claims of Virginia and of other members of our political family, to the public lands, were warmly resisted by the States of New Jersey, Delaware, and Maryland, as soon as those claims were avowed after the rupture with the mother country. The articles of Confederation were not signed on the part of New Jersey until the 25th of November, 1778, although she had bled freely in the cause of American liberty from the commencement of the struggle. One of the principal objections which caused this delay in the ratification of those articles will be found in the able representation of her Legislature, presented by her Delegates to Congress, before she acceded to the Union. "The ninth article," said they, "provides that no State shall be deprived of territory for the benefit of the United States. Whether we are to understand that by territory is intended any land, the property of which was heretofore vested in the crown of Great Britain, or that no mention of such land is made in the Confederation, we are constrained to observe that the present war, as we always apprehended, was undertaken for the general defence and interest of the confederating Colonies, now the United States. It was ever the confident expectation of this State, that the benefits derived from a successful contest were to be *general and proportionate*; and that the property of the common enemy, failing in consequence of a prosperous issue of the war, would belong to the United States, and be appropriated to their use. We are therefore greatly disappointed in finding no provision made in the Confederation for empowering the Congress to dispose of such property, but especially the vacant and unpatented lands, commonly called the crown lands, for defraying the expenses of the war, and for such other public and general purposes. The jurisdiction ought, in every instance, to belong to the respective States within the charter or determined limits of which such lands may be seated; but reason and justice must decide, that the property which existed in the crown of Great Britain, previous to the present revolution, ought now to belong to the Congress in trust for the use and benefit of the United States. *They have fought and bled for it in proportion to their respective abilities; and therefore the reward ought not to be predilectionally distributed.*" And when in November, 1778, the Legislature of New Jersey determined to attach her to the Union, they did it, as they then expressed, "in firm reliance that the candor and justice of the several States would, in due time, remove the subsisting inequality," yet still insisting on the justice of their objections then "lately stated and sent to the General Congress." So too Delaware and Maryland, for the same reasons, refused to join the Confederation until a still later period, the former ratifying the articles on the 22d of February, 1779, and the latter on the 1st of March, 1781. The State which I have the honor in part to represent here had, on the 1st of February 1799, adopted the following resolutions to authorize her accession to the Union:

"*Resolved*, That this State considers it necessary for the peace and safety of the State to be included in the Union; that a moderate extent of limits should be assigned for such of these States as claim to the Mississippi or South Sea; and that the United States, in Congress assembled, should and ought to have power of fixing their Western limits.

"*Resolved also*, That this State considers herself justly entitled to a right, in common with the members of the Union, to that extensive tract of country which lies to the westward of the frontiers of the United States, the property of which was not vested in or granted to individuals at the commencement of the present war; that the same hath been or may be gained from the King of Great Britain or the native Indians, by the blood and treasure of all, and ought therefore to be a common estate to be granted out on terms beneficial to the United States."

But after the accession of Delaware with this protest, Maryland still persevered in her refusal to join the Confederation, solely on the ground "that she might thereby be stripped of the common interest and the common benefits derivable from the Western lands." She still insisted that some security for these lands was necessary for the happiness and tranquillity of the Union, denied the whole claim of Virginia to the territory northwest of the Ohio, and still pressed upon Congress "that policy and justice required, that a country unsettled at the commencement of the war, claimed by the British crown and ceded to it by the treaty of Paris, if wrested from the common enemy by the blood and treasure of the thirteen States, should be considered as common property." In February, 1780, New York made her cession to accelerate the Federal alliance, and declared the territory ceded should be for the use and benefit of such of the United States as should become members of that alliance, "and for no other use or purpose whatever." And although Virginia attempted for a while to vindicate her claim, yet other States, feeling a strong attachment to Maryland, and conscious of the justice of her representations, disliked a partial union which would throw out of the pale a people standing, as Marylanders have always stood, among the bravest and most patriotic of our countrymen. The ordinance of Congress then followed in October, 1780, declaring that the territory to be ceded by the States should be disposed of for the common benefit of the Union, and on the 2d of January, 1781, Virginia, in that spirit of magnanimity which has generally prevailed in her councils, yielded up her claim for the benefit of the whole Union. It is a remarkable circumstance that Maryland did not actually join the Union until after these cessions had been made by New York and Virginia, declaring at the very moment, and by the very terms of her accession, that she "did not release, nor intend to relinquish, any part of her right and interest, with the other confederating States, to the western territory." These facts, which have now become a part of the familiar history of the country, furnish curious reminiscences in these latter days, when a new light has broken in upon us to show that the new States have title to all the lands within their chartered limits, and when we are told it would be most magnanimous and becoming in us, who claim to have imbibed the spirit and sentiments

of our forefathers, to cede away our patrimony for a nominal consideration. Let it be remembered that the feeling on this subject manifested by
the two States of Delaware and Maryland, preventing their accession to
the confederation until so late a period, was with difficulty repressed, even
by that ardent attachment to the cause of liberty for which they were then
so much distinguished, and in which they have never been surpassed.
Their troops went through the whole contest together, flanking and supporting each other in battle; commonly led on by the same Commander;
generally the first to advance and the last to retreat, their bayonets, like the
pikes of the Macedonian phalanx, always glittering in front of one and the
same compact mass; and when they fell, they slept in death together on
the same part of the blood-stained field. It was that same spirit which
prompted the combined exertions of these people in the American cause
throughout the whole struggle, which also united them in their resistance
against every attempt on the part of any single section of the country to
appropriate for its exclusive benefit the territory which they were striving
to conquer from the British Crown. Sir, I think they will now combine
again; I think they will, when considering this subject, bestow some reflection upon the millions which have been expended in the subsequent purchase of the Southwestern portion of our public domain, on the sums
which have been profusely lavished in making and carrying into effect our
treaties for the extinguishment of the Indian title, in making the surveys
of these lands, and in the payment of officers and agents for the maintenance of our land system. From the feeling which formerly actuated them,
I judge that their co-operation on this subject will be such as to resist every
effort to bribe them with promises, or to sway them by means of political
excitement to give up that which could not be wrested from them by appeals to their strongest attachments in the darkest days of their adversity.
They will claim, I think, Sir, an equal portion of this territory under the
plain letter of the grants referred to—they may claim a large portion of it
by the paramount title of the right of conquest, which has never been by
them relinquished; and by that title they can successfully defend it. Whatever foundation there may be for the imputation of motives in other sections of the Union, to flatter and to woo the West by the offer to her of
this splendid dowry if she will transfer her influence to a candidate in a
Presidential election, we, I believe, shall not take part in any such bargain.
The gentleman from Tennessee (Mr. Grundy) says the West has been already wooed and won. It may be so, but we are not, and I think shall never
be, *sub potestate viri,* and if we could be bought for any consideration to

sign this release of our birth-right, we should never agree, like Esau, to sell it for a mess of pottage.

I come now, Sir, to consider a subject which has been discussed in connection with this—the right of a State to regulate her conduct by the judgment of her own self-constituted tribunals, upon the validity of an act of Congress in opposition to the solemn decisions of the Supreme Court of the United States: and my remarks upon it will be chiefly in reply to gentlemen who have gone before me. I confess I do not discover why the power of deciding any, and every question, growing out of any circumstances in which a State may conceive her sovereignty impugned, is not translated to her own tribunals by the same train of argument which induces the conclusion that she may nullify an act of the Federal Legislature without the aid of the Federal Judiciary. We know—we are so taught by memorials on our files—that the doctrine is very current in some States of the West, that the public territory within their limits is their own; and we have been threatened that when the population flowing westward has transferred the balance of power beyond the Alleghany, or when, as one in this debate has phrased it, "the sceptre has departed from the old thirteen forever," we shall find the rights of the new States asserted and maintained, if not by the force of numbers here, at least by the force of arms at home. In that case, too, it is said, that to us distance will be defeat. State sovereignty and State rights constitute the very war cry of a new party in this country. I would myself be among the last to infringe upon the constitutional powers of the States. But how far will the new doctrines on the subject carry us? Some who have engaged in this discussion have avowed the opinion that our claim to the public lands is inconsistent with the paramount rights of Western States, and that upon the fundamental principles of government, the domain within their chartered limits is the property of these new grantees. Others who stand among the boldest champions of the principle that a sovereign State may constitutionally and lawfully enforce her declarations against the validity of an act of Congress, and nullify it whenever by her judgment it is "deliberately, plainly, and palpably unconstitutional," repudiate the whole doctrine of State supremacy, and State title, when we touch these claims to the public lands. The rule works badly then. The two positions assumed by the same reasoner are repugnant to each other. You cannot claim by virtue of your State sovereignty to nullify an act of Congress, and yet deny to another State the right by a similar operation to tear out of your statute book the leaf containing the Virginia grant, as well as that which bears upon it the act of

Congress declaring the uses of that grant. By the grant and the act, the estate ceded is "for the common benefit." The new sovereigns, within whose dominions the estate is situated, asserting their power to decide all questions which, in their judgment, touch their sovereignty, may nullify both, and make the land theirs; or if they cannot, how can any other of these *sovereigns* nullify a tariff law or an act for internal improvement, which the Federal Judiciary adjudges to be valid! The gentleman from Tennessee says he will admit that the Supreme Court is the final arbiter in all cases in law and equity arising under the Constitution, and the laws of the United States *made in pursuance of it.* But I am not satisfied with this limitation. The words of the Constitution are, "the Judicial power of the United States shall be vested in one Supreme Court, and in such inferior Courts as the Congress may, from time to time, ordain and establish." Then this general transfer of power is explained by the second section of the same article: "The judicial power shall extend to all cases in law or equity arising under this Constitution, *the laws of the United States,* and treaties made, or which shall be made, under their authority; to all cases affecting Ambassadors, other public Ministers and Consuls; to all cases of admiralty and maritime jurisdiction; *to controversies to which the United States shall be a party; to controversies between two or more States,* between a State and citizens of another State, between citizens of different States, between citizens of the same State claiming lands under grants of different States, and between a State or the citizens thereof and foreign States, citizens or subjects." All these words of the deed are in full force, except so far as it has been altered by the single amendatory article to prevent suits against one of the United States by citizens of another State, or by citizens or subjects of any foreign State. The instrument then contains no qualification of the judicial power restricting its exercise to cases arising out of laws *made in pursuance of the constitution.*

The reservation is an inadvertent interpolation in the instrument, and the power granted extends to laws of the United States, whether constitutionally or unconstitutionally enacted. It will be seen, too, that the United States must *"be a party to controversies"* concerning a tariff law, as well as to those which affect the right to the public domain, or any other question touching State sovereignty; and that if there be no authority in the instrument by which the judicial power can be extended to the former class of controversies, there is none to extend it to the latter class, or any case which a single State may consider as presenting an infraction of her own powers. The gentleman from Kentucky (Mr. Rowan) and other Senators have contended that a State cannot surrender any portion of her sovereignty, and we have been asked to produce an instance in which sovereignty has submitted itself to any judicial tribunal. Those who formed the constitution, in their recommendatory letter signed by Washington on the 17th of September, 1787, inform us that "it is obviously impracticable in the federal government of these States to secure all the rights of INDEPENDENT SOVEREIGNTY to each, and yet provide for the interest and safety of all." The gentleman from Tennessee, in order to explain and construe the constitution, referred to the brief enumeration, contained in this letter, of the specific objects which made it necessary to establish this government. I refer to the same authority to overthrow the doctrine which regards all the rights of independent sovereignty in each of the States, and to prove that some of those rights were, in the view of the convention, ceded to provide for the general welfare. States are not self-existent: they are created by the people for their benefit. Those who have conferred state power, can take it away; and for their own good they have transferred a portion of this mysterious principle of sovereignty, which troubles gentlemen so much, to another place. They have transferred a portion of the Judicial power to the Supreme Court, which acts as an impartial umpire, and not as an adversary party deciding his own cause, as is erroneously supposed by some reasoners here. The gentleman from Tennessee says the Federal Judiciary is, when a question of State rights is before it, a portion or part of one of the parties, created by the Legislative and Executive branches of the general government, responsible to that government alone, and liable to the imposition of destructive burdens by that party. Even if all this were correct, it would be a sufficient answer to it, when discussing this question, to reply that the States had agreed that the arbiter should be thus created and thus responsible, having signed the arbitration bond deliberately and with a full knowledge of the consequences. But when we look into the instrument we find that the States, by their representatives in the Senate, must first consent to the appointment of the arbiter, or he is not lawfully chosen. They can challenge for cause, and they can challenge peremptorily. By refusing to consent to appointments, they might in time vacate every seat on the whole tribunal. By the Legislative power of their immediate representatives in the Senate, responsible to the States as their only masters, they can always prevent the imposition of oppressive burdens on their common arbiters. They alone can try these arbiters on impeachment for misbehaviour, and without impeachment those arbiters cannot be removed from office. The Senator from Kentucky objects to the Federal Judiciary, that a majority in Congress may by law increase the number of judges, and thus oppress the minority when they please. It has been said, too, that large States, with a great representation in Congress, such as New York and Pennsylvania, combining with others, may by their superior vote so far increase the number on the bench as to oppress and destroy the sovereignty of the lesser States. If the objection has any weight, it is one which could be made to our whole system of republican government. We are ruled by majorities; and if the majority of this nation should become radically corrupt, I admit that the government will soon fall. But I have sufficient reliance on the virtue and good sense of the people, whether living in large or small States, to believe that no attempt will ever be deliberately made by a majority in either, to destroy the independence and legitimate powers of the other. And I feel no apprehensions on this subject, for other reasons. Let us inquire into the mode of operating. Supposing now (to make out the gentleman's case) that the large States wickedly conspire to ruin the small ones. New York, Kentucky, Ohio, Pennsylvania, Virginia and North Carolina, being (as would be so probable!) united for this end, carry a bill through the other House to double the number of judges. Suppose, too, that they had by their votes elected a President who would second their views. When the bill comes before the Senate, if the small States understand your object, they, having an equal representation here, secured by the only provision in the constitution which numbers can never change, vote you down at once; and your combination (as other combinations may be) is consigned to

———— "that same ancient vault,
Where all the kindred of the Capulets lie."

But suppose the Senators representing the small States here, not suspecting mischief, but relying on your integrity, suffer the bill to pass. Your President being in the plot, as we will for the sake of argument suppose, it becomes a law. What then? The bench is not yet filled. The "modus operandi" requires that he should nominate, and we should consent to the appointment of the men who are to adjudge away our independence. We might be slow to suspect our old friends of dishonest purposes, but we can learn some things if you give us time. When you bring out your nominations, we cannot fail to understand your plan. You are caught at once, *flagrante delicto*, and we check you in the Senate, by rejecting all nominations which do not please us. We have two chances to put an effectual *veto* on your plot, and our *veto* is a very different affair from your *State veto* on an act of Congress. However thankful, therefore, we may be for the kindly apprehensions expressed for our welfare, we say that we are not yet alarmed. We cannot see, with the honorable gentleman from Tennessee, that the States have been guilty of either folly or weakness in creating such a tribunal as we conceive the Supreme Court of the United States to be—nor do we think with him, that by the easiest operations imaginable this creature is so competent to the destruction of its creators.

But whatever may have been, in the opinion of honorable gentlemen, the folly of the people of these States in creating such a tribunal, or however incompetent it may appear to decide these matters, the question still recurs—Is there any other forum established with co-extensive, or with appellate powers? If so, what is it? There ought not to be a wrong without a remedy, and the interest and safety of all require the existence of some arbiter to grant a remedy. We are warned, however, that if by the Constitution there be not some express grant of power for this purpose, the States and the people still reserve it. On the other hand, if the grant to the Federal Judiciary be express, the States have not reserved it, and can create no other without forming a new Constitution or violating this. Sir, I listened with deep interest to the developement of what I thought was announced as a new discovery on this subject. I will consider that adverted to, and recommended, by the gentleman from Tennessee, (Mr. Grundy.) After conceding to the Federal Judiciary the powers of a common umpire, to decide on the constitutionality of all Congressional enactments made *in pursuance* of the Constitution, he informed us that there was another tribunal to which a State might resort when oppressed by what she considered to be a plain, palpable, and dangerous violation of the Constitution, without throwing herself out of the Union. He admitted that the Legislature of the State was not this tribunal. That might be misled. He beats the ground then which was occupied by the gentleman from South Carolina, (Mr. Hayne,) but himself takes a new position, not less dangerous. For he informed us that a State Convention might be called, and *that* might nullify the oppressive law—after which, he thought Congress must acquiesce by abandoning the power. The amount of this is, that one State is to govern all the rest whenever she may choose to declare, by Convention, that a law is unconstitutional. The end of this, we say, is war—civil war. We admit that a State Convention may *pronounce* any law unconstitutional, as Virginia did in '98. But the mere declaration comes to nothing, unless it can be enforced. You may declare a law unconstitutional, and so can I. But what of that? It amounts only to this—we have full freedom of speech in this country, may advocate what opinions we please, and peaceably endeavor to impress them upon others. But the gentleman says this doctrine does not lead to war. If Congress will not submit to the State, he thinks there is still a complete political salvo in another tribunal, and that is *a Convention of the States* to be called under the provisions of the Constitution. The State then must exert herself until Congress, two thirds deeming it necessary under the fifth article, shall propose amendments to the Constitution; or, on the application of the Legislatures of two thirds of the several States, shall call a Convention for proposing amendments, which, when ratified by the Legislatures of three-fourths of the several States, or by Conventions in three-fourths of them, shall be valid to all intents and purposes as part of the Constitution. So far this does not contravene the doctrine which we advocate, and which the Senator from New Hampshire, if I rightly understood him, after much preface, and with some "slips of prolixity," finally settled down upon as a part of the true orthodox creed. The right to amend the Constitution has never been denied. This was a part of the political platform upon which my honorable friend from Missouri, (Mr. Barton,) invited you to come and stand with us. If the Convention of the States should assemble and decide by a majority of three fourths against the State, the gentleman from Tennessee says the State must submit. But if they decide otherwise, or do not decide at all, Congress must submit to the State. Without assenting to this last conclusion, which appears to be arbitrarily assumed, I will only inquire, if this be so, how is this tribunal to save us from civil war? The answer is, only by so amending the Constitution as to warp it to suit the declarations of the State Convention. This is an excellent remedy for the complaint of the State, but rather difficult to procure. If this is the sovereign panacea which the honorable Senator from Tennessee has discovered for healing the diseases of the South—Sir, I fancy she will agree with me in commending her physician for his ingenuity in finding out the ingredients of the bolus, but she will still think they are too hard to be obtained to render the prescription valuable to her. With less experience, I would recommend to a State groaning under the operation of a law which she deems unconstitutional, to apply first to the Federal Judiciary, where she will generally obtain relief, if her complaint be not hypochondria or imaginary ill. If she fail there, let her pour her complaints into the ears of her sisters, and use all constitutional means to procure a *repeal* of the obnoxious law. A bare *majority* of Congress will be sufficient to give her relief in this way. Do you object that Congress will probably persevere in their course, and refuse to repeal the law they have enacted? It may be so—and if so, their constituents, being a majority of the people, must concur with them, that the law is not only constitutional but salutary, or they would, by the exercise of the elective franchise, remove such unworthy agents of their sovereign will. If they do concur with their representatives, and uphold them in their refusal to repeal the law, no matter how often by any other power than the Federal Judiciary declared to be unconstitutional, in my humble judgment you will hardly persuade three-fourths of them to assemble for the purpose of altering their Constitution, and depriving their own agents of the power of acting on the subject.

It comes at last then to this—that we have no other direct resource, in the cases we have been considering, to save us from the horrors of anarchy, than the Supreme Court of the United States. That tribunal has decided a hundred such cases, and many under the most menacing circumstances. Several States have occasionally made great opposition to it. Indeed it would seem that in their turn most of the Sisters of this great family have fretted for a time, sometimes threatening to break the connection and form others—but in the end nearly all have been restored, by the dignified and impartial conduct of our common umpire, to perfect good humour. Should that umpire ever lose its high character for justice and impartiality, we have a corrective in the form of our government; but if it is to be had only by a calm and temperate appeal to the judgment and feelings of the whole American people, it can never be obtained by such addresses and resolutions as those of Colleton or Abbeville. Reason receives not in place of argument violent denunciations or furious appeals to party and passion. During a period of four or five years past, the complaints of the South have for this reason met with a cold reception in almost every other section of the Union. They have been loud and deep—but they have been evidently regarded as the transient effusions of party feeling, coming, as they too often did, couched in language of bitter vituperation, with the now stale and despicable charges of "coalition, bargain and corruption," that vile and putrescent stuff which has at length, as the Senator from Massachusetts truly stated, sloughed off and gone down into the kennel forever. The course pursued was exactly that which was best calculated to make the whole alleged grievances, if real, irremediable. Those who loved and admired the character of the Statesman of the West, indignant at the calumnies with which he, as they saw, was so unjustly assailed, often regarded the complaints which came with them as mere secondary considerations, brought in to aid a personal attack. On the other hand, many of those who affected to accredit these calumnies for political effect, in their hearts never sincerely believed any part of the story of southern sufferings, thinking perhaps that they knew best what weight was to be attached to the political falsehoods which commonly accompanied them. However different their objects, they were really on the same chase, but to the southern huntsman the game taken has been of no benefit. From a recent demonstration, we perceive the Southern complaint is *now* not even deemed worthy of a hearing. Sir, when I witnessed the manly and candid manner in which the Honorable Senator from South Carolina on my right (Mr. SMITH) spoke of the grievances of his constituents, when I saw him evidently soaring above mere party feeling, menacing none, denouncing none, and touching with all the delicacy which characterizes him the subjects in difference between us, the reflection forced itself irresistibly on my mind—how different might have been the reception of these complaints, had they always come thus recommended. South Carolina, though erring in a controversy with her sisters, would by all have been believed to have been *honestly* wrong; and if under such circumstances she should ever throw herself out of the pale of the Union in consequence of such a misconception of the constitution as we have endeavoured to prevent, I would rather see my own constituents stripped of the property acquired under the protection furnished by the government to their honest industry, than compelled by any vote of mine here to drive the steel with which we should arm our citizens into the bosoms of that gallant people. And I will now say, without meaning to express any further opinion on this delicate subject, that, for myself, whenever pounds, shillings and pence alone shall be arrayed against the infinite blessings of the Union, I shall unhesitatingly prefer the latter—for the simple reason, that I can never learn how to "calculate its value."

The honorable member from New Hampshire, in the progress of his very ingenious remarks, discussed, in connection with the constitutional power of the Judiciary, the whole doctrine of internal improvement, as well as the tariff. He denounced both as aggressions of the Federal government on the rights of the States, as measures evincive of and flowing from a disposition on the part of some, to claim for that government unlimited powers; and endeavoured to make it appear that these acts for internal improvement were and ever had been *Federal* heresies, while the opposite and restrictive tenets, limiting us to the strict exercise of certain enumerated and specific powers, had always distinguished your genuine democrat and only true republican. The honorable member informed us that by the prevalence of his strict construction of the constitution over the latitudinarian doctrines, the great political revolution of 1800 was effected, and that his mode of construction had ever since remained "the watch-word of democracy" and the strongest "test of political orthodoxy." He showed us by these means how "the matchless spirit of the West," the great advocate of the principles so denounced, had always been a federalist, while on the other hand he barely intimated that a matchless spirit in the South had perhaps been misrepresented on the same subject. The intimation, that the views of one statesman had been misunderstood, was accompanied by the admission that there might be differences, and possibly honest differences, on the same subject, in the same party. This was all well—and my only reason for adverting to it, is to express my regret that so charitable a *salvo* was not extended beyond the party line. But we were afterwards told by the honourable member, that the resemblance between the political character of the opposition and administration parties, in 1798, 1812, and 1828, confers upon him, and his political friends, "a title to old fashioned democracy, as the same democratic States, with one or two exceptions only, are found, (he says,) at each era, side by side, in favour of Jefferson, Madison, and the hero of Orleans. On one side Virginia, and Pennsylvania, Carolina and Georgia, Tennessee and Kentucky. On the other Delaware and Massachussetts, Connecticut, and divided Maryland." I shall hereafter take leave to present to the view of the honourable member some coincidences much more striking than that which here appears to have caught his fancy. Keeping in view now the position assumed by him, in regard to the federalism of the Western statesman, and other advocates of internal improvement, I would enquire into the title to "old fashioned democracy" of Georgia, Carolina, and other Southern States, here designated by him, on the 14th of March 1818, when twenty one of their representatives in the other House carried the resolution which fully established this "federal" heresy—declaring "that Congress has power, under the constitution, to appropriate money for the construction of post roads, military and other roads, and for the improvement of watercourses." Four of the seven representatives from South Carolina, Mr. Lowndes, Mr. Simkins, Mr. Middleton, and Mr. Erwin, voted for this resolution, the two first named gentlemen advocating, in the debate to which it gave rise, the power of Congress to construct Roads and Canals. When the resolution was adopted, Mr. Lowndes declared that the decision then made had settled the whole question. Two thirds of the Georgia delegation, Mr. Abbott, Mr. J. Crawford, Mr. Terrill, and Mr. Forsyth now an honourable Senator from that State, supported the same resolution. Did Carolina and Georgia then forfeit their "title to old fashioned democracy?" Shall we not try them too, as well as Delaware and Massachusetts, by the "strongest test of political orthodoxy." If Delaware is here to be put on trial, she will stand his test admirably. Though generally Federal until 1826, when the new parties were formed, she was almost uniformly represented in this Senate, up to that period, by Federal gentlemen holding on this subject the very tenets of the honourable member himself, always confining the powers of the government to the specific and enumerated objects; and opposed alike to these acts for internal improvement and tariff laws. In 1827 and 1828, she was represented here by two able Statesmen of the opposite and latitudinarian creed, both of whom had been federalists; but at that time, Sir, they were dyed in the wool by the Jackson process, and, of course, were genuine republicans, as the honourable member will admit. They neither changed or concealed their opinions. Were they not "orthodox?" One of them, standing conspicuous for his talents in the ranks of the orthodox party, now, by their appointment, represents us at the proudest court in Europe. It cannot be necessary to follow out the inquiry further, to try the truth of his test by a reference to musty records and by gone events. If the honourable member will pursue it, he will soon find himself, by the aid of such a test, involved in the mazes of a labyrinth, from which he could not escape in safety, even with the thread of an Ariadne to guide him. Sir, the whole of this part of the gentleman's ingenious argument is admirably calculated, *ad captandum*, as it makes all our Canals, Rail Roads, and Turnpikes, which have been made by the assistance of Congress, the works of that anathematized "peace party in war," which, as we have been told here, has been thus struggling, since the earliest period of our history, to confer upon our rulers absolute power; and I will now dismiss it, that it may perform the duties of its mission, with this single remark, that you may perceive, peeping through its foregone conclusions, how the bent of the gentleman's mind, in condemning Southern votes, is evidently at this time inclining with a breeze to the North North-East—though I still suppose that, "when the wind is southerly, he will know a hawk from a hand-saw."

So far as the State which I have the honor in part to represent here, can furnish evidence to illustrate the title of the honorable member, and his political associates, to "old fashioned democracy," by the fact that a party odious to them has always prevailed there, he is welcome to the evidence for his own uses. It will never redound to her discredit. It can never be a cause of exultation to any man who knows the history of his own country, and values his own reputation, to find her always arrayed against him. And as the honorable member has called my attention to the subject, I will remind him what kind of a "peace party in war" we have always had in Delaware. We have ever had such a party there as "bewares of entrance to a quarrel," but, being once engaged in it, puts forth all its energies of body and soul in the controversy, and for the love of peace fairly *fights out of it*. We had a party of this kind at the bloody era of the American revolution, contending against the usurpations of the British Crown—a party which supplied more warriors in the cause of American liberty, in proportion to our limited means and population, than were furnished by any other State in the whole confederation. The bones of many of that old party were buried on Long Island, and at White Plains, at Princeton, at Brandywine, at Germantown, at Camden, at Guilford, at Eutaw, and at Yorktown; and your pension rolls now show but fourteen of them alive and dependent on your bounty. Many of that party were at Fort Mifflin too; and the gentleman from Maryland, (General SMITH,) the father of the American Senate, (himself one of the most distinguished patriots of the revolution,) who commanded there, when referring in debate a few days since to the conduct of one of them, (Captain Hazzard,) bore testimony to that kind of peace-loving disposition in war which we cherish, when, almost overpowered by the emotion caused by a recurrence to the sad history of the sufferings of his gallant comrades, he described our old peace party troops as soldiers than whom better or braver had never existed. I am told that we had Federalists who opposed the declaration of the last war; but those very Federalists, like their brethren of the opposite party, supported the cause of their country through the whole war with unbending firmness and devoted patriotism. We have national republicans, I am now told; but as they are made up of the same kind of *materials* which composed the peace parties I have been describing, I shall be pardoned if I defer to other judgment than that of the gentleman from New Hampshire, and say that I am proud to represent them here, even though, by so doing, I am placed in opposition to an administration which claims to be exclusively democratic, and yet appoints more Federalists to office than all its predecessors have done since the revolution of 1801—always, nevertheless, keeping steadily in view this indispensable qualification, that every Federalist so appointed must be of the Jackson stamp. I shall ever feel attachment for that party which seeks in peace to prepare for war, by extending the beneficent action of this government to increase the means of our defence, makes roads and canals to transport our munitions in time of need, fortifies our coast, improves our harbours, protects our commerce, and has already built up a navy which is the glory of our country and the admiration of the world.

Sir, I must be pardoned for dwelling at length in reply to other remarks of the honorable member from New Hampshire, whose opinions and reasoning are regarded, by some of his political friends here, as laying down the law and fixing the standard of political orthodoxy. When he had closed his remarks, the Senator from Missouri near him (Mr. BENTON) arose in his place, and pronounced the honorable gentleman to be his Peter, the rock on which he would build the great democratic Church.

[Mr. BENTON having risen to explain, Mr. CLAYTON gave way for the purpose.

Mr. BENTON.—I did not say "this is MY Peter. I said—yes, this is Peter, and this Peter is the rock on which the Church of New England democracy shall be built. This is what I said aloud, and what the Senate heard. What I said in a lower tone, and not intended for the Senate, was this, "and the gates of hell shall not prevail against him."]

Mr. CLAYTON resumed. Sir, I accept his modification, and wish to present fairly, not only all the words, whether spoken on a high or a low key, but the action which was so admirably adapted to them. The gentleman from Missouri then, in the face of the Senate, extended his right arm over the head of the gentleman from New Hampshire, with all the majesty of a Cardinal, or a full robed Bishop, about to pronounce a benediction on a new monarch, or to install a new incumbent of the papal see, and, as he now says, did not merely declare him to be *his* Peter, but announced him to the world as the great Pontiff of New England democracy; and, of course, I suppose, (as *that,* by his former admissions, is as good as *any,*) of all other democracy under the whole Heavens. Sir, I had the right to suppose that he who thus inducted him to office had full powers, or he would not have performed the ceremony. Give me leave to say, that when I heard the new Pontiff lay down his law in conformity with my old-fashioned notions of the powers of the Judiciary, abjuring, as a political heresy, all the new "Carolina doctrine," though seemingly endorsed by the Senator from Missouri himself, I thought that I should stand at least one of the new "tests of political orthodoxy," and I sincerely hoped that, on this subject, nothing might prevail against him. When he issued this, his first bull, I felt disposed to register all his rescripts, and I certainly have preached the very doctrine which it inculcated. But when I heard the American System denounced as a mere federal measure; when I heard, too, from the same source, that a good officer ought to be removed before the regular expiration of his term, for party motives, or personal aggrandizement, and the whole proscriptive system of the new administration thus justified and extolled,—then, Sir, I confess (meaning nothing irreverent by my allusions) that I became a DISSENTER AND A PROTESTANT, and although I expect indulgence for such transgressions, I strongly suspect that I shall carry my abominable heresies to the grave.

The Senator from Missouri, (Mr. BARTON,) having, in the range of this debate, invited the concurrence of others in certain fundamental principles and important objects, enumerated among the number the preservation of the freedom and purity of elections, unawed by official punishments, and uncorrupted by official rewards, in opposition to removals from office for the exercise of the great elective franchise, or to make room for the reward of partisans in our Presidential Elections, by the bestowal of public employments. He submitted that the power of removal from office by the President was a high legal trust, to be exercised for the public benefit, in sound discretion, for cause relating to the official conduct or fitness of the incumbent; that the Senate of the United States had restraining powers in the matter of displacing, as well as of appointing Federal officers; and that, by the Constitution, the Executive power could never be arbitrarily exercised. He advocated "the freedom of inquiry into the exercise of Executive discretion and official trust, in opposition to Executive irresponsibility and unsearchableness, and to the suppression of free inquiry into our political affairs." The Senator from Maine (Mr. HOLMES) merely adverted to the general proscription in New England. In reply to these gentlemen, the Senator from New Hampshire says he will not accept the invitation of the Senator from Missouri, (Mr. BARTON,) to stand on his new political platform, composed, as he considers it, of articles of opposition to the present administration—defends the whole course of that administration as "democratic and constitutional," and informs us that, in the principle of removal from office, for even political motives, their policy only follows up the doctrines of the great revolution in 1800. He speaks of these removals as mere rotation in office, first made by the people themselves in the highest office in the land, the Chief Executive of the Union, for political cause, then inquires, triumphantly, if the same cause should not affect the active deputies and subordinates, as well as the principal. "Whatever disappointments and suffering by removal, (says he,) some individuals may sustain; *yet they knew the legal tenure of their offices.*" He, therefore, thinks the agents of the people cannot fear the cry of cruelty or persecution, because the power of removal, as now exercised, only "changes one good man," (that is, for political opinions,) "for another good man," and, therefore, does no injury to the public. He then proceeds to say these agents need not dread the discussion of the constitutionality of their exercise of this power, thus plainly avowed by him to have been levelled at the right of opinion. Sir, the honorable Senator from Tennessee, (Mr. GRUNDY,) if I rightly understood him, avowed the same opinions; for he denied the right of the Senate to inquire into the causes of removal, and insisted that the present administration had not gone beyond his principles on this subject. He contended that the Senate would transcend their constitutional power, and thus violate the instrument which it is their interest to preserve, by examining into and judging of the propriety of removals from office, or by controlling the Executive in the discharge of this branch of his authority. He entered into a full discussion of the rights of the President with great ingenuity, and manfully challenged us "to come out boldly, and discuss this subject with his friends freely and frankly." The honorable gentleman is a formidable antagonist. He wields a long knife with a strong arm, in defence of his friends; but when he throws down his gauntlet to what is here called the opposition, and defies them to a contest *with these principles of this Administration,* he will be met freely, frankly, and boldly too.

Mr. PRESIDENT: Another year has rolled away. Our ides of March are come. This day, which is the anniversary of the Chief Magistrate's Inauguration, brings with it some strange reminiscences of the past, and some still stranger anticipations of the future. On the last 4th of March, and at about this very hour of the day, the American Senate followed the American President in the progress of his stately triumph to that scene where, in the presence of assembled thousands of his countrymen, he proclaimed to the world the principles upon which he intended to administer the government. Independently of the fact, that the whole subject has been thrust into this debate, as I have stated, there seems to be some propriety in devoting a portion of the passing hour to the consideration of the extent and influence of executive authority. These on this day would be proper subjects of reflection for the Chief Magistrate himself; and as we are his constitutional advisers, exercising, in one sense, a portion of the executive power, we may learn our own duty better by the temperate examination of his. I concur with the gentleman that in discussing this, or any other subject, involving a question of constitutional law, passion and feeling are to be regarded as poor auxiliaries. We should go for nobler game than mere party interests. Principles are to be first settled here; but then the application of them must be fearlessly made. The first inquiry ought to be, what *are* the true principles;—not what is the interest of any party. It will be found that my view of those principles differs, as much, in some respects, from those of some to whose judgment I usually defer, as it does, in others, from those of some who profess to be politically arrayed against me.

The power of removal is no where *expressly* conferred by the Constitution, except in the section which provides that all civil officers of the United States shall be removed from office on impeachment for, or on conviction of, treason, bribery, or other high crimes and misdemeanors. A Judge, the tenure of whose office is *dum bene se gesserit*, is removeable only by this means. But where good behaviour is not the tenure of office, the power of removal is properly and generally incident to, and a consequence of, the power of appointment. The power to destroy is ordinarily implied from the power to create. It is a common axiom of our jurisprudence, that the authority to dissolve a thing must be as high as that which formed it. The Legislature which has the express power to pass a law for raising revenue, for example, has the necessary power to *repeal* it. The Governors of many of the States enjoy, by express provisions in their respective constitutions, the power of appointment to office, and yet exercise by construction, and by implication only, the power of removal from it, their State Constitutions being silent on that subject. The Post Master General, who, *harmonizing* with this administration, has removed, within the last year, his thousand deputies, agents, and clerks, though vested by law with the express right of appointing them, can point you to no statute conferring upon him the right to remove one of them. The numerous clerks and agents appointed under express *legal* provisions, by other Heads of Departments here, are removeable only by the same construction. The law has conferred upon the Supreme Court the power of appointing its Clerk, and, although considered removeable by it, yet no law has thus limited the tenure of his office in express terms. But then this authority, thus derived from implication and construction, if kept within the spirit of the Constitution and the laws, instead of being used arbitrarily or tyrannically, can be exercised only for the public welfare.

In two classes of cases the power of appointment is exercised by the President alone:—first, where Congress have, by law, vested in him the appointment of such inferior officers as they thought proper; and, secondly, where he is empowered to make appointments by virtue of the last clause in the second section of the second article. There are some peculiar considerations growing out of the manner in which the power of removal in the first of these classes has been exercised, which it is unnecessary to enter into now, as they are not immediately connected with the executive rights of the Senate. Appointments of the second class are *temporary* only by the express provisions of the clause which authorizes them. "The President shall have power to fill up all vacancies that may happen during the recess of the Senate, by granting commissions which *shall expire at the end of their next session.*" With these exceptions, the second section referred to expressly confers the power of appointment upon the President *and Senate,* by the words "he shall nominate, and, by and with the advice and consent of the Senate, shall appoint."

Although the Constitution has thus recognised the Senate as an essential component part of the appointing authority, yet the power of removal has been uniformly exercised by the President alone since the Constitution was established. This then has been a deviation from the general principle, that the right to remove can be exercised only where the right to appoint exists. But I do not concur with the honorable gentlemen who have viewed this power as unlimited by the spirit of the Constitution, and having arrived at the conclusion that *sic volo* is the legal tenure of office, would leave it to become the sport of a spirit not less arbitrary and tyrannical than that of absolute despotism. Every administration preceding this has professed to exercise this power within certain established constitutional limitations, regarding removals as expedients to be resorted to by the President only for the purpose of securing a faithful execution of the laws, or when really necessary for the general welfare. And if a single instance can be shown in which any President before this has ever prostituted this authority to party uses, or for personal aggrandizement, it will be found that he has, at least in terms, assumed the virtue of administering the government on different principles, and denied that he intended to invade the right of opinion, or pervert his power from its legitimate object. The history as well of the precedent upon which the Senator from Tennessee so much relies, as of others to which he has not adverted, shows that this constructive power would have never been acknowledged if it had not been supposed to have been strictly limited and distinctly defined.

When the bill "for establishing an Executive Department, to be called the Department of Foreign Affairs," was under the consideration of the House of Representatives, during the first session of Congress after the adoption of the Constitution, the debate to which the gentleman from Tennessee has referred, arose upon one of its provisions granting to the President the right of removing the Secretary to whom our foreign relations were to be principally entrusted. That provision was then so modified as not to carry with it the appearance of a grant of something not before given, but to recognise a constitutional power of removal already subsisting in the President. The power was strongly denied by Mr. Gerry and Mr. Roger Sherman, and maintained by Mr. Madison and Mr. Baldwin. These gentlemen had all been members of the Convention that made the Constitution, and yet were thus equally divided in opinion on the construction of the very instrument which they had, so recently before that, assisted in forming. The point then was regarded as extremely doubtful. There were others, who had not been members of the Convention, who engaged on different sides with equal zeal in the contest, until at length a construction implying the existence of the power was established, so far as a tribunal which had no jurisdiction over the subject could do it, by a vote of thirty four to twenty. It has often been observed, and I apprehend it is unquestionably true, that the character of Washington, then President of the United States, had great influence in producing this decision. Add to this, too, that the question arose in the very strongest case which could have been presented for the advocates of the Executive—the case of a Secretary, between whom and the President it was absolutely necessary that the most confidential relations should subsist. These supporters of Executive authority were then, as men will ever be, influenced in some degree by the circumstances immediately around them. The statesmen of the day literally vied with each other in expressions of their high confidence in the man who then filled the Chair of State, beloved by all, and distrusted by none; and it is but too evident from the arguments advanced on this occasion, that they were beguiled by the imagination that none but beings of such exalted virtue and spotless purity would ever be elected to succeed him. They reasoned from an illusion to which human nature is at all times liable. Under such circumstances, a principle was decided, which forms a distinct exception to an established general rule; and it cannot escape observation that under other auspices a very different result would probably have been produced by the deliberations of 1789. The discussion to sustain this power mainly rested on these brief positions—that the Constitution had conferred upon the President the Executive power—that the general concession of Executive authority embraced removals, as well as appointments—that the power granted to the Senate, being an exception to this general provision, ought therefore to be construed strictly, and could not be extended beyond the express right (with its necessary incidents) of negativing appointments—and, above all, that the President, being bound to "take care that the laws be faithfully executed," must therefore remove whenever the public interest imperiously requires it. The last position, aided by all the extraneous considerations referred to, was successful. Every reasoner dwelt upon it as the keystone of the argument. It was not then contended by the fathers of the republic, that the general grant of Executive power was to be construed alone by the strict specifications of it, subsequently entered in the same instrument. True, our modern reasoners revolt at the thought of extending the powers of Congress beyond the specific enumeration of them, by a general grant of "all legislative power;" and although the honourable gentleman from New Hampshire has informed us that the friends of this administration, claiming the authority to remove in its utmost latitude, need not dread the discussion of their right to do so, yet he has, in this very debate, stoutly denied a construction, to the general delegation of power to Congress in the Constitution "to provide for the general welfare," similar to the one placed in 1789 upon the general delegation of Executive power "to take care that the laws shall be faithfully executed." Without this latitudinarian interpretation, the power of removal would have remained forever, on the general principle, in the President *and* Senate. But it was not urged in 1789, by any man, that this constructive power was unlimited and absolute; on the contrary, gauging it by the strict standard of the rule which defined while it conferred it, they declared that it was given to the President only for the purpose of "*securing a faithful execution of the laws,*" as an incident to his great prerogative to preside over his country for his country's good. They pointed out the very cases for its proper exercise: They said it was necessary to remove a traitor from office, "to secure a faithful execution of the laws:" They urged that an officer who should become insane, corrupt, disabled, or in any manner or by any means unfaithful or disqualified to serve the public to the public advantage, ought to be, and was of right removable, in order "to secure a faithful execution of the laws;" and having thus measured and marked down the length, the breadth, and the depth of the whole principle recognised by them, they doubtless little expected that any opinion given, or precedent set by them, would ever be adduced to sanction the exercise of uncontrolled and despotic power. The honourable gentleman from Tennessee, who has filled the office of a Judge with great credit to himself, says that he loves precedents; and having informed us that "Mr. Madison understood the Constitution and structure of the government as well as any man that ever lived," holds up the Congressional Register of that day, points to the opinion of that able statesman there given, and triumphantly announces that there we may see his doctrines, and there *his constitutional lawyer.* Sir, we may venture here, I think, to meet the gentleman on his own grounds. I say, too, that, like others from the schools of forensic disputation, I love precedents; and that Mr. Madison on this subject is also *my constitutional lawyer.* But then, when I like the opinion of a constitutional lawyer so well, I take the whole, and not merely a part of it. I do not gratuitously reject one half of it, while I rely so much upon the other. I read from the same volume Mr. Madison's words, uttered on that same occasion, that "the dismission of a meritorious officer was an abuse of power ABOVE HIS CONCEPTION, and would merit impeachment." Again, he qualifies the power he advocates, and explains it thus: "The danger, then, consists in this: the President can displace from office a man whose merits require that he should be continued in it. What will be the motives which the President can feel for such *abuse of his power,* and the restraints to operate to prevent it? In the first place, he will be impeachable by this House, before the Senate, for SUCH AN ACT OF MAL-ADMINISTRATION; for I contend, that the wanton removal of meritorious officers would subject him to impeachment, and removal from his own high trust." *Our* constitutional lawyer then thinks your President ought to be removed from office, if he has acted on the principles avowed by his friends here, and says—the kind of power you contend for is ABOVE HIS CONCEPTION. This does not seem to work well; and perhaps you may now think our constitutional lawyer, "who understood the constitution and structure of the government as well as any man that ever lived," in an error. Then let us look into the opinions of others, expressed on the same occasion, who were aiding in the establishment of this precedent, admired so much. Mr. Lawrence, though an advocate of the same power, denied that, according to his understanding of it, it was ever to be exercised "in a wanton manner, or from capricious motives;" and, with a view to silence the apprehensions of those who were alarmed lest it might be exercised without restraint, he puts to them the question which had been answered by Mr. Madison—"would he (the President) not be liable to impeachment for displacing a worthy and able man, who enjoyed the confidence of the people?" Mr. Vining, on the same side, remarked "that if the President should remove a valuable officer, it would be an act of TYRANNY which the good sense of the nation would never forget." Such were the views of all the prominent advocates of this right at that time. Do I go an inch, then, beyond your own authority when I infer, from the opinions of the very men upon whose judgment you now build, that the system of removing meritorious officers before the regular expiration of their terms of service, for either personal or party motives, is hostile to the spirit of the constitution, an "impeachable mal-administration" of the government, and a "tyrannical" encroachment on the liberties of the people?

But when we trace the history of the same bill in its progress through the Senate, it seems not to admit of a doubt that, but for the extraordinary concurrence of extraneous circumstances then co-operating to produce this construction, the right of removal would never have been recognised. While that bill was under consideration in this House, on the 18th July, 1789, a motion was made to strike out of the clause, implying the existence of the right, the words "by the President of the United States," the object of which was to deny that right altogether. The Senate then sat with closed doors, and we have no account of the discussion. But we see from the records how the vote stood. Mr. Madison's constitutional opinions were then unpopular in Virginia, as being too latitudinarian; in consequence of which he had lost his election to the Senate, that State being, at the period referred to, represented here by William Grayson and Richard Henry Lee. Both those gentlemen voted against the power and in favor of the motion to strike out; and I suppose that the doctrine of strict constructions of executive power was at that time, as it often since has been, the prevailing sentiment of the State. Georgia, South Carolina, and New Hampshire, were all united against the power, and they were supported by Johnson of Connecticut, and Maclay of Pennsylvania. Among the friends of the motion we find Johnson, Few of Georgia, Butler of South Carolina, and Langdon of New Hampshire, who had all been members of the Federal Convention. *Nine voted for the striking out,* and *nine against it;* and Mr. Adams, the Vice President, having given a casting vote in favor of the power, the words were retained. So the honorable gentleman from Tennessee will perceive that he owes the whole of his favorite precedent at last to that same "elder Adams," the "tendencies of whose opinions" were, if we are to rely on his friend from New Hampshire, "to consolidation and monarchy." I do not call his attention to this fact, however, because I concur in any of these sweeping denunciations of that great patriot. The same question arose again in the Senate on the 4th of August, 1789, on a motion to strike out of the bill "to establish an Executive Department to be denominated the Department of War," the words, "and who whenever the said principal officer shall be removed from office by the President of the United States;" and again on the same day, pending the bill "to provide for the government of a territory North West of the Ohio," which contained a clause recognising the right to remove the Governor of the territory. Similar decisions followed in each of these cases; so that the question was within three weeks thrice decided here; and these decisions form the grounds upon which the power, under its proper constitutional restraints, has ever since been claimed for the Executive. These facts, I submit, leave not a shadow of a doubt that, without the influence which the character of the Father of his Country was calculated to produce upon the minds of the Senators, many of whom were his old compatriots and most intimate friends, and without the powerful co-operation of Mr. Adams, the decisions would have been different. Under such circumstances, I would pause to inquire whether it is reasonable to suppose that the understanding of those Senators who so established this power, was, that the President, upon whom it was conferred, was to exercise it without limitation? Is it probable that uncontrolled and absolute authority would have been acknowledged then, and that, too, by a body of men whose patriotism and devotion to the cause of liberty have never been surpassed?

The opinions of Mr. Adams, on this subject, are probably in a great measure attributable to a belief which he had indulged in opposition to the Federal Convention, that the power of the Senate, in regard to appointments, ought to have been entrusted to "a council selected by the President himself *at his pleasure*"—in fact, a mere privy council without the authority to check him. He thought that the people would be jealous that the influence of the Senate, if it were entrusted with appointments, would "be employed to *conceal, connive* at, and *defend* guilt in Executive officers, instead of being a guard and watch upon them, and a terror to them." These opinions are disclosed in a correspondence which took place between him and Roger Sherman, in the summer of 1789. With these opinions, thus known to have been entertained by him at the very time when he decided by his casting vote, he went far, we now find, to destroy the rights of the Senate, and to reduce it to a mere privy council without any effective power. In that correspondence Mr. Sherman, who had been a member of the Convention, urged against such opinions the views of that Convention, which ought to have been decisive in favor of the rights of the Senate. "But," said he, "if the President was left to select a council for himself, though he may be supposed to be actuated by the best motives,— yet he would be surrounded by flatterers who would assume the character of friends and patriots, though they had no attachment to the public good, no regard to the laws of their country, but, influenced wholly by self-interest, would wish to extend the power of the Executive in order to increase their own; they would often advise him to dispense with laws that should thwart their schemes, and in excuse plead that it was done from necessity to promote the public good—they will use their own influence, induce the President to use his to get laws repealed, or the Constitution altered to extend his powers and prerogatives, under pretext of advancing the public good, *and gradually render the government a despotism.* This seems to be according to the course of human affairs, and what may be expected from the nature of things." The views of Mr. Adams on this subject appear to have been different from those of any other man who participated in the decisions in 1789, of which we have any information now, as well as from those of the Federal Convention itself.

It is true that Washington exercised this power during his administration. The gentleman from Tennessee produced *nine* cases as the result of his industrious researches, which had occurred during the whole eight years in which Washington presided, to justify the hundreds which have been made in the first year of this administration. But, in every instance, Washington's removals were made (and it will not be denied) only when necessary for the public good, exactly complying with the rule which had been established. In announcing the exercise of this right to the Senate, he used the word "superseded" instead of "removed" or "dismissed," which were subsequently adopted by his successors. But whether he did or did not consider the removals as provisional, and dependent on the future action of the Senate, we have no distinct information. On all occasions he manifested the highest respect for its concurrent powers in the business of Executive appointment, and prescribed a duty for a President, which has certainly not been regarded as such by *one* of his successors, when in his message of the 9th of February, 1790, containing a few nominations to supply vacancies which had been temporarily filled in the recess, he says, "these appointments will expire with your present session, and, indeed, *ought not to endure longer than until others can be regularly made.*"

The gentleman from Tennessee informed us of twenty three cases in which Mr. Jefferson had removed; and then read, to justify the immense proscription now made, his answer of the 12th July, 1801, to a remonstrance of the committee of the merchants of New Haven, on the appointment of Samuel Bishop to the office of Collector at New Haven, then lately vacated by the death of David Austin. That letter was doubtless written under some excitement, caused by the memorial itself; and the fame of Mr. Jefferson is rescued from the imputation now attempted to be cast upon it by better evidence. Yet, even in this answer, he places his removal upon the ground that it was for the public good, and to secure the necessary co-operation with the government, expressly stating, too, that his general object was to remedy the very evil now complained of. "During the late administration," says he, "the whole offices of the United States were monopolized by a sect." He considered that the former incumbents had been appointed merely for party and personal aggrandizement, and not for the public welfare. Try the present abuses of power by the standard of that letter, and you find yourselves standing on the very doctrine which he repudiated, and the deleterious effects of which he says he endeavored to correct. "I shall correct the procedure; but that done, return *with joy* to that state of things when the only question concerning a candidate shall be, is he honest?—is he capable?—is he faithful to the Constitution?" The last Administration removed no man for party motives, before the regular expiration of his term, and even went beyond the line prescribed by Mr. Jefferson, by regularly reappointing political opponents when their offices had expired. You now rest, therefore, on the principles which Mr. Jefferson attributed to the elder Adams, and your policy, as avowed here by the Senator from New Hampshire, does not "follow up the doctrines of the great revolution of 1800." This construction of the answer to the New Haven remonstrance makes Mr. Jefferson consistent with himself. In his letter to Mr. Gerry of the 29th March, 1801, he says—"officers who have been guilty of *gross abuses* of office, such as marshals, *packing juries*, &c. I shall now remove, as my predecessors ought in justice to have done. The instances will be few, and guided by STRICT RULE, and not party passion. The right of opinion shall suffer no invasion from me. Those who have acted well have nothing to fear, however they may have differed from me in opinion." In other parts of his correspondence we see the same view taken of his constitutional power. On the 6th of July, 1802, in a letter to David Hall, then Governor of Delaware, he acknowledges the receipt of communications covering two addresses, the one from a democratic republican meeting at Dover, and the other from the grand and general juries of the Circuit Court of the United States, both of them praying a removal of Allen McLane, the father of our present Minister to England, from the office of Collector of the Customs at Wilmington. It appears that Mr. McLane was objected to by them, on the ground of personal dislike, and for the alleged warmth of his federal opinions. Mr. Jefferson, in this letter, replying to those addresses, refuses to remove the incumbent for such reasons, "lest he should bring a just censure on his administration." He says, "we are not acting for ourselves alone, but for the whole human race. We must not, by any *departure from principle*, dishearten the mass of our fellow citizens." He then lays down the very principle on which this power can be constitutionally and properly exercised. "If Colonel McLane has done any act *inconsistent with his duty* as an officer, or as an agent of this administration, *this* would be *legitimate* ground for inquiry, into which I should consider myself free to enter." He takes a distinction between refusing to appoint a political opponent, and removing him during his term, the last of which he refuses to do:—thus leaving your thousand removals from the Post Office and other Departments of the government under the full reprobation of the "doctrines of 1801," upon which you have attempted to justify them.

The next President whose removals were referred to by the gentleman from Tennessee, was Mr. Madison, our "constitutional lawyer" under whose opinions we have already seen there is no shelter to be found for this administration. Then came Mr. Monroe, who not only disavowed such policy as is now pursued, but practised political tolerance in its widest signification. He had a great constitutional lawyer to advise him—one whose precepts ought to be now adhered to, even as strongly as the gentleman from Tennessee grasped those of Mr. Madison. That constitutional lawyer, Sir, was Andrew Jackson, whose advice on any question should not be slightingly passed over by the gentleman from Tennessee, and especially when we are considering the special force and efficacy of the second section of this article, in the Constitution. On the 12th of November, 1816, before Mr. Monroe's election had been officially announced, he gives this magnanimous view of the duties of a Chief Magistrate: "In every selection, party and party feelings should be avoided. Now is the time to exterminate that monster, called party spirit. By selecting characters most conspicuous for their probity, virtue, capacity and firmness, without any regard to party, you will go far to, if not entirely eradicate, those feelings which on former occasions threw so many obstacles in the way of government, and perhaps have the pleasure and honour of uniting a people heretofore politically divided. The Chief Magistrate of a great and powerful nation should never indulge in party feeling. His conduct should be liberal and disinterested, *always* bearing in mind that he acts for the whole, and not a part of the community. By this course you will exalt the national character, and acquire for yourself a name as imperishable as monumental marble. Consult *no party* in your choice: pursue the dictates of that unerring judgment which has so long and so often benefitted our country, and rendered conspicuous its rulers. These are the sentiments of a friend; they are the feelings, if I know my own heart, of an undissembled patriot." It may be said, Sir, that this constitutional lawyer has since abandoned these views as unsound. But I ask when? Why, as late as May, 1824, he maintained the same moral and mental elevation, confirming the same opinions, and imprinting them more deeply by the increased authoritative sanction of his own great name. In a letter to the Hon. George Kremer, of that date, so far from retracting them, he says, "My advice to the President was, that he should act upon principles like these:—Consider himself the head of the Nation, not of a party; that he should have around him the best talents the country could afford, without regard to sectional divisions; and should, in his selection, seek after men of probity, virtue, capacity and firmness; and, in this way, he would go far to eradicate those feelings which, on former occasions, threw so many obstacles in the way of government, and be enabled perhaps to unite a people heretofore politically divided." Those who delight to view the result of the last Presidential election as a verdict rendered by the people on an issue joined, can best inform us how far these sentiments and constitutional opinions should be viewed as having formed a part of that issue, and how far they were sanctioned by the then expression of popular approbation.

These opinions and precedents of great constitutional lawyers lead us to other reflections upon the general expediency of the two doctrines, and the probable reasoning of those who made our constitution. By the old articles of confederation, the power of appointment was vested in Congress. Under the present Constitution the same power was transferred to the President and Senate. The House of Representatives, chosen biennially, was not entrusted with any portion of this important power. Why not? Honorable gentlemen have strongly pressed the importance of what they call the principle of rotation or change in office, to comply with the popular will. The House of Representatives being entirely subject to the mutability of popular opinion, would be most apt to change with every popular breeze, and give effect to that opinion. Did this escape the intellects of the fathers of the Republic? Sir, if we are to accredit their contemporaneous expositions of the Constitution, and the very writings which procured its ratification, their reason for not investing the Representatives with this power, was to prevent the removal of valuable officers with every popular change, and to give stability to the administration of the government. Moreover, when the gentleman from New Hampshire states here, that the same political causes which induce the people to change their Chief Magistrate, should operate upon all the subordinates, agents and deputies, he forgets that the popular attention never is, and never can be, while absorbed by the consideration of the merits and demerits of contending candidates for the first office in their gift, sufficiently diverted to decide upon all the officers in the country. In a State or a small territory where the people know all their officers, they may act with a view to them. But hundreds of thousands voted, during the last great political contest, for men politically opposed to officers whom they had never seen, and of whom they knew nothing—nay, to their dearest friends whom they neither wished nor expected should be removed. You cannot justify your course, then, by saying it is the popular will, and especially when your President, with his election in full view, and with a knowledge of the effect of the sentiment of the public, told us that "the Chief Magistrate of a great and powerful nation should never indulge in party feeling." Under such circumstances, is it not fair to conclude, that if his election must be regarded as any expression of popular will, in regard to subordinate officers, that will was in favor of his sentiment, and against the indulgence of party feeling to remove them. Still I admit that although the great mass of the nation know little, and care less, in the election of a President, about the qualifications of inferior officers, yet they have in recent practice been too much guided in their choice by the hopes of Executive patronage, and the love of office. And it is time to lay before them the true principles of their Constitution, which teach that for the gratification of personal ambition or the mere elevation of a party, for private pique or for personal vengeance, for the free exercise of the right of opinion, for hatred or for favoritism, or for any other cause than to secure a faithful discharge of public service for the public good, Executive power cannot be legitimately exercised; and shall now and forever after be effectually and fearlessly restrained. The expectants "for dead men's shoes" will then disappear. The elective franchise will be restored to its pristine purity. Executive patronage will no longer teach us at the polls that "power over a man's support is power over his will," and the action of our government will, by thus cleansing the very spring from which it flows, become henceforth refined, healthful, and vigorous. But if these principles be now disregarded, despised and prostrated, our people will be converted into office hunters, the contest for power will be every where conducted without reference to principle, the elective franchise will sink under the influence of personal hopes and personal fears, universal corruption will be substituted for that virtue without which a republic cannot exist, and at the expiration of every four years the tumult will swell, and the venality will fester, until, the depravity of the whole system of government being no longer tolerable,—disgusted, dejected, and dispirited by the complete failure of our attempt at self-government, we shall sink into the arms of the first Caesar who shall be willing to strike a mortal blow at the liberties of his country. Let me not be told, then, that the most sacred of our constitutional privileges is to become the victim of any slovenly draftsman of a commission or a statute, confounding Executive power with Executive pleasure. By the paramount law of the land, a President can officially know no pleasure but the people's interest, and when you suffer him to sink the officer in the man, you violate its simplest and most salutary restrictions.

With this view of the duties of a Chief Magistrate, and of his constitutional power, it must occur that as his authority to remove can be exercised only for cause, there must be some tribunal to inquire into and ascertain that cause. I regard this right, though denied by the gentleman from Tennessee, as a necessary incident of the advisory power of the Senate. We know well that here is a great dividing line between us in this body. One party here denies our constitutional right to put such troublesome questions, or to test any part of the groundwork of our "great and glorious *reform*." We want to learn a little of the *rationale* of this operation. We have been all along, as you tell us, benighted and in the dark. Give us light, then, we say. We consider ourselves bound to advise the Chief Magistrate in his appointments. We are not restricted to a mere expression of consent to, or dissent from, his nomination. We may, aye, *must* go further. If you ask me whether I will consent to a choice which you alone can make, I may answer, yes. But if you ask me whether I will *advise* you so to choose, I might point you to a better. The words *advice* and *consent* are not synonymous—their meaning is essentially different. *Consent* is the mere agreement of the mind to what is proposed by another. *Advice* ordinarily implies the recommendation of some opinion, or the offering of some information worthy to be weighed and acted upon by another. The gentleman from Tennessee, expressing an opinion current, as we all know, among his political friends here, denies the constitutional right of the Senate to examine into and judge of the propriety of removals from office, and declares that *our power is confined to the question of fitness or unfitness of the person nominated to succeed.* Now, if A be removed from office, and B nominated to supply the vacancy, were only our *consent* asked on the appointment of B, we might possibly, adopting his construction, vote aye;

when, if we are asked whether we would *advise* as well as consent to the appointment, we might answer, "no; we know a thousand better men, though we do not think the nominee absolutely unfit. We think the man removed is a better man." It is said, however, that we must restrict our advice to the nomination before us, and that, if we go beyond that, it is advice unasked. I answer that even if I am, as his adviser, to consult the interests of the President alone, I cannot always know whether B will really suit his purposes, until I learn why A has been removed, and thus ascertain what his purposes are. He may be deceived either in the character or qualifications of his nominee, and we knowing, perhaps, more about them than the President, if bound to look to his interests alone, ought to advise him of his error. Is it our object to advise him to appoint such persons as will aggrandize himself or sustain his party? He may have recommended one of the opposite party to supply the vacancy created by the removal of his own party man. With a view to his interest then, as his *adviser*, we ought, I suppose, to tell him so. Well, I inform him of it, and he tells me in reply that he knew that, but has dismissed his old friend because he has lost his influence. Then, if I know it to be a fact that his nominee has lost his influence too, I should tell him so—should I not? How then, even according to the views of those who think the President is to consult his own *pleasure,* can we be faithful advisers without asking in our confidential way here, what that pleasure is, or ferreting out the causes of his removals? On the other hand, if I am to advise with an eye single to the public good, which I take to be my true standard, I ought not to advise him to appoint B when I know that A, whom he has removed, and can reappoint, is a better man for the office. Is it not then expedient for us—nay, is it not sometimes absolutely necessary to the proper discharge of our advisory duties, to learn why our servants have been dismissed? And if so, where is the clause in the Constitution which limits us in the exercise of these duties? If we have, as gentlemen say, no constitutional right to inquire into the causes of these removals, we have no power to investigate the propriety of appointments to fill the vacancies; for the first of these principles being conceded, the other will flow as a consequence from the concession. This makes the President independent of the Senate in his appointing power, and of course of any other tribunal established by the Constitution. And the Senator from New Hampshire has reminded us, in discussing another topic of this debate, that Mr. Jefferson's "axiom of eternal truth in politics" was, "that whatever power in any government is independent is absolute also." I apprehend, too, that this new restrictive construction of our constitutional duties differs entirely from that adopted by all our predecessors. True, their Executive records show that the subject has not been moved on every nomination; yet the right to exercise the power appears not to have been denied before, and those records show us that the Senate has often inquired into the propriety of nominations and of removals also. When Robert Purdy memorialized this body on the 15th of January, 1822, representing, as he did, that his removal from the army had been improperly made, and even charging, expressly, that favoritism, with the President, "had superseded the claims of merit," the Senate, instead of deciding against their own power, or branding it as inquisitorial, appointed a committee to investigate the whole subject; and on the 13th of April afterwards, they, by resolution, called for the report of the board of general officers upon which the reduction and new arrangement of the army had been predicated. When Mr. Monroe nominated Gadsden as Adjutant General, and Towson and Fenwick as Colonels, the Senate looked behind the nominations, and took cognisance of the fact that other officers were superseded and disbanded as supernumeraries; and although, as appears by the able reports of the committee which investigated the causes and the legality of the arrangement, they did ample justice to the merits of these gallant officers, *and admitted them to be fully competent for the stations to supply which the President had named them to the Senate*, yet the nominations were not confirmed. Gadsden and Towson were rejected here on the 16th of March, 1822, and the nomination of Fenwick was then withdrawn. The President afterwards re-nominated them to the Senate, when the same investigation was again made; the committee called on the War Department for more full information; the President assigned *all his reasons* in an elaborate message to the Senate; the committee reported against those reasons, with a full argument to refute them, and the Senate a second time rejected all these appointments, on the ground that other persons were entitled to them. Here was no cry of inquisitorial power, nor did the Senate consider, as the gentleman from Tennessee now does, that their power was *confined to the question of fitness or unfitness of the nominees*. On the 10th of April, 1822, the Senate, by resolution, instructed the Secretary of the Navy, among other things, to communicate to them, in Executive session, "in what situations and *for what reasons* acting appointments of officers are made in the Navy Department." It will not be pretended that the mere fact, that the call was not directly on the Chief Magistrate, impairs the force of the precedent, as a demand of the causes of Executive action. Cases in which the Senate has inquired into the causes of appointments have often occurred. On the 4th of January, 1826, the Senate, by resolution, called "for any information *tending to show the propriety* of sending Ministers to Panama;" and it does not appear by the Journal that the majority, so much reproached for their defence of the then administration, made any objection to the resolution, but it *does* appear that the resolution was on that day offered by Mr. Macon, and was immediately adopted. In the case of William B. Irish, who was nominated by Mr. Monroe as Marshal of the Western District of Pennsylvania, the Senate called, by resolution, on "*the President of the United States,* to cause to be laid before them all such letters and petitions, or other papers, as were presented to him relative to the appointment, *as well those which opposed his appointment,* as those which requested it," and the President complied with the call, without complaining against the Senate for having exercised power unconstitutionally or improperly. The first President of the United States, who was also the President of the Convention that made the Constitution, considered the Senate as entitled to the utmost latitude of inquiry. When they rejected his nomination of Benjamin Fishbourne, for the place of Naval Officer of the Port of Savannah, Washington, in his message nominating Lachlan McIntosh for the place, says—"Permit me to submit to your consideration, whether on occasions where the propriety of nominations may appear questionable to you, it would not be expedient to communicate that circumstance to me, and thereby avail yourselves of the information which led me to make them, *and which I would with pleasure lay before you.*" A committee was then appointed to wait on the President, and confer with him on the mode of communication proper to be observed between him and the Senate, in the formation of treaties and making appointments to offices. This committee, by their chairman, Mr. Izzard, on the 21st of August after, reported the very rule of the Senate now to be found in our manual as No. 36, which, with the very view to give time for these inquiries, provides that when nominations shall be made, a future day shall be assigned, unless the Senate unanimously direct otherwise, for taking them into consideration—prescribes the form of arrangement, when the President shall meet the Senate to give or to receive information, and even directs their own attendance at any other place where he may convene them for such purposes. With this history of that rule, which has been carefully preserved by all our predecessors, but appears now to be forgotten, who can doubt that, in their opinion, the utmost latitude of inquiry was to be allowed to the Senate on all Presidential nominations? We have high authority in favor of our constitutional right to inquiry, in the report of the committee on Executive patronage made in this body on the 4th of May, 1826—a committee which then thought, as they informed the world, that they were "*acting in the spirit of the Constitution* in laboring to multiply the guards, and to strengthen the barriers, against the possible abuse of power." The second section of the second bill reported by that committee provides, "That, in all nominations made by the President to the Senate, to fill vacancies occasioned by an exercise of the President's power to remove from office, the fact of the removal shall be stated to the Senate, at the same time that the nomination is made, *with a statement of the reasons for which such officer may have been removed.*" Now, Sir, would that committee* have reported an unconstitutional provision for the adoption of the Senate? The proposition in it was to exercise the right of inquiry in *every case,* and thus by one sweeping clause to supersede the necessity of any future resolutions for that purpose in particular cases. Why *now* consider the doctrine unconstitutional which was thus supported? So highly were the principles of this report then approved, that six thousand copies were ordered to be printed, and the arguments contained in it were *then* declared to be unanswerable.† These inquiries were all right *then,* and the thought that it was wrong "to establish a court of inquiry" did not occur to the Committee. So, too, the House of Representatives, in the exercise of its legislative powers, has scrutinized the motives of the Heads of Executive Departments. That House demanded, by resolution, on the 8th of May, 1822, from the Secretary of the Treasury, "a particular and minute account of each transfer of the public money from one Bank to another, which had been made after the first of January, 1817, *and the reasons and motives for making the same;*" and in March, 1822, they obtained the information demanded, in a report. By us the right to look into the causes of executive action is not claimed as an incident of the mere legislative power of the Senate, but of its executive authority, and therefore stands on much stronger grounds.

In 1821, the Senate thinking a *charge d'affaires* not a proper representative of this government at Rio de Janeiro, interfered to recommend the appointment of a Minister. Their opinion on that subject had not been requested, when, by their resolution of the 3d of March of that year, they

---

*The names of those who composed the Committee on Executive patronage, are Messrs. Benton, (chairman,) Macon, Van Buren, White, Findlay, Dickerson, Holmes, Hayne, and Johnson of Kentucky.

†By Mr. Randolph.

advised the President to appoint such a minister. The act was voluntary and gratuitous. They did not then regard it as an objection that their advice was unasked, nor consider themselves confined to the fitness or unfitness of the *charge d'affaires*. They did not feel bound to remain silent, like the slaves around the throne of a despot, and answer only when spoken to. And it appears to me that on subjects connected with either treaties or appointments, before the election of the present Chief Magistrate, they have considered themselves, in the spirit of the Constitution, and under the solemn obligation to advise the President which it imposed upon them, equally bound to warn him of approaching danger to the country, and to consult with him on the means of averting it; equally bound to give him information which could tend to increase the welfare and prosperity of that country, and to discuss with him the means of securing and promoting it, whether he had or had not first asked their advice. Would you, Sir, regard him as a faithful adviser, and a true friend, who should never warn you of danger, or give you information until you asked him to do so? And if not, are we acting in the spirit of the Constitution when we restrict our advice to the President to the mere fitness or unfitness of his nominee?

The treaty making, as well as the appointing power, is vested in the President and Senate. The advice and consent of this body is an indispensable prerequisite to the ratification of all treaties, and is an essential component part of the power to make them. It necessarily looks as well to the annulled as to the annulling stipulations with other nations; has always rejected new treaties, when preferring old ones; and though indulging the utmost latitude of inquiry into all the reasons, and all the facts connected with both, it has never yet been met with objections to the most ample exercise of these powers.

It is well understood, Sir, that within the year of which this day completes the circle, a great revolution has been effected, in the public offices, by the discharge of the former incumbents, and that the representatives of many of the States are anxious to spread upon the records here, for the benefit of posterity, as well as of the present age, the latent cause of this great Executive *reform*. We have another motive to make the effort to effect this. We desire that the simple facts should appear, in justice to all those who have been dismissed from the public service without charge or accusation against them. We consider this necessary as an act of justice, not only to the sufferers, but to their families, their friends and their posterity. We seek to distinguish the innocent from the guilty, to exhibit to public view, among the searching operations of this government, how many have been removed on the representations of secret foes, or vindictive political opponents; how many have been dismissed on suspicion, and how many without suspicion; and how many have been condemned without having been suffered to learn the nature of the accusations against them. If rumours, founded in many cases on the statements of the victims of the proscriptive system, be true, many have been hurled from stations, which they have filled with honour to themselves, and with advantage to the public, without the assignment of any reason for the act; and in many instances, it is said, the files of departments here have been filled with foul calumnies, by aspirants to office, and their secret agents, without giving the accused even the formality of a trial. If this be so, here is a real inquisition, to rack and torture, not the bodies indeed, but the characters of men. Is it more than an act of justice, to the victims, that the truth should appear? The accusations against them, though strictly *ex parte*, are yet the avowed foundation of official acts of departments here, and are matters of record on file, in those departments, which may be resorted to, by all future generations, to blacken the memory of these men, and to disgrace their families, when they shall be laid in their graves. In a government of laws properly administered, the discharge of a public servant, without any assigned reason for the act, must ordinarily cast some imputation upon his character. No matter how innocent he may be—no matter whether any charge has or has not been preferred against him, yet the existence of such charges will be presumed. Under such circumstances, the breath of calumny is sure to stain his reputation, even though acquired by a long life of faithful public service, and exemplary private conduct. The hireling libeller, the prostituted wretch, who may have gained the very office from which he has been removed, will sound the tocsin of slander, and if the press has been generally subsidized by the government, surmises of official delinquency will be carefully propagated, as "proved on file," until the victim loses character, as well as office, by the action of Executive vengeance. To what tribunal then should he appeal for justice? I answer, to the Senate of his country, a party to the contract by which he was employed, and which, by fairly showing the causes of his dismissal, may repel the imputations resting on his reputation, and "set history right;" thus forming a barrier against the influence of a spirit of malevolence, which in these latter days, as we have seen, can pursue a man to his grave for vengeance on his posterity. No good or honorable man will dismiss a faithful servant from his private employment, without furnishing him at his request with a certificate of his fidelity. The same justice, which we dispense in private life, should be yielded to a faithful public servant, when dismissed from public employment; and unless as public men we intend to abandon those principles which govern us in our social and domestic relations, we are in my humble judgment, bound to entertain these inquiries. They can do no injustice to the Executive. If its power has not been wantonly abused, the conduct of the government will be presented to the people in an unexceptionable point of view. But, on the other hand, if the President's authority has been perverted entirely to party and personal purposes, are we not bound to correct the evil, and should we refuse to present him to this nation in his proper character, at the expense of the reputation of all our fellow citizens, who have been trampled under foot by the arbitrary and despotic exercise of power? Will it not be said that, by shrinking from the investigation, we have distrusted his integrity, and have shown a belief that his security was in concealment? If all has been rightly done, do we not treat him ungenerously by refusing him an opportunity of presenting the evidence for his acquittal at the bar of public opinion—aye, Sir, at the bar of public opinion; for at that bar he must stand and await his sentence; and his direst foe could not wish him a more certain condemnation than inevitably awaits him unless he is heard in his defence.

If I am right in my views of the constitutional powers of the President and Senate thus far presented, the former can never properly remove an officer before the expiration of his term, but for cause connected only with the public interest; while the latter can investigate that cause, and ascertain by the facts how far the Constitution has been complied with; and, if this authority has been abused, or extended beyond its constitutional limits, the House may impeach the author of such abuses before the Senate, and the Senate may remove him and all his minions. An impeachment, however, requiring a majority of the House to prefer it, and two-thirds of the Senate to sustain it, can rarely, perhaps never, prevail against the exercise of Executive patronage directly on Congress and the influence of party spirit. Then suppose that a President, regardless of his duty, and of the consequences either of exposure or impeachment, should remove all our public servants who would not assent to his usurpation of the sovereignty of the people, and fill their places with favorites and parasites who should seek to robe him with the imperial purple? We have been told that such a case may occur—that Aaron Burr was once on the verge of this high office, and it has been said that he would have filled every office in this way. I do not say so myself, nor do I pretend to decide upon that. But the question now arises—what checks have the people upon a usurper who should do these things for his own advancement, immediately after his accession to the Presidency? It is certain that, until the expiration of his four years' term, a period long enough for the achievement of a revolution, the people have no check upon him *except through the instrumentality of the Senate;* and in such a case the question *what control has the Senate upon this power* becomes one of intense interest to the American people.

We have seen that, by the terms of the Constitution, the President is authorized to fill up all vacancies *happening* in the recess of the Senate, by granting commissions which shall expire *at* the end of their next Session. When a vacancy is created by a removal, the question arises, can the officer removed be reinstated by the direct action of the Senate?

There are many who maintain the affirmative of this question. Some for whose judgments I feel great deference, and with whom I usually act here, have so expressed themselves; and there are certainly strong opinions to support them. That of Alexander Hamilton, expressed in the 77th number of the Federalist, is urged with much force as being in accordance with this construction. After enumerating there, as one of the advantages to be expected from the co-operation of the Senate in the business of appointments, that it would contribute to the *stability* of the administration, he adds, "the consent of that body will be necessary to *displace* as well as to *appoint.*" It is insisted that the displacing here referred to, is indicated by the context to be, not a temporary removal by a temporary appointment, amounting only to an "attempt to change," but that the power denied by him to exist in the President alone, was such a displacing power as could defy the "discountenance of the Senate"—and that, therefore, this great statesman pressed it upon his countrymen as one of the highest recommendations of the Constitution, that "a change of the Chief Magistrate would not occasion so violent or so general a revolution in the officers of government as might be expected, if he were the *sole disposer* of offices. Where a man in any station has given satisfactory evidence of his fitness for it, a new President would be restrained from *attempting a change* in favor of a person more agreeable to him, by the apprehension that the discountenance of the Senate might frustrate the attempt. Those who can best estimate the value of a steady administration, will be most disposed to prize a provision which connects the official existence of public men with the approbation or disapprobation of that body, which, from the greater permanency of its own composition, will, in all probability, be less subject to inconstancy than any other member of the government." The weight of Hamilton's opinion is here set in full array against the advocates of constructive power; and it is true that his exposition of the Constitution was cotemporaneous with its ratification; that it was then given to, and pressed upon, our countrymen, for the purpose of effecting that ratification; that it was viewed at the time as obviating all objections to the extent of Executive influence; and that, perhaps, the only censure which has ever been cast upon his political writings, charges that he was too much disposed not to curtail, but to extend and increase the powers of the Federal Government. Yet, this doctrine, at least to the extent contended for, was not recognised by the House of Representatives in 1789; and if the decisions of that day, which have been referred to, are to be regarded as obligatory upon us, the Senate has no *direct* action upon the removals of the President. The question recurs then, by what constitutional mode can it maintain any check upon these abuses of Executive power?

I take the true difference, between the present advocates of that power and myself, to consist in *this:*—they consider the Senate as standing in the relation of a *quasi* privy council to the President, who may or may not abide by their advice, as to him shall seem most expedient. They deny the doctrine of Hamilton, that "the Constitution connects the official existence of public men with the approbation or disapprobation of the Senate." They deny the whole and every part of it. They deny it in every view which can be taken of it. I consider the Senate as possessing certain Executive powers, to be exercised in co-operation with the President when they approve of the Administration of his co-ordinate powers, or in opposition to, and as a salutary check upon him when he has abused such powers; and that, as officers of a certain grade cannot be appointed without their advice and consent, so if those officers be removed to reward partisans, or for any other unjustifiable purpose, the Senate can reject nominations to supply the vacancies thus occasioned, and thus either compel the President to reinstate those removed, or leave vacancies *which he cannot supply after the expiration of their session.* If this view be sound, the Senate, by its legitimate, though indirect action upon every removal, has a check upon the abuse of power, which, if exercised when the public interest really demands it, will destroy the motives for that abuse, and may hereafter save the Republic in her hour of greatest peril. The objects to be attained by an ambitious and designing President, through the instrumentality of these removals, will be to displace the real friends of the people, and to fill up the vacancies with his own creatures, subservient to his will, and independent of all other control; and if the Senate have the virtue to reject his propositions to effect these ends, he may be compelled to retract his removals, or to leave the places vacant. This right of rejecting appointments, with the express design of acting upon the removals, should be exercised whenever the removing power has been abused—because every such abuse is an act of tyranny, and the first approaches of usurpation, or oppressive and arbitrary power, should be repulsed by those who ought to stand as the most vigilant and intrepid among the sentinels of liberty. Ordinarily, he who accepts an appointment to fill a vacancy occasioned by such an abuse of power, is cognisant of the fact, and consenting to the abuse. Moreover, this check should be interposed whenever the public interest demands the restoration of a meritorious officer, whether removed through inadvertent error or intentional injustice. The Senate thought it important to exercise this right in the cases of the military nominations in 1822; but the privilege becomes inestimably valuable whenever the removing power of a President is exerted for the purposes of personal ambition, and in utter contempt of the public interest. It is infinitely better to go without an officer than to submit to "*an act of tyranny*" in any shape. We have no right to originate bills for raising revenue—we cannot nominate or propose in the first instance the sums to be levied on the people; but when the other House sends here such bills, we can amend or reject them. Now, whenever we believe that the sum to be raised is destined for any purpose which is tyrannical or oppressive, or not really necessary for the public interest, we are bound to negative the whole bill, if we are not allowed to amend it to suit that interest. We should, doubtless, refuse any appropriation of public money if we believed it destined to advance the interests of an usurper, although satisfied at the same time that a real evil might grow out of the want of funds to disburse the ordinary expenses of government. In these and all similar cases the question must be weighed and decided, whether the object to be achieved is worthy of the sacrifice it may occasion; and so long as the spirit of our ancestors dwells within these walls, we shall rarely think any sacrifice too great, if made in a successful resistance to the oppressive exercise of arbitrary power.

But there are some here who maintain that we have no such check on the Executive, and that the President is authorized to fill all vacancies *existing* in the recess of the Senate; so that when we have rejected such appointments as have been proposed to us, and, having been informed by the President that our services are no longer necessary here; shall have adjourned without day, he may fill the *vacancies then existing*. If this be true, he can fill such vacancies as well with one person as another, and of course can, and will generally, re-appoint the very man whom we have rejected;

or, he may entirely dispense with future nominations to the Senate, granting, on the day after each session, commissions which shall expire with the
next, and thus take away from this co-ordinate branch of power even the
miserable subordinate privilege of the old French Parliament whose only
glory was to register the mandates of the sovereign.

The commentator on Justinian, who has been alluded to, as a jurist, in
terms of high commendation, in the range of this debate, (Mr. COOPER,)
after animadverting upon the removing power as formerly exercised by the
Governor of Pennsylvania, says, the analogy between the rights of the
Governor and those of the President, in this respect, will not hold, "considering that under the constitution of the United States the exercise of
the right of removal is subject to the formidable check of the Senate's concurrence in the successor of the President—a difference so important as to
destroy the force of all reasoning from the one to the other. *A power in
every instance controlled in its exercise by the Senate, cannot be compared with
a power in every instance uncontrolled*, and exercised as the caprice of the
Governor for the time being, heated by recent opposition, and goaded by
revenge, may dictate." The distinction lies here,—every vacancy existing in
the recess is not a vacancy *happening* within the true construction of the
second article. The appointments to supply such vacancies must be made
"by granting commissions which shall expire *at* the end of the next session"—not *after* the expiration of that session. The commissions granted
during the last recess expire, *eo instanti*, with the determination of the present session; and if the offices are not filled by the concurrence of the
Senate, vacancies will *exist* at the moment we adjourn, not in the recess—
for that moment can with no more propriety be said to be recess, than session—and those vacancies will not exist by reason of any *casualty* or
happening not provided for, but by the expressed will of a co-ordinate
branch of the appointing power. It has never been pretended that the
President alone could fill, by one of these temporary appointments, a vacancy happening during the session. In the celebrated report of the committee on military affairs, made here on the 25th of April, 1822, which, as I
have already stated, met with the sanction of the Senate in the rejection of
the military appointments, it is urged that "the word *happen* relates to
some casualty not provided for by law. If the Senate be in session when
offices are created by law which were not before filled, and nominations be
not made to them by the President, he cannot appoint after the adjournment of the Senate, unless specially authorized by law, such vacancy not
happening during the recess." The same construction was evidently

adopted by Congress, and by the President himself, when, in the act of the 22d of July, 1813, they thought it necessary to insert an express provision in the second section, to confer upon the President the power to appoint collectors of direct taxes and internal duties during the recess, if not before made by and with the consent of the Senate. Every vacancy existing in the recess, is not therefore a vacancy "happening in the recess." In the third section of the first article of the Constitution, touching the appointment of Senators, it is provided that, "if vacancies happen by resignation or otherwise, during the recess of the Legislature of any State, the Executive thereof may make temporary appointments, until the next meeting of the Legislature, which shall then fill such vacancies." These temporary appointments by the State Executive are analogous to temporary appointments by the National Executive. How, then, has this clause in the Constitution been construed? The first case which occurred, to test its construction, was decided on the 28th of March, 1794, on an appointment by the Executive of Delaware, which appears to have undergone a full investigation. The report of the committee appointed to examine it, sets forth, that a Senator from that State resigned his seat upon the 18th day of September, 1793, and during the recess of the Legislature; that the Legislature met in January, and adjourned in February, 1794; that upon the 19th day of March, and subsequently to the adjournment of the Legislature, another was appointed by the Governor to fill the vacancy occasioned by the resignation. With these facts, a resolution was reported by the committee, and adopted by a vote of twenty to seven, that the appointee was not entitled to a seat here, "because a session of the Legislature of the said State had intervened between the resignation and the appointment;" and among those who sustained this resolution, we find the names of Langdon, King, Ellsworth, Martin, and Butler, who had been members of the Convention. Such was the determination on this question, going the whole length of the principle we seek to establish. In the case of Mr. Lanman, a Senator from Connecticut, the Senate, on the 7th of March, 1825, went still further. His term expired on the 3d of March, 1825; after which, he produced here a certificate of appointment by Oliver Wolcot, then Governor of the State, dated the 8th of February, 1825—and although the Legislature of the State was not in session at the time, and did not sit until May, yet the Senate decided that there was not in this case a vacancy happening by any casualty not provided for, and therefore Mr. Lanman was not entitled to a seat. We find among the distinguished names then recorded in favour of this construction, those of Messrs. Benton, Berrien,

Dickerson, *Eaton*, Gaillard, Hayne, JACKSON (now President,) King, Lloyd of Maryland, Macon, Tazewell, and *Van Buren*. It is not for me to pronounce upon the correctness of a decision thus established; but if it was right, it not only covers, but goes beyond my position. It is true that in some similar cases Senators have been permitted to sit here; but they all passed without consideration, except that of Mr. Tracy, who was held entitled to a seat, by a party vote, in a period of high excitement—all those who were called *federalists* voting for, and all those who were called *democrats*, against him. *Tempora mutantur.* However we may be branded as the federalists of this day, our doctrine appears to have been the Republican doctrine of that period. The constitutions of each of the States, in the cases referred to, provided that their governors *should see that their laws were faithfully executed;* and their laws directed those governors "to fill up all vacancies happening in the recess" of their respective legislatures by temporary appointments; so that there exists no ground upon which to build up a construction in favor of the power of the Federal Executive, which does not equally sustain that of the State Executive in each of these instances. Without further discussion of the principles connected with this subject, we might regard it as never to be shaken while the Constitution lasts, that the President alone can not fill any vacancy occasioned by the refusal of the Senate to concur in his nominations; and that if he, having had a fair opportunity to consult his constitutional advisers, should refuse or neglect to do so in any case where their consent to the appointment is required, he has no power to supply the vacancy existing at the expiration of their session.

Before I close my remarks upon the constitutional rights of the President and Senate, suffer me to say, Sir, that there cannot be, in a free government, a more dangerous principle than that of implied executive power. To control it, we cannot keep too steadily in view, that delegated authority of this character, should always be either strictly construed, or strictly defined, and that by the terms of the Constitution power, not expressly ceded, is reserved *to the people or the States.* I shall be gratified to see some farther evidences than any yet developed, to make good the remark of the gentleman from Tennessee, when he expressed his pleasure at beholding the administration majority of the American Senate "contending against all those doctrines which are calculated to increase the authority of men in office." We have also been informed, that we live in an age when STATE RIGHTS are the great objects of regard—when a predominating party has taken them into its especial keeping—when the President himself is their grand protector—when our hearts shall be gladdened, and our eyes blessed with the glorious vision of a party in power no longer warping the Constitution from its legitimate construction to increase the strength of the Federal head, but paring down all forced implications of authority, and restoring to their pristine purity and vigour the sovereign and independent powers of the twenty four States. Such, we are told, Sir, is the primary object of modern reform. But the example of this administration is a sad commentary on so fine a text; and the principles advanced in this debate to sustain it, sap the whole foundation of these lofty pretensions. Reverencing, as I sincerely do, *the constitutional rights of the States*, I view the avowed principles of the Executive as subversive of the most important powers of that very body where alone the States, as such, are represented. Rob the Senate of these, and of what avail is their mere Legislative authority, when the very laws themselves are to be passed upon by judges, and executed by officers, in whose appointment they have substantially no concern? An English King boasted that while he could appoint the Bishops and Judges, he could have what religion and laws he pleased; and it was the opinion of Roger Sherman, in adverting to that remark, that if the President was vested with the power of appointing to and removing from office at his pleasure, like the English monarch, he could render himself despotic: A blow at the rights of the States, is a blow at the liberties of the people; and whenever the period shall arrive for destroying the latter, the first aim will be to prostrate the powers of the former, in the Senate. Those who framed the Constitution foresaw this, and, so far as human wisdom could guard against the evil, they provided for it, by ordaining that no State shall ever be deprived of her equal suffrage, in this body, by any change of Constitution. *Hic murus aheneus esto!* Here lies the bulwark against consolidation of the government—the barrier for the protection of the States against the encroachments of Executive power; and the American who shall succeed in breaking down this defence, will bury in its ruins the liberties, with the Constitution of his country. The effort to destroy it, in order to be successful, will never be made in open and avowed hostility, but the first approaches of the enemy will be gradual, crafty, and disguised. Many a Semipronius will thunder "war to the knife's blade" against the foe whom he secretly encourages, until, by successive restrictions upon the rights of the Senate, the salutary powers of the States are stolen imperceptibly away, and most probably under this very pretence of enabling the Executive to see that the laws are faithfully executed.

Let us now, Sir, briefly, in conclusion, while we commemorate the day which inducted our Chief Magistrate to office, review his administration of the past year, apply to it the test of these principles, and calmly inquire whether any constitutional interposition of the Senate be requisite to check the abuses of power. This anniversary recalls the pledges of the inaugural address, to keep steadily in view the limitations as well as the extent of the Executive authority, to respect and preserve the rights of the sovereign members of our Union, to manage by certain searching operations the public revenue, to observe a strict and faithful economy, to counteract that tendency to private and public profligacy which a profuse expenditure of money by the government is but too apt to engender, to depend for the advancement of the public service more on the integrity and zeal of the public officers than on their numbers, and particularly to correct those abuses which, it was then charged, had brought the patronage of the Federal government into conflict with the freedom of elections, and counteract those causes which had placed or continued power in unfaithful or incompetent hands. The lateness of the hour warns me that I ought not to trespass on your attention, by inquiring how far *all* these pledges have been redeemed; and the examination of all the topics presented by such a general inquiry might lead me beyond the "exiguo fine" within which I am admonished that an American Senator should confine himself, when speaking of an American President. But it is true, and ought to be observed on this day, that our public officers are increased in number, and not diminished in salary; that the promised retrenchment has terminated in a recommendation to establish additional bureaus, with *more* public agents, and increased demands on the Treasury, to swell to an almost boundless extent the influence of the Executive by a general extension of the law which limits appointments to four years, and by the establishment of a government bank; and that a general system of proscription for a manly exercise of the right of opinion, under the pretence of rotation in office, has brought the patronage of the Executive into full conflict with the freedom of elections. Turning from the investigation of minor subjects which might by possibility be considered as mere topics for partisan effect, and with a nobler purpose than to subserve the petty interests of any sect, or any party, our attention is forcibly arrested by some instances in which these pledges have been so violated, that their tendency, if not immediately, at least consequentially, and by the force of example, is subversive of the dearest interests of our people, and of the most sacred institutions of our republic.

When we look to the manner in which the pledge to observe a strict and faithful economy has been redeemed, we find the expenses of government increase, through the instrumentality of these rewards and punishments for political opinion. Outfits, salaries, and all the incidental expenses attending the recall of nearly the whole of our diplomatic corps, and the appointment of others to supply their places, have caused large drafts upon the Treasury, and laid the foundation for increasing demands upon it. But without dwelling to estimate how many tens, or hundreds of thousands of dollars have been expended in punishing opponents, or inquiring how profusely the public bounty has been lavished upon favourites, we have something more important to consider. We know that if funds for such purposes have been taken from the strong box without appropriations, the President must have dipped his hands into the nation's treasure in opposition to the Constitution, which it is our duty to support. Money cannot be drawn from the Treasury except in consequence of appropriations made by law, and the radical act of the first of May, 1820, after limiting the powers of the President, in relation to transfers of appropriations in the Army and Navy, provides, in the fifth section, "that no transfers of appropriation from or to other branches of expenditure shall thereafter be made." May we not inquire now, from what fund the money has been drawn to defray the greatly increased expenses of our foreign missions? These expenses were not provided for during the last session of Congress by any law, for they were not foreseen or anticipated. If then the diplomatic fund was insufficient for these purposes, either the nation has been brought in debt to accomplish them, or the Constitution and the law have been violated by unauthorized drafts on the Treasury. It is certain that we are now called upon to appropriate largely, either to pay a debt incurred, or to supply a deficiency in some other fund not appropriated for these expenses. If the Executive can recall our foreign agents for party purposes, or to promote friends, even where no Legislative appropriation has been made for these objects, Congress has virtually no control over our foreign intercourse, and we may hereafter expect that our ministers abroad will be withdrawn on the accession of every new incumbent of the Presidency; that new men will be sent to supply their places, and that the whole relations of the country with foreign powers will be changed, or thrown into confusion, at the end of every four years. Admit the power of the Executive, without appropriation, to recall and to appoint Ministers, and by the operation to bring the nation in debt, *for the public good*,—yet show us how the public good required this increased expense. Take a case for example, and let some ingenious advocate of the administration assign a reason why our late Minister near the Court of St. James' was recalled. Mr. Barbour had acquitted himself faithfully in every public trust which had ever before been confided to him, and was at the time of his recall discharging with honour to himself and his country the high duties of his mission. In what respect was he thought to be either incompetent or unfaithful? Was any new policy to be adopted in our relations with England which he would not espouse? Take another case, and inform us why the gallant Harrison, the hero of Fort Meigs, the victor at Tippecanoe, and the Thames; a veteran in council, as well as in the field, distinguished for his virtues in all the relations of the citizen, the soldier, and the statesman—why, I ask, was he proscribed as unfit to represent his country abroad, and withdrawn from Colombia, to make room for Thomas P. Moore? He had scarcely arrived at Bogota—the ink was still fresh on the Executive record which informed the President that it was the advice of the Senate that he should represent us there, when the order for his removal was announced. This could not have been done for any official misconduct. There had been no time to inquire into that. Was his fidelity distrusted then? Or how did the public good require his dismissal? Think you it will tell well in the annals of history, that he who had so often periled life and limb, in the vigour of manhood, to secure the blessings of liberty to others, was punished for the exercise of the elective franchise in his old age? Sir, it was an act, disguise it as we may, which, by holding out the idea that he had lost the confidence of his country, might tend to bring down his gray hairs with sorrow to the grave. But the glory he acquired by the campaign on the Wabash, and by those hard earned victories for which he received the warmest acknowledgments of merit from the Legislature of Kentucky, and the full measure of a nation's thanks in the resolutions of Congress, can never be effaced; and any effort to degrade their honoured object will recoil on those who make it, until other men in better days shall properly estimate his worth, and again cheer his declining years with proofs of his country's confidence and gratitude. If then these acts, and others of a similar character, be hostile to the spirit of the Constitution, can we regard the expenditure of public money they have occasioned as a proper redemption of those pledges which on this day last year so much delighted us, "to observe a strict and faithful economy," and to keep steadily in view the *limitations* as well as the extent of the Executive power?

The pledge to preserve the rights of the sovereign members of our Union, as well as the defence of the administration made by the gentleman from Tennessee, lead us to the reflection that more members of Congress who were friendly to the election of the present Chief Magistrate, have been appointed to office by him, within the compass of a single year, than have been appointed by any other President during the whole course of an administration of *eight* years. The consequences of this were foreseen and deprecated by the founders of our government; but the provision which they inserted in the Constitution to prevent them has proved inadequate to its object. Such was the opinion of a favorite constitutional lawyer, who, in an address to the Tennessee Legislature on the 7th of October, 1825, explained this subject so fully that I shall be pardoned for producing a large extract from that valuable state paper—especially after the gentleman from Tennessee has adverted to it, and made an argument upon it. "With a view," says he, "to sustain more effectually in practice the axiom which divides the three great classes of power into independent constitutional checks, I would impose a provision, rendering *any member of Congress* ineligible to office under the general government during the term for which he was elected, and two years thereafter, except in cases of judicial office. The effect of such a constitutional provision is obvious. By it Congress, in a considerable degree, would be free from that connection with the Executive Department, which at present gives strong ground of apprehension and jealousy on the part of the people. Members, instead of being liable to be withdrawn from legislating on the great interests of the nation, through prospects of Executive patronage, would be more liberally confided in by their constituents; while their vigilance would be less interrupted by party feelings and party excitements. Calculations from intrigue or management would fail; nor would their deliberations or their investigation of subjects consume so much time. The morals of the country would be improved, and virtue, uniting with the labors of the representatives, and with the official ministers of the law, would tend to perpetuate the honor and glory of the government.

"But, if this change in the Constitution should not be obtained, and important appointments continue to devolve on the representatives in Congress, it requires no depth of thought to perceive that corruption will become the order of the day; and that, under the garb of conscientious sacrifices to establish precedents for the public good, evils of serious importance to the freedom and prosperity of the republic may arise. It is through this channel that the people may expect to be attacked in their constitutional sovereignty, and where tyranny may well be apprehended to spring up, in some favorable emergency. Against such inroads *every guard ought to be interposed*, and none better occurs than that of closing the suspected avenue with some necessary constitutional restriction."

It is interesting to examine how far this administration has actually practised on these maxims. Why, within the very first year six members of the Senate,* being one eighth of the whole body as it was composed during the twentieth Congress, have been appointed to some of the most important offices within the gift of the Executive. And yet the message of this session reiterates the principles of the Tennessee letter, with a slight reservation by way of covering the case as it now exists. By that letter judges alone might be selected from the members of Congress. By the late message we are informed that "the necessity of *securing in the Cabinet,* and *in diplomatic stations of the highest rank,* the best talents and political experience, should *perhaps* (even here we have a *quere*) except these from the exclusion." If it be "perhaps" necessary to change the Constitution to save us from doing wrong, why not do right without the change? The new reservation is a flat departure from the maxims of 1825, and still even that does not cover the acts of the Executive, for we have not only diplomatists and cabinet ministers (important officers!) chosen from the members of Congress "within the term for which they were elected, and two years thereafter," but *important* appointments of a very different character, even in the Post Office and the customs, continue to devolve on them, convincing those who have become proselytes to the Tennessee doctrine, without any great depth of thought, that corruption may become the order of the day, and that, under the garb of conscientious sacrifices for the public good, evils of serious importance to the freedom and prosperity of the republic may arise. But the gentleman from Tennessee, who called our attention to the letter, and without whose notice of it I should hardly have adverted to it, says—

[Here Mr. GRUNDY explained. He stated that he had alluded to the letter in reply to the Senator from Indiana (General NOBLE).]

Mr. CLAYTON continued. Sir, the honorable gentleman's reply was, that the people ought to have changed the Constitution, but that, without some constitutional restraint, the President was under no obligation to practise what he formerly preached. However valid that defence may appear, it is not the opinion of my constitutional lawyer, for in that same letter he says, "It is due to myself to practise upon the maxims recommended to others." These, and similar pledges, obtained for him thousands of votes during the canvass of 1828, and ought to have been redeemed.

*Mr. Van Buren, Secretary of State; Mr. Branch, Secretary of the Navy; Mr. Berrien, Attorney General; Mr. Eaton, Secretary of War; Mr. McLane, Minister to England; and Mr. Chandler, Collector at Portland.

"When the blood burns, how prodigal the soul
Lends the tongue vows."

Moreover, it will require much "depth of thought" to convince us that a President cannot do what he thinks right without some constitutional restriction to prevent him from doing what he knows to be wrong;—or that a man of sound mind and good disposition cannot avoid the destruction of his own family, unless you treat him like a madman, by tying his arms and depriving him of the means of doing injury.

There was, however, no pledge in the inaugural so striking or so important as the recognition of that obligation, then said to be inscribed on the list of Executive duties by the recent demonstration of public sentiment, to counteract those causes which brought the patronage of the General Government into conflict with the freedom of elections. Sir, your Postmaster General, wielding the patronage of his Department over clerks, deputies, contractors and agents, in numbers amounting to nearly eight thousand men, has for political effect removed from public employment, in pursuance of a general system, so vast a proportion of the old and faithful public servants connected with that immense establishment, that its resources and its energies are impaired, public confidence is diminished, and suspicion, darkening this great avenue to light, as she spreads her dusky pinions over it, whispers that some of its recesses have been converted for political purposes into *posts of espial* on the private intercourse of your citizens. The public press, too, by the instrumentality of which alone this republic might be prostrated; by the influence of which a President might be swelled into a Monarch, has been—not shackled by a gag-law— no, Sir, but subsidized by sums approximating to the interest on a million of dollars granted in the way of salaries, jobs and pensions to partisan editors, printers, proprietors, and all the host directly and indirectly connected with and controlling it. The appointment of editors to office is not casual, but systematic. They were appointed *because they were Editors*. In the days of the French Revolution, when the press was bought up with the public funds, the country was flooded with envenomed effusions from the Jacobin prints. The post of profit was then erected in the kennel where a venal pack bayed like blood-hounds for murder. Marat was distinguished, as the Editor of a Revolutionary journal, for violence and vituperation; and having published his demand of two hundred and sixty thousand heads as a sacrifice to liberty, was soon elevated to one of the highest offices of the Republic, where, as a member of the infernal triumvirate which deluged

France in tears and blood, he combined the cunning malice of Robespierre with the native ferocity of Danton. He was a compound of the vices of both his coadjutors—of all that on earth was flagitious, mean, inhuman and inexorable; for he came from the schools of a faction which trained its disciples to cry havoc without mercy when bounty lured them up the path to blood and death. The examples of that day teach us how easy is the transition from the hireling libeller to the brutal murderer; and that he whose habits have long accustomed him to live upon the ruins of private reputation, would shed the blood of his victim with pleasure, if paid to do the deed of death. An independent, able, high-minded Editor, is an honor to his country and to the age in which he lives. He is the guardian of the public welfare, the sentinel of liberty, the conservator of morals; and every attempt to allure or to coerce him to desertion from his duty should be re-garded as an insult and an injury to the nation whose interests he is bound to defend. It is less manly in an assailant, and not less indicative of hostil-ity, to bribe the sentry on the walls of your citadel, than to gag him and hurl him from its battlements. It is more dangerous to corrupt the press by the prospect of office, than absolutely to silence it by sedition laws; be-cause, although by the latter course it may be destroyed, yet by the former it may be made the engine of tyranny. The charge of an undisguised effort to subdue its energies in the days of the elder Adams, brought down upon the heads of all who were friendly to the sedition act the full measure of public condemnation; and it yet remains to be seen what will be the effect produced by an attempt to buy and prostitute it. We have a pack in full cry upon the trail of every man whose integrity of purpose will not suffer him to bend before power; and friends, and character, and happiness, are torn from him by them, with as little remorse as was felt by the blood-hounds of the old French litter. Can all these things be justified by the examples of the illustrious Jefferson? Sir, his real friends will at all times spurn the im-putation which the very question conveys. They will remind you that the first prominent act of his administration was to disembarrass and untram-mel the press, to disengage that "chartered libertine" from the shackles of authority, and leave him free as mountain air. They will tell you that the great maxim he adhered to till the latest period of life, was, that "error of opinion should always be tolerated while reason was left free to combat it;" that he rewarded the office hunting libeller who had slandered his prede-cessors with a view to gain by his election, with his unconcealed and un-mitigated scorn and contempt—that he bought no man's services with gold, adopted no system of pensioning presses with office, offered no lures to libellers, employed no assassins of character. Three years ago, when the great Western Statesman who has, for his independence, been hunted like a wild beast, filled with honour to his country the office of Secretary of State, he became an object of the bitterest vituperation, by discharging some half a dozen printers from the petty job of publishing the laws; and although the whole extent of this exercise of *patronage*, as it was then called, did not amount to more than a few hundred dollars, yet it was considered as an exertion of power vitally dangerous to the country, as *tending* to establish a government press. Such a press was said to be more alarming to the liberties of the people than a palace guard of six thousand men, and the acts of the Secretary were denounced, as being calculated to "sap the vigour, degrade the independence, and enfeeble the vigilance of the sentinels on the watchtower of liberty, whose beacon lights should blaze with pure and undying lustre." But now, when so many of those very sentinels have been subsidized by office, and the new stipendiaries have formed in battalia about the throne, presenting their pikes, in close array and forty deep, for its defence, the lofty eloquence of these patriot orators is heard no more within our walls; their harps hang on the willows, and instead of ringing an alarm through the land, they are hushed into the deepest silence, and the most tranquil repose.

Mr. PRESIDENT, in this brief and hasty review of the prominent characteristics of the first year of this administration, we have observed those acts which in the opinion of the honourable member from Tennessee will have no more effect upon the American public than "an attempt to agitate the ocean by throwing pebbles on its surface." We find, however, that the removals to which he referred have not amounted only to the dismissal of a "few subordinate officers," but to a thorough revolution among the most important and most faithful functionaries of the government; and it ought to be remembered that even the subordinate officers alluded to were FREEMEN. I may know less of this world than the able and experienced member from Tennessee—but I still think this nation will look to an act of tyranny which tramples a faithful servant under foot, or turns him out with scoffs and contempt, however humble his condition may have been, with feelings very different from those manifested by the advocates of power. They may not care for the *little salaries*,—but they will look to the *principle* of Executive action—to the *motive* which makes that action *dangerous*. Does the honorable gentleman recollect the reason for which John Hampden refused to pay the ship money? The sum for which he contended amounted only to a few pence, yet the claim of a British monarch to it was resisted to the utmost; and the feelings of an English public were agitated like the ocean in a storm, not on account of the sums to be paid under the illegal exaction, but because it was an encroachment on their rights, and an abuse of power. Every GENUINE AMERICAN REPUBLICAN carries the spirit of John Hampden in his bosom. Surely the honorable member's own high estimate of national character will not suffer him to entertain the degrading idea that an English public, under an English monarch, cherished a loftier sense of liberty, or a more determined spirit of resistance to the abuses of authority, than his own countrymen. Has he forgotten the reason which induced our ancestors to resist the tea duties and the stamp tax? Was it only the sum to be levied which set this continent in a flame, or was it the oppressive *principle* upon which those claims were founded? If the mal-administration of Executive power has been such as even to *"exceed the conception"* of that great patriot whose opinions we both reverence so highly, why is it that the honorable member views with such contempt the sum of the salaries awarded to Executive partisans, and all the distress and anguish inflicted on the sufferers by proscription, while he overlooks the principles which have been violated, and the Constitution which has been trampled under foot? Here is the ground on which we have arraigned your administration; and although its friends may laugh its victims to scorn, they should recollect that what is theirs to day may shortly be in the power of another; though they now consider this as a mere gossamer floating in the political atmosphere, and have even told us it is a feather which can weigh nothing with the People, they should recollect that this feather is torn from the plumage of the American Eagle, and that the transgression which they now regard as so venial, may be a precedent to sanction the usurpation of power for the destruction of the liberties of the People.

Having closed my remarks in reply to honorable gentlemen, suffer me now to say, sir, that it has been no part of my object to embitter the feelings of my associates by personal allusions to them, although I have intended, upon the challenge of the gentleman from Tennessee, to speak out as 'boldly, frankly and freely,' as he might reasonably desire. But if any luckless arrow of mine, inadvertently shot, rankles in the bosom of any member here, he is welcome to send it back with his best force, provided he does not poison its point. My objects, I trust, however, have been above such warfare. I have endeavored to preserve unimpaired the rights of the tribunal established by our forefathers as the only common umpire for the decision of those controversies which must arise in the best regulated political families, and to show that without the aid of such a tribunal we must sink back into that anarchy which, among all other nations and in all former ages, has been the sure harbinger of tyranny. I have labored to sustain what I believe to be the right and duty of the Senate—to interpose a barrier against the improper exercise of executive power which now controls, either directly or indirectly, nearly every avenue to every station, whether of honor or profit, within the gift of twelve millions of people. But if the sentiments which have been avowed by gentlemen of the majority on this floor should be supported by the American people, their giant party, which has already borne upon its shoulders a weight greater than the gates of Gaza, will, in the overthrow of both these objects, wrench the very pillars of the government from their foundations. Then we shall find how dreadful are the consequences of such doctrines. Upon their construction of executive power, should one possessed of the temper and ability which have so often characterized the Consuls and Chiefs of other republics, obtain the Presidency—such a man as Napoleon meant to describe when he spoke of the Russian "with a beard on his chin"—exercising, as he may, in the spirit of oriental despotism, perfect command over the army, the navy, the press, and an overflowing treasury, the merest driveller may foresee that our liberties will fare like the "partridge in the falcon's clutch." The very sentinels of our freedom will be bribed by him, with our own gold; and even many of those who have so triumphantly borne aloft the stripes and stars amidst the thunders of battle, will be compelled to "beg bitter bread," or to turn the steel which we have placed in their hands, against our own bosoms. He will readily gain to his purposes a flock of those voracious office hunters, whom we have seen brooding over the spoils of victory after a political contest, like so many vultures after a battle, perched on every dead bough about the field, snuffing the breeze, and so eager for their prey that even the cries of the widow and the orphan cannot drive them from the roost. It has been said, and I believe truly, that we can never fall without a struggle; but in the contest with such a man, thus furnished by ourselves with "all appliances and means to boot" against us, we must finally sink. For a time our valleys will echo with the roar of artillery, and our mountains will ring with the reports of the rifle. The storm of civil war will howl fearfully through the land, from the Atlantic border to the wildest recesses of the West, covering with desolation every field which has been crowned with verdure by the culture of freemen, and now resounding with the echoes of our happiness and industry. But the tempest must subside, and be succeeded by the deep calm and sullen gloom of despotism:—after which, the voice of a freeman shall never again be heard within our borders, unless in the fearful and suppressed whispers of the traveller from some distant land who shall visit the scene of our destruction to gaze in sorrow on the melancholy ruin.

EDWARD LIVINGSTON

Edward Livingston was born in New York in 1764, the younger brother of the revolutionary statesman Robert R. Livingston. Educated at Princeton College, he studied law and began the practice of law in 1785. He entered politics as a Republican, serving in the United States House of Representatives from 1795 to 1801. He voted for Thomas Jefferson for president when the election was thrown into the House of Representatives in 1801. He was appointed United States attorney for the district of New York and was elected mayor of New York in 1801. He got into legal and financial difficulty in 1803 when a custom house clerk misappropriated public funds. Livingston, held responsible, sold his property to pay back the money and moved to Louisiana. There he practiced law and invested in a land development project that brought him into conflict with the Jefferson administration and that drove him more deeply into debt. In the War of 1812, he served on the staff of General Andrew Jackson. Livingston was elected to the Louisiana legislature in 1820, and to the United States House of Representatives in 1822, where he served three terms. A supporter of Andrew Jackson, Livingston was elected to the Senate in 1829 and was appointed Secretary of State in 1831. He wrote Jackson's proclamation on nullification in 1832. He served as minister to France from 1833 to 1835. Throughout his career, Livingston made contributions to legal and penal reform that won him international acclaim. He died in 1836.

Speech of Mr. Livingston,

of Louisiana

[March 9, 1830]

The resolution of Mr. Foot, of Connecticut, relative to the
public lands, being under consideration, Mr. Livingston
addressed the Chair as follows:

Mr. President: The important topics that have been presented to
our consideration, and the ability with which the questions arising
out of them have been hitherto discussed, cannot but have excited a very
considerable interest; which I regret exceedingly that I shall be obliged to
interrupt, and greatly disappoint those who look for a continuance of "the
popular harangue, the tart reply, the logic, and the wisdom, and the wit,"
with which we have been entertained. For, sir, you can expect nothing
from me but a very plain, and, I fear, a very dull exposition of my views on
some of the subjects comprised in this excursive debate—unembellished
by eloquence, unseasoned by the pungency of personal allusions. For I
have no accusations to make of sectional hostility to the State I represent,
and, of consequence, no recriminations to urge in its behalf, no personal
animosity to indulge, and but one—yes, sir, I have *one* personal defence to
make; a necessary defence against a grave accusation; but that will be as
moderate as I know it will be complete, satisfactory, and, I had almost
said, triumphant.

The multiplicity and nature of the subjects that have been considered
in debating a resolution with which none of them seem to have the slightest connection, and the addition of new subjects which every speaker has
thought it proper to increase the former stock, has given me, I confess,
some uneasiness. I feared an irruption of the Cherokees, and was not
without apprehensions that we should be called on to terminate the question of Sunday mails; or, if the Anti-Masonic Convention should take
offence at the secrecy of our Executive session, or insist on the expulsion of

all the initiated from our councils, that we should be obliged to contend with them for our seats. Indeed, I had myself serious thoughts of introducing the reformation of our National code, and a plan for the gradual increase of the Navy, and am not yet quite decided whether, before I sit down, I shall not urge the abolition of capital punishments. In truth, Mr. President, the whole brought forcibly to my recollection an anecdote told in one of the numerous memoirs written during the reign of Louis XIV, too trivial, perhaps, to be introduced into this grave debate, but which, perhaps, may be excused. A young lady had been educated in all the learning of the times, and her progress had been so much to the satisfaction of the princess who had directed her studies, that, on her first introduction, her patroness used to address her thus: "Come, miss! discourse with these ladies and gentlemen on the subject of theology; so, that will do. Now talk of geography; after that, you will converse on the subjects of astronomy and metaphysics, and then give your ideas on logic and belle lettres." And thus the poor girl, to her great annoyance, and the greater of her auditors, was put through the whole circle of the sciences in which she had been instructed. Sir, might not a hearer of our debates for some days past, have concluded that we, too, had been directed in a similar way, and that you had said, to each of the speakers, "Sir, please to rise and speak on the disposition of the public lands; after that, you may talk to the tariff; let us know all you think on the subject of internal improvement; and, before you sit down, discuss the powers of the Senate in relation to appointments, and the right of a State to recede from the Union; and finish by letting us know whether you approve or oppose the measures of the present, or the six preceding administrations." The approximation, Sir, of so many heterogeneous materials for discussion, must provoke a smile; and most of those who have addressed you, while they lamented that subjects, unconnected with the resolution, had been introduced into debate, rarely sat down without adding to the number. For my own part, I think the discussion may be turned to useful purposes. It may, by the interchange of opinion, increase our own information on all the important points which have been examined, while, not being called on for a vote, we may weigh them at leisure, and come to a conclusion, without being influenced by the warmth of debate.

The publication of what has been said, will spread useful information on topics highly proper to be understood in the community at large.

The recurrence which has necessarily been had to first principles is of incalculable use. The nature, form, history, and changes of our Government, imperceptible or disregarded at the time of their occurrence, are remarked; abuses are pointed out; and the people are brought to reflect on the past, and provide for the future.

It affords a favorable opportunity, by explanations that would not otherwise have been made, to remove prejudice and doubts as to political character and conduct. For instance, Sir, it has already produced one which has given me, individually, sincere pleasure. The Senator from Massachusetts, who so eloquently engaged the attention of his auditors in the beginning of the debate, took that occasion to disavow any connexion with the Hartford Convention; to declare, in unequivocal terms, that he "had nothing to do with the Hartford Convention." Sir, I repeat, I heard this explicit declaration with great pleasure, because, on my arrival here as a member of the other House, in which I first had the satisfaction of being acquainted, and associating with that Senator, I received an impression (from whom, or how, or where, it would be impossible for me now to tell,) that, although not a member of that Convention, he had, in some sort, favored, promoted, or approved of its meeting; and, being only on such terms of social intercourse as one gentleman has with another, without that intimacy which would have justified my making a personal inquiry on the subject, I heard, and doubtless all who had received the same impressions, heard, with great satisfaction, a declaration which has so completely eradicated every suspicion that the Senator from Massachusetts lent his countenance to that injudicious, ill-timed, and dangerous measure, to which others have given stronger epithets of disapprobation. Sir, I happen to know something, not of the proceedings or views of that body, but of the effect its existence had in encouraging our enemy in exciting hopes of disunion, nay, of disgraceful adherence to their cause. While these worthy citizens were occupied in deliberating on the plans, whatever they were, which drew them together in the East; while they and others associated with them in party feeling, were devising means of putting an end to the war, by vilifying those who declared, and detracting from the merit of those who conducted it, by opposing every measure for prosecuting it with vigor, and obstructing our means of defence, by denouncing the war itself as unjust, and the gallant exploits of our Army and Navy as unfit subjects for rejoicing—while these men were thus employed at one extremity of the Union, others were differently engaged at the other. A small but gallant band, directed by their heroic leader, were striving also to put an end to the war, but by far different means; by means of brave, uncompromising, uncalculating resistance; their attacks were made upon the enemies of their country, not upon its Government; among them were militiamen, who, without any constitutional scruples about passing the boundary of their State, had marched more than a thousand miles beyond those boundaries in search of the enemy. They found him, and glorious victory at the same moment; joined to my brave constituents, they gave a most signal defeat to more than three times their number; and signalized the close of the war by an action in itself capable of putting an end to the contest. Immediately after this great event, I was sent on a mission to the British fleet. Circumstances protracted my stay on board the Admiral's ship for several days; during which, having been formerly acquainted with an officer high in command, I discovered, not only from his conversation, but that of almost all the officers, that the utmost reliance was placed on the Hartford Convention, for effecting a dissolution of the Union, and the neutrality of New England. I have no evidence that these hopes and expectations were derived from any communication with any member of that body. But I know that the enemy were, as must naturally have been the case, encouraged by the appearance of division which that meeting was calculated to produce; it was made the topic of conversation as often as civility to me would allow. An assembly, on whose deliberations were founded such insolent expectations, so injurious to the patriotism and integrity of a part of my country, whose inhabitants I had always been taught to respect—such an assembly could not but have raised the most unfavorable impressions of its object; and the suspicion of having favored or promoted its meeting, necessarily derogated from the high opinion which might otherwise have been entertained of the discretion or patriotism of any one to whom it attached.

As this debate has offered an occasion of making a declaration which I am sure must have been heard with equal satisfaction by all who, like me, were under impressions which that declaration completely removed, so, if it should (as I sincerely hope it may) produce a similar disclaimer of that construction of the Constitution which gives all powers to Congress under the general expression of *providing for the general welfare;* if it should produce this effect, it will completely annihilate one of the most dangerous party dogmas, and verify what has been so frequently said, that federalism was extinct; and, on the other hand, an open avowal of that doctrine will have the effect of putting us on our guard against its operation, so that the frank interchange of sentiment that may be expected, must, in every view, be beneficial.

Yet, Sir, I should, notwithstanding these ideas of the utility of the debate, have taken no part in it but for these considerations:

The importance of the subject of the resolution to the State I represent;

The appeals that have been made to my recollection, in the course of the discussion;

And the necessity of repelling a charge implicating me, and others with whom I acted, in a charge of hostility to the Father of his Country.

The original resolution, now completely abandoned, and only incidentally referred to, must form a prominent figure in the observation I shall address to the Senate. The subject it involves is one of deep interest to my State; and the policy of the General Government, with respect to its public land within our boundaries, shall be freely canvassed. Representing, with my worthy colleague, the interests of that State, I should betray those interests were I not to seize this favorable opportunity of making known the true state of our claims on the justice of the Union. I confine myself to my own State—the others are too ably represented to need my aid. Some of them have thought that they could trace the measures of which they complain to particular sections of the Union, and I must not be understood as censuring this course. Though I do not think it necessary for my State, other gentlemen, who undoubtedly understand this subject better than I do, think it is so for them. It is not for me to blame them. My friend from Missouri has, with his characteristic diligence, collected a mass of evidence on this subject, which is perhaps conclusive; but this it does not suit my purpose to examine; I will not attempt any such research. The measures of which I shall complain are those of the nation. I should bewilder myself, do injustice to others, and cause useless irritation, were I to seek, in old journals or forgotten documents, for the names of those who voted for or against the measures of which I am forced to complain, or try to discover what river or what geographical line divided them. All those votes I am bound to believe were given from proper motives, though from erroneous views. I feel no sectional or personal hostility, and will endeavor to excite none. In avowing this course, I am far from arraigning that which some of my friends have pursued; they are the best judges of their own griefs, and the best mode of redressing them. For my own part, I repeat, that all of which I shall complain are the acts and omissions of the whole Government; and I state them, because I hope and believe that, when they shall be fully known, compensation for injuries and injurious omissions will be offered, and all stipulations faithfully performed.

Louisiana was ceded by France to the United States in 1803. By the treaty of cession the United States acquired all the vacant lands within the province, and the sovereignty over it; but under the following conditions:

To maintain the inhabitants in the enjoyment of their property;

To admit them as soon as possible into the Union, according to the principles of the Federal Constitution.

Neither of these conditions have been faithfully performed, according to the spirit of the stipulation.

To maintain the inhabitants in the enjoyment of their property, it was essential that all disputed claims to it should be submitted to the decision of a court, whether such claims were made by individuals or the Government. Yet all the titles disallowed by the Government were directed to be decided by Commissioners of its own choosing, holding their offices at the will of the President. This was not only doing injustice to us, but was an infringement on the constitutional distribution of power, by which the judicial powers of the United States are vested in a Supreme and inferior Courts, of which the Judges are to hold their offices during good behavior, who are to take cognizance of all controversies to which the United States are parties, and from the decisions of the latter of which, an appeal lies to the former. Now, no one can deny that, to decide on the validity of a title to land, is a judicial function; that the United States are parties to all the controversies in relation to their titles to public lands; and that the Commissioners are not such judges as are intended by the Constitution. Yet, Sir, you refuse to give us the enjoyment of two millions, and more, of acres claimed by citizens of my State, under perfect grants, made by the former sovereigns of the province, because your Commissioners, under the *instructions* of an Executive Department, have refused to ratify them. Year after year, for more than twenty years, they have petitioned for their right under the treaty, or for a judicial inquiry into their title; year after year you have refused this just and reasonable demand. You have partially granted it to the adjoining States and Territory of Missouri, Alabama, and Arkansas, but have pertinaciously, unjustly, and cruelly refused it to us. We have, also, in common with the adjoining States of Missouri, Mississippi, and Alabama, (all in part or in the whole taken out of the territory ceded by treaty) been deprived of the benefits of the judiciary system of the United States. Lives and fortunes submitted to the legal decision of a single man. Lives without appeal—fortunes, under 2000 dollars, without appeal. Both, in my opinion, have been more than once illegally sacrificed to this cruel neglect of our rights.

To understand the next grievance of which I complain, the attention of the Senate must be drawn to the topographical features of the country, as well as its statistics and geographical position. In the short distance of four degrees of latitude, the extent of this State on one side of the Mississippi and two on the other, that river, by its meandering course, and the division of its waters in the Delta, presents banks of near 1500 miles on both its sides—the other rivers falling into it nearly as much more. All these are subject to annual inundation; and in the whole alluvial soil the banks of the river are the highest ground, which descends in an inclined plane to the level of the ocean. It follows from this configuration that the banks of the river must be secured by dikes, or that the whole of the alluvial country must be submerged during every annual rise of the river. The construction of these dikes was a duty imposed on the first settlers of the province, as a condition of their grants; and this mighty river, encased in high and solid embankments for near two hundred miles of its course, attests how faithfully this condition was fulfilled. A wonderful work, when compared with the slender population by which it was effected. By the terms of the cession, the United States became proprietor of all the vacant lands; but they have not considered themselves liable to any of the duties that would have attached to the property had it been in private hands: they expressly exempt themselves, and even those to whom they may sell, during five years, from taxes or any contribution to Government; and, practically, have refused to make any of the improvements necessary, not only for reclaiming their own lands, but for protecting their inhabitants from the effects of the inundation which has been described; and, in numerous instances, parishes have been obliged, in their own defence, to perform this expensive operation for you. Now, Sir, the State contains 36,000,000 of acres, of which your Commissioners have confirmed, and you have granted and sold, only 5,000,000; so that you now own six-sevenths of the whole State. That one-seventh, which is in private hands, supports a population of more than 200,000 souls, and raises an agricultural produce, beyond its own consumption, of 8,000,000 of dollars. Yet, with this evident advantage, resulting from a settlement of the old titles, and the sale of the lands in the State, which, at the same rate, would give a population of more than a million, and an export nearly equal to that of all the rest of the States, you have only sold 250,000 acres of the public land; you refuse to try or to allow just claims to the amount of two millions of acres, and, with the richest soil in the world, we are condemned to a scanty population, and to see the owners of six-sevenths of our soil refusing to contribute to the expenses of our Government, forcing us to defend their property, as well as ours, from destructive inundations and more destructive invasions, and for more than a quarter of a century, by delaying the disposition of the lands, breaking that which I shall prove was the most important condition on which they received the country.

That condition was not only security to property, but "that the inhabitants should be incorporated in the Union, as soon as possible, according to the principles of the Federal Constitution;" that is to say, that the country should be erected into a State, as soon as it could be done according to the principles of the Constitution; but there was no principle to oppose its being done instantly. Yet, notwithstanding the most spirited remonstrance made in the first year after the cession—a remonstrance now on your files, and which testifies not only the desire to enjoy the privilege, but the ability to exercise it, you kept them in the subordinate grade of a territory for more than eight years, and you lopped off the greater part of the province, out of which, without their consent, you have made an extensive territory, and a more extensive State. It is true, sir, that, at this late period, you brought Louisiana into the Union; you assigned their boundaries; you approved of their Constitution; and you admitted their Senators and Representatives in the councils of the nation. But is this all that is necessarily implied by the obligation of the treaty? Is an extent of territorial limit all that is required? In contracting to create a State, you promised to promote its population. In stipulating that it should become one of a confederacy of free republics, you promised the means of making that population worthy of the name, and capable of exercising the duties of freemen; you promised them the means of moral, religious, and scientific education; you promised such a disposition of the lands as would fill the space assigned the new member of the Union with independent freeholders, the product of whose labors, after supporting themselves in comfort, would contribute to the necessary expenses of the local Government, and increase, by their consumption, the revenues of yours. Unless you did this, you did nothing. Your assignment of boundaries, your statutory provisions, would have been a mockery, if we had not, by almost miraculous exertions, broke the shackles imposed on our progress, and supplied, by the energy of our scanty population, the want of numbers, which your laws denied us. You forgot that population, as well as soil, was necessary. You forgot the lesson taught by a Greek, and elegantly paraphrased by a British poet—

"What constitutes a STATE?
    Not high raised battlement, nor labored mound,
  Thick wall or moated gate.

Not cities fair with spires and turrets crown'd,
Not bays and broad armed ports,
    Where, laughing at the storm, rich navies ride!
Not starr'd and spangled courts,
    Where low bowed baseness wafts perfume to pride!
No! MEN! high minded MEN!
    MEN who their duties know;
But know their rights, and, knowing, dare maintain,
    Prevent the long aimed blow.
And crush the tyrant when they burst the chain—
THESE CONSTITUTE A STATE!"

These your policy would have refused; but these Heaven had provided, by inspiring the little band which our scanty population could afford, and their few associates, with the energy, patriotism, and self devotion, which the moment of danger required. Think you, sir, that, if my constituents, instead of the noble minded men who flew to the standard of the country the moment its soil was invaded—who heroically and successfully contended against odds in discipline and numbers, and braved dangers, before which even high courage might quail—who can boast of having gained for the State the honor of that resolution on your statute book, which records, in terms to which they and their posterity may look with pride, that "the brave Louisianians are entitled to the thanks, and deserve well of the whole people of the United States"—an honor which, as yet, no other State has attained; if, instead of the enlightened people who gave the first example to their sister States, of providing a written code of laws, and will be the last to give them an example of dishonor, or want of attachment to the Union; if, instead of these, they had been the degraded vassals of arbitrary power, hugging rather than bursting their chain, incapable of appreciating the advantages of liberty and self government, such as their calumniators in and out of Congress represented them to be; I ask, sir, whether all the laws you could have passed would have enabled them to become a State, unless those laws, by rendering the acquisition of lands easy, should have supplied us with a race of independent, well informed cultivators of the soil—the bone and sinew of every State?

You have left us for this, to our own resources; you have done worse; by denying the power of trying our titles, you have deprived us of those to which we are legally entitled, independently of your laws; and you have for twenty-five years forced the proprietors of grants to contribute to the support of the State Government according to the value of their lands, while you, by unfounded claims, prevent them making any use of them.

In these, as is the case in most unjust measures, the interest of those who adopt them has been most materially injured. If our titles had been confirmed; if the lands had been surveyed and disposed of at low prices to actual settlers; if large allowances had been made out of them for public education and other useful institutions; if, while the lands remained unsold, the Government had subjected itself to the duties required of other land holders, it is no extravagant calculation to say that the State would have, at this day, contained a million of inhabitants, producing from the soil an excess above their own consumption of forty millions of dollars, and, if there be any truth in the calculations of political economy, paying annually, by the duties on their consumption, according to the present rates, more than ten times as much as the aggregate sales of all your lands have produced in any one year.

As I said, sir, I confine my remarks to my own State, and I consider the policy pursued with respect to the lands it contains as unjust, narrow, unwise, and in the highest degree injurious to the Union. If, twenty years ago, the lands had been parcelled out to actual settlers according to the policy pursued by the French and Spanish possessors of the province, without exacting any consideration, I have not the slightest doubt that, in a mere pecuniary point of view, it would have been the wisest measure, and that, through your Custom-house, you would, as long as you chose to continue your duties, receive more dollars and cents twenty fold than you will annually receive in the comparatively few years that your lands in the State will be on sale. It is because I think it not too late to change this policy that I have seized this occasion to expose it. Confirm all our just titles, submit those of which you doubt to the Judiciary, endow all our public institutions liberally, remember that you deprive us of laying taxes for this purpose by condemning to sterility six-sevenths of the land in the State. Supply this defect, rescue your own lands, and those of our citizens which adjoin yours, from the destructive effects of inundation, and connect us by canals and roads with the rest of the Union. Give, if you cannot sell, your lands to settlers, who will become consumers, and add to your revenue; who will be hardy and independent, and add to your strength; and who will form an iron frontier on your Southern and Western boundary, that will set invasion at defiance.

In asserting their rights, I address my just complaints to the Representatives of the people and the States. I trace our injuries to no section of country, to no party, to no particular men. I can make proper allowance for opinions that may have actuated all who advocated the different measures of which we complain, without imputing them to a marked and improper hostility. Constitutional scruples were entertained to our admission; they are removed. Doubts existed of our attachment to the Union, of our courage to defend it; they have been triumphantly destroyed. Our ability for self-government was made a question, but our legislation has long since solved it. Now, therefore, we look for justice, and I trust, Sir, that we shall not look in vain.

Having finished what I thought myself obliged to say on the policy pursued with respect to the State, I have tried to find some chain by which this subject might be connected with another, to which frequent allusions have been made—the existence of present, and the history of past parties in our Legislature. This I have found it difficult to do, unless from the consideration that, in popular governments, party connects itself with every thing;—nothing too high or too low, too grave or too trivial; from a construction of the Constitution to the merits of an actor; from the election of a president to that of a constable. It is not surprising, therefore, that party views may at times have mixed themselves with the measures pursued by the General Government towards the Western States. But I cannot willingly bring myself to believe that there is a party permanently, and on principle, hostile to the prosperity of those States. Allusions have been made to those which formerly divided us, and which are still, under other names, supposed to exist. It may be useful to examine their nature, and refer to their history. It is quite obvious that parties must exist in all popular governments, and not less so, that they are, when not carried to excess, useful, and even necessary; but we must carefully observe their different kinds. The first and most important is that which divides the supporters of general tenets on the construction of the powers of government, or of any of its branches, from the opposers of those tenets; these being from their nature permanent, and occurring in almost every operation of the Government, form, until their doctrines are fully established, or finally given up, a marked line of division between all who take any part in public affairs; there can be in the nature of things no neutrals; every man who has any opinion, or even acts on those of others, must be united with one or the other of these parties; and when they are thus arrayed, great sacrifices of individual opinion must be made in matters of minor importance, in order to secure strength in those which regard the great question. Hence we find, that, whenever the country is divided by a permanent party of this kind, it brings within its vortex every measure of government, and that useful laws are opposed by the one party, and injurious measures favored by the other, from the effect that the one or the other will have in gaining proselytes, or preserving friends.

Whenever such great party division ceases to exist, it is generally replaced by those which are formed for the elevation or depression of particular men, or the support or opposition to particular measures. These last having no permanent principle to rest upon, continually change with the men, and the operations which they purport to favor or oppose. Opposition in both these parties is extremely useful; the first, to preserve the Government pure in its organization, the other in its operations.

The establishment of our present happy Constitution (happy unless corrupted by false constructions, or torn by mad and ruinous resistance,) was preceded by the contest of two parties, whose names (not a common occurrence) designated their principles, and the object for which they respectively contended. It was general, and founded on principle; the one contending for a radical change in the confederation of the States—these were designated as federalists; the other, opposed to this change—who were styled anti-federalists. When the States had agreed to the Constitution, this party became extinct; the object on the one side having been completely established, and the opposition on the other generally abandoned. Coeval with the operations of the new government, arose a new party, of the same general permanent kind, because it was founded on a contrariety of opinion on the powers of the new government. Among those who had most zealously promoted its adoption, were men of high talents, who strove in its formation to give it a character of greater energy, and increase its powers at the expense of those of the States; being obliged to yield many of their ideas to those of others, who thought it too energetic as it was, they compromised with their opponents, and agreed to the Constitution as it is, or, rather, as it was before the amendments. It was natural that men entertaining those ideas, should put every construction on the words of the compact that would bring it nearer to, what they thought, the point of perfection. Men of equal eminence and abilities had co-operated as indefatigably in procuring the adoption, but from a conviction that the powers given to the Federal Government, strictly construed, were sufficient for all national purposes; that any extension of them would be injurious, if not ruinous; and that no construction or direct change should be permitted that would lessen the power or influence of the State Governments. These last description of federalists were naturally joined by the individuals who had formed the extinct party of anti-federalists; and, together, under the name of the REPUBLICAN PARTY, they watched the movements, and opposed the suspicious measures of those whom I have first designated, and who retained the name of FEDERALISTS.

The first and most dangerous principle, sometimes avowed by the federal party, but generally acted upon, was that under the construction of the words in the preamble, that the object of the Constitution was to promote the *general welfare*, and the use of the same phrase in the power to lay taxes on any object which promoted the general welfare of the United States, unless expressly inhibited, was included. The direct operation of this interpretation in consolidating the General Government, and annihilating the power of the States, was evident, and the avowal of it alarming. Besides this, there were many incidents which, to minds already excited by more important opinions and events, created suspicions of a design to change the forms, as well as the substance, of the new Government; and which, although by one party considered "trifles light as air," were by the other thought to be "confirmation strong as proofs from holy writ." The President having opened the session by a speech to both Houses, as was then, and for twelve years continued to be, the mode, one of the first subjects of deliberation in the Senate was the style by which he should be addressed in their answer. A committee was appointed to consider this subject, and they reported that the President should be styled HIS HIGHNESS. The democratic branch, however, insisted on calling him simply what the people had made him—the President of the United States; and the Senate, yielding to the necessity of the moment, came to the following resolution:

IN THE SENATE OF THE UNITED STATES, MAY 14, 1789.

The committee, appointed the 9th instant, "to consider and report under what title it will be proper for the Senate to address the President of the United States of America," reported, that, in the opinion of the committee, it will be proper thus to address the President: HIS HIGHNESS THE PRESIDENT OF THE UNITED STATES OF AMERICA, AND PROTECTOR OF THEIR LIBERTIES.

Which report was postponed, and the following resolve was agreed to, to wit:

From a decent respect for the opinion and practice of civilized nations, whether under monarchical or republican forms of government, whose custom is to annex titles of respectability to the office of their Chief Magistrates; and that, on intercourse with foreign nations, a due respect for the majesty of the people of the United States may not be hazarded by an appearance of singularity, the Senate have been induced to be of opinion, that it would be proper to annex a respectable title to the office of the President of the United States; but the Senate, desirous of preserving harmony with the House of Representatives, where the practice lately observed in presenting an address to the President was without the addition of titles, think it proper, *for the present*, to act in conformity with the practice of that House. Therefore,

Resolved, That the *present* address be *"To the President of the United States,"* without addition of title.

A motion was made to strike out the preamble as far as the words "but the Senate;" which passed in the negative; and, on motion for the main question, it passed in the affirmative.

By which you will perceive that, as the resolution has never been further acted upon, we may to-morrow confirm the report of the committee, and decorate our President with the princely title of Highness, and the ominous appellation of *Protector*. One other incident which I remember, took place in the gay world of which my youth then made me a denizen. The citizens of New York, among other marks of hospitality and desire to show a proper attention to the Great Man, who had just reluctantly given up his retirement at the unanimous voice of his fellow citizens, gave a grand inauguration ball; on the ceremonial of which it was said one, at least, of those who afterwards composed his cabinet, was consulted. But though he came from the Eastward, I do not mean to say that this was an Eastern measure. In a conspicuous part of the large ball room was erected a superb canopy, and under the canopy was placed what the ill-natured democrats called a throne; whether it was or not, not having had the honor to see one, I cannot tell. Napoleon said, a throne is a block of wood covered with velvet. This was a small sofa or a large chair, covered with some costly material, and on it they induced the President to sit; and when the music sounded for the dance, every couple, before they took their station in the long column of the country dances, then in fashion, were directed to go up and make a low obeisance, to the great annoyance of the President, who is said, when he quitted the seat, (in which he had thus reluctantly and by surprise been placed) thus to have addressed the contrivers of the ceremonial, with some warmth: "You have made a fool of me once; but I will take care you never do it again." Such fooleries, Sir, are hardly worth relating, but they are characteristic of the views of parties—at least they were thought so then. *Hae nugae*, said the democrats, (or such of them as understood Latin) *seria ducent*, and many of the more apprehensive thought they saw royalty typified in these signs of the times. These imaginary fears soon gave way; but others of greater reality succeeded them. Circumstances of historical notoriety influenced the minds of both parties with foreign predilections and animosities; and the federal party, which had constantly been predominant in Congress, sealed their construction of the powers of the General Government by the passage of the alien law and the sedition law. Nothing could exceed the indignation which these practical applications of the federal doctrine excited in the minds of their opponents. An attack on the liberty of the press, not only unauthorized, but forbidden by the Constitution by the one act, the arbitrary power vested in the President by the other, opened the eyes of the people to the principles of the party by which they were passed, and, at the very next election, they were deprived of a power they had so grossly abused. Having mentioned the alien law, let me stop to perform an act of justice to deceased worth. In the first stages of that bill, for it was hurried through the House, I was absent from the seat with which I was then honored in the House of Representatives. I returned on the day set for its third reading. Before I went to the House, I met with a Senator from Virginia,* who, notwithstanding the disparity of our years, honored me with his friendship, sometimes instructed me by his advice, and always stimulated me by his example. The conversation naturally turned on the measure depending before the House; and he detailed to me its provisions, spoke with his usual animation of its unconstitutional features, and inspired me with his own indignation against its attack on the liberty of the nation. Warmed with this conversation, I went to the House and made a speech in opposition to the bill, which was at the time spoken of with applause, and sometimes attracts attention even now; but whatever of merit it had, was owing to the circumstance I have related; and I might address him who urged me to declare my sentiments on the occasion, in the words of the poet to his muse—

Quod spiro et placeo (si placeo) tuum est.

The country has since been deprived of the services of that Senator, but she has the consolation to know that the mantle of his patriotism, talents, and virtues, has fallen on his son and successor in this body.

I have given you, Sir, so much of the history and state of parties as was necessary for the understanding of the refutation I must make of a charge

---

* The late Mr. Tazewell. [Henry Tazewell served as a Senator from Virginia from December 29, 1794, until his death, January 24, 1799.]

brought against me, and those with whom it was my happiness to associate, and will always be my pride to have acted in those times. I repeat the charge, verbatim, from the printed speech of the Senator from Massachusetts (Mr. WEBSTER.) Speaking of the merits of New England, which I, at least, have never attempted to lessen, he says he "will not rake into the rubbish of by-gone times to blot the escutcheon of any State, any party, or any part of the country;" yet, Sir, in the same page, he endeavors to fix a blot of the blackest ingratitude on a party, on men (I do not speak, Sir, of myself,) who have rendered most important services to the country, to one of whom it has given the highest mark of its confidence and esteem, and all of whom were, in the transaction alluded to, much more sinned against than sinning. The honorable gentleman goes on to say: "Gen. Washington's administration was steadily and zealously maintained, as we all know, by New England. It was violently opposed elsewhere. We know in what quarter he had most earnest, constant, and persevering support in all his great and leading measures. We know where his private and personal character was held in the highest degree of attachment and veneration; and we know too where his measures were opposed, his services slighted, and his character vilified. We know, or we might know, if we turn to the journals, who expressed respect, gratitude, and regret, when he retired from the Chief Magistracy; and who refused to express respect, gratitude, or regret—I shall not open these journals."

Sir, the honorable gentleman would have done well to open the journals, or not to have referred to them. If he had opened them, he would have found the name of the individual who addresses you arrayed with those of men more worthy of note, in the vote to which he alludes. If he had opened the debates which led to that vote, as I think he ought to have done, he would have seen how utterly void of foundation is the charge he has brought. I do not think the gentleman intended any personal allusion to me; the terms of civility on which we are, forbid it—the consciousness of having said nothing to provoke the attack forbids it; but, Sir, the individual, who cannot arrogate to himself sufficient importance to justify the supposition that he was the object intended, was, at that time, the representative, the sole representative, of the first commercial city in the Union. That individual is now one of the members of this body, representing a sovereign State. He owes it, therefore, to those who have offered him these marks of their confidence, to show that they were not unworthily bestowed; he owes it to himself to disprove the reflection which the allegation casts on his character. Suffer me, also, Mr. President, to remark, that this very charge was used during the late election; and that the refutation I am about to give was so widely diffused that it is somewhat singular it should never have come to the Senator's knowledge, or that he should have forgotten it if it had. Yet one or the other must have been the case, or he would not now have repeated the tale, nor, by incorporating it in his eloquent harangue, have given new currency to a refuted calumny which had long before been nailed to the counter. Since the honorable gentleman believes the tale to be true, and surely he would not otherwise repeat it, hundreds of others must give it the like credit; and it increases the obligation I am under to explain all the circumstances attending it.

I have shown, Sir, what were the doctrines and measures of the federal party at that time; during the whole of the Presidency of Washington they were predominant in both Houses; and as Washington was the head of the Government, one of their greatest objects was, to cover all their proceedings with the popularity of his name; to represent all opposition to their measures, as personal hostility to him; and to force the republican party either to approve all their measures, or, by opposing them, incur the odium of being unfriendly to the Father of his Country. In this they were for the most part defeated. The universal confidence reposed in the high character of Washington, the gratitude felt for his services, the veneration for his name, had practically produced the effect, in our Government, which a constitutional maxim has in that of England. He could not, it was believed, do wrong—most certainly he never meant wrong—most certainly his ardent wishes were for the happiness of the country he had conducted through so many perils, and the preservation of that form of government which had been adopted under his auspices. Yet measures were adopted, during his Presidency, which a very large proportion of the country thought injurious to their interests, and, on one occasion, a majority of their Representatives deemed them to be an infringement on their privileges. None of these were ascribed to the President; a practice which he introduced, enabled us to ascribe to his administration (to which in truth they belonged) all the measures of which we disapproved. The practice alluded to, was that of assembling the Heads of Department in a Cabinet Council, and being guided, as was generally understood, by the opinion of a majority in all important concerns. Hence the official acts of the President came to be considered as those of his Cabinet, and were, in common parlance, called the acts of the administration, and they were opposed, when it was deemed necessary, and canvassed, and freely spoken of in debate, without any hostility being felt, or supposed to be felt, towards the

President. Indeed, several of those most prominent in opposition to acts of the administration, were men for whom Washington had the highest esteem, and who were among those who most admired and revered *him*.

Of the acts to which the republican party were opposed, it may be necessary to specify some, in order to show that the opposition was not a frivolous or a personal one.

The Chief Justice of the United States was sent as a Minister Plenipotentiary to England, while he held his Judicial office, which he retained until after his return. Thus, in our opinion, blending the Executive and Judicial departments, directed by the Constitution to be separated, and setting an example which might create an undue influence on the bench, in favor of the Executive.

This minister negotiated a treaty which contained stipulations requiring the agency of the House of Representatives, in the exercise of their constitutional powers over the subject of them, to carry into effect. To enable them discreetly to exercise these powers, the House respectfully requested the communication of such papers, in relation to the treaty, as could, without injury to our foreign relations, be made public. This request, the President was advised to refuse; and the refusal was grounded on a denial of the constitutional right of the House to exercise any discretion in carrying the treaty into effect. On this refusal, the House of Representatives passed a resolution declaratory of the right which the President had denied. I will not trouble the Senate with adverting to any other measures which I, and those who acted with me, opposed. We opposed them, Sir, without, in any instance, forgetting the sentiments of respect, gratitude, and high admiration, which were due to the name and character of Washington. We believed that it would have been a dereliction of duty to give up the independent expression of that opinion, because it was contrary to measures falsely ascribed to a name they revered; and conscious of the weight of that name. I may, without vanity, say, there was some degree of merit in stemming the tide of popularity that was attached to it.

The mission of Mr. Jay took place after the second election of General Washington, and the discussion on the treaty, in the first session of the fourth Congress, the seventh year of his Presidency. In his speech on the opening of the second session of the same Congress, (I repeat, sir, what I formerly wrote on this occasion) he alluded in affecting terms to his approaching retirement from office. I can solemnly say for myself, that, on this occasion, so far from any ill feeling towards the President, none among those who arrogated to themselves the title of his exclusive friends,

could feel more sincerely, or were more disposed to express every sentiment of gratitude for his services, admiration for his character, or wishes
for his happiness, than I was. These were ideas that had grown up with me
from childhood. I had never heard the name of Washington pronounced
but with veneration by those near relatives who were engaged with him in
the same perilous struggle. Independence, liberty, and victory, were associated with it in my mind; and the awful admiration with which, when yet a
boy, I was first admitted to his presence, yielded only to the more rational
sentiments of gratitude and national pride, when, at a maturer age, I could
appreciate his services, and estimate the honor his virtues and character
had conferred on the nation. I had seen him in the hour of peril, when the
contest was doubtful, and when his life and reputation, as well as the liberties of the country, depended on the issue. I had seen him in the moment of triumph, when the surrender of a hostile army had secured that
independence. My admiration followed him in his first retreat, and was
not lessened by his quitting it to give the aid of his name and influence to
the union of the States under an efficient government. In addition to this,
he had received me with kindness in my youthful visits to his camp; and,
without having it in my power to boast of any particular intimacy, circumstances had thrown me frequently in the way of receiving from him such
attentions as indicated some degree of regard. With these motives for
joining in the most energetic expressions of gratitude, with a heart filled
with sentiments of veneration, and desirous of recording them, my concern can scarcely be expressed, when I found that I must be debarred from
joining my voice with those of my fellow-citizens in expressing those feelings, unless, in the same breath, I should pronounce a recantation of principles which I then thought, and still think, were well founded, and
declare that I approved measures which I had just solemnly declared I
thought injurious to the country.

Thus, Sir, it was contrived. At that period, the President opened the
session by a speech, (the more convenient mode of sending a message having been introduced five years afterwards by Mr. Jefferson,) and the House
made an answer, which they presented in a body. The answer on this occasion was most artfully and most ably drawn. It was the work of a federal
committee, and was supported by a federal majority. It contained, as it
ought to have contained, every expression that gratitude, veneration, and
affectionate regret, could suggest; and to the adoption of these there would
not have been a dissenting voice; it would have been carried, not only
unanimously, but by acclamation. But the dominant party had other

views; it was to be made the instrument of degrading their opponents, if they could vote for it, or of holding them up to all posterity as opposers of the Saviour of his Country if they refused to pronounce their own condemnation. They preferred a paltry party triumph to the glory of the man they professed to honor, and deprived him of the expression of an unanimous vote, that they might have some pretence to stigmatize their opponents with ingratitude. The press, sir, the omnipotent press, and the publicity of our debates, have enabled me, even at this distant day, to defeat this unworthy end—unworthy of the honorable men who contrived and executed it, and which nothing but the madness of party would have suggested to them.

To understand this fully, Sir, I should read to you the whole of the address. Its general character I have stated. But I will confine myself to one or two passages, which show what was endeavored to be forced upon us, and the amendments offered will show what we were willing to say; and I will then ask who it was that refused a unanimous expression of gratitude, respect, and merit?

The debates of that period were very concisely taken down; but (in Carpenter's debate, p. 62) we find enough for our purpose. It is there stated that Mr. Livingston expressed his sorrow "that the answer was not so drawn as to avoid this debate, and his sincere hope that parties would so unite as to make it agreeable to all. He moved some amendments, first, to correct an error in the phraseology, which were adopted; and, in the course of his remarks, used these expressions: 'He hoped, notwithstanding the tenacity of adherence to words, that all might agree in the address; he would be extremely hurt, he said, could he conceive *that we differed in sentiments of gratitude and admiration for that great man*; but, while he was desirous to express this, he could not do it at the expense of his feelings and principles. The former he might sacrifice, but the latter he could not to any man.' "

I invite the particular attention of the Senate to the passage which I proposed to alter as it stood in the address; it was in these words:

"And while we entertain a grateful conviction that your *wise, firm,* and *patriotic administration* has been signally conducive to the success of the present form of government, we cannot forbear to express the deep sensations of REGRET with which we contemplate your intended retirement from office." Now, sir, mark what were the words objected to in this sentence; bear in mind the distinctions that have been drawn between the character of the President, and that of his *administration;*—remember what was the sense in which that word was universally used at the day; recollect, too, what I have just said of the opposition to one of the leading measures of that *administration*, and you will then be enabled to judge whether I, and those with whom I acted, could give our assent to this passage as it stood. To show, however, that, while we could not, with consistency or truth, say, that the measures of the cabinet were wise and patriotic, but that we were perfectly willing to use these epithets as applied to the President, I moved to strike out the words "wise, firm, and patriotic administration," and insert "your wisdom, firmness, and patriotism;" the sentence then would have read thus: "while we entertain a grateful conviction, that *your wisdom, firmness, and patriotism,* have been signally conducive to the success of the present form of Government, we cannot forbear to express the DEEP sensations of REGRET, with which we contemplate your intended retirement from office." Now, sir, compare this clause, which we were all ready to vote for, and did vote for, with that which was supported by the majority; and say which of them expresses the greatest veneration for the person, and the personal character of Washington— that which ascribes wisdom, firmness, and patriotism, to the measures of his cabinet, or that which attaches them to himself. Say whether we refused to express *regret* at his retirement, when that word, accompanied by an epithet most expressive of its intensity, is readily adopted. Say who were the real friends to the glory of our great leader in war, and director in peace—those who, for a paltry party triumph, deprived him of an unanimous expression of thanks and admiration, who forced him to appear rather as the chief of a party, than in his true character of the man uniting all affections, regretted, beloved, venerated by all his fellow citizens; or those who intreated that, on this occasion at least, party considerations should be laid aside, and that they might be permitted to join their voice to that of their country, and of the world, in expressing the sentiments with which their hearts were filled. Say, finally, Sir, whether the Senator from Massachusetts is justified in the allegation, that we refused to express respect, gratitude, and regret, on the retirement of Washington; or what is more than insinuated, that we slighted his services and vilified his character. Sir, the register I have quoted shows, that I supported my amendment by expressing the very sentiments you have just heard; and I must add, that, shortly after this transaction, while my votes, speeches, and conduct, were fresh in the recollection of my constituents, my term of service expired, and I was re-elected by an increased majority. Would a man, entertaining the sentiments of Washington that have been ascribed to me, have received the votes of a city where his name was adored. Nay, more sir; one of the most conspicuous of those who have incurred the reproach of the Senator from Massachusetts, and for whose sole use it was perhaps designed—the President of the United States—was not long since selected, by the veteran reliques of the Revolutionary war; the chosen companions in arms of their venerated commander; the New York Society of Cincinnati—as one of the very few honorary members to whom that distinction has been bestowed. They have, since that, done me the same honor. Would the venerable remnant of the friends and companions of Washington, associated under his auspices for the purpose of cherishing the friendships contracted during the contest he so gloriously conducted, and watching over his fame, so inseparably connected with their own—would they have conferred this distinction on two men, who had, at any period of their lives, shown themselves his enemies or detractors? Me, sir, they knew from my childhood; my whole life was before them. At the time these votes were given, I was their immediate representative. Many of them were opposed to me in the politics of the day, but they knew my conduct to have been such as I have described, and they did justice to my motives; and most assuredly, would not have joined in my unanimous association to their honorable body, had they doubted the purity of either.

In the course of this defensive part of my address to the Senate, I have been obliged to refer, with some minuteness, to the state of parties at a remote period. I have done so with no desire to renew forgotten animosities, or impute injurious designs to the living or the dead. The latter consideration has induced me to stop short of the scenes which occurred in this place, in the first session that was held here; much of what I know, more of what I heard, would have this tendency if detailed. Designs of the most violent and disorganizing kind were ascribed to some of the Federal party, in a letter bearing the signature of one of its distinguished members; but which was attributed to mistake by another, a no less respectable leading man of the same party, both of them since deceased. It does not enter into my purpose to determine between them. I had a high respect for both, and an intimacy with one, which was never interrupted by our difference in political tenets; in truth, I had, during the whole course of those violent times, the good fortune to preserve the most friendly intercourse with most of my principal political opponents. I thought their political principles dangerous; and they thought my ideas of government inefficient; but we did justice to the purity of each other's motives, and preserved social harmony amid party discord. It is far, therefore, I repeat, from my intention, to renew heats which are now allayed by a reference to the olden times of party; but I referred to them because they were necessary to my defence. Because, having left the Atlantic states soon after the triumph of the republican party in 1800, I thought, on my return to public life, after a retirement of more than twenty years—I thought I discovered some of the great dogmas of federalism prevailing in our public councils; and thinking them always dangerous, I felt it a duty to take this occasion to guard against their revival. Engaged during my absence in professional pursuits, and wholly absorbed by them, I had not marked the changes of political parties or events. I knew not even the appellations by which they were distinguished; but in whatever shape the old dangerous federal doctrine of assuming all power under the claim of providing for the general welfare, may have appeared; under whatever colors its partisans may enroll themselves, *quocunque nomine gaudent,* federalists, federal republican, or *national* federalists, I now do and ever will hold it a paramount duty to discover and oppose their doctrines. I know that many who belonged to the federal party, never did entertain this dangerous opinion; I believe that many who did entertain, have abjured it; I most sincerely hope they all have; and thinking this a favorable occasion to produce a disclaimer of them, I have seized it to submit the propriety of doing so. Should this doctrine be formally abandoned here, one great source of suspicion and ill feeling will be destroyed; and when that is done, enough will remain to satisfy the most zealous lover of party.

These, Mr. President, were some of my reasons for speaking of the history of party under our Government. I had another. It was to mark the difference between the necessary, and, if I may so express it, the legitimate parties existing in all free Governments, founded on differences of opinion in fundamental principles, or an attachment to, or dislike of, particular measures and particular men; between these and that spirit of dissension into which they are apt to degenerate: to throw the weight of my experience, and the little my opinions may have, in the scale, and lift up a warning voice against the indulgence of the passions which lead to them, the allusions that irritate, the personal reflections that embitter debate, and the altercations that debase it. The spirit of which I speak originates in the most trifling as well as the most important circumstances. The liberties of a nation or the color of a cockade are sufficient to excite it. It creates imaginary, and magnifies real causes of complaint; arrogates to itself every virtue—denies every merit to its opponents; secretly entertains the worst designs—publicly imputes them to its adversaries: poisons domestic happiness with its dissensions; assails the character of the living with calumny, and, invading the very secrets of the grave with its viperous slanders, destroys the reputations of the dead; harangues in the market place; disputes at the social board; distracts public councils with unprincipled propositions and intrigues; embitters their discussions with invective and recrimination, and degrades them by personalities and vulgar abuse; seats itself on the bench; clothes itself in the robes of justice; soils the purity of the ermine, and poisons the administration of justice in its source; mounts the pulpit, and, in the name of a God of mercy and peace, preaches discord and vengeance; invokes the worst scourges of Heaven, war, pestilence, and famine, as preferable alternatives to party defeat: blind, vindictive, cruel, remorseless, unprincipled, and at last frantic, it communicates its madness to friends as well as foes; respects nothing, fears nothing; rushes on the sword; braves the dangers of the ocean; and would not be turned from its mad career by the majesty of Heaven itself, armed with its tremendous thunders.

The *tristes irae* of the poet—

> ———Quas neque noricus
> Deterret ensis, nec mare naufragum,
> Nec saevus ignis, nec tremendo
> Jupiter ipse ruens tumultu.

And to which, with an elegance of expression and profundity of thought rarely united, he ascribes the ruin of republics—

> ———Et altis urbibus ultimae
> Stetere causae cur perirent
> Funditus, imprimeretque muris
> Hostile aratrum exercitus insolens.

Yes, sir, the poet tells us true. These few lines contain a most important lesson. Not long before he wrote them, there existed a confederacy of independent States, united, as ours are, by the same religion, language, manners, and laws. Fair cities, adorned with noble edifices, decorated by the miracles of the imitative arts, governed by wise magistrates, and defended by intrepid warriors—where sages gave lessons of morality and wisdom—poured forth their numerous inhabitants at stated seasons to assist at solemn games, where poets sung, and historians read their instructive pages, to admiring crowds; where the young contended for the prize of agility or strength, and the old recounted their former exploits; where the wisdom, and valor, and talent, and beauty, of each State, were the boast and pride of the whole. What followed? Civil dissension breathed its poisonous influence over them, and they met to contend, not for the peaceful prizes of dexterity or genius, but in the deadly strife of civil war. Where are their magnificent temples, their theatres, their statues of gods and heroes? They have vanished: they have been swept by the besom of destruction! The ploughshare of devastation has been driven over their walls, and their mighty ruins remain as monumental warnings to free States, of the danger of falling into the excess of party rage.

From these evils may Heaven, in its mercy, preserve our beloved country: but, that this prayer may be heard, we must begin by correcting in ourselves every approach of the passions which lead to them. Is there no danger? Have no symptoms appeared to justify a fear that too great an excitement has been already produced by no sufficient cause? I am no censor of the conduct of others: it is sufficient for me to watch over my own. The wisdom of gentlemen must be their guide in the sentiments they entertain, and their discretion in the language in which they utter them. No doubt they think the occasion calls for the warmth they have shown; but of this the people must judge; and, that they may judge with impartiality, let the facts which have drawn forth the invectives we have heard, be fairly submitted to them.

We have heard much of supposed lines of division in this body. "This side of the House" and "the other side," "majority" and "minority," "opposition" and "administration," are as familiarly mentioned as if they were universally understood. Now, sir, I profess my ignorance. In what cause have the Senators of the United States arranged themselves into different bodies, and arrayed themselves under adverse banners? If the dangerous doctrine of undefined and undefinable powers in the General Government be assumed as the watchword; if the dormant—I had thought the extinct—principles of persecuting federalism are to be revived let it be declared; and I, for one, will not hesitate on which side of the party line I shall be found. As yet, sir, I see no constitutional question of a permanent nature to divide us. We undoubtedly think differently of particular measures, and have our preferences for particular men: these, surely, can not arrange us into any but temporary divisions, lasting no longer than while the election of the man is pending, or the debate on the measure continues. The election has been long decided. Do gentlemen understand that, because they preferred

another candidate, they are to form an opposition to all measures he recommends, or to all appointments he has made? Do they imagine that those
who supported him in his election are, in this House, to form a separate
party for the indiscriminate approbation of all he may advise or do? Of
their own intentions, gentlemen are the best judges: they must think for
themselves, and draw what lines they choose for their own conduct; but, for
one, sir, I inform them they cannot do so for me. I shall now, as I have always done, exercise my own judgment, guided by the instruction I receive
from debate, on all important measures. I gave to the election of the present
Chief Magistrate all the aid which my vote and little influence could give.
My own knowledge of facts enabled me to refute many slanders: my intimate acquaintance with his character and services gave some weight to the
testimony by which I cleared them from misrepresentation. I thought him
entitled to the place, because he possessed talents which eminently qualified him to execute its duties; because he had rendered services such as but
one man had ever before rendered to the country: because I had witnessed
the energy, courage, prudence, and talent, by which he saved the State I
represent from the worst of desolations. These were my inducements for
his support during the first election when he was a candidate. The decision
of that election, in favor of a man having a fewer number of votes, was calculated to embitter the minds of his friends, and make them hostile to the
successful candidate. Yet, Sir, during his Presidency, I gave a practical proof
of the profession I now make: a measure of great importance was proposed
by his administration—I mean the Panama mission; I thought great good
might result from it, and, although it was violently opposed by those with
whom I had acted in the election, I not only voted for, but supported it by
argument, I then thought, and I still think, that its nature and object were
both of them misrepresented or misunderstood; and that, if the assembly
had taken place as it was first proposed, our envoys attending in a diplomatic, not a representative character, might, by their influence and advice,
have prevented many dissensions that have since distracted those republics;
might have introduced stipulations favorable to commerce, social intercourse, and the great interests of humanity. My reasons for that vote are
published. And the fact, that, although one of the warmest friends of the
unsuccessful candidate, and one of those who felt the deepest regret when
his opponent was declared to be elected, I yet supported such measures of
his administration as I approved when they were opposed by my political
friends, ought to be a sure pledge of my sincerity when I say, that I will support no important measure that I disapprove, merely because it is one of the

present administration. I have not, however, the passions avowed by the honorable Senator from Maine, (Mr. HOLMES) who told us, if I understood him, that he had always been and always wished to be, in a minority. [Mr. HOLMES explained, he did not say he desired to be in a minority, but that he believed he always would be.] Mr. LIVINGSTON continued: It seems I have not repeated the words used by the honorable Senator, which I regret; but the sense is the same. If he has always been in a minority it must have been a matter of choice, otherwise, in the ups and downs of his congressional life, in the turns of the political wheel, it must have so happened, that, for a short time, at least, he must have been uppermost; if so, it struck me as a singular predilection. But there is no disputing about tastes; and the Senator has, at least, one great precedent for his:

Victrix causa diis placuit, sed victa Catoni.

and I am sure he cannot be offended by my classing him with the stern republican, who would not survive the liberties of his country, as a fitter associate than the nameless one offered to him by my friend from Tennessee. But, Sir, neither the example of Cato nor of the Senator tempt me. I am contented with the *victrix causa;* contending for what I think right, I like to see it succeed. On this occasion I have as yet had no cause to repent my choice; nor have the charges, urged with so much warmth against the measures of the President, changed the opinion I had formed of his talents to conduct the affairs of the nation with honor, advantage, and success. I listened to them attentively, resolved to weigh calmly, and determine impartially on all that could be urged. Sir, I expected a like disposition in those who have expressed their disapprobation; I expected a detail of facts supported by proof, and of calm and clear deductions from those facts; need I say that I have been mistaken? When I heard from the Senator from Maine, "that this administration had glutted its vengeance upon the purest patriots on earth; that no *age, condition,* or *sex,* had escaped; that the sins of the fathers had been visited upon the children to the third and fourth generation; that innocence, virtue, patriotism, had *all, all* been swept into the gulf of misery," and listened to the impressive tone in which the eloquent Senator from Delaware reprobated the spirit of *oriental despotism,* which had displaced deputy postmasters, and recalled unoffending ministers from abroad, need I repeat that I was disappointed? Now I ask—will not the country ask—what is there to justify such exaggerated invective?—language that might be applied to the tyranny of Nero or

Caracalla, but which is evidence of nothing but a heated imagination when used to express disapprobation of removals from, and appointments to, office. But let us, Sir, before we catch the infection of this fever, while our pulse still beats evenly, and our heads are cool, examine calmly into the oppressions of the Executive which have excited this patriotic fervor. The honourable Senator from Maine did not deign a single specification, except one, which I confess I cannot fully comprehend—this bloody administration which, in its savage warfare, spares neither *men, women,* nor *children,* has visited, in its vengeance, the sins of the fathers upon the *third* and *fourth generation* of their descendants. Now, Sir, I cannot comprehend what offence the *great great grandfather* of any one of the removed officers, who must have lived in the reign of Queen Ann, could have given to the President, or any one in his administration—this, I confess, puzzles me.

The Senator from Delaware has been more explicit: and from his address, to which I listened with great pleasure, I gathered that these were the grounds of complaint.

That the principles of the administration are destructive of the liberties of the country. Such were the words used, as I noted them, and not without much surprise.

That the public treasure has been extravagantly and illegally expended.

That the press has been *subsidized* for party purposes.

That persons have been removed from office without the advice and consent of the Senate; the President having no constitutional right to do so.

That if there be such a right, it is illegal to exercise it without giving to the Senate the reasons for which the removals were made.

That removals have been made for no other cause than to satisfy the vengeance of the President, or for the purpose of rewarding his friends.

That he has made appointments out of the two Houses of Congress, and particularly out of the Senate, for the purpose of rewarding his friends.

Of each of these grave charges in its order.

First, (says the Senator from Delaware) the principles of the administration are destructive of the liberties of the people. By administration the Senator must mean here, and on other occasions, where he uses the term, the President: for, as far as I have understood, there is now no cabinet in the sense in which that word has been usually taken. If my information be correct, the words of the Constitution, and what I have always believed to be its true intent on this subject, have been pursued, rather than the example of former Presidents. The Constitution, in enumerating the rights and duties of the President, says, "he may require the opinion in writing of the principal officers in each of the Executive Departments, upon any subject relating to the duties of their respective offices." Instead of this, from the first organization of the Government, the Heads of Departments have been convened and converted into a cabinet council, not where, according to the Constitution, each was to give his opinion on the affairs of his own department, but where all were consulted on every difficult question relating to the affairs of each, or of the Government in general; and where, it has been generally understood, particularly during the presidency of Washington, that the President was guided by the voice of the majority and the responsibility of the Executive, so far as regarded public opinion, was, if not thrown on the cabinet, at least divided with them. Indeed, Sir, I know, that, at a long subsequent period, a most illegal and oppressive act, by which I was deeply injured, was justified as being done by the advice of the cabinet. Now, Sir, as I have said, there is no such cloak for Executive acts; the President performs the duties of his office and assumes the responsibility they incur. The *Cabinet,* a body unknown to the Constitution, does not exist. The chiefs of the Departments are consulted on the business of their respective offices; they are answerable to the President; and he, so far as he sanctions their acts, to the country. Of this, however, I have no further information than any other Senator has obtained, or may obtain.

In speaking of the administration of the Executive Department, therefore, it must be understood that gentlemen mean the acts of the President, or of his officers, sanctioned by him.

His principles, then, according to the charge, are subversive of the liberties of the people.

The only modes by which the principles of a man may be known, are either by his professions, or by a long course of action evincive of them. Submit the principles of the Executive to these tests. First, his professions. He has made two communications to us, and to the country—his inaugural address and his message at the opening of this session. Surely the gentleman does not mean to apply the epithet he has used to the principles avowed in either of these instruments; if he does, the voice of the whole people of the United States, re-echoed from foreign nations, will contradict him; the principles there announced, as those by which he will be guided, are, an adherence to the Constitution of the United States, a respect for those of the individual States, economy, justice, liberty, equal protection to industry, manufactures, and trade, and a strict enforcement of the laws at home, and the extension of commerce; the observance of treaties, the assertion of our rights, and the establishment of a good understanding with all nations abroad. Which of these principles, thus professed, are subversive of the liberties of the people? if any, let them be pointed out. The charge then is not justified by any principle openly professed. Examine the other source. Can those principles be discovered by his course of conduct? Observe, Sir, that this is a sweeping accusation of evincing dangerous principles; any single improper act, even if it could be substantiated, would not justify it; it may be in contradiction to his professions, it may be injurious, but, unless persevered in, or followed up by others, they can be accounted for only by supposing that they were dictated by such principles, it does not justify the charge.

The present Chief Magistrate has been in office a year. During that time, he has assumed no new power; he has evinced no desire to enlarge those confided to him by the Constitution; and if, in their exercise, he has not exactly followed the march which the Senator thinks the proper one; if he has selected for office those in whom he, and not the Senator, had confidence; if he has consulted his own, and not the Senator's, discretion; surely he ought not to be denounced as entertaining principles destructive of the liberties of the people. In examining the Constitution for the rules which were to direct his duties, he certainly found nothing written there by which he was bound to conform his own opinion to that of any Senator or any party. Where discretion is given to him, he has used it on his responsibility to the people; and the exercise of this discretion, even if it be not conformable to that which would have been suggested by the superior wisdom of those who arraign his conduct, cannot authorize them to call his *principles* in question. Where no discretion was given him, he has confined himself, as far as I have heard or observed, to the strictest rule of the Constitution and law.

Enough, then, and more than enough, in refutation of this vague and general charge. Let us come to those that are more specific.

The public treasure has been extravagantly and illegally expended.

It is not, under this head, even pretended that any other or greater sum has been taken or paid to any individual, than that which was due by law for the service or salary for which it was given. But comparisons are made between the amount of expenditure made under the last, and that made under the present administration. As applied to our Government, there cannot be a more fallacious rule for measuring the true economy or wisdom of the exercise of Executive functions. What has the President to do with the extravagance of the general expenditure? These are directed by legislative wisdom. But he must approve all laws! True, he must approve them; but remember, that, if there was any extravagance in the expenditures of the last year, his predecessor, not he, is answerable for it. He has not approved a single law under which a dollar was disbursed in the year 1829; and all of the contracts for the service of that year were made before he came into office. But, Sir, there was no extravagance in the appropriations; (for the contracts I will not vouch, because I am uninformed,) on the contrary, there was a marked, I will not say a designed, reduction of a usual and necessary appropriation for the contingent expenses of the foreign missions. In former estimates, this had been put at $25,000: in the estimate for 1829, it will be found, by deducting the salaries and outfits provided for, it was only $11,000.

But although I protest against his mode of testing the economy or profusion of the Executive, yet, as it has been relied on, let it be looked into, and it will be found that the expenditure of the year 1828 exceeded that of 1829 by more than $400,000; it is true that near $700,000, properly chargeable to the year '27, was expended in '28, for awards under the Convention with England, but this was balanced again by a payment of nearly the same sum in 1829, for expenditures for objects of internal improvement directed in the year 1828, and properly chargeable to that year.

But, Sir, I have done with these irrelevant calculations. If the criterion contended for was the true one, it would make in favor of the present Executive; but, in truth, it shows neither extravagance or profusion in that Department. It shows what the united legislative wisdom of the Union thought necessary to be expended, and it shows nothing more; and the truest economy is frequently found in the largest expenditure. This depends altogether on the object for which it is incurred.

There is, however, one branch of expenditure more immediately under the President's direction; which, indeed, like all other expenditures, must be provided for by law, but which, from its peculiar nature, demands a greater degree of confidence in the Executive than any other—I mean the expenses of our foreign intercourse. All negotiations with foreign Powers, being a part of Executive duty vested in the President, the nature of the service frequently forbids that previous disclosure, which is expected in every other case; and the estimates for this service, furnished by the Executive, are most generally followed by appropriations; in the estimates, the existing missions are enumerated, and if any new one is contemplated, which requires no secrecy, it is also mentioned, and, to provide for unforeseen cases, an appropriation for the contingent fund of missions abroad, made, and placed at the President's order; besides this, if the interest of the country should require that there should be an expense which the contingent fund should not cover, it must be left, as in the case of all other excess of expenditure over the appropriation, to be provided for under the head of "deficiencies in the appropriations" of the preceding year—an item to be found very frequently in the estimates; and, if well founded, always provided for by an appropriation. Here, again, the same reasoning which I have used with respect to the general annual expenditure, will apply to this particular head. It may be large, and not extravagant. The occasion must determine whether it was judicious or not; and, therefore, though again the comparison is greatly in favor of the present administration, yet I am, in candor, obliged to admit that this circumstance alone will not decide the question in favor of its economy as compared with that of its predecessors. That depends on other circumstances, and other inquiries must be made to determine their weight. But it would seem that, if the same number of missions be kept up, and some of them of an increased rank and expense; if additional expenditures have been incurred by the necessary change of ministers; and yet the whole expenditure is less than under the preceding missions, it would seem to follow, that, if all this now is done at a less expense than formerly occurred, there must have been a saving in some part of the expenditure under the present that did not exist under former administrations. Figures cannot deceive us; let us bring the question to that test, and compare the years 1817 and 1818 the two first of Mr. Monroe's administration; 1825 and 1826, the two first of Mr. Adams', and the last and the present years, the two first of General Jackson's. To the comparative view of the expenses of foreign intercourse, let us add that of the contingent expenses of the Department of State during the same years. From which it results that the expenditures for foreign intercourse in the year 1829, added to the whole appropriation asked for for the year 1830, supposing the whole to be expended, are less than those of the two first years of Mr. Monroe's administration by $233,065.56, and less than the two first years of Mr. Adams' presidency by $134,024.98. That the contingent expenses of the Department of State, in the last and present years, is less than the two corresponding years of Mr. Adams' administration by $10,280.45, and exceeds that of Mr. Monroe's only two hundred and nineteen dollars—an excess more than counterbalanced by the increased expense of printing the biennial calendar. But as a part of this excess consists of items of occasional and temporary occurrence only, we must bring the comparison to bear only on the permanent items, consisting of—

The diplomatic department, strictly so called;

The contingent expenses of foreign intercourse;

And treaties with the Mediterranean Powers.

On comparing these, the balances will stand thus:

The expenditure in the two first years of the present administration, falls short of that in the two first years of Mr. Monroe, by the sum of $38,258; and of that in the corresponding years of Mr. J. Q. Adams, by 5,302, notwithstanding the additional expense of outfits incurred in the last year.

[Mr. L. here read an abstract of the expenses of foreign intercourse for the several years above referred to—(see note A.) He then proceeded.]

For the full understanding of the accounts I have just referred to, it may be necessary to state, that previous to the year 1801, the accounts of our foreign relations were kept at the Treasury, under the head "Intercourse with Foreign Nations," and included every charge in relation to our foreign relations—even the "contingent expenses of foreign intercourse," commonly known by the appellation of the "Secret Service Fund." In 1801, according to an arrangement made by Mr. Gallatin, the bankers of the United States in Europe were directed to open an account headed "the Diplomatic Department;" a correspondent account was of course opened at the Treasury, and, under this head, until the year 1814, were brought every item which had formerly been comprehended under the head of the intercourse with foreign nations; and this fund was provided, by general appropriation, in the same words. In 1814, the appropriations became more specific "for the salaries, allowances, and contingent expenses, of Ministers to foreign nations, and for Secretaries of Legation;" and in 1818, the present form of appropriation, designating the several missions, was first adopted. But, from the date I have mentioned, 1801, until the present day, the accounts have been kept in the Treasury, under the general head of the "diplomatic department." And the course has been, to remit to our bankers in Europe, and charge to this fund, the moneys necessary for the payment of the salaries and allowed expenses of our foreign agents. These bankers are sometimes in advance to the United States, when unforeseen occurrences oblige the President, during the recess, to increase the expenses of our foreign intercourse, by new missions; and in those cases, appropriations are asked for, and made at the next session of Congress to reimburse them. This was the case in the year 1816, to the amount of $50,000; in the year 1818, to the amount of $20,000; and probably, other instances may be found by a more careful examination than I have been able to give to the subject.

In the last year, owing to the insufficiency of the contingent fund for *the expenses of foreign missions,* which must not be confounded with the *contingent expenses of foreign intercourse,* (the secret service fund) there was a deficiency of about $40,000, which was included in the estimates for the current year, and, as I stated in the debate on the appropriation, would have been more accordant with form; to have been asked for as a *deficiency* in the appropriations of the last year. But the effect is precisely the same; by appropriating for the salaries and outfits of foreign ministers, &c. as it stands in the bill, it is carried to the credit of the diplomatic fund, and will be remitted to our bankers to make good their advances.

After having shown that the sum expended for our foreign intercourse is actually much less than in former administrations, the statement I have just made of the mode of keeping the accounts, may be necessary, when we consider another charge, loudly made out of the House, and confidently and with a triumphant air repeated on this floor, that the laws which forbid a transfer of one appropriation to meet a deficiency on another, have been violated by the President. The Senator from Delaware, who most earnestly urged this charge, added, that the President had appropriated money for outfits *contrary to law.* Now, sir, the honorable Senator, in the charge of an illegal transfer, must have been ill informed, or he would not have hazarded it. No transfer whatever has been made. The balance in the Treasury to the credit of the "Diplomatic Department" was applied to outfits that have been paid; that balance was what remained unremitted to our bankers in Europe. If our Ministers there have drawn upon them for their quarter's salaries, due on the first of January last, they of course are in advance; because, as I have stated, the appropriation of 1829 fell short of the expenditure about the sum of $40,000. The appropriation for the contingent expenses of missions abroad always formed part of the *"Diplomatic Fund,"* and without any exception has been made liable to the drafts on that fund; therefore, there was no *illegal transfer.* The other contingent fund (that for foreign intercourse, the secret service fund,) might consistently with former usage, have been applied to this use; but with a scrupulous regard to the directions of the law, the President suffered it to remain untouched, and to the amount of $13,900, it has been carried to the Surplus Fund, having been more than two years appropriated. There has been, therefore, no illegal transfer of appropriations—there has been no transfer whatever. And this charge also falls under the investigation, which the President should rejoice has been provoked here, where it must meet its final overthrow. Now to the one connected with it, and urged with equal warmth, (I will not say violence.) Outfits have been paid, for which there was no specific appropriations. Can the gentleman have calculated the consequences of the doctrine implied in this charge? Can he have reflected on the blot its establishment would fix on the characters of men whose memory I know he reveres? Surely not. But as to the consequences of the doctrine. If it be true, the President cannot, in time of war, send a Minister to make peace in the recess, when no previous appropriation has been made for an outfit. He must lose the most favorable opportunities for negotiation, and suffer the ravages of war to go on until he can call Congress, at the expense of more than $100,000, to get an appropriation of $9000. Observe, sir, that, if our bankers were ready to advance the sum—nay, if he were ready to advance it himself, the doctrine contended for would make it equally illegal. How comes it that gentlemen who agree with the Senator from Delaware in this doctrine, have ever voted an appropriation to supply the deficiencies of former years? Why have they not censured the Presidents under whose authority they were created? No, sir; they were silent under Madison, silent under Monroe, when deficiencies in this department were voted for without a word of dissatisfaction. They, and all our predecessors were silent; and it was reserved for the present occasion to discover that an outfit could not be legally paid until there was a specific appropriation. General Washington appointed Mr. Charles Cotesworth Pinckney to France; Mr. Jefferson appointed Mr. Charles Pinkney to Spain, Mr. Monroe to England, Mr. Armstrong to France, Mr. Monroe again to Spain, Mr. William Pinkney to England, and Mr. Erving to Denmark; Mr. Madison appointed Mr. Crawford to France, and Mr. Irving to Spain; Mr. Monroe appointed Mr. Rush to England, and Mr. Everett to the Netherlands; and Mr. J. Q. Adams appointed Mr. Tudor to Brazil. All these appointments were made in the recess, and without any specific appropriations. Their salaries and outfits were paid out of the Diplomatic fund generally, and when that fund was indebted to our bankers, provision, as we have seen, was made to reimburse them.

Now, Sir, let the gentleman, and those who join him in the crimination of the Executive, determine whether they are willing to incur the ruinous consequences attending the establishment of their doctrine, and the inculpation of every former President, the Father of his Country included, in their sweeping charge. And I pray the Senate also to remark, that, if these appointments and outfits in the recess, without a special appropriation, were proper by former Presidents, (as they undoubtedly were) even in the cases where the appropriations were specified for particular missions,

without providing for outfits in the recess, the present case must be infinitely more justifiable: for the appropriation for 1828 gives a gross sum for
salaries, outfits, and contingencies, without specifying how much was intended for each, thereby creating a general fund, applicable to all such objects; but, being inadequate to the exigencies of the year, an appropriation
has been asked for to provide for the deficiency, as has been usual in this
and in every other department of the Government. This deficiency was
provided for in the House of Representatives without any opposition, and
in the Senate with only, I think, three or four dissenting votes. And this,
Sir, is the whole extent of the affair of the outfits, and the illegal appropriations and transfers, which has been made the ground of so much serious
accusation against the President. I hope we shall hear no more of this
groundless charge. Now, Sir, to another connected with it: the missions for
which these outfits were expended were totally unnecessary. The men
whose recall occasioned them were fit persons to be entrusted with the
business they were charged with; they ought to have been left; their recall
was not only unnecessary, but, in the opinion of the Senator, a *proscription*.
Now, Sir, what means the Senator may have of judging on this point, I
cannot tell; all I know is, that I have none that would justify me in believing that all these gentlemen possessed just such qualities and talents as
ought to have induced the President to constitute them his agents in the
important negotiations we have with foreign Powers. And if I had brought
myself to this belief, there are certain considerations that would induce me
to think that a man selected by the people of the nation to manage for
them this very concern, might, possibly, have rather more information,
and must be much better qualified than I was to form a proper opinion. I
might say, as I do say, although these are very estimable men, in my opinion, yet the President, possibly, may have reasons to believe that others
may succeed where they have failed. He may not unreasonably think that,
in addition to a Minister's being a man of ability and integrity, he ought to
possess the perfect confidence of the First Magistrate, whose views he is to
carry into effect. These reflections, Sir, would probably occur to me did I
disapprove of the nominations which have been made, and would prevent
my expressing any warm disapprobation of measures, of the propriety of
which I had not the means of judging. Much more would this induce me
to refrain from stigmatising them as illegal usurpations of power, and cruel
proscriptions.

Do gentlemen really suppose that, by applying to the recall of a Minister a word which leads the mind to the murders and assassinations of

Marius and Sylla, and the Triumvirate, they can identify the two cases? Sir, the attempt is not very complimentary to our understanding; and the approximation only tends to show the ridiculous disparity of the cases.

What are these proscriptions? Five Ministers Plenipotentiary, at one *"fell swoop!"*—incarcerated? banished? decapitated? No, Sir! Invited to return to their country, to their friends! Let us see, Sir, who were the sufferers, whose fate excites so much commiseration?

First, Sir, our late Minister to France. I can, fortunately, lessen the gentleman's distress on his account, at least: for, having had the happiness to enjoy an intimate and uninterrupted friendship with him for many years, I know that he returned by his own desire, after having faithfully and ably represented his country, with honor to himself, and possessing the esteem and the confidence of the first Magistrate, who acceded to his request.

The Senator from Delaware will not find fault with the mission to the Netherlands, when he knows that it was provided for under the administration of Mr. Adams. And the Senators from Maine, I am sure, cannot object to the selection of the distinguished citizen from their State, who so thoroughly understood the important question submitted to the decision of the Court to which he has gone; a question so vitally interesting to their constituents.

Our Minister to Spain had been there for five years, the usual period for them to remain abroad; during that time, as far as has been made public, he had been able to effect nothing, and the important claims of our citizens remained unsettled; it was not extraordinary, therefore, in any view, (doing full justice to that gentleman's assiduity and ability) that the efficacy of a new mission should be tried.

There remain our Ministers to England and Colombia, and their cases seem particularly to have excited the sympathy of the Senator from Delaware. He pathetically exclaims, What had General Harrison done? What had Mr. Barbour done? that they should be proscribed. Sir, I cannot answer this question; I know not what they have done. But I do not consider their recall as a punishment. As far as the individuals are concerned, I presume they do not think it any great hardship: each of them, for a year's service, has received eighteen thousand dollars; and one of them has returned from a country which is, from all accounts, no very agreeable residence in its present unsettled state. I esteem both of these gentlemen; with the former I have an acquaintance of a very old date, and although I think highly of his character, and as highly of his military services as the Senator can, yet I scarcely expected from that quarter to hear these last insisted on as a qualification for diplomatic duties. But because I have this opinion, am I to join in the lamentations that are uttered over their recall, as if the act were an offence and the consequences of it a public calamity? The President, for aught I know, may have as high an opinion of them as the Senator has, and yet he may very properly have chosen others to replace them; and if we may judge from what we hear, his choice has not been injudicious or unsuccessful. Sir, I disavow any invidious comparisons, but it cannot escape observation, that, in one of these missions, so loudly reprobated, Mr. Moore has already completed an arrangement for compensation to our fellow citizens, which his predecessor was unable to obtain; and, in the other, under Mr. McLane, a gentleman well known to all of us, and highly esteemed wherever he is known—the important negotiations with which he was charged, and which had so long slumbered, were, from the moment of his arrival, revived. They were begun and have been continued with his characteristic activity, talent, and perseverance; they may fail, for there are some errors which it is a most difficult task to repair. But, whatever be the event, neither the honor of the country, nor the reputation of its minister, will have suffered by the change. But, Mr. President, I feel as if I had been led astray by the example of the gentleman, to whose argument I am replying, and were treading on unconstitutional ground. Both of us, Sir, have a right, as individuals, to form an opinion, and freely to express it, in such terms as our sense of propriety will permit, on appointments, removals, or any other measures of Government. As Senators, we have a duty to perform in relation to appointments; but, in our legislative capacity, I am at a loss to discover what duty requires, or what right permits us to pass upon the propriety of acts which the Constitution has vested exclusively in the Executive hands; and that, too, without knowing the reasons or circumstances which induced them. Whether we accuse or defend, it must be in the dark; to know whether a Minister has been properly recalled or appointed, we must know the precise object which the Executive had in view. We do not know it. We must know what particular talents or qualities were necessary to be employed. We do not know it. We must know what were the instructions of the recalled Minister, and whether he had obeyed them. We do not know it. We must peruse his correspondence and know the whole progress of the pending negotiation. These we have not perused, and this we do not know. We must know the difficulties which prevented his success, and whether his successor may be better enabled to overcome them; and of this too, we are ignorant, and must be ignorant, and ought to be so until the

Constitution is changed, and the Executive power is taken from the President and placed in our hands; for without totally subverting it, we cannot arrogate to ourselves the rights claimed in this argument.

So much for the despotism, and oppression, and illegality, alleged in our foreign relations. Let us now come to the domestic corruption: for such is the charge. The public treasure has been employed in destroying the liberty of the press, and subsidizing its venal conductors; the interest of a million of dollars (I think that was the calculation) employed for this corrupt purpose. There are, I believe, on a moderate computation, above one thousand newspapers printed in the United States; of these seventy-two are employed to print the laws of the United States, and the advertisements and notices issued by the Departments, for which they receive, I believe, on an average, about one hundred and twenty dollars each. Now, Sir, suppose, instead of eight thousand dollars, the sum mentioned by the gentleman, or even a greater, for these necessary objects, were expended, would that incur the charge made? The printing must be executed. Who is to do it, the men designated by the proper officer, or those selected by the gentleman and his friend? One tenth or one twelfth of the printers in the United States are paid a very small price for doing a necessary duty, and this is called subsidizing the press for corrupt purposes. I have not inquired, but I take it for granted, that, at the expiration of the year, the Secretary of State has restored the public printing to those presses which were deprived of it for opposing the election of Mr. Adams; that he has not given, or continued it, to these who manufactured or published the vile slanders by which the present Chief Magistrate and his dearest connexions were assailed; and that, in making the selection, he has taken care to choose such papers as had a proper circulation. This is a business confided to the Secretary of State—not to us, or even to the President; a proposition was made some sessions ago to give it another destination, but it was violently opposed by the friends of the gentleman who then filled that office; a similar proposition is, I believe, now before the other House. The subsidies then are paid to seventy-two printers out of a thousand, and amount to one hundred and twenty dollars each, for which they perform a service of equal value. Those who make this grave accusation must go further, if they mean to support it; they must show that these presses are employed in some other service; that a part of the consideration is the promoting some object hostile to the interest or liberties of the country; that they are undermining the Constitution, or preparing the minds of the people for revolt; and that this condition was written in their bond. No,

Sir, the sin is, that they do not join in the clamor which restless, disappointed men, out of doors, are raising against the Chief Magistrate of the People. While they are independent, those men will call them corrupt.

Having exhibited what I think must be an abundant refutation of the charge of extravagance, so perseveringly made against the present administration in the expenditure of the public moneys, let us now see whether there is not some evidence, not only that there is no illegal or extravagant expenditure, but of a system which has already effected some savings, and promises greater, by the application of greater vigilance, and the introduction of new checks in the administration of the revenue. I speak only facts that are notorious; but I have reason to believe that others of the same nature exist which will be developed when time is given to put the system in complete operation. One collector, whose accounts had been frequently examined under the late administration, without the detection of any fraud or error, was, in the course of the Summer, found to have abstracted the sum of $80,000; another, nearly under the same circumstances, was found in arrears to the amount of $30,000, and both have absconded; a minor defect was found in the accounts of the Patent Office, also undiscovered, from the want of official superintendence; and, by the introduction of a simple system of checks, losses can never again occur without detection before the amount becomes considerable.

In the office of the Treasurer a most material and highly important check has been provided. Heretofore, the Treasurer might, by his own draught on the banks, with no other guard than its registry, command all the moneys in the Treasury. The highly respectable character of the venerable officer who held that place from the first institution of the Government, rendered every check of his draughts unnecessary, and the integrity of his successors has secured the public against any loss, and forbid the suspicion of any. But the Senate will perceive how necessary it was to introduce a different system, as well to guard the reputation of the officers from unjust suspicions, as the Treasury of the Nation from embezzlement; one has been provided, which, by requiring the signatures of different officers and registers in their respective offices, effectually answers the end. The value of this single regulation can scarcely be too highly appreciated. Seeing these evidences of regularity and economy, and hearing of many others, that either have already taken place, or are projected, I cannot but consider the charge of extravagance as entirely undeserved. Whenever it shall be again made and supported by proof, I promise the gentleman that no one will go further to blame or to correct the evil than I will. But, if I dared to offer my advice to men who want it so little, I would say, reserve your invective against extravagance until you have clear proof of its existence; by making it without reason, now, you lessen the weight of your testimony hereafter, when, perhaps, it may exist.

My friend and worthy colleague seems to have transferred this charge from the President to those in this House who favored his election; he has taken up the report of a Committee of Retrenchment at a former session, and rebukes us for not following up the plan traced out in that report, some of which reforms he has honored with his approbation. If this is meant as a reproach upon the administration, it is hardly a fair one; for I know of no means, of no influence, by which they could induce the members of this body to pursue the course of reform, other than that which has been pursued; the President's message, if acted on in the spirit which dictated it, will certainly satisfy the severest economist; and although I am not prepared to say that I should adopt all the measures he recommends, yet he sufficiently indicates a desire to advise and approve every plan for reforming abuses that the wisdom of the Legislature might devise. Let my colleague, therefore, give his aid in the work; let him select the measures he approves from the report of the committee, support them with the ability he is known to possess, and there is no doubt they will be adopted; in the mean time, a little patience will show perhaps that others are laboring in the same cause, and it is hoped their labors will be successful.

The remaining charges are so connected with the constitutional question of the right of removal from office, that it will be necessary to examine the several doctrines now resuscitated after having been at rest forty years. The first position (I do the Senator from Delaware the justice to say that this strange construction is not his) is, that the power of removal from office is annexed to the appointing power, from its very nature; and that the Constitution having vested the right of appointment in the President, by the advice and consent of the Senate, the same advice and consent is necessary to effect a removal. There is so much color for this argument, that, at the outset of the Constitution, men of much discernment were deceived by the fallacy it contains, and argued strenuously for the joint power; it was, however, differently, and, as I hope to show, rightfully decided in the year 1789; and from that time to this has not, as I hope also to show, been departed from.

One error of the argument lies in the first position assumed, that the power of removal, where there is no constitutional contrary provision, is inherent in that of appointment. It has no connexion whatever with it.

The power of creating a vacancy might, certainly, not without great inconvenience, be vested in one Department, and that of filling it in another; but they are not inseparable. The Constitution has no express clause declaratory *in terms* that the President shall have the power of removal; but it gives it to him by a necessary inference, when it declares that he shall have the *Executive power*—the signification of which is amplified in the subsequent clause, declaring it to be his duty to "see that the laws are faithfully executed." Here the power of removal is as fully granted as if it had been developed by the clearest paraphrase. No principle is clearer than that the grant of a power or the requisition of a duty, implies a grant of all those necessary for its execution; and it is equally clear that the power and the duty of causing the laws to be executed must carry with it that of selecting those persons necessary and proper to carry them into effect. But if, after having selected them, they are found unfit for the purpose, the same necessity exists of changing the selection which has been made; but this cannot be done in any other way than by removal; therefore, the power of removal is a power necessary for the due execution of the laws; and, being necessary, must be presumed to have been given with, and annexed to, the power of executing the laws; which is the Executive power of the President alone, and cannot be divided with the power associated with him in making appointments. If my mind be capable of appreciating the force of reasoning by deductions, this is conclusive against the participation claimed by the Senate in the right of removal. But this is not all. Supposing the position were true, that the power which appoints must, of necessity, remove: how would the case stand? Who is it appoints? The President: he alone appoints. But, because there is a restriction on the one branch of his power, by making the advice of the Senate necessary to an appointment, does it follow that he cannot execute the other branch without that assent also. He has two powers by the argument—to appoint and to remove: surely the Constitution might reasonably provide that the Senate should have a veto on the first, without having it necessarily implied that they gave it in the second. Let it be remembered that the Senate do not appoint: they can never select: they can only approve or disapprove: they can advise, or refuse to advise. But, independent of abstract reasoning, let us examine, from practical results, what the Constitution really intended. The wise framers of that instrument could not be ignorant of the great republican principle, that, to every grant of power, responsibility ought to be annexed—responsibility to the laws for its wilful abuse or neglect—responsibility to public opinion for its indiscreet or erroneous exercise. If there were then, even a doubt of the construction in this case, to what solution ought this principle to lead us? When the President removes, his act is known: should he act from corrupt motives, he is liable to impeachment. Should he act from indiscretion only, public opinion, from which there is no escape, will pass upon his conduct. But admit the co-operation of the Senate: what happens? First, the perfect irresponsibility of the President, both at the bar of this House and at that of the public. Having co-operated in the offence, by advising the removal, how could we punish it as a crime? And with the public, our confirmation of the act would be a complete cloak to cover the indiscretion, if there were one in the measure. There would then be no responsibility whatever attached to the President. Would it be shifted upon us? As little. Our sittings are secret: our opinions and votes must necessarily be so. The act of the Senate is known: a majority have advised the removal, or, by refusing to do so, have kept a negligent, or incapable, or unfaithful officer in his post. Who is chargeable with this? When our terms of service expire, will the Legislatures of our respective States know which of us have disappointed the expectations they had formed of the prudence, discretion, or judgment of their Senators, so that they may continue or withdraw their confidence? No, sir! the whole plan would present the anomaly of most important powers exercised in a free Government without any check from the fear of punishment or of popular disfavor.

If it were possible then for the Senate to participate in this power, it would be not only contrary to the true construction of the words of our social compact, but would be destructive of one of the most important principles on which it is founded. But it is totally impracticable, morally and physically impracticable, in its exercise, consistently with the existence of the Government. Take the case of a Minister to a foreign Court, charged with a negotiation of the most important kind, on the subject of which the commercial prosperity, perhaps the peace of the country depends; he becomes negligent in his correspondence, he addicts himself to play, to pleasure, to intemperance; he becomes unworthy of his trust from these or other causes; or from malady, mental or bodily, becomes incapable of performing his duties; or, he makes himself so obnoxious to the Court to which he is sent that it demands his recall. The knowledge of these facts is brought to the President, soon after the adjournment of Congress; he cannot recall this Minister, because he has been appointed by the advice and consent of the Senate, and, by this newly vamped doctrine, the same advice is necessary to displace him. The President must then convene the Senate: sixty days, at least, is necessary for this operation. All this while the unworthy, or inefficient, or obnoxious Minister must remain, to betray or disgrace his country, or irritate the Power which he was sent to conciliate. The Senate are at length convened, and the President communicates the information he has received. But here another new principle stands in the way of his recall. The Minister, like all other officers, (such is the doctrine of the day) has an interest in his office, which it is *injustice, tyranny,* and PROSCRIPTION, to deprive him of without cause. He ought not then to be deprived of this interest unheard; he must have a copy of the charges, the names of the witnesses, time to reply, and a right to examine his evidence in discharge. Gentlemen must acknowledge this, or they must give up their favorite cry of oriental despotism and cruel proscription. The examination of ex parte evidence here is quite as fatal to the vested interest they contend for, as any removal the President has made. These formalities are gone through, and at the end of three or four months the charges are substantiated, and the Minister is recalled or, the proof is not deemed satisfactory, and he remains, having lost the confidence of the President, who is forced, however, to retain him, and he himself irritated by the accusation, and endeavoring to defeat every negotiation that will reflect credit on the administration of his country. Ten days after this trial is concluded, before the members from the distant States have reached their homes, advice is received that a collector is speculating with the funds committed to his charge; the same operation is to be renewed, the same delay incurred, the same waste of public money, the same vexation to the members of this body, the same impossibility—let us come to the conclusion at once—the same utter impossibility of carrying on the operations of Government with such machinery.

This was seen, felt, and acknowledged, as I have said, in the outset of our Government, and, from that time to the present, it has never been made a serious question. Why is it raised now? Doubtless from conscientious motives by those who advocate it here. But out of this House it has been (in the total absence of better matters, for a reproach to the President) made a party cry, which will be hushed as soon as the matter is examined by an enlightened people. The gentleman from Delaware does not go this length; his doctrine is this:

The President has the right of removal for just causes. If he abuses it for corrupt or party purposes, he is liable to impeachment.

Whenever the Senate suspect that a removal has been made without cause, or from such improper or corrupt motives, they may ask for the reason of the removal.

The President is bound to communicate the cause whenever it may be demanded by the Senate.

The Senate, if he should refuse to give any, or give an unsatisfactory answer, may, and ought to reject, successively, all the nominations he may make.

And the conclusion to which the gentleman is brought by this series of positions, is, that the temporary appointment made by the President, being in force only until the end of the session, the vacancy that is thus created is not one occurring in the recess, and therefore cannot be filled by the President, but the office must remain vacant.

These are, as accurately as I could note them, the positions laid down by the Senator from Delaware.

Let us inquire whether they are more tenable than the general doctrine I have just examined.

The first position I accede to. The President has the right of removal, and he is liable to impeachment for corruption and malconduct in the exercise of this, as well as any other of his functions. But this true position is fatal to all the errors which the Senator has built upon it.

He admits the right of removal to be in the President, without the advice of the Senate. As it is no where in terms given by the Constitution, it must exist as a necessary means of executing some power which is expressly given. What is that power? Clearly the Executive; or, as more fully expressed, the duty of "seeing that the laws shall be faithfully executed." He has it then, amply, completely, solely, and the second member of this proposition proves it; he is impeachable for corruption in its exercise; he has the power without participation, and must bear the responsibility, without any one to share in it.

Having seen that the President derives the power he is admitted to possess from a legitimate constitutional source, and that this gives it to him without any other limitation than that of his own responsibility, we must inquire from whence the Senate derives the control with which they are, gratuitously, I think, invested by the argument. They may call on the President for the reasons of the removal; and if they have the right, the obligation to comply with it follows of course. But in what part of the Constitution is this right given? It is not pretended that there is any express provision. From what part is it a necessary inference? To the execution of what power, vested in the Senate, is it the necessary means? Not to the power of advising on the fitness of a candidate proposed to fill the vacancy, because the vacancy must be created before that advisory power can be exercised, and the argument admits that the President has the right to create the vacancy by a removal. Of what power, then, I ask, vested in the Senate, is this the necessary appendage? Or where is it expressly given as a distinct power? If given neither expressly, nor by implication, it cannot exist.

But for what purpose should it exist? What is the advantage to be derived from it that should make us solicitous to give a construction that should admit it? Remember in this inquiry the first position which is assumed by the argument, and which I admit, that the President is impeachable for a corrupt removal, and remember also that we are the judges of fact and of law on an impeachment. The power, then, is one that makes us accusers as well as judges, and judges who have predetermined the guilt of the accused: for, if on the inquiry, the corruption appear, and we make it the ground of refusing to confirm the President's nomination, do we not prejudge the question on the impeachment that must follow? This is an insuperable objection, which the doctrine of the Senator entirely overlooks in zeal to apply his remedy. And what is that remedy? One surely worse than the disease, although that should have all the bad symptoms ascribed to it. The evil complained of is, the removal of one good officer, to be replaced by another as good. Observe, Sir, that I grant the fact in dispute. I admit, for the sake of showing the weakness of the argument, that all the removals have been of men well qualified for their offices; and all I ask in return is, a similar admission that the Senate, for whose powers they contend, will consent to no nomination of a person not qualified. This is the evil. What is the remedy? It is contained in the Senator's last position, that, if the President refuse to give his reasons, or the Senate are not satisfied with them, they may refuse to confirm his nominations, and suffer the appointment to expire by its limitation, at the end of the session: and then it is the opinion of the Senator that the office can no longer be filled; because, according to his reasoning, it is not one that accrues during the recess. This is his remedy: for this you are to suppose powers that are no where given. For this admirable result you are to strain the construction of the Constitution until it breaks. For this you are to add the accusing to your judicial power. For this you are to leave the laws unexecuted, and disjoint the whole machinery of Government. No matter whether the offices to be filled are the Commanders of your Army, or the Captains of your fleet in time of war, or the Heads of Departments, or Collectors of Revenue, or Marshals to execute the decrees of your courts in time of peace—all must remain vacant. This is the remedy. Apply it in the present case. A number of removals in every Department has been made. Suppose the Senate should have asked for the causes, and the President, as he most probably would, should have declined to comply with the request, what would have followed? All our diplomatic relations would have at once ceased: for all the Ministers appointed in the recess would cease their functions at the end of the session. The revenue in some of our largest ports would be uncollected. The administration of justice in most of the districts would be stopped for want of District Attorneys and Marshals. This is the remedy for an evil, perhaps of doubtful existence in any case, but certainly much aggravated in all.

But suppose this right in the Senate to call for the causes of removal, and an acknowledgment by the President of an obligation to comply. He sends us his reasons, and in one case they are that he has no confidence in the man he has dismissed. Confidence can not be commanded; it is the result of observation on character and conduct; on a thousand indescribable impressions. But a majority of the Senate say we have confidence in him. What is to be the result? Is he to be restored to office? No one pretends it. What then? The grand remedy to punish the President for his want of confidence in an officer whom he has not appointed, is to adopt the plan of the Senator from Delaware, and leave the office vacant. The whole reasoning on the general question of the right of the Senate to participate in removals, applies with the same force to this power of inquiring into the causes of removal; both are gratuitously assumed in argument; both are destitute of either express or implied authority in the Constitution; both lead to absurd consequences, and to impracticable results; ruinous, if they were practicable.

But I deny that the remedy proposed (ruinous and extraordinary as it is) could be applied. The offices would not, in my opinion, remain vacant. The President would have a right to fill them, and would certainly exercise that right; the expressions used in the Constitution are general: he shall have a right to "fill all vacancies that *may happen during the recess of the Senate.*" Now, Sir, in the case supposed, the vacancy arises when the commission expires—when is that? At the end of the session. When is the end of the session? Certainly not before the beginning of the recess; not at any moment while the session continues. An official act, done at the last instant of the session, would be well done. The vacancy then happens at the first instant of the recess: but the Constitution makes no distinction whatever; whether at the first moment, or the last day, is immaterial. When I use this argument, I am free to admit that I do not think the framers of the Constitution did intend to provide for so extraordinary a case as that which the ingenuity of the Senator from Delaware has imagined, of the

Senate rejecting all the nominations of the President, successively, because they might be dissatisfied with a removal. But the words of the Constitution permit the exercise of his powers to fill all vacancies, whenever they should occur—with the advice of the Senate, if in session; without it, by a temporary appointment, when they are not. The exercise of the extraordinary and destructive power contended for, never certainly entered into their minds; it was left for the ingenuity of our times to discover. But, it has been said that this power is liable to abuse; the President may remove from caprice, prejudice, or a worse motive. No doubt, Sir, he may; he may do worse; he may embroil you with foreign nations, by his abuse of the treaty making power; he may cause your fortifications to be dismantled and your army to be dispersed in time of war; he may destroy your revenue by the appointment of corrupt men in the management of the treasury: but what argument can be drawn from this? That he has not the constitutional power? Certainly not. But if the President might abuse the power of removal, may not the Senate abuse the control with which it is attempted to invest them? If he has enemies to displace, may not they have friends to keep in? If he is liable to be actuated by political feelings, are bodies, constituted as this is, at all times free from their influence? The President has the power to remove, it is said, again, but only for just cause; but who is to judge of what is just cause—not the Senate, or if so, the power would be theirs, not the President's; he must himself be the judge, or else it would be a solecism to say that he has the power; he must judge and he must act, as I have said, uncontrolled but by his responsibility to the laws for corrupt acts; to his country for those which are indiscreet or erroneous.

This, Sir, is my view of the Constitutional power of the President in relation to removals—a power, in my view of it, vested solely in him, and for the due exercise of which he must bear the sole responsibility. I will not consent to divide it with him. No terms seem sufficiently energetic for gentlemen to express their disapprobation of the manner in which the President has exercised this power. As it is their only subject for declamation and invective, it would be cruel to deprive them of it; but, by their own showing, are they not accusing without evidence? Why all these attempts to call on the President for his reasons of removal, if they already know that he has none? Why call for evidence if they already have it? If these proofs of corruption, of favoritism, of persecution, are sufficient, plead the cause before the people, or prefer accusations of impeachment in the other House; but do not render yourselves, by prejudging the cause, liable to be challenged for the favor, or, by bold accusation, endeavor to influence the minds of your fellow judges with your own prejudices. If their doctrine be true, as it undoubtedly is, that, for corruption in the exercise of this as well as any other function, the first magistrate is liable to impeachment; and if they believe, as they repeatedly allege, that there is evidence of it in the late removals; I put it to them, whether they are correct in showing a feeling inconsistent with the calm investigation that becomes a judge. If, on the contrary, as I am more inclined to believe, the warmth that has been expressed arises only from a feeling for political friends, who have lost their places, are not the expressions they have used highly exaggerated? and ought they not to have been suppressed? But if there has been, in their opinion, an indiscreet use of the power, let them plead the cause before the people, who have the power to apply the remedy. To them the President is responsible, and to them, I have little doubt, his conduct will appear, as on other occasions it has done, correct, upright, disinterested, and intended for their best advantage. Yet, Sir, if the contrary be proved, I shall, as a Senator and an individual, hold myself open to the conviction that evidence may produce.

I now approach a graver subject, one, on the true understanding of which the Union, and of course the happiness of our country, depends. The question presented is that of the true sense of that Constitution which it is made our first duty to preserve in its purity. Its true construction is put in doubt—not on a question of power between its several departments, but on the very basis upon which the whole rests; and which, if erroneously decided, must topple down the fabric, raised with so much pain, framed with so much wisdom, established with so much persevering labor, and for more than forty years the shelter and protection of our liberties, the proud monument of the patriotism and talent of those who devised it, and which, we fondly hoped, would remain to after ages as a model for the imitation of every nation that wished to be free. Is that, Sir, to be its destiny? The answer to that question may be influenced by this debate. How strong the motive, then, to conduct it calmly; when the mind is not heated by opposition, depressed by defeat, or elate with fancied victory, to discuss it with a sincere desire, not to obtain a paltry triumph in argument, to gain applause by tart reply, to carry away the victory by addressing the passions, or gain proselytes by specious fallacies, but, with a mind open to conviction, seriously to search after truth, earnestly, when found, to impress it on others. What we say on this subject will remain; it is not an every day question; it will remain for good or for evil. As our views are correct or erroneous; as they tend to promote the lasting welfare, or accelerate the dissolution of our

Union; so will our opinions be cited as those which placed the Constitution on a firm basis, when it was shaken or deprecated, if they should have formed doctrines which led to its destruction.

With this temper, and these impressions of the importance of the subject, I have given it the most profound, the most anxious and painful attention; and differing, as I have the misfortune to do, in a greater or less degree, from all the Senators who have preceded me, I feel an obligation to give my views of the subject. Could I have coincided in the opinions given by my friends, I should most certainly have been silent; from a conviction, that neither my authority nor my expositions could add any weight to the arguments they have delivered.

My learned and honorable friend, the Senator near me, from South Carolina, (Mr. HAYNE) comes, in the eloquent arguments he has made, to the conclusion, that whenever, in the language of the Virginia resolutions, (which he adopts) there is, in the opinion of any one State, "a palpable, deliberate, and dangerous violation of the Constitution by a law of Congress," such State may, without ceasing to be a member of the Union, declare the law to be unconstitutional, and prevent its execution within the State; that this is a constitutional right, and that its exercise will produce a constitutional remedy, by obliging Congress either to repeal the law, or to obtain an explicit grant of the power which is denied by the State, by submitting an amendment to the several States; and that, by the decision of the requisite number, the State, as well as the Union, would be bound. It would be doing injustice, both to my friend and to his argument, if I did not add, that this resort to the *nullifying* power, as it has been termed, ought to be had only in the last resort, where the grievance was intolerable, and all other means of remonstrance and appeal to the other States had failed.

In this opinion I understand the honorable and learned chairman of the Judiciary Committee substantially to agree, particularly in the constitutional right of preventing the execution of the obnoxious law.

The Senator from Tennessee, in his speech, which was listened to with so much attention and pleasure, very justly denies the right of declaring the nullity of a law, and preventing its execution, to the ordinary Legislature, but erroneously, in my opinion, gives it to a Convention.

My friend from New Hampshire, of whose luminous argument I cannot speak too highly, and to the greatest part of which I accord, does not coincide in the assertion of a constitutional right of preventing the execution of a law believed to be unconstitutional, but refers opposition to the unalienable right of resistance to oppression.

All these Senators consider the Constitution as a compact between the States in their sovereign capacity; and one of them, (Mr. Rowan) has contended that sovereignty cannot be divided, from which it may be inferred that no part of the sovereign power has been transferred to the General Government.

The Senator from Massachusetts, in his very eloquent and justly admired address on this subject, considers the Federal Constitution as entirely popular, and not created by compact, and, from this position, very naturally shows, that there can be no constitutional right of actual *resistance* to a law of that Government, but that intolerable and illegal acts may justify it on first principles.

However these opinions may differ, there is one consolatory reflection, that none of them justify a violent opposition given to an unconstitutional law, until an extreme case of suffering has occurred. Still less do any of them suppose the actual existence of such a case.

But the danger of establishing on the one hand a constitutional veto in each of the States, upon any act of the whole, to be exercised whenever, in the opinion of the Legislature of such State, the act they complain of is contrary to the Constitution; and, on the other, the dangers which result to the State Governments by considering that of the Union as entirely popular, and denying the existence of any compact; seem both of them to be so great, as to justify, and indeed demand, an expression of my dissent from both.

The arguments on the one side, to show that the Constitution is the result of a compact between the States, cannot, I think, be controverted; and those which go to show that it is founded on the consent of the people, and in one sense of the word, a popular government, are equally incontrovertible. Both of the positions, seemingly so contradictory, are true, and both of them are false—true, as respects one feature in the Constitution; erroneous, if applied to the whole.

These States, during the short period of the contest with Great Britain, which preceded the Declaration of Independence, although colonies in name, were, in fact, independent States, and, even at that early period, their political existence partook of this mixed character.

By a popular or consolidated government, I understand one that is founded on the consent, express or implied, of the people of the whole nation; and which operates in all its departments directly upon the people.

By a federative government, as contradistinguished from the former, I mean one composed of several independent States, bound together for specific national purposes, and relying for the efficiency of its operations on its action upon the different States in their political capacity, not individually upon their citizens.

In the incipient state of our political existence, we find traces of both of these features. When the oppressive acts of the mother country had excited the spirit of resistance, we find the Colonies sending delegates to a General Congress; and, without any formal federative contract, that Congress assumed, by general consent, and exercised, powers which could strictly be classed only under the head of such as belong to a consolidated Government. In order to effect a non-importation of goods from Great Britain, instead of operating through the agency of the separate Colonies, and recommending that they should use their influence or authority to effect the object, the Congress address their recommendation to the merchants of all the United Colonies *individually*. It is true this was only in the shape of a recommendation, not an imperative order; but this makes no difference in the argument: it was still an action of the Government, addressed to individuals of the Colonies, not through the medium of the Colonial authority, as would have been the case under a strictly federative compact. This was on the 19th of September, 1774. On the 27th of the same month, they proceeded more directly, and *resolved* that there *should be* no goods imported after a certain day, and that those so imported *should not* be *used* or *sold*; and a few days after, a *resolution* of non-exportation was entered into; the negotiation of British bills was prohibited; and besides levying and equipping a naval and land force on the *Continental* establishment, they erected a Post Office Department, emitted money, and declared that persons refusing to receive the bills, on conviction, be deemed, published, and treated as *enemies of the country*. All these acts were, in a greater or less degree, direct operations of the general temporary Government upon the citizens, and, in that degree, were proofs of its character as a mixture of popular with a federative Government. After all these acts, and many more of the same nature, came the Declaration of Independence, in which they *jointly* declare themselves independent States, but still, it would seem, as one nation. In the preamble they assert the right, as *"one people,"* to take the *station*, not the *stations*, to which they are entitled. The whole instrument complains of illegal and oppressive acts against them jointly.

After this decisive act, for more than two years the States, thus declared free, remained connected by no other bond than their common love of liberty and common danger, under the same authority of a general

Congress, which continued to exercise all the powers of a mixed kind, which, if they had been formally conferred, would have constituted a Government which could not properly be called either purely a federation of States, retaining all their sovereignty, or a consolidated Government to which it had been surrendered.

The Confederation was at length entered into. This was certainly a compact between the States; but, among a number of stipulations strictly federative, contained others which gave to the Congress powers which trenched upon the State sovereignties; to declare war and make peace; enter into treaties binding on the whole; to establish courts of admiralty, with power to bind the citizens of the States individually, in cases coming under that jurisdiction; to raise armies; equip fleets; coin money; emit bills of credit, and other similar powers. The defects of this bond of union are well known; among these the most prominent was the want of a power, acting directly on the citizens, to raise a revenue independent of the agency of the States. And it is a most instructive fact, that the common danger, though at times extremely imminent, during the continuance of the war, could never produce any kind of attention to the requisitions of Congress; yet there was no want of patriotism or attachment to the cause. Each State then possessed, in the subject of the requisition, the practical power of giving a veto to the operations they disliked, by refusing its quota, and the power was abused and will always be abused, whenever it is the interest of the State possessing it to exercise that right.

In the Federal Constitution this combination of the two characteristics of Government is more apparent. It was framed by delegates appointed by the States; it was ratified by conventions of the people of each State, convened according to the laws of the respective States. It guaranties the existence of the States, which are necessary to its own; the States are represented in one branch by Senators, chosen by the Legislatures; and in the other, by Representatives taken from the people, but chosen by a rule which may be made and varied by the States, not by Congress—the qualification of electors being different in different States. They may make amendments to the Constitution. In short, the Government had its inception with them; it depends on their political existence for its operation; and its duration cannot go beyond theirs. The States existed before the Constitution; they parted only with such powers as are specified in that instrument; they continue still to exist, with all the powers they have not ceded, and the present Government would never, itself, have gone into operation, had not the States, in their political capacity, have consented. That consent is a compact of each one with the whole, not, (as has been argued, in order to throw a kind of ridicule on this convincing part of the argument of my friend from South Carolina,) with the Government which was made by such compact. It is difficult, therefore, it would appear, with all these characters of a federative nature, to deny to the present Government the description of one founded on compacts to which each State was a party; and a conclusive proof, if any more were wanted, would be in the fact, that the States adopted the Constitution at different times, and many of them on conditions which were afterwards complied with by amendments. If it were strictly a popular Government, in the sense that is contended for, the moment a majority of the people of the United States had consented, it would have bound the rest; and yet, after all the others, except one, had adopted the Constitution, the smallest still held out; and if Rhode Island had not consented to enter into the confederacy, she would, perhaps, at this time, have been unconnected with us.

But with all these proofs (and I think them incontrovertible) that the Government could not have been brought into being without a compact, yet, I am far from admitting, that, because this entered so largely into its origin, therefore there are no characteristics of another kind, which impress on it strongly the marks of a more intimate union and amalgamation of the interests of the citizens of the different States, which gives to them the general character of citizens of the United Nation. This single fact would show, that the entire sovereignty of the States, individually, has not been retained: the relation of citizen and sovereign is reciprocal. To whatever power the citizen owes allegiance, that power is his sovereign. There cannot be a double, altho' there may be a subordinate fealty. The Government, also, for the most part, (except in the election of Senators, Representatives, and President, and some others,) acts in the exercise of its legitimate powers directly upon individuals, and not through the medium of State authorities. This is an essential character of a popular Government.

I place little reliance on the argument which has been mostly depended on to show that this is a popular Government—I mean the preamble; which begins with the words, "We, the people." It proves nothing more than the fact, that the people of the several States had been consulted and had given their consent to the instrument. To give these words any other construction, would be to make them an assertion directly contrary to the fact. We know, and it never has been imagined or asserted that the people of the United States collectively, as a whole people, gave their assent or were consulted in that capacity; the people of each State *were* consulted to know whether *that State* would form a part of the United States under the articles of the Constitution, and to that they gave their assent, simply as citizens of that State.

This Government, then, is neither such a federative one, founded on a compact, as leaves to all the parties their full sovereignty, nor such a consolidated popular government, as deprives them of the whole of that sovereign power. It is a compact by which the people of each State have consented to take from their own Legislatures some of the powers they had conferred upon them, and to transfer them, with other enumerated powers, to the Government of the United States, created by that compact; these powers, so conferred, are some of those exercised by the sovereign power of the country in which they reside. I do not mean here, the ultimate sovereign power residing under all governments, democratic or despotic, in the people—a sovereignty which must always in theory exist, however its exercise may by foreign or domestic power be repressed—but I mean that power to regulate the affairs of a nation, which resides in its government, whatever the form of that government may be; this may be, and generally is, distributed into several hands. As to all these attributes of sovereignty, which, by the federal compact, were transferred to the General Government, that Government is sovereign and supreme; the States have abandoned, and can never reclaim them.

As to all other sovereign powers, the States retain them.

But the States have not only given certain powers to the General Government, but they have expressly given the right of enforcing obedience to the exercise of those powers. They have declared that "the Constitution, and the laws which shall be made in pursuance thereof, shall be the supreme law of the land, any thing in the Constitution or laws of any State to the contrary notwithstanding." And they have also expressly consented that the Judiciary of the United States shall have cognizance of all cases coming under those laws. Here the words of the compact provide for the means by which controversies coming under it are to be decided; but this must be taken with the understanding, that they are controversies arising not only under the laws of the United States, (including the Constitution and treaties) but they must be between parties over whom the Constitution has given jurisdiction to the courts. Every case, then, of this description, must be submitted to the Judiciary of the United States; and as in all cases, the Constitution of the United States is paramount in authority to a law of the United States, and as both of them are so to a law of the State, the Supreme Court of the United States must, of necessity, when a contrariety between these authorities is alleged, in any case legally before it, determine that question, and its determination must be final; the parties must be bound; the State to which they belong, must be bound; for they in this compact have agreed that their citizens shall be so. But it is asked, suppose the law of Congress is palpably contrary to the Constitution, and endangers the liberties of the country, must the State submit? If the question be whether the State can *constitutionally* resist, there is but one answer. She has by the Constitution consented that the Supreme Court shall finally decide whether this be constitutional or not. If the question be, of the right which all people have to resist ruinous oppression, the answer is as clear, and I should be the last man in the world to contravene the existence of that inalienable right. But that is not the question; it is of a constitutional right, whenever, in the opinion of the Legislature, (or as some think, of a convention of the people of any one State) a law of Congress is palpably unconstitutional, such State has a right, under the Constitution, not only to declare the act void, but to prevent its execution within the State, until Congress shall propose a declaratory amendment to the States, and their decision shall be obtained; and all this without quitting their place in the Union—without disturbing its peace it is said; but, on the contrary, it is contended, for the purpose of preserving the general compact inviolate. Now, Sir, independently of the argument drawn from the express consent of the people of the several States, that in all matters where the Supreme Court have jurisdiction between individuals, they should determine, and must determine, whether a law be unconstitutional—independently of this, and supposing no such powers given to the court, can it be supposed that so essential a feature in the Government, as a positive *veto* given to, or reserved by each State, upon the operations of the whole, would have been left not only unprovided for by express words, but without even an ambiguous phrase—a single doubtful word to hang the argument upon? It is derived solely from the rights attached to the sovereignty of the States, unimpaired by its accession to the Union, *indivisible*, according to the argument of my learned friend from Kentucky, and always alive and active, (not one of those which he expressively says will *keep cold*) and ready to go into operation whenever it is attacked.

I have called it a positive *veto* on the operations of the whole Government. Is it not so in effect? That the right, when exercised by a single State, can only prevent the execution of the obnoxious law in the State alone, which objects to it, does not take from the power the character I have given to it, is apparent from the double consideration that, if the General Government were under an obligation to desist from executing the law in the opposing State, they must, of necessity, refrain from putting it in force in the others; if it were a tax, because they must be equal; if any other subject of legislation, imposing a burthen or restriction, they could not, in justice, force the others to bear what one was relieved from, nor would the other States submit to so unequal an imposition. The argument, then, supposes a feature in the Constitution, which certainly is not expressed in it; which, most assuredly, would have been expressed, if it had been intended: for it totally alters its character; puts the power of the Union at the will of any one of its members; and allows it, without risque, to throw off all the burthens of Government at its pleasure. Remember, Sir, that I am speaking of a *constitutional right*, (for that is the one claimed)—a right under the Constitution, not over it—a power that may be exercised without incurring any risque or committing any offence— without forfeiting a place in the Union, or any right or privilege under it. The State has only to resolve, by its ordinary Legislature, or, according to others, in a convention of its citizens, that a law enacted by the General Government is palpably unconstitutional and dangerous, and that it shall cease to operate, and it must cease to operate; and as an inevitable consequence, it may be resisted by force; as another consequence, if death ensues, it is murder in those who act under the General Government— justifiable homicide in those who resist. Now, Sir, would not these serious consequences have presented themselves to the enlightened men who framed this Constitution? and, if they did, would not some provision have been made to prevent any illegal exertion of power by the Executive, fraught with such danger? If they had supposed that this was a right reserved, would they not have declared the correlative obligation in the General Government to respect it: for, Sir, it is needless to say that every right carries with it its correspondent obligation, and that there cannot be two conflicting rights. If, then, the States have a right to prevent the execution of a law, the General Government are under an obligation to refrain from enforcing it; yet, instead of declaring this obligation to respect this reserved right, not the slightest allusion is made to it. On the contrary, when a law is once passed, it is made the duty of the President to execute it. But by the argument, the law has been passed as constitutional by both Houses of Congress; it has been approved as such by the president; and a judgment has been given by the Supreme Court, declaring it to be constitutional, and directing that, in the particular case before them, it shall be executed. The State against whose citizen the judgment is given, declares it to be palpably and dangerously contrary to the Constitution, and that it is null and void, and shall not be executed. What is to be done? The right of the State, says the gentleman, must be respected; but, unfortunately for the argument, the Constitution does not say so; unfortunately, it says directly the contrary. The President is bound by his oath to cause every constitutional law to be executed. But he has approved this law, therefore he believes it to be constitutional: but both Houses have passed it, therefore they believed it so; but the judges have decreed that it shall be executed; therefore, they, too, have believed it to be constitutional. Must the President yield his own conviction, fortified as it is by these authorities, to the opinion of a majority—perhaps a small majority—in the Legislature of a single State? If he must, again I ask, show me the written authority? I cannot find it. I cannot conceive it. I am not asking for the expression of the reserved right; I know that they are not enumerated. But I ask for the obligation to obey that right; I ask for the written instruction to the Executive to respect it; I ask for a provision, that nothing but the grossest inattention, or the most consummate folly, could have omitted, if the doctrine contended for be true.

This might have been done by an article in these words: "Whenever, in the opinion of any one State, a law passed by the Congress shall be deemed unconstitutional and dangerous, such State may prevent its execution, and the President and the courts shall forbear to enforce the same; but Congress shall, in that case, if they persevere in thinking the law expedient, submit the question as an amendment to Conventions of the States, in the manner prescribed by the Constitution." Now, Sir, the inquiry cannot be too often repeated, if such had been the intention of those who framed our form of Government, or of those who adopted it, and considered and amended it, would not some expression of this kind have been inserted? and, if inserted, would it have been recommended or adopted? and, if adopted, how long would it have continued in operation? how many vetos would have been interposed? how many Conventions would have been assembled? Not an embargo—not a restriction—not a declaration of war—not a measure for defence—not a tax or an impost, but would produce a stoppage in the wheels of the political machine; the most pressing operations of Government must be suspended until the amendments are proposed by Congress; until Conventions are called in all the States, and they have made their decisions. It is unfortunately no answer to say that this power would not be abused; that the argument supposes it to accrue only in palpable cases. Let the constitutional right be acknowledged, let it be known that it may be exercised without risk, and local interest will always be strong enough to suggest constitutional scruples; nor will common interest, the incalculable interest of our Union, be a sufficient argument. When was the interest of union more apparent than during the latter years of the Revolutionary war, and those which immediately succeeded the peace? Yet, when was the apathy of the States more apparent to the considerations of common good? When were local interests more consulted? When was it more difficult to procure the slender contributions which each State was bound to furnish to the common fund? It is a most important truth, that the existence of the General Government must depend on that feature which permits the exercise of all its legitimate powers directly upon the people, without the intervention of the States. Make that intervention necessary for the execution of those legitimate powers, or permit it to arrest them in cases which the States may deem illegal, and your Government is gone; it changes its character; it becomes, whatever other features you give to it, essentially an inefficient confederation, without union at home, without consideration abroad, and must soon fall a prey to domestic wars, in which foreign alliances will necessarily intervene to complete its ruin. No, Sir; adopt this as a part of our Constitution, and we need no prophet to predict its fall. The oldest of us may live long enough to weep over its ruins; to deplore the failure of the fairest experiment that was ever made, of securing public prosperity and private happiness, based on equal rights and fair representation; to die with the expiring liberties of our country, and transmit to our children, instead of the fair inheritance of freedom, received from our fathers, a legacy of war, slavery, and contention.

But it is asked, Will you deny to the States every portion of their former sovereignty? Will you call this, with the Senator from Massachusetts, a strictly popular Government? Will you deny them all right of intervention, and reduce them to the condition of mere corporations? Do you renounce the doctrines for which you contended in 1798, and consider the Supreme Court as the umpire provided in all cases to determine on the extent of State rights? God forbid that I should hold such doctrines. If my friends had stopped at the declaration that they adopted the resolutions of the Virginia Legislature, I should not, perhaps, have thought the difference between us of sufficient consequence to have troubled the Senate with my opinions. For the most part, I coincide in the sentiments of those resolutions; but my friends carried them out into their practical consequences further than, I think, they warrant; further, certainly, than I am willing to follow them.

As I understand them, they assert the right of a State, in the case of a law palpably unconstitutional and dangerous, to remonstrate against it, to call on the other States to co-operate in procuring its repeal, and, in doing this, they must, of necessity, call it unconstitutional, and, if so, in their opinion null and void. Thus far I agree entirely with the language and substance of the resolutions. This, I suppose, is meant by the expression *interpose for arresting the progress of the evil*. I see in those resolutions no assertion of the right contended for, as a constitutional and peaceable exercise of a veto, followed out by the doctrine that it is to continue until, on the application of Congress for an amendment, the States are to decide. If these are the true deductions from the Virginia resolutions, I cannot agree to them, much as I revere the authority of the great statesman whose production they are. I cannot assent to them; and it is because I revere him, and admire his talents, that I cannot believe he intended to go this length. I cannot believe it, also, for another reason. He thought, and he conclusively proved, the alien and sedition laws to be deliberate, unconstitutional, and dangerous acts; he declared them so in his resolutions. Yet, Sir, he never proposed that their execution should be resisted; he never uttered or wrote a word that looked like this doctrine, now contended for, of a constitutional right to arrest the execution of the law until amendments could be proposed. The right he asserted, when he alludes to resistance, was one that all acknowledge—that of opposition to intolerable and unconstitutional oppression. Mr. Jefferson, in the Kentucky resolutions, has used a word of equivocal authority, as well as signification; he asserts the right of a State to *"nullify"* an unconstitutional act. If he means by this any thing more than is contained in the Virginia resolutions, he must apply it to the extreme case of resistance, on the right of which, there can be no contrariety of opinion: for Mr. Jefferson does not, if I read him aright, avow, any more than Mr. Madison does, the right now contended for, of a State veto with its consequences. This, it appears to me, is a more modern invention, and, as I think I have proved, utterly incompatible with the nature of our Government. Was it ever conceived, before the present day, to form a part of it? If it was, why is it not alluded to in any of the debates of the Federal Convention which framed, or the State Conventions which adopted it? Surely it is of sufficient importance to have attracted attention, either as an advantage or an objection; yet not a word is said about it. Nay, more, if we refer to that luminous exposition of the whole character of the

General Government, and of its expected operation, "The Federalist," not a word can be found that favors this idea of a *veto,* now, for the first time, set up as a part of our Constitution. The Constitution, its advocates, its opposers, the great cotemporary exposition of its character, the practice under it for forty years, all silent on so important, so fundamental a doctrine. Is not this a fair, I might say a conclusive argument that it does not exist—that it is what I have indicated it to be, a modern invention. But this is not all: the case of a conflict of authority between the General and State authorities, under the new Government, was one that could not escape the foresight of the authors of "The Federalist." A series of chapters on this, and subjects connected with it, are found in that collection, written by Mr. Madison. Here would have been the place, certainly, to have developed the character and operation of this legal *veto,* if, in his opinion, it had existed. He could not have been silent on the subject. It is impossible that he could then have held the doctrines which are erroneously, in my opinion, said to be those of his Virginia resolutions. In the 44th number, in arguing the necessity of the article which makes the laws of the United States, made in pursuance of the Constitution, paramount to the State Constitutions, he says, if the State sovereignty had been left complete in this particular, among other absurd and dangerous consequences, "The world would have seen, for the first time, a system of government founded on an inversion of the fundamental principles of all governments; it would have seen the authority of the whole society every where subordinate to the authority of the parts; it would have seen a monster, in which the head was under the direction of the members." And, as more immediately applicable to the present subject, in the 46th number, he gives expressly what he supposes the only remedy for an *"unwarrantable,"* by which he must mean unconstitutional, measure. "On the other hand, (he says) should an unwarrantable measure of the Federal Government be unpopular in particular States, which would seldom fail to be the case, or even a warrantable measure be so, which may sometimes be the case, the means of opposition to it are powerful and at hand." Now, Sir, if the new doctrine were the true one, if the veto were a constitutional measure, now we should hear of it! What more *powerful!* What more *at hand!* What more effectual! Why look for any other? Yet this constitutional right, so clearly deducible from the very terms of our national compact, never occurred to the very man whose doctrines, in 1798, are said, erroneously, I again repeat, to embrace it. What are the remedies which he there points out? "The disquietude of the people, their repugnance, and, perhaps, refusal to co-operate with the officers of the Union, the frowns of the executive magistracy of the State, the embarrassments created by legislative devices, which would often be added on such occasions, would oppose, in any State, difficulties not to be despised; would form in a large State very serious impediments; and where the sentiments of several adjoining States happened to be in unison, would present obstructions which the Federal Government would be hardly willing to encounter." These were the sentiments of Mr. Madison in 1787. And such, I think, is the true construction of his language in 1798. For he goes on in the same paper to follow up the consequences of a perseverance of the Federal Government in unconstitutional measures, into the only result that all agree must, in *extreme cases*, happen—a resistance by force; and that he may not be misunderstood, makes it analogous to the case of the Colonial resistance to Great Britain.

Although, in my opinion, in every case which can lawfully be brought within the jurisdiction of the Supreme Court, that tribunal must judge of the constitutionality of laws on which the question before them depends, and its decrees must be final, whether they affect State rights or not; and, as a necessary consequence, that no State has any right to impede or prevent the execution of such sentence; yet, I am far from thinking that this Court is created an umpire to judge between the General and State Governments. I do not see it recorded in the instrument, but I see it recorded that every right not given is retained. In an extreme case that has been put, of the United States declaring that a particular State should have but one Senator, or should be deprived of its representation, I see nothing to oblige the State to submit this case to the Supreme Court; on the contrary, I see, by the enumeration of the cases and persons which may be brought within their jurisdiction, that this is not included; in this the injured State would have a right at once to declare that it would no longer be bound by a compact which had been thus grossly violated.

I consider the existence of the States, with that portion of their sovereignty which they have reserved, to be a most invaluable part of our Government; their rights should be most zealously watched over and preserved—preserved, but not enlarged. An organized body, ready to resist either Legislative or Executive encroachment, round which the people, whenever oppressed, may rally, will always keep oppression in awe; they are an intermediate corps between the people and the Federal Government; and, being a permanent one, they answer the same end in our Government that a hereditary aristocracy does in some others. They check the power of the federative head, while they themselves are kept within constitutional bounds by the direct operation of the general laws on their citizens through the Judiciary. Their agency and its effective utility were shown in 1798, in the stand which Virginia and some other States took against the obnoxious alien and sedition laws. They reasoned, they remonstrated, they appealed to the high feelings of patriotism and freedom, as well as to the understanding of the people; they demonstrated the usurpation of the power which had enacted these laws; they proved to conviction that they were void; and this had the desired effect. But they did not declare that the laws should not be executed; they did not array the force of the State against the decrees of the Judiciary; they did not interpose, or threaten to interpose, their constitutional *veto*.

But if the power contended for on the one side be dangerous, the doctrine by which it is opposed on the other seems no less so. If this be strictly a popular government, as contended for by the Senator from Massachusetts, that is to say, a government formed by the people of the United States, considered in one mass, without any consideration of the relation in which they stand to each other as citizens of different States, then the following important consequences follow. Not a denial of State rights, as has, I think, been incorrectly and unjustly, in and out of the House, charged to the Senator's argument; he expressly, as I understand him, acknowledges that they retain all that are not given to the General Government. But, Sir, although his argument acknowledged the existence of the reserved rights, yet it took away the means of preserving them. If it be a popular Government in the sense I have described, then what a majority of the whole people will, must be executed, and rightfully executed. If this be the true construction of our fundamental compact, then, in any future changes that our situation may call for, the people of a few large States, making a majority of the whole number of voters, must give the law to the greater number of States, and may materially and injuriously alter, or totally destroy, the Union, which the argument supposes not to be a compact between the States, but the work of the people, that is to say, the whole people of the United States. It will be no answer to this to say, that alterations cannot be made in the Constitution but by the assent of the *States,* because, if there is no *compact* there is no injury to the States, any more than there would be by altering the boundaries, or the representation; or giving to or taking from a county, advantages which it enjoyed under a State constitution. The majority of the people in a State may do this at their pleasure, with regard to a county; so might a majority of the people of the United States do, with regard to a State, if the Government has the same popular character in the one instance that it has in the other. As to the impediments imposed by the Constitution to the power of making alterations, by the clause which designates the mode in which they are to be made, by the assent of a requisite number of States, it affords no insurmountable difficulty. If the Government was made by the People, the same people have the right to alter it, and a majority may alter that clause with the same ease and the same right that they change any other in the Constitution. It is plain, therefore, that this argument places three-fourths of the States at the mercy of one-fourth of their number. Six States having on an average a million of inhabitants each, form a majority of the population. In a popular Government, the will of the majority must be obeyed in making or altering constitutions as well as laws; therefore, if this be a popular Government, without any feature of compact in it, there is plainly no security for even the existence of the State governments under it. It is true, that the argument allows to them certain rights; but if those rights were the result of the will of the People, expressed by their adoption of a popular Government, is it not clear, that, whenever that will changes, and another kind of government is preferred by a majority, the rights are gone, and rightfully gone? In short, the doctrine puts the States precisely in the situation of counties, or any other political division of a consolidated government.

It is true, that, while the present form of government exists, States are necessary for its organization; but if it be simply popular—if no compact enters into its composition—the State agency may be easily dispensed with in the new changes that a majority may deem expedient.

Observe, Sir, that, by popular government, the Senator does not mean one adopted or made by the people of each State, acting separately in their State capacity; if he did, there would be no dispute: for it cannot be denied, that the Constitution was adopted by the people of each State in its separate convention. This would not contravene the idea of a compact, which his argument totally denies. He means, and so I understand him clearly to express, a government framed by the people of all the States, acting in their aggregate capacity; and this doctrine, for the reasons I have stated, I think dangerous in the highest degree. Even if no attempt be made under it, it will, if acknowledged, lessen the dignity and utility of the State Governments; they will be considered as mere tenants of their power at the will of the Federal head; which will be looked to as the source of all honor and all profit. State rights will be disregarded, when held by so precarious a tenure; encroachments will be submitted to that would not be otherwise hazarded, until, gradually, we are prepared for a consolidated government, which, on experiment, will be found to require more energy for its support over the extensive country which it must embrace; and then the dormant resolution on your Journals will be called up, and HIS HIGHNESS the President of the United States will be invested with dictatorial or protectorate powers, for an enlarged term, for life—and at last with reversion to his children. Sir, this is the natural consequence of the doctrine, should it be acquiesced in as correct, but not carried into effect in an immediate attempt against the State sovereignties. Suppose, however, the reverse should take place, and the citizens of a number of States, sufficient to constitute a large majority of the inhabitants of the Union, should become converts to the Senator's doctrine, and determine to exercise the lawful right which a majority of every consolidated government has, to change the Constitution. The minority of numbers constituting, perhaps, two-thirds of the number of States, are incredulous, and entertain the heretical opinion that there were certain portions of their State sovereignty never surrendered, and which they deem it a duty to defend. Can no case be imagined that may, by a diversity of local interests, produce such a state of things? and can the consequences be calmly considered by any lover of his country?

The most dangerous of all errors are those which give false impressions of fundamental political rights. When firmly convinced that they are true, it is thought a duty to defend them at the risk of life—at the expense of fortune. The tranquillity of the country is sacrificed, its institutions destroyed, and its dearest interests disregarded by men, who, with the purest intentions, have adopted on trust the opinions of others, in whom they have confidence; and who are taught to believe, that disobedience to legitimate authority is resistance to oppression, or the exercise of an unauthorized power is the assertion of a constitutional right. This consideration alone, it appears to me, should make us most tremblingly apprehensive of inculcating any new doctrine of this character; and it has made me scan with greater attention those which have been offered in this important branch of the debate. But with a becoming distrust of my own judgment, and a proper respect for that of the Senators who have preceded me, I cannot but see, in the doctrines of all excepting only those of my friend from New Hampshire, (Mr. WOODBURY) dangers of the gravest cast. Those I have endeavored respectfully but decidedly to point out, and to state what are my own views on the subject, that they may be weighed and compared. I resume them.

I think that the Constitution is the result of a compact entered into by the several States, by which they surrendered a part of their sovereignty to the Union, and vested the part so surrendered in a General Government.

That this Government is partly popular, acting directly on the citizens of the several States; partly federative, depending for its existence and action on the existence and action of the several States.

That, by the institution of this Government, the States have unequivocally surrendered every constitutional right of impeding or resisting the execution of any decree or judgment of the Supreme Court in any case of law or equity between persons or on matters of whom or on which, that court has jurisdiction, even if such decree or judgment should, in the opinion of the States, be unconstitutional.

That, in cases in which a law of the United States may infringe the constitutional right of a State, but which, in its operation, cannot be brought before the Supreme Court, under the terms of the jurisdiction expressly given to it over particular persons or matters, that court is not created the umpire between a State that may deem itself aggrieved and the General Government.

That, among the attributes of sovereignty retained by the States, is that of watching over the operations of the General Government, and protecting its citizens against their unconstitutional abuse; and that this can be legally done—

First, in the case of an act in the opinion of the State palpably unconstitutional, but affirmed in the Supreme Court in the legal exercise of its functions;

By remonstrating against it to Congress;

By an address to the People in their elective functions to charge or instruct their Representatives;

By a similar address to the other States, in which they will have a right to declare that they consider the act as unconstitutional and therefore void;

By proposing amendments to the Constitution in the manner pointed out by that instrument;

And finally, if the act be intolerably oppressive, and they find the General Government persevere in enforcing it, by a resort to the extreme right which every people have to resist oppression.

Secondly, if the act be one of those few which, in its operation, cannot be submitted to the Supreme Court, and be one that will, in the opinion of the State, justify the risque of a withdrawal from the Union, that this last extreme remedy may at once be resorted to.

That the right of resistance to the operation of an act of Congress, in the extreme cases above alluded to, is not a right derived from the Constitution, but whenever resorted to, can be justified only on the supposition that the Constitution has been broken, and the State absolved from its obligation.

That the alleged right of a State to put a *veto* on the execution of a law of the United States, which such State may declare to be unconstitutional, attended (as, if it exist, it must be) with a correlative obligation on the part of the General Government, to refrain from executing it; and the further alleged obligation on the part of that Government, to submit the question to the States, by proposing amendments, are not given by the Constitution, nor do they grow out of any of the reserved powers.

That the exercise of the powers last mentioned, would introduce a feature in our Government, not expressed in the Constitution, not implied from any right of sovereignty reserved to the States, not suspected to exist by the friends or enemies of the Constitution when it was framed or adopted, not warranted by practice or cotemporaneous exposition, nor implied by the true construction of the Virginia resolutions in '98.

That the introduction of this feature in our Government would totally change its nature, make it inefficient, invite to dissension, and end, at no distant period, in separation; and that, if it had been proposed in the form of an explicit provision in the Constitution, it would have been unanimously rejected, both in the Convention which framed that instrument, and in those which adopted it.

That the theory of the Federal Government, being the result of the general will of the People of the United States in their aggregate capacity, and founded, in no degree, on compact between the States, would tend to the most disastrous practical results; that it would place three-fourths of the States at the mercy of one-fourth, and lead inevitably to a consolidated Government, and, finally to monarchy, if the doctrine were generally admitted; and if partially so, and opposed to civil dissension.

These being my deliberate opinions on the nature and consequences of the constructions hitherto given of the Federal compact, and the obligations and rights of the States under it; deeming those constructions erroneous, and in the highest degree dangerous to the Union, I felt it a duty to my place and to my country to say so. Having done this, I ought perhaps to stop. But, Sir, I dare not! I dare not stifle the expression of apprehensions, which have fastened upon my mind.

It would be useless affectation to pretend ignorance of the discontent that prevails in an important section of the Union; its language is too loud, too decisive, too menacing, not to have been heard, and heard with the deepest concern. It has already been more than once alluded to in this debate, in terms of severest censure. I shall not assume that tone, although I cannot but deprecate the light manner in which the greatest evil that can befall us is spoken of, as if it were an every day occurrence. Arguments for and against the dissolution of the Union are canvassed in the public papers; form the topic of dinner speeches; are condensed into toasts; and treated in every respect as if it were "a knot of policy that might be unloosed familiar as a garter." Sir, it is a Gordian knot, that can be severed only by the sword. The band cannot be unloosed until it is wet with the blood of brothers. I cannot, therefore, conscientiously, be silent; and, humbly as I think of my influence or powers of persuasion, I should feel myself guilty if they were not exerted in admonition to both parties in this eventful controversy. The tariff is the prominent grievance that excites the discontents in some of the Southern States, and particularly in South Carolina. It is denounced as unconstitutional, injurious to the whole country, ruinous to the South, and beneficial only to a particular interest in the North and East. My sentiments on this subject may be expressed in very few words. A decided convert to the free trade system, I think it may be departed from in the few cases in which restrictions may be used, with the hope of producing a relaxation of similar restrictions by a foreign Power. I therefore believe the present tariff unwise, unequal, and oppressive in its operations, but I cannot think it unconstitutional. And I consider one of its worst consequences to be, that, when it has been long persisted in, and considered as the settled policy of the nation, so much of the capital and population of the country may be employed, in the manufactures protected by it, as to make it a matter of serious calculation whether a sudden and total abandonment of the policy, may not produce greater evil to the whole nation than the benefit to be expected from throwing open the trade. With these opinions on the subject of the Southern discontents, I enter largely into their feelings, and join them in their lamenting a policy which operates so distressingly on their prosperity.

There is no doubt, that, for some years past, the pecuniary difficulties of that part of the country have increased; that the value of property has diminished; and that, from a state of affluence, many of the citizens are, without extravagance or individual misfortune, greatly reduced in circumstances. But, would it not be prudent, calmly to consider whether all this distress is to be attributed to this one cause—whether the low price of the staples of that district (the immediate cause) has been produced by that measure; whether the actual price of imported goods paying the duty, or the same kind of goods protected by it, have not, from other causes, been kept down nearly to their former value? And that, therefore, although they may lose the advantage which the fall of prices would have given, independent of the tariff, whether the actual expenditure is increased beyond that of former years; and, if this should be the result, whether the evil is not of such a nature as may be borne without recurring to extremities—in the hope, in the certain hope, that it will not be of long continuance?

For, Sir, let them also consider the powerful agents that are at work for their relief. First, in point of efficiency, is the press. It may spread errors, but it also diffuses truths; and, with an intelligent, an educated people, such as ours, these last will ultimately prevail. Political economy was but lately with us considered as a science; a false, but specious, and now exploded policy, usurped its place, under the imposing title of the American system. The true science was the subject of idle sneers and jests by those who found it easier to adopt an old error, than to study a new science; and to found political combinations upon sectional interest, than to acquire popularity on the broad basis of general interest. These doctrines are in a course of examination; they cannot stand the test of theory, still less of practice. Sir, the professor is in his chair, the press is at work, and a powerful but demoralizing agent is demonstrating the truth of their science. The smuggler is abroad—his boats and cutters are in all your bays, and inlets, and rivers, on the Atlantic; his canoes are on your lakes; he is lurking in the woods of your frontier; and presently, Sir, when your oppressive laws have become unpopular, he will come in at noon day, in defiance of them. You may seize, and sue, and prosecute; but when the feelings of the people, in such a Government as ours, are enlisted against the laws, you cannot execute them; and this is one of the worst consequences of the restrictive system—an unavoidable consequence. Oaths are disregarded, evasions of the law considered as proofs of genius, and the agent or captain who has most address in defeating the officers of the customs, is sure to be the most employed. Let any one who doubts this, look back to times of the non-intercourse and embargo. How many vessels, bound from Charleston or New Orleans to New York, blown by irresistible gales from Sandy Hook to Liverpool; how many false log books, how many perjured protests, how many acquittals against evidence; presenting a mass of perjury, fraud, and combination, to defeat the laws, perpetrated by men in every other view respectable, but who have become contaminated by the corrupt influence of these demoralizing laws. In every country in the world, high duties have been defeated by illicit trade; it is inevitable; no cause is more certain of producing its effect; it will be so forever. If the morals of the country are correct, it will corrupt them. If the frontier is small and guarded, the officers will be bribed; if it is extensive, their vigilance will be avoided. If France with 13,000 men, and England with a fleet of revenue cutters, cannot prevent it, what can be expected from our insignificant revenue force, on a coast of more than 2000 miles, and an inland frontier of the same extent? These causes will disgust those for whose exclusive use the system was intended, with its operation, and at the same time, convince the People of its injustice. It is possible, also, that the improvements in machinery, and the competition fostered by the protection, may reduce the price of some of the domestic articles, so as materially to lessen the evil.

But, if these should fail, I cannot but place great reliance on an address to the justice of the nation, and do not believe, when, in the confidence of private correspondence, the venerable Jefferson, in a moment of warmth and irritation, said of the Representatives of the nation, that "you might as well reason with the marble columns which surround them," that he uttered the cool dictates of his judgment. No, Sir! he had a higher idea of the value of representation in Government. In a debate like this, on the importance of the Union, his genius would have drawn a different illustration from those objects which surround us and sustain the dome under which we deliberate. What were they originally?* Worthless heaps of unconnected sand and pebbles; washed apart by every wave; blown asunder by every wind. What are they now? Bound together by an indissoluble cement of nature; fashioned by the hand of skill, they are changed into lofty columns, the component parts and the support of a noble edifice—symbols of the Union and strength on which alone our Government can rest—solid within, polished without; standing firm only by the rectitude of their position, they are emblems of what Senators of the United States should be, and teach us, that the slightest obliquity of position, would prostrate the structure, and draw with their own fall, that of all they support and protect, in one mighty ruin.

A distrust of the justice and good feeling of one part of the Union by another, is a most dangerous symptom; it ought not to be indulged even when occasional circumstances justify it. A distrust of the justice of the whole is still more fatal. How can we hope for ready obedience to our laws,

---

* The interior columns of the Capitol are of a beautiful marble, composed of variegated pebbles, united by a natural calcareous cement.

if the people are taught to believe in a permanent hostility of one part of the Union towards another; and that every appeal made by reason and argument to their common head, is vain? Perseverance will do much; for even if the illustration which has been made, of party obduracy, were just, we should remember that the hardest marble is worn by a succession of drops; much more may we hope that prejudice, however strong, will yield to the claims of justice, frequently enforced by a repetition of sound arguments.

Menace is unwise, because it is generally ineffectual; and of all menaces, that which strikes at the existence of the Union is the most irritating. Have those who thus rashly use it, who endeavor to familiarize the people to the idea, have they, themselves, ever done what they recommend? Have they calculated, have they considered, what one, two, or three States would be disjointed from the rest? Are they sure they would not be disjointed themselves? That parts of any State, that might try the hazardous experiment, might not prefer their allegiance to the whole? Even if civil war should not be the consequence of such disunion—an exemption of which I cannot conceive the possibility. What must be the state of such detached parts of the mighty whole? Dependence on foreign alliances for protection against brothers and friends; degradation in the scale of nations; disposed of by the protocols of allied monarchs to one of their dependents, like the defenceless Greeks. But I will not enlarge on this topic, so fruitful of the most appalling apprehensions—Disunion! the thought itself—the means by which it may be effected—its frightful and degrading consequences— the idea, the very mention of it, ought to be banished from our debates— from our minds. God deliver us from this worst, this greatest evil. All others we can resist and overcome; encroachments on individual or State rights cannot, under our representative government, be long or oppressively persevered in. There are legitimate and effectual means to correct any palpable infraction of our Constitution. Try them all before recourse is had to the menace of this worst of evils. But when an honest difference of construction exists, surely such extreme means or arguments ought not to be resorted to. Let the cry of unconstitutional oppression be justly raised within these walls, and it will be heard abroad—it will be examined; the people are intelligent, the people are just, and in time these characteristics must have an effect on their Representatives. But let the cry of danger to the Union be heard, and it will be echoed from the White to the Rocky Mountains; every patriotic heart will beat high with indignation; every hand will draw a sword in its defence. Be assured, on both sides of this argument, that the people will not submit to consolidation, nor suffer disunion, and that their good sense will detect the fallacy of arguments which lead to either.

Sir, I have done. I have uttered the sincere dictates of my best judgment, on topics closely connected with our dearest interest. I have, because it was my duty, uttered them freely—without reserve, but I hope without offence; with the respect that was due to the opinion of others, and with a becoming diffidence of my own. It would be a cause of great regret if I should have misapprehended the tendency of any of the doctrines of which I have spoken. It would have been a greater, if, thinking of them as I do, I had omitted the animadversions which I thought their consequences required.

Gentlemen have spoken, with patriotic enthusiasm, of the consolation they would receive, at their last moments, in seeing the flag of their country displaying to their dying eyes its emblems of union and glory. The period when mine must be closed in night, is too near to refer to it the duration of my country's happiness. But I can anticipate for it a continuance of freedom and prosperity long after the distant, I hope, the far distant day, when the last of those honorable men shall have finished his useful career. I can apprehend for it the worst of evils before one of them shall quit the stage.

These hopes are founded on a continuance of the Union;

These fears, on the madness of party that may destroy it.

NOTE.

Extracts from the printed Public Accounts, which are published, including 1828, since that date, from manuscript in Register's Office, or in the Department of State.

For the first two years of James Monroe's administration:

1817,	"Foreign Intercourse,"..	$ 281,995 97
1818,	Do. do...	420,429 90
		$ 702,425 87

Abstracts of the above.

1817,	Diplomatic Department,.......................................	107,738 38
1818,	Do. do..	103,652 04
1817,	Contingent expenses Foreign Intercourse, ...	35,953 39
1818,	Do. do. do.......................................	98,856 09
1817,	Treaties with Mediterranean Powers,..................	28,721 57
1818,	Do. do. do.......................................	51,412 21
		$426,333 68

Civil List.

1817,	Contingent expenses Department of State, (excluding expenses of publishing laws)	9,784 85
1818,	Do. do.......................................	12,515 00
		$ 22,299 85

For the first two years of John Q. Adams' administration.

1825,	"Foreign Intercourse,"..	$ 371,666 25
1826,	Do. do...	232,719 08
		$ 604,385 33

Abstract of the above.

1825,	Diplomatic Department, ...	159,603 82
1826,	Do. do..	152,476 90
1825,	Contingent expenses Foreign Intercourse,..........	25,474 95
1826,	Do. do. do.......................................	18,627 07
1825,	Treaties with Mediterranean Powers, ...	26,108 67
1826,	Do. do. do.......................................	2,086 08
1826,	Panama Mission, ...	9,000 00
		$ 393,377 49

Civil List.

1825, Contingent expenses Department of State,
(excluding publishing of laws) 16,800 00

1826, Do. do. 16,000 00

$ 32,800 00

First two years of Andrew Jackson's administration.

1829, "Foreign Intercourse," 207,060 35

1830, The whole estimate asked for the above, ... 263,300 00

$ 470,360 35

Abstracts of the above.

1829, Diplomatic Department, ... 121,667 99

1830, Whole estimate of the above, ... 180,000 00

1829, Contingent expenses Foreign Intercourse, ... 14,469 12

1830, Whole estimate of the above, ... 30,000 00

1829, Treaties with Mediterranean Powers, ... 11,938 88

1830, Whole estimate of the above, ... 30,000 00

$388,075 99

Civil List.

1829, Contingent expenses Department of State,
(excluding publishing of laws,) taken from
manuscript in Department of State, ... 10,819 55

1830, Whole estimate, ... 10,700
And Biennial Register 1,000

11,700 00

$ 22,519 55

Index

A NOTE ON THE TYPE

The typeface used in this book is Adobe Caslon, a modern interpretation of the classic faces cut in the 1720s by the English typographer William Caslon (1692–1766). Caslon was trained as an engraver but turned increasingly to type design and cutting, setting up his own type foundry in 1720. Caslon's design became the first major native English typeface to achieve wide popularity. It displays the small lowercase height and the relatively restrained contrast typical of what are now called "old style" fonts. Modern taste and technology have smoothed out many of the idiosyncrasies of William Caslon's original cutting, but the modern version retains some of the warmth and much of the straightforward honesty that have made Caslon a good and dependable friend of the typographer for more than 250 years.

This book is printed on paper that is acid-free and meets the requirements of the American National Standard for Permanence of Paper for Printed Library Materials, z39.48-1992. ∞

Book design by Martin Lubin Graphic Design, Jackson Heights, New York

Typography by Monotype Composition Company, Inc., Baltimore, Maryland

Printed and bound by Edwards Brothers, Inc., Ann Arbor, Michigan